MAYA ART AND CIVILIZATION

PAINTED CAPSTONE FROM THE TEMPLE OF THE OWLS
AT CHICHEN ITZA

MAYA ART
AND CIVILIZATION

REVISED AND ENLARGED WITH ADDED ILLUSTRATIONS

BY

HERBERT JOSEPH SPINDEN

Curator Emeritus,
American Indian Art & Primitive Cultures,
The Brooklyn Museum;
President Emeritus, Explorers Club

Part I
A STUDY OF MAYA ART
Part II
THE NUCLEAR CIVILIZATION OF THE MAYA
AND RELATED CULTURES

THE FALCON'S WING PRESS

To Ailes and Jody
For Their Understanding Love

TO THE MAYA*

About us range abodes of nameless priests and kings;
We climb to temples of forgotten gods and pause
Before fantastic sculptures, half effaced, that deck
The inner shrine. What teasing riddle must we read?
O'er crumbling walls the vine and lizard run: the tree
Sends forth her prying roots to wreck the warrior's tomb,
And year by year the sun and rain undo the toil
Of patient builders working toward a common dream.

Strange faith that reared the serpent to the skies and made
A fearful god of Death himself, whom we bewail
In faint equivocations! On the temple front
Are monstrous shapes foretelling doom: yet beauty's touch
Softens the rigor of barbaric thought and leaves
A tender sadness. What hopes flared up to die again!
These secret writings on the mouldered stone may tell
A boast of splendid triumph. This alone we know:
That, standing in the dark, the swarthy Indian seers
Clutched at eternity and won instead the count
Of wheeling stars: cities unnumbered rose and fell,
Till changing course of empire left the land forlorn
And kings were turned to clay with all their captive trains.
Little we pity kings: rather the world's warm heart
Gives heed to children's prattle or to pleasing quest
Of tremulous love on tropic nights. Gods come and go
And men who make them out of fear and doubt are still
The victims of their own emprise. Mankind is one;
And this the crown of all: the artist breathing on
The senseless stone, the dreamer who makes good his dream.

HERBERT JOSEPH SPINDEN

* Written longhand on the flyleaf of the first copy of *Maya Art*, presented to the Demings in their
McDougall Alley Studio, March 6, 1913.

CONTENTS

PART I

	PAGE
DEDICATION	v
TO THE MAYA	vii
LIST OF PLATES, PART I	xiii
LIST OF PLATES, PART II	xv
LIST OF FIGURES, PART I	xix
LIST OF FIGURES, PART II	xxix
FOREWORD	xxxi
EDITORIAL NOTE TO THE FIRST EDITION	xli
PREFACE TO THE FIRST EDITION	xliii
INTRODUCTION	1
Area	1
Relation to Surrounding Cultures	1
Natural Divisions	2
Early Notices	3
Native Accounts	10
Political and Religious Ideas	11
Present Population	12
Materials Available for Study	12
Previous Studies	13
GENERAL CONSIDERATION OF MAYA ART	15
Homogeneity of Maya Art	16
The Human Form	21
Subjects Represented	21
Poses and Groupings	24
Foreshortening and Perspective	27
Expression	31
Composition	31
The Serpent	32
The Origin of the Serpent in Art	32
Zoölogical Observations	33
Idealization	34
The Serpent in Design	36
Simplification	39
Elaboration	41
Elimination	43
Substitution	46
The Serpent and Geometric Art	46
The Serpent in some of its Religious Aspects	49
The Ceremonial Bar	49

PAGE

The Manikin Scepter 50
The Two-headed Dragon 53
Composite Types and Miscellaneous Variations 56
The Serpent Bird 60
The Long-nosed God 61
The Roman-nosed God 69
Other Subjects 76
The Jaguar 76
Birds and Feathers 77
Miscellaneous Animals 82
Bones and Death 85
Grotesque Figures 87
The Maize God 88
Other Divinities 90
Astronomical Signs 91

CONSIDERATION OF THE MATERIAL ARTS 96
Architecture 96
Assemblage 96
Function of Buildings 98
Ground-plans 99
Elevation Plans 102
Correlation of Buildings 103
Substructures 105
Walls 107
Vaults 108
Roof Structures 110
Columns 113
Cornices 114
Doorways and Wall Openings 115
Application of Decoration 115
Realistic Decoration 116
Mask Panel 118
Profile Mask Panel 124
Geometric Decoration 127
Stelae 129
Altars 130
Color 131
Prototype of the Maya Temple 132
Minor Arts 133
Ceramics 133
Precious Stones 142
Metal Working 145
Basketry 146
Textiles 147
Tattooing 150
Minor Carvings 150
Illuminated Manuscripts 152

CHRONOLOGICAL SEQUENCE 155
First Epoch 155

PAGE

Statement of the Problem 155
Copan 155
Table I. Chronological Sequence of Copan Monuments, *facing* . . 164
Tikal 165
Earliest dated Objects 170
Quirigua 173
Naranjo 177
Seibal 183
Yaxchilan 184
Piedras Negras 189
Palenque 192
Other Sites 195
Summary of the First Epoch 198
Second Epoch 198
The Period of the Transition 199
The Period of the League of Mayapan 202
The Period of Influence from the Valley of Mexico 205
Correlation of Maya and Christian Chronology 215
Table II. Historical Correlation of Inscriptions and Chronicles,
facing 216
Connection with other Cultures 219
Maya Influence in Nahua and Zapotecan Art 219
Chronological Sequence of Art in Mexico 225
Problems of Cultural Connection outside of Mexico 231
Pyramids 232
Religious Ideas Connected with the Serpent 236
Symbolism and Art 237
Conclusion 247

TABLE OF NOMENCLATURE 249
Ruins and Monuments 249
Codices 260

PLATES, PART I [Plates follow page 264] 1–30

PART II

INTRODUCTORY NOTE 265

INTRODUCTION 267

THE ARCHAIC HORIZON 281

THE MAYAN CIVILIZATION 291

THE MIDDLE CIVILIZATIONS 327

THE AZTECS 346

EPILOGUE 369

PLATES, PART II [Plates follow page 398] 1–68

BIBLIOGRAPHIES 399

INDEX, PART I 417

INDEX, PART II 427

LIST OF PLATES, PART I
[Plates follow page 264]

FRONTISPIECE. Painted Capstone from Chichen Itza

PLATE 1. Quirigua sculptures: Fig. 1, Altar G, viewed from the northwest; fig. 2, Altar G, west side; fig. 3, Altar B, south side; fig. 4, Altar B, east side. Photographs by Peabody Museum Expeditions (Gordon).

PLATE 2. Quirigua sculptures: Fig. 1, Altar P, west side; fig. 2, Altar P, detail of east side. Photographs by Peabody Museum Expeditions (Gordon).

PLATE 3. Copan structures: Fig. 1, Mound 21, view looking north; fig. 2, portions of Structures 21a and 22, view looking west. Photographs by Peabody Museum Expeditions (Saville).

PLATE 4. Vault construction: Fig. 1, Copan, small vaulted chamber; fig. 2, Labna, view of a portion of the Temple. Photographs by Peabody Museum Expeditions (Fig. 1, Saville, fig. 2, Sweet).

PLATE 5. Maya construction: Fig. 1, Chichen Itza, partial view of a structure belonging to the Group of the Columns; fig. 2, Uxmal sealed portal vault of the House of the Governor. Photographs by Peabody Museum Expeditions (Fig. 1, Thompson; fig. 2, Sweet).

PLATE 6. Roof structures: Fig. 1, Uxmal, general view of the roof comb, House of the Doves; fig. 2, Sabacche, small temple with flying façade. Photographs by Peabody Museum Expeditions (Sweet).

PLATE 7. Columns: Fig. 1, Chacmultun, portion of Edifice 1; fig. 2, Chichen Itza, structure belonging to the Group of the Columns. Photographs by Peabody Museum Expeditions (Thompson).

PLATE 8. Mask panels: Fig. 1, Kabah, portion of the façade of Structure 1; fig. 2, Uxmal, portion of the façade of the House of the Governor. Photographs by Peabody Museum Expeditions (Sweet).

PLATE 9. Mask panels: Fig. 1, Uxmal, portion of the façade of the Western Range of the Nunnery Quadrangle; fig. 2, Labna, East Wing of Upper Range of the Palace. Photographs by Peabody Museum Expeditions (Fig. 1, Sweet, fig. 2, Thompson).

PLATE 10. Mask panels: Fig. 1, Labna, West Wing of Lower Range of the Palace; fig. 2, Labna, building north of the Portal. Photographs by Peabody Museum Expeditions (Sweet).

PLATE 11. Mask panels and profile panels: Fig. 1, Hochob, Left Wing of Principal Structure; fig. 2, Hochob, Middle portion of Principal Structure. Photographs by T. Maler.

PLATE 12. Mask panels and profile panels: Fig. 1, Tabasqueño, North Façade of Temple; fig. 2, Dsibilnocac (Iturbide) Temple with Sealed Doorway. Photographs by T. Maler.

PLATE 13. Mask panels and profile panels: Fig. 1, Uxmal, House of the Magician; fig. 2, Chichen Itza, Eastern façade of the East Wing of the Monjas. Photographs by Peabody Museum Expeditions (Fig. 1, Sweet, fig. 2, Thompson).

PLATE 14. Geometric decoration and mask panels: Fig. 1, Uxmal, House of the Governor; fig. 2, Uxmal, Eastern Range of Nunnery Quadrangle. Photographs by Peabody Museum Expeditions (Sweet).

PLATE 15. Geometric decoration and mask panels: Fig. 1, Chichen Itza, Iglesia; fig. 2, Labna, Portal arch from the southeast; fig. 3, Sabacche, Principal Structure, East Façade. Photographs by Peabody Museum Expeditions (Sweet).

PLATE 16. Contrasted styles of decoration: Fig. 1, Kabah, Structure 3; fig. 2, Xlabpak of Maler, Façade of Principal Temple; fig. 3, Uxmal, North Range of the Nunnery Quadrangle. Photographs by Peabody Museum Expeditions (Sweet).

PLATE 17. Terra cotta figurines: Figs. 1–3, whistles from Uloa Valley, Honduras; figs. 4 and 7, whistle and figurine from Jonuta, Tabasco, Mexico; figs. 5 and 6, figurines

from mounds at Kamela, Rio Salinas (Chixoy), Guatemala; fig. 8, modèrn cast from
terra cotta mould, Rio Salinas, Guatemala; All the above figurines are in the collections
of the Peabody Museum. Photographs by the Museum. Figs. 9–12, figurines from the
Island of Jaina, Campeche, Mexico, in the collection of Mrs. W. M. James, Merida,
Yucatan. Photographs by T. Maler.

PLATE 18. Copan: Series of archaic stelae: Fig. 1, Stela 7; fig. 2, Stela E; fig. 3, Stela P;
fig. 4, Stela 6. Photographs by Peabody Museum Expeditions (Saville and Gordon).

PLATE 19. Copan: Series showing later development of sculpture: Figs. 1–2, fragments of
Stela 5 showing sculpture on opposite sides; fig. 3, Stela 3; fig. 4, Stela N; fig. 5, Stela H.
Photographs by Peabody Museum Expeditions (Saville and Gordon).

PLATE 20. Series showing development of hieroglyphs. Copan: Fig. 1, fragment of an old
altar found in the Hieroglyphic Stairway; fig. 2, one side of Altar K; figs. 3–4, blocks
from the Hieroglyphic Stairway; fig. 5, part of inscription on back of Stela 9; fig. 6,
inscription on back of Stela 6; fig. 7, hieroglyphs on back of Stela A; fig. 8, hieroglyphs
on back of Stela D; Quirigua; fig. 9, hieroglyphs on east side of Stela D; fig. 10, hieroglyphs on the east side of Stela F. Photographs by Peabody Museum Expeditions
(Gordon).

PLATE 21. Tikal: Series showing development of sculpture: Fig. 1, Stela 7; fig. 2, Stela 9;
fig. 3, Stela 1; fig. 4, Stela 16. Photographs by Peabody Museum Expeditions (Maler).

PLATE 22. Tikal sculptures: Fig. 1, Stela 5; fig. 2, three hieroglyphs on west side of Stela 13;
fig. 3, three hieroglyphs on east side of Stela 9; fig. 4, eight hieroglyphs, some incomplete
on north side of Stela 1; fig. 5, part of hieroglyphic inscription of west side of Stela 5.
Photographs by Peabody Museum Expeditions (Maler).

PLATE 23. Early and late stelae. Quirigua: Figs. 1 and 3, front and back of Stela I; Copan:
fig. 2, one side of Stela 15 bearing initial series inscription. Photographs by Peabody
Museum Expeditions (Gordon).

PLATE 24. Naranjo: Series showing development of sculpture: Fig. 1, Stela 25; fig. 2, Stela
30; fig. 3, Stela 12. Photographs by Peabody Museum Expeditions (Maler).

PLATE 25. Miscellaneous sculptures. Seibal: Fig. 1, Stela 7; fig. 2, Stela 10; Piedras Negras: fig. 3, Stela 13; Ocosingo; fig. 4, lower portion of Stela 1; fig. 5, portion of Stela 2;
Cankuen: fig. 6, lower portion of Stela 1. Photographs by Peabody Museum Expeditions (Figs. 1, 2, 3 and 6, Maler, figs. 4 and 5, Tozzer).

PLATE 26. Sculptured heads. Copan: Fig. 1, stone head from Mound 32; fig. 2, stone head
from Mound 41; fig. 3, stone head from débris of Temple 22. Photographs by Peabody
Museum. Palenque: Figs. 4 to 6, three views of a stone head, after Maudslay.

PLATE 27. Chichen Itza: Fig. 1, Casa de Monjas, Second or Main Range of rooms; fig. 2,
Casa de Monjas, East Wing, from the north. Photographs by Peabody Museum Expeditions (Sweet).

PLATE 28. Chichen Itza: Details of Casa de Monjas: Fig. 1, reused stones in wall of Upper
Chamber; fig. 2, geometric panel, Second Range; figs. 3 and 4, mask panel in frieze of
the Foundation; fig. 5, mask panel, East Façade of East Wing; fig. 6, corner masks on
northeast corner of East Façade of East Wing. Photographs by H. J. Spinden.

PLATE 29. Fig. 1, Sculptured Column, North Temple of Ball Court; fig. 2, Fresco Painting,
Temple of the Jaguars; fig. 3, Pilaster, Temple of the Tables; fig. 4, Atlantean Figure;
fig. 5, Chacmool Figure at San Salvador; fig. 6, Sculptured Columns, Temple of the
Tables; fig. 7, Jaguar Relief, Mausoleum, Mound 13; all except fig. 5 are Chichen Itza.
Photographs by F. M. Chapman (fig. 2); E. Mosonyi (fig. 5); T. Maler (fig. 7); H. J.
Spinden (figs. 1, 3, 4 and 6).

PLATE 30. Map of the Principal Archaeological Sites of the Maya Area. Compiled from
various sources by H. J. Spinden. Drawn by L. M. Hendrick.

LIST OF PLATES, PART II

[Plates follow page 398]

PAGE

Funerary Urn from a Zapotecan Tomb . . . . *Facing* 267
Map of Mexico and Central America showing the Principal Archaeological Sites with
a Detail Insert of the Valley of Mexico . . . . *Facing* 280
Diagram of American Chronology 396

PLATES

I. *a*, Village Scene in Arid Mexico; *b*, In the Humid Lowlands.

II. *a*, Site of Pueblo Viejo, the First Capital of Guatemala; *b*, A Spanish Church at the Village of Camotan on the Road to Copan.

III. *a*, View of the Island Town of Flores in Lake Peten; *b*, The Sacred *Cenote* at Chichen Itza.

IV. *a*, A Guatemalan *huipili*; *b*, Pouches of the Valiente Indians.

V. *a*, Zapotecan Girl from the State of Oaxaca; *b*, Lacandone Man from Southern Mexico.

VI. *a*, Cuicuilco. A view showing cobblestone facing of mound and lava in contact with apron or causeway; *b*, Archaic Site under Lava Flow near Mexico City.

VII. Large Archaic Figures found in Graves and offering Evidence of Ancient Customs and Arts and also showing a Quality of Caricature or possibly Portraiture.

VIII. Two Stages in the Stone Sculptures of Costa Rica.

IX. *a*, Stone Sculptures of the Archaic Period; *b*, Typical Site of the Archaic Period.

X. Widely Distributed Female Figurines.

XI. Distribution of the Archaic Culture.

XII. Distribution of Agriculture in the New World.

XIII. A General View of the Ceremonial Center of Copan.

XIV. *a*, View of the Plaza at Copan from the Northwestern Corner; *b*, View Across the Artificial Acropolis at Copan.

XV. *a*, Model of the Temple of the Cross, Palenque, designed to show the Construction; *b*, Detail of Frieze on the Temple of the Cross.

XVI. A Temple at Hochob showing Elaborate Facade Decorations in Stucco.

XVII. A Sealed Portal Vault in the House of the Governor at Uxmal.

XVIII. *a*, Realistic Designs on Vases from Chamá, Guatemala; *b*, The Quetzal as represented on a Painted Cylindrical Vase from Copan.

XIX. Stela 13, Piedras Negras.

XX. *a*, Top of Stela 1 at Yaxchilan; *b*, Analogous Detail of Stela 4, Yaxchilan.

XXI. Development in Style of Carving at Copan.

XXII. Scheme of the Mayan Calendar as presented in the Codex Tro-Cortesianus.

XXIII. Typical Mayan Inscription.

XXIV. Page 24 Dresden Codex.

XXV. *a*, Detail of the Dresden Codex showing *Tzolkin* used in Divination; *b*, Analysis of the above *Tzolkin*, according to Förstemann.

XXVI. General View of Monte Alban from the North.

XXVII. Detail of Monte Alban showing Wall Foundations and Small Cell-like Rooms.

XXVIII. Zapotecan Art: Incense Burners, Funerary Vases of Portrait Type, Cruciform Tomb with Geometric Decoration.

XXIX. *a*, Sculpture of Stone of the Early Zapotecan Period; *b*, Jade Tablets pierced for Suspension.

XXX. Laughing Head of the Totonacs.

XXXI. *a*, An Elaborately Carved Stone Collar; *b*, A Palmate Stone from the State of Vera Cruz.

XXXII. The Temple of Xochicalco before Restoration.

XXXIII. Two Views of the Principal Pyramid in the Citadel at Teotihuacan.

XXXIV. *a*, Partial View of the Great Pyramid at Cholula; *b*, A View at La Quemada.

XXXV. Stone Slab from an Ancient Sepulcher in the State of Guerrero.

XXXVI. *a*, Finely Carved Ceremonial Slab found at Mercedes, Costa Rica; *b*, Stone Figure from Costa Rica; *c*, Ceremonial Slab decorated with Monkeys, Mercedes, Costa Rica.

XXXVII. *a*, The Gold Work of the Ancient Mexicans; *b*, Ornament of Gold from Costa Rica.

XXXVIII. A Page from the Tribute Roll of Moctezuma.

XXXIX. A Page from the Codex Telleriano-Remensis.

XL. Serpent Head at Bottom of Balustrade, Great Pyramid, Mexico City.

XLI. Sahagun's Plan of the Tecpan in Mexico City.

XLII. The Calendar Stone of the Aztecs.

XLIII. The Shield Stone at Cuernavaca.

XLIV. The Newly Discovered "National Stone" of Mexico.

XLV. Sculpture representing Coatlicue, the Serpent-Skirted Goddess.

XLVI. Page from the *Tonalamatl* Section of the Codex Borbonicus.

XLVII. *a*, Pictures of Tlaloc, the God of Rain, and of Ehecatl, the God of Winds, in the Codex Magliabecchiano; *b*, Mexican Genealogical Table on Amatl Paper.

XLVIII. Non-Theocratic Art of Farming Communities.

XLIX. Development of the Maya Temple.

L. Great Theocratic Art: *a*, Stela at Piedras Negras on the Usumacinta; *b*, Part of Sculptured Wooden Lintel at Tikal, Guatemala.

LI. *a*, The Celestial Canopy; *b*, The Ecliptic Strip, for Male Theocrat; *c*, The Ecliptic Strip, for Female Theocrat.

LII. Maya Renaissance Architecture.

LIII. The Sun God turns Warrior: *a*, Rain Mask at Iximche near Hopelchen, Campeche; *b*, Jaguar Sun as a Warrior. Dzecabtun, Campeche; *c*, Jaguar Sun as a Warrior. Dzecabtun, Campeche; *d*, Rain Mask of Venus at Xkichmul, Campeche.

LIV. The Thirteen Animal Constellations in the Maya Zodiac.

LV. *a*, Huetzin's Temple, Chichen Itza; *b*, The Temple of Reinterment (Holmul), Peten, Guatemala.

LVI. Aftermath of Figurines and Portrait Statues: *a*, Bat Patron of Cylinder Painting; *b*, Two Zapotecan Aristocrats; *c*, An Olmec Jade; *d*, Mixtec Gold Jewel from Tomb 7 at Monte Alban.

LVII. The Final Maya Revival: *a*, Temple at San Antonio Muyil, Yucatan Peninsula; *b*, Two-Storied Building at San Antonio Muyil.

LVIII. Two Priests Engaged in Ritual, Bas-relief at Yaxchilan.

LVIX. *a*, A Painful Ceremony at Yaxchilan; *b*, Sacrificial Jade in the Codex Vienna.

LX. *a*, The Sun in the Ecliptic, Aztec Carving, Fifteenth Century; *b*, The Confraternity of the Eagle and the Jaguar War Societies, Aztec Carving, Fifteenth Century.

LXI. Bas-relief from Yaxchilan.

LXII. *a*, Toltec Bat from Acanceh, Yucatan; *b*, Chichimec Sculpture, Guatemala, Jaguar with Cacao Pods attached to the Body; *c*, The Plumed Serpent, Chichen Itza; *d*, A Jaguar Warrior of the Aztecs.

LXIII. *a* and *b*, Maya Carvings of the Head of a Central American Sun God with a Symbol of the Planet Venus; *c*, Jade Breastplate, carved about 500 A.D.; *d*, Divine Serpent, Yaxchilan.

LXIV. *a*, Man's Ascent from the Underworld. Design from Ancient Pottery found in

New Mexico; *b*, Mixtec Place Names, Codex of the Seven Caves; *c*, The
Snail Man, Peru and Mexico.

LXV. Faces, Places, and Dates make Mixtec History: *a*, The Marriage of Twelve
Vulture and Twelve Lizard unites Two cities; *b*, Gruesome Woman makes
War; *c* and *d*, The Fatal Results of the War; *e*, Sun Worship of the Toltecs;
f, Carved Cylindrical Vases, Highlands of Guatemala.

LXVI. Tabular View of Maya Chronology. Traditional History: Fixed Astronomy.

LXVII. Tabular View of Maya Chronology. How Correlations Affect Dates.

LIST OF FIGURES, PART I

PAGE

FIGURE 1. Heads with curled nose ornament: *a*, Sun shield on the tablet of the
   Temple of the Sun, Palenque; *b*, Stone head with a tenon at back, from Copan,
   original in the Peabody Museum; *c*, Sculptured stone block from Pyramid 37,
   Quen Santo, Seler,[1] 1901, *c*, p. 112; *d*, Sculptured stone head from Labna, in the
   Peabody Museum; *e*, Pottery vessel from near Coban, in the collection of Mr.
   E. P. Dieseldorff, Seler, 1901, *c*, p. 178; *f*, Pottery mask from Panzamalá, Seler,
   1901, *c*, p. 179 17

FIGURE 2. Plant motive: *a*, Chichen Itza, Lower Chamber, Temple of the Jaguars,
   Maudslay, III, pl. 47; *b*, Palenque, Palace, House D, Maudslay, IV, pl. 37; *c*,
   Madrid Stela, Léon de Rosny, 1882, pl. 2 18

FIGURE 3. Plant and fish motive: *a*, Copan, Altar T, Maudslay, I, pl. 96; *b*, Palenque,
   Palace, House A, Maudslay, IV, pl. 10; *c*, Chajcar, Maudslay, IV, pl. 93; 1; *d*,
   Chichen Itza, Lower Chamber, Temple of the Jaguars; *e* and *f*, Palenque, Temple
   of the Cross, Maudslay, IV, pl. 71; *g*, Ixkun, Stela 1, Maudslay, II, pl. 69; *h*,
   Palenque, Frieze of Temple of the Cross, Maudslay, IV, pl. 68, a; *i*, Copan,
   Stela N, Maudslay, I, pl. 82; *j*, Chichen Itza, Lower Chamber, Temple of the
   Jaguars, Maudslay, III, pl. 51; *k*, Nebaj, on a pottery vessel reproduced by Seler,
   1902-1908, III, p. 718 19

FIGURE 4. God B wading in water, Dresden Codex, p. 67 19

FIGURE 5. Astronomical signs in bands: *a*, Uxmal, Façade of the Annex to the House
   of the Magician; *b* and *c*, Pottery fragments from Alta Vera Paz, Seler, 1902-1908,
   III, p. 615; *d*, Chichen Itza, East facade of East Wing, Monjas, Maudslay, III,
   p. 13, b 19

FIGURE 6. Astronomical signs combined with bird and animal heads: *a*, Quirigua,
   back of Stela I, Plate 23, fig. 3; *b*, Copan, Stela H, Maudslay, I, pl. 61; *c*, *d* and *f*,
   Peresianus Codex, Léon de Rosny, 1888, pls. 3, 5, and 22; *e*, Dresden Codex, p. 46;
   f, Naranjo, Stela 32 20

FIGURE 7. Detail showing a kneeling worshiper, Yaxchilan, Stela 7, after a photograph by Maler 21

FIGURE 8. Presiding priest, Palenque, Tablet of the Temple of the Sun, Maudslay,
   IV, pl. 88 22

FIGURE 9. Man wearing mask, Yaxchilan, Stela 11 22

FIGURE 10. Memorial of conquest, Yaxchilan, Lintel 12, drawn from photograph by
   Maler and a cast in the Peabody Museum 23

FIGURE 11. Atlantean figures on pilasters, Temple of the Tables, Chichen Itza . . 26

FIGURE 12. Warrior from the frescos of the Inner Chamber of the Temple of the
   Jaguars, Chichen Itza 26

FIGURE 13. Group of figures, Dresden Codex, p. 60 27

FIGURE 14. Seated worshiper in profile, Palenque, Palace, House A, see Maudslay, IV,
   pls. 8 and 11 27

FIGURE 15. Elaborated aprons: *a*, Copan, Stela N, Maudslay, I, pl. 82; *b*, Quirigua,
   Stela F, Maudslay, II, pl. 36, a; *c*, Ixkun, Stela 1, Maudslay, II, pl. 69; *d*, Tikal,
   Stela 11; *e*, Palenque, Temple of the Inscriptions, Maudslay, IV, pl. 55 28

[1] References to author and year are according to the Bibliography given at the end of the
volume. All references to Maudslay are to the archæological portion of the Biologia Centrali-
Americana, 1889-1902. Where the name of the site or monument is stated but no reference to a
publication is given the reader may ordinarily gain additional information by consulting the
Table of Nomenclature beginning on page 249. Here the sites are arranged alphabetically and
the principal contributions to our knowledge of each site is noted and correlated.

PAGE

FIGURE 16. Ornament suspended from headdress, Tikal, Stela 5, Plate 22, fig. 1 . .   28
FIGURE 17. Drawing of sculpture, Yaxchilan, Lintel 8 . . . . ; . .   29
FIGURE 18. Kneeling figures, La Mar, Stela 1   30
FIGURE 19. Representation of drapery, Palenque, Temple of the Cross, Maudslay,
    IV, p. 76   30
FIGURE 20. Realistic serpents in Dresden Codex: a, p. 23; b, p. 36   34
FIGURE 21. Idealized serpent, Chichen Itza, frescos of the Inner Chamber of the
    Temple of the Jaguars, after Miss A. Breton, 1906, pl. 8, fig. 1   34
FIGURE 22. Feathered serpent, Chichen Itza, Lower Temple of the Jaguars, Maud-
    slay, III, pl. 49   34
FIGURE 23. Serpents with grotesque heads in their mouths, Copan, Stela D, Maud-
    slay, I, pl. 45   35
FIGURE 24. Divine serpent with human head in the mouth, Yaxchilan, Lintel 15,
    Maudslay, II, pl. 83   35
FIGURE 25. Details showing influence of serpentine forms: a–d, Tro-Cortesianus
    Codex, pp. 14, 30 and 35; e, Palenque, Palace, House A, Maudslay, IV, pl. 11;
    f, Palenque, Temple of the Foliated Cross, Maudslay, IV, pl. 81; g, Chichen Itza,
    Lower Chamber, Temple of the Jaguars, Maudslay, III, pl. 46; h, Palenque,
    Temple of the Cross, Maudslay, IV, pl. 72; i, Quirigua, Altar P, Maudslay, II,
    pl. 60, b; j, Detail of a glyph, Copan; k, Quirigua, Altar P, Maudslay II, pl. 61;
    l, Tikal, Lintel of Temple IV, Maudslay, III, pl. 78; m, Quirigua, Part of initial
    glyph Stela E, Maudslay, II, pl. 32; n, Quirigua, Part of initial glyph Stela J,
    Maudslay, II, pl. 46; o, Tikal, Lintel of Temple II, Maudslay, III, pl. 73; p, Labna,
    Ear plug of mask panel   37
FIGURE 26. Plumed serpent with elaborated head, Altar O, Copan   38
FIGURE 27. Reptilian radicles, H. Allen, 1881, p. 315   39
FIGURE 28. Drawing of rattlesnake's head   39
FIGURE 29. Serpent heads with tenons, Mound 14, Chichen Itza   39
FIGURE 30. Typical conventionalized serpent head   40
FIGURE 31. Part of underlying design, Altar P, Quirigua   41
FIGURE 32. Part of overlying design, Altar P, Quirigua   42
FIGURE 33. Elaborated serpent head, Altar P, Quirigua   43
FIGURE 34. Modified serpent heads: Copan, a and d, Stela H, Maudslay, I, pls. 61
    and 59; Palenque: b, Temple of the Cross, Maudslay, IV, pl. 68; c, Palace, House
    E, Maudslay, IV, pl. 43   44
FIGURE 35. Serpent heads at sides of aprons: a, Ixkun, Stela 1, Maudslay, II, pl. 69;
    b, Quirigua, Stela F, Maudslay, II, pl. 36; c, Copan, Stela B, Maudslay, I, pl. 34;
    d, Copan, Stela N, Maudslay, I, pl. 82; e, Naranjo, Stela 6; f, Seibal, Stela 10;
    g, Copan, Stela A, Maudslay, I, pl. 26   44
FIGURE 36. Serpent heads conventionalized in the flamboyant manner: Chichen Itza,
    Temple of the Jaguars, Maudslay, III, pl. 35   45
FIGURE 37. Nose plug representing a conventionalized serpent head, Piedras Negras,
    Stela 14   45
FIGURE 38. Plant form modified by serpent features, Palenque, Palace, House D,
    Maudslay, IV, pl. 35   45
FIGURE 39. Plant form modified by serpent features, Chichen Itza, Lower Chamber,
    Temple of the Jaguars, Maudslay, III, pl. 45   45
FIGURE 40. Plant form with stem modified into a serpent's head, Quirigua, Altar P,
    Maudslay, II, pl. 62   45
FIGURE 41. Detail of an ear plug with attached serpent heads, Copan, Stela 2 . . .   46
FIGURE 42. Serpent heads showing multiplication of nose plugs, Chichen Itza, Lower
    Chamber, Temple of the Jaguars, Maudslay, III, pls. 49, 51 and 47   46
FIGURE 43. Breast ornaments, Copan: a, b, d, e and g, from interior step of Temple
    11, Maudslay, I, pl. 8; c and f, Altar Q, Maudslay, I, pl. 92   47

PAGE

FIGURE 44. Serpent head modified by a fret turning down, Copan, Southern stairway
of Temple 11   47

FIGURE 45. The Ceremonial Bar, Leiden Plate   50

FIGURE 46. The Ceremonial Bar, Copan: a, Stela P, Maudslay, I, pl. 87; b, Stela N,
Maudslay, I, pl. 82   50

FIGURE 47. The Manikin Scepter: a, Yaxchilan, Lintel 1; b, Quirigua, Altar P, Maudslay, II, pl. 62   51

FIGURE 48. The Manikin Scepter on potsherd from Santa Cruz Quiché, Guatemala.
Original in Peabody Museum   51

FIGURE 49. The Manikin Scepter as a new-born child (?), Palenque: a, Temple of
the Inscriptions, Maudslay, IV, pl. 55; b, Temple of the Foliated Cross, Maudslay, IV, pl. 81   52

FIGURE 50. The Manikin Scepter with body reduced to a staff, Ruins of Tzendales.
After a field sketch by Dr. Tozzer   52

FIGURE 51. The Manikin head on a staff, Palenque, Palace, House A, Maudslay, IV,
pl. 10   52

FIGURE 52. The Two-headed Dragon, simplest form on an oblong block of stone,
Copan, Maudslay, I, pl. 114   53

FIGURE 53. View of central portion of Altar M, Copan   53

FIGURE 54. Trefoil scroll on joints of Two-headed Dragon   53

FIGURE 55. Rear head of Altar M, Copan   54

FIGURE 56. Rear head of Altar D, Copan   54

FIGURE 57. The Two-headed Dragon with elongated body: a to c, Palenque, Palace,
House E, Maudslay, IV, pl. 43; d, Piedras Negras, Stela 25   55

FIGURE 58. Manikin Scepter combined with Ceremonial Bar, Tikal, Stela 1   56

FIGURE 59. Rear end of modified Ceremonial Bar, Seibal, Stela 10   56

FIGURE 60. Fragment of carved bone from the river front, Copan. Original in the
Peabody Museum   56

FIGURE 61. Ceremonial Bar held in tilted position, Yaxchilan, Stela 1   57

FIGURE 62. Man holding two-headed serpent of flexible type, Yaxchilan, Lintel 39 .   57

FIGURE 63. Ceremonial Bar on pottery box from Coban, Dieseldorff Collection . .   58

FIGURE 64. Degenerate form of Ceremonial Bar, Copan, Stela 11, Maudslay, I,
pl. 112   58

FIGURE 65. Substitute for Ceremonial Bar, Tikal, Stela 16   58

FIGURE 66. Substitute for Ceremonial Bar, serpent heads attached to chain-like objects: a, Quirigua, Stela F, Maudslay, II, p. 36, a; b, Palenque, Temple of the
Cross, Maudslay, IV, pl. 67   59

FIGURE 67. Two-headed Dragon, degenerate form, Yaxchilan, Lintel 25, Maudslay,
II, pls. 87 and 88   60

FIGURE 68. Serpent Bird, Palenque, Temple of the Foliated Cross, Maudslay, IV,
pl. 81   60

FIGURE 69. Staff representing a bird on a tree, Yaxchilan, Lintel 2   60

FIGURE 70. Serpent Bird, Copan, Stela H, Maudslay, I, pl. 61   61

FIGURE 71. Small clay head with serpent wing panel attached to ear plug. Dieseldorff
Collection   61

FIGURE 72. The Wing Panel: a, Copan, Stela H; b, Yaxchilan, Lintel 1; c, Quirigua,
Stela Q; d, Quirigua, Stela F   62

FIGURE 73. God B and the serpent: a, God B issues from serpent, Dresden Codex,
p. 33; b, God B with serpent body, Dresden Codex, p. 35   62

FIGURE 74. God B holding serpent in his hand, Dresden Codex, p. 40   63

FIGURE 75. Head of Long-nosed God as secondary ornamentation, Quirigua, Altar P,
Maudslay, II, pl. 64   63

FIGURE 76. Head with elaborated nose, Quirigua, Stela F, Maudslay, II, pl. 36 . .   64

FIGURE 77. God K in his relation to the serpent and to God B: a, God B attached to
serpent with the head of God K, Tro-Cortesianus Codex, p. 31; b, God K, Dresden

PAGE

Codex, p. 12; *c*, God B wearing head of God K, Dresden Codex, p. 34   64

FIGURE 78.   God B, the Long-nosed God, in relation to rain and corn growing: *a*, scattering seeds in the rain (?), Tro-Cortesianus Codex, p. 10; *b*, holding sign for corn in hand, Tro-Cortesianus Codex, p. 8; *c*, falling with sprouting corn in hand and leaves attached to body, Dresden Codex, p. 15   65

FIGURE 79.   The Long-nosed God as incised decoration on a bowl. Original in American Museum of Natural History   65

FIGURE 80.   The Long-nosed God with the sun sign on forehead, Copan, Stela D, Maudslay, I, pl. 46   66

FIGURE 81.   Long-nosed death heads attached to serpent tails:*a*, Copan, Stela D, Maudslay, I, pl. 46; *b*, Yaxchilan, Lintel 14 (design reversed), Maudslay, I, pl. 23   66

FIGURE 82.   Hieroglyphs of the rear head of the Two-headed Dragon, Palenque, Temple of the Inscriptions, Maudslay, IV, pl. 61   66

FIGURE 83.   The rear head of the Two-headed Dragon attached to band of astronomical symbols, Palenque, Temple of the Cross, Maudslay, IV, pl. 76   67

FIGURE 84.   Objects that may represent falling water: *a*, Quirigua, Stela H; *b* to *c*, Palenque, Temple of the Cross, Maudslay, IV, pls. 75 and 71   67

FIGURE 85.   Object falling from hands, Yaxchilan, Stela 7   67

FIGURE 86.   The Long-nosed Death God as a period glyph, Copan, Stela D, Maudslay, I, pl. 46   68

FIGURE 87.   The inverted head of Long-nosed Death God, Copan, Stela B, Maudslay, I, pl. 37   68

FIGURE 88.   Head in serpent mouth, Tikal, Stela 1   68

FIGURE 89.   The Roman-nosed God as Sky God: *a*, Yaxchilan, Stela 1, *b*, Yaxchilan, Stela 4; *c*, Dresden Codex, p. 56; *d*, Dresden Codex, p. 55   69

FIGURE 90.   Two-headed monster with face of God D, Dresden Codex, pp. 4 and 5 .   71

FIGURE 91.   The Kin period glyph and the Roman-nosed God as Sun God: *a*, Copan, Stela 9, Maudslay, I, pl. 110; *b*, Copan, Stela I, Maudslay, I, pl. 31; *c*, Yaxchilan, Lintel 23, Maudslay, II, pl. 98; *d*, Chichen Itza, Casa Colorada, Maudslay, III, p. 24; *e*, Copan, Stela A, Maudslay, I, pl. 24; *f*, Palenque, Temple of the Sun, Maudslay, IV, pl. 88; *g*, Copan, Stela M, Maudslay, I, pl. 74   72

FIGURE 92.   Conventionalized head of Roman-nosed God, Piedras Negras, Stela 14 .   73

FIGURE 93.   Sculptured block showing Two-headed Dragon and the face of the Roman-nosed God, Northeast group, Copan   73

FIGURE 94.   Pottery flask with face of Roman-nosed God, Uloa Valley, Gordon, 1898, *a*, p. 19. Original in Peabody Museum   74

FIGURE 95.   Jadeite slab representing a Sun God, Ocosingo. Squier collection, American Museum of Natural History   74

FIGURE 96.   Intermediate series: Long-nosed God and Roman-nosed God: *a*, Copan, Stela D, Maudslay, I, pl. 46; *b*, Copan, Altar O, Maudslay, I, pl. 85; *c*, Copan, Stela A, Maudslay, I, pl. 26; *d*, Copan, Stela 2, Maudslay, I, pl. 101; *e*, Palenque, Temple of the Cross, Maudslay, IV, pl. 71; *f*, Copan, Stela H; *g*, Tikal, Lintel of Temple III, Maudslay, III, pl. 78; *h*, Copan, Stela I, Maudslay, I, pl. 63 . . .   75

FIGURE 97.   Close association of God B and God D: *a* and *b*, Dresden Codex, pp. 41 and 12   75

FIGURE 98.   God G, the Sun God, Dresden Codex, p. 15   75

FIGURE 99.   Altar of Stela F, Copan, Maudslay, I, pl. 114   76

FIGURE 100.   Realistic drawing of a jaguar, Dresden Codex, p. 8   77

FIGURE 101.   Jaguar on a potsherd from Mound 36, Copan. Original in Peabody Museum   77

FIGURE 102.   Various representations of birds: *a*, Copan, back of Stela B; *b*, Copan, sculptured stone from Hieroglyphic Stairway; *c*, Copan, detail from front of Stela B, Maudslay, I, pl. 37; *d*, Codex Borgia, p. 51; *e*, Palenque, Temple of the Cross, Maudslay, IV, pl. 71; *f*, Codex Peresianus, pl. 6; *g*, Dresden Codex, p. 36; *h*, Quirigua, Altar B, Maudslay, II, pl. 14; *i*, Tro-Cortesianus Codex, p. 85; Codex

PAGE

Peresianus, pl. 4; *k*, Palenque, Palace, House C, Maudslay, IV, pl. 28 . . . · . . .   78

FIGURE 103. Quetzal bird on conventionalized tree, Yaxchilan, Lintel 5   79

FIGURE 104. The Moan bird, Dresden Codex, p. 11   79

FIGURE 105. Highly modified birds as period glyphs: *a*, *d* and *g*, Copan, Stela D, Maudslay, I, pl. 48; *b*, *e* and *h*, Quirigua, Stela D, Maudslay, II, pl. 25; *c*, *j* and *i*, Quirigua, Altar B, Maudslay, II, pl. 14   80

FIGURE 106. Examples of sculptured feathers: *a*, Copan, Stela A, Maudslay, I, pl. 26; *b*, Copan, Stela D, Maudslay, I, pl. 45; *c*, Piedras Negras, Stela 7; *d*, Copan, Stela D, Maudslay, I, pl. 46; *e* and *f*, Copan, Stela H, Maudslay, I, pls. 61 and 56; *g*, Copan, moulding representing feathers, original stone in Peabody Museum; *h*, Seibal, Stela 10; *i*, Piedras Negras, Stela 7; Uxmal, House of the Turtles, Stephens, 1843, I, pp. 311   81

FIGURE 107. Head showing manipulation of feathers, Yaxchilan, Lintel 16, Maudslay, II, pl. 84   82

FIGURE 108. Shells and figures associated with them: *a*, Codex Peresianus, pl. 6; *b*, engraved pot from Chama, Dieseldorff, 1893, p. 378; *c*, Dresden Codex, p. 41; *d*, Dresden Codex, p. 37; *e*, Tikal, Lintel of Temple III, Maudslay, III, pl. 78; *f*, Codex Nuttall, p. 75; *g*, Codex Borgia, p. 8; *h*, Palenque, Temple of the Foliated Cross, Maudslay, IV, pl. 81 . . . . •   83

FIGURE 109. God N, Dresden Codex, p. 23   84

FIGURE 110. Man with shell attached, Chichen Itza, Seler, 1908, p. 197   84

FIGURE 111. Girdle ornaments of shell: *a*, Palenque, Temple of the Inscriptions, Maudslay, IV, pl. 5; *b*, Ixkun, Stela 1, Maudslay, II, pl. 69; *c*, Copan, Stela B, Maudslay, I, pl. 34; *d*, Copan, Stela P, Maudslay, I, pl. 87   84

FIGURE 112. Anthropomorphic bat, Copan: *a*, Stela D, Maudslay, I, pl. 48; *b*, Stela D, Maudslay, I, pl. 46; *c*, Altar T, Maudslay, I, pl. 96   85

FIGURE 113. Realistic drawing of a deer, Dresden Codex, p. 60   85

FIGURE 114. Representation of human sacrifice, Piedras Negras, Stela 11   85

FIGURE 115. Various representations of bones and death: *a*, Chichen Itza, Temple of the Jaguars, Lower Chamber, Maudslay, III, pl. 45; *b*, Copan, Altar G1; *c*, Copan, Altar R, Maudslay, I, pl. 95; *d*, Tikal, Altar 16; *e*, Tikal, Lintel of Temple III, Maudslay, III, pl. 78; *f*, Copan, Stela H, Maudslay, I, pl. 56; *g*, Palenque, Temple of the Cross, Maudslay, IV, pl. 72; *h*, Tro-Cortesianus Codex, p. 33; *i*, Copan, Back of Stela B; *j*, Copan, Stela I, Maudslay, I, pl. 63; *k*, Palenque, Palace, House D, Maudslay, IV, pl. 37; *l*, Uxmal, Torso from the House of the Governor, collected by Le Plongeon, original in the American Museum of Natural History; *m*, Dresden Codex, p. 53; *n*, Tikal, Detail of frieze, Temple 55; *o*, Sculptured stone, environs of Uxmal, Stephens, 1843, I, p. 367; *p*, Palenque, Palace, House D, Maudslay, IV, pl. 37; *q*, Mexican Codex   86

FIGURE 116. Death God, Dresden Codex, p. 12   87

FIGURE 117. Glyphs indicating death: *a*, Dresden Codex, p. 63; *b*, Dresden Codex, 10; *c*, Quirigua, Stela F, east side, Maudslay, II, pl. 40; *d*, Copan, Stela I, Maudslay, I, pl. 65   87

FIGURE 118. Grotesque heads: *a*, Palenque, Temple of the Foliated Cross, Maudslay, IV, pl. 81; *b*, Quirigua, Altar P, Maudslay, II, pl. 60 a   88

FIGURE 119. Fish with a face on its back, attached to shell. Collection of E. P. Dieseldorff   88

FIGURE 120. Girdle strap wrappings modified into an inverted face, Copan, Stela B, Maudslay, I, pl. 34   88

FIGURE 121. Glyphs of the day Kan: *a*, Tro-Cortesianus, p. 83; *b*, Tro-Cortesianus, p. 24; *c*, Yaxchilan, Lintel 21; *d*, Palenque, Temple of the Cross, Maudslay, IV, pl. 77   88

FIGURE 122. Various representations of the Maize God: *a*, Dresden Codex, p. 14; *b*, Dresden Codex, p. 12; *c* to *e*, Peresianus Codex, pl. 19 . . . . 0 .   89

FIGURE 123. The Maize God in the sculptures: *a*, Palenque, Palace, Enclosed Corridor, sculpture over vault in passage; *b*, Tikal, Lintel of Temple IV, Maudslay, III, pl. 78; *c*, Copan, Interior step of Temple 11, Maudslay, I, pl. 8; *d*, Palenque, Temple of the Foliated Cross, Maudslay, IV, pl. 81; *e*, Copan, Stela H, Maudslay, I, pl. 59; *f*, Quirigua, Stela M 89

FIGURE 124. God C and his hieroglyph, Dresden Codex, p. 5 90

FIGURE 125. God C with a mottled green body, Codex Peresianus, pl. 18 90

FIGURE 126. God C, Tro-Cortesianus Codex, p. 10 90

FIGURE 127. Hieroglyphs containing face of God C: *a*, Palenque, Palace, House C, Maudslay, IV, pl. 24; *b*, Copan, Stela A, Maudslay, I, pl. 30; *c* to *e*, Tro-Cortesianus Codex, pp. 21, 74 and 78 90

FIGURE 128. Sun symbols: *a*, Palenque, Palace, House A, IV, pl. 10; *b*, Yaxchilan, Stela 4; *c* and *d*, Dresden Codex, pp. 66 and 55 91

FIGURE 129. Sun disk represented in fresco, Chichen Itza, Inner Chamber of the Temple of the Jaguars 92

FIGURE 130. Symbols that may represent the moon: *a*, Dresden Codex, p. 55; *b*, Palenque, Palace, House E, Maudslay, IV, pl. 43; *c*, Palenque, Palace, House A, Maudslay, IV, pl. 11 92

FIGURE 131. Venus symbols: *a*, Palenque, Palace, House E, Maudslay, IV, pl. 43; *b*, Copan, Altar R, Maudslay, I, pl. 94; Dresden Codex, p. 56 93

FIGURE 132. Astronomical symbols: *a*, Copan, Stela N, Maudslay, I, pl. 82; *b*, Dresden Codex, p. 68; *c*, Palenque, Temple of the Inscriptions, Maudslay, IV, pl. 56; *d*, Dresden Codex, p. 53; *e*, Dresden Codex, p. 54; *f, j* and *k*, Palenque, Temple of the Inscriptions, Maudslay, IV, pls. 54, 55 and 56; *g*, Palenque, Palace, House A, Maudslay, IV, pl. 11; *h*, Dresden Codex, p. 52; *i*, Dresden Codex, p. 53 . . . 93

FIGURE 133. Composite monster and its glyph, Dresden Codex, p. 45 94

FIGURE 134. Series showing modifications of glyphs: *a*, Peresianus Codex, pl. 24; *b*, Dresden Codex, p. 6; *c*, Tro-Cortesianus Codex, p. 17; *d*, Landa, 1864, p. 244; *e*, Copan, Interior step of Temple 11, Maudslay, I, pl. 8; *f*, Quirigua, Stela E, Maudslay, II, pl. 31; *g*, Quirigua, Stela F, Maudslay, II, pl. 40; *h*, Quirigua, Stela E, Maudslay, II, pl. 31; *i*, Quirigua, Stela F, Maudslay, II, pl. 40; *j*, Quirigua, Stela D, Maudslay, II, pl. 26 94

FIGURE 135. Hieroglyph with entire figures, Copan, Stela D, Maudslay, I, pl. 48 . 95

FIGURE 136. Representations of Indian huts in fresco, Chichen Itza 99

FIGURE 137. Series showing development of the sanctuary: *a*, Copan, Temple 22*a*; *b*, Tikal, Temple I; *c*, Copan, Temple 22; *d*, Chichen Itza, Castillo; *e*, Palenque, Temple of the Sun 99

FIGURE 138. Structures showing the extreme development of the portico, Chichen Itza, Group of the Columns 100

FIGURE 139. Partial ground-plan of the Group of the Monjas, Chichen Itza, Maudslay, III, pl. 3 101

FIGURE 140. Ground-plan, House of the Turtles, Uxmal 101

FIGURE 141. Ground-plan of Akat'cib, Chichen Itza 102

FIGURE 142. Ground-plan, Santa Rosa Xlabpak, Maler, 1902, p. 226 102

FIGURE 143. Elevations, Santa Rosa Xlabpak: *a* and *b*, cross-section, Maler, 1902, p. 226 103

FIGURE 144. Assemblage of Edifice 5, Chacmultun, Thompson, 1904, p. 19 104

FIGURE 145. Restoration of balustrade, Hieroglyphic Stairway, Gordon, 1902, p. 13 109

FIGURE 146. Typical cross-section of an interior wall 107

FIGURE 147. Cross-section of Temple 5, Tozzer, 1911, p. 122 110

FIGURE 148. Plans of Yaxchilan temples: *a*, Structure 25, Maudslay, II, pl. 77; *b*, Cross-section of Structure 33, Maudslay, II, pl. 77; *c*, Ground-plan of Structure 33, Maudslay, II, pl. 77 112

FIGURE 149. Plans of the Casa Colorada, Chichen Itza 113

FIGURE 150. Cornice forms: *a*, Southern area; *b*, Usumacinta area; *c*, Northern area; *d*, Lower cornice of the Iglesia, Chichen Itza; *e*, Palenque, Temple of the Cross;

PAGE

f, Palenque, Palace; *h*, Second Range, Monjas, Chichen Itza; *i*, Caracol, Chichen
Itza; *j*, Monjas, Chichen Itza; *k*, Labna; *l*, Chacmultun   114
FIGURE 151. Modifications of door jamb: *a*, common form; *b*, Uxmal; *c*, Chichen Itza   115
FIGURE 152. Gargoyle in form of serpent head, Copan, Gordon, 1896, p. 7   117
FIGURE 153. Ornamental niche on façade, Uxmal, The Nunnery, North Range,
Catherwood, 1844, pl. 15   118
FIGURE 154. Faces limited to rectangular spaces, Chichen Itza: *a*, Temple of the
Jaguars, Lower Chamber; *b*, Temple with two pilasters made of re-used blocks,
Group of the Columns   118
FIGURE 155. Face in profile, Stela B, Copan, Maudslay, I, pl. 37   118
FIGURE 156. Mask panel at base of Stela 4, Yaxchilan   119
FIGURE 157. Mask panel at base of stela, La Hondradez   119
FIGURE 158. Mask panel on tower, La Hondradez. After sketch by Dr. Tozzer . .   119
FIGURE 159. Mask panel, partly restored, Nakum. After sketch by Dr. Tozzer . .   119
FIGURE 160. Mask panel, partly restored, Nakum. After sketch by Dr. Tozzer . .   120
FIGURE 161. Corner mask built up mosaic fashion, Palace, Labna   120
FIGURE 162. Mask panel, Palace, Labna   120
FIGURE 163. Mask panel over doorway, Xkichmook   121
FIGURE 164. Simplified mask panel   121
FIGURE 165. Superimposed mask panels showing elaboration, East Range of the
Nunnery, Uxmal   122
FIGURE 166. Mask panel over doorway, showing extreme elimination, Palace, Labna   123
FIGURE 167. Mask panel, East Range of the Nunnery, Uxmal, Catherwood, 1844,
pl. 15   123
FIGURE 168. Mask panel showing substitution, House of the Dwarf, Uxmal, Cather-
wood, 1844, pl. 13   124
FIGURE 169. Geometric panel, Dsibiltun   124
FIGURE 170. Geometric panel, Dsibiltun   124
FIGURE 171. Profile panel, Yaxchilan, Stela 7   125
FIGURE 172. Panel at base of Stela 6, Yaxha   125
FIGURE 173. Profile at side of doorway, Copan, Temple 11   125
FIGURE 174. Remains of wall decoration, Nakum. After a sketch by Dr. Tozzer .   126
FIGURE 175. Profile mask panel, Hochob, Principal Structure   126
FIGURE 176. Assemblage of profile and front view mask panels, ruined temple, Hochob   126
FIGURE 177. Mosaic elements, Labna. Original stones in Peabody Museum   128
FIGURE 178. Mosaic elements with examples of their development. Chichen Itza .   128
FIGURE 179. The shield as a mosaic element, Labna   128
FIGURE 180. Mosaic elements used in façade decorations, Labna. Original stones in
Peabody Museum   129
FIGURE 181. Typical banded section of the banded column, Labna   129
FIGURE 182. Richly ornamented wall with projecting sculpture, Uxmal, Temple of
the Magician. The sculptured head now removed to Museo Nacional, Mexico City   129
FIGURE 183. Detail of façade decoration of banded columns, Tantah   130
FIGURE 184. Potsherds showing different processes of ornamentation: *a*, *b*, *c*, and *e*,
Copan; *d*, Peten region. Original specimens in Peabody Museum   134
FIGURE 185. Decoration on bowl from near Peto. Original in Peabody Museum .   135
FIGURE 186. Bowl from Calcetok. Collection of Señor Enrique Camara   136
FIGURE 187. Bowl from the Island of Jaina. Musée de Trocadéro, Hamy, 1897, pl. 27   136
FIGURE 188. Engraved potsherd from Santa Cruz Quiché. Original in Peabody
Museum   136
FIGURE 189. Potsherds showing applied relief decoration. Quen Santo, Seler, 1901,
c. pp. 140 and 171   137
FIGURE 190. Jaguar head vase, Copan, Tomb 1, Gordon, 1896, p. 48. Original in
Peabody Museum   137
FIGURE 191. Crude painted figures on food bowls, Copan   138

PAGE

FIGURE 192. Design on finely painted bowl from Copan. Original in Peabody Museum 139
FIGURE 193. Design on bowl, El Jicaro, Guatemala. Original in Peabody Museum . . 140
FIGURE 194. Geometric motives used in pottery decoration 141
FIGURE 195. Carved jadeite amulet with inscription. Bishop Collection, Metropolitan Museum of Fine Arts 143
FIGURE 196. Jadeite amulet with inscription on back, Island of Jaina. In American Museum of Natural History 144
FIGURE 197. Perforations of a jadeite amulet. In Field Museum of Natural History . 144
FIGURE 198. Jadeite amulet, Chichen Itza. In Field Museum of Natural History . . 144
FIGURE 199. Jadeite ear plug, Ocosingo. Squier Collection, American Museum of Natural History 145
FIGURE 200. Clay figurine showing use of jadeite ear plugs, Coban, Seler, 1895, d, p. 34 145
FIGURE 201. Portion of design on marble vase from Honduras. Squier Collection, American Museum of Natural History 145
FIGURE 202. Copper bell with coarse wire decoration, Honduras. In American Museum of Natural History 146
FIGURE 203. Baskets represented on sculptures: a, Yaxchilan, Lintel 24; b, Chichen Itza, Lower Chamber of the Jaguars, Maudslay, III, pl. 49 146
FIGURE 204. Imitation of basket weaves on painted potsherds, Uloa Valley. In Peabody Museum 147
FIGURE 205. Details of textile ornamentation from the sculptures: a, Copan, Hieroglyphic Stairway; b, f, g, Piedras Negras Stelae 35, 1 and 14; c and d, Details of lace work; e and h, Yaxchilan, Lintel 25 148
FIGURE 206. Garments represented in sculptures and codices: a and b, Chichen Itza, Lower Chamber Temple of the Jaguars; c–e, Dresden Codex, pp. 5, 23, 27 . . . 149
FIGURE 207. Woman richly attired, Yaxchilan, Lintel 15 149
FIGURE 208. Facial tattooing: a–f, Details mostly from figurines, Schellhas, 1890, p. 213; f, g, Yaxchilan, Lintel 24 150
FIGURE 209. Pottery whistle in shape of head showing tattooing, Tecolpa, Tabasco. In American Museum of Natural History 150
FIGURE 210. Peccary skull with incised drawings, Copan. In Peabody Museum . . 151
FIGURE 211. Ceremonial staff ending in a hand: a, Dresden Codex, p. 27; b, Codex Borgia 153
FIGURE 212. Cross-sections of Copan stelae 157
FIGURE 213. Proportions of the body on Copan stelae 158
FIGURE 214. Altar 14, Copan 161
FIGURE 215. Altar of Stela I, Copan 161
FIGURE 216. Rectangular altar, Copan, Sculpture Y, Gordon, 1902, b, pl. 14 . . . 161
FIGURE 217. Glyphs from jadeite statuette, San Andrés Tuxtla, Holmes, 1907, pl. 36 171
FIGURE 218. Introducing glyph on Leiden Plate 171
FIGURE 219. Head of jadeite statuette, San Andrés Tuxtla, Holmes, 1907, pl. 34 . . 172
FIGURE 220. Foot of figure on Leiden Plate showing serpent-head ankle ornament . . 173
FIGURE 221. Feet of Copan stelae showing serpent-head ankle ornaments: a and b, Stela D, Maudslay, I, pls. 45 and 47; c, Stela N, Maudslay, I, pl. 82 173
FIGURE 222. Foot showing conical ankle ornament, Quirigua, Stela F, Maudslay, II, pl. 36 176
FIGURE 223. Altar N, Quirigua 177
FIGURE 224. Plan of Main Temple, Naranjo, showing locations of stelae 178
FIGURE 225. One end of Ceremonial Bar of Stela 32 179
FIGURE 226. Ceremonial Bar, Stela 6, Naranjo 179
FIGURE 227. Ceremonial Bar, Stela 7, Naranjo 182
FIGURE 228. Bound captive, Stela 1, Ixkun, Maudslay, II, pl. 69 182
FIGURE 229. Ceremonial spears: a and b, Chichen Itza, Temple of the Jaguars, Maudslay, III, pls. 47 and 48; c, Palenque, Temple of the Sun, Maudslay, IV, pl. 88 . 183
FIGURE 230. Head on fragment of Lintel 41, Yaxchilan 188

PAGE

FIGURE 231. Short wands with head of the Long-nosed God: *a*, Palenque, Temple of the Foliated Cross, Maudslay, III, pl. 81; *b*, Yaxchilan, Lintel 14   193
FIGURE 232. Stela at ruins of Tzendales. After a field sketch by Dr. Tozzer   197
FIGURE 233. Diagram showing growth of the Substructure of the Casa de Monjas, Chichen Itza   203
FIGURE 234. Details of re-used mask panels, Chichen Itza: *a*, Lateral mouth ornament of mask panel of frieze of the Substructure of the Casa de Monjas; *b* and *c*, Details from center mask of the flying façade of the Iglesia   204
FIGURE 235. Serpent head with human head in its mouth, Uxmal, Nunnery Quadrangle, West Range   205
FIGURE 236. Atlantean figure, Temple of the Initial Series, Chichen Itza   207
FIGURE 238. Atlantean figure, Tlascala, Seler, 1902–1903, p. 92   207
FIGURE 238. Breast ornaments representing birds, Chichen Itza: *a* to *d*, Temple of the Jaguars, Maudslay, pls. 49 and 50   208
FIGURE 239. Sun and star symbols of the Nahua type: *a*, Mitla, Seler, 1895, *c*, pl. 1; *b*, Totonacan area, Strebel; *c*, Santa Rita, Gann, 1897–1898, pl. 29; *d*, Santa Rita, Gann, 1897–1898, pl. 31; *e*, Codex Porfirio Diaz; *f*, Codex Fejérváry-Mayer, p. 25; *g*, Vienna Codex; *h*, Chichen Itza, Temple of the Jaguars, Maudslay, III, pl. 38; *i*, Mitla, Seler, 1895, *c*, pl. 1   209
FIGURE 240. Speech scrolls: *a*, Hieroglyph for Cuernavaca (Cuauhnahuac), Peñafiel, 1885, pl. 91; *b*, Hieroglyph for Cuicatlan, Peñafiel, 1897, pl. 30; *c* and *d*, Xochicalco, Peñafiel, 1890, pl. 190; *e*, Santa Lucia Cosumahwalpa, Habel, 1878, pl. 5; *f*, *h*, *i*, *k*, *l*, *m*, *n*, Chichen Itza, Temple of the Jaguars, Maudslay, III, pls. 46, 49 and 50; *g*, Dresden Codex, p. 34; *j*, San Juan Teotihuacan, Peñafiel, 1899, pl. 82; *o*, Chavero, 1900–1901, Pt. I   210
FIGURE 241. Speech scroll representing Long-nosed God, Chichen Itza, Temple of the Jaguars, Maudslay, III, pl. 51   211
FIGURE 242. Terra cotta tile from Tezcoco. In American Museum of Natural History   211
FIGURE 243. Nahua subjects similar to those of Chichen Itza: *a*, Codex Vaticanus, 3773, p. 14; *b*, Codex Borbonicus, p. 17   212
FIGURE 244. Design showing Maya style, Chichen Itza, Temple of the Jaguars, Maudslay, III, pl. 46   212
FIGURE 245. A stucco panel at Acanceh   213
FIGURE 246. Figure that may represent Manikin God, Santa Rita, Gann, 1897–1898, pl. 30   213
FIGURE 247. Head of Roman-nosed Sun God, Santa Rita, Gann, 1897–1898, pl. 31 .   214
FIGURE 248. Head of figurine with animal headdress, Santa Rita, Gann, 1897–1898, pl. 32   214
FIGURE 249. Figurine from Cerro de los Idolos, Tabasco. In Musée de Trocadéro. Hamy, 1897, pl. 24   215
FIGURE 250. Typical Lacandone incense burner   215
FIGURE 251. Human heads in animal jaws: *a*, Piedras Negras, Stela 26; *b* and *c*, Figurine from Oaxaca; *d*, Stone sculpture from Oaxaca, Seler, 1901–1902, p. 41; *e*, Piedras Negras, Stela 7; *f*, Onyx slab, Chalco, in Field Museum of Natural History, Holmes, 1895–1897, *m*, p. 305; *g*, Chichen Itza, Temple of the Jaguars, Maudslay, III, pl. 51; *h*, Sculptured bowlder, in Field Museum of Natural History, Holmes, 1895–1897, pl. 56   221
FIGURE 252. Human head in animal jaws, Oaxaca, Teotitlan del Camino, Seler, 1895, *c*, pl. 13 . . . :   222
FIGURE 253. Human head in jaws of serpent, Calendar Stone, Museo Nacional, Mexico   222
FIGURE 254. Serpent head on pottery, Cholula, Seler, 1902–1908, II, p. 297   222
FIGURE 255. Serpent head on engraved bowl from Cholula. In American Museum of Natural History   222
FIGURE 256. Serpent head on bowl from Cholula. Museo de la Academia de Bellas

PAGE

Artes, Puebla 223
FIGURE 257. Serpent heads on Cholula pottery: a, Seler, 1902–1908, vol. 2, p. 296; b, Museo Nacional, Mexico; c, In American Museum of Natural History; d, Museo Nacional, Mexico 223
FIGURE 258. Conventionalized serpent heads arranged in a swastika, Museo Nacional, Mexico 223
FIGURE 259. Lineal forms derived from serpent head, Cholula pottery; a, American Museum of Natural History; b and c, Museo Nacional 223
FIGURE 260. Serpent, curvilinear style, Codex Vaticanus, 3773, p. 49 224
FIGURE 261. Serpent head, angular style, Codex Vaticanus, 3773, p. 71 224
FIGURE 262. Double-headed serpent forming a bowl, Codex Vaticanus, 3773, p. 55 . 224
FIGURE 263. Serpent heads painted on pottery, State of Vera Cruz, Strebel, 1899, pl. 9 224
FIGURE 264. Detail of stone yoke, State of Vera Cruz, Holmes, 1895–1897, p. 211 . . 225
FIGURE 265. Reptile head on stone yoke, State of Vera Cruz, Holmes, 1895–1897, p. 316 225
FIGURE 266. Human figure, Xochicalco, Peñafiel, 1890, pl. 190 225
FIGURE 267. Small pottery objects of earliest type, Mexico. In American Museum of Natural History: a–c, Atzcapotzalco; d, San Juan Teotihuacan; e, Tuxpan, Jalisco; f, Zapotlan, Jalisco; g, Cuernavaca 228
FIGURE 268. Design on interior of bowl, Calchaqui area, Argentine. In Field Museum of Natural History 239
FIGURE 269. Snakes on vessels from Chimbote, Peru. In American Museum of Natural History 239
FIGURE 270. Fragment of a garment, Pachacamac, Peru, Uhle, 1903, pl. 4 239
FIGURE 271. Detail on pot from Pachacamac, Peru. In American Museum of Natural History 240
FIGURE 272. Serpent heads on pottery from Nicaragua. In American Museum of Natural History 240
FIGURE 273. Nahua sculptures, Nicaragua: a, Subiaba, Squier, 1852, I, p. 319; b, Zapatero, Squier, 1852, II, p. 52; c, Pensacola, Squier, 1852, II, p. 36 240
FIGURE 274. Head of basalt from near Tegucigalpa, Hamy, 1896, pl. 1 241
FIGURE 275. Plumed serpents on Casas Grandes pottery. In American Museum of Natural History 241
FIGURE 276. Reclining figure with animal headdress, Casas Grandes pottery. In American Museum of Natural History 241
FIGURE 277. Plumed serpent of Zuñi: a, Cushing, 1882–1883, p. 515; b, National Museum, Washington 242
FIGURE 278. Horned serpent on prehistoric bowl from Puye, New Mexico. In Museum of the Southwest, Santa Fe 242
FIGURE 279. Horned serpent and cloud symbols on prayer meal bowl from Perige (Old San Ildefonso). In Museum of the Southwest, Santa Fe 242
FIGURE 280. Shell gorget with rattlesnake design, Tennessee, Holmes, 1880–1881, pl. 65 242
FIGURE 281. Winged and horned snakes: a, Alabama, Moore, 1905, p. 229; b, Arkansas, Holmes, 1898–1899, p. 91 243
FIGURE 282. Serpent engraved on a vase from Georgia, Holmes 243
FIGURE 282. Copper plates from the Mound Area: a, Illinois, Thomas, 1890–1891, p. 309; b, Georgia, Thomas, 1890–1891, pl. 17; c, Thomas, 1890–1891, p. 304; d, Thomas, 1890–1891, p. 305; e, Thomas, 1890–1891, pl. 17 244
FIGURE 284. Designs on shell gorgets: a, Kentucky, Moorehead, 1910, II, p. 130; b, Alabama, Moore, 1907, p. 398 245
FIGURE 285. Shell masks: a, Tennessee, Holmes, 1880–1881, pl. 69; b and c, Virginia, Holmes, 1880–1881, pl. 69 246
FIGURE 286. Horned snake on buffalo skin lodge, Dakota Indians, Weygold, 1903 . 246

LIST OF FIGURES, PART II

PAGE

1. The Great Snowstorm of 1447 shown in the Pictographic Record of the Aztecs . 267
2. A Mexican Picture of a Volcanic Eruption 268
3. Yucatan Deer caught in a Snare 270
4. The Moan Bird, or Yucatan Owl, personified as a Demigod 270
5. Spanish Ship in the Aubin Codex 271
6. Cortez arrives with Sword and Cross and Moctezuma brings him Gold 272
7. Aztecan Canoe. Lienzo de Tlaxcala 273
8. Design on Modern Huichol Ribbon 277
9. Woven Pouch of the Huichol Indians 277
10. Atzcapotzalco Destroyed 282
11. Diagram of Culture Strata at Atzcapotzalco 283
12. *Teocentli* or Mexican Fodder Grass 284
13. Archaic Figurines from Central Mexico 285
14. Archaic Figurines—Zapotlan, Jalisco; Tampico, Vera Cruz; and Cuesta Blanca,
    Salvador 285
15. Archaic Figurine from Salvador 286
16. Types of Eyes of Archaic Figurines 286
17. Textile Designs painted on Archaic Effigies 287
18. Typical Tripod Vessels of the Archaic Period, from Morelos, Mexico 287
19. Series showing the Modification of a Celt into a Stone Amulet 288
20. Groundplans of Yaxchilan Temples 292
21. Cross-section of Typical Mayan Temple in Northern Yucatan 293
22. Mask Panel over Doorway at Xkichmook. Yucatan 294
23. Design on Engraved Pot representing a Tiger seated in a Wreath of Water Lilies.
    Northern Yucatan 295
24. Painted Design on Cylindrical Bowl showing Serpent issuing from a Shell. Sal-
    vador 295
25. Mayan Basket represented in Stone Sculpture 296
26. Typical Elaborated Serpents of the Mayas 297
27. Conventional Serpent of the Mayas used for Decorative Purposes 298
28. Upper Part of Serpent Head made into a Fret Ornament 299
29. Sculpture on Front of Lintel at Yaxchilan 299
30. Types of Human Heads on the Lintels of Yaxchilan 299
31. Sculpture on Upper Part of Stela 11, Seibal 301
32. The Ceremonial Bar 302
33. The Manikin Scepter 303
34. The Two-Headed Dragon 303
35. Gods in the Dresden Codex 304
36. The Front Head of the Two-Headed Dragon on Stelae at Piedras Negras showing
    the Increase in Flamboyant Treatment 305
37. Grotesque Face on the Back of Stela B, Copan 306
38. Jaguar in Dresden Codex with a Water Lily attached to Forehead 306
39. Late Sculpture from Chichen Itza 308
40. The Twenty Day Signs 308
41. The Nineteen Month Signs of the Mayan Year 310
42. Bar and Dot Numerals of the Mayas 312
43. Face Numerals found in Mayan Inscriptions 313
44. The Normal Forms of the Period Glyphs 313

PAGE

45. Face Forms of Period Glyphs   313
46. Hieroglyphs of the Four Directions   315
47. Hieroglyphs containing the Phonetic Element *kin*   315
48. Mayan Ceremony as represented in the Dresden Codex   317
49. Diagram of the Astronomical Base Line at Copan giving Readings at April 9 and
        September 2   319
50. Representations of the Moon   321
51. The Last Glyph of the Supplementary Series   322
52. Comparison of Mayan and Zapotecan Serpent Heads   328
53. Bar and Dot Numerals combined with Hieroglyphs on Zapotecan Monuments .   328
54. Detail of Wall Construction at Mitla   329
55. Wall Paintings of Mitla   330
56. The Eyes of Totonacan Figurines   331
57. Jointed Doll of Clay from San Juan Teotihuacan   336
58. Pottery Plates from Cholula with Decorations in Several Colors   337
59. Vessel with "Cloisonné" Decoration in Heavy Pigments   338
60. The Turtle Motive as developed in Negative Painting with Wax at Totoate,
        Jalisco   339
61. Jaguar Head on Disk-Shaped Stone. Salvador   340
62. Front View and Profile View Serpent Heads in Chorotegan Art   341
63. Jaguar Design associated with Figurines that still retain Archaic Characters.
        Costa Rica   342
64. Jaguars from painted Nicoyan Vases   342
65. Highly Conventionalized Jaguar Motive   342
66. Simple Crocodile Figures in Red Lines on Dishes from Mercedes, Costa Rica . .   343
67. Panels containing Crocodiles painted in White Lines on Large Tripod Bowls from
        Mercedes, Costa Rica   343
68. Simplified Crocodile Heads in the Yellow Line Ware of Mercedes, Costa Rica .   343
69. Conventional Crocodiles from Costa Rica and Panama   345
70. Pictographic Record of Fighting near the Springs of Chapultepec   348
71. Details from the Stone of Tizoc   352
72. Detail showing the Construction of the Face of Coatlicue   353
73. Hieroglyphs of Precious Materials   353
74. Phonetic Elements derived from Pictures and used in Mexican Place Name
        Hieroglyphs   354
75. Aztecan Place Names   354
76. Aztecan Day Signs   355
77. Variant Forms of Aztecan Day Signs   355
78. Aztecan Numbers and Objects of Commerce   356
79. Analysis of Mexican Record   357
80. Chalchuihtlicue, Aztecan Goddess of Water   358
81. A Mexican Orchestra   362
82. Mexican Blanket with the Design that represents interlacing Sand and Water
        called "Spider Water"   363
83. The Year Symbol of Southern Mexico   364
84. Year Bearers in the Codex Porfirio Diaz ascribed to the Cuicatecan Tribe . . .   364
85. A Page from the Codex Nuttall, recording the Conquest of a Town situated on
        an Island of the Sea   365
86. The God Macuilxochitl, Five Flower, as shown in a Mexican Codex and in Pot-
        tery from southern Mexico   366

FOREWORD

No longer is history a simple narrative of marching facts. We learn so much about so many things that knowledge becomes a blended background like the myriad noises of a tropical night or the city's unremitting overtone. These form a sort of vibrant silence as awareness is lost in the multiplicity of its own receptions.

Historical research in America is now carried into remote Arctic reaches, along with geological and biological studies, explorations over ice or under ice, and of course by air as well. Sensitivities of personal attention merge to form a matrix, cosmopolitan in scope and inductive in quality. Perhaps a layer of thin volcanic ash will become a date line. Perhaps a muted voice of Kipling's explorer will remonstrate: "By the lost campfires I lighted they will tell me how I got there." Over all the world a similar tendency is felt as rejudgments make for harmony.

New dimensions in New World history, and their significance to the Old, need brief retainer proofs. One reason for making these so prominently and so soon is precisely to emphasize the independence of great developments in the eastern and western halves of the world as regards the upper registers of civilization. The lower registers are everywhere, humble but potentially strong.

Present man in every land is Homo sapiens, admittedly a biologic species. That embracing human oneness stretches like a cold-drawn wire across Bering Strait just short of the Arctic Circle. It means an equality of first immigration for human beings on the self-reliant stage of big-game hunters. These emerged in Europe during the Fourth Glaciation as the Neanderthal type of man purged himself for cultural advancement by accepting climatic harshness for the sake of a red-meat diet. This was a generalizing experience which eliminated defects and emphasized resourceful normality. Wearing animal skins, man became at will an Arctic animal, able to resist the cold as he slept on the trail.

If at that time specifically lower types of human beings, beyond redemption by crossbreeding, still existed (which may be doubted), they do not exist now. The present races are now mutually prolific, except that individuals may be eliminated. Nevertheless, a homogeneous lot of immigrants chose the long, hard road across northern Europe and Siberia to America as nomads of the strongest kind.

One smiles at the Rocky Mountain slogan: "Only the brave went West, and the weak died on the way." While the far-northern hunters, dressed in stolen furs, had small capital in hand beyond a kit of tools, it is significant that they had retained an old tropical inheritance; their natural bodies were able to withstand the heat.

Man's extensions of management outside the body explain his meteoric rise to dominion over animals who mostly achieved their specializations slowly within themselves and at a risk of narrowing over-all efficiency.

When the first primates left the ground and took to the friendly trees, they freed their limbs and enlarged their brains while their eyes gained stereoscopic vision from arboreal security. Continuing in this vein, one finds it easy to enumerate a succession of advantages which historically clears the way for human evolution—as though that alone were pertinent. It is true that the biped animal has recently explored the psychic front and named its promontories. Should his discovery of what is what give him title to truths he did not compose but merely discerned?

Natural intelligence there surely is, as high-powered knowledge that comes to man through organs of sensitivity traceable in long stages of animal evolution. These anticipate all utterances of direct human intelligence. By matching nature in static machines, we discover that natural eyes, for instance, are lenses which operate dynamically against a sensitive screen. Having that screen, or retina, we can substitute a static lens and get vision which successfully transmits and transmutes illusion. But let us moderns not be too proud and assertive.

Discovering Dynamics

For one great advance we must give credit to the New World, not the Old. To the Maya of Central America we owe the first conception and measurement of time in a truly dynamic sense, and to them we owe mathematics capable of expressing the sheer idea that time is movement in a living universe. When, in the eighth century before Christ, the Maya began to wonder what eclipses meant, they set about to find out in a thoroughly scientific manner. They knotted a string, and against the knot they dropped a bead to count from a notable phenomenon. This was a solar eclipse total in their territory. After 177 days another solar eclipse was of ring-form type. Then, 872 days after the first event, a total eclipse of the moon took place. Here was a synchronization with natural phenomena of the universe.

The Maya doubtless reasoned that, as regards the sun, earth, and moon, the latter two were getting in each other's way. In other words, they argued that eclipses are perfect gunsight alignments. At other times of new and full moons, the alignment misses its mark. The explanation must have been that the moon goes around the earth, and the earth goes around the sun, from which both obtain their light. Wisely, the Maya decided that close timing might be the answer to important truths. At that first event of November 10, 752 B.C., they inaugurated an ephemeris or astronomical journal, which they kept without amendment until October 14, 58 A.D.

Time out for basic comparisons. We speak of time counts and calendars as straws whirled in a torment of intelligence, now natural, now man-made. In Europe, time was taken and mistaken in so many senses that it became the great rogue of logic. It is duration, as all of us now agree. But even figuratively, it is not a river that flows tumultuously from nowhere to nowhere without beginning and without end, Marcus Aurelius and Jerome Kern—in words and music, respectively—notwithstanding. Instead, for us worldlings, time is a continuity of astronomical days. In conformity with the order of these days are months, years, and other natural and artificial periods which may be rectified into the sequence on common multiples.

Not hitting upon that simple method, the Babylonian, Assyrian, Greek,

Roman, and Persian calendar makers spent 3,000 years in futile statics. What they really needed was not irresponsible fluidity, nor the neutrality of a squirrel's treadmill, but the mutuality of action which spells progress. This clearly happens for better or for worse. The continuity of time and space holds the footprints of evolution, or artful living, while discontinuity is artless inaction or death, which leaves no footprints. Calendarial continuity is, indeed, a cultural sublimation which expresses itself dynamically and proves the cosmos.

The outward evidences of counted units of time are old in both the Old World and the New in calendars and the regnal years of kings, yet everywhere recorded eclipses give us the oldest exact dates. After coinage was invented in Sardis, there were numismatic city dates in abundance in the Near East. This system spread both ways, to China and Spain.

City dates ceased in Phoenician ports with Alexander's conquest; those towns simply accepted a dire event and made a fresh start of Alexandrian years as a trade convenience. When Alexander died, his eastern general, Seleucus Nicator, began his system of lunisolar years with the first new moon after the autumnal equinox in 311 B.C. This formal calendar did not quiet the differences. The long-sought rule for the lunisolar year produced many patched-up cycles, one being that of Omar Khayyám, who exclaimed:

> Ah, but my Computations, People say,
> Reduced the Year to better reckoning, Nay!
> 'Twas only striking from the Calendar
> Unborn Tomorrow and dead Yesterday!

It is strange that, with all the Old World emphasis on "make use of the day," *carpe diem*, no Old World people ever tried to count days Maya fashion, in a seriation of strictly natural happenings. If only they had done this with the same thoroughness that they recorded social and business happenings in their diaries, journals, and account books!

To be sure, a certified number now connects day counts of America and the Old World with many classical eclipses which we read in a rectified chronology. This accomplishment is credited to Joseph Scaliger, "Father of Chronology." But ideas which stimulated him must be explained as radiations from America by ship after the voyage of Columbus. Other radiations, out of hundreds, material in quality, are maize, potatoes, and tobacco. Intellectual ones are concepts not formerly a part of Old World philosophy.

Joseph Scaliger was born up the Garonne River from Bordeaux, where he went to school. He absorbed knowledge from any and all sources, and in religion became a Huguenot. The famous *Emendation of Time* was published in 1583, the year after the Gregorian correction reaffirmed old errors, albeit with curious modifications. The Huguenot's conclusions had been accomplished in 1575, it seems, when he edited a Roman work on astronomy, recognizing the error of its ways. The reforms in thinking which he introduced were ancient among the Maya, but unknown previously in the Old World. First came the day count to replace year counts; second, a point of time from which to count; third, a method of reaching this point of time by tripodal convergence of existing year counts; fourth, an adaptation of Julius Caesar's essentially Egyptian year.

All three chronological requisites had been developed by the Maya many centuries before Columbus' time. After that, ways were soon opened for thought transference from America to Europe—by piecemeal, if not coherently. The Spanish churchmen were intent on destroying native civilizations around the world for replacement by the sovereignty of Christendom. The proof is very clear that when the Franciscans established themselves in Mexico and Central America, the New World time machine was in day-for-day adjustment with the heavens. Also, knowledge of ancient sciences still existed. A call went out from authority for the total suppression of Indian calendars and beliefs. Facts new to the Spaniards were retained for such new uses as might appear feasible. The original ecclesiastical purpose of time reform had been to correct the error for Easter on the tropical year back to the Council of Nicaea (325 A.D.), which amounted to ten days. In the end this purpose was shifted by adding ten days to October 4 to reach October 14, the tropical anniversary of Maya zero. The Gregorian shift was static ordination with a new twist, for the Maya point of time was identified with the birthday of St. Francis of Assisi, founder of the Franciscan Order, then managing the native demolition in Yucatan and the Valley of Mexico. Even cosmic problems became administrative and political as information not wanted for public consumption was censored. And as Shakespeare says, "Lilies that fester smell far worse than weeds."

The continuity adopted by Scaliger after American priming produced the Julian Era and the equation Maya Day Number +489,384 = Julian Day Number. The convergent point of time involved the fifteen separate years of the Roman Indiction, the nineteen years of the Metonic Cycle, and the twenty-eight years of the Cycle of the Sun, all carried back to a common Year One. Then the pattern of the Julian Year of $365\frac{1}{4}$ days gave dates.

What of Man and Nature?

With early man in America a big-game hunter who had his fling in two continents for five millennia, it often is assumed that a human carnivorous cycle closed here with the extinction of at least three sorts of elephants, the mammoth, the mastodon, and the imperial beast that flourished southward from Mexico. There was extinction also for giant sloths, giant armadillos, giant beavers, etc. Horses and large camels apparently perished in droves in the continents of their generic origin. There were exceptions, one being that four small camels survived in South America, two of them wild and two others now in a domesticated state. In the tropics, the tapir and the manatee somehow continued to exist, and life in abundance in ocean rivers. As for North America, a numerous holarctic fauna enjoyed easy exit and entrance across Bering Strait during mild interglacial climates of the Pleistocene—bears, reindeer, bison, musk oxen, etc. Even at the end, when man appeared, armed with knife and spear, opinions differ whether he played a leading part in animal extinctions. Personally, I think he did and still continues to do so, to his own great disadvantage, failing to maintain a proper balance.

Before that, other roads are now demonstrable which antedate the rise of man. These made terrestrial transfer possible for land animals, while aqueous life was seldom actually terminated in dead sea areas. Oceans were free-moving waters in spite of occasional land bridges between the continents. Natural history, as now determined along many lines, is first and last consistently logical in evolutionary retractions and expansions as natural intelligence speaks through continuing operations. These take an upward trend in betterments as adventurous forms pass from water to land, then from land to air, under the guidance of organic instrumentation. To be sure, there were dinosaurs before industrialists—and they died.

Sapient man long ago seized control. He has tried to hold that control for twenty thousand years, but with doubtful success, since nature is not always in agreement with the inflexible intentions of human management, and nature generally has the last say. The question is this: Does the long succession of plotted causes and results in natural history, as developed on this our earth, under our visible heaven, justify the record of interventions by self-constituted human authority? Gods, worthy of reverence wherever found, are indeed the noblest expression of human art—but sometimes the worst. And god-makers are limited, as all things individually human are limited, by incapacity for omniscience and omnipotence, and by incapacity, too, for wise rectifications of error, as static arguments have been used so naively.

Is the conclusion justified that old-American perceptions present a better record? I think they do, to this extent: in the New World, integration, as final honesty, is repeatedly acclaimed through a superior accounting of time in relation to recurring events of natural rather than human management.

We find in America no Joshua commanding the sun to stand still, no Canute setting up his throne on the beach to halt the tide. Those are but straws, for dictators know that time and tide wait for no man. Only the Toltecs, as the Romans of America, claimed to bring the dawn of civilization by conquest. But let us look at general American expressions of respect for nature, with conservation demonstrated by the fact of unwasted wealth and domesticated resources in foods and materials before the white man came with sword and cross.

Alfred Kroeber tells us that a Yokuts Indian with whom he worked in California addressed this petition to seven deities:

> My words are tied in one
> With the great mountains,
> With the great rocks,
> With the great trees,
> In one with my body
> And my heart.
> Do you help me
> With supernatural power,
> And you, Day,
> And you, Night!
> All of you see me
> One with this world!

This is integration, pure and simple, as a principle of understanding. It represents the outcome of natural intelligence which works upward through the senses. Awareness seeks reality. This fundamental truth was imparted to Clark Wissler by a Pawnee informant in these words:

> Let me see if this be real,
> Let me see if this be real,
> Let me see if this be real,

> Let me see if this be real,
> This life I am living?
> Ye who possess the skies,
> Let me see if this be real,
> This life I am living.

Quite similar in cosmology are lines in a Peruvian hymn to Viracocha, Lord of the Universe:

> The Sun, the Moon,
> The Day, the Night,
> Summer, Winter,
> Not vainly in proper order
> Do they march to the destined place.

There is a fourth step to be considered in the attainment of integration as a universal ideal; that is the identification of cosmos with goodness, and conversely, though not to that extent, of chaos with evil. The Great Mystery or the Great Spirit of our western Indians is called Wakonda, a word which definitely means goodness in Siouan speech, protective goodness, evidencing sincerity. The quest of goodness is part, it seems, of the Guardian Spirit Religion, a tolerant type of worship, especially prevalent among tribes beyond the agricultural limits. There useful skills are exemplified in birds, animals, insects, etc., which stand ready to help if approached in friendly fashion. If some skills have a dangerous quality, that may be remedied by a culture hero. We find many such reformations in American and Old World mythology. Nevertheless, to many rationalists of modern times, who are also wholehearted believers in man's infallible superiority, nothing is worse than what they call the pathetic fallacy. Even "Go to the ant, thou sluggard" leaves them unmoved. Yet sympathetic magic flourished under the noses of Aesculapius and Galen. The art of suggestion, whether directed to fellow men or imagined gods, is not content with realism: it embroiders.

I myself took down from the lips of Ignacio Aguilar, dedicated summer cacique of San Ildefonso, the Song of the Sky Loom.

> Oh our Mother the Earth, oh our Father the Sky,
> Your children are we, and with tired backs
> We bring you the gifts that you love.
> Then weave for us a garment of brightness;
> May the warp be the white light of morning,
> May the weft be the red light of evening,
> May the fringes be the falling rain,
> May the border be the standing rainbow.
> Thus weave for us a garment of brightness
> That we may walk fittingly where birds sing,
> That we may walk fittingly where grass is green,
> Oh our Mother the Earth, oh our Father the Sky!

To sign a compact of sympathy, Ignacio gave me his name, Tse Tsire Anyi— the Yellow Bird Bobs Up and Down—which I have not been able to live up to!

The Cult of the Dead goes around the world, and the hope of resurrection too. The obligation of the dead to help the living is just as strong in Peru of the Incas as it was in Egypt of the Pharaohs. This means that the fabric of sympathetic magic has great vitality. With the organs of judgment separately individual, the schemes of judgment are communal, belonging to social oversouls with the continuity of language and other going concerns of immaterial culture. Mankind is, then, an animal entity with a natural title to group equality. Individuals are not equal, of course, but societies should be so in potentialities: collectively man is at his best when self-governments are democratic.

Words are streams that overflow their banks and often subside in backwaters and swamps. Their derivations in many cases may be traced with perfect clarity, but not so easily their associations en route and the swamp flowers that safely grow within their final sinks. Such a good word surreptitiously changed is concept, conception; another not so good is abstract, abstraction. They were not intended to be opposites, as art and inertia are opposites, yet concept is creative and forward-pressing, while abstract is delinquent and destructive. Thus they end as opposites. Absolute, absolution, as another word in philosophic company, has no strings and should be perfect and self-contained. Under present associations, absolutism in many applications has a bottom, not a summit, meaning. The absolute zeros we seek are inaction; the absolute positives, where must lie performance and energy, are beyond us. Can we trust ourselves, I wonder? Even when the Maya or Egyptian theocrats turned to apotheosis as a transfer from finite to infinite existence, they nevertheless died, to every outward seeming.

We think of radioactivity today as a sort of cooling off, a let-down transformation of original power, for chemical elements first, in slow diminution; for plants and animals next, in dwindling quantities. If there is really an all-time conservatism within the universe, it may be invoked by colliding bodies which make new energy through the holocaustic remedy of cosmic rays.

It is customary to speak of physics and metaphysics with the former applying to external nature and the latter to the underlying gist of nature. Both words were subject to great social pressure among the Greeks and Romans, a tension that still is felt. A difference in method separates classical philosophy and modern science, the former being essentially a static analysis and the latter a dynamic appreciation. Before the classical ordering of the eighth century before Christ, which put emphasis on measurements and mechanics, sound judgments had long been in force through the instrumentality of sensory organs. In the life of man these were culturalized into arts of expression as an extension of animal physiology and psychology. This may be described as existing on social rather than individual planes. An awareness to environment approaching intellectuality came into being long before the advent of the superior creature called Homo sapiens advanced command through tools and weapons. When within the horde additional management was needed to supply co-operation, this was reached through the authority of the father, the strong man, the master of constructions, and the holder of magic powers, always supposedly for the common good. Regulated marriage was a binding force in politics, as all the skills of animals were sources of instruction, with the world an institution of contact education. Clearly, in his bodily evolution man improved himself to attain the freedom of action necessary to speak clearly, move adroitly, and act co-operatively. His rise was through the generalization of his mind and body. Now, through specialization and overspecialization, he prepares to destroy himself.

HERBERT J. SPINDEN

Carmel, New York, 1956

PART I

MAYA ART

EDITORIAL NOTE TO THE FIRST EDITION

THIS Memoir is the result of researches by Dr. Spinden in the Peabody Museum while a graduate student in the Division of Anthropology of Harvard University during the years 1906–1909. He presented the substance of the Memoir as a thesis for the degree of Doctor of Philosophy on May 1, 1909. During these researches he discovered and worked out the chronological sequence of the ancient monuments in Honduras and Guatemala, and in Yucatan and other portions of Mexico. Later in making a comparison with the Maya dates included in the hieroglyphic inscriptions on the monuments he found a remarkable correspondence between the dates and the several periods as determined by the character of the art itself. This important discovery was pointed out by Dr. Spinden to other workers in the Museum and to students in the Division. Thus this correlation between Maya art and Maya dates became generally known long before Dr. Spinden, at the suggestion of his friends in the Museum, presented a paper "On the Historical Development of Art at Copan," before the International Congress of Americanists, held in the City of Mexico in September, 1910.

After his graduation, and on leaving Cambridge to take the position as Assistant Curator in Anthropology in the American Museum of Natural History, Dr. Spinden continued his studies of the ancient art of Central America and Mexico, and made trips to Mexico, Honduras and Guatemala for the purpose of confirming, from the original monuments, some points which were not perfectly clear in the casts and photographs that he had studied. The results of his later studies are incorporated in this Memoir.

With two or three exceptions the illustrations in the text are from drawings by the author, either from the original sculptures or from photographs and illustrations.

Dr. Spinden is the first Maya scholar who has devoted himself to a thorough study of the ancient art of Central America as shown by the architecture, the sculptured monuments and other objects found in the ruined cities of the ancient Maya people.

The Museum is indebted to the Committee on Central American Research for the publication of this Memoir.

F. W. PUTNAM.

PEABODY MUSEUM OF HARVARD UNIVERSITY,
  Cambridge, November 28, 1912.

PREFACE TO THE FIRST EDITION

THE study of Maya art, here presented, is based upon a thesis for the degree of Doctor of Philosophy submitted May 1, 1909, in Harvard University. While the matter has expanded greatly under further study, still the thesis presented contained an exposition of the chronological sequence of the monuments, which the writer considers the most noteworthy contribution, as well as chapters on the analysis of the designs and the principles of the architecture. It was thought wise to present the portion relating to the historical development of art at Copan before the Congress of Americanists at Mexico City in September, 1910, otherwise the subject matter has not been given to the public. The attempt has been made to be precise and exoteric in the discussion of this most involved subject.

It is with gratitude that the writer acknowledges his indebtedness to the many persons who have aided and encouraged him in this work. The inception of this research took place in Anthropology 9, a course on Mexican and Central American archaeology offered in Harvard University by Dr. A. M. Tozzer. Its continuance has been largely due to the support and coöperation of the small band of students of Maya culture headed by Mr. C. P. Bowditch. Thanks are also due to Mrs. Zelia Nuttall of Mexico City, to Mr. E. H. Thompson of Chichen Itza, Yucatan, and to Mrs. W. M. James of Merida, Yucatan, as well as to many other persons in Mexico, Guatemala and Honduras.

In the revision of the manuscript the writer received valued assistance from Dr. Tozzer. For the revision of the proof he is indebted to Professor Putnam and to Miss Mead and to the latter also for the preparation of the index. Mr. C. C. Willoughby has given his kind attention to the preparation of the plates and to the making of the blocks for the illustrations in the text. The map of the region covered by the Maya civilization was drawn by Mr. L. M. Hendrick, Jr., according to data compiled from several sources.

Since his connection with the American Museum of Natural History the writer has been greatly indebted to his superiors in the Museum, who have done everything in their power to further his labors in this field.

H. J. S.

AMERICAN MUSEUM OF NATURAL HISTORY,
New York, November 28, 1912.

MAYA ART

INTRODUCTION

Area. The region in which remains of the pre-Columbian Maya civilization are found corresponds closely with that still inhabited by Indians speaking dialects of the Maya linguistic stock. Roughly it lies between 87° and 94° west longitude and 14° and 22° north latitude. More exactly it comprises, in Mexico, the states of Tabasco and Chiapas and the peninsula of Yucatan (with the states of Campeche and Yucatan and the territory of Quintana Roo), in addition to the whole of British Honduras, the two-thirds of Guatemala lying north of the Motagua River, and a considerable portion of Honduras including the head-waters of the Copan River, the lower course of the Uloa, and, in all probability, the rich central valley of Comayagua.

Relation to Surrounding Cultures. Upon the west the Maya area adjoins those of the Zapotecan and Nahua cultures. Although there is hardly a doubt concerning the common origin of these three most important civilizations of Mexico and Central America, yet environmental, chronological and linguistic differences have made them at least superficially distinct. In all three there were apparently two or more periods of widespread high culture, each followed by a period of disintegration and lower culture.

It has been argued that all were branches of an early civilization located on the plateau of Mexico and referable to the legendary Toltecs. A detailed discussion of this question will be taken up further on, after evidence has been presented. In this place it is only necessary to point out that, owing to the imperfections of Nahua reckoning, all dates before 1325, the year generally accepted for the founding of Tenochtitlan, the Aztec capital, must be regarded as largely fictitious. It will be shown that the Toltec or pre-Aztec remains were for the most part contemporary with the brilliant period of the cities of northern Yucatan, but much later than the first florescence of southern Maya art. The Zapotecan and Nahua cities, found in a flourishing condition by the Spaniards, apparently rose after the Maya culture had declined.

It seems unnecessary to consider at length the various wild speculations concerning Old World origins of New World civilizations. Lord Kingsborough's attempt to identify the nations of America with the lost tribes of Israel was in keeping with the speculative age in which he wrote. The far-fetched theories of Dr. Le Plongeon must be laid to an over vivid imagination, although there is no gainsaying the painstaking enthusiasm of this unfortunate student. But no reasonable excuse can now be found for writers who, on the strength of this or that similarity, cheerfully leap the bounds of space, time and reason to derive the religious and artistic conceptions of the Maya from Egypt, India or China. The evidence these writers present is always insufficient and usually wrong.

Where real similarities exist they probably can be explained by pure chance or by psychic unity.

In determining origins, however, account may well be taken of the single outlying group of the Maya-speaking peoples, the Huasteca, who inhabit the low coast region north of Vera Cruz, and in whose territory many remains of cities as yet undescribed are known to occur. It is possible but not likely that a careful study of this disconnected group will indicate a northern origin for Maya arts. An origin to the south of the stated limits is hardly conceivable, owing to the great and sudden falling off in handicraft and ideas once the southern frontier has been crossed. Such similarities as do exist may easily be accredited to the Nahua colonies which, in the last centuries before the coming of Europeans, were planted even farther south than Lake Nicaragua. No matter, however, to what other region fuller investigation may refer the humble beginnings of Maya art, the indisputable fact remains that in all essential and characteristic features it was developed upon its own ground.

Natural Divisions. The Maya area, as above defined, contains three principal natural divisions. In each of these the differences in climate, in natural resources, and in topography are marked enough to have had a decided effect upon the material culture of the inhabitants. The first of these divisions comprises the peninsula of Yucatan; the second, the great central valley; the third, the cordilleran plateau on the south and west. Since the entire region lies south of 22°, it is distinctly tropical except where the altitude counteracts, and is subject to the doldrum rains under the high sun. The duration of this summer rainy season is less in Yucatan than in the two other regions of greater land relief.

The peninsula of Yucatan is a limestone plain of recent geological formation, with its highest ridges but a few hundred feet above the sea.[1] It has no river valleys because, owing to the porous and soluble nature of the limestone, the drainage [2] is subterranean. There are many caverns and sink-holes. The caverns seldom show signs of former habitation and then only as retreats.[3] The sink-holes are often very large and form natural wells or cenotes. These cenotes determined the location of most ancient and modern towns. Often, however, artificial reservoirs and cisterns, called chultunes,[4] were constructed. In the southeast several large lakes occur, Lake Peten being the most important. The soil of Yucatan is shallow, and although trees grow rapidly and in dense masses they seldom attain great height. The universal building stone is limestone, which also is burned for lime.

The wide valley plain of the meandering Usumacinta and its maze of tributary streams is a region little known and poorly mapped. It supports at present a small, roving population of wood-cutters and a few hundred squalid Lacandone Indians, though it must formerly have been the seat of wealth and power, to judge from its ruined cities, such as Yaxchilan, Piedras Negras, and Seibal. Like Yucatan, the rocks are young and calcareous. Maler is probably in error when he refers to sandstone at Piedras Negras. In the great alluvial valley stone may be had at but a few points where the hills come close to the river. Consequently many sites show now only the earthen foundation mounds from which the wooden superstructures have long since vanished. Timber is plentiful, the

---

[1] For a discussion of the geology see Sapper, 1896.
[2] Casares, 1905; Mercer, 1896, p. 21, footnote.
[3] Thompson, 1897, a; Mercer, 1896.
[4] Thompson, 1897, b; Stephens, 1843, II, p. 227.

whole region being covered with a dense tropical forest of mahogany and other large trees. The rivers form the highways of travel. The surface of the land is marked by extensive swamps and a number of lakes; hills of moderate elevation vary the topography, and on the southern and western margin the land rises suddenly to the continental plateau.

This plateau attains an average height above the sea of about 8000 feet, but is deeply dissected by the Chiapas, Usumacinta and Motagua river systems. The crest of the continental range lies so close to the Pacific that no large streams flow into that ocean. The plateau swings to the east round the head of the Usumacinta basin and reaches the shores of Lake Izabel in long narrow spurs, while outlying ridges extend well into British Honduras. The flora of the plateau region is characterized by the oak and the pine, but much of the country is fairly open and well adapted to agriculture. These uplands formed the highway for migrations north and south, and supported a large heterogeneous population, but were apparently never the seat of such high culture as obtained in the lowlands. Copan and Quirigua are both situated on valley floors. Ledges of old blue limestone and of a soft volcanic tuff furnished an abundant supply of excellent building material at the former, while at the latter city a much harder stone of similar volcanic origin was encountered.

Early Notices. The number of early historical references to the Maya Indians is small, partly due to the fact that the principal theatre of action for the Spaniards lay in the valley of Mexico. Few of the soldiers of those strenuous days found time to lay aside the sword. As for the Spanish priests, most were as deeply imbued with fanaticism as were the natives whose culture they sought to destroy. They were incapable of comprehending the real character of the native religion, which they summed up as devil worship. They were true iconoclasts, and went about throwing down idols, burning ancient chronicles and destroying everything that would keep alive the remembrance of old times. Most of the first-hand information on the culture of the Maya must be gleaned from the writings of Cogolludo, Landa, Lizana and the "Relations of Yucatan" which consist of reports sent in by the heads of various towns and provinces. Excellent second-hand information is found in the works of the great historians, Herrera, Oviedo and Villagutierre.

The first expeditions from Cuba to the mainland made a number of landings along the coast of Yucatan,[1] where the Spaniards met bands of natives and visited their towns. Bernal Dias del Castillo, who sailed and fought with Francisco Hernandez de Cordoba in 1517, with Juan de Grijalva in 1518 and with the redoubtable captain Hernando Cortes in 1519 and for many years afterwards, describes Maya temples and sculptures. Dias [2] writes as follows:

"They led us to some large houses very well built of masonry, which were the Temples of their Idols, and on the walls were figured the bodies of many great serpents and snakes and other pictures of evil looking Idols. These walls surrounded a sort of altar covered with clotted blood. On the other side of the Idols were symbols like crosses, and all were coloured. At all this we stood wondering, as they were things never seen or heard of before."

At first reading this might be considered an adequate description, from the blunt pen of a sixteenth-century soldier, of the run of Maya architecture and

---

[1] For an early map see Valentini, 1902.　　　　[2] Dias del Castillo, 1908, I p. 1

art. But on examining the ruins [1] of the buildings referred to in this and similar notices (on Cozumel Island, near Cape Catoche, etc.), it is evident that they must have been decidedly inferior to the great temple structures of interior Yucatan. Though the same principles of construction were applied in both localities, yet the workmanship of the temples on the seacoast was much cruder, and the ornamentation of the façades much less permanent. Beyond doubt, the same people erected all these buildings but during different stages of culture.

It is possible that Tuloom, on the east shore of Yucatan, was visited or observed from the sea by the expedition of Juan de Grijalva. His chaplain, Juan Dias, speaks [2] enthusiastically of a city facing the sea and having great walls and towers. He compares this city to Seville, and mentions that it was inhabited by a large population. Unfortunately Tuloom has since been visited only by Stephens, who found it in ruins, and by Dr. Howe in 1911, who was forced to limit his stay to two days. Stephens [3] comments on the fresh appearance of the walls, and expresses his belief that Tuloom was inhabited until after the Conquest. This may be the case, because in several architectural features Tuloom varies from cities known to be early.

In regard to the inland cities of Yucatan there are early notices of Chichen Itza and Uxmal that are worthy of consideration. These passages indicate that both cities were fallen from their ancient glory, although still the centers for certain religious rites. There is no evidence that the stone buildings of either city were actually inhabited at the time of the Spanish conquest.

Bishop Diego de Landa,[4] writing about 1566, says of Chichen Itza:

"The elders among the Indians say that they remember to have heard from their ancestors that in that place there once reigned three Lords who were brothers, and who came to that land from the west. And they brought together in these cities a great number of towns and people, and ruled them for some years with justice and in peace . . . that soon they split into factions, so wanton and licentious in their ways, that the people came so greatly to loathe them that they killed them, laid the town waste and themselves dispersed, abandoning the buildings and this beautiful site . . ."

Landa [5] also gives a fairly accurate description and a crude plan of the famous Castillo, and mentions survivals of the ancient religious practices in connection with the sacred cenote.

Stephens [6] quotes at length from the title paper to the land upon which the ruin of Uxmal is situated. It appears that the Regidor received by royal grant certain meadows and places, uncultivated and useless except for pasturage, whereby a great service would be done to God because "it would prevent the Indians in those places from worshiping the devil in the ancient buildings which are there, having in them idols, to which they burn copal, and performing other detestable sacrifices, as they are doing every day notoriously and publicly." This grant having been contested by an Indian claimant, the matter was settled by payment. A later document runs as follows: "In the place called the edifices

---

[1] Le Plongeon, quoted in Salisbury, 1878, pp. 76–84; Stephens, 1843, II, pp. 365–378, 415–417; Holmes, 1895–1897, pp. 57–78.

[2] Dias, Juan, 1838, pp. 11–12.

[3] 1843, II, p. 406.

[4] Landa, 1864, p. 340. Passage translated by Maudslay, 1889–1902, III, pp. 6–7.

[5] 1864, pp. 342–344.

[6] 1843, I, pp. 322–325.

of Uxmal and its lands, the third day of the month of January, 1688, . . . he walked with me all over Uxmal and its buildings, opened and shut some doors, etc." The last statement, in regard to the opening and shutting of doors, seems a mere legal formula to indicate acts of possession. Maya temples, in all probability, never had doors that opened and shut. While these passages prove conclusively that the buildings were still held sacred by the natives, they cast little light upon the question when Uxmal ceased to be a real city.

Of more value in deciding this vexatious question is an account of Uxmal dated a full century earlier (1586). This account,[1] written by one of the companions of Alonzo Ponce, a Franciscan delegate, is so accurate and detailed that it deserves to be given in full. Not all the buildings of the city were examined and described by this early traveler, yet one can recognize with ease each structure taken up, for the descriptions of the outward appearances apply to-day with hardly the change of a word. The curious reader may compare this passage with the excellent modern description of the same buildings by Mr. Holmes.[2]

The earlier description is as follows:

"On the north of the ranchos where the father delegate was lodged, as has been seen, which is about twenty leagues from Merida, to the south of that city, stands a *ku* or *mul* [artificial pyramid], very tall and made by hand. It is very difficult to ascend this by its 150 stone steps, which are very steep and which, from their being very old, are very dilapidated. On the top of this *mul* a large building [House of the Magician] has been built, consisting of two[3] vaulted rooms, made of stone and lime, the stones being carved with great care on the outside. In old times they took the Indians who were to be sacrificed to these rooms, and there they killed them and offered them to the idols. The father delegate went up this *mul* as soon as he arrived there, and this surprised the others greatly, since many others did not dare to go up and could not have done so if they had tried. Close to this *mul* and behind it on the west, there are lower down many other buildings built in the same way with stone and lime and with arches. The stones are carved with wonderful delicacy, some of them having fallen and others badly injured and ruined, while others can still be seen, and there is much in them worth examining. Among these there are four very large and handsome buildings [Nunnery Quadrangle] set in a square form, and in the middle is a square plaza, in which grew a thicket of large and small trees, and even on top of the building there were very large and dense trees growing. The building [South Range of the Nunnery Quadrangle] which faces the south, has on the outside four[4] rooms, and on the inside eight others, all arched with cut stone, and as carefully joined and put together as if very skillful workers of the present had built them. These arches, and all the other old arches which have been found in this province, are not rounded over in the form of a cupola nor like those which are made in Spain, but are tapered as the funnels of chimneys are made when built in the middle of a room, before the flue begins, since

[1] Relacion Breve, 1872, LVIII, pp. 455–461.

[2] 1895–1897, pp. 86–96, and panoramic drawing. Comparison may also be made with Stephens, 1843, I, pp. 166–180; 299–308; 312–318.

[3] It should be noted that the padre ascended this pyramid by the main stairway on the eastern side. He thus could gain access only to the two end rooms of the main temple. The center room of this building has its only doorway on the west, looking out upon the roof of the two-chambered annex. For the names given to these buildings the reader is referred to the table of nomenclature at the end of this volume, p. 252.

[4] Here again the numbering of the rooms is slightly at fault. This building has eight rooms on the outside as well as the inside. There are also two rooms at either end. Such minor inaccuracies need not be wondered at when one considers the luxuriant tropical vegetation which covered everything. The padre properly noted that this building faced outward as well as inward. It served, in fact, as the façade of the entire group of four correlated structures.

both sides draw together little by little and the space between becomes more narrow, till on the top one wall is separated from the other by about two feet and there they place a layer, which extends inwards four or five inches on each side, and over this they place flags or thin flat stones in a level position, and with these the arch is closed, so that there is no key to the arch, but with the great weight of stone and mortar, which is placed on top and which strengthens the sides, the arch is closed and remains fixed and strong. The ends of this arched building are continuous and straight from top to bottom. At the door of each of the rooms of this building on the inside, there are four rings of stone, two on one side and two on the other, — two of them being high up and two lower down and all coming out of the same wall. The Indians say that from these rings those who lived in these buildings hung curtains and portières, and it was to be noticed that no one of these rooms, nor of all the others, which we found there, had any window, small or large. The rooms were therefore rather dark, especially when they were made double, one behind the other, so that even in this, this idolatrous race gave evidence of the darkness and obscurity of the error in which it was enshrouded. The high lintels of all these doors were made of the wood of the chico zapote, which is very strong and slow to decay, as could well be seen, since most of them were whole and sound, although they had been in position from time immemorial, according to the statements of the old Indians. The door jambs were of stone carved with great delicacy.[1] On the façades of the building, both on those which face the plaza or courtyard, as well as on those which face outward, there are many figures of serpents, idols and shields, many screens or latticework, and many other carvings which are very beautiful and fine, especially if one look at them from a distance like a painting of Flanders, and they are all carved from the same kind of stone. In the middle of this building a great arch is made, so that it takes in all the depth of the building, and therefore it is the entrance to the courtyard or the above-mentioned plaza. It would appear that this entrance had been plastered and that on the plaster paintings had been made in blue, red and yellow color, since even now some of them remain and can be seen. Nearly all the rest of the stones had been plastered but not painted.

"The building [Eastern Range of the Nunnery Quadrangle] which stands at the west, behind the previously mentioned mound of sacrifices, was in the best condition and uninjured. It had four doors which opened on to the courtyard or plaza with as many rooms, arched in the same way as the others, and beyond each room was another, so that there were eight in all. Between these four doors, two on one side and two on the other, there was still another door which opened on the patio, and within this was a very large hall, long and broad, with two small rooms on the sides; and beyond this hall there was another — a little smaller, with two other small rooms — one on each side, so that inside of this one door there were six rooms, four small and two large, making, with the other eight, fourteen rooms which this building contained. On the inside façades and ends of this building, there were carved many serpents in stone, and heads of savages and other figures in the manner of shields, and at the four corners (since each building stood by itself and not joined or connected with the other) there were many other carvings cut in the round like a half curve, with tips, which looked like serpent heads, and which stood at half a vara from the rest of the carvings.

"The building on the north [North Range of the Nunnery Quadrangle] is the tallest, and has more carvings and figures of idols, serpents and shields and other very beautiful things about it, but it is very much injured and the most

---

[1] Stephens states, 1843, I, p. 308, that the doorways of the central group of chambers in the Eastern Range are ornamented with sculptures, the only instances of interior decoration at Uxmal. No reproductions of these sculptures are known.

of it has fallen. It has ten [1] doors which open on the plaza and another which opens on the eastern end, and inside each one there are two rooms, and so among them all there are twenty-two rooms in that building made of stone and lime, and arched like the others, but the most of them, especially those inside, have fallen. Before the ten doors above mentioned there has been made a terrace, *paseo*, or walking-place, somewhat broad and open on all sides, to which one ascends from the plaza by steps which are now half in ruins. All this terrace has below it other arched rooms with doors opening on the same plaza, and these are covered and stopped up with stones and earth and with large trees which have grown there.

"The building on the west [Western Range of the Nunnery Quadrangle] is very elegant and beautiful on the outside façade, which looks on the plaza, since serpents made of stone extend over the whole of it so as to enclose it from end to end, making many turns and knots, and they finally end with the head of one of them, on one end of the building, joined with the tail of the other, and the same thing happens on the other end of the building. There are also many figures of men and idols, other figures of monkeys, and of skulls and different kinds of shields — all carved in stone. There are also over the doors of the rooms some statues of stone with maces or sticks in their hands, as if they were mace-bearers, and there are bodies of naked Indians with their *masteles* (which are the old-fashioned loin-clothes of all New Spain, like breeches), by which it is shown that these buildings were built by Indians. In this building are seven doors,[2] of which six open on the patio and the seventh on the end which faces the north, and inside of each door are two rooms, so that there are fourteen rooms in all, arched like the others.

"Besides these four buildings there is on the south of them distant from them about an arquebus shot, another very large building [House of the Governor] built on a *mul* or hill made by hand, with abundance of buttresses on the corners, made of massive carved stones. The ascent of this *mul* is made with difficulty, since the staircase by which the ascent is made is now almost destroyed. The building, which is raised on this *mul*, is of extraordinary sumptuousness and grandeur, and, like the others, very fine and beautiful. It has on its front, which faces the east, many figures and bodies of men and of shields and of forms like the eagles which are found on the arms of the Mexicans, as well as of certain characters and letters which the Maya Indians used in old times — all carved with so great dexterity as surely to excite admiration. The other façade, which faces the west, showed the same carving, although more than half the carved part had fallen. The ends stood firm and whole with their four corners much carved in the round, like those of the other building below. There are in this building fifteen doors, of which eleven face the east, two the west [3] and one each face the north and south, and within these doors there are twenty-four rooms arched like the others. Two of these rooms are in the northern end, and two others in the southern end, while two are in the west front, and all the rest in the eastern front — all made with special accuracy and skill.

"The Indians do not know surely who built these buildings nor when they were built, though some of them did their best in trying to explain the matter, but in doing so showed foolish fancies and dreams, and nothing fitted into the facts or was satisfactory. The truth is that to-day the place is called Uxmal, and an intelligent old Indian declared to the father delegate that, according to what the ancients had said, it was known that it was more than nine hundred

---

[1] According to the plans of Mr. Holmes this building has twelve doors which open on the plaza and one door at each end, making fourteen in all. All the rooms are double.

[2] According to Holmes all seven doors open on the court.

[3] The small chambers under the great arches of this building must have been counted on both the eastern and western face. The central chamber of the eastern front has three doors; apparently only one of these was counted.

years since the buildings were built.   Very beautiful and strong they must have
been in their time, and it is well known from this that many people worked to
build them, as it is clear that the buildings were occupied, and that all about
them was a great population, since this is now evident from the ruins and remains
of many other buildings, which are seen from afar; but the father delegate
did not go to these ruins, since the thicket was very close and dense, and there
was no opportunity to open and clear out a path so as to reach them.   And now
they all serve only as dwellings and nests for bats and swallows and other birds,
whose droppings fill the rooms with an odor more disgusting than delightful.
There is no well there, and the farmers of the vicinity carry their drinking water
from some little pools of rain-water which there are in that region.   It may be
easily suspected that these buildings were depopulated for want of water, although others say that this is not so, but that the inhabitants departed for another country, leaving the wells which were there choked up."

Similar notices of the evident antiquity of Tiho[1] (Merida), Izamal,[2] and
other cities might be quoted.   The complete silence in regard to other important
centers of northern Yucatan, such as Labna and Kabah, tells the same story of
desertion and desolation.[3]

Cortes, during his wonderful march from Vera Cruz to Honduras, seems to
have found none of the stone-built cities of the Usumacinta region inhabited.
The identifying of the village of Teutiercar with Palenque is surely incomplete.
"This village," says Cortes,[4] "is very pretty, and is called Teutiercar by the
natives.   There are in it very handsome mosques or idol-houses, where we took
up our abode, casting out their gods, at which the natives showed no great dis-
content . . ."   There is no reason to suppose that the idol-houses were built
of stone.   Indeed, in speaking of a near-by village of equal importance, he writes: [5]
"Cagoatespan was entirely burnt down, even to the mosques and idol-houses."
Many passages indicate that the idols of this region were carved of wood and
not of stone.   When more permanent structures are suggested, there are no
modern remains to test conclusions.   Bernal Dias[6] thus describes a town on
Lake Peten: "We proceeded towards a place named Tayasal, situated on an
island, the white temples, turrets and houses of which glistened from a distance."
Although this town was a capital of a province, no noteworthy remains are
found on its site.[7]   At the end of the journey, had Quirigua still been the center
of such wealth and power as its monuments bear witness to, Cortes would probably have found food there and would not have been forced to ascend to the
highlands.   As Maudslay[8] points out, the praise that Cortes bestows on the
town of Chacujal, where the present remains are of the most meager sort, is a
pretty sure indication that he visited none of the really great cities.   Yet, had
these great cities still been maintained, he could hardly have missed them all.

Copan was visited in 1576 by Diego Garcia de Palacio,[9] who saw there "ruins
and vestiges of a great population and of superb edifices, of such skill and splendor that it appears that they could never have been built by the natives of that
province."   The natives informed him "that in ancient times there came from

[1] Bienvenida, 1877, p. 71.
[2] Lizana, pp. 3 et seq., and Landa, 1864, p. 32.
[3] Charnay, 1885, p. 329, is evidently in error in
thinking Landa refers to these cities as recently
abandoned.
[4] 1868, p. 36.   See also, Seler, 1895, c, p. 22.
[5] Cortes, 1868, p. 25.

[6] Dias del Castillo, 1803, pp. 117 et seq.
[7] Maler, 1910, p. 169.   For an account of the destruction of Tayasal in 1697 see Villagutierre, 1701,
pp. 481–483.
[8] 1889–1902, II, p. 29.
[9] Gordon, 1896, pp. 47–48.

Yucatan a great Lord, who built these edifices, but at the end of some years returned to his native country, leaving them entirely deserted."

Maler [1] is doubtless right in identifying Yaxchilan with the ruined city discovered by Alzayaga during the Lacandone wars. It is described [2] thus: "They arrived at a place, where it was plain that there must have been once a very ancient city, owing to the great number of stone foundation-walls, and enormous ancient ruins of edifices which they found; which city must have measured more than a league in circumference." The fact that the wild and untaught Lacandone Indians to this day bring offerings of copal to the old ruined temples of Yaxchilan is worthy of note in weighing the evidence above quoted in regard to Uxmal.

Regarding Comalcalco, perhaps the westernmost Maya city of importance, the ruins of which lie on the right bank of the Rio Seco about forty miles west of Frontera, there is also credible evidence of desolation. Charnay [3] attempts to identify this city with the historical Cintla, where Cortes fought his first great battle, but all his arguments are signally refuted by the independent researches of Rovirosa [4] and Brinton.[5] At the coming of the Spaniards the inhabitants of this portion of Tabasco spoke a Maya dialect and probably belonged to the Tzendal tribe. But they had evidently fallen away from the high culture of their ancestors.

Upon the highlands of Guatemala and southern Mexico certain large towns are known to have been occupied at the time of the conquest. Alvarado,[6] in a dispatch to Cortes, describes Utatlan. In this description the Spanish captain pays special attention to fortifications and leaves the bare impression that the town consisted of inflammable buildings crowded together. The ruins found on the site of this old town show small mounds, one of which in Stephens' [7] time still retained part of its stone facing and traces of frescos. There is nothing here, however, fit to be compared with the monumental remains in the lowlands. Indeed, it appears that at no period, historic or prehistoric, did architecture on the plateau reach a high stage of development. But the ceramic and other remains [8] of minor arts prove undoubtable connection at some time with the lowland civilization. Since, however, this open plateau lies upon the frontier of the Maya area and upon the main road for migration north and south, it is but natural that it should be the first to feel the effects of an ascendant neighboring culture. It will be shown that influence from the Nahua cities to the north was marked.

The above and similar notices from the accounts of the first European observers, referring to the various parts of the Maya area, make it pretty evident that when white men set foot on the shores of Mexico the golden age of Maya civilization had long since passed. Not a single great city was maintained in its ancient splendor. It is equally evident that certain phases of the ancient culture, such as referred to religious ideas, were still kept up and that the art of writing and recording time were still understood at least by a portion of the people. The decadent culture was surely a survival of the higher and earlier

[1] 1903, pp. 106–108.
[2] Villagutierre, 1701, p. 362.
[3] 1885, pp. 163–177.
[4] 1897, pp. 16 *et seq.*
[5] 1896, pp. 262–264.
[6] 1838, p. 112.
[7] 1841, II, p. 184; Maudslay, 1889–1902, II, pp. 30–38.
[8] Bulletin 28, pp. 77–121 and 639–670.

one in the same area, and the Maya of historical times were the descendants of the builders of the monuments.

Native Accounts. The conclusions stated in the preceding paragraph are borne out by certain native literary material. This native material is of two kinds, pre-Columbian and post-Columbian; the one written in hieroglyphs and the other in European script but with Maya words.

As is well known, the Indians of Mexico and Central America possessed a compound system of ideographic and phonetic writing and were on the very threshold of the alphabet. The Nahua hieroglyphs of personal and place names are readily solved; first, because the glyphs are so strongly pictographic that the component parts may be recognized; secondly, because the method of writing was maintained after the conquest and in part mastered and described by the Spanish priests. The Mexican place name glyphs or cartouches show an elaboration of the rebus method in which advantage was taken of the position, color and all the possibilities of punning pictures. The system of writing in vogue among the Maya was probably the same, but with a greater degree of conventionalization.

Only three pre-Columbian Maya books or illuminated manuscripts are known to exist. They are known by the names of, 1st, the Dresden Codex;[1] 2d, the Tro-Cortesianus;[2] 3d, the Peresianus.[3] These treat subjects much more complex than many of the Nahua codices and afford no easy beginnings for their elucidation. Thus far it has only been possible to work out their meanings in a general way, except where numbers are concerned. They treat of the calendar and of associated religious ceremonies.[4]

Among the books destroyed by the zealous Spanish priests there are said to have been some on civil and religious history and some on rites, magic and medicine. They seem to have been held in great veneration, and in all probability had either been handed down from former times or else carefully copied from earlier originals. The manuscripts were capable of withstanding wear and tear, being written on both sides of strips of prepared deerskin or stout paper of maguey fiber sized with fine lime.[5] These strips were folded screenwise between boards.

Although most of these invaluable records had been lost, yet educated natives attempted to save something from the wreck of ancient culture by writing down in European script certain digests of chronicles. These make up the so-called Books of Chilan Balam.[6] The different redactions from different towns vary in details, but all agree in carrying back Maya history many hundred years.

Two Maya tribes from the highlands of Guatemala have preserved somewhat similar ancient accounts. Both in the Annals of the Cakchiquels[7] and in

[1] Förstemann, 1880 and 1892.

[2] Codex Troano published by Brasseur de Bourbourg, 1869–70, and the Codex Cortesianus by Rady y Delgado in 1892. For convenience the two parts are usually put together and the numbering of the pages made consecutive as is shown in the Table of Nomenclature at the end of this volume.

[3] Codex Peresianus reproduced by Léon de Rosny, 1887 and 1888. The pagination was probably as shown in the Nomenclature but references are made to the plates as numbered by de Rosny.

[4] By far the most important single contribution to the study of the codices is Förstemann's Commentary on the Dresden Codex.

[5] Important early references to codices are Peter Martyr in Brasseur de Bourbourg, 1869–70, I, pp. 2–3; Aguilar, 1639, p. 88; Alonzo Ponce, Relacion breve, LVIII, p. 392; Landa, 1864, p. 44; Villaguticrre, 1701, pp. 393–394.

[6] Brinton, 1882, b and d.

[7] Brinton, 1885, a.

the Popol Vuh [1] of the Quiché there is a mythological preamble identical in regard to certain place names (Zuiva, Nonoual, etc.) with that which introduces the definite historical sequence in the Books of Chilan Balam. Without doubt a careful study of these three accounts — considerable portions of which are still unpublished — will make possible a valuable outline of the ancient history of the Maya.

Political and Religious Ideas. The Spaniards found the Maya-speaking people divided into many small tribes, each independent of the others and under the direction of its hereditary chief. About twenty such tribes are recorded for the peninsula of Yucatan alone.[2] There was an organized priesthood and a well-marked nobility with strict regard for descent. Probably the priesthood and the nobility were more or less closely joined. Nepotism was apparently the prevailing system under which the chiefs assigned secondary political offices such as that of headman of a village. Practically nothing is known regarding the qualifications of the priests or their divisions into classes. It is clear, however, that the priesthood and the nobility held a monopoly of learning.

It seems necessary to postulate for the period of national greatness a much more centralized form of government than existed at the time of the conquest in order to account for the magnitude and splendor of the temples and public buildings. These could have been built only at great expense of wealth and labor and under a highly organized system of superintendence. Tradition, however, refers to confederacies and not to a united empire. It seems possible that the Maya, like the Greeks, were religiously and artistically a nation while politically a number of sovereign states. Under the powerful stimulus of a religious and artistic awakening of national scope, city after city may have arisen, in influence and wealth. Conquest, colonization, abandonment of old sites and migration to new ones may be inferred from striking similarities in the remains of certain cities. But, whatever the political conditions under which the Maya flourished, there were doubtless intervals of decadent culture due to civil strife. Finally, perhaps a scant century before the coming of Europeans, the entire political fabric fell apart.

Little is known concerning the details of Maya religious ideas. A list of divinities is given by Cogolludo [3] and other information added by Lizana [4] and Landa.[5] There seems to have been belief in a supreme deity without form or substance. Outwardly religion was greatly concerned with the plumed serpent, especially in the personification known as Kukulcan. There were, however, many lesser divinities.[6] Some of these were closely connected with the plumed serpent, and seem to have been merely individual or functional expressions of this more generalised godhead. An idea of the symbolical complications which probably prevailed throughout Maya religion may be gained from the Popol Vuh, the cosmogonic myth of the Quiché.

The ceremonials seem to have been characterized by pageants and processions, by incense burning, and to some extent by human sacrifice. It is clear that human sacrifice never reached among the Maya the horrible extreme that it held among the Nahua in Mexico City. For incense, both rubber and copal

[1] Brasseur de Bourbourg, 1861.
[2] Brinton, 1882, *b*, pp. 25–26.
[3] 1680, pp. 196–198.
[4] 1893, pp. 4–5.
[5] 1864, pp. 144–168; 206–232, etc.
[6] Schellhas, 1904, and Brinton, 1894, *b*, pp. 37–68.

gum, the latter burning with a cloud of white smoke and a pleasant perfume, were used. This feature of incense burning, coupled with the prescribed making of the pottery burners, was purely ritualistic. Consequently it was practiced by the mass of the people and has survived to this day, while the complex theology died with the priests and nobles. Thus Dr. Tozzer[1] has been able to connect the chief ceremonies of the pagan Lacandone Indians of the present day with the yearly renewal of the incense burners, as described by Landa in the sixteenth century.

The insufficient direct knowledge of gods and ceremonies has been pieced out by the study of the ancient codices, and of the sculptured representations on stelae and on temple walls. Apparently astronomy, the understanding of which made possible the calendar, was of first importance. Planets and stars, as well as the sun and moon, were represented by divinities. The forces of nature, such as the rain, the wind, and fertility in its various forms, were conceived as individual or as variant gods. That warfare had its strong religious aspects is seen in the prevalence of bound captives in the sculptured groups and in the use of spears and shields in the ceremonial regalia. Many particulars regarding sacrifice are also to be gathered from these sources. These particulars support the conclusion that human sacrifice played but a minor rôle in the religious practice of the Maya.

Present Population. The present population of the Maya area is largely made up of Indians of the original stock, showing no great amount of race mixture. In many regions tribal distinctions are still clear. The range of culture is remarkable. In northern Yucatan the Maya have long been civilized and under the sway of the Catholic church. Even here, however, they still use their native language in almost entire purity, while a careful observer can detect in the modern religious rites many remnants of ancient custom and superstition. There is no chance that an understanding of the ancient hieroglyphs now exists among any of the Indians here or elsewhere in the area. Along the southern coast of Yucatan, in the territory of Quintana Roo, some of the tribes are at present independent of the Mexican rule. The ruins of Tuloom and others in this region are practically closed to investigation. These wild Indians and the tribes of British Honduras and the Peten department of Guatemala show only a moderate degree of culture.[2] The status of the Lacandone Indians[3] of the Usumacinta Valley is lower yet. Scattered thinly in family groups, these people have indeed reverted to the wild. Although their religion is now of the primitive spiritual guardian type, the ritual still preserves features that point upward to the past, as also does the making of pottery and cloth. On the highlands the Quiché and other tribes live in agricultural communities and possess an interesting decorative art, making excellent textiles. This art seems to be quite distinct from the ancient Maya art.

The estimates of numbers by the Spanish historians were doubtless excessive, but the country is capable of supporting a large population. The Maya-speaking tribes number to-day several hundred thousand. Large tracts of territory that show abundant remains of habitation are now entirely deserted.

Materials Available for Study. Remains of Maya art are for some branches of the subject quite extensive, while for others they are wofully lacking. Tak-

[1] 1907, pp. 106 *et seq.*   [2] Sapper, 1895, *b.*   [3] Tozzer, 1907.

ing all in all, however, there is no reason to complain, because the mass of material preserved for study is probably greater than that which has survived from the great art of Greece. The remains may be considered under two heads: first, architecture; second, minor arts.

The entire Maya area is dotted with groups of structures, great and small, some admirably preserved, others ruined beyond repair. Some of these structures were temples, while others may have been for secular use. Probably more domestic architecture has all passed away. Some of the complicated structures may have been chiefs' palaces, but it is more probable that they resembled monasteries. The church and state were one. These structures still show much of the original embellishment in stone carving, wood carving, frescos and stucco work.

The minor arts include ceramics, textiles — most of the data on which must be taken second hand from the sculptures — ornaments carved in semi-precious stones, a little metal work, and, most noteworthy of all, the ancient illuminated manuscripts.

Previous Studies. Recent study in the field of Maya culture has been directed mostly towards the elucidation of the codices and the decipherment of the hieroglyphic inscriptions. As a result of the labors of Bowditch, Goodman and Thomas, the calendar system has been worked out in many of its finer details, while Förstemann, Seler and Schellhas have collected much data upon the nature of the gods and the ceremonies. The facts brought out by these investigators are of great value to the student of art, because they furnish a basis for the chronological sequence of forms and for the interpretation of designs and sculptures.

Descriptions of the buildings and other monuments may be gleaned from early and modern writings. The scanty notices of the Spanish conquerors have already been considered. The first travelers to draw the attention of the world to the wonderful structures of Central America were Stephens and Catherwood. The detailed accounts of the former and the accurate drawings of the latter are still of the greatest service to the student. The drawings of Waldeck are beautiful but inaccurate. The voluminous writings of Brasseur de Bourbourg contain many valuable references, but most of the theories and conclusions are untenable. The same may be said of the works of Le Plongeon. The era of enthusiastic travelers was followed by that of trained observers. Holmes,[1] in particular, has explained the process of Maya construction, and prepared admirable panoramic views of Chichen Itza, Uxmal and Palenque. For overshadowing importance, however, first place must be given to Maudslay's[2] elaborate publication. In the four volumes of plates are figured, both by photographic reproduction and by clear drawings, the most important sculptures and buildings of Copan, Quirigua, Tikal, Yaxchilan, Palenque and Chichen Itza. The text, however, gives little more than brief descriptions of the monuments, with hardly any stylistic comparison, the author apparently being content to let his splendid illustrations speak for themselves. With these deserve to be mentioned the accounts of explorations at Copan and along the Uloa River by Gordon, and explorations in Yucatan and in the Valley of the Usumacinta by Maler, as well as the more popular narratives of Charnay. All of the latter works deal only ob-

[1] 1895–1897.   [2] 1889–1902.

jectively with Maya art, and are in reality hardly more than storehouses of selected material. Unselected material of equal value may be found in the collections of photographs and maps which constitute the field reports of various expeditions of the Peabody Museum. Such reports include much unpublished material, as, for instance, Thompson's explorations of Labna, Kabah and other sites in northern Yucatan. Miss Breton's reproduction[1] of the frescos of Chichen Itza in color is of the greatest value, because it preserves a splendid example of a kind of perishable art that has survived in few places, and that is peculiar in giving intimate glimpses of the ordinary life of the people. It is to be hoped that this excellent work may soon be published to the world.

Among institutions who have supported field work in the Maya area, first place must be accorded to the Peabody Museum which has sent out many expeditions both to explore and to excavate. The results are seen in the splendid collections in this museum and in the many publications by Thompson, Gordon, Maler and Tozzer, mostly appearing in the Memoirs. Dr. Seler[2] conducted the only systematic field work that has taken place on the highlands of Guatemala. Excavations were also made by Maudslay, Dieseldorff and others.

Special notice must be given Dr. Gordon's paper on the Serpent Motive in the Ancient Art of Central America and Mexico,[3] because this is the only attempt at a general consideration that has been made.

The modern ethnology of Maya-speaking tribes has been covered by Stoll,[4] Starr,[5] Tozzer,[6] and Sapper.[7] In general, however, the survivals of the ancient art are apparently slight, and little has been done in collecting myths. Maya art is on a much higher scale than any art in America except possibly the textile art of Peru. It deserves earnest study for the contributions which it is able to make to comparative religion and to comparative art.

[1] A complete reproduction of these paintings is on exhibition in the Peabody Museum.
[2] 1901, c.   [3] 1905.   [4] 1889.   [5] 1900–1904.   [6] 1907.   [7] 1905.

GENERAL CONSIDERATION OF MAYA ART

THE influence of a national religion upon a national art was never more unmistakable than in the case of the Maya. But, indeed, it is universally important. Religion is able to furnish the deepest and truest inspiration which the human mind is capable of receiving. Being ideal in itself, it develops the imagination so that this in turn finds secret meanings in common things. Moreover religion, as a communal element in the life of the nation, turns the attention of all artists to a common purpose. Through this focusing of the attention religion leads inevitably to an intensive rather than a diffuse development of art. But once this intensive development has exhausted the possibilities of the established ideas, then religion throws its powerful influence against further disorganizing change. Thus religion enriches art and makes it permanent.

In the case of the Maya the art might almost be termed the concrete expression of the religion, since all the great monuments were apparently connected with religious practices and no minor object was too humble to receive decorations with religious significance. Clearly this wonderful art rose under the communal inspiration of a great religious awakening and was conserved by the persistence of ritual. Doubtless the art reacted strongly upon the religion which gave it birth, filling that religion with symbolism and imagery. The two worked hand in hand. The spreading of the religion meant a spreading of the art, and the graphic representations of the art rendered the religion intelligible. It was probably through the objective ritual on the one hand and the objective art on the other, that the religion of the Maya was enabled to leap the bounds of language and impress itself so strongly upon the Nahua and Zapotecan peoples.

The student finds in the ancient masterpieces of Yucatan and Central America a fine technique and an admirable artistic sense largely given over to the expression of barbarous religious concepts. Upon the scale of development the art is many points higher than the religion, in spite of the close connection between them. At first glance too exotic and unique to be compared with the art of the Old World, nevertheless Maya art furnishes upon examination many analogies to the early products of the classic Mediterranean lands. Indeed upon technological grounds — such as the knowledge displayed of foreshortening, composition and design — Maya art may be placed in advance of the art of Assyria and Egypt and only below that of Greece in the list of great national achievements.

The representation of the body of man himself was not all-important to the Maya as to the Greeks, for a good and sufficient reason, although it received a very considerable share of attention. The Greeks conceived and represented their divinites and mythical heroes in human form. Hence they idealized this form till it embodied the finest possible conception of strength and grace. Now the gods and culture heroes of the Maya had fundamentally the physical characteristics of reptiles, birds and lower mammals, or were, at best, grotesque figures of composite origin. However, these brute gods, as we shall see, were often more or less humanized, resembling in a general way the half-animal, half-human gods of Egypt and Assyria. Human beings appear only in the mundane guise of priests, worshipers, rulers, warriors, and captives. The strange subject matter of Maya art should not militate against its real artistic merits, for the finest products of an inspired imagination are always worthy of respectful study.

The principal methods employed by the Maya in the graphic and plastic arts differed little from those of classic lands. Delineation and painting upon a variety of substances including paper and plaster, carving in wood and stone and modeling in clay and stucco were widely practiced. Terra cotta figurines made from moulds are very common. Metal working was highly developed as far as the technical processes are concerned, but the scarcity of materials was such that only ornaments were commonly made. The stones used in the temples and monuments were cut and carved with stone implements. The Maya might have accomplished greater wonders if they had had fine-grained marble instead of coarse and uneven limestone, and iron or bronze chisels instead of stone knives.

In Maya plastic art the three usual divisions may be made; namely, low relief, high relief and full round. Much of the high relief, however, shows no more modeling than does the low relief, the figures being simply blocked out in high relief, but still retaining a comparatively flat outer surface. Sometimes high relief shows flat sculpture upon two or more planes. Fine examples of blocked-out high relief of these two sorts are found at Copan and Yaxchilan. But high relief with excellent modeling also occurs, particularly in the stucco work of Palenque. Sculpture in the full round reaches its highest development at Copan, probably because the stone found there was very easy to work. There may have been another reason. The habit of representing faces and bodies in front view seems to lead directly to the full round treatment, especially of the face. Profile figures, on the other hand, appear best in low relief. At Copan the majority of figures are presented in front view, and there is a steady progression from low relief, through high relief, to the exact reproduction of the human body. At Quirigua and Piedras Negras, where other front-view figures occur, the greater part of the body is shown in low relief, but the face is generally carved in high relief or in the natural roundness. The full round method of representation is also accorded to figures seated in a niche that occur at the two cities just referred to. But low relief is by far the most common mode of sculpture in wood, stone and stucco, and may be studied to advantage in all the principal Maya cities.

Homogeneity of Maya Art. The homogeneity of Maya art, in spite of the many necessary differences due to time and place, will prove itself as the description proceeds. In the following pages the aim will be to give a general explanation of the most widespread phenomena. Illustrations on particular points will be taken from all parts of the area, and from both major and minor arts. For instance, the pottery decoration of the uplands will show features similar to the architectural decoration of the lowlands, or the drawings of gods in the codices will agree with stone and stucco figures on monoliths and temple walls.

Simply by way of illustration two or three series of particular similarities that cover nearly the entire Maya area may be given in detail. Fig. 1 presents a number of faces of diverse forms. Most are strikingly grotesque, and all possess the curious feature of a cruller-like ornament over the nose. This ornament is adventitious and unnatural, and, although apparently insignificant, yet it furnishes the strongest kind of proof of cultural unity, because it is in the nature

FIG. 1. — Heads with curled nose ornament: a, Palenque; b, Copan; c, Quen Santo; d, Labna; e, Coban; f, Panzamala.

of an unconscious admission. The first specimen, a, is a representation of the so-called sun shield on the tablet of the Temple of the Sun at Palenque; b, is a somewhat similar design from Copan. It is carved upon a block of stone with a tenon at the back so that it could be set into a temple wall. Shields having decorative faces of the same general type as these are represented as worn on the left arms of many of the warlike figures on the monuments. Noteworthy examples occur at Tikal, lintel of Temple II,[1] Naranjo, Stela 21,[2] and Yaxchilan, Stela 11.[3] The same device appears on faces in other situations, that may or

[1] Maudslay, 1889–1902, III, pl. 73.   [2] Maler, 1908, b, pl. 35.   [3] Maler, 1903, pl. 74.

may not represent the same thing. In *c* we have a simple face crudely carved upon a rectangular block of stone. This object was found by Dr. Seler at Quen Santo on the highlands of western Guatemala.[1] Object *d* comes from the opposite side of the Maya area: it is a corner-stone from the ruins of Labna in northern Yucatan. A clay figurine (Plate 17, fig. 12) from the Island of Jaina near Campeche likewise has a face with the twisted nose ornament incised or stamped upon it. Reverting again to the distant highlands, we see in *e* a remarkable

vase in the collection of Mr. E. P. Dieseldorff of Coban,[2] with applied ornament in the form of an excellently modeled face. This vase was excavated from ruins near Coban. The last specimen, *f*, comes from Panzamala,[3] some distance east of Coban. Other examples of this peculiar feature might be given.[4] Most, if not all the faces which

FIG. 2. — Plant motive showing flowers and leaves: *a*, Chichen Itza; *b*, Palenque; *c*, Madrid Stela.

have been described probably represent some form of the Sun God. This point will be discussed later.

Other examples of widespread similarities may be given to include certain important cities where the face with the twisted nose ornament is not known to occur. The representation of plants is rarely seen in Maya art, except in a very peculiar motive that Maudslay[5] has worked out rather fully and which he calls the water-plant motive. This water plant as used in decorative bands is shown in Fig. 2, *a* and *b*, while *c* offers a more realistic presentation from the so-called Madrid Stela.[6] The design frequently occurs on pottery. The flower has somewhat the appearance of the water lily, and in many instances a fish is shown seemingly in the act of feeding upon the petals. Examples of the fish and water-plant design present much stronger proof of culture affinity among the cities where they occur than do the simple water-plant forms, for designs analogous to the latter are universal, whereas the association of fish and flower is very unusual. In Fig. 3 are given examples, taken from different parts of the Maya area, that illustrate this peculiar motive. It occurs in full vigor at Copan, Palenque and Chichen Itza, as well as at many other sites, both on the highlands and lowlands. Its exact meaning is somewhat difficult to determine, but it apparently carries the idea of water. It is attached as an ornamental detail to the bodies of animals and to the heads of divinities that are probably asso-

[1] Seler, 1901, *c*, p. 112.
[2] Seler, p. 1901, *c*, p. 178.
[3] Seler, 1901, *c*, p. 179.
[4] For instance, the feature seems to occur on a head from Bellote on the coast of Tabasco, Char-

nay, 1885, p. 162, and on a vase from San Salvador, Seler, 1901, *c*, pp. 180–181.
[5] 1889–1902, IV, pp. 37–38 and pl. 93.
[6] Léon de Rosny, 1882, pl. 2.

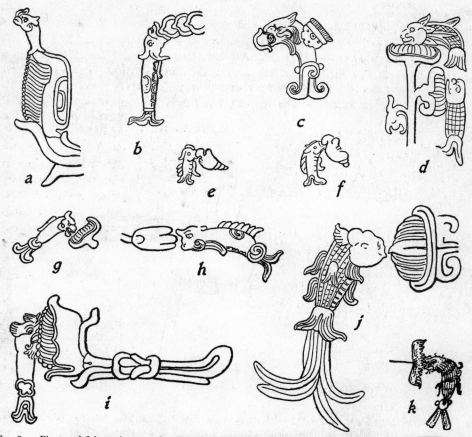

FIG. 3. — Plant and fish motive: *a* and *i*, Copan; *b*, *e*, *f* and *h*, Palenque; *c*, Chajcar; *d* and *j*, Chichen Itza; *g*, Ixkun; *k*, Nebaj.

ciated with water. Fig. 4, from the Dresden Codex, represents one of the Maya gods — known as God B or the Long-nosed God — wading into the water and

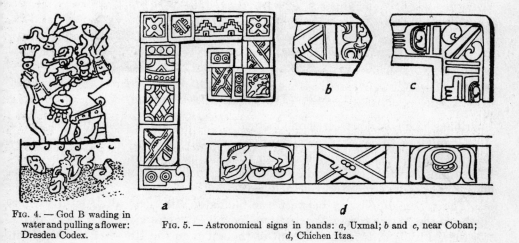

FIG. 4. — God B wading in water and pulling a flower: Dresden Codex.

FIG. 5. — Astronomical signs in bands: *a*, Uxmal; *b* and *c*, near Coban; *d*, Chichen Itza.

pulling up a water plant. Fish and shells are shown in the water, the lower depths of which are colored green.

The planets and other astronomical bodies are generally represented by simple oblong hieroglyphs arranged in strips or bands. These signs occur as details of ornamentation on the dress of human figures, particularly on the belts, as

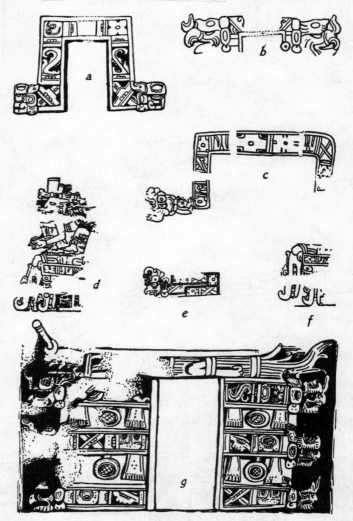

Fig. 6. — Astronomical signs combined with bird and animal heads: *a*, Quirigua; *b*, Copan; *c*, *d*, and *f*, Codex Peresianus; *e*, Dresden Codex; *g*, Naranjo.

markings upon various ceremonial objects and upon the elongated bodies of monstrous creatures, as general motives of architectural enrichment, as well as in connection with many gods and with intricate astronomical calculations. The forms written in the codices are similar to those carved upon the monuments, but show a more cursive delineation.

The general similarity between the bands of astronomical signs in various parts of the Maya area is brought out by the examples given in Figs. 5 and 6. Of these Fig. 5, *a*, is from the front of the annex to the House of the Magician at Uxmal, *b* and *c* are pottery fragments from the neighborhood of Coban on the highlands of Guatemala, and *c* is from the eastern façade of the Monjas at Chichen Itza.

Fig. 6 presents a second series showing the astronomical signs combined with birds' heads and upon seats or thrones across which are bound grotesque animals. A very close parallel is evidenced in *a* and *c*, the first from the back of a monolith at Quirigua, the second from the Peresianus Codex. In neither of these specimens is the head very distinct. Often bands of astronomical signs are terminated by birds' heads, as may be seen from *b* on the back of Stela H at Copan, *e* in the Dresden Codex and *g*, the base of the splendidly carved Stela 32 at Naranjo. The latter sculpture really represents an elaborate throne, but the human figure seated upon it is so badly mutilated that it was not reproduced in the drawing. Across the top of this throne is a grotesque animal trussed and bound. The same sort of thing is represented by drawings in the Peresianus Codex (*d* and *f*), likewise connected with astronomical signs. This grotesque animal will be discussed more fully in a later section, where many other objects combined with star symbols will come up for consideration. The interpretation of the particular signs will also be postponed.

As stated, the only reason for giving the preceding examples at this time is simply to remove all possible doubt concerning the homogeneity of the ancient art within the limits ascribed to the Maya culture. This is seen in important things as well as in the relatively unimportant ones just given. The latter, however,

FIG. 7. — Detail showing kneeling worshiper: Yaxchilan.

have the unusual quality of covering not only all the geographical range but most of the chronological range as well.

THE HUMAN FORM

An easy understanding of Maya art may be had by starting with subjects least opposed to the familiar ones of the Old World and proceeding thence into the labyrinth of fantastic conceptions peculiar to the New World.

Subjects Represented. The representation of the human figure seldom served as an end in itself. The men and women shown in the sculptures are seemingly engaged in religious ceremonies and acts of adoration. The divinities which they worshiped are more or less clearly indicated. As a rule, the human figures are those of priests or warriors. But even in the case of the latter the religious motive is rarely absent and human beings free from the artistic domination of gods of lower nature. There are, however, a number of sculptures which apparently memorialize success in war, and in these none of the usual religious paraphernalia appears.

An example of adoration is seen in Fig. 7 that reproduces part of the beautifully carved but badly broken Stela 7 at Yaxchilan. This kneeling worshiper wears a loose cloak over the shoulders, a light garment that covers the thighs and a rather elaborate headdress in the form of a somewhat grotesque animal head. His face is turned upward and his hands are lifted to receive whatever the being above may care to bestow. From a pair of hands above him, that belong to a standing figure so badly shattered that it cannot be reproduced, descend certain objects that may indicate an answering of his prayer. Immediately above the face of the kneeling figure is a sign resembling that for corn or maize, lower down is the symbol of the sun, while the scroll-work of small circles may represent rain or, perhaps, fruitfulness. This tableau, then, might be considered to represent a prayer for the corn crop and the sun and rain most necessary for its welfare. Such an interpretation would be in keeping with the principles of sympathetic magic according to which the thing desired is usually represented either pictographically or dramatically.

FIG. 8.—A presiding priest: Palenque.

Very often a human figure holds in his arms or hands one or more ceremonial objects. In the next drawing (Fig. 8) a man in simple attire stands upon the back of a grotesque being and supports upon his uplifted palms a manikin. He is one of two priest-like figures sculptured on the justly famous tablet of the Temple of the Sun at Palenque.[1] Many other examples of human beings engaged in religious services will be given in other places.

Many sculptures show human beings seated upon thrones before which are standing or kneeling worshipers. These seated persons may represent rulers or high priests who were worshiped as the embodiments of gods. The divinities themselves were of a low animal order. But the government as well as the religion of the Maya was probably of totemic origin, and so might be expected to emphasize close relationships between the temporal and spiritual rulers and the animal gods. These seated figures frequently hold the same ceremonial objects as the standing ones, while in other

FIG. 9. — Man wearing mask: Yaxchilan.

cases the ceremonial objects are held aloft by attendants. The human overlord as the agent of the god is clearly shown on Stela 11 at Yaxchilan.[2] On this monument is a standing human figure wearing the mask of a grotesque god (see Fig. 9 for the mask) who threatens with his baton several bound captives kneeling before him.

    [1] Maudslay, 1889–1902, IV, pl. 88.   [2] Maler, 1903, pl. 74.

A sculpture that seems to refer only to war and conquest is reproduced in Fig. 10. This is Lintel 12 at Yaxchilan. In the center is a chief with spear and shield and in full regalia. The head of a slain enemy hangs hair down from his breast, and cross bones decorate his dress. At the left is one of his assistants, likewise armed. Kneeling on the ground are four captives bound with rope. Upon the bodies of these captives are glyphs which may record their names and the date of their capture. At the upper part of the stone are two bands of glyphs, left blank in the drawing, which possibly contain the narrative of the

Fig. 10. — Memorial of conquest: Lintel 12, Yaxchilan.

victory or other information of historical interest. Several analogous sculptures might be described if space warranted.

It is exceedingly doubtful whether any sculptures were seriously intended as portraits of individual chiefs or priests. To be sure, there are a number of face types depending upon variation in form of features and in expression. Usually one type prevails in each city. On the stelae of Quirigua several types are to be seen, but the degree of individualism is slight. Possibly, as was the case in Egypt, the faces of portrait statues varied slightly, while individualism was expressed in dress, ornament or inscription.

The general physiognomy represented on Maya sculptures differs widely from the accepted European types of beauty. It seems pretty clear that artificial flattening of the head was practiced and that straightened foreheads and retreating chins were held to be marks of beauty. The nose is usually prominent and of a somewhat Hebraic cast. The lower lip is protruding and pendulous and the mouth kept slightly open. / This type is not characteristic of the modern Maya Indians, who, however, do not retain the ancient practice of deformation. Hamy [1] compares the faces carved at Palenque with those of two Mexican microcephalic freaks on exhibition in Europe about 1850. The striking resemblance he notes seems to be purely the result of chance. Besides cranial deformation other modifications of the natural form were in vogue. Filed teeth and teeth inlaid with jade and other minerals have been found in a number of burial sites, as well as cumbersome nose and ear plugs.

In regard to evidence of style which may be associated with particular sculptors, it is by no means lacking. There is a widely advocated theory that primitive art is purely communal. To be sure, the first artists did not ordinarily sign their works, but strict regard for ownership of designs or of songs is no rare thing among primitive people. What reason is there to hold that artistic genius among the Maya was not essentially the same as in our own land, simply because the social organization of the nation and the subject matter furnished by the religion are different? Real contributions to human culture are always referable to individuals, and the fact that the records are lost matters not. But the individual lives and works within the mode of his nation and his epoch. He adds something of his own to art, theology or what not, and that something is more noticeable in present view than in retrospect. Upon analysis that something frequently resolves itself into a new imaginative reconciliation of previously known elements. Rarely, indeed, the individual may strike back to real origins and make a radical departure from traditional habits of thought and expression. The works of the most flagrant individualist of to-day will to-morrow fall into an inevitable scheme of evolution. It is reasonable to suppose that each of the various groups into which the stelae of Copan may be divided was the work of a single sculptor, or of a school under the direction of a single artist. Each group shows, as we shall see, a conscious and typical arrangement of common elements. But through all the groups runs a thread of change and development of which the artists themselves may well have been entirely unconscious, except in its more obvious features.

Poses and Groupings. The poses as exemplified on the monolithic monuments, commonly called stelae, most of which present a single human figure, or a single figure on the front and another on the back, will be taken up first. Then the more unusual poses and the complex groupings on the monuments and elsewhere will be briefly considered.

In the case of the Copan stelae the pose is practically uniform throughout the long series. The priest, chief, or whoever it is that is represented, stands in an erect attitude, with his heels together, and holds an object called the Ceremonial Bar against his breast. The body shows perfect bilateral symmetry. Certain changes in the pose, which, in a later section, will be co-ordinated with changes in manner of carving to establish in part the chronological sequence of the monuments, may here be mentioned. In the earliest stelae the upper arms lie close to the side and the forearms rise almost vertically. In the later stelae the forearms are almost horizontal. Again, on the greater number of the monuments, the feet are represented as turned directly outward, forming a straight

[1] 1875.

angle. But at the end of what we will call the Archaic Period, the sculptors began to take advantage of the increased relief, furnished by the heavy apron, to turn the feet inwards, till in the latest examples the pose became almost natural. Some of these stelae are reproduced in Plates 18 and 19.

On a few of the stelae at Quirigua the feet are likewise set at less than a straight angle. It may be noted that in general the stelae of Quirigua are later than those of Copan, but that they show a reversion to less laborious construction. The poses are much the same, though on some of the monuments a manikin figure on a staff, commonly called the Manikin Scepter, replaces the Ceremonial Bar. This substitution breaks up the bilateral symmetry, since the staff is held diagonally across the body and not horizontally.

As before stated, low relief practically necessitates the profile view of the face. Many stelae at Tikal, Naranjo, etc. (Plate 21, figs. 1–4; Plate 24, figs. 1–3 and Plate 25, figs. 1–2) show the same pose as those of Copan except that the face is turned in profile. With the feet turned straight out this pose is an awkward one. Often, however, the body appears in profile as well as the face (Plate 22, fig. 1). In such cases the Ceremonial Bar is replaced by other ceremonial objects. Frequently a staff or scepter is held before the face with one hand, while the other holds a decorated pouch at the side. Sometimes spear and shield replace the ceremonial objects. The feet are either one behind the other, as though the person were taking a short step, or else the outer foot covers and conceals the inner one. The bodies are represented as erect and motionless.

In a few instances two standing figures are brought face to face with each other, as on Stela 11 at Yaxchilan.[1] More often a warlike figure stands above or beside a bound captive. In other cases where two persons are shown one is seated while the other stands.

Seated figures are rather common on stelae in the Peten and Usumacinta cities. The most important type of monument, especially at Piedras Negras, shows a figure in high relief seated cross-legged in a niche with the hands upon the knees. There seems little doubt but that the niche really represents a canopied throne. Such a throne in profile with a seated personage is seen on Stela 5[2] at this city. As a rule, however, the royal thrones, while richly upholstered, do not have canopies. It is worthy of note that on most of the stelae presenting a tableau of several persons, the interest centers in a seated figure. A good example of this is the remarkable Stela 12[3] at Piedras Negras on which a number of individuals, including priests or warriors, and bound captives are arrayed before a seated being that may represent either a chief or a divinity, but more probably the former.

As to the disposition of the legs in seated poses, there is considerable variety. Usually they are crossed Turkish fashion and represented either in front or side views. Sometimes only one leg is drawn up, while the other extends downward, the result being a free, graceful pose. Seated figures are also shown with both feet on the ground in the usual attitude. But when this method of sitting is represented in front view the knees are bent outward and the heels raised, as on Stela 2 at Cankuen.[4]

[1] Maler, 1903, pl. 74, fig. 2.
[2] Maler, 1901, pl. 15, fig. 2.
[3] Maler, 1901, pl. 21.
[4] Maler, 1908, a, pl. 12, fig. 2.

Poses which show motion are rather rare on the stelae. Of course the mere act of offering is common enough. One monument at San Juan de Motul [1] apparently shows two heavily dressed beings in the act of dancing. The knees are turned outward and the heels are raised so that the figures seem to stand on tiptoe in a somewhat squatting attitude. But it is probable that this peculiar pose is intended to represent sitting rather than dancing, as indicated by the

Fig. 11. — Atlantean figures on pilasters: Chichen Itza.

Cankuen stela referred to above and by the principal figure on the lintel of Temple IV at Tikal.[2] The sprinkling of maize or other small grains upon the ground is represented on Stela 13 at Piedras Negras (Plate 25, fig. 3). Various gesticulations are clearly shown on Stela 2 [3] of La Mar. Here the poses exhibit unusual freedom.

The poses and groupings on sculptured lintels, panels, steps, etc., show so much variety that it seems almost impossible to treat them in a general way. At Copan there are a number of sculptures which show small seated figures arranged in rows. The best examples are Altar Q [4] and the interior step of Temple 11.[5] The pose is slightly different in each case, the variety being more marked upon the last-mentioned monument.

Most of the lintels of Yaxchilan show two figures facing each other, one with the body in front view and the face in profile and the other with both body and face in profile. As a rule, one figure is somewhat subordinated to the other. A number of lintels show more than two figures each, as, for instance, Lintel 12, which has already been presented (Fig. 9) as an example of a memorial of conquest. The panels and tablets of Palenque exhibit a great variety of grouping, but no remarkable departures from the poses of other cities. The processional arrangement of human figures so highly developed at Chichen Itza [6] is un-Maya and belongs, as we shall see, to the very latest period of Maya art, when influence from the highlands of Mexico had set in strongly. In these representations there is crude delineation, but often an admirable sense of action. Muscular effort also appears in the strained poses of the small atlantean figures carved on columns and door jambs at this city (Fig. 11).

Fig. 12. — Warrior in fresco paintings: Chichen Itza.

In the codices and frescos action is usually indicated, and the body is represented in many positions. Warriors depicted on the walls of the inner chamber of the Temple of the Jaguars at Chichen Itza are especially active, as may be seen from the one reproduced in Fig. 12. A portion of this fresco represents a spirited battle with much lifelike detail. Part of page 60 of the Dresden Codex

[1] Maler, 1910, pl. 45.
[2] Maudslay, 1889–1902, III, pl. 78. For notation see Table of Nomenclature, p. 256.
[3] Maler, 1903, pl. 36.
[4] Maudslay, 1889–1902, I, pl. 92.
[5] Maudslay, 1889–1902, I, pl. 8.
[6] Maudslay, 1889–1902, III, pls. 44 et seq.

is reproduced in Fig. 13, from which an idea of the more complicated poses and groupings in this wonderful manuscript may be obtained. Other illustrations of the points so far covered will appear as the discussion proceeds.

Foreshortening and Perspective. As may be gathered from the foregoing description of poses and groupings, the Maya had a considerable but by no means complete mastery of the technical difficulties of representing objects with three dimensions upon a surface with only two. High and low relief form something of a transition for this process. In foreshortening they greatly excelled the Egyptians and Assyrians, since they became sufficiently skilled to draw the entire body in pure profile, besides representing the legs and feet with ease and precision in a variety of sitting and

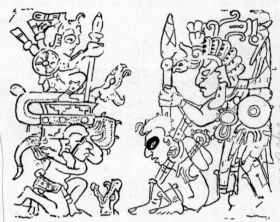

FIG. 13. — Example of complicated grouping: Dresden Codex.

reclining positions. The real difficulty in the development of perspective is that the artist's previous knowledge of the object interferes with his visual impressions. He cannot let the hand draw the picture as the eye sees it. He knows that a man possesses two arms and so feels constrained always to draw two arms in plain view. The Maya artists established a sort of compromise between appearance and reality. When they could not find a way to correct the drawing, they at least succeeded by graceful and pleasing treatment in distracting attention from the errors in delineation. The historical development of skill in foreshortening will be demonstrated in another section. Only the more perfect phases will be treated here.

FIG. 14. — Seated figure in pure profile: Palenque.

The mastery of the pure profile may be studied to advantage at Palenque. A good example from this city is given in Fig. 14, which represents a seated individual with very little clothing to conceal the body. It will be noted that the upper part of the breast is drawn in profile, as well as the head and legs, and that the more distant arm does not appear in the picture.

When, however, the body was covered with heavy drapery or elaborate ornaments, the difficulties of foreshortening all the details were sometimes beyond the skill of the artists, especially when the profile pose was adopted. This ineffectiveness is best seen in the braided breast ornaments which seem to project outwards when they should lie flat on the breast. Examples may be seen in the right-hand priestly figure of the tablet of the Foliated Cross at Palenque [1] and in the drawing which Maler [2] gives of part of the incised tablet at Xupa. In all fairness to the Maya sculptors it must be stated that the difficulty with this detail seems to have been overcome on other monuments at Palenque.

[1] Maudslay, 1889–1902, IV, pl. 81.   [2] 1903, p. 21.

A change in pose of an exact 90 degrees, that is, from front view to profile or *vice versa*, was for the most part readily accomplished. Among the complicating details of the more elaborate dresses worn by human beings were small heads, probably of stone, with appendages of one sort or another. These heads were placed on the breast and on the middle and sides of the girdle. When the body was in front view, the head on the breast and the one on the front of the

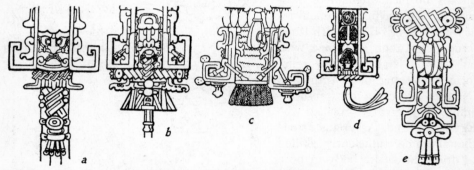

Fig. 15. — Elaborated aprons on the monuments: *a*, Copan; *b*, Quirigua; *c*, Ixkun; *d*, Tikal; *e*, Palenque.

girdle were likewise drawn in the full face, while those at the sides of the girdle were presented in profile view. When the pose was shifted to the profile, the small heads on the breast and on the front of the girdle were likewise shifted into the profile. One of the heads at the side of the girdle was thrown into the front view, and the other disappeared behind the body. Other objects, such as disk-shaped and bar-shaped breast ornaments, aprons, shields, etc., that appeared

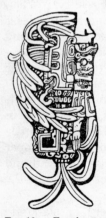

entire in front view were ordinarily divided vertically in halves, and only the nearer half drawn when the pose was turned in another direction. The circle seems never to have been foreshortened into an ellipse, but instead was divided vertically as above. The modifications in circular breast ornaments when viewed from the side are easily seen on some of the lintels of Yaxchilan which show both profile and front-view figures with the same style of dress.[1] Shields in half view are worn by the sculptured warriors of the Temple of the Jaguars at Chichen Itza.[2]

Fig. 15 presents a series of elaborate aprons of a wide-spread type. There is a grotesque face in the middle and a fret at each side. The latter, as we shall see, is really a highly modified serpent head. At the top are usually shell pendants, in groups of three, which project out over the rest of the apron. At the bottom are plumes, braided strips and

Fig. 16. — Foreshortening of feathers: Tikal.

tassels. Aprons of this sort are occasionally represented on human beings in side view, and in these cases the face in the center becomes converted into a profile face. The adjacent fret is retained without change, and the more distant one disappears from view. Fig. 16 represents an object in side view, the lower part being very similar to the aprons we have just examined. This

[1] See, for instance, Lintels 2 and 3 (Maler, 1903, pls. 47 and 48).

[2] Maudslay, 1889–1902, III, pls. 38, 49 and 50.

object is attached to the headdress and hangs down at the back of a human figure (Plate 22, fig. 1). The fret is readily seen, and the face in profile in front of it can be made out after a little study. Higher up appears the group of three shell pendants. But the feathers that issue from the side of this object are splendidly foreshortened by the use of sweeping curves. The front view of feather projections on similar objects attached to headdresses may be examined

FIG. 17. — Low relief composition: Lintel 8, Yaxchilan.

for comparison on Lintels 1, 2, 3, 5, 33, etc.,[1] at Yaxchilan and Lintel 2[2] at Piedras Negras.

The human body is seldom represented in what might be called quarter-view, but there are a few interesting departures from the prevailing front and profile studies that deserve note. One of these is seen in the left-hand person on Lintel 8 at Yaxchilan (Fig. 17). This sculpture pictures two warriors bending over and grasping two partially fallen captives. The attitudes are all excep-tionally free, but the figure to which special attention has been called has few parallels in this respect. The face is in profile, but the rest of the body is twisted almost but not quite into front view. One foot is partially raised from the ground. Altogether the drawing shows with considerable success a

[1] Maler, 1903, pls. 46–48 and 63.   [2] Maler, 1901, pl. 31.

pose having many difficulties. The carving on this lintel is, however, in such low relief that it appears to be hardly more than an incised sketch.

On Stela 13 at Piedras Negras (Plate 25, fig. 3) is carved a superb figure apparently in the act of scattering grains of some sort. The shoulders in this instance are likewise twisted around, but not to so great an extent as in the drawing we have just examined. Other representations of the human body in more or less twisted attitudes are seen on the stucco panels of House D of the Palace at Palenque.[1]

FIG. 18. — Kneeling figures: Stela 1, La Mar.

The manipulation of drapery does not appear to any great extent in Maya art. As a rule, the dresses of both male and female subjects are covered with stiff and inflexible ornament. Some of the crouching women at Yaxchilan[2] have the lower borders of their dresses extended over the ground in a rather picturesque manner. Two simply draped persons are presented in Fig. 18. The folds of the garments are represented by incised lines. Better examples yet may be seen on Stela 1 at Cankuen (Plate 25, fig. 6) and on Stela 7 at Yaxchilan (Fig. 7). But the highest development of drapery in the Maya area occurs at Palenque. One of the most interesting examples is given in Fig. 19. The apron and cloak fall in free and graceful folds, and a sort of twisted scarf hangs down behind the back.

Perspective in its application to many objects, such as a crowd or a landscape, the Maya seem scarcely to have considered at all. Figures in different planes of perspective may have been intended when they are shown in tiers one above the other. When two or more human beings are placed together, there is usually no unnatural difference in size, to express kingly qualities as is so common in Egyptian scenes. On some of the stelae the captives and kneeling figures are clearly supplementary and are crowded into the available space. The small figures of men and animals interwoven so gracefully into the scroll ornaments of many of the Copan stelae seem to be primarily decorative.

The frescos of Chichen Itza are about the only known attempt to handle a crowd or to portray everyday life. On the best one of these, against a green field, are shown many warriors of equal size engaged in combat. At the top of the picture, and apparently in the middle distance, are houses

FIG. 19. — Representation of drapery: Palenque.

[1] Maudslay, 1889–1902, IV, pls. 32–37.

[2] Maudslay, 1889–1902, II, pl. 87.

near which are women preparing for flight. The scene is very natural, as if viewed from a considerable height, and the absence of perspective does not make itself felt. A group of trees in a corner of the scene is drawn with much decorative effect.[1] When, however, the artist puts his hand to drawing a mountain or hill with men clambering over it, he goes quite beyond his power. One or two such attempts are very crude.

Expression. Except in the more or less grotesque figures, there is very little in the way of expression. The drooping eye in profile faces gives a certain air of sadness, and the finest faces in the full round have perfect serenity (Plate 26, fig. 3). Sometimes, however, there is a sullen expression upon the faces of the captives that is probably intentional, as may be seen from the four kneeling persons in Fig. 10. In grotesque conceptions, however, grimaces and scowls are admirably portrayed.

Perhaps the best example of characterization is the old man smoking a tubular pipe, who adorns one side of the doorway to the shrine of the Temple of the Cross at Palenque.[2] The thin lips, stooped back and weak knees of old age are extremely well presented.

Composition. Composition in simple and in subtle kind finds high expression in Maya art. Not only the direct opposition of practically equal figures, as on Stela 1 of Ixkun,[3] but also balance secured by difficult modes and measures, distinguishes the work of the Central American people. Long feathers drooping in graceful curves as well as strips and blocks of glyphs are commonly employed to fill out corners and carry the lines of interest.

The tablets of Palenque might serve as models of composition in which the most intricate methods are used. In the three tablets of the Sun, the Cross, and the Foliated Cross[4] the balance is across the vertical, medial axis. The attendant priests in each instance are of different heights, and blocks of glyphs and other devices are employed to give equal weight to the two sides of the picture. The pyramidal type of composition is illustrated in the stucco panels of House A of the Palace.[5] Here there is in each case a central standing figure who holds before himself a ceremonial staff. The staff balances the headdress of this principal subject. In each of the lower corners is a seated figure who looks upward. This arrangement gives weight and stability to the design as a whole. Many other examples of pyramidal grouping might be mentioned. The two lintels of Yaxchilan reproduced in Figs. 10 and 17 show agreeable composition. In both designs the bottom is made much heavier than the top, although the pyramid is not very obvious. Composition on the diagonal is not so common among the Maya as some other forms. This may be explained by the abhorrence of blank spaces. Still in some sculptures a diagonal line of interest is maintained. Attention might be called in this regard to one of the most remarkable works of art that the Maya produced in the matter of composition and execution. The splendid lintel taken by Maudslay[6] from Yaxchilan and deposited in the British Museum represents a divine serpent which towers above a crouching female worshiper who holds up a basket of offerings. In the mouth

---

[1] Maudslay has reproduced this but without entire success, 1889–1902, III, pl. 40.
[2] Maudslay, 1889–1902, IV, pl. 72.
[3] Maudslay, 1889–1902, II, pl. 69.

[4] Maudslay, 1889–1902, IV, pls. 76, 81 and 88.
[5] Maudslay, 1889–1902, IV, pls. 8–11.
[6] Maudslay, 1889–1902, II, pl. 87.

of the serpent appears the upper part of a being in human form — probably an anthropomorphic god — who threatens the woman below with a spear. The top of this picture possesses a heavier interest than the bottom, and the diagonal line of division is well marked.

It has been frequently pointed out that the Maya did not subordinate sufficiently for our tastes and that they did not understand the contrast value of blank space. Of course it is probable that most of the more complicated designs were painted in different colors. Under this treatment much of the complexity would disappear.[1] After all, the principal reason the drawings seem involved to European eyes is because they are utterly unintelligible. But it might here be noted that there was a tendency to simplify and to limit the field of vision toward the end of the first Great Period. This tendency is mostly in evidence at Piedras Negras and Palenque. The principal figures or groups are often carefully framed in by strips of astronomical signs, etc., and considerable blank space preserved as a background.

The sense of careful and accurate composition was probably developed along with the carving of hieroglyphs. Each glyph is indeed a careful bit of composition and design limited to a definite and uniform space. The matter represented in a single glyph ranges from whole figures of men and animals to cryptic abbreviations. Examination shows that the spaces were nicely divided and mapped out before the finer details were added.

A number of monuments have unfinished figures and inscriptions that show the preliminary blocking out in the rough. Altar L at Copan and Stela 1 at Tikal (Plate 22, fig. 4) may be given as examples. Rough free-hand drawings found on walls at Tikal[2] and elsewhere give some idea of the artists' preliminary studies.

THE SERPENT

The Origin of the Serpent in Art. The unique character of Maya art comes from the treatment of the serpent. Indeed, the trail of the serpent is over all the civilizations of Central America and southern Mexico. Any attempt to explain the origin of the serpent in Maya art must take note of the following facts concerning the religion and social organization of the Maya:

1st. The belief in many animal gods, some being more powerful than others.

2nd. The association of these powerful gods with natural phenomena.

3rd. The marked progression of these animal gods towards anthropomorphism.

4th. A strong political structure almost amounting to theocracy.

5th. A ruling class with careful regard for inheritance.

6th. The number and magnitude of public works of a religious nature.

All of these conditions may be explained as direct indigenous outgrowths of generalized totemism. This is widespread among the American Indians as well as among primitive peoples in almost all parts of the world.

Totemism, which as a religious and social institution varies widely in many details, may be said to have as its basis a primitive philosophical conception of

---

[1] A fine instance of this is seen in Miss Breton's restoration of the painted sculptures of the Lower Chamber of the Temple of the Jaguar at Chichen Itza now installed in the Museum of the University of Pennsylvania.

[2] Maler, 1911, pp. 56–63.

the world. According to this conception all, or at least a part, of the objects of man's physical environment, such as animals, plants, heavenly bodies, and various sorts of natural phenomena, are his equals or even his superiors in the possession of skill and intelligence and a will to help or hinder. The individual chooses from these his best friend in the society of nature. The methods by which the choice is made are legion, but fasting, revery and self-hypnotism are common features. The religious side of totemism concerns the worship of the acquired guardian spirit of the individual or the inherited guardian spirits of the clan. Of course this worship does not constitute the whole of the religion of any people unless the powers of the totems are extended to cover the more general activities and phenomena of nature. The governmental side of totemism is of even greater importance than the religious, from which, however, it is derived. Principally through its relation to ideas of inheritance totemism tends to emphasize the importance of the family or clan and gives rise to a strong and stable society with well-defined leadership.

In a progressive community the different clan protectors do not long maintain an equal status. An unusual or striking ritual, a popular myth or a change in the condition of life may elevate one clan totem over the totem of other clans of the same tribe. Or the political fortunes of a family may redound to the credit of the being worshiped by that family. When a god, as when a man, rises from the ruck of the commonplace, he attracts to himself the strong qualities of his inferiors, for even among gods nothing succeeds like success. Such a process of survival and absorption may partially account for the importance of the serpent and other animal forms in Maya religion and art.

But there is good reason to suspect that the serpent was more potent in art than in religion and that its importance in the latter was partly reflected from the former. The peculiar form of the serpent's body was able to furnish a richer theme and one with more obvious possibilities of artistic development than could that of any other animal in the early list of totemic divinities. Most of the more or less anthropomorphic gods of the historic Maya pantheon are distinct enough in powers and attributes and seem to have successfully cast off some earlier animal nature only to be endowed afresh with ophidian characters. On the other hand, there is no single god that can safely be called the serpent god to the exclusion of all others. As a result of its artistic extension the serpent seems to have lost its earlier religious intention and to have become merely a sign or an attribute of divinity in general.

Zoölogical Observations. In any analytical study of this most complicated subject it is necessary to distinguish three aspects. The first aspect concerns the physical or zoölogical basis or explanation for any representation. The second aspect concerns methods of idealization or evidences of the reaction of religious ideas and inspiration upon the given natural form. The third aspect concerns conventionalization, so called, or the modifications brought about by a sense of pure design. More briefly these three aspects are, 1st, physical, 2nd, religious, 3rd, decorative.

The serpent is seldom represented realistically, but we may safely infer that the rattlesnake was the prevailing model. The common rattlesnake of Central America and southward is the *Crotalus durissus*, which has been thus described [1]

[1] Ditmars, 1910, pp. 353–354.

as to its coloration: ". . . the ground color is rich yellow or pale olive; a chain of large brown rhombs, bordered with light yellow, extends along the back."

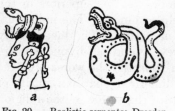

a   b

Fig. 20. — Realistic serpents: Dresden Codex.

Rarely, indeed, did the Maya draw snakes with the markings given above. Rattles are sometimes shown, but in many cases these too are omitted. Usually the picture conveys merely a general suggestion of the snake with every feature more or less modified. Still the lack of realism was not owing to the inability of the artist, as may be seen from a number of excellent drawings in the codices (Fig. 20).

Parts of other creatures are frequently added to the body of the snake, but it is usually difficult to make a zoölogical identification of these additions. The most important are the plumes of the quetzal bird and ornaments and features taken from the human form. The jaguar is also a close associate of the snake in Maya art. Clawed forefeet are often seen on some of the more complicated representations. Other animals make occasional contributions to the more or less grotesque conceptions, while some features appear that apparently have no zoölogical explanation. It will be shown that in the composite figures now one component and now

Fig. 21. — Idealized serpent: Fresco painting: Chichen Itza.

another comes to the front, but that all are artistically controlled by the suggestion of the snake. The unnatural combinations are doubtless attempts to figure characters that appear in the mythology and religion.

Idealization. But while the religion provided the gross composites just noted, as subjects for artistic expression, it also inspired a fine, spiritual idealization of them. This idealization was achieved by two methods which, although fundamentally distinct, nevertheless worked hand in hand.

According to the first method of idealization the body and head of the serpent were elaborated by the additions of scrolls, spirals, undulating lines and other elements essentially serpentine. Sinuosity received its ultimate expression. Thus the serpent of religion was distinguished from the serpent of nature by being made more ideally serpentine. Fig. 21 presents an example of such elaboration from the frescos of Chichen Itza.

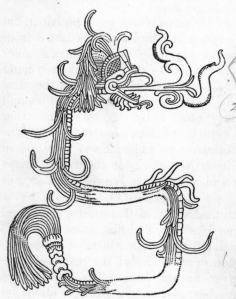

Fig. 22. — Feathered serpent: Chichen Itza.

The second method followed in the idealization of the serpent was progressively anthropomorphic. The serpent was endowed with certain human aspects by the addition, in the first stage, of ornaments worn by human beings. Nose and ear plugs appear on comparatively unelaborated representations. Fig. 22 shows a plumed serpent whose head is decorated by nose plugs and by a feather headdress. The plumes on the body curve outward in much the same manner as the scrolls just considered. As a final stage in the evolution of the divine serpent, a human or grotesquely human head was placed in the wide-open jaws. This device is well illustrated in Fig. 23. This latter addition is perhaps the most striking and original feature of Maya art and has, as we shall see, a most significant development.

FIG. 23. — Serpents with grotesque heads in their mouths: Copan.

Fig. 24 shows a beautiful representation of the divine serpent from Yaxchilan in which both the above-described methods of idealization receive lucid expression. In this example the body markings of the serpent are also brought into play.

FIG. 24. — Divine serpent with human head and hand in mouth: Yaxchilan.

The explanation of this progressive anthropomorphism is simple and dependent upon universal principles. It is but the graphic record of a process that takes place in all religions, from totemism upwards, in which the supernatural relations between men and animals are intensified.

In gods, as in men, there is always the union of a body and a mind. The body of the god may be any natural form, vegetable, animal or human, but the mind is always like that of man himself. It is impossible for man, savage or civilized, to conceive of a divinity with an intellect essentially different from his own although the powers may be magnified or extended. When the body of the god is imagined as that of an animal, there comes, with increase of culture, a growing sense of incongruity or inadequacy in the association of a superior mind with an animal body. As a first stage, the animal-like body of the god becomes larger or more mysterious than that of the every-day wild animal of the same species. Such a stage may be seen, for instance, in the totem gods and clan ancestors of the tribes of the northwest coast of America. Gradually the divinities assume human form and manners. The half-animal, half-human gods of Egypt, Assyria, India and Peru, as well as the deities of the Maya, show the middle stage. Complete anthropomorphism is seen in the gods of Greece. Even here, however, there are many scholars who maintain that an earlier animal nature of these gods is disclosed by the peculiar epithets, by sacred animals, plants, etc., and by sacrifices. Be this as it may, it is clear that after they had achieved human form the gods had to struggle to keep up with the ethical progress of their worshipers.

It was, as before remarked, the special quality of human form in the Greek gods which directed Greek artists toward the human form as a principal subject for artistic treatment.

Aside from human associations, the human body possesses little, if any, more absolute beauty than does the most humble object shaped by the refining hand of nature, be it bird, flower or stone. In any really great national art the choice of subjects from such a wide field is usually directed by the specialized enthusiasm of religious fervor.

The Serpent in Design. It is necessary to consider the serpent in regard to modifications which result from its constant repetition as a decorative and symbolical motive. In this aspect of art the serpent combines with diverse objects, natural and artificial, and presents many phases of so-called conventionalization.

The character of the delineation of any figure in decorative art is determined by a sort of survival of the fittest. These surviving forms show certain qualities of order — especially harmony of measures and dominant directions, or parallelism of lines — that constitute the basis for any successful appeal to the esthetic sense. The suggestion has already been made that the artistic success of the reptilian motive in design probably had much to do with making the same motive strong in religion. Many divinities of diverse animal natures seem to have been overcast by the serpent, and the actual intrusion of ophidian features into distinct representations can often be demonstrated.

Any national or regional design is, of course, finite. Its scope is limited by one or more modes wherein it is intensively developed. Now, in the case of the Maya the physical nature of the serpent reacted strongly upon the national sense of beauty. Not that they saw beauty where there was none, but that they accepted the special beauty of the serpent and neglected the other kinds. The serpent appeared to them the ultimate expression of grace.

It must be admitted that the snake's body has a very simple but exceedingly graceful outline. Good artistic values can be obtained with little difficulty with this as a motive. The body swells and tapers. Within a little distance the body can bend upon itself, and the curves produced by such bending are almost capable of being plotted by formulas, so simple are the factors which govern them. But the snake's body does not ordinarily fall into the simple and uniform wave forms with which it is commonly associated. Instead, it makes a succession of quick curves which merge into tangents or into long, slow curves.

The characteristic lines of the snake's body in repose or motion seem, upon careful study, to be as nearly angular as the physical limitations allow. A snake will stretch out along a wall and fold itself as closely as it can into a corner.

In Maya design the serpentine alternation of quick and slow curves strikes the dominant note. Fig. 25 presents a collection of parts of designs chosen from many different situations. In all of these examples the angular shaping of the curves is manifest. The angular drawing of the serpent itself appears in a to d, while the remaining figures show the use of comparable lines in a variety of other instances. The striking development of vertical or horizontal lines of interest should also be noted. This is not due to the suggestion of the serpent, but rather to the universal principle of harmony of directions. The skill with which tapering masses are handled must elicit admiration. Here is a relation of lines directly opposed to parallelism, yet the sense of the parallel is preserved, while the grace and variety of converging lines only lend a subtle interest.

The prevalence of tapering, flamelike masses is characteristic of Maya art (Fig. 24, *e*, *f*, *h*, *l*, etc.). These forms were doubtless suggested by the representations of the snake's body. Two other prominent characters may have

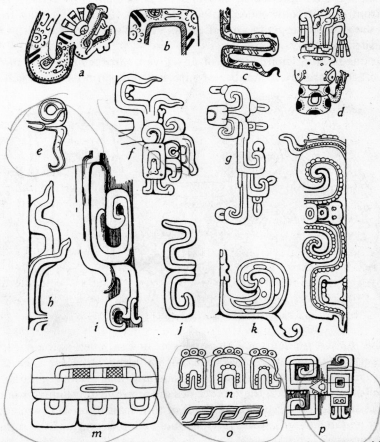

FIG. 25. — Details showing influence of serpentine forms: *a–d*, Tro-Cortesianus Codex; *e*, *f*, and *h*, Palenque; *g*, Chichen Itza; *i*, *k*, *m*, and *n*, Quirigua; *j*, Copan; *l* and *o*, Tikal; *p*, Labna.

had a similar origin. One of these is the use of the double outline and other applications of parallel lines. Parallelism of lines introduces into any design an emphasis of contours and a harmony of measures. The origin of the double outline may be traced to the common method of drawing the belly of the snake so as to distinguish the area of large ventral scale plates from the rest of the body. This demarcation may be seen in the first four examples given in Fig. 25. In *m* is given one of the important factors of the great glyph that introduces the so-called Initial Series dates. The three loops at the bottom and the single loop at the top may represent in a vague and symbolical manner a portion of a serpent's body. But if the device of the double outline comes from this natural source its application was greatly extended, as may be seen from its occurrence

in the remaining examples in the collection above noted. The suggestion may
also have come from drawing the midribs of feathers, but this seems less likely.

The common use of rows or series of small circles is another pleasing feature
of many drawings. These circles are probably derived by suggestion from the
small scales on the body of the snake. Altar O at Copan (Fig. 26) shows these
body scales, but it must be admitted that they seldom appear on important
works of art. A fine application of this decorative element is seen in Fig. 25, *l*,
a detail from one of the wooden lintels of Tikal. Groups of circles frequently
decorate the eyes of serpents and of gods. They are also used as symbols of
water and fruitfulness.

In the imaginative modification of any given natural figure, for purposes of
decorative art, there are a number of rather definite processes. Each of these

FIG. 26. — Plumed serpent with elaborated head: Altar O, Copan.

is amenable to the fundamental principles of design, such as balance, rhythm
and harmony, as these terms have been elucidated by Dr. Ross.[1] Each process
may show, moreover, the phases of conscious and unconscious manipulation of
the subject matter. Lastly, these processes of intensive development of a design
motive, like the already described methods of the idealization of the serpent, work
both singly and in combination. It is possible to detect much of the counterplay.

The processes are:

1. Simplification.   2. Elaboration.   3. Elimination.   4. Substitution.

Careful analysis of one group of designs after another, during which special
attention is paid to the changes in homologous parts, makes pretty clear the
manner in which the imagination works. In the first place, imagination does
not create, it merely reshapes and recombines, taking suggestions and material
from any thing lying within the field of experience. It may be likened to a
kaleidoscope. Instead of bits of vari-colored glass are shaken up elements disassociated from originally composite ideas. Through some agent of order these
are rearranged symmetrically, so that the result satisfies the logical sense. In
any developed decorative art the student may find a graphic record of the progress of imagination.

The term "conventionalized art" comprises a number of diverse mani-

[1] 1907; see also Batchelder, 1910.

festations. To be exact, all art is conventionalized of necessity. In any representation there is always a compromise with truth and a mental allowance for inadequacy. But when any idea other than that of giving the most realistic representation possible is uppermost in the mind of the artist, the result may without any quibble be termed conventionalized. As a rule the decorative idea is more important than the realistic, and is achieved by limiting the field of the design and by modifying the lines of the model in a purely formal manner.

Simplification. In an early paper that has not received the attention it merits, Dr. Harrison Allen[1] discusses the relations between natural forms and art forms. He finds that the tendencies of conventional art are:

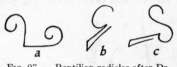

1st, to repeat the normal lines of the model;

2nd, to diminish the normal lines of the model;

3rd, to modify according to a symbol;

FIG. 27. — Reptilian radicles after Dr. Harrison Allen.

4th, to modify according to mythic or religious ideas.

FIG. 28. — Drawing of rattlesnake's head, showing the parts.

The primitive designs given in paintings, etc., he calls "primals"; the final forms which result from a series of variants he calls "ultimates"; and the more or less ideographic figures that preserve the essential lines of a natural series of variants he calls "radicals." In the art of Mexico and Central America he finds a very common radical which he terms the "crotalian curve," because it preserves the supposedly essential lines of the profile of the rattlesnake. Examples of this crotalian curve are given in Fig. 27. It may be pointed out that this radical is more characteristic of Nahua than of Maya art. Maya art was vital, original and constructive, while Nahua art was largely devoted to imitations and to derived forms. The phrase, "normal lines of the model," must be allowed a very liberal interpretation. In almost all kinds of realistic art among people of low culture the normal lines of any natural form are at best roughly approached.

In Fig. 28 is given a sketch of a rattlesnake head. When the mouth is wide open, the forked tongue does not naturally protrude as it does in this drawing. Note particularly the dentition. At the top are two backward curving fangs, while at the bottom are a number of small raking teeth.

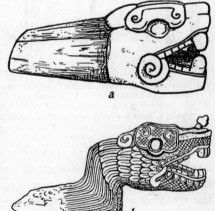

FIG. 29. — Serpent heads with tenons: Chichen Itza.

Note also that immediately above the eye is a scale plate somewhat more prominent than the other scales that cover the face.

The nearest approach to this natural head in sculptural, decorative art occurs at Chichen Itza in carvings in the full round (Fig. 29, a and b). These ex-

[1] 1881, pp. 289 *et seq.*

amples show dentition quite different from the natural form. At the front of the mouth are several teeth resembling incisors, and behind these are a number of molar teeth. The tongue hangs out at the back of the mouth. In *b* the prominent scales around the mouth are clearly indicated, but the scales on the rear part of the head resemble feathers and in fact upon the neck are unmistakably so represented. The supraorbital scale plate is greatly enlarged, and a nose plug is added.

In Fig. 30 is shown a typical serpent head in profile as developed by the Maya for decorative purposes, with the parts lettered and named. The nose

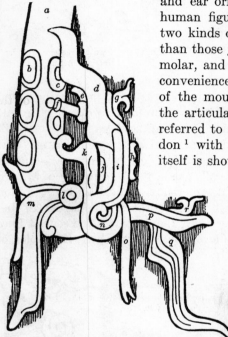

and ear ornaments have been taken over from the human figure and perhaps the beard as well. The two kinds of teeth shown are more fanciful in shape than those just examined. One kind is pretty clearly molar, and the other kind may be called incisor for convenience. The spiral-shaped object at the back of the mouth (*n*) may have originally represented the articulation of the jaw, although it is commonly referred to as a curled fang and is identified by Gordon [1] with the sheath of the tongue. The tongue itself is shown in front of this object. Of the added features one of the most important is the small object (*e*), extending along the top of the nose, that is labeled the "nose scroll" for want of a better name. Through it is thrust the nose plug, which usually represents a bone. To the circular ear plug (*l*) is attached a flowing ornament divided into three parts. This head exhibits all the parts that characteristically belong to the developed serpent head in Maya decorative art. As can be seen, it is very different from the head of a natural snake. All the scales on the head are omitted in the conventional form except the large scale above the eyes (*k*), and this is greatly en-

FIG. 30. — Typical conventionalized serpent head: *a*, body; *b*, belly markings; *c*, back markings; *d*, nose; *e*, nose scroll; *f*, nose plug; *g*, incisor tooth; *h*, molar tooth; *i*, jaw; *j*, eye; *k*, supraorbital plate; *l*, ear plug; *m*, ear ornaments; *n*, curled fang; *o*, tongue; *p*, lower jaw; *q*, beard; *r*, incisor tooth.

larged. The nose is elongated and the upper jaw made considerably longer than the lower one. To sum up, the head lacks prominent natural features, the remaining natural features are greatly modified and a number of unnatural features are added.

The delineation of this head shows, however, artistic skill of no mean merit. The lines of interest are either vertical or horizontal, although the masses themselves are of varied contours. The subtle and skillful use of sinuous shapes is deserving of note.

This head is an excellent example of simplification. All the details are represented economically in few lines, and there is a splendid harmony of parts that defies analysis. Of course the simplification could be carried further by

[1] 1905, p. 138.

omitting the extraneous features. Indeed, a sort of factoring out could be carried on till the irreducible characteristic was reached. According to Dr. Allen's nomenclature, such an irreducible characteristic would be a "radical."

Elaboration. Of less real worth in the development of art but of more common occurrence is the process of elaboration. This process amplifies rather than reduces and by means of adventitious ornament renders the original form more complex. The unnatural features that appear on the typical serpent head just described are evidences of elaboration of a sort. But the most interesting elaboration does not add new features so much as it makes the old ones more complex. In Fig. 26 is reproduced a plumed serpent from Copan. The head

FIG. 31. — Part of underlying design, Altar P, Quirigua: *a*, incisor teeth; *b*, molar tooth; *c*, eye; *d*, nose scroll; *e*, supraorbital plate; *f*, fang of supplementary head.

shows most of the features already noted. The three divisions of the ear ornament hang down over the neck, but the ear plug itself is not visible. The nose turns up and then back. The nose plug is seen directly over the supraorbital plate. The short lower jaw with the beard and the long upper jaw with the large teeth are easily made out. The flame-like object that issues from the mouth may represent breath. So far little evidence of elaboration has been mentioned. This, however, appears in the treatment of the upturned nose and the tongue. The end of the nose, that turns back horizontally, is modified into a grotesque face, best seen by turning the picture on end with the head down. The tongue, which hangs out at the back of the mouth just behind the two molar teeth, is itself the upper jaw of a serpent possessing nose plug, supraorbital plate, and teeth of two kinds.

Extreme types of the elaboration of the serpent head are found on Altar P of Quirigua (Plate 2). This altar, as will be shown later, represents a curious and grotesque conception known as the Two-headed Dragon. The ornamentation that overlies the body of this monster is several layers deep. In particular, on each side of the body, are two pendent serpent heads lacking the

lower jaws. Each serpent head is elaborated to the last degree, but the manner
of enrichment is different in each case.

Fig. 31 offers in a simplified and partial drawing the first of these heads.
In *a* and *b* we see the incisor and molar teeth, respectively, in *c* the eye decorated with feather-like markings, in *d* the nose scroll, and in *e* the remains of
the supraorbital plate which projects farther forward than usual. The upturned nose of this serpent head, part of which appears at the left of the drawing, really lies along the ground on the great sculptured boulder. The details
are so modified by the irregularities of the stone and so concealed by other
overlying figures that they can be made out only with the greatest difficulty.
This nose itself consists of two small superimposed faces of which the eyes are

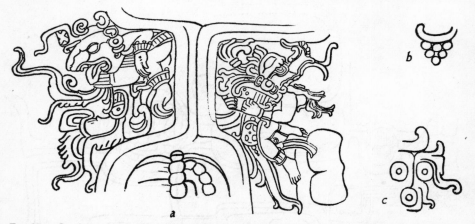

Fig. 32. — Overlying ornament, Altar P, Quirigua: *a*, ornament above the eye; *b* and *c*, water symbols.

the only obvious features. The lower one is partly reconstructed in the drawing. The detail marked *f* is the curled fang at the back of the mouth of this
subordinate face.

But the elaboration of the great serpent head does not stop with this. The
larger spaces are overlaid with grotesques, as may be seen from Fig. 32, *a*, which
gives the two designs decorating the back part of the eye. Another grotesque
occupies the nose scroll and the space above the incisor teeth. The smaller
spaces are filled up with motives that seem to be modifications, for the most
part, of a very common water symbol (Fig. 32, *b* and *c*). This incrustation of
ornament would seem to have no relationship with the serpent heads beneath,
or with the Two-headed Dragon which the serpent heads themselves overlie,
except to embellish.

A second serpent head from Altar P occupies a similar and adjacent position to the one just examined, which, in fact, it partly conceals. It is given in
Fig. 33, *a*. The original parts of the serpent are here much more difficult to
distinguish, for the ornamental details are more closely incorporated. A human face, bearing a peculiar forehead ornament and a prominent nose plug, is
readily seen in front of the serpent's upper jaw. This human face and the serpent jaws that partially enclose it are upside down on the monument, but are
set right side up in the drawing. Curling locks of hair are seen at the side of
the face. Perhaps the forehead ornament is intended for a tuft of knotted hair

The eye of the serpent is indicated by the sunken space in the center of the design just back of the human forehead. The teeth project from the angles of the jaw in the form of double scrolls. The upturned nose ends in a grotesque and highly modified face, redrawn in *b*. As a whole, the face is comparable to the one already noted on Altar O at Copan (Fig. 26). It possesses a forehead ornament analogous to that of the human face beneath (Fig. 33,*a*). The back or top of what was originally the supraorbital plate consists of a face greatly modified, the

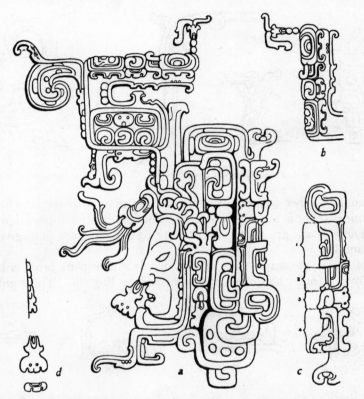

Fig. 33. — Elaborated serpent head, Altar P, Quirigua: *a*, entire head; *b*, grotesque face terminating the nose; *c*, grotesque bead at the back; *d*, details representing bones.

parts of which are indicated in *c*. The mouth of this face incloses a second one. Note also on various parts of the representation the use of the motive given in *d*, frequently in partial form and in connection with circles. This motive apparently represents the end of a bone. As we shall see in another section, the rather grewsome use of bones is highly developed in the art of the Maya.

In connection with these two elaborated heads on the side of Altar P it must be emphasized that they themselves merely serve to elaborate the body of the so-called Two-headed Dragon.

Elimination. Elimination of one feature after another of a natural motive till only one or two survive is a common phenomena the world over in decorative art. In Maya art the process is frequently observed in the case of the serpent. Very often the entire lower jaw is omitted, as in the examples of elaborated heads we have just examined. In fact, the upper part of the serpent head adapts itself to many situations, usually with little change in the relative positions of the different features but with much change in their configuration. More complete elimination, leading to the survival of but one or two details, is rather rare in the best period. It is more frequent in ceramic decoration and in the sculptures of Chichen Itza and other late cities in northern Yucatan. Examples of incomplete and highly modified heads running the gamut of change will now be given. In Fig. 34 are shown serpent heads that lack the lower jaw

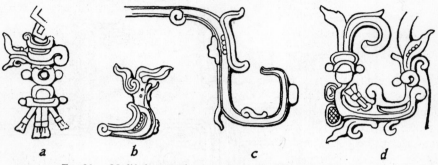

FIG. 34. — Modified serpent heads: *a* and *d*, Copan; *b* and *c*, Palenque.

and occasionally other features such as the ear plug with its attachments. In some instances there is a compensation for the loss by the application of foreign bodies. These heads are parts of elaborate figures, but are here given as individual examples.

Very often the elongated nose of the incomplete serpent head is bent backward to form a fret. Examples are furnished in Fig. 35. The significance of

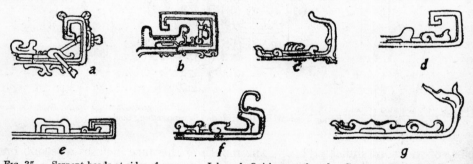

FIG. 35. — Serpent heads at sides of aprons: *a*, Ixkun; *b*, Quirigua; *c*, *d*, and *g*, Copan; *e*, Naranjo; *f*, Seibal.

this and other geometric modifications will be discussed at length in another place. Heads of this type occur particularly as enrichment of a widespread form of apron that is seen on many of the heroic sculptures. This apron (Fig. 15) has characteristically a front-view face in the middle and a profile serpent head at each side. In Fig. 35, *a* and *b*, the serpent heads retain the eye with its supraorbital plate, the nose scroll pierced by a single or double nose plug, and both the molar and incisor types of teeth. In *c* of the same series the nose plug is eliminated and in *d* to *g* both the teeth and the nose plug are wanting. Formal heads of this character also occur in other situations. Sometimes ear and nose plugs of human beings are modified into serpent heads with the nose turned back in a fret.[1] The detail also is found in some of the elaborate head-dresses represented on stelae and lintels.[2]

In marked contrast to the angular development just described there are many incomplete serpent heads cast into flamboyant lines. Examples of these

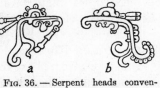

FIG. 36. — Serpent heads conventionalized in flamboyant manner: Chichen Itza.

FIG. 37. — Nose plug representing a conventionalized serpent head: Piedras Negras.

are given in Fig. 36. In *a* the eye is seen at the top, and in front of this is the double nose plug. The nose turns downward in a flamelike scroll. The inner division of the nose represents the incisor tooth, while the molar tooth is shown below and to the right of the eye. The ear plug survives in the object at the extreme right. A somewhat similar head looking in the opposite direction is given in *b*.

The reptilian motive is very intrusive and is much used for the enrichment of all manner of objects. In fact, most of the examples of incomplete serpent heads given above are themselves details that serve to complicate other conceptions. Fig. 37 illustrates the fanciful development of the nose plug of an elaborate bird, while Fig. 34, *c*, is one side of a comparable nose plug upon a similar bird head. Fig. 38 probably represents some sort of plant growth. Each branch, however, is modified by the addition of an incomplete serpent head and by other foreign details. The so-called crosses on the tablets of Palenque probably represent trees. The branches are greatly modified by reptilian details. Fig. 39 reproduces a section of a vinelike decoration at Chichen Itza that is limited to a narrow band. Flowers, fruits and fish are clearly represented. Serpent fea-

FIG. 38. — Vegetal form modified by serpent features: Palenque.

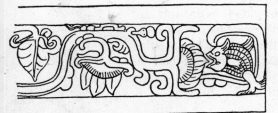

FIG. 39. — Vegetal form with the stem modified by serpent features: Chichen Itza.

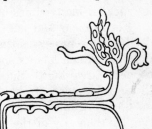

FIG. 40. — Plant form with stem modified into a serpent head: Quirigua.

tures are attached to the stems in some places. In this example the eye, the nose plug and the teeth are readily seen on the upper bend of the vine. Another example of the same sort of modification in a floral motive by adding certain serpentine features is seen in Fig. 40, taken from the Altar P at Quirigua.

[1] For example, Maler, 1903, pl. 72, fig. 3.   [2] Maler, 1903, pls. 46 and 47.

The stelae of Copan and Quirigua are notable examples of reptilian enrichment. Fig. 41 reproduces an ear plug with which are connected no less than four more or less complete serpent heads. The one which shows the greatest elimination is that which issues from the side of the ear plug. Only the tip of the nose survives in this instance. Examples might be multiplied, but enough have been given to make clear the various processes and stages of change.

Fig. 41. — Detail of an ear plug with attached serpent heads: Copan.

Substitution. The process of substitution likewise plays a great part in all highly developed art, whether barbaric or civilized. The substitution of new and striking details for old and commonplace ones — even at the cost of the first meaning of the design — is one of the simplest and most natural ways by which the imagination can reconstruct and revivify worn-out subjects. The creative effort is much less in making a parody than an original production. For the parody preserves, in greater or lesser degree, the fundamental composition upon which much of the esthetic interest of the original depends. Especially in decorative art, details of a composition realistic or geometric may be progressively replaced by other quite different details until in the end only a trace of the original setting remains. The true history of the design is made clear only through a study of the homologous parts of a series of stages.

Occasionally, as in the series of three heads given in Fig. 42, there is a sort of degenerate modification due to the redoubling or displacing of some feature. In *a* we see a rather simple serpent head with the nose plug projecting forward from the front of the eye. In *b* this object is doubled and projects from the top of the eye, while in *c* it is repeated many times upon the eye and in front of it.

Elaboration and substitution are closely akin, but, indeed, all the processes that have been described work hand in hand. Each has its special field where it may be studied to best advantage. Substitution may be studied best in the development of the Mask Panel, which will be taken up under Architecture. Since, in principle, this process is simpler than any of the others, the illustration of it will be postponed till the consideration of the latter subject.

Fig. 42. — Serpent heads modified largely by multiplication of nose plugs: Chichen Itza.

Lest a false idea concerning the relation of the realistic motive to the geometric should follow from the examples of development and modifications that have just been given, it seems best to take up at this time a brief discussion of geometric art in its relation to the serpent and other life forms.

The Serpent and Geometric Art. It has for some years been the vogue among students of primitive art to derive all geometrical elements in decorative art from realistic forms through increasing conventionalization. Even in so elaborate an art as that of the Maya there have been attempts to derive the fret, the spiral, the guilloche, etc., from the serpent.[1] The usual method adopted to show such derivation is to arrange the designs in a "series" with a recognizable life form at one end and a pure geometric form at the other, and between these extremes to place a number of highly modified figures which show increasing similarity with one or other of the extremes. Such a method of study is highly useful and suggestive. But there are three possible lines of explanation.

The change might be considered to move from the realistic to the geometric, from the geometric to the realistic, or from both the extremes inward. In order to prove either of the first two processes it is necessary to establish two things: first, chronological sequence, for the derived form must come after its original in point of time; second, a reasonable explanation why the change occurred.

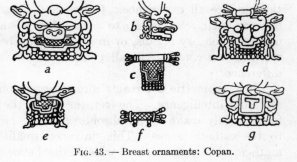

FIG. 43. — Breast ornaments: Copan.

As regards the first point, it is often upon the same object that all the stages of change are represented, as, for instance, in the case in the carved paddles of the Hervey Islands, the study of which by Stolpe really led to the derivative method of explanation. Such a series in Maya art might be taken from the breastplates of the small human figures on the step of Temple 11 at Copan (Fig. 43), to prove beyond doubt that the tau sign is derived from the mouth of the jaguar. The successive elimination of one feature after another till only the opening of the mouth remains is so obvious that it needs no comment. All the stages of change here given are shown on this one monument, with the exception of c and f that illustrate another departure and are taken from Altar Q, showing the same style of sculpture. Few students would insist that any historical significance could be attached to the phenomenon under such circumstances. But chronological sequence from lost sculptures might be assumed and the possibility of survivals invoked. At least it is reasonable to ask why the change took place. What natural quality is present in a jaguar's face that would lead to the survival of the mouth in the form of a tau sign? And why should the cross hatching within this mouth (a) survive on a bar-shaped breast ornament (f) and not on the tau sign (g)? We have seen that the nose of the serpent in Maya design is frequently elongated and turned back to form a fret. What is there about a serpent's nose that would ever suggest a fret? And if a reason is forthcoming would it also explain how the process might proceed in the opposite direction, as shown in Fig. 44, or in no particular direction at all, as in the majority of cases? Why were two serpent bodies placed head to tail in the first place and so twisted that they could conveniently develop into the

FIG. 44. — Serpent head modified by a fret turning down: Copan, back stairway of Temple 11.

[1] In particular, Gordon, 1905.

guilloche? There remains for consideration the third explanation, namely, that of the working inward from the two extremes. This process might be termed involution.

It is almost self-evident that all kinds of art are of a twofold nature and depend for their effect upon two sorts of appeal. The first of these is physiological and the second psychological — the one absolute, the other varying from man to man or nation to nation. Pleasure is produced by an invariable physical reaction such as may come from two wires tuned, we will say, an octave apart, or from more subtle combination of sounds which awaken the imagination and recall experience. Colors and lines and masses may please simply because their relationship to each other is such that they react harmoniously upon the sensory organs, or in a larger way because they epitomize experiences more or less common to all persons, but still with an element of individual difference.

Pure geometric art reacts directly upon our senses and does not appeal at all to our intelligence. The fret, the spiral, the guilloche, and many other simple forms, really make up an absolute art that is universal in its successful appeal to the esthetic sense. This universal quality apparently depends upon the mathematical relationships which exist between the parts of each figure. The fret, like the diatonic scale, contains a definite series of measures.

Now natural objects, animals, plants, crystals, human beings or landscapes, present in their forms a resultant of many complex forces each operating infallibly and invariably. While the erosive refinement is in many cases incomplete or imperfect, yet it is true that nature approximates true and orderly types. The utilitarian and the esthetic processes go back to the very origins of life and perhaps even before that to the economics of chemical combination. According to the stern law of nature only the fittest forms survive, but the test of fitness is at once mechanical and social. Ultimate utility is expressed in good lines and in forms that appeal to the sense of the beautiful. It will be granted that the natural lines of all objects of natural origin contain many elements of beauty. But these natural lines are so subtle that the rude hand of man is not at first able to imitate them, even when his eye perceives them clearly. Man can, however, express the fundamental harmony of parts in a simpler system. He can do this by throwing his crude drawings of natural forms into a geometric mould. By doing this he gives his realistic art, already quick with life as he perceives it, a certain absolute power to react upon other men who may not know the thing he saw. This fusion of the realistic and geometric is called conventionalized art. It may occur at any stage of cultural development. But the higher the stage the more successfully is the artist able to keep his harmonic qualities and at the same time approach the ultimate natural form. For illustration let us say the ultimate form is a circle. Rather than make an imperfect circle the artist draws a square, which he is able to make faultless. Then, by a process of lopping off corners in a perfectly orderly way, he is finally able to approximate the unattainable circle. In the highest form of realistic art, that subtle relation of parts which leads to the sense of balance, or rest, and which we call composition, is indeed due to the primary training of man in the school of geometric expression.

At a much lower stage of culture than that which obtained among the Maya, textile and ceramic decoration lead to the working out of simple geometric forms through the necessary limitations of method and material. Among the Maya the guilloche, occurring on pottery decoration of the Uloa Valley, antedates by centuries the same motive of decoration on buildings in northern Yucatan. Similarly the fret appears as a textile design on the dress of figures carved upon stelae and lintels of Piedras Negras and Yaxchilan long before it was developed as a pattern for façade embellishment at Uxmal and Chichen Itza. The same early use of the geometric figures in minor art that were later transferred to architecture has been noted in Egypt and in Greece. But while it may be possible to demonstrate a later development of the same motives in architecture than in minor art, yet it must be noted that these forms existed throughout the entire period and constituted a national treasury of ideas from which anyone could take what he chose and apply it where he desired. These and other geometric forms were to the Maya artist merely modes of order into which he could throw his serpent forms. By this fusion the geometric forms were rendered more interesting and the serpent forms more orderly. The general theory of involution given above accounts for realistic, geometric and conventionalized art existing side by side; the different degrees of modification according to this method of change do not require a time sequence.

Of course time brings many and important changes. There is often a marked tendency for rich conventionalisms to degenerate into meager geometric moulds. But this is simply an evidence of dissolution when the unstable compound of conventional art breaks down into its original components. The determination of the real sequence of Maya art will be attempted in another part of this work. It will then be shown that there were two or more periods of decadence when the fabric of Maya art stood in a fair way to be destroyed.

Typical geometric patterns will be given under the sections on architecture, textiles and ceramics.

The Serpent in some of its Religious Aspects. There are many classes of objects and figures of religious import that are intimately connected with the serpent. Several plainly defined series will be considered in order. Then intermediate forms will be presented to show how all these classes, which are at first sight distinct, really merge and blend into one another in a most surprising manner. The objects and figures of the monuments will be correlated with those of the codices when such a correlation is possible. Finally the representations of the principal gods will be taken up in some detail.

The Ceremonial Bar. The Ceremonial Bar is the name given to a peculiar object of unknown use that is commonly held in the arms of the priest-like figures represented in the sculptures. It occurs at a number of cities in the southern part of the Maya area, usually upon stelae, but in two or three known instances upon minor works of art. It is particularly important at Copan, where its development can be most clearly traced. This object does not occur in recognizable form in any of the manuscripts.

In its first phase the Ceremonial Bar is composed of a double-headed serpent with a flexible, drooping body. In the wide-open jaws of each serpent head may be seen a human or grotesque face. The most primitive example is found on the Leiden Plate. A portion of the incised drawing on this jadeite slab is reproduced in Fig. 45, showing the double-headed serpent with the grotesque heads and the arms that support it. Other examples are found on the following stelae at Copan: E, I, P, 1, 2, 3, 5, 6 and 7, all of which, as will be demonstrated in another section, belong to the earlier period of that city. The Ceremonial Bar of Stela P which is reproduced in Fig. 46, a, shows the type in

FIG. 45. — The Ceremonial Bar: Leiden Plate.

its greatest richness of detail. The Ceremonial Bar of Stela I is interesting because it represents a dead snake. The pendent body consists only of vertebrae and on the jaws are the characteristic markings that indicate death.

In the second phase (Fig. 46, b) the central portion of the Ceremonial Bar is no longer pendent, but is transformed into a straight panel usually decorated with astronomical signs. The serpent jaws are often much enlarged. Ceremonial Bars of this general type have a notable distribution. They occur upon all the later stelae of Copan as well as upon stelae at Naranjo, Tikal, Yaxha, Quirigua, Yaxchilan, Ocosingo and uncertain sites on the highlands of Guatemala. They apparently do not occur at Piedras Negras and Palenque, or at any of the cities of northern Yucatan.

At Copan the Ceremonial Bar is always held in a horizontal position against the breast of a standing figure in front view. In other cities it is sometimes held diagonally, and the resulting asymmetry may have been a powerful factor in causing it to be greatly modified. Composite and variant forms of this object will be taken up presently and treated in some detail.

The Manikin Scepter. A second important ceremonial object, of strikingly different character, will next be considered. After its commonest phase this object has been called the Manikin Scepter, but this catch phrase does not apply equally well to all appearances. The Manikin

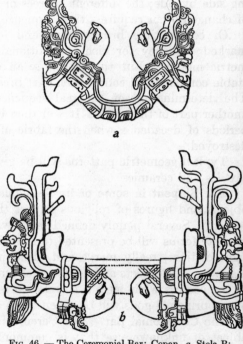

FIG. 46. — The Ceremonial Bar: Copan, a, Stela P; b, Stela N.

Scepter is a small grotesque figure that is usually, as the name implies, held out in one hand of the priest or ruler. A flexible appendage in the form of a serpent serves as a handle. Fig. 47 shows two examples of the Manikin Scepter, a from Yaxchilan and b from Quirigua. Representations of this general type have a wide distribution among the cities of the southern Maya area and even occur at Sayil [1] and Santa Rosa Xlabpak [2] in northern Yucatan.

[1] Maler, 1895, p. 278.　　　　[2] Maler, 1902, p. 223.

The face of the manikin varies considerably, but is characterized by a long turned-up nose and a wide-open mouth which has in its upper jaw a prominent flame-shaped tooth. The lower jaw is usually much shorter than the upper one. These grotesque features are decidedly reptilian according to the Maya standard for such things. Indeed, the upper part of the face will bear comparison part for part with the typical serpent head. Often a long celt-shaped object projects from the forehead. The body of the small figure has, as a rule, no covering except a belt with apron attached and such minor ornaments as arm bands and necklaces. There are usually oval markings on the legs, back and arms that may be intended to represent the scales of snakes or other reptiles. The provenance of the appendage is an interesting problem and several explanations may be given. Its purpose was doubtless to indicate still more clearly the ser-

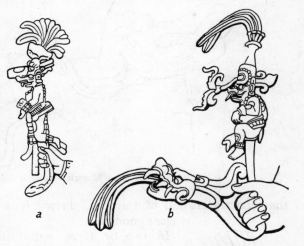

FIG. 47. — The Manikin Scepter: a, Yaxchilan; b, Quirigua.

pentine nature of the figure, but there is great uncertainty whether it is a modified leg or phallus or even the umbilical cord. Only one leg is shown on the examples that are clear enough for detailed study, and it seems probable that the pendent serpent takes the place of the more distant leg. The general lack of sex significance in Maya art is an argument against phallic origin. It may, of course, represent the umbilical cord, but it does not begin at the right point.

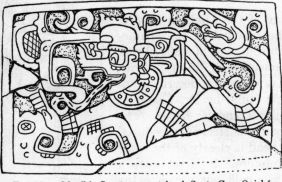

FIG. 48. — Manikin Scepter on potsherd, Santa Cruz Quiché.

In Fig. 48 is reproduced a potsherd from the highlands of Guatemala, that has an incised representation of the Manikin Scepter so modified as to fill an oblong space. The serpent appendage is seen at the right. Unfortunately the design is not complete, but the decorative band on the base of the appendage resembles a leg or arm band and may indicate that the serpent appendage is really a modified leg.

The same manikin type of figure appears in the guise of a newly born child at Palenque. In the Temple of the Inscriptions are four panels with stucco relief which show a human being holding a child in one arm, while the other arm is stretched out to support the ophidian appendage (see Fig. 49, a). The faces on all these representations are unfortunately destroyed.   Maudslay's drawings give both feet of the child, but a study of the photographs shows

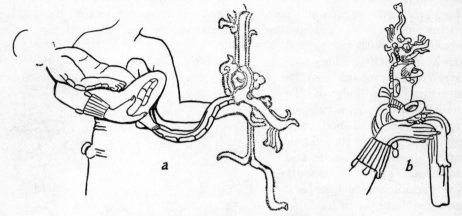

FIG. 49. — Manikin Scepter as child: Palenque.

that the restoration of the more distant foot is doubtful, although the knee is clear enough.

In two or three sculptures at Yaxchilan [1] the manikin figure with the flexible appendage is seated upon an inverted basket-like object on the top of a pole.

Manikin figures without the flexible appendage are sculptured upon the tablets of the Temple of the Cross, the Foliated Cross and the Sun at Palenque.[2] They are represented either in a sitting or reclining attitude upon a folded cloth supported by the outstretched hands of a priest. The best preserved example is given in Fig. 49, b.

The final stage of the Manikin Scepter is marked by the survival of the characteristic head upon some sort of staff. Proof of the actual connection of this type with the more complete ones just described appears upon a stela found by Dr. Tozzer at a ruin on the upper Tzendales River. The object carved upon this stela is reproduced in Fig. 50. The head is clearly of the same character as heretofore. It is set upon a short staff which is held out opposite the face of the principal personage in the manner already noted. The body, however, is entirely eliminated. The staff itself is rigid for the greater part of its length, but the

FIG. 51. — The Manikin head on a staff: Palenque.

FIG. 50.—The Manikin Scepter with body reduced to a staff: Tzendales.

lower end bends outward and terminates in a serpent head.   This staff, then, is clearly a survival of the ventral appendage. Examples of the head upon

[1] Maler, 1903, pls. 50 and 67.   [2] Maudslay, |1889–1902, IV, pls. 76, 81, and 88.

a simple staff occur at Tikal,[1] Piedras Negras[2] and Palenque. Fig. 51 shows one from the last-named city.

Two-headed Dragon. The monstrous creature to which Maudslay has given the name "Two-headed Dragon" will next be considered. This grotesque ani-

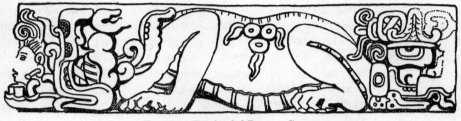

FIG. 52. — Two-headed Dragon: Copan.

mal is seen in its simplest form on the side of a small rectangular altar at Copan (Fig. 52). The principal characters are as follows. There are two heads, one of which distinctly belongs to the front and the other to the rear, as may

be seen from the direction in which the feet are pointed. The markings on the legs and belly are reptilian, and there is a prominent water symbol on the side. The feet in this example are clawlike, but in many other cases they resemble the cloven hoofs of deer or peccary. The front head is hard to characterize, but as a rule the face or snout is long and shaped somewhat like that of a crocodile. Often the eye is feathered and decorated with a diagonal cross. In the specimen before us a human head is seen in the open jaws, but this feature is out of

FIG. 53. — Middle part of Altar M: Copan.

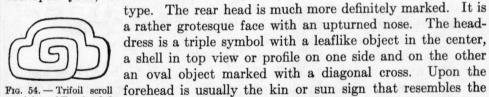

FIG. 54. — Trifoil scroll on joints of Two-headed Dragon.

type. The rear head is much more definitely marked. It is a rather grotesque face with an upturned nose. The head-dress is a triple symbol with a leaflike object in the center, a shell in top view or profile on one side and on the other an oval object marked with a diagonal cross. Upon the forehead is usually the kin or sun sign that resembles the common ring and cross symbol. The lower jaw is represented as a bleached bone, and sometimes the nose has a cavity that likewise indicates death.

A more elaborate treatment of this motive is seen in a number of altars at Copan and Quirigua. The central portion of the Altar of Stela M is presented in Fig. 53. In this instance the body of the monster is carved on one huge block of stone, but the front and rear heads are each carved on a smaller block. The feet are all pointed the same way and are of the cloven type. The joints of the legs, on this example and many others, are marked with a peculiar scroll which generally assumes the trifoil form given in Fig. 54. A grotesque face bearing water symbols occupies each side between the front and hind legs, and another similar

[1] Maudslay, 1889–1902, III, pl. 73.   [2] Maler, 1901, pl. 15, fig. 2.

face adorns the top. Thus we have on this specimen five faces, three of which may be accounted for by the process of elaboration that has already been explained. The separate blocks upon which the front and back faces of the monster are carved have unfortunately suffered mutilation. A sketch of the rear face is given in Fig. 55. The three signs of the headdress are rather hard to make out excepting the middle member, but the kin sign on the forehead is very clear as well as the characteristic grotesque face with the bone grooves and crescents on the lower jaw. The front block shows a widely extended reptilian mouth enclosing a human head. In the effort of the Peabody Museum Expedition to

Fig. 55. — Rear head of Altar M: Copan.

set the two supplementary blocks of this altar in position they were unfortunately turned around so that the rear head appears at the front of the animal in the photographic reproduction and *vice versa*.[1]

The Altar of Stela N [2] is somewhat similar, but lacks the upper face and is carved from a single block. Upon the top of this altar is the trifoil scroll that characteristically occurs on the joints. The Altar of Stela D is interesting on account of the syncopation that it shows. This monument is a more or less cubical block bearing two faces on diagonally opposite corners. One of these faces represents the front head of the Two-headed Dragon and the other the rear one. On each intermediate corner is a vertical bone with two clawed feet attached. These two leg bones with their double feet are all that remain of the body of the monster. The face that corresponds to the front is ornamented with water symbols. The rear face is given in Fig. 56. This clearly represents a death's head, as may be seen by the nose and by the circles, crescents and wavy lines on the jaws. The peculiar triple symbol is absent, but the eyes are modified into the shape of the kin sign.

Fig. 56. — Rear head of Altar D: Copan.

Altar B of Quirigua (Plate 1, figs. 3 and 4) presents far greater elaboration than any specimen so far considered. A more or less irregular boulder is completely covered with carvings in low relief and of very great detail. The front head has feathered eyes marked with the diagonal cross. In the open jaws is a human head with an animal headdress. The legs are doubled upon themselves frog fashion and have the trifoil scroll at the joints. The feet are reptilian in appearance. The rear head is crowded into an irregular space and is represented in profile in a horizontal position looking downward. The sun symbol is carved upon the forehead, and the middle element of the triple headdress is given in an elaborated style. The entire top of the altar is covered with a complicated scroll-work face. The legs conceal so much of the sides that there is no room for additional faces in these positions. These legs, however, are themselves overlaid with large hieroglyphs of the most elaborate type.

Altars O and P at Quirigua belong to the same series as the preceding sculptures. The first of these is not in a very good state of preservation and the de-

---

[1] Gordon, 1902, *a*, pl. 17.   [2] Maudslay, 1889–1902, I, pl. 83.

tails are difficult to make out. Altar P (Plate 2), sometimes called the "Great Turtle Altar," is perhaps the most complicated as well as the best preserved piece of sculpture in the entire Maya area. It is a natural boulder of great size and of hard stone, with carvings in fairly high but delicately modeled relief. Maudslay [1] regards this sculpture as a representation of a turtle, but a comparison of details shows that it belongs to the Two-headed Dragon group, although much modified by the several layers of ornament that conceal the animal form beneath. The front face shows a richly attired human figure in front view seated cross-legged upon the lower jaw of a great, open mouth. This human figure resembles very closely those carved on the stelae. In the right hand he holds the Manikin Scepter and in the left a shield. Concerning the great head that

FIG. 57. — Two-headed Dragon with elongated body: *a–c*, Palenque; *d*, Piedras Negras.

contains this figure little can be said. The pointed teeth in both the lower and upper jaw are easily discernible. The eye is decorated with feathers and with the diagonal cross. The rear head bears evidences of death and is of a grotesque type, but the sun sign and the triple headdress are absent. The head on the top of the monument resembles that on Stela M at Copan, and is marked with many water symbols. The sides of this great altar are ornamented by conventionalized serpent heads that hang down from the sides of the face above and partly overlie each other. These heads have already been explained in some detail as examples of artistic elaboration (Figs. 31 to 33).

A return to less labored presentation of the Two-headed Dragon is now in order. At Copan this motive is used in the adornment of the inner doorway

[1] 1889–1902, II, p. 17.

of Temple 22. The partly destroyed design has been restored by Maudslay.[1] The pendent heads of the monster rest upon the hands of two seated human figures and the body stretches across the doorway. In the significant details of heads and legs this representation agrees with the type specimen that was described first. The feet are of the cloven type. The parts of the body adjacent to the heads show ventral scale plates, but the rest of it consists of a number of S-shaped devices in which are entangled small human figures with grotesque faces.

FIG. 58. — Manikin Scepter and portion of Ceremonial Bar: Tikal.

Fig. 57, a–c, gives an example of the Two-headed Dragon with the body still further modified. This design stretches over the doorway and along each side of a room at Palenque, and is executed in stucco. The heads are fairly true to type and the legs as well, but the body is conventionalized into a long band of astronomical symbols. Upon the center of this band and directly over the doorway is perched a bird with wings extended, the head very much out of proportion to the rest of the body. The rear head of the monster is turned upside down, perhaps to emphasize its inferior position. The phase of the Two-headed Dragon shown in this figure is well established. Several fine examples occur on the stelae of Piedras Negras, one of which is given in Fig. 57, d. Here the astronomical band forms a framework for a human being seated in a niche, and the two heads are brought close together at the bottom just in front of a sort of throne. Note the legs with cloven feet and with trifoil scrolls at the knees. Other forms related to the Two-headed Dragon will be given pres-ently.

FIG. 59.—Rear end of Ceremonial Bar: Siebal.

FIG. 60. — Fragment of carved bone: Copan.

Composite Types and Miscellaneous Variations. The three objects or conceptions whose principal developments have just been described certainly appear distinct enough at first glance. But as a matter of fact each is more or less connected with the other, and all break down into variant types and gradually lose their individual characters. The intermediate stages will be presented first, in order, and then the decadent stages will be treated.

The connecting link between the Ceremonial Bar and the Manikin Scepter appears at Tikal upon Stelae 1 and 2. The human beings represented on these

[1] 1889–1902, I, pl. 12.

monuments hold against their breasts unmistakable Ceremonial Bars of the second or straight-bodied phase. But sitting on the lower jaws of the serpent heads that terminate the bars is the complete Manikin Scepter, ventral append-age and all (Fig. 58). This little figure has quite evidently replaced the head or bust that usually appears in the serpent's mouth on other repre-sentations of the Ceremonial Bar. Many of these heads or busts are found upon examination to re-semble the physiognomy of the manikin, but others are of a very different type. The Manikin Scepter is a common substitute for the Ceremonial Bar. It probably is not derived from this object but from the more generalized body of the serpent.

FIG. 61. — Ceremonial Bar held in tilted position: Yaxchilan.

At Seibal the Ceremonial Bar seems to have fallen under the influence of the elongated phase of the Two-headed Dragon as may be seen on Stela 9,[1] and Stela 10 (Plate 25, fig. 2). This object is held in the arms of the human being in a tilted position. The upper or forward end is developed into a curious head with flamboyant details. The head that usually appears in the jaws of the serpent has in this case been moved upward and attached to the serpent's nose. This same feature appears on the Cere-monial Bar of Stela 7 at Naranjo.[2] The lower or backward end of the Seibal specimen, reproduced in Fig. 59, is modified into a likeness of the inverted rear head of the Two-headed Dragon. The details are represented in a flam-boyant style, but the triple headdress with the shell, the leaflike object and the saltire are discernible as well as the typical grotesque face with the kin sign on the forehead and the bleached bone for a lower jaw.

The connection between the Manikin Scepter and the Two-headed Dragon is more difficult to demonstrate. Altar P at Quirigua represents, as we have seen, a very much elaborated Two-headed Dragon that has in the mouth of

FIG. 62. — Man holding two-headed serpent of flexible type: Yaxchilan.

the front head a human figure carrying a Manikin Scepter. But this circum-stance may have no special significance. The real connection between these two concepts is shown through the general similarity of the rear head of the monster to the head of the manikin. Aside from the symbols indicating special powers that are marked upon the rear head the physiognomy of the two figures is almost identical. It will be shown presently that these heads may be classed as different manifestations of a generalized god. In the meantime a more defi-

[1] Maler, 1908, *a*, pl. 10, fig. 2.   [2] Maler, 1908, *b*, pl. 22, fig. 1.

nite idea of the affinity may be gathered from Fig. 60. This reproduces a carved fragment of bone, formerly painted red, that was picked up on the river front at Copan and is now in the Peabody Museum. The design shows a part of a reptilian monster with scaly legs and a head that is very similar to the manikin

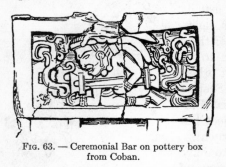

FIG. 63. — Ceremonial Bar on pottery box from Coban.

head. Although this head is most easily explained as the rear head of the Two-headed Dragon, still all the noted symbols are absent.

The Ceremonial Bar is seen in a number of variant and decadent forms. When held in a tilted rather than horizontal position, its symmetry begins to break down. Such a tilted bar is given in Fig. 61 from one of the Yaxchilan stelae. Note the dislocation of the lower head. A reversion of type to the original flexible serpent may be seen in Fig. 62, which likewise is found at Yaxchilan. The body of the bar is a flexible snake body that folds over the arm of the seated human figure. In the open jaws are likenesses to the head of the Manikin Scepter. Fig. 63 reproduces a piece of finely modeled pottery from the uplands of Guatemala upon which the Ceremonial Bar is represented in a simple manner with a knife blade instead of a head in the serpent jaws. The same feature appears on Stela 25[1] at Naranjo. On the small stelae at Ocosingo (Plate 25, fig. 5) the Ceremonial Bar appears to end in serpent heads without any object in the mouth. On Stelae A and C at Quirigua[2]

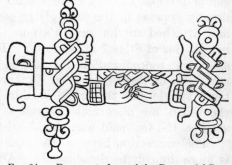

FIG. 64. — Degenerate form of the Ceremonial Bar: Copan.

the Ceremonial Bar ends in small incomplete heads. The lower jaws are lacking and a long pendent object seems to be attached in their stead. A very decadent form of the bar is seen on Stela 11 at Copan (Fig. 64).

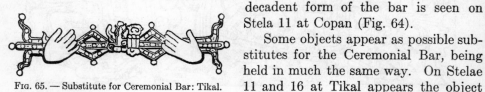

FIG. 65. — Substitute for Ceremonial Bar: Tikal.

Some objects appear as possible substitutes for the Ceremonial Bar, being held in much the same way. On Stelae 11 and 16 at Tikal appears the object shown in Fig. 65. In the center of an openwork staff is set a grotesque head of familiar type. On the south face of Stela F at Quirigua the human figure is represented with his hands held against his breast in the attitude taken when holding the Ceremonial Bar. However, no such object is in evidence. Below each hand is a serpent head that is suspended from a chain attached well up on the headdress. These two serpent heads may be survivals of the old order. It is interesting to note that an almost identical arrangement is seen at Palenque, as is made clear by the two

¹ Maler, 1908, *b*, pl. 40, fig. 1.   ² Maudslay, 1889–1902, II, pls. 4 and 16.

drawings given in Fig. 66, *a* and *b*. The decadent forms and the possible survivals above noted are of great value in determining chronological sequence:

There are a number of curious sculptures that are perhaps related to the Two-headed Dragon group. The most important are Altars G 1, G 2, G 3[1] and O[2] at Copan. These are vertical slabs of stone that are carved into reptilian forms. They make a series midway between the Two-headed Dragon and the ordinary representations of the Feathered Serpent.

The Feathered Serpent on one side of Altar O has already been figured and described (Fig. 26). The design on the opposite side shows two serpents with greatly enlarged heads and small intertwined bodies, ending in "Ahau" symbols. The heads are similar in detail to the head on the opposite side of the altar,

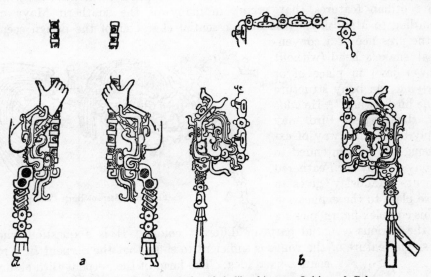

FIG. 66. — Serpent heads attached to chain-like objects: *a*, Quirigua; *b*, Palenque.

and the upturned noses end in the same grotesque face. But under each head is a leg with a clawed foot. In the space enclosed by the intertwined bodies is a bunch of feathers.

Altars G 2 and G 3 represent a double-headed serpent (the two heads being uniform in all particulars) with an arched body decorated by triangular and circular markings and by a mane of feathers. There are no legs on either of these reptilian forms. Altar G 1 is more elaborate. It also has two heads, one being smaller than the other; and a short body concealed beneath feather fringes and a double column of glyphs. The smaller head is similar to the heads of Altars G 2 and G 3 except that it has a Venus symbol marked on the eye and a grotesque bust in the mouth. Under this head is a leg, the character of which does not appear very clearly. The larger head also has a grotesque figure in the mouth. The lower jaw of this mouth consists of a bleached bone. The leg under the head also has bones marked by circles and wavy lines.

From this description it is apparent that the last head comes pretty close to the type of the Two-headed Dragon, and that the series as a whole simply

[1] Maudslay, 1889–1902, I, pls. 116–117.   [2] Maudslay, 1889–1902, I, pls. 84–85.

emphasizes the lack of definite demarcation between the various conceptions
in Maya art. Minor details on headdresses, etc., show two-headed reptile forms
of a nondescript type, an example appearing in Fig. 67. Other phases of two-
headed animals, now approaching
the type of the Ceremonial Bar
and now the Two-headed Dragon,
will receive still further consideration in connection with material
in the codices and the representations of certain gods.

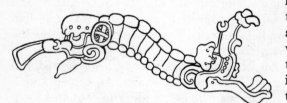

FIG. 67. — Two-headed figure: Yaxchilan.

The Serpent Bird. This name
is applied to a bird motive with cer-
tain reptilian features that occurs in many of the southern Maya cities.
According to Maudslay,[1] "the most essential character of the design seems to
be the presence of a conven-
tional snake's head (without
a lower jaw) in place of or
overlying the bony structure
of the bird's wing." He adds
that the Serpent Bird may
simply be another way of expressing the idea intended to
be conveyed by the Feathered
Serpent. Maudslay[2] gives an
entire plate to the explication
of this complex figure, picking
out the various essential parts in different colors. It is a question whether
the single feature of the wings is sufficient to show that the Serpent Bird represents a fixed idea. The head of the Serpent Bird assumes a
number of distinct forms, and the head is usually the part
that expresses the real individuality.

FIG. 68. — Serpent Bird: Palenque.

FIG. 69.—Staff representing
a bird on a tree: Yaxchilan.

This bird is seen in profile at Palenque and Piedras
Negras. In the former city it is represented in two cases
on the tops of the ceremonial trees, which so closely resemble crosses that they have caused much foolish speculation. The heads of these two birds are similar to the
long-nosed grotesque heads of the manikin figures which
are represented elsewhere on the same tablets. One of
these birds is reproduced in Fig. 68. The conventionalized
serpent head may be easily seen on the under side of the
wing in an inverted position.

The general idea of a bird upon a cross-shaped tree
occurs rather widely, but in other instances the serpent
head on the wing does not make its appearance. For
instance, the idea is embodied in a sort of ceremonial
wand that is seen a number of times at Yaxchilan (Fig. 69). Likewise in
the illuminated manuscripts from the neighboring Zapotecan area, the bird

[1] 1889–1902, I, p. 63.   [2] 1899–1902, I, pl. 99.

on the cross-shaped tree plays an important part, but the bird is without reptilian features.[1]

The Serpent Bird of Piedras Negras is perched upon the top of a grotesque head that forms a sort of canopy over a seated personage on Stela 5.[2] The face of this bird is not of the long-nosed variety, but is much more nearly human. The plumage, however, is much the same as that of the Palenque examples and doubtless imitates that of the quetzal.

The front view representation of the Serpent Bird is much more common than the profile view. Fine examples may be seen on the back of Stela H at Copan (Fig. 70)[3] and at the top of the lintel of Temple IV at Tikal.[4] The serpent heads are arranged vertically on the inner sides of the wings in the Copan specimen and horizontally on the under sides of the wings at Tikal. In both cases long bones in pairs project outward from these serpent heads and extend across the fringe of

Fig. 70. — Serpent Bird. Stela H: Copan.

feathers. In the last example the bird is really perched upon the arched body of the Two-headed Dragon. This same association is seen in Fig. 57, *a* and *d*, already described. In these cases the wings are fully spread, with the serpent heads in an inverted horizontal position. A stucco ornament over a door at Ocosingo represented a Serpent Bird of this type. An incomplete drawing of this by Catherwood[5] has been repeatedly miscalled a Winged Globe in various labored attempts to connect the civilization of the Maya with Egypt.

Objects similar to the wings of the Serpent Bird are widely found on stelae and other sculptures as lateral ear ornaments of the richly dressed human figures. This device might be called the Wing Panel. A rather realistic instance of it is given in Fig. 71, and more conventionalized forms in Fig. 72. Of the examples given here *a* and *b* show a single serpent head at the side of the wing, while *c* and *d* show one head at the top and another at the bottom.

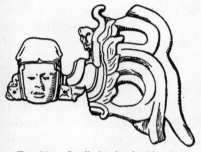

Fig. 71. — Small clay head with wing attached to ear plug: Copan.

It is quite possible that the Wing Panel was invented and developed as an independent ornament and was later used in the artistic elaboration of any sort of bird figure. We have seen throughout this study that the serpent was a very active element in art and was able to force itself into all sorts of designs. Birds in their more natural aspects will be taken up separately, when further evidence concerning the serpent head on the wing will be offered.

The Long-nosed God. Having examined in some detail certain of the more important religious objects shown in the sculptures, we are now in a position to

[1] Seler, 1902–1903, pp. 77–81; Nuttall, 1901, pp. 187–190.

[2] Maler, 1901, pl. 15, fig. 2.

[3] Maudslay, 1889–1902, I, pl. 61.

[4] Maudslay, 1889–1902, III, pl. 78.

[5] Stephens, 1841, II, p. 259.

attempt a correlation of the material on the monuments with that in the codices. The objective method gives safer results than the subjective and will be employed in most cases. We will first consider the multifold character and phases of a figure that must represent one of the principal Maya gods. From a persistently characteristic feature this deity is termed the Long-nosed God.

Because of the natural exuberance of Maya art identification even of gods is far from easy. Fewkes [1] declares that in any attempt to classify the Maya

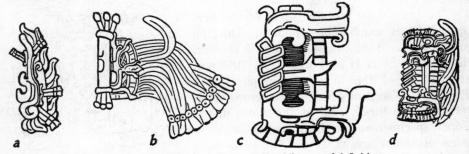

FIG. 72. — The Wing Panel: *a*, Copan; *b*, Yaxchilan; *c* and *d*, Quirigua.

deities the character of the head must be taken as the basis. This statement is true within certain limits, simply because characterization is more easily expressed in the head than elsewhere, especially when the figures are largely anthropomorphic. But in many cases the character and decoration of the body are also significant and should be examined. It was remarked in the preliminary explanation that the more or less human head or bust in the mouth of the divine serpent was intended to express the fundamentally human intelligence of an animal divinity. More detailed study has shown that the serpent itself is merely a badge and cloak of godship. The personality and special powers of the individual gods who have more or less of the serpent character are expressed largely by symbols and by grotesque modifications of the face and body.

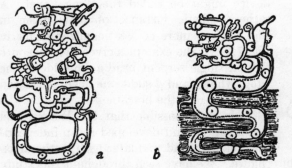

FIG. 73. — God B, issuing from serpent and with serpent body: Dresden Codex.

Schellhas, in his well-known paper on the "Representation of Deities of the Maya Manuscripts," calls the most common figure in the codices God B. He declares [2] that this god is "a universal deity to whom the most varied elements, natural phenomena and activities are subject." Many authorities consider God B to represent Kukulcan, the Feathered Serpent, whose Aztec equivalent is Quetzalcoatl. Others identify him with Itzamna, the Serpent God of the East, or with Chac, the Rain God of the four quarters and the equivalent of Tlaloc of the Mexicans.

Typical examples of this god are shown in Figs. 73 and 74. The nose is, after

[1] 1894, pp. 260–262.   [2] 1904, p. 16.

all, the most characteristic feature. This is long and usually rather pendulous, with a curled object attached to the top. The mouth shows a flame-shaped tooth at the front and frequently a somewhat similar object at the back. The representations of this god in the Tro-Cortesianus Codex are similar to those in the Dresden Codex as far as features are concerned, but the style of delineation is much coarser in the former manuscript. The general similarity of the face of this god to the face of the serpent is apparent: the former is simply the latter shortened and humanized to a slight extent. The curled object above the nose is clearly the homologue of the nose scroll of the serpent (Fig. 30), through which the nose plugs are thrust. On some of the faces of God B in the Dresden Codex the nose plugs are still attached to this object.

Fig. 74. — God B holding serpent in his hand: Dresden Codex.

A personage so important in the manuscripts as is God B could hardly escape representation in the sculptures. Indeed, with slight chance of error, he may be identified with a number of figures, characterized by a long nose, that occur in many situations. In fact, some of the phases of a Long-nosed God of the sculptures have already been discussed under the title of the Manikin Scepter. We have seen the head of this grotesque deity thrust forth from the gaping jaws of the serpent, and we have seen the entire body — with its peculiar serpentine appendage that declares over and again the ophidian nature of the god — seated upon the under jaw of the serpent head on the Ceremonial Bar, or held up as a sacred thing before worshipers. In representations in the Dresden Codex God B likewise issues from the jaws of the serpent (Fig. 73, a). In other representations he sits cross-legged upon the open mouth. He even appears in some drawings with the body of a serpent (Fig. 73, b). But in the majority of cases he has the body and the dress of a man.

Reverting again to the long-nosed manikin god of the sculptures, it has been noted that the ventral appendage disappears in the more advanced stages and that the face expresses the exact nature of the divinity by its striking reptilian features. God B likewise has reptilian features, as has already been shown. A comparison of the two discloses a remarkable similarity of parts. The following features of the face are practically identical: 1st, long, sinuous nose with the nose scroll at the top; 2d, long, single or double tooth at front of mouth; 3d, curled fang at back of mouth; 4th, lower jaw much shorter than upper jaw. Besides these similarities in the face there are often comparable oval markings on the limbs and torso. In Fig. 74 we see God B holding up a snake in the exact manner that the Manikin Scepter is held in the sculptures.

Fig. 75.— Head of Long-nosed God as secondary ornamentation: Quirigua.

On the monuments many long-nosed grotesque faces occur as details of artistic enrichment (Fig. 75) on human figures and other objects as well as in the mouths of serpents on the Ceremonial Bar and in other connections. The range of form is remarkable and the transitions smooth and without a

break. In some cases the long-nosed faces receive a decidedly elaborate
treatment (Fig. 76).

In the codices there is a second kind of long-nosed figure with an extremely
elaborate face who is called God K (Fig. 77, b). According to Schellhas,[1] God
K is closely related to God B and yet distinct from him. He suggests that
this god has some astronomical significance. Brinton [2] and Fewkes [3] consider
him simply a special manifestation of God B, and Förstemann[4]
holds that he is a storm god. The close relation between God
B and God K is indicated in many ways. For instance, the
former sometimes wears the latter's head on the top of his
own (Fig. 77, c).

The face of God K seems to be derived from the face of
the elaborated serpent that is often associated with God B.
In the Tro-Cortesianus codex we find the body of God B
attached to the middle portion of a snake bearing the head
of God K (Fig. 77, a). In the Dresden Codex the serpent,
from the mouth of which God B issues and upon the jaws of which he sits,
has a remarkable likeness to the same god (Fig. 73, a). We have already seen
that the face of God B itself resembles the serpent face, but the resemblance
is not so striking as in the case of God K. Anthropomorphism is more complete in the case of the more important deity.

FIG. 76. — Head with
elaborated nose:
Quirigua.

It might be well before proceeding on another line of inquiry to consider
briefly the functions of
the Long-nosed God in
the phases so far pre-
sented (including Gods
B and K of the codi-
ces and the Manikin
Scepter God and cer-
tain similar forms on
the monuments). This
generalized deity is
prominently associated
with water and vegeta-
tion. Leaflike objects,
water plants, fish and
shells are frequently re-
presented in connection
with him. In the codi-
ces in the guise of God
B, he is seen in the

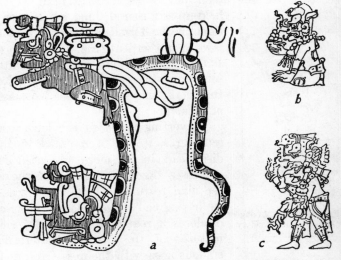

FIG. 77. — God K in his relation to the serpent and to God B:
a, Tro-Cortesianus Codex; b and c, Dresden Codex.

pouring rain (Fig. 78, a) or near bodies of water (Fig. 4). Sometimes he
appears in the form of the water serpent (Fig. 73, b). Fig. 78, b, shows him
associated with the kan or maize sign, and c represents him with leaves attached to his body and the growing maize plant in his hand. In the form of
God K he appears in connection with a sacrifice the apparent object of which

is to obtain good crops.[1] Drawings from other sources than the codices connecting the Long-nosed God with leaves, flowers and water are very common. A cylindrical terra cotta vase in the American Museum of Natural History bears an interesting design which is represented rolled out in Fig. 79. The principal subject is a head of the Long-nosed God, lacking the lower jaw. Bulblike

FIG. 78. — The Long-nosed God in relation to rain and corn growing: *a* and *b*, Tro-Cortesianus Codex; *c*, Dresden Codex.

objects and flowers that resemble water lilies are attached to the forehead and to the ear plug. Nearby is a curious bird which probably is intended for a pelican. The association of water seems to be pretty clear in this instance.

The Manikin Scepter and the Ceremonial Bar are evidences of worship, but offer little information concerning the powers of the object worshiped. On Stela 11[2] at Yaxchilan a human figure wearing a mask with an elaborated nose

FIG. 79. — The Long-nosed God combined with flowers and other objects.

(Fig. 9) holds in one hand the Manikin Scepter and in the other a club with which he appears to threaten three bound captives who kneel before him. It seems possible that this universal deity may have also been concerned with war. The astronomical significance of the Long-nosed God is not clear. In the codices neither God B nor God K seems to be connected with the sun, but such a

[1] Förstemann, 1906, pp. 59–60.   [2] Maler, 1903, pl. 74, fig. 1.

connection is indicated in Fig. 80 by the kin sign on the forehead of the Long-nosed God in the serpent mouth. The grotesque being here represented holds in his hand a leaflike object. In the phases so far considered it is most signifi-

cant that the Long-nosed God seems to be entirely beneficent, since death signs do not occur in connection with him.

There is another large group of representations that shows a Long-nosed God with features indistinguishable from those of the god just considered, but who seems to be connected unchangeably with death. It seems possible that these figures may symbolize the destructive extremes to which the generally beneficent sky god may sometimes go in causing flood or drought. Or they may indicate a dualism, pure and simple, in which each power for good is directly opposed by a second one for evil.

FIG. 80. — The Long-nosed God with the sun sign on his forehead: Copan.

Sometimes when the head of the Long-nosed God of the first type appears in the mouth of the serpent, the death's head of the second type is attached to the serpent tail (Fig. 81, a and b). Examples of such an opposition of good and bad are fairly common.

A somewhat similar appearance of this Long-nosed God with the attributes of death has already been considered in connection with the Two-headed Dragon. The rear head of this monster, it will be remembered, is characterized by a long nose and by symbols that have been interpreted as referring to the sun, to water and to death. This head occurs in many situations detached from the body of the monster. Frequently it serves as a headdress for human figures on stelae, lintels and other monuments.[1] Its

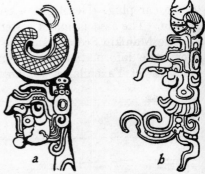

FIG. 81. — Long-nosed death heads attached to serpent tails: a, Copan; b, Yaxchilan.

hieroglyph is perhaps to be seen in Fig. 82, which gives the details of its own peculiar headdress. In Fig. 83 the head of this god with all its attributes is

placed in the center of a band of astronomical symbols, possibly to indicate that the powers of this god are of a heavenly nature.

Fig. 84, a to c, furnishes examples of a peculiar object that in the first instance comes out of the end of a Ceremonial Bar where the bust of the manikin god with shield and spear is also featured, and in the next two instances is attached to the head of the

FIG. 82. — Hieroglyphs of the rear head of the Two-headed Dragon: Palenque.

other similar Long-nosed God, just considered, with the three signs as a headdress. This second god has in c the kin sign upon his forehead, but in b he has

---

[1] For instance, Copan, Stelae H and I, Maudslay, 1889–1902, I, pls. 61 and 63; Palenque, Palace, House A, Maudslay, 1889–1902, IV, pl. 10, and Yax- chilan, Lintel 14, Maler, 1903, pl. 55, and Piedras Negras, Stela 3, Maler, 1901, pl. 13.

the sign which Seler [1] considers the general sign for all heavenly bodies. The pendent object with the symbols attached may indicate water descending in a flood. In Fig. 85 we have a somewhat similar object descending from the hands of a priest or deity. The kan or perhaps the imix symbol is seen as well as

FIG. 83. — The rear head of the Two-headed Dragon attached to a band of astronomical symbols: Palenque.

the sun sign. These representations deserve comparison with the last page of the Dresden Codex, where is depicted, according to Förstemann, the destruction of the world. In this picture a great flood of water gushes forth from the mouth

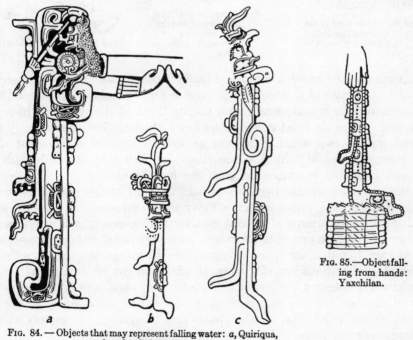

FIG. 85.—Object falling from hands: Yaxchilan.

FIG. 84. — Objects that may represent falling water: *a*, Quiriqua, *b* and *c*, Palenque.

of the composite monster that terminates the band of astronomical signs. Water also descends from the signs of the sun and moon that are attached to the lower side of the astronomical band. An old woman with a serpent upon her head, with crossbones on her skirt, and with jaguar feet inverts a bowl of water.

[1] 1901–1902, pp. 169–170.

Upon the water that pours out of the bowl is the sign of the unlucky day, Eb, and the sign for zero, or completion.[1] At the bottom of the picture is a black god with the ominous moan bird perched upon his head. The old woman with the serpent upon her head will be reconsidered presently.

There are many representations of the Long-nosed God that possess the bleached bone for a lower jaw and sometimes the kin sign on the forehead, but lack the characteristic shell, leaf and saltire symbols. Often heads of this type appear as hieroglyphs with numerals in connection (Fig. 86). Still other examples fulfill some unknown function of symbolism or suggestion in the enrichment of stelae. Fig. 87 shows a small inverted head, attached to a vinelike object. The lower jaw, as before, is fleshless. When the head of the Long-nosed God appears as a headdress the lower jaw is often lacking, but when such is the case it is often possible to find other symbols of death upon the face.

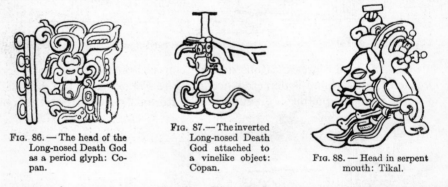

FIG. 86. — The head of the Long-nosed Death God as a period glyph: Copan.

FIG. 87. — The inverted Long-nosed Death God attached to a vinelike object: Copan.

FIG. 88. — Head in serpent mouth: Tikal.

Let us examine one more example. Fig. 88 shows a more or less human head enclosed in the jaws of a snake. The nose is not elongated, but the flamelike teeth seem to place this representation among those of the deity we have been considering. Upon the head itself are no death symbols, but immediately below the head we see two bonelike objects as well as another object that almost surely represents a leaf. In this case, then, attributes of life and death seem to be both indicated in connection with one individual.

A mass of evidence has been presented in regard to the general conception of a Long-nosed God with constant affinity to the serpent. It has been shown that there are two groups of special manifestations, one of which is good and the other bad. Each one of these groups presents several distinct phases which, however, are found upon fuller investigation to merge into one another. A number of explanations for this state of affairs might be advanced: 1st, that each phase represents a distinct divinity; 2d, that each group represents a divinity of diverse interests who is directly opposed to the divinity of the other group of interests; 3d, that all the phases and the groups are merely attempts to differentiate the powers of one general and universal god.

It is too early to make a choice of these explanations or of others that might be advanced in their stead. The study of primitive religions shows that in general the line of change is from many gods towards fewer gods and finally to one god. Assimilation is a much more common phenomenon than differentiation. Very often one god or a group of gods rises above the others and gradually absorbs

[1] This picture is not on the last page in revised numbering. See the Nomenclature, p. 261.

or assimilates the less fortunate rivals. Such may have happened in the case of the Maya. The phases and the groups of phases that have just been described may represent many gods merged into one.

The Roman-nosed God. One of the most important gods in the codices is God D, whose face seems likewise to be recognizable in the sculptures. In the codices he takes the form of an old man with a Roman nose and an eye ornamented with a scroll, beneath which are small circles. The corners of his mouth are drawn back and surrounded by deep wrinkles. Sometimes a single tooth projects forward from the front part of the upper jaw, and when this is absent a stub tooth may appear in the lower jaw. But as often as not both jaws are toothless. Frequently he wears a flowing beard.

According to Schellhas,[1] God D is a Moon and Night God; Fewkes,[2] as well as Thomas, Seler and Förstemann, consider this figure to represent Itzamna,

FIG. 89. — The Roman-nosed God as Sky God: *a* and *b*, Yaxchilan; *c* and *d*, Dresden Codex.

while Brinton[3] thinks he is Kukulcan. It can be pretty definitely demonstrated that God D is a universal sky divinity with powers extending over the day as well as the night. He is not so obviously connected with the serpent as is God B. The weight of evidence seems to incline towards the interpretation of this divinity as Itzamna rather than Kukulcan. Both God B and God D have the strongly deformed teeth which Cogolludo gives as the characteristic of Itzamna. Until the indentification is complete, however, it seems best to employ titles that are without prejudice.

Some connection between God D and the sun is indicated by the kin sign that occasionally appears on the forehead of this god. The general connection with all the heavenly bodies is made clear by several passages in the Dresden Codex. In Fig. 89, *c*, we see the head of God D inclosed in a figure half white and half black that may symbolize alternating night and day. Over the head of the god is the usual sun sign, while above this is a strip of astronomical signs.

[1] 1904, pp. 22–28.　　[2] 1895, *b*, pp. 208–216.　　[3] 1894, *b*, p. 56.

A variant of the above appears in *d*, where the sun sign is placed on the forehead of the god.

Let us now turn for a moment to the monuments. Fig. 89, *a* and *b*, presents two examples of a very complicated design, occurring several times at Yaxchilan, that resembles the familiar Two-headed Dragon. The legs of the more complete specimen (*a*) have trifoil scrolls at the joints and cloven feet exactly like those of the Two-headed Dragon figures of the elongated phase shown on page 55. Also the body consists of a band of astronomical symbols. The two heads, however, are similar to each other rather than strongly differentiated, and other heads of more or less human forms are seen in the mouths and elsewhere in connection with the body.

On the original monument from which *a* is taken (Stela 1) [1] there is a bust of a human being or of a god directly over the center of the planet strip that forms the body of the two-headed monster, and its resemblance to God D of the codices is evident at the first glance. The Roman nose, the open mouth with the lips drawn back, the wrinkles on the cheek, the peculiar tooth projecting outward, the ornamented eye and the flowing hair and beard are all features that occur in the codices in connection with God D. The air of old age is admirably characterized.

At either side of this central bust are representations of small human beings. Each of these figures is seated in a device which in one case is circular and possibly represents the sun and in the other is crescent-shaped and may represent the moon. Each figure holds in his arms a Ceremonial Bar. At both ends of the Ceremonial Bars appear small faces of the principal deity in the mouths of the serpent heads (Fig. 61).

Reverting to Fig. 89, *a* and *b*, it hardly needs pointing out that the face which so closely resembles God D likewise appears in the jaws of these two-headed monsters. As if this were not enough repetition, it occurs twice more on the under side of each one of the bodies. The latter examples are worthy of examination. The faces look directly downward, but one is the obverse of the other, so that the lower parts of the heads are in conjunction. In *a* the two heads amalgamate into one, but in *b* they are separate and easily seen.

The two heads of God D of the codices (*c* and *d*) that are attached to the planet signs and sun symbols acquire a new significance in the light of these sculptured pictures.

It is impossible to state what connection exists between the Two-headed Dragon and the grotesque creature just discussed that is so completely loaded down with the faces that resemble God D. There is some reason, however, for believing that the Roman-nosed God is associated with the front head of this curious monster in somewhat the same way that the Long-nosed God is associated with the rear head.

On pages 4 and 5 of the Dresden Codex is represented a scaly green monster with a head at each end (Fig. 90). In the open mouth of the front head is the face of God D.[2] Above this monster are the glyphs of a number of the principal gods, but no glyph that belongs exclusively to the monster itself. This monster may represent the same conception as the Two-headed Dragon that takes so many forms in the sculptures.

[1] Maler, 1903, pl. 69.   [2] Förstemann, 1906, p. 68.

God D, according to Schellhas,[1] appears as a benevolent deity in the codices, but it seems certain that, like God B, he either has dual aspects or else is directly opposed by another divinity of similar form.   In his benevolent appearance he assumes a close connection with maize, but his other powers and relationships are not clear.   God E, who is the Maize God, seems to be rather lacking in real power and dependent upon the aid of other gods.   He receives this aid from God B as benevolent rain god and God D as benevolent sun god.

FIG. 90. — Two-headed monster with face of God D: Dresden Codex.

The malevolent aspect of God D — or the evil-minded deity that assumes his form — is seen in the female figure that Schellhas [2] has named by the letter I and which he further describes as a destructive Water Goddess.   It may be remarked at this time that sex seems to be a shifting and uncertain attribute among the Maya gods.   Although generally masculine, nevertheless the principal deities sometimes assume female form.

The Goddess I has already been brought before the reader in connection with the destructive flood symbols discussed on page 67.   It seems clear that this deity has some affinity to the composite monster with the astronomical symbols on its narrow body that appears at the top of page 74 of the Dresden Codex.   The floods that issue from the body of this monster are augmented by the water from an inverted bowl that the goddess holds in her hands.   Goddess I appears several times more in conjunction with gushing streams of water, both in the Dresden Codex and in the Tro-Cortesianus, and shows an indefinite relationship to God D.   Her hieroglyph is uncertain, but the hieroglyph of God D is used in one instance where her picture occurs.   The physiognomy of this goddess resembles strikingly that of God D.   A constant and peculiar feature is a headdress consisting of a knotted serpent.

Perhaps the natural opposition intended to be conveyed by God D and Goddess I is that which exists in nature between the clear sky in which appear the sun and stars, and the black storm clouds which blot out these orbs and deluge the earth with destructive floods.   Fewkes, who offers much evidence of the close connection existing between Gods B, D and G, seems to be inclined to accept [3] the relationship implied in the Dresden Codex between God D and Goddess I.

To return to the sculptures, the face of the Roman-nosed God — which is

[1] 1904, pp. 22–23.   [2] 1904, pp. 31–32.   [3] 1895, b, p. 210.

perhaps a safer title than God D for the general appearance of this divinity —
appears frequently in the serpent mouths that terminate the Ceremonial Bar.
Reference has already been made to one example of this at Yaxchilan. At
Copan good examples are seen on Stelae P, 2 and I, and at Naranjo on Stelae 6,
7, 20 and 32, while numerous other citations from different cities might easily
be given. In fact, it may be stated with some assurance that the heads on the
Ceremonial Bar are nearly equally divided between representations of the Long-
nosed God and of the Roman-nosed God. While the extreme types are clear and
well fixed, the two types of heads blend into each other by almost insensible
gradations.

Still another manifestation of the Roman-nosed God is probably seen in the
face form of the kin glyph, which, as every one knows, is the period glyph of
the lowest order in the calendarical
inscriptions, representing one day.
If this god is, as we surmise, a god
of both night and day but with the
idea of the sun god uppermost, his
face would serve nicely as a sign
for the period, one day. The kin
glyph is fairly uniform, examples
from diverse monuments and cities
being given in Fig. 91, a to d. Sometimes the kin sign appears on the
face, usually the nose is of the
Roman type, a peculiar terraced
tooth that is commonly described
as filed projects from the front of
the upper jaw, and a flowing beard
is often present. The eye likewise
shows similarities to the eye of the
god we have been studying. The
so-called normal form of the glyph

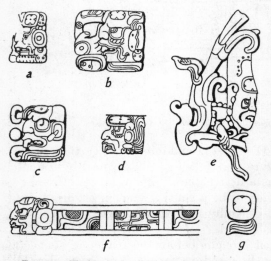

FIG. 91.—The kin glyph and the Roman-nosed God as
Sun God: a, b, e and g, Copan; c, Yaxchilan; d,
Chichen Itza; f, Palenque.

simply abbreviates the above-described face to the kin sign and the flowing
beard (Fig. 91, g). This glyph occurs in other situations than the initial series
inscriptions. It is one of the common glyphs in the so-called supplementary
series that follows the initial series.

The face numeral for four, which occurs only in the inscriptions, is likewise
probably a variant form of the Roman-nosed God. The kin sign is usually placed
on the cheek in front of the ear ornament. The face numeral for fourteen is
similar except for some indication of death such as a bone for the lower jaw.
The glyph of the month Yaxkin, in at least one instance [1] in the inscriptions,
also offers evidence of the use of the face in question.

One of the common astronomical signs shows the face of the Roman-nosed
God curiously conventionalized. This has been interpreted by Seler [2] as a
symbol of the sun. Fig. 91, f, gives a portion of the strip of planet signs at the
base of the Tablet of the Sun at Palenque. This strip ends in the god's face in
the phase most common as the day period glyph. Back of this face is a rectan-

[1] Bowditch, 1910, pl. IX, 9.   [2] 1901–1902, p. 165.

gular panel containing a sign that resembles Caban and has been interpreted as referring to the moon. Next to this sign, and alternating with it during the entire course of this strip of symbols, is the conventionalized face of the Roman-nosed God looking upward. This type of face occurs many times at Yaxchilan, Piedras Negras and Palenque. A beautiful example greatly enlarged to frame in the entire side of a niche for a seated figure at Piedras Negras is given in Fig. 92.

While discussing the homogeneity of Maya art (pages 20–21) there was presented a series of strips of astronomical symbols, some of which are combined with bird heads. These bird heads are in profile at the ends of the strips (Fig. 6, *g*). Later, while elucidating the development of the Two-headed Dragon, the occasional presence of the Serpent Bird upon the central part of the elongated body was noted (page 61). It seems possible that some connection may be established between these bird heads and the multiform Roman-nosed God, but the results are ambiguous. The face of God D certainly appears on birds in the Peresianus Codex.[1] The so-called Serpent Bird on Stela 5[2] at Piedras Negras

FIG. 93. — Sculptured block, showing Two-headed Dragon and Roman-nosed God: Copan.

presents a face of the same type. The front view example of the Serpent Bird from Palenque (Fig. 57, *a*) likewise shows similar features. An interesting sculpture from the northeastern group of mounds at Copan is sketched in Fig. 93. This sculpture is an abbreviated form of the Two-headed Dragon. The front head is true to type, while the rear head has the features of the Long-nosed God, but lacks the usual symbol of the shell, etc., on the forehead. In place of the monster's body is a somewhat damaged face in front view that probably represents the Roman-nosed God. An analogous design is found as the headdress of the principal figure on the north side of Stela N[3] of the same city.

FIG. 92. — Conventionalized head of Roman-nosed God: Piedras Negras.

But these examples, after all, may not indicate the survival of the Serpent Bird that in other cases is perched upon the body of the Two-headed Dragon. Nearly all the animal altars of Copan of the Two-headed Dragon type are elaborated by the intrusion of grotesque heads between the legs and upon the back. The real explanation of these anomalous conditions may be artistic exuberance rather than complication of religious ideas.

The representations of the Roman-nosed God that are executed in the full

[1] Léon de Rosny, 1888, pls. 4 and 8.   [2] Maler, 1901, pl. 15, fig. 2.   [3] Maudslay, 1889–1902, I, pls. 77 and 79.

round show the same features as the more common profile studies and at the same time make possible the identification of the front view representations in low relief. Small heads on the belts of Stelae I and H at Copan likewise show the transition between profile and front-view faces. A large block of stone on the northeast corner of Mound 16 at Copan [1] is carved into an excellent portrait of the divinity. Upon the forehead is the usual kin sign. A tassel-like nose ornament hangs down over the mouth, and at either side of the latter is a deep crease or wrinkle. Another similar head adorns the Jaguar Stairway.[2] In the Peabody Museum are a number of excellent original carvings from Copan that represent the Roman-nosed God with the terrace-shaped tooth (Plate 26, fig. 1).

In the same collection there are several heads with the twisted or cruller-shaped ornament over the nose. Examples of faces of this type have already been presented in Fig. 1, and the wide distribution has received due notice. A re-examination of these faces will bring out many points of resemblance to one or another of the phases of this important god. It seems possible that this definite manifestation may refer directly to the sun disk, the Tonatiuh of the Nahua. Seler,[3] however, considers the face with the twisted nose ornament to represent the god of the Evening Star.

The face glyphs for seven and seventeen show this god in profile with the twisted ornament in view. On one of the wooden lintels at Tikal [4] is carved a human figure with this nose ornament and with the number seven on his cheek. Examples of the face glyphs for seven and seventeen agree with the face on this tablet in the matter of the twisted ornament over the nose. The sign for seventeen has in addition the fleshless jaw bone, as is usual for numbers above ten. The twisted element appears also on heads in the Ceremonial Bar, an instance being Stela 2 at Copan.

FIG. 94. — Pottery flask with face of Roman-nosed God: Uloa Valley.

Many other representations, in the light of the variations and developments that have been noted, seem to represent the generalized Roman-nosed God. Among others may be mentioned the atlantean figures that support the altar as well as those on whose backs stand the officiating priests on the tablet of the Sun Temple at Palenque.[5] The old man smoking a tubular pipe from the same city is another case in point.[6] The same face stamped upon a pottery flask in the Peabody Museum is shown in Fig. 94.

Let us now consider briefly some of the indeterminate representations that lie between the Long-nosed God and the Roman-nosed God. Fig. 95 is a drawing of a thin jadeite plate from Ocosingo which is alike on the two sides and has some features indicated by stencil-like perforations and others by low relief carving. The diagonal cross on the fore-

FIG. 95. — Jadeite slab representing a Sun God: Ocosingo.

[1] Maudslay, 1889–1902, I, pl. 10, b.
[2] Maudslay, 1889–1902, I, pl. 18, a, and Stephens, 1841, I, p. 143.
[3] 1902–1903, I, p. 317.
[4] Maudslay, 1889–1902, III, pl. 73.
[5] Maudslay, 1889–1902, IV, pl. 88.
[6] Maudslay, 1888–1902, IV, pl. 72.

head probably represents the sun symbol. The nose is slightly broken, but it is evident that it never projected much farther than now. It is impossible to say with assurance whether this face represents the Long-nosed God or the Roman-nosed God. In Fig. 96 we see eight heads. Some of these, such as *a* and *e*, are good examples of the Long-nosed God; others, such as *d* and *h*, represent the opposite conception. The remaining heads are much more ambiguous, although it seems likely that *b* and *f* fall in the Long-nosed group and *c* and *g* in the Roman-nosed group. The heads which terminate the upturned noses of elaborated serpents (see Fig. 26 and Fig. 33, *b* and *c*) almost all belong to an ambiguous middle series. In fact, Fig. 96, *b* and *g*, already discussed, are found in such positions.

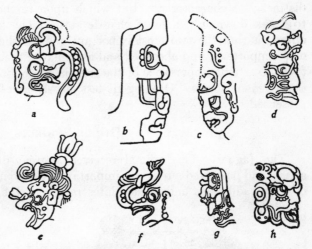

FIG. 96.—Intermediate series. Long-nosed God and Roman-nosed God: *a–d*, *f* and *h*, Copan; *e*, Palenque; *g*, Tikal.

Aside from these intermediate types there is abundant evidence of a close connection between the two generalized forms. Fig. 97 shows two drawings from the Dresden Codex in which the two deities are combined. In *a* we find God B, the principal phase of the Long-nosed God, seated upon the head of God D, the principal phase of the Roman-nosed God. This latter head is marked with bunches of circles which have been interpreted as water symbols. In *b*, on the other hand, we see God D, with a sun symbol in his hand, wearing the head of God B as a headdress.

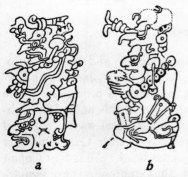

FIG. 97.—Close association of God B and God D: Dresden Codex.

FIG. 98.—God G, the Sun God: Dresden Codex.

We have observed that both the Long-nosed God and the Roman-nosed God occasionally bear the sun symbol. Now the Sun God, *par excellence*, of the Dresden Codex is God G according to the classification of Schellhas. This god takes the form of an old man with a Roman nose and a body marked with sun symbols (Fig. 98). The feature that distinguishes him from God D is an ornamental hook that is attached to his nose. It is possible to see in this characterization a sort of compromise between the natural nose of God D and the fantastic serpentine nose of God B. Schellhas[1] finds that God G is closely connected with God B. Fewkes[2] goes farther and groups Gods B, D and G together. God N may also belong here.

[1] 1904, p. 28. [2] 1895, *b*, pp. 216–218.

In closing this discussion it seems best to reiterate the most significant point of all. Both the Long-nosed God and the Roman-nosed God are distinct enough in their general appearances and yet each blends into the other. Moreover each divinity is presented in a number of phases, which at first glance seem to be distinct and characteristic, but which upon further examination are all found to break down into a most chaotic state. The best explanation that can be offered is that the two most important gods in the pantheon became more and more important, and absorbed and assimilated their less powerful rivals. Then, too, the artistic importance of the serpent undoubtedly led to convergent evolution of many forms. Other gods less closely allied to the serpent will soon be presented.

OTHER SUBJECTS

The Jaguar. This animal received a great deal of attention from Maya artists and possessed a religious importance secondary only to the serpent. Many of the headdresses and breastplates represent the face of the jaguar. A fine

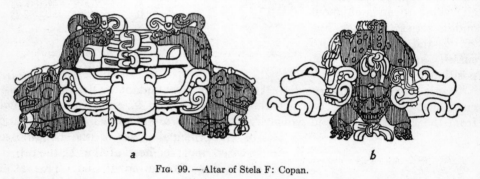

a   *b*

FIG. 99. — Altar of Stela F: Copan.

series of such breastplates are shown on Altars Q, L and T, and on the sculptured interior step of Temple 11 at Copan. The Temple of the Jaguars at Chichen Itza gets its name from a frieze representing jaguars in a procession. The Jaguar Stairway at Copan is another notable occurrence of this animal in architectural design. The jaguar seems to have served in a general way as a model for some of the animal altars of Copan and Quirigua. Altar G at Quirigua (Plate 1, figs. 1 and 2) presents a particularly fine jaguar head. Altar F at Copan consists of several carved stones fitted together that represent two jaguars bound to the side of two grotesque heads. Two views of this altar are reproduced in Fig. 99, *a* and *b*. A possible combination of the jaguar and the serpent in monstrous and grotesque creations may be seen in some of the altars of the Two-headed Dragon type. In particular the clawed feet seemed to be derived in some instances from this animal.

Double-headed jaguar seats are represented at a number of sites, particularly Palenque [1] and Uxmal [2] and Chichen Itza.[3] Perhaps the finest example was the throne modeled in stucco upon the Tablet of the Beau Relief at the former city. This famous panel is now destroyed, but its original features are preserved more

---

[1] Maudslay, 1889–1902, IV, pl. 44.   [2] Stephens, 1843, I, p. 183.

[3] Maudslay, 1889–1902, III, pl. 35, *b*, and pl. 50.

or less exactly in the drawing of Waldeck.[1] Jaguar seats occur at Chichen Itza on the carved lintels.

The Chacs or Rain Gods of the Four Quarters were conceived in the form of jaguars, and the Balam or Jaguar Priests were an important religious institution among the Maya. Jaguar priests which may or may not correspond to the Balam priests are represented upon Stela A [2] at Quirigua, Stela 10 [3] at Piedras Negras and Stela 8 [4] at Siebal. They are in human form and dress with the exception.of the hands and feet, which have the claws and markings of the jaguar.

Many references to the jaguar occur in the codices, but their meanings are uncertain. Fig. 100 reproduces a drawing in the Dresden Codex where the animal is realistically represented. The only unnatural feature is a flower resembling a waterlily that is attached to the fore-head. A jaguar design engraved upon a vase from Peto in northern Yucatan is figured in a later section of this paper (Fig. 185). This remarkable specimen shows a jaguar sitting in a floral circlet and wearing a cloak and breech cloth, not to mention arm and leg bands, nose plugs, etc. His headdress consists of the head of the Long-Nosed God and a small flower similar to that shown in the Dresden Codex specimen. A painted potsherd from Copan (Fig. 101) presents an analogous drawing of an elaborately dressed jaguar, with a so-called

FIG. 100.— Realistic drawing of a jaguar: Dresden Codex.

speech scroll issuing from his mouth, who wears over his forehead a leaflike ornament. The same leaflike design occurs again on one of the lintels of Tikal.[5]

FIG. 101.— Jaguar on a potsherd: Copan.

It seems possible that some connection may be established between the water plant and fish motive (page 18) that has already been described and this powerful beast of the jungle.

The jaguar skin is frequently represented as a garment. Skirts showing the typical jaguar markings prevail on the figures at Copan and are common elsewhere. Sometimes the entire skin [6] with head and tail attached is represented as thrown over the shoulder or about the waist.

Birds and Feathers. The ceremonial and artistic importance of birds and feathers in Maya art can hardly be overestimated. Representations of the former occur in the glyphs and codices and upon the sculptured monuments in connection with some of the more recondite and peculiar features of religion and design. Feathers form a common motive for decoration on stelae and the façades of buildings and are, as well, an integral part of the gala and everyday dress of the people as represented by sculptures and frescos.

The Feathered Serpent and its reciprocal concept the Serpent Bird have

[1] Waldeck, 1866, pl. 42.
[2] Maudslay, 1889–1902, II, pl. 8.
[3] Maler, 1901, pl. 19.
[4] Maler, 1908, a, pl. 7.
[5] Maudslay, 1889–1902, III, pl. 71.
[6] For a good example see Maudslay, 1889–1902, IV, pl. 72.

already been discussed at some length. It was indicated that both simply form a general basis for a large part of the peculiarly involved art of this people and that further definite characterization was accomplished by adding specific details of one kind or another. It was pointed out that several species of birds (judg-

ing by the head) might have the unnatural feature of a conventionalized serpent jaw lying along the wing, and that this unnatural feature was the only fixed characteristic of the so-called Serpent Bird. It was shown that this peculiar wing might even occur separately in the device known as the Wing Panel, and that, as such, it frequently served as lateral ear ornaments for the more complicated figures on the monuments.

The natural characters of birds are sometimes clearly given, but more often the representation is vague and grotesque. Many bird faces approach now the serpent and now the human type. Most of the more elaborate specimens have ear plugs, nose plugs and teeth. The teeth are of the same two kinds as seen on the serpent jaws,

FIG. 102. — Various representations of birds: *a–c*, Copan; *d*, Codex Borgia; *e* and *k*, Palenque; *f* and *j*, Codex Peresianus; *g*, Dresden Codex; *h*, Quirigua; *i*, Codex Tro-Cortesianus.

namely, a rather realistic molar and a curious flame-shaped incisor usually divided into two parts. Very often the curled object at the back of the mouth likewise appears.

Among the birds represented in the Maya codices Drs. Tozzer and Allen [1] have identified the following: herons, probably of several species, frigate bird, ocellated turkey, king vulture, black vulture, harpy eagle, Yucatan horned owl and screech owl, coppery-tailed trogan or quetzal, blue macaw and perhaps a few others. The bird reproduced in Fig. 79 doubtless represents the pelican, as

[1] 1910, pp. 324–346. See also Seler, 1909–1910, pp. 427–457, 784–846.

may be seen from the character of the greatly enlarged bill which shows the knot that appears during the mating season.

The length to which the Maya artist would go in representing a single species is shown in Fig. 102, *a–c*. Of these, *a* is a glyph carved on the back of Stela B at Copan, the first part of which gives the head of the blue macaw, while *b* is a sculpture in the full round representing the same bird and coming from the same city. Note the nostril at the top of the bill, the eyes surrounded by a circlet of small knobs as well as the hook-shaped appendage to the base of the eye, likewise composed of knobs. In *c* the short lower bill and the tongue are omitted and a more or less human ear with characteristic decoration is introduced at the side of the face. The upper bill is lengthened and enlarged. This last figure occurs twice on the front of Stela B at Copan and has often been explained as an elephant trunk. The true explanation has been worked out independently by a number of students.[1] Drawing *d* reproduces a bird with a similar head from one of the Mexican codices.

Birds, either entire or in part, are frequently found on the more elaborate headdresses of the priests and warriors on the monuments. An interesting example from Palenque is given as Fig. 102, *e*, which represents a heron with a fish in its mouth. The same idea with only the upper part of the bird in view appears at Seibal on Stela 10 (Plate 25, fig. 2) and a second variant (*g*) may be seen in the Dresden Codex.

Flying birds of various sorts flutter before priests who perform certain ceremonies in the Peresianus Codex from which *f* is taken. Other carefully drawn birds are perched upon the backs of seated women in the Dresden Codex.[2] A black vulture attacking a snake is very realistically represented on page 36 of the same manuscript. Other vultures are shown devouring sacrificial victims, etc. Birds, among which the ocellated turkey is prominent, are themselves decapitated and given as offerings to one god or another.

FIG. 103. — Quetzal bird on a conventionalized tree: Yaxchilan.

Particularly fine examples of this may be found on pages 25–28 of the Dresden Codex. A quetzal bird on a conventionalized tree is shown in Fig. 103. A variant form has already been presented and discussed (Fig. 69 and page 60).

FIG. 104.—The moan bird; Dresden Codex.

Anthropomorphic birds which may represent minor deities are found in the manuscripts. An officiating priest in the guise of an ocellated turkey with human body is the principal figure on page 8 of the Peresianus Codex. The Yucatan screech owl, known as the Moan bird and popularly associated with death by the Maya, is characteristically represented in the drawing reproduced in Fig. 104. In this case the sprouting maize plant appears as a headdress, the association probably indicating a failure of the crops. The glyph of this bird occurs very frequently in the codices, usually with evil intent. The vulture and the harpy eagle are also represented with features

[1] Parry, 1893, p. 166. Gordon, 1909, pp. 193–195. Tozzer and Allen, 1910, p. 343.
[2] For example, pp. 16–18.

drawn from the figure and ornamentation of man. The possible connection between the Roman-nosed God and a bird of some sort has already been mentioned.

Bird heads are prominent in the hieroglyphs, but the features are usually modified towards the serpent or the human type. In particular the higher period glyphs, including the cycle, katun and tun, commonly show birdlike hooked noses. As is well known, these glyphs are of two types, the face type and the so-called normal type. With the latter we have at present no concern. The face type is the more usual, but it is very difficult to determine the signifi-

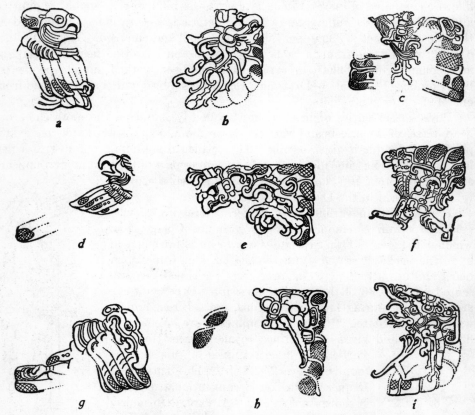

Fig. 105. — Highly modified birds as period glyphs: *a, d* and *g*, Stela D, Copan; *b, e* and *h*, Stela D, Quirigua; *c, f* and *i*, Altar B, Quirigua.

cant feature from which the meaning of the face is drawn. Fortunately there are four examples of initial series which show bodies as well as heads. The earliest and clearest of these is on Stela D at Copan. On this monument each number is represented as a human being who carries the period upon his back. Two other instances of full-form glyphs occur on Stela D at Quirigua and the fourth upon Altar B at the same city. These latter examples of picture writing show a contest between the being who represents the number and the one who represents the period. The complexities and involutions of these sculptures are almost beyond solution. In the series given here for comparison only the period forms are shown.

The cycle according to the Copan example is represented by a parrotlike bird (Fig. 105, *a*), but in two Quirigua drawings (*b* and *c*) this resemblance is lost. In all three the lower jaw consists of an open hand with thumb pointing forward, but in the first example this feature is somewhat disguised. In the Quirigua specimens the serpent head on the wing greatly complicates the design. It will be seen at once that this is the adventitious feature that has already been discussed under the caption, the Serpent Bird. Unfortunately nothing appears in these drawings to fix the species of bird unless we accept the suggestion of the parrot offered by the Copan example. In the simple face forms of the cycle glyph, as may be seen in the series given by Mr. Bowditch,[1] the hand that replaces the lower jaw is a fairly constant feature. Most of the faces have beaked noses, but, aside from this and the hand just mentioned, they are exceedingly divergent.

Fig. 105, d, e and f give the bird figures that appear in the katun glyphs, and g, h and i those of the tun glyphs. Both these series are unintelligible as far as definite interpretation is concerned. The subject of the former may indeed be an eagle, as suggested by Mr. Bowditch. The subject of the latter is in all cases an extremely grotesque bird. The bird beak is pretty clearly shown in many of the abbreviated glyphs, and in these the frequent presence of a

FIG. 106. — Examples of sculptured feathers: a, b, d, e, f, g, Copan; c and i, Piedras Negras; h, Seibal; j, Uxmal.

peculiar ornament in front of the forehead and back of the ear suggests the Yucatan screech owl or Moan bird. This bird is closely connected with the idea of death. In harmony with the interpretation is the bone that appears on the lower jaw of many of the heads where the bird element is wanting.

Perhaps the clearest and most consistent use of a bird head is in the hieroglyph for the month Kayab.[2] This glyph has been explained as the head of a turtle, but a careful comparison of all the forms shows that it really represents a macaw. The short under bill and the tongue are clearly marked, as well as the nostrils at the base of the bill. Often the feathers at the back of the head can be easily distinguished.

[1] 1910, pl. 12.   [2] Bowditch, 1910, pls. 8 and 10.

Fig. 106 shows typical examples of the use of feathers in decoration. In *a* is given the first appearance of independent feather-work decoration on a Copan stela. Previous stelae in this city do not show feather drapery, although it subsequently was magnificently developed, as may be seen from details given in *d* and *e*. The handling is very free, and frequent use is made of a sort of rosette that loops or binds the feathers together. Long plumes with these circular ornaments occur widely on headdresses (Copan, Tikal, Ixkun, Yaxchilan, Kabah, Chichen Itza, etc.) and in simplified form are used as motives for mouldings on the façades of buildings from Copan to the cities of northern Yucatan. Feather drapery without such binding is likewise common. The flowing headdresses of the Seibal stelae furnish good examples, as may be seen from *h*. This free feather-work is represented in architecture by the example figured in *j* that occurs, according to Stephens,[1] on the House of the Birds at Uxmal. Occasionally attempts were made to give the finer details of feathers, as appears in *c*, which may represent a turkey plume. Notched margins are likewise seen on some representations of long feathers occurring on the monuments. Feather cloaks and aprons are commonly worn by the elaborately attired figures on the stelae. Specially beautiful examples of these are found at Piedras Negras and Naranjo.[2] The apron of Stela D at Copan is reproduced in *b*, while in *i* is given the more elaborate one of Stela 7 at Piedras Negras.

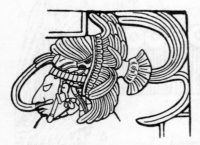

FIG. 107. — Head showing manipulations of feathers to fill out corners: Yaxchilan.

One of the most noteworthy features of feather-work is the service it pays to composition. The Maya artists frequently balanced their designs by sweeping plumes. Fig. 107 illustrates the use of feathers in filling up corners. The feather-work of the Maya never becomes stiff and heavy. The curves are those natural to drooping feathers and quite in contrast to the rather tortuous curves derived from the serpent.

Miscellaneous Animals. Besides the classes of figures that have already been considered, examples may be given of many other animals, of bats, of fish and shells and of plants. Some of these play very minor rôles and are presented without elaboration. Others were apparently of some religious significance and show modifications towards anthropomorphism. It is possible that some of the latter were of ancient totemic importance.

According to Förstemann,[3] the snail denoted the winter solstice and the tortoise the corresponding period of the summer. Both are represented in the codices and the sculptures, but under somewhat different conditions. The hieroglyph for the month Kayab, in which the summer solstice falls, is explained by Förstemann as the head of the tortoise; but it seems almost certain that this head represents the blue macaw, as may be seen by the spiral hook under the eye, the dotted circle around the eye and the nasal opening at the upper part of the bill (compare the typical glyphs[4] with Fig. 102, *a* and *b*). The tortoise

[1] 1843, I, p. 311.
[2] Maler, 1901, pl. 21, seated figure, and Maler, 1908, *b*, pls. 30, fig. 2, and 35, fig. 2.
[3] 1902, p. 27, and 1906, p. 161, etc.
[4] Bowditch, 1910, pls. 8 and 10.

clearly occurs in connection with astronomical signs in the codices,[1] but its exact significance is open to some doubt. The snail does not seem to have any clearly defined meaning of an astronomical nature.

The Altar of Stela C at Copan is carved in the form of a tortoise or turtle,[2] but the so-called Great Turtle Altar at Quirigua is not properly a turtle but an extremely elaborate example of the composite animal aready described as the Two-headed Dragon. Small turtle carvings form a sort of frieze on the House of the Turtles at Uxmal. The most striking use of this reptile in art is seen at Chichen Itza, where it reaches the anthropomorphic stage. Here the carapace of the turtle incloses the middle part of the human body. This figure may be studied on the façade of the Iglesia, where it is represented in high relief, and on columns and jambs of the Castillo, the Temple of the Tables and other buildings, where it occurs as an atlantean or caryatid motive in low relief. The turtle is drawn realistically on the piers of the Lower Chamber of the Temple of the Jaguars.

The snail, so called, is represented in combination with human form

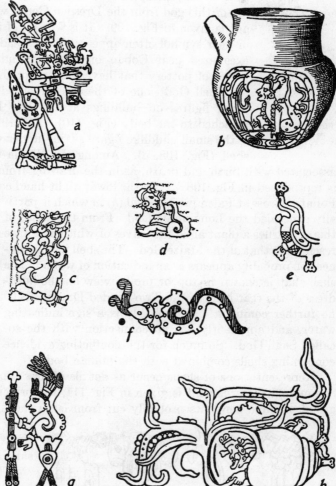

Fig. 108. — Shells and figures associated with them: a, Codex Peresianus; b, Chama; c and d, Dresden Codex; e, Tikal; f, Codex Nuttall; g, Codex Borgia; h, Palenque.

much more often than the tortoise, and occurs not only on the buildings at Chichen Itza just referred to, but also in the codices and on objects of minor art such as pottery. The word "snail" is commonly used, but there are no means of telling whether the shell represented belongs to the snail or to some other mollusk. According to Tozzer and Allen[3] the shell is probably that of the *Fasciolaria gigantia*, which is the largest known American shell and is found along the coast of Yucatan.

In Fig. 108 are given a number of representations of the human form com-

[1] For instance, Tro-Cortesianus, p. 37; Peresianus, pl. 24.   [2] Gordon, 1896, p. 40.   [3] 1910, p. 296.

bined with a shell. The first example is from the Peresianus Codex, and shows the personage which Schellhas [1] calls God N, the God of the End of the Year. Seler,[2] however, names him the Old Bald-headed God, and suggests that he governed the moon. He is probably related to God D, the principal Roman-nosed God. Usually, but not always, this God N wears a large shell from which the upper part of his body seems to emerge. A drawing of this god from the Dresden Codex without the shell appendage is given in Fig. 109. It is worthy of note that the tun glyph or year symbol often appears on the headdress. Mr. Dieseldorff excavated near Coban on the highlands of Guatemala several pieces of pottery that have painted or incised representations of the Shell God: one of these is presented in Fig. 108, *b*. Sculptured figures on buildings at Chichen Itza often have a shell attached to the body (Fig. 110). Differing somewhat from these is the small childlike figure sitting under water with his feet in a shell (Fig. 108, *d*). Among the Nahua the snail was commonly associated with birth and death, as in the drawing from a Mexican codex that is reproduced in Fig. 108, *g*. In the lower, right-hand corner of the Tablet of the

FIG. 109. — God N: Dresden Codex.

Foliated Cross at Palenque is a shell (*h*) in which is partially concealed the Long-nosed God. From the hands of this god issues a plant amid the leaves of which is a face resembling that of the Maize God. The shell in this connection probably appears as an indication of water. The shell that is shown in top or profile view on the headdress of the rear head of the Two-headed Dragon needs no further comment. It probably is a sign indicating water, and apparently has no connection with the so-called Snail God. So much for this conflicting evidence concerning shells combined with the human body.

FIG. 110. — Man with shell attached: Chichen Itza.

Representations of shells occur as details of dress on many of the stelae. A common girdle ornament is given in Fig. 111, the principal part being a central group of three pendants probably cut from large shells. Smaller shells, resembling the olive shell, sometimes form a fringe at either side, as in *b* and *c*.

The head of the leaf-nosed bat makes the hieroglyph for the month Zotz,[3] which means bat in the Maya language.

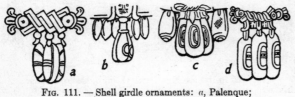

FIG. 111. — Shell girdle ornaments: *a*, Palenque; *b*, Ixkun; *c* and *d*, Copan.

Upon the back of Stela D at Copan this month glyph (Fig. 112, *a*) is given its full form and the membranous wings clearly represented. The Bat God was probably a deity of considerable importance[4] both among the Maya and the surrounding nations. Elsewhere at Copan he is represented with a human body but with the same upturned nose (Fig. 112, *b* and *c*). The more or less humanized figure of the bat with wings outstretched occurs as a painted decoration upon pottery from the Uloa

[1] 1904, pp. 37–38.   [3] Bowditch, 1910, pls. 7 and 9.
[2] 1902–1908, III, pp. 593–595.   [4] Seler, 1902–1903, pp. 112–115.

Valley [1] and from the highlands of Guatemala.[2] A fine example is also found on the remarkable stucco reliefs of Acanceh in northern Yucatan.

Animals such as the deer, the dog, the peccary, etc., are usually represented with little variation from the natural form. The first-mentioned occurs rather

FIG. 112. — Anthropomorphic figures of the bat: Copan.

frequently in both the sculptures and the manuscripts (Fig. 113). The dog is given a ceremonial importance in the codices. From the body markings it has been determined that a domesticated species is represented. Other animals are not of enough interest to be presented in a detailed study at this time.

The principal occurrence of vegetable life has already been noticed under the discussion of the fish and water-plant motive.

FIG. 113. — Realistic drawing of a deer: Dresden Codex.

Bones and Death. The frequent representation of death and its attributes is responsible for the more gruesome aspects of Maya art. Symbols of death are found everywhere in the codices and sculptures. Bones and death's heads even occur as motives for architectural embellishment. Maya religion seems to have been strongly dualistic and to have been concerned with the unceasing conflict between good and evil, life and death. If we may

FIG. 114. — Representation of human sacrifice: Piedras Negras.

credit the evidence of the art, repeated many times over, the Death God rode supreme over all the other deities. Perhaps the explanation is that death and destruction were within the sphere of every god if he cared to extend his powers beyond a given point. The dual natures of the general divinities called the Long-nosed God and the Roman-nosed God have been explained by examples. The power of the Death God over good crops and over women in childbirth is strikingly represented in the codices. Propitiation against death was accomplished at the cost of life. Although human sacrifice was not so excessive as among the Mexicans, still it existed and is clearly represented on page 3 of the Dresden Codex as well as in Fig. 114 from Piedras Negras and in a number of cases at Chichen Itza.

The usual representations of skulls, skeletons and separate bones show some curious and characteristic features. A typical collection is given in

---

[1] Gordon, 1898, a, pls. 1, fig. 11, and 3, b. [2] Dieseldorff, 1894, b.

Fig. 115. In *a*, *b*, *d* and *h* are shown long bones. As a rule, they have knobbed ends, the knobs being two or three in number. On the enlargement at each end of the bone are usually two circles or crescents, while a wavy line runs along the middle of the shaft. Most ear and nose plugs as they occur on the monuments of the southern Maya cities appear to represent bones. In *g* the ear plug of an old man (the Roman-nosed God?) upon a tablet at Palenque shows three bones

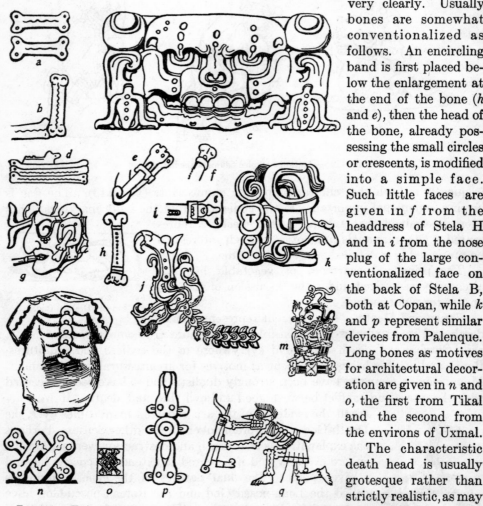

very clearly. Usually bones are somewhat conventionalized as follows. An encircling band is first placed below the enlargement at the end of the bone (*h* and *e*), then the head of the bone, already possessing the small circles or crescents, is modified into a simple face. Such little faces are given in *f* from the headdress of Stela H and in *i* from the nose plug of the large conventionalized face on the back of Stela B, both at Copan, while *k* and *p* represent similar devices from Palenque. Long bones as motives for architectural decoration are given in *n* and *o*, the first from Tikal and the second from the environs of Uxmal.

The characteristic death head is usually grotesque rather than strictly realistic, as may be seen from *c* taken from Altar R at Copan. Here death is indicated

FIG. 115. — Various representations of bones and death: *a*, Chichen Itza; *b*, *c*, *f*, *i* and *j*, Copan; *d*, *e* and *n*, Tikal; *g*, *k* and *p*, Palenque; *l* and *o*, Uxmal; *m*, Dresden Codex; *q*, Mexican codex.

principally by the presence of circles, ovals and crescents on the forehead, the jaws, etc. The eyes show little modification, while the nasal cavity of the skull is inadequately represented. The setting of the teeth in bone rather than in the gums is indicated by the use of double and triple outlines. Although the face seems intended to represent a bleached skull, yet the ears are drawn in full flesh. Similarly in many other delineations the hands and feet are represented entire, while the legs, arms and other parts are bare bone. The torso of a skeletal figure from Uxmal that is now in the American Museum of Natural History is reproduced in *l*. Often bodies are represented practically entire yet with certain symbols which indicate death. A device resembling a percentage sign and often called the maggot symbol surely indicates death. Dotted lines connecting small circles as well as black spots and closed eyes appear to do the same.

The Death God has been called God A by Schellhas,[1] who gives full information concerning his attributes and associations. An elaborate representation of the Death God seated on a throne made of bones is given in *m* of Fig. 115. Note the use of lines or circles and dots along the limbs and the full-fleshed hands and feet. A frequent characteristic of the Death God is a spiny back, made so by projecting vertebrae (Fig. 116). The hieroglyphs of the Death God have been definitely determined. They are found in many places where the figure is absent and seem to indicate misfortune and failure. The attributes of the Death God appear in connection with many conceptions represented on the monuments. In particular the rear head of the Two-headed Dragon has, as we have seen, a bone for the lower jaw. Many other figures of the Long-nosed God are also characterized by this gruesome feature. On Stela I at Copan the double-headed serpent that forms the Ceremonial Bar is a thing of dry bones, as may be seen from Fig. 115, *j*, which reproduces part of it. The heads in the mouths of this object represent the Roman-nosed God.

FIG. 116.—Death God: Dresden Codex.

The importance of the death element in the hieroglyphs is easily illustrated. The day Cimi and the number ten are represented in the four ways shown in Fig. 117: *a* is the face of a dead person characterized by the closed eye, *b* is the so-called maggot sign, *c* is a face bearing this sign and *d* is a skull. The face glyphs for numbers from 11 to 19 are often merely the faces from 1 to 9 with added death symbols such as a bone for the lower jaw. The same feature usually occurs in the face forms of the tun glyph.

a   *b*   *c*   *d*

FIG. 117.—Glyphs indicating death: *a* and *b*, Dresden Codex; *c*, Quirigua; *d*, Copan.

Grotesque Figures. Figures which according to European standards would be termed grotesque occur frequently in Maya representative art. In some cases the grotesque character seems to have been taken seriously as a means of expressing a supernatural quality. Most of the representations of gods in the codices are grotesque in many of their features. The manikin figure derived from the serpent is certainly grotesque, and by this grotesqueness the reptilian nature of this god in human form is made evident to anyone. The methods used by Maya artists to produce grotesque figures and effects are much the same as prevail elsewhere. Some are true composites, while others show purely fanciful exaggeration.

The elaborate bird forms in some of the initial series inscriptions have already been commented upon. Very similar forms appear on various parts of the so-called Great Turtle Altar at Quirigua (Plate 2). At first it seemed possible that some cryptic inscription was contained in these figures, but the possibility of this is slight. Examples of these grotesques have been given in Fig. 32.

[1] 1904, pp. 10–15.

Conscious manipulation on the part of the artist is shown in faces which might be described as reversible. Fig. 118, *b*, presents such a face from the Great Turtle Altar. As it stands, this represents a grotesque human face with a knob nose, a protruding tongue and a fringe of beard. When this face is inverted, it becomes an elaborate but typical bird head. A small figurine of a fish attached

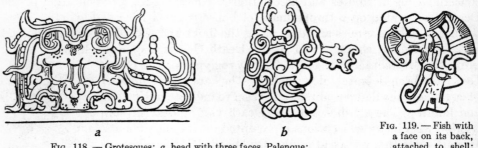

FIG. 118. — Grotesques: *a*, head with three faces, Palenque;
b, inverted bird's head, Quirigua.

FIG. 119. — Fish with a face on its back, attached to shell: Chajcar.

to a shell is shown in Fig. 119. A very good likeness of the Long-nosed God may be seen along the back, facing in the opposite direction, the posterior dorsal fin of the fish forming the nose of the god. The breast ornament of Stela N of Copan is also a reversible face. Maudslay[1] has commented on the straps that hang from the girdles of stelae at Copan. In a number of cases the wrapping at the top of the straps forms part of an inverted head (Fig. 120).

Facial expression is more highly developed in grotesque than in realistic sculpture. The elaborated initial series glyphs, already referred to, have many figures showing grimaces and other violent distortions of the face.

Maize God. The Maize God which Schellhas[2] has termed God E usually bears upon his head the kan sign, which represents a grain of maize. To the latter is ordinarily attached a growth of some sort that may either represent an ear of maize surrounded by leaves or a young sprout. The simple kan sign is basis of the glyph for the day, Kan (Fig. 121), and likewise occurs in many other situations. Offerings of maize cakes are indicated

FIG. 120. — Girdle strap wrappings modified into an inverted face.

in the codices by bowls containing kan signs. The sign is also placed in juxtaposition with some of the gods to indicate powers favorable or unfavorable to good crops. The kan sign in connection with the ear of maize or the sprout, whichever it may be, is shown in Fig. 122, *d*. This latter object is sometimes represented as a curiously conventionalized serpent head of which the eye at the top is the most conspicuous feature. According to Schellhas the head of

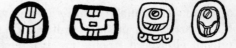

FIG. 121. — Glyphs of the day Kan.

the Maize God was itself evolved out of this object. In this statement, however, he probably goes too far. Sometimes, as in Fig. 122, *b*, the face and the headdress are very closely combined or even fused together. Sometimes the face is divided into a forward and a backward part and the two divisions differentiated in color. But as often as not the face and form of the Maize God is

[1] 1889–1902, I, p. 37.   [2] 1904, pp. 24–25.

youthful, beautiful and of a purely human type (Fig. 122, *a* and *b*). The Maize
God, apparently represented as
newly born, and with the umbilical cord still attached, may be
seen on Plate 19 of the Peresianus Codex (Fig. 122, *c*).

On the monuments the rep-
resentation of this god may be
discerned in the youthful figure
with a leafy headdress, examples
of which are given in Fig. 123.
It occupies a secondary position
on the monuments, but the characters are constant and are,
moreover, consistent with those
appearing on the figures in the
codices. On Stela H at Copan

FIG. 122. — Various representations of the Maize God: *a* and *b*,
Dresden Codex; *c–e*, Codex Peresianus.

several small human beings of this type, Fig. 123, *e*, may be seen climbing
round and over the interwoven bodies of serpents. At Quirigua the occurrence

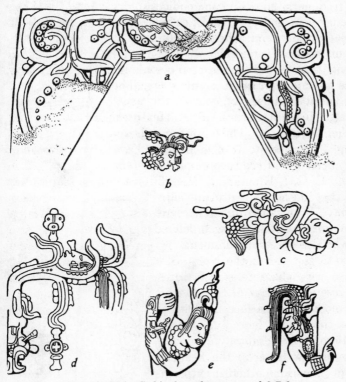

FIG. 123. — The Maize God in the sculptures: *a* and *d*, Palenque;
b, Tikal; *c* and *e*, Copan; *f*, Quirigua.

is similar (*f*), while at
Tikal the head shown
in *b* thrusts itself out of
the eye of a richly em-
bellished serpent head,
the upturned nose of
which is shaped into
the face of the Roman-
nosed God (Fig. 96, *g*).
In all these drawings
the determining feature
is the bunches of circles
enclosed in leaflike ob-
jects that may repre-
sent the ear of maize or
bursting seed pods. In
an interesting stucco
decoration in the Pal-
ace at Palenque (Fig.
123, *a*) are shown com-
parable circular details
as well as maize ears
rather realistically
drawn, while the god
himself appears at the
top of the design. De-

tails which seem to represent ears of maize or bursting pods are recorded in a
drawing by Waldeck[1] of one of the now lost tablets of Palenque. The maize

[1] Maudslay, 1889–1902, IV, pl. 86.

ears in this instance seem to depend from the inverted head of the Long-nosed God. The form of the Maize God in all these instances is distinctly human and in marked contrast to the other deities so far considered. The beautiful sculp-

FIG. 124.—God C and his hieroglyph: Dresden Codex.

ture[1] from the façade of Temple 22 at Copan which Maudslay calls a "singing girl" may represent the youthful Maize God. Other comparable figures from the same building are in the Peabody Museum (Plate 26, fig. 3). The headdress resembles that of this deity as given in the codices. There is clear enough evidence that the faces and figures of the Long-nosed God, the Roman-nosed God and the Death God were used to decorate the façades of temples in this city, and the usage may have included other deities as well. Two sculptured stones from the terrace east of the Great Plaza at Copan doubtless bear representations of the Maize God.[2] The figures are human. The headdress has the usual sign of the growing plant surmounted by a small face of the Long-nosed God.

The Maize God seems to have been a divinity with little absolute power. He is frequently shown in the codices under the protection of the benevolent gods, B and D, or under the malign control of the Death God whom Schellhas calls God A.

The Maize God seems to bear some relation to the numbers eight and eighteen,[3] because his face occurs in some instances as the glyph for these numbers. The higher number shows, of course, the usual death signs in addition to the natural features.

FIG. 125.—God C with a mottled green body: Codex Peresianus.

Other Divinities. The following gods according to the system of Schellhas have already been considered in more or less detail: A, B, D, E, G, I, K and N. In addition to these many other

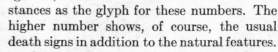

forms that do not fall into this category have been taken up. There remain a number of fairly well-defined gods who deserve brief comment.

God C, the god of the North Star

FIG. 126.—God C: Tro-Cortesianus Codex.

or the northern sky, has very characteristic features. Figs. 124, 125 and 126 present drawings of God C from each of the three Maya codices. The face of this god was found a number of times as a hieroglyph during the exploration of the Hieroglyphic Stairway at Copan, one of the original stones now being in the Peabody Museum. It also occurs in various other inscriptions (Fig. 127) and in astronomical bands on several of the monuments. No extensive use of this god's figure has come to light in the larger sculptures.

FIG. 127.—Hieroglyphs containing face of God C: a, Palenque; b, Copan; c–e, Tro-Cortesianus Codex.

Gods F and H have not been clearly identified in the sculptures. The first

[1] Maudslay, 1889–1902, I, pl. 17, a and b.　　　[2] Gordon, 1896, p. 2.　　　[3] Bowditch, 1910, pls. 16 and 17.

is a god of war who has human form. It is possible, of course, this portrait appears in some of the sculptures that deal with warfare and conquest. The second god is called the Chicchan God because he has certain markings on his face that resemble the markings on the serpent body and on the glyph for the day Chicchan. He also seems to be a warlike divinity. Seler calls this god the Young God. He may perhaps be identified with the head having purely human features that rarely appears in the serpent mouth (Fig. 24). As a rule, the head in the serpent mouth belongs to the Long-nosed God group or to the allied group of the Roman-nosed God.

Gods L and M are represented in the manuscripts with black bodies. The latter according to Schellhas may be identified with Ekchuah, the black god of the traveling merchants. Goddess O represents an old woman; few representations of her occur. God P has been called the Frog God. The frog is represented with some frequency on the monuments and seems to be the original of the uinal glyph that represents the month. This connection appears to be purely phonetic, however, since "uo" means frog and "u" month.[1]

Astronomical Signs. Bands of astronomical symbols have already been many times referred to and compared in a general way. There is considerable uncertainty concerning the exact significance of many of the individual symbols. It is probable that the sun and moon, the important planets, and the larger constellations were represented specifically and that there were other signs that were general and inclusive in their meaning.

It has already been demonstrated that one of the so-called astronomical symbols is the conventionalized face of the Roman-nosed God (Fig. 128, a). The sign probably signifies either the sun

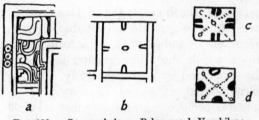

Fig. 128. — Sun symbols: a, Palenque; b, Yaxchilan; c and d, Dresden Codex.

specifically or the more general idea of day or light. Its importance is indicated by the fact that in one case it occupies the entire space at the side of a monument (Fig. 92) and in another alternates with the unusual Caban sign (Fig. 91, f) that may represent its opposite, which might be the moon, or perhaps darkness.

The usual form for the sun is the normal kin sign (Fig. 128, b), which consists of an oval or oblong with one or more marks extending inward from the middle of each side. Sometimes a circle occurs in the center.

Dr. Seler [2] includes in this group of sun symbols the forms with dotted diagonals (Fig. 128, c and d), which Förstemann considers to be symbols for the planet Mercury. Mr. Bowditch,[3] however, shows that the calculations in the Dresden Codex upon which the supposition is based do not agree very closely with the periods of revolution of this planet. The sign is of very frequent occurrence, both in the sculptures and in the manuscripts.

Another form which may represent the sun is less commonly encountered. It is more or less circular, with a normal kin sign in the center and a serpent head projecting outward at four points. As an astronomical symbol it may be seen on Stela 10 at Piedras Negras[4] and perhaps in the upper division of Stela 1

[1] Bowditch, 1910, pp. 257–258. [2] 1901–1902, pp. 165–166. [3] 1910, p. 228. [4] Maler, 1901, pl. 19.

and in the upper left-hand corner of Stela 4 at Yaxchilan.[1] As a medallion decoration on piers it occurs at Palenque,[2] where it incloses a head. It likewise is found in the Peresianus Codex.[3] In the frescos of Chichen Itza a sun disk is represented with a serpent head projecting on the four diagonals (Fig. 129). This sun disk is itself a Nahua and not a Maya concept, but the four serpent heads in connection with it may hark back to a genuinely native origin.

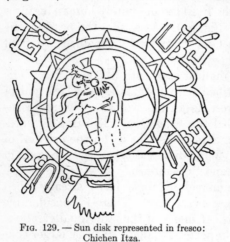

FIG. 129. — Sun disk represented in fresco: Chichen Itza.

A symbol which Förstemann considers a moon symbol (Fig. 130, a) occurs very frequently in the codices on terms of equality with the kin sign in the heraldic shields which are attached to the under sides of astronomical bands. It represents in a cursive and a demotic manner an ornamented eye or a partial face. This symbol is very similar to the sign for twenty in the codices as well as to the hieroglyph for God D, the principal phase of the Roman-nosed God in the manuscripts. Dr. Seler[4] considers these signs to represent the bloody sockets of gouged-out eyes, the hieroglyphs of Itzamna, whom he considers Lord of Life and of the Milky Way. He is probably right in the general conclusion that the face represents a god who takes the form and features of an old man. But the points upon which the interpretation is made appear highly fanciful and hardly to be supported by objective study. Ornamented eyes are of very general occurrence, and in most cases where circles are drawn beneath them there is no other evidence of "gouged sockets." It seems probable that this cursive face should be correlated with the rectangular presentation of the Roman-nosed God that has just been considered (Fig. 128, a). This symbol that occupies so prominent a place in the monuments does not appear in the manuscripts unless under the present guise.

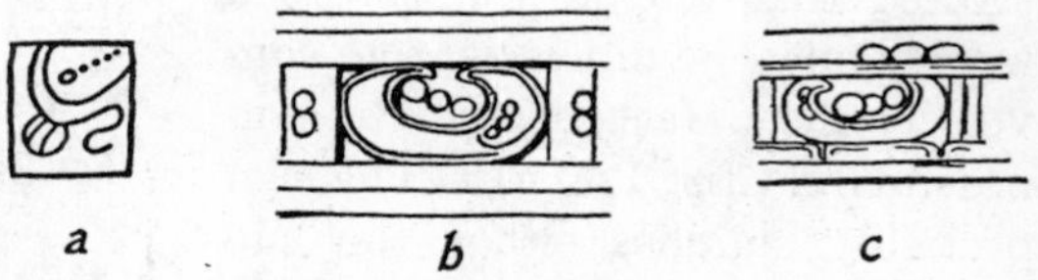

FIG. 130. — Symbols that may represent the moon: a, Dresden Codex; b and c, Palenque.

As for the crescent-shaped symbols (Fig. 130, b and c) which Dr. Seler in the same passage associates with the symbol of the ornamented eye, just considered, a comparison of other forms does not seem to support his conclusions. The form occurring on Stela 10 at Piedras Negras[5] clearly shows a head inclosed in the deep crescent. The most interesting example of this figure is seen in the upper right-hand figure of Stela 4 at Yaxchilan, where it is in a position of opposition to the circular sign with the four serpent heads. It is of course quite possible that these crescent symbols should represent the moon. They also resemble one of the glyphs of the so-called Supplementary Series.[6] The symbols of the planet Venus are pretty well ascertained. There are two principal forms, as

[1] Maler, 1903, pls. 69 and 70.
[2] Maudslay, 1889–1902, IV, pl. 6.
[3] De Rosny, 1887, pl. 21.
[4] 1901–1902, pp. 166–167.
[5] Maler, 1901, pl. 19.
[6] Bowditch, 1910, p. 244.

shown in Fig. 131, *a* and *b*. Also there are many irregular or unusual forms that include one of these simple signs combined with an animal or some other object. Venus symbols are of very common occurrence not only in astronomical bands but also as details on various sculptured figures and in the hieroglyphic inscriptions. In fact, some of the most extensive inscriptions may refer largely to the correlation of the solar and Venus years. An extended passage in the Dresden Codex is given over to this

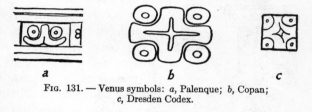

subject.[1] Some of the variant signs of the Venus symbol doubtless refer to different appearances and conjunctions of this planet. Gordon[2] derives the Venus symbol of the first type from the con-

FIG. 131. — Venus symbols: *a*, Palenque; *b*, Copan; *c*, Dresden Codex.

ventionalized jaws of the serpent. But the stages of this development are not very clear if you omit the doubtful forms that occur in Nahua art. The second type seems, however, to have developed from the first by a simple folding over or reduplication.

Another sign which is pretty well settled as to its significance represents the face of God C, the divinity who rules the North Star or the entire northern sky. This sign occurs more frequently in the codices than on the monuments.

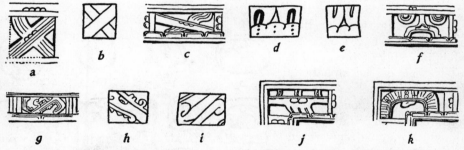

FIG. 132. — Planet symbols: *a*, Copan; *c*, *f*, *g*, *j* and *k*, Palenque; *b*, *d*, *e* and *i*, Dresden Codex.

A symbol in the form of a cross (Fig. 132, *a–c*) is exceedingly common. It probably has some very general meaning such as the sky as a whole. This sign frequently occurs as a hieroglyph and upon headdresses. The symbol which resembles Akbal may mean night or it may have some more specific meaning. Comparable forms in the manuscripts and monuments are given in the text (Fig. 132, *d–f*). This symbol has been referred to the planet Jupiter on rather doubtful grounds.[3] The symbol which shows a serpent head arranged diagonally in the oblong panel (Fig. 132, *g–i*) has been similarly ascribed to Saturn. Other symbols of less frequent use are shown in Fig. 132, *j* and *k*, as well as in Figs. 5, 6, 83 and 89.

Hieroglyphs. The Maya hieroglyphs have been so many times referred to in the text that it seems hardly necessary to accord them here more than a general treatment. Although at the present time few of the hieroglyphs have been deciphered, the task does not seem to be an insurmountable one. A large part of

---

[1] Bowditch, 1909.   [2] 1905, pl. 6.   [3] Bowditch, 1910, pp. 229–231.

the inscriptions have to do with astronomical calculations which introduce certain absolute factors. In fact, the glyphs connected with numbers and the calendar are now pretty well ascertained, including the so-called period glyphs and the numerals from one to twenty, and the signs for each of the twenty days and for each of the eighteen months. The hieroglyph for the extra period of five days used to complete the annual calendar is also known as well as the signs

FIG. 133. — Composite monster and its glyph: Dresden Codex.

for zero or completion. Some of the hieroglyphs which refer to certain heavenly bodies and to certain gods have been isolated. The symbols for the four directions have been determined with considerable certainty as well as a few other signs of lesser importance. It may be remarked, *en passant*, that the results of Le Plongeon[1] and Brasseur de Bourbourg[2] are of very little value so far as the decipherings of inscriptions are concerned. Nor has the so-called alphabet of Landa[3] proved of much service, although it was evidently taken down in good faith.

Most of the Maya hieroglyphics are probably ideographic and consist of abbreviated pictures of the thing intended or of some object connected with it. In Fig. 133 we see a representation of some mythological conception and the glyph which refers to it. The glyph that probably stands for the rear head of the Two-headed Dragon contains, as we have seen (Fig. 82), the three peculiar signs of the headdress and the sun sign on the forehead.

It seems pretty clear that certain symbols have a phonetic value, probably of the syllabic rather than of the alphabetic type. This phonetic character is particularly demonstrable in words containing the syllable *kin*, which may be represented by the sun symbol. But it is extremely doubtful if there was a complete syllabary adapted to narrative texts. The general status of writing was probably much like that of the Valley of Mexico, which has been explained by Brinton, Peñafiel and others, although it is possible that the range of subjects was somewhat greater. The

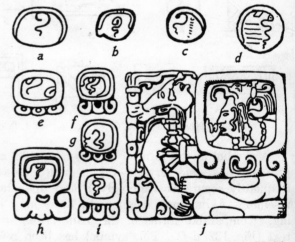

FIG. 134. — Series showing modifications of glyphs: *a* and *b*, Cib; *c–j*, Caban; *a*, Peresianus Codex; *b*, Dresden Codex; *c*, Tro-Cortesianus Codex; *d*, Landa; *e*, Copan; *f–j*, Quirigua.

Nahua seem to have learned this valuable art from their southern neighbors. Many points of divergence in the two areas must be ascribed to the differences in organic structure in the two languages as well as to the different standards of art.

In addition to what is now known we may expect to find in the Maya inscrip-

[1] 1886 and 1896.   [2] 1869–1870.   [3] 1864, pp. 316 *et seq.*; Valentini, 1880; Brinton, 1894, *b*.

tions some hieroglyphs that give the names of individuals, cities and political divisions and others that represent feasts, sacrifices, tributes and common objects of trade as well as signs referring to birth, death, establishment, conquest, destruction and other such fundamentals of individual and social existence. Juxtaposition of these hieroglyphs together with directive signs and dates would make possible records of considerable accuracy. On many of the monuments the small number of hieroglyphs left, once all the dates have been eliminated, suggests that such an abbreviated system of writing was in vogue.

As to names of individuals or cities, it is worthy of note that several of the sculptures show hieroglyphs over the heads or upon the bodies of human beings. These might very well be names (Figs. 10 and 17). The hieroglyphs over the heads of the warriors in the processions shown on the walls of the Lower Temple of the Jaguars at Chichen Itza may represent cities rather than individuals. They are of Nahua rather than Maya type, however.

FIG. 135. — Hieroglyph with entire figures: Stela D, Copan.

The degree of variation in the Maya hieroglyphs that have been ascertained is very great, as may be seen from the series collected by Mr. Bowditch.[1] Fig. 134 presents a series of glyphs of the day Caban which are unusually consistent. The characteristic feature is the corkscrew curl. But even this feature reappears in other glyphs, particularly in the forms for the day, Cib, from the codices. An example of elaboration is given in Fig. 135 from Stela D at Copan. The essential features of the hieroglyph seem to be those that are carried in the arms of the two human figures. Other examples of complicated hieroglyphs have received comment. It is apparent from these examples that the study of the art is very necessary if one is to arrive at an understanding of the subject matter expressed in these abbreviated or elaborated pictures.

[1] 1910.

CONSIDERATION OF THE MATERIAL ARTS

ARCHITECTURE

Assemblage. The mapping of the principal Maya ruins has disclosed several styles of assemblage of the city as a whole, each of which seems to have a fairly definite geographical distribution and at the same time a topographical explanation. The clear types will here be briefly described as well as some of the apparent transitions.

Most of the Maya cities were built upon level ground, either extensive plains or valley floors. Where such was the case the assemblage was unhampered and followed the fashion of the region or perhaps of the period. But in some instances — particularly in the western part of the Maya area — the cities were hemmed in by hills and streams. Here the assemblage had to adapt itself to surroundings, but doubtless the builders attempted to preserve as much of the usual order as they could.

Perhaps the most careful and elaborate grouping of the city as a whole is seen at Copan.[1] In this place there is a massive platform mound, a sort of artificial acropolis, with terraces and sunken courts at various levels. Rising from the flat of this principal mound are small pyramids of the usual type crowned with temples. The great mound overlooks an extensive plaza in which are set up stelae. The plaza is surrounded by a stepped wall as if it were a sort of theater. The so-called sunken courts are also inclosed by stepped walls and are drained by tunnels that pass under the walls. Most of the small mounds which mark the domiciliary structures lie on the opposite side of the great mound from the plaza.

This elaborate mode of grouping may have been intended to obtain a broad architectural effect. While there is apparently no definite orientation, there is an orderly alignment of the buildings and terraces. At Quirigua[2] a very similar assemblage is found, both as regards the form of the artificial acropolis and the use of the plazas in which were set up stelae.

The use of the great platform mound to serve as a base for a number of smaller substructures also characterizes the great ruins of the Peten region. But in these cities the artificial acropolis is perhaps not so conspicuous as in the cities just named. A plan of Ixkun by Maudslay[3] shows an artificial acropolis on which are several pyramids arranged around courts. At Naranjo,[4] near the western end of the city, is a large rectangular mound with a lower adjoining terrace. Upon this large mound are remains of six structures very much destroyed. At the eastern end of the city there is, in all probability, a low but extensive mound which serves as a foundation for the three principal courts with their inclosing structures.

[1] Maudslay, 1889–1902, I, pl. 1; Gordon, 1896, pl. 1.
[2] Maudslay, 1889–1902, II, pl. 2.
[3] 1889–1902, II, pl. 67.
[4] Maler, 1908, b, p. 83.

At Tikal there are, according to the recent explorations of Dr. Tozzer [1] and Mr. Merwin, no less than three great foundation mounds that mark out the civic and religious centers of this most important city. These mounds are of considerable height, but do not compare with the great mound of Copan. Upon these mounds are many closely connected courts surrounded by temple and palace structures. The artificial acropolis also occurs at Nakum, La Hondradez and other sites in the Peten region. [2]

The orientation of courts and buildings with strict regard for the four directions prevails among the cities of southern Yucatan that have just been mentioned as well as at Siebal [3] and doubtless other places. It does not occur at Copan and Quirigua, although at these sites there is an orderly alignment of walls and mounds. At Copan an east and west line passing directly across the city seems to have been surveyed with tolerable accuracy and marked by two stelae placed on hills on opposite sides of the valley. [4] Perhaps the most interesting point concerning the use of closely connected and carefully oriented courts is that each court with its associated buildings naturally served as a unit of city growth and that the sequence is more or less exactly indicated by position.

The ruins of northern Yucatan, [5] although situated in a level country, show neither the artificial acropolis nor the careful orientation that distinguishes the cities of the south. Occasionally advantage was taken of slight natural elevations, as at Labna. The irregular platform mounds that serve as foundations for the larger structures may perhaps be considered decadent examples of the early artificial acropolis. The assemblage may be termed haphazard. There are, as a rule, several independent groups of correlated buildings. These independent groups may represent different periods of city growth. In the correlations of buildings within these groups the principle of arrangement is very often that of the rectangular court with one or more buildings on each side.

Yaxchilan, [6] Piedras Negras [7] and Palenque [8] are examples of cities situated in narrow valleys where the topography modified the assemblage. In the first two sites natural hills or ridges were leveled off and terraced. But the buildings erected upon these hills have little exact and premeditated grouping. The same may be said of Palenque. No natural or artificial acropolis occurs at this site, unless the mound that supports the Palace is considered one, but instead a narrow valley, the sides of which were terraced to a considerable height. There is good reason to believe that the artificial acropolis would have prevailed at these cities if the topography had permitted. At Comalcalco, which is even farther west than Palenque, there is, according to Charnay, [9] a massive mound upon which are the ruins of several buildings. The same occurs at Ocosingo or Tonina. [10]

Certain minor features of assemblage will now be presented principally in

[1] Tozzer, 1911, pls. 29 and 30.
[2] Sapper, 1897, p. 360 (Ixtinta) and p. 362 (S. Clemente).
[3] Maler, 1908, a, p. 13.
[4] Gordon, 1898, b, p. 4, gives a map of the environs of Copan, as does Maudslay, 1886.
[5] For plans of Chichen Itza see Maudslay, 1889–1902, III, pl. 2, and Holmes, 1895–1897, pls. 17 and 18. For Uxmal see Holmes, 1895–1907, pls. 8 and 9, and Stephens, 1843, I, p. 165. For Labna see Stephens, 1843, II, frontispiece showing panorama, and an unpublished map made by the Peabody

Museum under Mr. Thompson. For Kabah see Stephens, 1843, I, p. 385. For Ake see Charnay, 1885, p. 249. For Tuloom see Stephens, 1843, II, p. 396.
[6] Maudslay, 1889–1902, II, pl. 76; Maler, 1903, pl. 39.
[7] Maler, 1901, pl. 33.
[8] Holmes, 1895–1897, pls. 24 and 25; Maudslay, 1889–1902, IV, pl. 1.
[9] 1885, p. 167.
[10] Sapper, 1897, p. 361.

connection with frontier ruins. Along the Uloa River [1] the influence of Copan and Quirigua may be seen in the arrangement of mounds and courts. At one of the ancient ruins a crude stela appears in front of the principal mound. The use of sunken courts and of plazas with stelae extends up the Motagua River and over the highlands of Guatemala as far as the Chiapas Valley. Many of the plans of ancient settlements given by Sapper [2] and Seler [3] show similarities to the lowland sites. Careful orientation was not observed. These outlying towns were doubtless provincial in character, and most of them seem to have flourished at a later period than the great cities of the Peten region. The elaborate artificial acropolis is not seen, while the parallel walls of the so-called ball courts present a new and probably un-Maya feature.

Many of the frontier settlements offer definite evidence of fortification that is lacking elsewhere. Tenampua [4] in central Honduras is described as occupying an impregnable position upon a lofty hill and as being further strengthened by surrounding walls. A number of towns in the highlands of Guatemala [5] were placed between barrancas and in other easily defended positions. Of course the artificial acropolis in the great cities may have been partly intended for defense. There is no doubt that warfare was highly and scientifically developed. Stephens [6] describes a wall at Tuloom that seems to have surrounded the city. Upon the frescos of Chichen Itza are represented earthworks behind which warriors are fighting, as well as what may be taken for scaling ladders.

Function of Buildings. Little is known concerning the function of Maya buildings other than that they were largely of a religious nature.

It is possible to distinguish between buildings for strictly ceremonial uses, such as the small temples on lofty pyramids, and other buildings, usually larger and situated on lower terraces, which may have served as dwellings for the priests and the nobility. This latter group includes the great rambling collections of rooms, usually arranged around courts and commonly called palaces. Evidence concerning the differentiation and development of the temple and the palace will appear under various headings.

Towers of several stories were sometimes built, but their use is unknown. The square tower at Palenque, four stories in height, has often been described. [7] A similar structure, not so high, is found at Comalcalco. [8] Maler [9] figures a tower-like structure, with a great stucco face on one side, that occurs at Nocuchich, as well as another tower of more slender dimensions. Round towers occur at Mayapan [10] and at Chichen Itza, the example from the latter city being the famous Carocol. [11] It seems pretty clear that these towers were not intended for observation. None of the towers have pyramidal substructures, and in each city where examples are found there are other buildings that exceed the tower in elevation. The round towers are said to have been associated with the worship of Kukulcan.

[1] Gordon, 1898, *a*, p. 11.

[2] 1895, *a*. Map No. 5 (Hacienda Grande); No. 6 (Las Quebradas); No. 8 (Cakiha); No. 9 (Chacujal); No. 11 (Sacramento); No. 12 (Bolonchac); No. 13 (Saculeu); No. 17 (Kalamté); No. 18 (Comitancillo); No. 20 (Sajcabaja).

[3] 1901, *c*, pp. 100 and 131 (Quen Santo).

[4] Squier, 1858, pp. 133–138, and Bancroft, 1875–1876, IV, pp. 72–77.

[5] Maudslay, 1889–1902, II, pls. 70 (Rabinal), 72 (Utatlan) and 73 (Iximché).

[6] 1843, II, pp. 395–396.

[7] Maudslay, 1889–1902, IV, pl. 39; Holmes, 1895–1897, pp. 179–186.

[8] Charnay, 1885, p. 170.

[9] 1895, pp. 281 *et seq.*

[10] Stephens, 1843, I, p. 136.

[11] Maudslay, 1889–1902, III, pl. 20.

The ball court or gymnasium seems to have a foreign origin and will be discussed in that connection, together with certain other imported ideas, architectural, decorative and religious. This structure is found in none of the early Maya cities.

The dwellings of the common people in ancient times were probably not essentially different from the huts still made and used by the natives of Yucatan.[1]

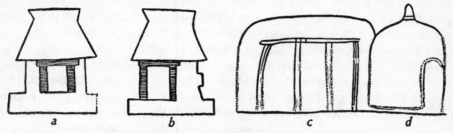

Fig. 136. — Representations of Indian huts in fresco: Chichen Itza.

These huts are generally oval in plan, containing a single room. The framework is of light poles skillfully bound together by withes. The walls are of wattle and mud, while the roofs are heavily thatched with the leaves of the Sabal and other palms. Mural paintings in the Temple of the Jaguars at Chichen Itza represent the ancient dwellings of the lower classes. Examples of these are reproduced in Fig. 136. Near most of the remains of stone temples and palaces there are, according to Mr. Thompson,[2] many evidences of these poorer dwellings. The outlines of the huts may be traced out by the uneven surface of the ground and the three-stone fireplaces uncovered by slight excavation.

Ground-Plans. Some idea of the uses to which buildings were put may be obtained from a study of the ground-plans. The simple room, with the door in

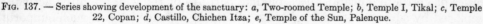

Fig. 137. — Series showing development of the sanctuary: a, Two-roomed Temple; b, Temple I, Tikal; c, Temple 22, Copan; d, Castillo, Chichen Itza; e, Temple of the Sun, Palenque.

the center of one of its long sides, seems to have been the common starting-point for both the temple and the palace type of structures. In the case of the temple this simple room was modified by interior partitions until there was a clear development of the sanctuary or inner sacred chamber, while in the growth of the palace structures there was an agglutinative process by which one room, with or without interior divisions, was simply set up against another. Rarely indeed is there a series of interior doorways connecting the different room units of a large building.

The development of the sanctuary in the temple is indicated in the series of temple ground-plans shown in Fig. 137. The simple two-chambered temple, a step in advance of the single room that served as a starting-point, is shown in a. Here

---

[1] Thompson, 1892, a, p. 262. [2] 1892, a, pp. 263 et seq.

the inner room, getting only the diffused light from the outer door, might fittingly have been considered the holy of holies and the mysterious abode of divinity. Often the floor of this interior room is raised a foot or more above that of the outer room and the doorway and inner walls adorned with sculptures. The temples of Tikal have very massive walls and small cell-like rooms, sometimes three in number one behind the other (Fig. 137, *b*). The wooden lintels over the doorways are in some cases splendidly carved. The ground-plan of Temple 22, at Copan, is given in *c* of this series. The ceremonial importance of the inner chamber of this temple is emphasized by elaborate carvings, representing the Two-headed Dragon supported by kneeling atlantean figures. This design enclosed the doorway. The entrance to the inner chamber of Temple 11, at Copan, is also elaborately ornamented by carvings. The highest form of the sanctuary is seen at Palenque (*e*), in the Temples of the Sun, the Cross and the Foliated Cross. The sanctuaries here are little temples in themselves, roofs and all, and

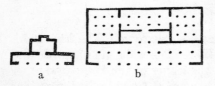

a   b

Fig. 138. — Structures showing the extreme development of the portico: Group of the Columns, Chichen Itza.

are adorned with the most wonderful native bas-relief carvings of the New World. Some of the temples of Chichen Itza also have well-defined sanctuaries, as may be seen from *d*, the ground-plan of the Castillo. In many temples there is a built-up bench in the sanctuary which may have served as an altar. In some cases table altars have been found in position in the outer room directly in front of the door to the sanctuary.

Closely paralleling the development of the inner division of the simple temple into a true sanctuary, the outer division becomes a portico. At Copan, Quirigua and Tikal, where the walls are exceedingly massive, the temple façades are broken by but one doorway. As one proceeds toward the north, the walls become much lighter, although at best cumbersome, and two or more doorways, symmetrically placed, give entrance to the outer chamber of the temple. At Yaxchilan nearly all the temples have several doorways. At Palenque the doorways are placed so closely together that the portions of the wall remaining between them are hardly more than piers. At Labna, Chichen Itza and other cities of northern Yucatan these pierlike portions of the wall are often actually replaced by square or round columns. With the extended use of such supports the front room of the temple becomes more and more open. Fig. 138 gives two ground-plans that illustrate this ultimate development of the outer chamber into a light and airy portico. In *a* the sanctuary is a small cell behind a wide open chamber and in *b* the portico has a double row of columns. The buildings showing double rows of columns are found only in northern Yucatan and are of late date. It will be shown in a later treatment that the development of the sanctuary and the portico, that has just been sketched out, is really historical and covers practically the entire chronological range of Maya art.

Some structures, not properly of the one-room origin just described, but consisting of two or more independent rooms, were probably used as temples and not for civil or domiciliary purpose. The House of the Magician at Uxmal is an example. The main temple has three rooms in a row without connecting doorways. The middle chamber of this temple opens in the direction opposite to the doorways of the end chambers and is, in fact, rendered inaccessible by the Annex built apparently at a later date. The steep and lofty substructure of the House of the Magician would have made it an inconvenient abode. But as a temple it is exceedingly impressive, looking down as it does upon the Nunnery Quadrangle.

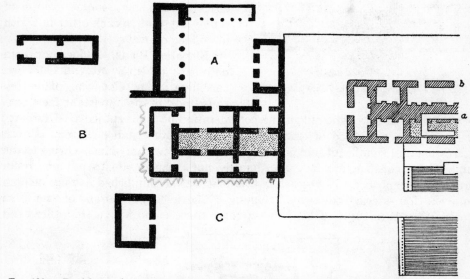

FIG. 139. — Partial ground-plan of the Group of the Monjas: Chichen Itza. Ground-level buildings in black; *b*, second range structures; *a*, third range.

It is difficult, if not impossible, to draw any definite line between the temple and the palace; for it is likely that even in buildings clearly of the latter type there were certain rooms given over to religious rites. A partial plan of the Group of the Monjas at Chichen Itza, after Maudslay, is presented in Fig. 139. This group shows several distinct periods of growth. Moreover, some of the parts seem to show differentiation in use. In particular the small closed court marked A in the plan appears almost necessarily domiciliary. The elaborate frieze decoration of grotesque masks, that characterizes the north and east façade of the eastern ground-level wing, stops abruptly after turning the corner on the south side. The rest is plain. The two buildings which completed the square were of unusually light construction and may even have had wooden roofs. They are in complete ruin and the amount of debris is not great. This secluded

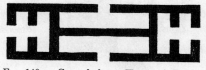

FIG. 140. — Ground-plan: House of Turtles, Uxmal.

court may well have been the abode of the temple attendants. On the other hand, the elaborate decoration of the eastern façade indicates a religious significance for the end chamber. The third story of this building must also have had purely religious uses. A wide stairway leads up to a small single-room structure with an altar-like object in front. The small detached building known as the Iglesia was probably for purely religious uses. The other chambers of this group might have served as a religious college or monastery, or as a chief's palace.

The remarkable symmetry in plan as well as the agglutination of independent room-units of the larger structures is well brought out in the ground-plans of the House of the Turtles (Fig. 140) and of the Governor at Uxmal [1] and of the Akat'cib at Chichen Itza (Fig. 141). The rooms are either strung out or clustered. The palace structures at Palenque [2] and some of the southern cities often show several groups of rooms adjacent to each other but with disconnected walls.

FIG. 141. — Ground-plan: Akat'cib, Chichen Itza.

Elevation Plans. It does not seem necessary to enter into an extended consideration of elevation plans, because most of the important facts concerning them are brought out in the consideration of other subjects. However, the usual Maya method of erecting buildings of more than one story is both interesting and significant and is readily seen from elevation plans. Owing to the cumbersome construction it was ordinarily not deemed safe to put one room directly over another. Nevertheless this feat was accomplished as may be seen from the four-storied tower at Palenque. The so-called Temple of the Five Stories (Structure 10) at Tikal [3] shows three stories, one above the other, and

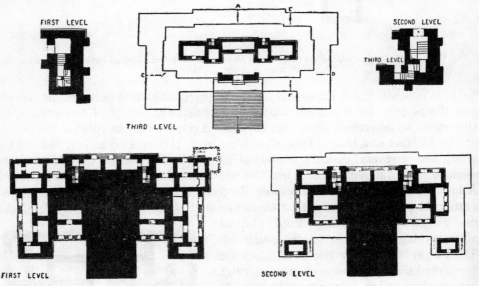

FIG. 142. — Ground-plans: Santa Rosa Xlabpak.

two lower stories at the side of the foundation mound. As a rule, however, the second story was built upon a solid substructure immediately behind the room or rooms of the first story and on a level with its roof. As a development of this method a series of rooms was sometimes constructed entirely around or at either end of a solid mass of masonry. Upon this mass of masonry was built the second story, which might in turn have a smaller core of solid masonry to support the third range of rooms. The principal building of Santa Rosa Xlabpak is a most interesting example of symmetry and fine construction. In Fig. 142 are repro-

[1] Holmes, 1895–1897, pl. VIII.   [2] Maudslay, 1889–1902, IV, pl. 3.   [3] Tozzer, 1911, pp. 112–113.

duced the careful drawings of Maler giving the floor plans of the three stories of the Palace-temple Tampak, as he calls it, and in Fig. 143 are three typical elevation cross-sections. The masses of solid masonry are shown in black. The first story is on a level with the ground. The rooms open out on all four sides of the buildings and are generally double, one chamber being behind the other. The second story covers a somewhat greater area than the solid core of the first story. The outer walls of the second range of rooms fall in some cases over the interior walls of the first. The third story faces the east and is approached by a broad flight of stairs, at the top of which stands a portal arch. The narrow winding stairway at the back also ascends to the third story (Fig. 142). The rooms at this high level are all single. Stephen [1] calls this building "the grandest structure that now rears its ruined head in the forests of Yucatan."

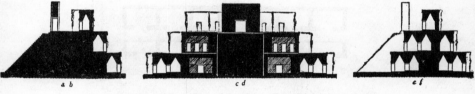

FIG. 143. — Elevations: Santa Rosa Xlabpak.

The Akat'cib at Chichen Itza (Fig. 141) may be compared in certain details to this building. Here the ground-level rooms are finished and the solid mass that was probably intended to support the upper stories is in place, but no second and third story was ever begun. The principal building at Sayil [2] shows all three stories, and is perhaps the most extensive single structure in the Maya area. Other examples of two or three stories built according to the same principle of an interior core might be named.

A peculiar feature of many Maya structures that has frequently been commented upon is the occurrence of rooms that have been filled with earth and stone and sealed up. In almost all cases this seems to have been a preliminary to the construction of second-story rooms immediately above. Examples of such filled rooms are seen in the Monjas at Chichen Itza (ground-plan in Fig. 139). Apparently it was the purpose of the builders to erect a second range of rooms over the East Wing, but this intention was never carried out. The single room of the third story is directly over a filled-up chamber.

Correlation of Buildings. It has been stated that assemblage in northern Yucatan is haphazard as far as the city as a whole is concerned, but that correlation is frequently shown between a number of structures. Of course this is also true in the south, where the cities are generally divided into courts. The grouping of structures around a court likewise occurs in northern Yucatan, but with certain differences. The ground-plan of the Monjas group at Chichen Itza has already been presented. In this group there are several buildings carefully aligned that partially enclose two or more courts. The principal façade is on the north side.

At Uxmal correlation is shown in more unmistakable ways. In the case of the grand Nunnery Quadrangle the group as a whole faces the south. The stairways are on the south side and in the middle of the South Range of rooms is a portal arch. The North Range is on a higher substructure, and the walls of the building itself are carried higher than usual and are very richly decorated. As

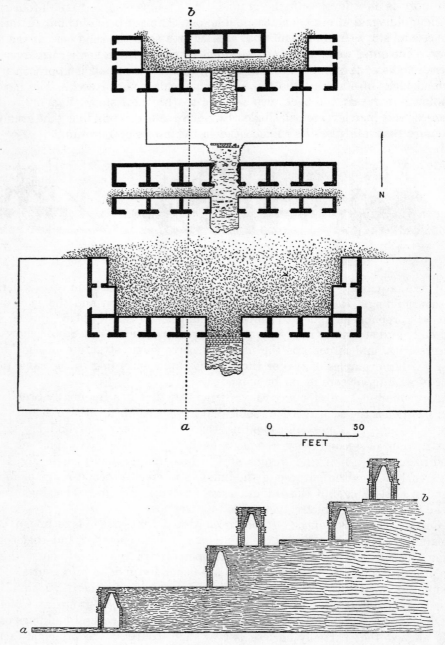

Fig. 144. — Assemblage of Edifice 5, Chacmultun.

a result, this building is visible over the top of the South Range from any point of vantage. The House of the Magician seems to be attached to the southeast corner of the Nunnery Quadrangle, the transition being affected according to

Holmes' plan [1] by two small buildings. It seems likely that the House of the Magician proper is an older building than the Nunnery, since it faces in the opposite direction, but that the Annex to it was built in connection with the latter structure.

The Southwest Group at Uxmal has been clearly presented by Mr. Morley.[2] This group has a four-roomed temple at the southern end, toward which the terraces gradually rise in several levels. Most of the ranges of rooms are built against the side of the next higher terrace. Across the middle of the group extends the House of the Pigeons, with its castellated roof comb and its portal arch (Plate 6, fig. 1). A still more striking development of this idea in a group of much smaller size is seen at Chacmultun (Fig. 144).

The details of Maya construction have been so clearly and admirably described by Mr. Holmes, in his "Archaeological Studies among the Ancient Cities of Mexico," that it is here only necessary to recapitulate the main features. Where, however, a somewhat different interpretation of accepted evidence may have important bearing upon the development of the architectural decoration or upon the connection of the Maya building art with an earlier, more primitive type, then the matter will be discussed more fully.

Substructures. The stone buildings of the Maya, as we have seen, were seldom erected upon ground level, but instead upon artificial mounds. These substructures were apparently not built with an eye to defense (although more or less adaptable to such purposes), but seem to have been purely architectural in function. A large part of the Maya area is without much natural relief, and it might be imagined that the fact led to the use of lofty substructures. But it must be pointed out that these foundation mounds were used as much in hilly country as on the level plain, not only in the Maya area but also in the neighboring Zapotecan and Nahua areas. Often natural elevations were entirely neglected and enormous mounds built up directly from the valley floor, as at Copan. At other sites where the topography was an inevitable factor in the laying out of the city, as at those of the Usumacinta Valley, the natural hills were leveled off or terraced and then artificial substructures reared upon these platforms. Thus it seems clear that the substructure was considered an architecturally valuable feature and one that made directly for grandeur and magnificence quite apart from the question of mere elevated outlook. The pyramid was part of the temple.

The artificial mounds vary much in size, height and shape, but are fairly similar from the point of construction. They usually consist of a solid mass of rubble, mortar and earth faced with cut stone. In many cases it is evident that they were built up by levels. Buried walls and pavements are occasionally found, as in the great acropolis mound at Copan. These may be the remains of the sides and crowns of earlier mounds, which, as the city grew, were found inadequate and so were deeply buried under the new acropolis, or they may be evidences of the method of construction.

It is possible to divide the mounds, as regards size and shape, into two general types, the platform mound and the pyramid. The platform mound includes a great range in contour and elevation, but is marked by the general presence of right-angled corners and irregular terracing. Usually rather low in elevation,

---

[1] Holmes, 1895–1897, pl. 8.   [2] Morley, 1910, a.

they have often several levels, both on the main mounds and on the ells, which are of frequent occurrence. These platform mounds serve as foundations for the larger and more irregular structures. The artificial acropolis that has already been described may perhaps be thrown into this class, although it is a communal rather than an individual substructure.

The pyramids are truncated, usually rectangular, although some have rounded corners, and rise in a series of either vertical steps or slanting terraces. Many

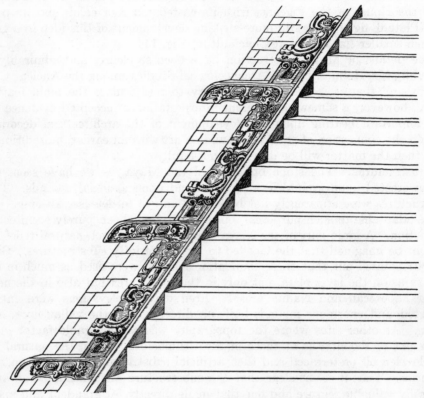

FIG. 145. — Restoration of balustrade of Hieroglyphic Stairway.

variations in form are found. In height the pyramids run from twenty to one hundred feet. The pyramids of Tikal are the highest and the steepest in the Maya area. There are many lofty pyramids in northern Yucatan. The temples of the Usumacinta region are placed, as a rule, on low pyramids.

A very effective decoration was obtained by the use of sunken panels in the stone casings of the various terraces, as may be seen on the pyramid of the Castillo [1] at Chichen Itza and on that Temple I at Tikal.[2] Ornamental stonework of simple but agreeable character may likewise be studied on the very steep pyramid at Rio Beque which has been described by the Comte de Périgny.[3] Sometimes each terrace wall was provided with a simple cornice. The upper part of the substructure of the Monjas at Chichen Itza bears a frieze of mask panels (Plate 28, figs. 3 and 4). Plastic decorations in stucco and painting upon

[1] Maudslay, 1889–1902, III, pl. 56.   [2] Maler, 1911, pl. 2.   [3] Périgny, 1908.

a plaster base may also have been used to adorn certain substructures. Scanty traces of such decorations are still to be seen.

Stairways were constructed on one or more sides of the pyramids and platform mounds. They were very steep, but usually projected somewhat at the base, and so were not so steep as the mounds themselves. Occasionally, as in the case of the Hierolgyphic Stairway at Copan, the steps were carved with glyphs and monuments were placed at intervals. Low balustrades were rather frequent. Sometimes they received considerable attention. Fig. 145 shows a restoration of the balustrades of the Hieroglyphic Stairway at Copan. A number of so-called serpent balustrades are found at Chichen Itza.[1] The heads of the serpents extend outward at the base of the balustrade, which may be said to represent the simplified serpent body. Serpent stairways seem to be restricted to a definite class of pyramids, namely, those with stairways on all four sides, and to a definite period of Maya art.

Walls. The ordinary wall construction resembles that of the Romans. It is not true masonry, but a rough concrete faced with cut stone. The universal lime rock of the country was the material that was broken up for rubble, burned for mortar and plaster, and cut

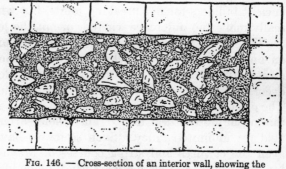

FIG. 146. — Cross-section of an interior wall, showing the hearting: Copan.

with flint chisels for surfacing stones or ornamental sculptured details. Walls made entirely of cut stone are rare.

Perhaps the nearest approach to true stone masonry occurs at Copan. Here rectangular blocks of fairly uniform size were laid in a neat and orderly manner. The joints were broken with fair regularity and the corner-stones were laid in a simple locking system. Plate 3 shows some of the best preserved walls at Copan in which these details are readily discerned. A heavy layer of mortar was used for floors and a thin coating for walls, but this material seems to have been seldom used to cement together the building stones.

The most peculiar and significant feature of the wall construction of Copan has yet to be mentioned. The temple walls are not made entirely of stone, but have a core or hearting of pounded earth or clay mixed with broken stone (Fig. 146). This impermanent filling could serve no useful purpose, except to give greater mass and weight to the wall should that be needed. The stonework is thereby converted into retaining walls for an earth embankment. The collapse inward of the stone retaining walls, such as may be seen in Plate 3, fig. 2, is perhaps due to the washing away of the earthen filling, although Professor Saville ascribes the destruction of the walls at Copan to earthquake action.[2] This peculiar method of construction may indicate that the prototype of the Maya temple was a mud-walled structure and that stonework was added as a veneer.

In the wall construction of Tikal, Yaxchilan, Palenque, etc., the use of irregular slabs of limestone set in a plentiful supply of mortar predominates. The

[1] Maudslay, 1889–1902, III, pl. 58.   [2] 1892, p. 273.

stones on the outer surfaces are roughly trimmed to shape and minor irregularities covered up under a liberal coating of stucco, which likewise formed the chief medium of ornamentation. The large stucco figures in high relief that served to ornament the roof combs were built up over stone skeletons, as shown by Mr. Holmes.[1]

In northern Yucatan, stucco surfacing is employed to a much less extent than in the south and west. As a rule, the walls are finished off with excellently dressed stones neatly fitted together. But these facing stones are not rectangular blocks such as are found at Copan. The outer face of each block is rectangular, while the inner part is roughly shaped into a tenon and set into the mortar and rubble hearting. The blocks come in contact only along the outer edges. Although having the general appearance of stone masonry, these facing stones have no real structural value. Much fault has been found with the ancient builders for not breaking joints, but with stonework of this character it really makes no difference whether or not the joints are broken.

The mosaic veneer character of the stone surfacing has an important bearing on any criticism of the architectural decoration. For if the stone facing had no structural character, and was frankly considered mere veneer, then the façade decorations were not limited in any way by considerations of mechanical fitness. The ornamental stones could be applied as mosaic without the necessity of maintaining any structural lines. The whole surface of the building became a fair field for unlimited fancy. Such seems to have been the understanding, since even the cornices and string courses of Maya buildings had no real virtue as binding stones, and were apparently intended for adornment alone. The mosaic elements used in façade decoration have roughly hewn tenons that were set into the walls.

Vaults. The Maya vault has usually been described as a corbelled or false arch, built not upon the side-thrust principle of the keystone, but upon the downward thrust of a load upon over-stepping stones. The principle of such a vault was doubtless understood by the Maya builders. Plate 4, fig. 1, reproduces a photograph of a small chamber at Copan that was formerly vaulted. The long neatly cut roof stones may still be clearly made out. Such stones are long enough and broad enough to allow considerable purchase along the contact planes, and the arch of this chamber was doubtless of the corbelled variety. But although the corbelled arch was known and used to a slight extent, the typical Maya vault was monolithic in character through the liberal use of cement, and was intended to be so by the builders. Plate 4, fig. 2, shows an excellent natural cross-section of a typical Maya vault of northern Yucatan. It will be noted that the stones are fairly well cut on the outer surface, but that they have no purchase upon each other, since only the merest edges come in contact. The stones are held in place by the mortar of the filling and the vault is in effect monolithic. The mortar used by the Maya seems to have been rather variable in quality. Sometimes the hearting was made exceedingly tight and resistent, but in other cases the mortar was badly mixed with earth and, after the outer coating of plaster had fallen away, the roots of trees were often able to force their way into the chinks, scale off the veneer and even disrupt the walls. But it is exceedingly doubtful if any kind of construction could have resisted better the

[1] 1895–1897, p. 198.

tropical conditions of heavy rainfall and luxurious vegetation than the mortar construction we have just examined.

Certain other features which increase the stability of Maya vaults deserve mention. The center of gravity for each half of the typical vaults of northern Yucatan often falls within the limits of the supporting walls. As a result, one half of a vault is frequently found standing when the other half is in ruins. The weight over the capstones that bridge the five or six inches between the two halves of the vault is usually very light. When the building is two rooms deep the center wall is very stable, since the overhang is equal on the two sides of the wall. This device of reducing the strain to a minimum has been interpreted by some as an understanding of the principle of the cantilever, but a careful examination will show that such is not the truth. The façades of the buildings of the Usumacinta region have a sloping upper zone, and as a result the front wall has nothing to balance the vault overhang.

The vaults in all Maya cities show one constant feature. Always, or at least in the vast majority of cases, there is a projection of a few inches at the springing of the vault on the inside, that is, the widest part of the vault is perhaps six inches narrower than the width of the room. Now this persistent fact doubtless reflects a universal method of construction. It seems probable that the vault was built over a wooden form, and that the shoulder projection at the spring of the vault was to give a few inches leeway to permit the ready removal of the false work. The walls may also have been made inside a wooden frame which held the veneer in position till the slacked lime mortar had set. Wooden struts were often used. Sometimes these are still found in place.[1]

The application of the monolithic arch to other uses than the roofing of rooms was rare, but a few interesting cases may be noted. It was not used for windows, but windows are an almost unknown feature in Maya buildings except in the roof structures. It was not ordinarily used in doorways. At Palenque, however, there are notable examples of vaults over interior doorways. Similar arched openings also occur in the medial walls above the spring of the vault. Several of these arches have a peculiar trifoil shape.

The half arch built against a façade was used in a number of sites to afford a narrow passage under a stairway. A well-preserved example is found at Chichen Itza under the stairway that ascends to the uppermost range of the Monjas. The arch was also used in aqueducts and small bridges.

But perhaps the most interesting employment is in the independent portal or triumphal arch, examples of which occur at Santa Rosa Xlabpak (Fig. 143), Kabah[2] and Labna. One view of the famous portal arch at the latter city is presented in Plate 15, fig. 2. Somewhat allied to this use of the arch are the vaulted passages in several long buildings at Uxmal, such as the House of the Pigeons, the South Range of the Nunnery and the House of the Governor. The arches in the last-named building (Plate 5, fig. 2) have been blocked up.

It is important to note that the vault as described in the preceding pages is peculiar to the Maya culture and is found in all parts of the area. Although very narrow vaulted chambers occur at Monte Alban and at a few other sites outside of the Maya area, yet the fundamental principles do not seem to have

---

[1] The interesting study of the Genesis of the Maya Arch by Mr. E. H. Thompson appeared too late to be of service in this discussion.

[2] Stephens, 1843, I, pp. 399–400.

been grasped by any of the neighboring peoples, although other details of construction were readily imitated or developed. Mrs. Nuttall[1] suggests that vaulted rooms of the Maya type may have been in use on the Island of Sacrifices in the harbor of Vera Cruz, but this point cannot be regarded as settled.

The photographs of buildings which are reproduced in Plates 3 to 16 offer an abundance of proof on the principal points that have been made con-

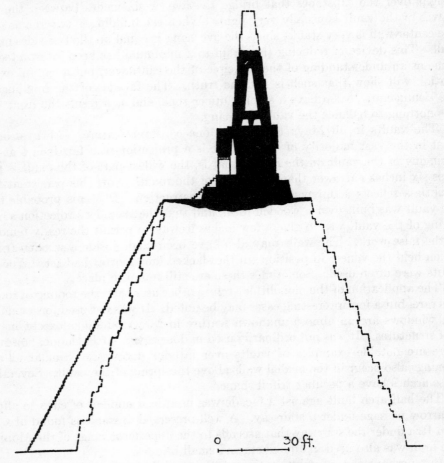

FIG. 147. — Cross-section of Temple V, Tikal.

cerning wall and vault construction. It is obvious that most of the surfacing stones do not support any weight, because other stones beneath them have fallen away. Nearly all of these structures show scaling off of the facing stones, now in the lower zone of the façade, now in the upper zone, and now in the vaults themselves. The inevitable conclusion is that the plain and sculptured blocks were purely and simply a veneer and a mosaic, and that once the mortar had hardened the entire structure was as a single stone.

Roof Structures. Not content with the amount of space for decorations afforded by the facade of the temple, the Maya builders greatly enlarged the area by raising a wall-like superstructure upon the roof. This superstructure is found

[1] 1910, p. 269.

in somewhat different forms in different cities, and from its most common type is often called a roof comb or roof crest. It will be described here in the probable order of the development.

This device for overloading temples with ornament probably was not used at Copan and Quirigua. To be sure, the buildings in these two cities are so completely dilapidated that little beside the floor plan can now be made out. But the amount of debris is not enough to justify the assumption that the buildings were of more than one story. Moreover, the number of sculptured stones, while considerable, does not demand more space than the upper walls of an ordinary façade could give. As a rule, the sculptures on roof structures were of stucco, a material little used in these southern cities.

At Tikal the principal temples, crowning very steep and high pyramids, were themselves topped by a lofty roof structure, which, like the pyramidal base, rose by a succession of narrow terraces. The back wall of the temple appears almost vertical and the greater part of the terrace recession is from the front. In order to support this massive superstructure the temple walls had to be made very thick indeed. The proportion of room space to wall space is much smaller in Tikal than in any other city. From its cumbersome nature we may reasonably conclude that the Tikal roof structures represent the first attempt in this direction by the Maya. The zones of the roof structures appear to have been ornamented with mask panels.

During the recent researches of Dr. Tozzer at Tikal he was fortunate enough to discover two sealed chambers in one of these roof structures. If the plan of the ancient builders was symmetrical, there must be two other similar chambers. A cross-section of this temple is shown in Fig. 147. The four rooms are in two stories and are entirely inclosed by the walls, so that no evidence of them appears on the outside. Their obvious purpose was to lighten the enormous load of the masonry. The temple where this discovery was made has only one very small open chamber and an almost unbelievable large proportion of solid wall. The other temples of the same type have two or three open chambers and a proportionally smaller volume of solid wall. It seems likely that these buildings are of somewhat later date and show an increase of skill in handling the mechanical difficulties.

At Nakum the roof structure on one of the temples appears as three massive towers. In each one of these towers is a small sealed room. At either side of the room, but not connecting with it, are three rectangular perforations, one above the other, that pass completely through from the front to the back of the towers. At La Hondradez roof towers also appear as well as an example of a continuous roof structure. The latter has one feature of peculiar interest. The chamber of the temple is directly under it, and the side walls of this chamber run up to a very great height inside of this lofty roof structure.

The roof structures of the Usumacinta region are typically of a much lighter and more airy construction. The simplest form is a vertical wall, pierced with windows, that rises from the center line of the roof. It seems possible to postulate the course of development of the roof comb at Yaxchilan from a comparison of the structural remains. Naturally the builders gained experience with each new attempt, and so the relative success with which the same problems of construction were met probably indicates time sequence in building. In the first place, there is the roof comb constructed over the single room. To bear the additional weight of the roof comb, interior buttresses were built which divided the room into a series of compartments, as may be seen in Fig. 148, *a* and *c*. In one group of such buildings it was apparently considered unsafe to put the roof comb directly over the ridgepole; it is therefore set somewhat back. In a second group the roof comb is over the center line, but the interior buttresses are still necessary. A third group shows the temple divided by a longitudinal partition into two rooms. The roof comb then arises with perfect safety over this central wall. After the discovery of this simple and economical device the builders must surely have dropped the old clumsy method. But the development was not yet complete. Heretofore the roof combs have been narrow, vertical walls pierced by windows.[1] In the fourth group the roof comb is made by

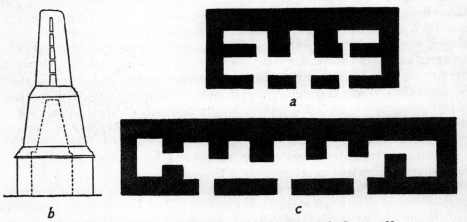

Fig. 148. — Plans of Yaxchilan Temples: *a*, Structure 25; *b* and *c*, Structure 33.

bonding together two walls which incline towards each other. These walls are pierced by windows, as before. The greater breadth and increased stability permitted these structures to be raised to a height of at least two stories. The lower story of the roof comb is like a long corridor. Fig. 148, *b*, reproduces a cross-section of a Yaxchilan temple of the single-room type crowned by a very cumbersome two-walled roof structure.

At a ruin on the Tzendales River there is a temple with a roof comb resembling an open corridor with six windows on each side. This structure and the ones at Yaxchilan that have just been considered are undoubtedly related to the roof structures of Tikal. The sealed rooms of the latter city in the course of development appear to have opened out into corridors with windows.

The roof combs of Palenque have often been described. Maudslay gives complete plans of them.[2] They show the highest refinement in the use of the two walls inclining inward, the mass being reduced to a minimum, so that the whole structure may be described as stone trellis work. The weight of these roof combs is borne by the medial longitudinal partition. In every constructural feature, particularly in economy and efficiency of support, and in artistic refinement, the temples of Palenque are superior to anything else in the Maya area.

[1] It must be admitted that Maler's plans and descriptions are not very definite in regard to the single-walled roof comb.

[2] 1889–1902, IV, pls. 65 and 85. See also Holmes 1895–1897, p. 201.

The roof structure in the cities of northern Yucatan received a sort of differential development. The double-wall type apparently does not occur. The castellated roof comb of the House of the Pigeons at Uxmal (Plate 6, fig. 1) shows a modification of the single-wall type. Roof crests more like those of the south are seen at Sayil [1] and Hochob.[2] A roof comb with rows of windows and cornice-like mouldings is seen upon the Casa Colorado at Chichen Itza (Fig. 149). Indeed, this building is somewhat unusual in that it has both a roof comb and a so-called flying façade.

The flying façade, which is the most common form of roof structure in northern Yucatan, is really a vertical extension of the front wall of the temple, giving a false impression of the height of the building. Although not so beautiful as the roof comb of the Palenque type, yet the flying façade served better to carry the mask panel decoration so common in northern Yucatan. Plate 15, fig. 1, pictures

FIG. 149. — Plans of Casa Colorada, Chichen Itza.

the Iglesia of Chichen Itza with its flying façade which is decorated on the front with mask panels and on the rear with a simple lattice design. A graceful flying façade of lattice work surviving upon a badly ruined temple at Sabacche (Plate 6, fig. 2) gives evidence of the excellent construction of this region.[3] In Plate 6, fig. 3, is shown a splendid building at Uxmal with tower-like elevations over the doorways instead of a continuous flying façade.

Columns. The development of the column is closely connected with the handling of doorways to allow for the admission of more light to the inner chambers. The column does not occur at all in the southern part of the Maya area and is none too common in the northern parts. At Palenque its prototype exists in the rectangular piers, all that remains of the front wall of the temple when three doorways are taken out. In northern Yucatan square columns occur, particularly at Chichen Itza, but round ones with a square capital are perhaps more common. The columns are made up of several drums or sections. Good examples of wide doorways with two or three columns occur at Labna,[4] Sayil,[5] Osehkabtun,[6] Chacmultun (Plate 7, fig. 1) and Tuloom.[7] In many buildings the use of round or square columns really turns the outer chamber into a portico, as has been already explained. Plate 7, fig. 2, shows an intricate interior at Chichen Itza, with rows of drum columns and other unusual features. Columns for interior roof support are rare, but occur at Chichen Itza if not at other cities. The highest development of the column is reached in the serpent columns of the Cas-

[1] Stephens, 1843, II, p. 25.
[2] Maler, 1895, p. 285, central building shown.
[3] For other examples see Stephens, 1843, II, pp. 0–53 (Labna), and Maler, 1895, p. 253 (Chunyáx-c) and p. 254 (Sabacche).

[4] Stephens, 1843, II, frontispiece.
[5] Stephens, 1843, II, p. 17.
[6] Maler, 1902, p. 227.
[7] Stephens, 1843, II, pp. 402–403.

tillo, the Temple of the Jaguars and the Temple of the Tables, all at Chichen Itza. These strongly resemble the serpent columns found by Charnay at Tula.

In the Court of the Columns at Chichen Itza are hundreds of columns, four or more abreast, in long alignments. Their purpose is unknown, but it seems certain that they did not support vaults. It is possible that they supported flat roofs and that the whole group formed a sort of open marketplace. The presence of temples in the group is an argument against this hypothesis. A number of similar groups of smaller size exist in northern Yucatan and will be discussed later in another connection.

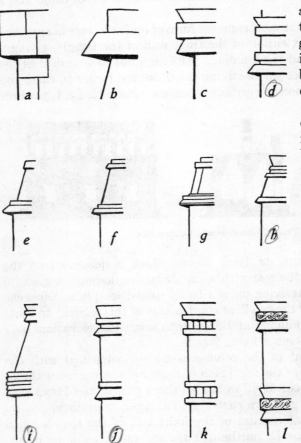

The small plain or banded columns so much used as a façade decoration in northern Yucatan must be clearly distinguished from the columns that serve as supports. The former have no structural character, but are simply mosaic elements used in architectural embellishment.

Cornices. The cornice is one of the most interesting features of the Maya building. The term must be used somewhat widely. Not only are the terraces of the pyramid and the upper portions of platform mounds ornamented by projecting tiers of stone which may be referred to by the term, but the buildings themselves often show cornicelike projections at several levels. The moulding commonly called the medial cornice separates the upper and lower zones of the façade.

Fig. 150.—Cornice forms: *a*, southern area; *b*, Usumacinta area; *c*, northern area; *d, h, i* and *j* Chichen Itza; *e, f* and *g*, Palenque; *k*, Labna; *l*, Chacmultun.

The cornice shows a refinement in form and an increase in variety from south to north. A series including the most important varieties of cornice forms is shown in Fig. 150. In the Copan substructures the cornices consist of a simple projection of two courses of stone (Fig. 150, *a*) at the tops of the terrace walls. In the cities of the Usumacinta Valley the type is varied in that the lower part is beveled and projects farther than the upper part, as in *b*. In northern Yucatan the main type is the three-part cornice shown in *c*.

Buildings with the sloping upper range have cornicelike projections at the eaves and also at the top of the sloping portion (Fig. 150, *e* to *i*).

The eaves cornice becomes the medial cornice when the wall becomes vertical (*j* to *l*).

The three-part cornice is much modified by the separation of its members and the introduction of a mosaic moulding of zigzags and other geometric elements (*d, k* and *l*). The Monjas and the Iglesia at Chichen Itza furnish examples of these modified cornices (Plate 13, fig. 2, and Plate 15, fig. 1). In the Carocol at Chichen Itza the three-part cornice is developed into a five-part cornice (*i*). It is worth noticing that the three-part cornice is identical in profile with the wrapping of the banded columns so common in the façade decorations of the buildings of northern Yucatan. Wooden poles used as vault struts sometimes have similar bands carved upon them.

Doorways and Wall Openings. The most interesting forms of doorways have already received an oblique presentation under the discussion of the development of the portico and the use of the vault and the column. Fundamentally, Maya doorways are of the simple post and lintel type, but after the concrete walls of the building had hardened there was very little weight upon the lintel. The stones that form the jambs are often of larger size than the usual run of building stones. The lintels are of the very durable zapote wood or of stone. The use of wooden lintels was a decided element of weakness, because after the decay of the lintel the mortar conglomerate over the doorway was often unable to bear up under its own weight. It is probable that no doors were hung in any of the wall openings, although curtains may have been used.

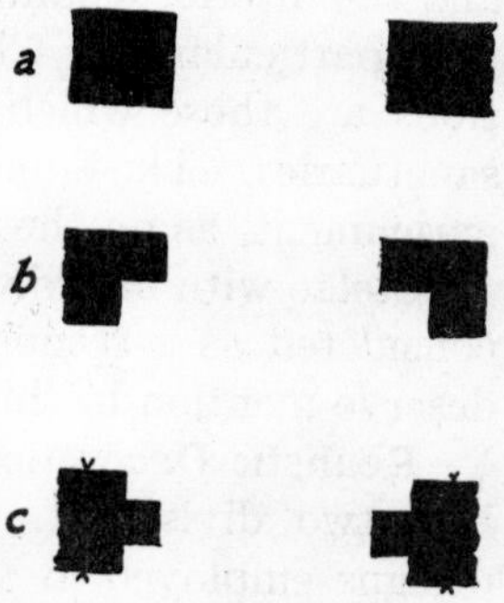

Fig. 151. — Modifications of door jambs; *a*, common form; *b*, Uxmal; *c*, Chichen Itza.

Occasionally the original three faces of each door jamb (Fig. 151, *a*) were increased by a simple modification. At Uxmal there are examples of doorways with the jambs modified as in *b*, while at Chichen Itza a pilaster was sometimes set up to carry a shorter under lintel so that the cross-section of the door jamb is like *c*. This device allowed seven vertical panels for decorative purposes. With the extended use of piers and columns, as we have already seen, doorways are widened until often the whole front of the building resembles an open portico. Typical doorways are shown in many of the photographic plates, and clear drawings of the different types are given by Mr. Holmes.[1] The use of a vault over an interior doorway is found at Palenque.[2]

Wall openings other than doorways are almost negligible when considering the Maya area as a whole. Small rectangular or tau-shaped windows occur. Perforations in the medial walls above the spring of the vaults are characteristic of Palenque, but are not found at most other sites.

Application of Decoration. In all parts of the Maya area the façades of buildings were richly decorated. The upper zone of the façade, whether of the sloping or the vertical type, seems to have been the favorite place for applying decoration. This zone was turned into a wide frieze for designs of many sorts expressed in high-relief stone sculpture, in stucco modeling and in realistic or geometric mosaics. Occasionally the lower zone was also covered with ornament.

[1] 1895–1897, pp. 40–44.   [2] Maudslay, 1889–1902, IV, pl. 5.

The surfaces of the roof combs and flying façades carried decoration of the same diverse character. In many cities these outside designs have been almost completely destroyed by the elements.

Some of the more complicated interior decorations were used to enhance the inner chamber which has been described as the sanctuary. Stone and wooden lintels over the outer and the inner doorways of temples were frequently carved with remarkable pictorial compositions. These sculptures were generally on the under side of the lintel and so directly overhead. They could not be viewed with comfort or accuracy. In a few cases the front of the lintel block was also ornamented. Carved lintels of wood or stone have been found at Tikal, Yaxchilan and other Usumacinta sites and at Kabah and Chichen Itza.

The front wall of the inner chamber was sometimes elaborately ornamented at Copan. The door jambs and the narrow spaces either side of the inner door and the interior columns were also sculptured in some of the more splendid temples, particularly at Chichen Itza. But the most successful and artistic decorations are those which in several instances were applied to the inner walls of sanctuaries. The famous tablets of Palenque belong to this type of architectural enrichment, as do the frescos of the Temple of the Jaguars at Chichen Itza.

Stelae with altars were correlated in many cases with temples and should be considered as a secondary architectural feature. Pyramids and stairways also deserve mention in this connection, although they are treated separately.

Realistic Decoration. Architectural decoration may be divided conveniently into two divisions. 1st, façade decoration; 2nd, interior decoration. The designs employed in the second division by the Maya do not lend themselves to comparative study from an architectural point of view. Those that emphasize the importance of the sanctuary have already been commented upon. Subjectively the range of the interior designs is wide and the manner of presentation realistic. The most striking door jamb, lintel, and sanctuary decorations have been treated already under different headings and do not deserve further discussion.

Façade ornamentation offers a rich field for comparative study. It may be subdivided, according to manner, into realistic, conventional and geometric, as these terms are commonly applied. The markedly conventional will be studied under the captions of "mask panel" and "profile panel," and the minor conventionalizations of the more realistic designs will not be considered.

Few buildings of the Maya area that were decorated in a free manner with realistic designs are now in a well-preserved condition. The method seems to have been more characteristic of the south than of the north. At Copan the façades were apparently decorated in a free manner with human and grotesque figures, the latter sometimes representing divinities, and with feather drapery. The arrangement of these sculptures on the walls is only known in part. The upper zone of the façade apparently carried most of the ornamentation. Temple 22 had a frieze of splendidly carved busts that were possibly arranged in a line with equal intervals of blank wall. At each corner of this building were two great heads, one above the other, made of several stones neatly fitted together. Temple 32, which is situated on a low mound just south of the acropolis, was decorated by more or less realistic carvings representing skulls, heads of the Roman-nosed God, serpent heads in profile, human figures and feather mouldings. The larger sculptures were made in several pieces, each with a long tenon that could be set in the wall.   On this building, as on others, the head and headdress of human figures were sometimes carved on one block, the bust or torso on another and the two legs on a third and fourth.   It is worthy of note that true gargoyles, serving as water spouts, occur at Copan.   An example is given in Fig. 152.

Judging by the debris, the temple on Mound 26, which is the one approached by the famous Hieroglyphic Stairway, was embellished by feather drapery sculptured in the freest manner imaginable.   There were also sculptured human bodies, as well as faces of both the Long-nosed God and the Roman-nosed God.

At Tikal less elaborate decoration limited to bands or friezes is still to be seen on two or more buildings.[1]   One frieze that is interesting is seen on the rear of the central temple of a row of seven temples (Structure 55).   The design con-

FIG. 152. — Gargoyle in form of serpent head: Copan.

sists of five parts.   At each end are two bones modified so as to form an over-locking pattern, next comes an object that probably represents a shield, while in the center is a much destroyed figure that may present some sort of face surrounded by feathers.

At Palenque free decoration executed in stucco is seen on the piers of the Temple of the Inscriptions and of some of the Palace structures.   The designs are presented in a most realistic manner in panels that are framed in by bands of astronomical and other symbols.   Some of these designs have already been presented and discussed in the General Consideration.   Maudslay[2] gives photographs and drawings of all these mural decorations.   He also gives a drawing[3] of the much destroyed stucco frieze on the sloping upper zone of the Temple of the Cross.   This frieze represents a dragon head in front view with a leg at each side and with fish attached to the headdress.   The stucco ornaments on the roof combs of Palenque are too badly destroyed for reproduction.   Waldeck[4] gives a drawing of one that shows atlantean figures supporting the cross beams.   Mr. Holmes[5] shows in a drawing the stone skeletons that were used for the larger stucco sculptures and the method of attachment to the walls.

In northern Yucatan the surviving use of the sculptures of human figures and other realistic motives on the façades of buildings is seen in a number of instances, although the general method of decoration here is very formal.   The Iglesia at Chichen Itza (Plate 15, fig. 1) has on its middle zone two panels each with two seated figures representing anthropomorphic gods.   Bodies attached to the wall by tenons occur at Uxmal.   On some of the flying façades at various sites in northern Yucatan the same style of sculptures seems to have been used. At intervals, in the geometric and conventionalized ornament that adorns the temples of Uxmal, are details that are strongly realistic.   A sculpture of the sort

[1] Maler, 1911, pl. 8.
[2] 1889–1902, IV, pls. 8–11, 27–28, 32–37 and 53–56.
[3] 1889–1902, IV, pl. 68.
[4] 1866, pl. 26.
[5] 1895–1897, p. 198.

may be seen in Plate 8, fig. 2. It represents a personage with a lofty feather headdress seated over the open jaws of a serpent. The carving is executed on several blocks which are fitted together. Plate 9, fig. 1 shows a portion of an

interesting façade at Uxmal, where the intertwined bodies of two serpents overlie the geometric and mask panel decoration. Realistic designs which are too indefinite for study are shown in Catherwood's views of Tuloom.

An interesting feature on many façades in northern Yucatan is the niche which was intended to protect or embellish a seated individual represented in stone or stucco. Slight remains of such seated figures can still be made out in some instances. The niches usually take the form of little houses, with two sides and a roof, and are

FIG. 153. — Ornamental niche in façade: Uxmal.

frequently decorated. An example after Catherwood is given in Fig. 153. The finest development of the niche is seen at Labna, Chacmultun and Uxmal (Plates 7, fig. 1, and 16, fig. 3). The niche is often placed over the doorway, and it seems likely that the figure enclosed in it was that of some deity.

Mask Panel. The use of the mask panel is the most noteworthy characteristic of Maya façade decoration. The mask panel is essentially a highly conventionalized face, represented in front view, with its details so modified as to fill an oblong panel. This panel either extends

a   b

FIG. 154. — Faces limited to rectangular spaces: Chichen Itza.

along the wall surface or folds around a corner. In the case of the corner masks the relief is ordinarily higher than in those on a flat wall.

Before considering the mask panel as it is used in architecture it might be well to examine the general application of faces to rectangular areas. Such areas frequently occur at the bases of stelae, on sculptured door jambs, etc. Fig. 154, a, shows a face occurring in a long decorative band. The sides of the face are not framed in, so the design as a result is not strictly rectangular. Another face with many similar features is given in b. This face is framed in on all four sides, and the parts extend into all the corners of the area.

The changes which occur when a face in profile is turned into front view is illustrated in Figs. 155 and 156. The profile face is taken from the side of Stela B at Copan. Note

FIG. 155. — Face in profile: Copan.

the pendent nose, the curled object at the side of the mouth, the oval ear plug with inferior and superior ornaments, the feathered eye and the hair or feathers on the forehead. The front-view face (Fig. 156), occurring on the base of Stela 4 at Yaxchilan, retains most of these features modified to suit a rectangular area.   The featherlike details of the forehead and the feathered eyes are easily seen.   The nose hangs down over the mouth.   The teeth are replaced by the tips of feathers, a rather unusual substitution.   The curled object at each side of the mouth occurs, however, as well as the oval ear plugs with decorative appendages above and below.   A somewhat similar panel at La Hondradez is given in Fig. 157. Others of the same type occur in this city, likewise on the bases of stelae.

The rectangular panels on the bases of the stelae of Quirigua are often much more complicated than

FIG. 156. — Mask panel at base of stela: Yaxchilan.

the examples just given.   They present two or three superimposed heads, the upper ones being the headdresses of the lower ones.[1]

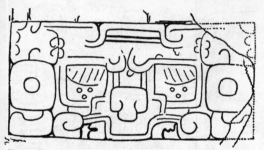

FIG. 157. — Mask panel on base of stela: La Hondradez.

In the southern portion of the Maya area the panel treatment of the façades of temples held a certain vogue, but the details were applied for the most part in stucco and so have since crumbled away.   At Copan there were apparently two superimposed mask panels on the corners of Temple 22.   These are now very incomplete, and the upper one is represented only by the ear ornaments in the photograph taken by Maudslay.[2]   Part of the lower mask on one of the other corners is shown in Plate 3, fig. 2.   Aside from this example the architectural decoration at Copan seems to have been in another and freer style than of the mask panel.

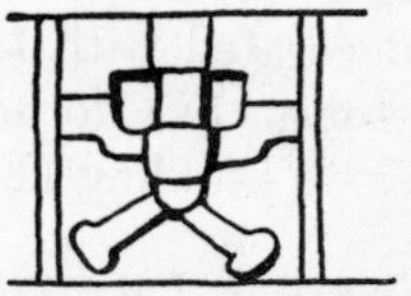

Portions of mask panels on the façades and roof structures of Tikal, Nakum, Yaxchilan and Palenque can still be made out.   The details of mask panels at Nakum and La Hondradez have been furnished by Dr. Tozzer.   Nearly all of these designs are incomplete, but they are decidedly interesting in showing a

FIG. 158. — Mask panel on tower: Nakum.

less trammeled hand than the analogous designs of the north.   Three of these panels are given in Figs. 158–160.   The most complete one (Fig. 158) is a detail on one of the towers of the roof structure.   The face is very simple, the most noticeable feature being the large nose

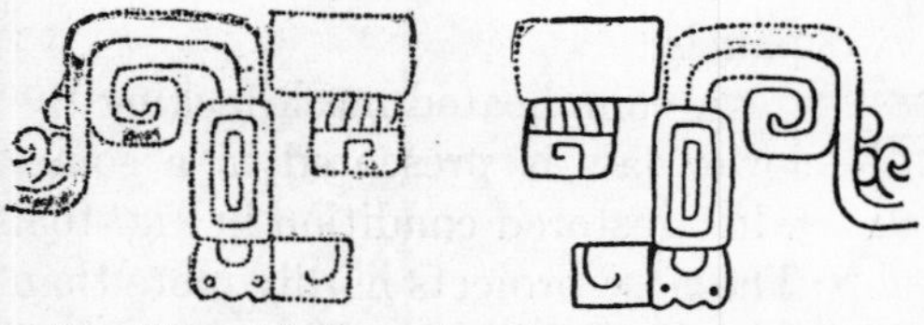

FIG. 159. — Mask panel partly restored: Nakum.

plugs at the base.   The second and third examples have the pupil of the eye represented by a spiral groove, while from the upper part of the ear plug ex-

[1] Maudslay, 1889–1902, II, p. 10.   [2] 1889–1902, I, pl. 17, c.

tends outward a bunch of feathers. These masks were built out of specially carved stones, but the finer details were expressed in stucco which was applied to the surface of the stones.

FIG. 160. — Mask panel: Nakum.

The mask panels at Tikal, Yaxchilan and Palenque were largely constructed of stucco. At the latter city, on the frieze of House C, of the Palace, a row of seven faces can still be made out.[1] These are less rectangular than the usual run of mask panels. On an inside wall of the same building are nine other faces in a much better state of preservation. Judging by the examples which Maudslay[2] gives, each one of these faces was different from the others. All were finely modeled in stucco.

Realism is not a marked characteristic of the mask panels, yet it seems likely that a number of conventionalized representations must be included under this general heading. Examples of two designs from Labna illustrate the most realistic panels, following the serpent model, encountered in northern Yucatan. The first of these (Fig. 161) is a corner mask, built up mosaic fashion out of many carved stones. In the open jaws at the front appears a small human head. Above the upper jaw the nose rises in a scroll, and back of this is seen the eye decorated with feathers. The rest of the face is a hodgepodge of sculptured stones that do not seem to represent natural features. The next mask on the same building (Fig. 162) is in front view. The jaws are much less prominent, although both protrude slightly. The nose is much enlarged. The ear ornaments at each side of the face are not complete, but the suggested forms are more in keeping with those on the more usual mask panels.

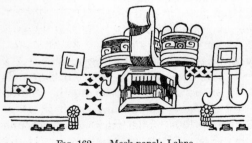

FIG. 161. — Corner mask built up mosaic fashion: Labna.

A complicated mask lacking the lower jaw is presented in a somewhat restored condition in Fig. 163. The nose projects hardly more than the teeth. The headdress is ornamented with checker-work. The ornaments at the side of the ear plugs are unusually elaborate for a mask with as much realism as this one shows. The mask is centered over a doorway which is the position first in importance to be filled by such designs.

FIG. 162. — Mask panel: Labna.

[1] Maudslay, 1899–1902, IV, pl. 20.　　　　[2] 1899–1902, IV, pl. 24.

Masks in which human features predominate are seen in the stucco panels of Izamal preserved in drawings by Catherwood [1] and Holmes.[2] A great human face modeled in stucco appears on the tower at Nocuchich, which has been described and photographed by Maler.[3]

From the examples so far presented the mask panel appears to have had a diverse origin. But, as a rule, it seems pretty clear that the mask represents the feathered serpent. The eyes often show feathered lids. The projecting curl represents the nose of the serpent, which, as has been observed, was commonly elongated. The serpentine head may of course have been intended for that of the Long-nosed God.

FIG. 163. — Mask panel: Xkichmook.

Fig. 164 gives an ideal mask in its most simplified form but with all the parts. It may be well to run over the main features of the complete mask. The head band usually represents a series of threaded disks or a line of rosettes, the middle and terminal ones being more ornate than the others. This head band extends over the eyes and ends above the ear ornaments. The eye consists normally of three parts, the upper and lower lids and the eyeball. There are two principal forms of the eye, one being round and the other rectangular. In the round eye the upper and lower lids are equal in height and shape, while in the rectangular eye the upper lid is a straight bar and the lower lid is trough-shaped and includes the sides. The eyeball is frequently represented with a forward and backward part, the former representing drooping feathers. The nose is curled in nearly all cases, but presents a considerable variety in profile. The superior nose ornament is usually either a roll-shaped

FIG. 164. — Simplified mask panel with all the usual parts.

body or a human face. The curious detail is the homologue of the nose scroll on the profile serpent head (Fig. 30, e). Through this object the nose plugs were thrust. Two of the masks on the flying façade of the Iglesia at Chichen Itza still show nose plugs (Plate 15, fig. 1), but they are usually omitted on mask panels. The mouth varies in many details. The lips are much reduced. The teeth are of two kinds; those at the side of the mouth correspond to molars and those on the front to incisors. These teeth have frequently been described as filed, but a comparison with those on the profile head of the serpent proves that the traditional method of representing teeth was followed in these architectural designs. The lateral mouth ornament corresponds to the curled fang at the back of the

[1] 1844, pl. 25.   [2] 1895–1897, p. 99; Charnay, 1885, p. 262.   [3] 1895, p. 289.

mouth on the more realistic representations. The ear plug is usually square and fitted with a peg in the center. The inferior ear ornament represents a pendant, while the superior one varies widely in form. The lateral ear ornament is very important in emphasizing the formal quality of the mask. It usually consists of two frets turned in opposite directions and separated by a horizontal object. These frets possibly symbolize feathers.

The general processes by which designs are modified, namely, simplification, elaboration, elimination and substitution, have already been explained. The general conceptions of the mask panel and its diverse origin have been touched upon, as well as the convergent results attained by the process of simplifying the original forms and throwing them into a geometric order. In the comparative study of the mask panel it is necessary to take strict account of the changes which take place in homologous parts. The ideal simplified mask may be made to serve as a standard for this comparison.

FIG. 165. — Superimposed mask panels: Uxmal.

Some of the mask panels of Chichen Itza are very simple, and others show adornment of the different features. Examples may be examined in Plates 13, fig. 2; 15, fig. 1; 27, fig. 2, and 28, figs. 3–6. Pleasing elaboration is shown in the last illustration. Better examples of highly elaborated masks are seen at Uxmal (Fig. 165 and Plates 8, fig. 2; 9, fig. 1; 14; 16, fig. 3). From the ebb-tide mask of greatest simplicity, the use of subsidiary ornament in elaborating each separate element becomes more and more prominent. The eyelids are ornamented with circles or other figures. Similarly the head band becomes a row of rosettes instead of simple disks. The nose takes on adventitious details, such as crosses and swastikas. The various ear ornaments assume a great variety of shapes, the lateral ones sometimes developing into serpent heads.

The same masks that show elaboration often show elimination as well. Elimination in the case of the mask panels seems to proceed by a pretty definite rule. The outer features are the ones that are cut off, but the process may continue till only the eyes and nose remain. Space considerations have something to do with elimination in many instances. The lateral ear ornaments are the most elastic features of the mask panel. The arms of the frets can be lengthened or shortened according to the space to be filled. If the space is very short, the lateral ornaments are left off entirely. Since the first consideration in placing a mask was to get it centered over the door, this elasticity counted. On the east wing of the Monjas at Chichen Itza (Plate 27, fig. 2) are five masks of varying width, three of which are placed over doors. The spaces not filled by the masks are given over to geometric decoration. On the east front of the same building the lateral ear ornaments are omitted entirely. The masks that cover the façade of Structure 1 at Kabah (Plate 8, fig. 1) evidence further elimination. Not only the lateral ear ornaments but also the head bands are omitted. In fact, except in the lower tier of masks, each ear plug is held in common by two masks. Examples might be multiplied. About the last stages of elimination are shown in

FIG. 166. — Mask panels over doorway, showing extreme elimination: Labna.

Fig. 166 and Plates 9, fig. 2, and 10, fig. 1. In the last photograph referred to the ear plugs and lateral ear ornaments are present but much reduced, and the teeth simplified to a notched line at the bottom of the face. In the other examples only the eyes and nose survive.

The process of substitution overlaps that of elaboration and is even seen in designs where elimination has had full play. An example of the latter is presented in Fig. 167. Here several features are wanting, and a simple geometric design consisting of a line of squares standing on their diagonals replaces the mouth. In Fig. 168 the mouth is replaced by a double fret, turning inward. Both of these figures are taken from the drawings of Catherwood. A more complete

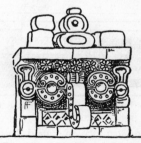

FIG. 167. — Mask panel showing elimination and substitution: Uxmal.

example of substitution is that given in Plate 10, fig. 2. On the lower zone of the façade of the building here depicted are two panels made, mosaic fashion, out of separately carved stones. The panels are on either side of a doorway, and while each is slightly asymmetrical the error is reversed from one panel to the other, so that the design as a whole is perfectly balanced. The motive that resembles a letter C recalls the shell beads of the more realistic head

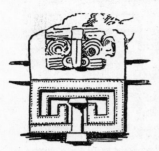

FIG. 168. — Mask panel showing substitution: Uxmal.

band. The fret at each side of the central part of the panel occupies the same position as the eyes, and the tau-shaped grouping of plain and banded columns corresponds to the nose. The teeth and the lateral mouth ornaments are also suggested at the base of the panel. It should be noted that there is no actual survival of a single feature, but simply a survival of the old characteristic order and assemblage. In Plate 28, fig. 2, is given a geometric panel from the upper range of the Monjas at Chichen Itza. The double frets at each side of the panel suggest the lateral frets of the complete masks on the lower range of the same structure. The face, however, is replaced by an arrangement of squares and drum columns. Characteristic geometric panels that offer only a vague suggestion of the mask panel are given in Figs. 169 and 170, and appear likewise on many of the buildings shown in the plates. The purely geometric decoration will be treated elsewhere.

Profile Panel. We have seen that the mask panel is merely a front-view face, of any sort, definitely limited to a rectangular space. Theoretically it is quite possible to develop artistically a profile face in much the same way. Examination proves that such designs actually occur in Maya art. They are much less common than the front-view panel, probably because of their necessary asymmetry. This is of course overcome by the opposition of two similar designs where such an arrangement is possible.

FIG. 169. — Geometric panel: Dsibiltun.

The rectangular spaces at the bases of stelae are sometimes decorated with profile faces. A particularly fine example is reproduced in Fig. 171. It represents the much elaborated face of the familiar Long-nosed God, looking toward

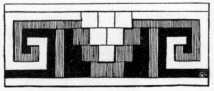

FIG. 170. — Geometric panel: Dsibiltun.

the left. From the feathered eye issue two strands which pass to the bottom of the panel and thence to either side, where each ends in an attractive vignette containing a small animal figure. In the circlet at the left is shown a rat, or some such animal, and in that at the right a deer. Much smaller and simpler profile heads may be seen on Stelae 2 and 3 at Naranjo.[1] On Stela A [2] at Quirigua the lower panel contains a face, looking upward, which has almost completely broken down into meaningless scroll-work. Upward-looking heads of a peculiar type are seen on the bottoms of Stelae 6 and 10 at Yaxha (Fig. 172). The human being above may be said to stand on the open jaws of the serpent below. The inverted face

---

[1] Maler, 1908, b, pl. 20.   [2] Maudslay, 1889–1902, II, pl. 8.

and the hands are hard to explain. While these examples carry us afield, they are evidences of the suggestions for profile heads to be used architecturally.

FIG. 171. — Profile panel: Yaxchilan.

In Temple 11 at Copan is represented a conventionalized serpent head, marked with death symbols, arranged vertically at the side of a door. Fig. 173 presents this design as it appears in one of Maudslay's photographs. It is probable that a similar head was placed at the opposite side of the door. Upon the façades of buildings in the Peten region elements taken from profile heads sometimes appear. A frieze on the so-called Palace of the Five Stories at Tikal (Structure 10) consists of a rectangular eye repeated with intervals of blank wall. At Nakum there are scanty remains of what may be regarded as profile heads, although they do not appear to have

FIG. 172. — Panel at base of stela: Yaxha.

been distinctly limited to rectangular spaces. The best preserved of these is given in Fig. 174, taken from photographs and drawings made in the field by Dr. Tozzer. It shows an open serpent mouth which contains a human head and an extended arm. The upper part of the serpent head has fallen away, but the rectangular ear plug with its pendant is still in position. A noteworthy feature of this decoration is that it is modeled in the stucco covering of the wall instead of being built up out of carved blocks in the manner of a mosaic. However, a second fragment at Nakum has carved stones fitted together.

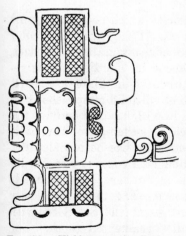

FIG. 173. — Highly conventionalized serpent head in profile: Copan.

Something of the uncertain genesis of the profile mask panel may be gathered from the preceding examples. But the principal occurrences where the geometric mould is unmistakable are in northern Yucatan. Here two profile panels assembled in opposition, one on each side of a doorway, unite with a front-view panel placed above the doorway to form a striking scheme for the decoration of an entire facade.

Plate XI gives views of two portions of the Palace at Hochob which has been explored and described by Maler.[1] The upper picture represents a small façade with the lower zone plain while the upper zone bears a somewhat elaborate mask

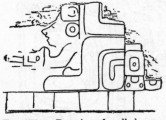

panel. The central part of the face has fallen away, but can be easily restored in the mind's eye. A row of teeth doubtless projected down over the lintel. The head band is particularly interesting since it consists of a double-headed snake surmounted by rosettes made of separate projecting stones. Locks of hair are apparently intended by the scroll-work between the eyes and the ear plugs. The lower picture shows a very similar face at the top. The principal difference lies in the wavelike figures that

FIG. 174. — Remains of wall decoration: Nakum.

represent hair above the two intertwined serpents of the headdress. Below this face and on either side of the door is an elaborated serpent face in profile, the whole cast into a strikingly rectangular mould. One of these profile heads is given in Fig. 175. It is an interesting example of elaboration, since the top of the eye is formed by a small complete serpent whose tail constitutes the nose plug of the greater head. The noteworthy features in the present connection are the teeth that project inward at the side of the door and the peculiar right-angled turn of the jaw. It should also be stated that the design does not completely fill a four-sided area and that details from other masks intrude into the open spaces.

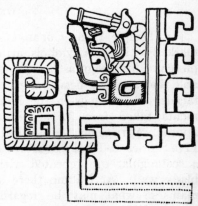

FIG. 175. — Profile mask panel: Hochob.

A drawing of a broken-down façade at the same city which shows the same elements treated in a simpler manner is given in Fig. 176. Another similar façade, admirably preserved, and from another site, is reproduced in Plate 12, fig. 1. The splendid temple shown in Plate 12, fig. 2, is perhaps the clearest example of any. The doorway has been sealed up, and as a consequence hardly a stone has fallen from its place. The upper face may represent the Sun God with the ornamented tooth. The profile faces are perhaps more

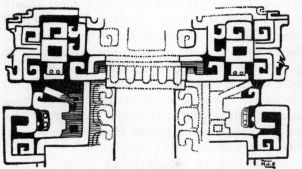

FIG. 176. — Assemblage of profile and front view mask panels: Hochob.

complete than any we have yet seen, since the short under-jaw is shown as well as the forked tongue which hangs below it.

Two other important façades of this type remain for consideration — one at

[1] 1895, pp. 278–279.

Uxmal and the other at Chichen Itza. The façade at Uxmal is that of the Annex to the House of the Magician (Plate 13, fig. 1). No near-by view of the building as a whole is obtainable. Catherwood [1] gives a drawing of the façade, which is accurate as far as it goes, but the upper front-view mask is merely suggested. Seler [2] reproduces this upper mask with all the details that now remain, and Le Plongeon [3] presents detailed photographs of the profile panels with which we are most concerned at this time.

The three principal faces are much complicated by bands of astronomical symbols which overlay the important features and fill in the blank spaces. The one above the doorway is readily made out on account of the eyes. The profile face at either side of the doorway harks back to a type of serpent head that has already been discussed, namely, the more or less modified head with the nose turned back into a fret. The eye is rectangular and is partly concealed by a small human figure attached to the wall by a tenon. This figure is now much destroyed. The teeth of the profile serpent head project inward toward the doorway. The lower jaw that appeared on the simpler examples is lacking. To sum up, the assemblage of three faces shows the effects of all four processes of modification, but especially those of elaboration and elimination.

The last façade to be examined is the justly famous one at the eastern end of the east wing of the Monjas at Chichen Itza (Plate 13, fig. 2), and here elimination and substitution have been carried much further. The only features of the mask panel over the door that survive in their original form are the lateral ear ornaments (see other mask panels on the northern side of the east wing, Plate 27, fig. 2). The face proper has been replaced by a seated human figure, in front view, with a drooping feather headdress. This figure is inclosed in an arch made mosaic fashion. Over the doorway is a row of projecting teeth separated by mouldings from the figure above.

Of the original side-view faces even fewer traces remain. The teeth at either side of the door are of the same character as the ones over it, but are homologous with the teeth of the profile faces in the earlier and more intelligible assemblage. The other features of the two profile heads are replaced by two front-view faces one above the other. The general outlines of the earlier grouping are pretty well maintained in the scheme presented in this façade. The devices that appear on the upper member of the cornice may survive from the earlier scroll work representing hair.

Maudslay [4] has expressed the opinion that the doorway represents an open mouth, but the series just given shows that it represents the surviving elements of an old arrangement of three heads, one in front view and two in profile. There is good reason to believe that the last two examples of architectural decoration in this series are later in point of time than the ones with easily recognizable features.

Geometric Decoration. Many motives which are purely geometric occur on the buildings of northern Yucatan. The geometric panels that show affiliations with the conventionalized faces through the process of substitution have already been considered in some detail. As a rule, geometric figures are not limited to panels, but are applied in string courses or in all-over patterns. Each geometric element is usually carved on a single stone and combined in different

[1] 1844, pl. 11.   [2] 1908, p. 162.   [3] 1896, pls. 71 and 73.   [4] 1889–1902, III, p. 17.

ways to form different designs. Typical design elements are given in Figs. 177 to 180. The element given in Fig. 177, *a*, is used to form zigzags or squares set on

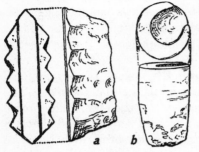

FIG. 177. — Mosaic elements: Labna.

the diagonal (Plates 8, fig. 1; 9, fig. 2; 13, fig. 2; 15, fig. 2; 27, fig. 1, and Fig. 178, *b*). The element with a cross (Figs. 178, *a*, and 180, *b*) is much used in imitation diagonal trellis work which often fills in the spaces between mask panels, but which is sometimes used as the sole motive, as in Plate 6, fig. 2. Squares with figures of different kinds carved on them, rosettes (Fig. 179) and stepped pyramids (Fig. 180, *a*) are of frequent occurrence as independent elements. In other motives, such as the guilloche, two or three repetitions of the figure may occur on the same stone. The fret is usually of large size and is built up out of many plain stones. As a rule, there is an outer and an inner fret, the latter more or less sunken below the former, but still in relief against the wall. An example of a fret with the planes differentiated by shading has already been given (Fig. 170). The plain and banded column motive (Fig. 181) will be treated in special detail because of its importance and frequent use.

Typical string courses follow the line of the medial cornice. Usually the design shows several motives in rows, one beneath the other. Fig. 182 presents an interesting combination of moulding on either side of a beautiful head that is now in the Museo Nacional at Mexico City. At the top are feathers, next comes a representation of vertebrae. The third row consists of banded columns, the fourth of assorted geometric motives, and the fifth of the stepped pyramid or wall of Troy motive in an inverted position. Frequently the cornice mouldings are

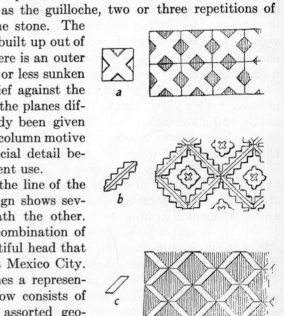

FIG. 178. — Mosaic elements with examples of their development: Chichen Itza.

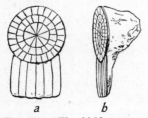

FIG. 179. — The shield as a mosaic element: Labna.

modified by the introduction of geometric ornament, such as zigzags, guilloches and short columns between the different members.

The rich combination of geometric, conventional and realistic elements that defies description is seen particularly on the buildings of the Nunnery Group at Uxmal and on the House of the Governor at the same city. Photographs of the structures are given in Plates 8, fig. 2; 9, fig. 1; 14, etc. The most striking single feature is the fret which does not form long meanders but is arranged singly or in groups of two or three.

The use of engaged columns, either plain or with simple banded ornament, is characteristic of a great many buildings in northern Yucatan. These columns are in sections, and each section may be considered a mosaic element. In fact the plain and banded sections of the decorative column are frequently intro-

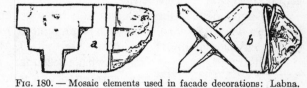

duced into cornice mould-ings or into mask panels that show substitution. One of the banded sections is shown in Fig. 181. The tenion at the back is not present in all instances.

FIG. 180. — Mosaic elements used in facade decorations: Labna.

Sometimes the entire upper range of a building is ornamented with banded columns placed close together between the medial and the true cornice mould-ings. Examples of such buildings are given in Plates 7, fig. 1, and 16, fig. 1. The columns may appear also in the lower zone, usually in groups and not in a continuous distribution. The detail of a façade decorated with banded columns is given in Fig. 183. In façades of this type the banded sections of the columns may occur at several heights. Three or more banded columns are frequently used to flank or frame in mask panels and doorways, the former in the upper and the latter in the lower zone of the façade. Examples of such uses are shown in Fig. 166 and Plates 9, fig. 2, and 10.

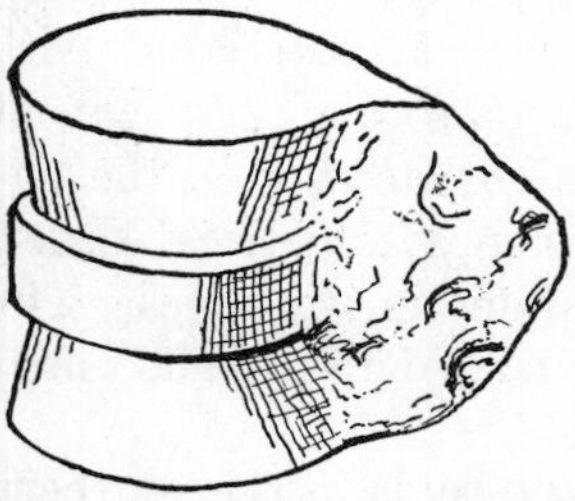

FIG. 181. — Typical banded sec-tion of the banded column.

Stelae. The great monolithic monuments of the Maya commonly called stelae may have served in some cases as grave monuments, but if so this was decidedly a minor pur-pose. Small cruciform chambers have been found under a few of them containing re-mains of what might have been a founda-tion offering. The prime purpose of the monuments is very uncertain. They may have been idols in the same sense that the representations of Buddha are idols. It seems unlikely that they were monuments to individuals, first, because they lack in in-dividuality; second, because most of them bear dates that fall on even, half, or quarter katuns which correspond to intervals of about five years. They may have been connected primarily with the completion of a time period and secondarily with the his-torical events that took place during that time period or the gods that governed it. Whatever their true significance, it seems clear that as objects of art they may be put into two groups. The first group includes those that are apparently independent of temple structures, and the second those that serve as auxiliary temple adornment.

FIG. 182. — Richly ornamented wall with pro-jecting sculpture: Uxmal.

The independent stelae prevail at Copan, Quirigua, Tikal and some other sites in the Peten region, where they were set up, as a rule, in a great paved court or plaza. Before each stela there was in most cases an altar. Stelae of the second group also occur at these cities.

The dependent stelae in Copan were likewise mostly set up in the Great Plaza, but were definitely correlated with some mound and generally placed at the foot of stairways leading to the temples. Stelae 3, D, M and N are examples of monuments with a secondary architectural character. Stela 3 is correlated to a mound in the Great Plaza, Stela 4 stands before a minor hieroglyphic stairway, Stela M is directly in front of the famous Hieroglyphic Stairway and Stela N is at the base of the wide stairway leading up to Temple 11.

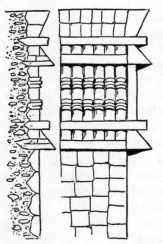

Fig. 183.—Detail of a façade decoration of banded columns: Tantah.

All the stelae at Naranjo, Seibal, Yaxchilan and Piedras Negras seem to have been correlated with temples. The arrangement is more complex than at Copan. The stelae were usually placed upon the terraces in front of the temples in symmetrical order, which, however, is hardly the same in two cases. The question of grouping will be considered again under chronological sequence.

Stelae occur at nearly all the ruins in the southern and western part of the Maya area. Only one has so far been noted at Palenque. In northern Yucatan stelae occur at a few sites, such as Sayil and Tabi, but they are very unusual and are rudely carved. At Sayil the three stelae described by Maler[1] were set up on a low platform. Crude sculptures as well as plain pillars are also found in Chiapas.[2]

The frequent occurrence of perfectly plain stelae in the Peten region has been noted by Dr. Tozzer. It seems possible that these may have been painted with figures instead of carved. It is not improbable that great wooden sculptures, comparable to the stelae, preceded these laborious monuments.

Altars. The most widespread type of altar is drum-shaped, either plain or sculptured. In many cities this is the only kind that occurs. In Copan and Quirigua the altar was especially developed. First came rectangular or drum-shaped altars with wrappings and knots sculptured upon them in addition to human figures and other designs.[3] Apparently this type of altar was intended to represent a bundle. A similar altar painted on a pottery vessel will be shown hereafter. The Altar of Stela 4, at Copan, represents a single knot.

The animal altars have been described. Most of them fall into the series of the Two-headed Dragon, but the Altar of Stela C[4] represents a turtle, and the Altar of Stela F represents two jaguars bound to the sides of two grotesque heads placed back to back (Fig. 99).

There are a number of sculptures at Copan independent of stelae that may be called altars. Some of these are rectangular blocks with beautiful carvings on the sides and tops representing seated figures in rows, grotesque faces of large

[1] 1895, pp. 277–278.
[2] Brinton, 1897.
[3] Gordon, 1902, b.
[4] Gordon, 1896, p. 40.

size and masses of hieroglyphs. Others are thin vertical slabs with sculptures of reptiles.

The animal altars of Quirigua (see Plates 1 and 2) seem for the most part to be independent of the stelae. They mostly belong to the series of the Two-headed Dragon, but one represents a jaguar and another a reptile's head. A drum-shaped altar is also to be seen at Quirigua.

At Tikal most of the altars are plain drum-shaped blocks. Altar 5, however, is finely sculptured on its upper surface. At the Usumacinta sites the altars are also usually drum-shaped and unsculptured, but there are one or two notable exceptions to both of these qualifications. Examples of more or less rectangular altars supported on carved blocks or sculptured heads may be seen at Piedras Negras. In northern Yucatan the table altar is highly developed at Chichen Itza. Here a flat stone is supported by from two to fifteen small stone sculptures. The low platforms or benches that are sometimes built against the wall in sanctuaries or at the heads of stairways may have served as altars. Portable incense-burners of pottery were much used and probably were placed on the altars.

Color. Like the Greeks, the Maya painted their stone sculptures and their stone buildings. There are still many vestiges of color. In some cases an entire monument or building seems to have been painted over by a single tint. In other cases details of ornament were picked out in contrasting tones. The colors were usually applied in a fairly definite way, red for flesh tones, blue and green for ornaments and green for feathers.

In the Peabody Museum are many examples of carved feather-work, grotesque figures, etc., which were used in architectural decoration at Copan. They appear to have been surfaced with smooth plaster and then painted red. Successive coatings seem to have become so thick that they may have seriously impaired the beauty of the original sculptures. Red apparently prevailed at Copan, for Stela 4 likewise shows traces of this pigment.

Maler notes many traces of color on the stelae of Piedras Negras. In this city there was considerable variety in the coloring, with the result that the details of the complex sculptures must have been rendered much more intelligible. Thus the color remains on Stela 1 showed:[1] face, arms and garment, bright red; background, dark red; edge of garment, blue; breast cape, blue; feathers in all cases, green.

Stela 7[2] showed the following color scheme: flesh parts and interior of serpent mouth, bright red; disks of head and breast ornaments, sky blue; feather-work, green; captive's body, red. The feathers were painted green to represent the plumage of the favorite quetzal bird, the sky-blue disks may have been intended for turquoise or jade, while red gave the body a more natural appearance. Maler could find no traces of black, yellow or white.

Maudslay[3] reproduces a painted stucco ornament from one of the rooms of the palace at Palenque, which shows decorative skill of no mean order. Miss Breton has recovered many of the vanishing traces of color on the reliefs of the Lower Temple of the Jaguars at Chichen Itza. They show a large variety of tones, by which the ornaments were clearly contrasted. The whole effect is one of rich tapestry. The bewildering detail which confuses when presented in one tone becomes perfectly intelligible when worked out in color. The remark-

[1] Maler, 1901, p. 46. [2] Maler, 1901, p. 51. [3] 1889–1902, IV, pl. 18.

able stucco reliefs of Acanceh were brilliantly painted when first uncovered. For preserving a record of the form and color of these reliefs thanks are due to Mrs. James, of Merida, and to Miss Breton.

Many instances of fresco paintings upon a flat base are given by Stephens.[1] The fragmentary frescos of Chacmultun have been preserved by Thompson.[2] These are probably purely Maya, while the better known frescos of the Upper Temple of the Jaguars at Chichen Itza may show some influences from Mexico, particularly in the use of speech scrolls. These remarkable paintings have been drawn in fac-simile by Miss Breton. They represent a variety of scenes from the unceremonial side of life. A large number of figures are painted with an astonishing brilliancy of coloring. There is no reproduction of light and shade, but the painting as a whole is in tone. The background is green or blue and thus makes an admirable contrast for the warmer flesh tints. From an examination of the tones, which are numerous but always laid on flat, it seems probable that the artist made color blends, mixing his paint fresh for each piece of color.[3]

In the main range of the Monjas at the same city are a few fragmentary paintings done in the same manner.

Frescos have also been discovered at Santa Rita,[4] near Corosal, in British Honduras. These are executed in a style rather similar to the well-known frescos of Mitla, and seem to show strong foreign influence both in the manner of drawing and in the subjects.

Prototype of the Maya Temple. The question of the probable prototype of the Maya temple deserves brief consideration. Viollet-le-Duc [5] finds evidence in the ornamentation of some of the stone temples of an earlier wooden construction. As is well known, decorative or utilitarian features developed in one material are frequently imitated in other materials, as, for instance, in pottery that sometimes takes over the designs used on baskets or textiles or imitates the natural forms of gourd vessels. It is also in evidence in the higher arts, for the Greek temples constructed of marble retained the shapes of earlier wooden parts as ornaments.

In the case of Maya architecture Viollet-le-Duc finds in the façade given in Plate 14, fig. 2, evidence of log-cribbing and lattice work. The analogy is close enough, but the ornamentation of this particular façade is unique. Lattice work made in stone is very widespread in northern Yucatan, where, however, the buildings are of a much later date than in the southern part of the area. The façades decorated with plain or banded columns (Plates 10 and 16, fig. 1) suggest a wooden construction of upright poles such as is still used in the huts of the natives. The bands might represent in an ideal way the withes which bind these poles together. Here, again, the established chronology interferes with the ready acceptance of this theory.

It seems reasonable to suppose that the original wall construction was of adobe, which was later faced with cut stone. Adobe bricks are widely used in ancient and modern construction from the Pueblo region on the north to Peru on the south. In many instances pyramids and other structures made of them are surfaced with a veneer of cement. This practice was clearly employed in the

---

[1] See, for instance, 1843, I, pp. 204–205, 409–410; II, pp. 73–75 and 92–93.

[2] 1904, pls. 8 and 9. Other examples recovered by Mr. Thompson are from Tzulá, 1904, pl. 2, and Xkichmook, 1898, pp. 226–227.

[3] Thompson, 1902; Breton, 1906, *a.*

[4] Gann, 1898–1899, pp. 655–673.

[5] Charnay and Viollet-le-Duc, 1863, pp. 64–68.

case of the great pyramid of Cholula and is seen in many modern houses. The use of adobe is common in the less humid parts of the Maya area. The wide occurrence of this simple form of wall construction points to the likelihood of its being of very early origin. The earthen filling in the walls of Copan may be explained as the surviving indication of an adobe prototype. Copan was one of the earliest Maya cities. The earthen core was a decided element of weakness which was turned into an element of strength in later Maya cities when mortar was substituted for the clay. Yet building stone was plentiful at Copan and could be cut in any required size. Lime of the finest quality was also close at hand, so that even if it were considered necessary to increase the thickness of the wall to give an adequate support to the overstepping roof stones, this need not have been done at the cost of efficient construction. At the same time there is no reason why wooden architecture should not have been developed by the people living in the forested areas where no stone was to be had. There are many mounds in the Usumacinta area from which the superstructures have entirely disappeared.[1]

MINOR ARTS

Ceramics. In the portions of the New World having the highest culture ceramics often rises to the importance of a major art, and pottery remains frequently constitute the principal results of archaeological research. In the Maya area this art, although finely developed, sinks into comparative insignificance in view of the sculptured monuments.

The art of making pottery had in pre-Columbian times a practically continuous distribution from central Argentina and Chili to southeastern Canada. But the materials and technique varied widely and there were many intensive developments in form and ornament. The art was in some respects most highly developed in the central portion of this vast area, particularly in Peru, Central America, Mexico and the Southwest. But even in these regions there were many fairly distinct ceramic provinces. Of course it is possible, and indeed probable, that there was an infiltration of culture from one province to another.

Certain structural features have a very wide distribution, such as, for instance, the use of ring base and tripod supports for round-bottomed pottery. Three legs furnish the simplest means of stability possible and are employed for a variety of objects the world over. It is but natural that the mechanical economy should be carried a step farther and the legs made hollow rather than solid.

The fundamental similarity in shape and construction, if not in decoration, between the ceramic products of Costa Rica and the Maya area suggests some sort of cultural connection. The art of Nicaragua seems to be more or less intermediate, and shows certain similarities to the Maya vessels in decoration as well as in form.

The ceramic remains found throughout the Maya area include a great variety of vessels for domestic and religious uses as well as figurines, whistles, moulds, stamps, etc. Certain forms are widespread, and possibly show commercial

[1] Mr. E. H. Thompson in a recent article (1912) derives the stone structures of northern Yucatan from the common thatched hut of the present Maya Indian. His explanations do not fit the facts in the earlier Maya cities of the south, however accurately they agree with conditions in the north. The importance of an historical perspective in this discussion will be more apparent after the problem of chronological sequence of style shall have been presented.

distribution from a definite center of manufacture. On the other hand, it is clear that some types of pottery can be referred to definite periods of time, so that the variety is in part explained by chronological sequence.

The pottery was shaped by hand and not by the potter's wheel. To be sure, in some places a block turned by heel and toe was used under the vessel while it was being formed. But this object cannot be called the potter's wheel, because the essential character of the latter comes from the development of centrifugal force. The block in question is still in use in northern Yucatan.[1] A small dish answering the same purpose is used to-day by the Pueblo Indians of the Rio Grande.

An effort will be made to consider briefly the different characteristic styles of Maya pottery, especially as regards ornamentation, illustrating each with a few noteworthy examples. No attempt will be made to distinguish the many variations in paste. Coarse heavy pottery for household purposes has usually no decoration and deserves little consideration here. It is commonly black or red in color, probably depending on whether the burning was done in a smothered fire or

Fig. 184. — Potsherds showing different processes of ornamentation: *a–c*, and *e*, Copan; *d*, Peten region.

an open one. The shapes are various, but flat-bottomed vessels with sides that flare outward seem to predominate.

The more artistic pottery falls naturally into groups according to the method of decoration:

1st. Vessels with incised decorations.
2d. Vessels with moulded or stamped decorations.
3d. Vessels with modeled relief decorations.
4th. Vessels made in the forms of animals, fruits, etc.
5th. Vessels with painted decorations.
6th. Figurines, stamps, moulds, spindle whorls, whistles, etc.

[1] Mercer, 1896, pp. 161–166, describes in detail modern pottery making in Yucatan; Tozzer, 1907, pp. 62–63 and pl. 13, fig. 3. Mr. Thompson has also collected material upon this subject.

Incised pottery made of a fine black or red paste is very widespread. Some-times the designs are geometric patterns or simplified hieroglyphs, incised in the soft clay with a sharp instrument, and sometimes they are elaborate draw-ings brought into relief by cutting away the background. Fig. 184, a, illustrates the simplest sort of incised black pottery. Such pottery is found throughout the Maya area. Some of the more graceful pieces of red or black pottery that come under this heading have vertical flutings (c) made probably by the finger while the clay is soft.

Fig. 185 reproduces a bowl, found near Peto in Yucatan, that is now in the Peabody Museum. The base is a pale yellow and there are traces of a red sizing.

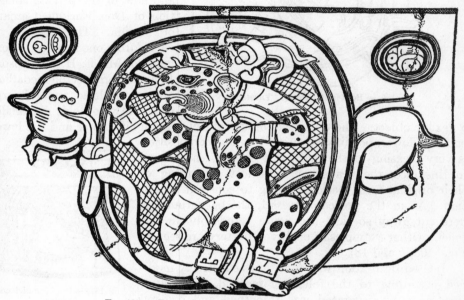

Fig. 185. — Decoration on bowl from near Peto, Yucatan.

The shape of the bowl is indicated diagrammatically in the drawing. The orna-mentation consists of a series of painted scrolls on one side and a carving in relief on the other. The carving which is shown in the drawing represents a jaguar seated within a closed ring that is made up of what probably represents a water-lily stem coiled and knotted. The stem has two buds or flowers branch-ing out at opposite sides of the circlet. The jaguar wears a cape tied round the shoulders and a loin cloth or skirt, as well as wrist and ankle bands, nose plugs and a headdress consisting of the well-known head of the Long-nosed God, in front of which is a small flower similar to the flowers at the side of the circlet. Seven oval glyphs are carved around the top of the bowl, two of these being shown in the drawing. The lines which delineate the coiled stem and the flowers are deeply incised.

The jaguar figure is brought into relief through the simple device of cutting away the background. The details of the dress upon the body of the animal are incised in delicate lines and there is little or no modeling. The spots of the jaguar are represented in black paint which has now largely disappeared. The sunken background is marked with incised cross lines which still retain traces of heavy red pigment.   The carving or engraving of this remarkable piece appears to have been done when the clay had become fairly hard and after the surface had been polished, but before burning.   It was certainly not modeled in soft clay.

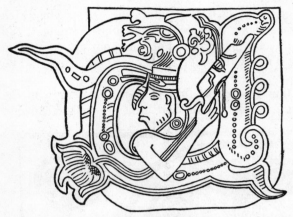

A somewhat similar style of decoration is shown in Fig. 186.   The bowl represented here is a fine piece of pottery coming from northern Yucatan and now in the private collection of Don Enrique Camara of Merida.   The drawing is copied from one made at the expense of Mr. E. H. Thompson. In an elaborate scroll medallion appear the head and left arm of a man who holds diagonally

FIG. 186. — Bowl from Calcetok, Yucatan.

a flexible object.   The upper end of this object is a simplified face and the lower end is a flower, possibly a water lily.   The composition is very pleasing to the eye.   But certain features as, for instance, the headdress, have lost something of their original form, perhaps owing to constant repetition.   As in the preceding vessel, the background is here cut away so that the figure stands out in flat relief.   Other examples of engraved pottery are seen in Figs. 108, b and 187.

FIG. 187. — Bowl from Island of Jaina.

Incised decoration was sometimes effectively modified according to the following method.   The outer surface to be decorated was smoothed and covered with a fine white or black sizing.   The vessel then appears to have been burned, after which the design, which was usually limited to a band or a panel, was incised with a sharp tool and the background cut away.   The lines of the design and the open spaces of the background thus show in dull red color, while the surface of the raised figures is white or black and more or less polished. In the Peabody Museum there are several interesting pieces of this ware from the environs of Santa Cruz Quiché, Guatemala. An example has been shown in Fig. 48, and another fragment of

FIG. 188. — Engraved potsherd from Santa Cruz Quiché.

the same vessel drawn in a manner that more nearly imitates the appearance of the original is given in Fig. 188.

Stamped pottery is somewhat unusual, but a number of interesting forms are encountered. A peculiar flask-shaped type of vessel made of a smooth white paste and bearing on both faces a stamped portrait of the Roman-nosed God and on each of the narrow sides a double column of stamped glyphs has already received comment (Fig. 94). Nearly identical examples of this ware have been found at Coban, Copan and in the Uloa Valley.[1] A rectangular bottle of the same paste and style of decoration is figured by Seler.[2]

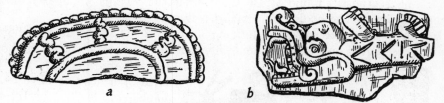

a   b

FIG. 189. — Potsherds showing applied relief decorations.

Other examples of stamped ware of dull red or yellow color are to be seen in the Peabody Museum collections from the Uloa Valley and from Santa Cruz Quiché, Guatemala. From the latter site come two interesting pieces, cylindrical in shape and decorated with stamped designs that are repeated several times around the outside. The stamped designs on these and other bowls are mostly fanciful heads limited to rectangular panels. In some cases tripod legs bear stamped patterns.

In Fig. 184, *d* and *e*, are given two potsherds with realistic designs modeled in relief. It is sometimes difficult to distinguish between this kind of decoration and the finer examples of stamped ware. Of course the arrangement of figures on the outside of a bowl of this sort is unrestrained, while stamped ware shows formal designs. The rounded character of the modeled relief is in marked contrast to the method of engraved or incised relief that has already been described.

Reliefs made by appliqué work are much commoner and, as a rule, cruder. The designs and figures that decorate this class of pottery are laid on or built up. Rolls of clay, ribbon-like strips, flat or pointed nodules, and modeled faces are the objects used

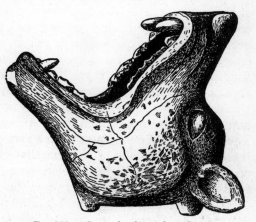

FIG. 190. — Jaguar head vase from Copan.

in making up the decoration. These are arranged on the sides and rims of plain vessels in a variety of ways, while the clay is yet soft, and they remain firmly attached after the firing. This process, although found widely, reached its highest development in the Maya area on the highlands of Guatemala. It seems to be related in a general way to the technique so finely exemplified in the Zapotecan funeral urns. Potsherds showing this method are given in Fig. 189. A beauti-

---

[1] Gordon, 1898, *a*, pp. 19–20; Seler, 1902–1908, III, pp. 685–686.   [2] 1902–1908, III, p. 682.

fully made vessel of this style has already been figured (Fig. 1, *b*).   Many others are described by Dr. Seler.[1]   Occasionally color was used upon certain details.

Vessels made in various natural forms are fairly common.   A remarkable vessel in the form of a jaguar head is given in Fig. 190.   A tripod vase with the body modified into a bird and a human face seen in the bird's open mouth was excavated at Copan.   Gourd-shaped pots are sometimes found.   A splendid example of such a pot, found at Acanceh is in the Museo Yucateco in Merida. The tall-necked bottles found by Dr. Gordon [2] in the caverns of Copan remotely resemble gourds.   The bodies are sometimes fluted.

Incense burners present many different forms.   Some of the more elaborate ones show a sitting or standing human figure attached to one side of the bowl.

a   *b*   *c*
FIG. 191. — Crude painted figures on food bowls: Copan.

Others are modeled into the form of a head or have heads joined to the rim.   Incense burners will be discussed more in detail at another time, because they furnish important evidence of the last phases of Maya art from an historical standpoint.

There are many different kinds of painted pottery.   Much of the common red or yellow ware evidently intended for domestic uses has painted designs running from crudely drawn monkeys and other animals (Fig. 191) to patterns of purely geometric bands.   There is also a red ware of exceeding fineness with designs in black or white.

The finest pottery of all is polychrome ware.   The paste is very smooth and of light weight.   The background sizing is usually a highly polished yellow-orange or red.   The applied colors are very rich and permanent, and include white and black and various shades of red, yellow, orange and brown.   Many of the finer pieces have the general appearance of lacquer ware, so glossy is the surface. But this glossy surface is really polished rather than glazed.   In fact, glazing does not seem to have been understood by any of the potters of the New World, although in two or more regions they were on the verge of the discovery.   A number of pieces from the Maya area show a thin and probably accidental glaze. This is seen on several vases from Finca Pompeya, Guatemala, that are now in the American Museum of Natural History, as well as on figurines from Jonuta, on the Usumacinta River, that are now in the Peabody Museum.   The former specimens have a greenish hue, while the latter are jet black.

It is interesting to note that a glazed paint was used by the natives in several parts of the Pueblo area, particularly in the valley of the Rio Grande.   The glaze in this case probably came from borax or other salts, which formed a flux upon moderate heating.   What may have originated by accident seems to have been developed purposely.   The art, however, was short-lived and is unknown to the present-day Indians.   It apparently came into general use shortly before the arrival of the Spaniards and may have lasted till the eighteenth century.[3]

[1] 1901, *c*, pp. 139–184.
[2] 1898, *b*, pl. 1.
[3] Pottery with glazed paint is found in New Mexican ruins near Ojo Caliente and in various sites in Pajarito Park, including Puye, Tcherigi and Rito de los Frijoles, all of which are believed to be prehistoric.   Potsherds with this kind of paint are found on nearly all the sites near the Rio Grande that are known to have been occupied at the coming of the Spaniards, from Taos and Picuris on the north

An excellent example of polychrome ware is given in Fig. 192. The base is orange color, which is represented by white in the drawing. The background of

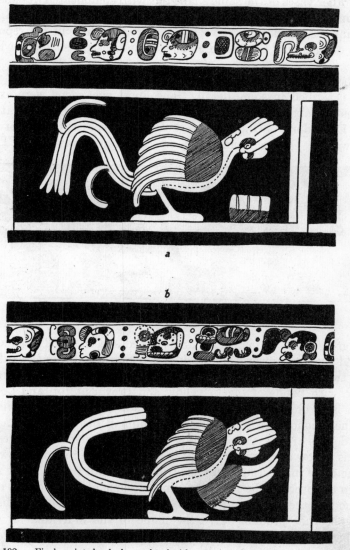

FIG. 192. — Finely painted polychrome bowl with representations of the quetzal: Copan.

the figures is black. The quetzal birds have light red markings on wings and head. In the glyphs there are details in several tones of red and brown. The

to Abo and Tabira on the south. The ware is particularly plentiful in the Galisteo Valley and in the Valley of the Jemez River. Occurrences have been noted as far west as the Little Colorado.

Castaneda, the historian of the Coronado Expedition, refers to the art as follows: " Some very beautiful glazed earthen-ware with many figures and different shapes. Here they also found many bowls full of a carefully selected shining metal with which they glazed the earthen-ware. This shows that

mines of silver would be found in that country." The last statement indicates that he believed the flux to be antimony. In a later passage he says: " In all these provinces they have earthen-ware glazed with antimony and jars of extraordinary labor and workmanship which are well worth seeing."

The glazed paint is usually black but thin applications are more or less translucent and colored by the tone of the background. In some instances the color is brownish with a slight yellowish tinge.

vase in question is cylindrical in shape, with a flat bottom and three short knobs instead of legs. It was excavated by the Peabody Museum Expedition at Copan.

Several other vases of the same shape but with complicated designs representing priests in ceremonial regalia were found by Dr. Gordon[1] in the Uloa Valley. The most interesting designs have been figured by him in his report. Many smaller pieces that may be classed as bowls have designs such as owls, bats and serpents.

A number of remarkable painted vases from the highlands of Guatemala have been described in some detail. The finest specimens were excavated in the environs of Coban. Of these the two most famous were found at Chama by Mr. E. P. Dieseldorff.[2] One of these bears two representations of a bat with outspread wings. On each wing is a crescent-shaped marking. The body of

Fig. 193. — Polychrome vessel: El Jecaro, Guatemala.

the bat is grotesquely human. A flame-shaped speech scroll begins in front of the face and twining upward divides into a forward and a backward part. Between the two figures are six excellently drawn glyphs. The background is a rich orange with bands of black, yellow and brown at top and bottom. The delineation is in black, and the interior areas are filled in with white, red and brown. The second vase represents seven human beings drawn in profile and with clear details of dress, upon a light yellow background. The flesh of five of the figures is yellow orange in color but in the case of the remaining two is painted black. The most interesting figure is striding forward with a spear in one hand and a fan in the other. The foreshortening of some of the bodies is rather poor, and the bodies themselves are gross. In connection with each figure are several glyphs that probably give the name of the individual or other information concerning him. Other vessels of the same general character might be mentioned.[3]

But as a rule the variations from black are towards green suggesting the use of borax. In fact, in some cases, the glaze is quite green while in others there are green spots or bubbles. Sometimes there are thin washes of green stain extending beyond the paint. The vessels were turned upside down in firing and in many instances the paint ran badly. Since it is an invariable rule to let the clay and the paint dry thoroughly before firing, it seems likely that the paint fused during the firing. In some cases it seems to have boiled or bubbled considerably. Blisters are seen on many specimens.

Glazed paint does not seem to have been limited to any one kind of ware, but to have been used on all wares that were burned in an open draft kiln (that is, all wares that are not black). It is commonest on a thin hard red ware which shows the use of red and orange sizing. It is also found on terra cotta ware and on ware with a cream coloring sizing.

[1] 1898, *a*, pls. 4 and 5.

[2] See collection of papers on this subject translated in Bull. 28, Bur. Am. Ethnol., pp. 639–666. For the original color reproductions see Dieseldorff, 1894, *a* and *b*, pls. 8 and 13.

[3] See Dieseldorff, 1893, *b*, pl. 14 (Chama); Seler, 1902–1908, III, pp. 629, 633 (Rio Hondo), 718 (Nebaj).

A small vessel of this type is given in Fig. 193. The persons represented wear flowers in their hair, as do those on the vases just described. They are seated and apparently engaged in conversation rather than in ceremonies. An interesting feature on this vase is the representation of an altar which is apparently a bundle tied by broad bands. The altar recalls the wrapped and knotted stone altars of Copan, as has already been pointed out. Upon the top of the altar shown on the vase is a human head, indicating sacrifice. The glyphs are apparently merely decorative, for all are approximately the same. The colors are orange for background, black for lines, and red, white and brown for masses. This vase was excavated at El Jicaro, near Zacapa, Guatemala, during the construction of the railroad, and was presented to the Peabody Museum by Dr. Lytle.

In the private collection of Don Enrique Camara of Merida, Yucatan, there is a remarkable vase of the same class. This specimen was found at Calcetok, between Merida and Campeche. The paste is very light in both color and weight. The background is a yellow orange sizing with a high polish. Upon this the figures were delineated in black, and certain details filled in in white, red and brown. The shape is cylindrical. The pictures on

FIG. 194. — Geometric motives used in pottery decorations.

this vase include three standing and two seated men, two deer, a jaguar, a tree, a serpent and a bird.

A description of the remarkable collection of pottery with painted and plastic decoration from eastern Peten, collected by Mr. Merwin for the Peabody Museum, will add much to our knowledge of the ceramic masterpieces of the Maya.

Many vessels that it is impossible to treat in detail show combinations of the different methods of decoration that have been described. A medallion decoration showing the combination of incised and painted design is given in Fig. 184, b.

The geometric units used in ceramic decoration embrace nearly all the more common ones. The fret and the spiral are finely developed, as may be seen from Fig. 194. As a rule, the geometric elements are applied in bands around the neck or rim of the vessel.

Small clay figurines occur very widely in Mexico and Central America, and in the Maya area especially are much diversified. Plate 17 shows human figurines of markedly different types, which give an excellent idea of the range in form and finish. Many interesting figurines come from the Uloa Valley on the southern frontier (1 to 3). The figurines from Jonuta on the lower Usumacinta (4 and 7) are among the finest from the Maya area. The last four specimens come from the Island of Jaina near Campeche and belong to the private collection of Mrs. W. M. James of Merida, Yucatan, through whose kindness they are here reproduced. The two smaller pieces, 9 and 12, exemplify very common forms, but the two larger ones are exceptional in several ways. One of them is really a tableau and presents three small figures grouped about the legs of a much larger figure. The other is a very unusual piece of modeling. It represents a man, naked except for a loin cloth and breast ornament. The right hand is raised and the left one hangs at the side. The right knee is also raised. The feet are missing. It is possible that this figure is only part of a group. A cast from an ancient terra cotta mould is reproduced in 8. This mould was obtained in the region of the Rio Chixoy in northern Guatemala. The type of face recalls the sculptures of Yaxchilan and Palenque.[1]

Many figurines in human and animal form were used as whistles with three or four notes. Others may have been used as household gods. Pottery stamps with geometric and conventionalized designs and many small objects of clay with ornamentations of various sorts are found in all parts of the Maya area.

Precious Stones. Jadeite and other semi-precious stones were much used for beads, ear plugs, nose plugs, amulets and other small carved objects whose use is unknown. Dr. G. F. Kunz,[2] an accepted authority on precious stones, writes as follows concerning the green stones of Mexico: "Chalchihuitl, a name celebrated in Mexican archaeology, was applied to certain green stones capable of high polish, which were carved in various ornamental forms and very highly valued. There has been much mystery and much discussion as to what this precious material really was, and whence it was obtained. It seems evident that several minerals were included under the name, among them a green quartz or prase, some of the deeper green varieties of techli or Mexican onyx (so called), and probably turquoise; but the precious chalchihuitl has now been proved to be jadeite, a stone which has possessed a singular charm for many aboriginal peoples in widely separated parts of the globe . . ." Nephrite apparently does not occur in Mexico and Central America.

Mrs. Nuttall[3] has been able to show, by the etymology of place names and by the tribute demanded from conquered cities by the Aztecs, that chalchihuitl was a product of definite regions in southern Mexico. Doubtless jadeite occurs in Guatemala and perhaps farther south. Hartmann describes jadeite objects from Costa Rica, which seem for the most part to be of local manufacture, and characteristic of the individualized art of Nicoya. A few specimens were probably acquired from the Maya region to the north. One piece in particular is almost surely Maya.[4] There is considerable similarity between the small human and animal figures crudely carved of green stone and possibly intended to be used as fetiches, that are common in western Guatemala[5] and in Costa

---

[1] For other examples of figurines see Blackiston, 1910, a and b; Seler, 1895, d; Batres, 1888, pls. 1–3.
[2] 1907, pp. 20–21.
[3] 1901, b.
[4] Hartmann, 1907, pl. 45, fig. 10. Plate 46 shows

crude jades from Oaxaca somewhat similar to many from Guatemala and Costa Rica.
[5] The localities represented in the American Museum of Natural History by these crude carvings are Zacualpa, Joyabaj and Sajcabaja.

Rica. This likeness may be due to similarity in technique which is characterized by the use of straight grooves to outline crudely either faces or entire figures. Of course this method is the simplest possible one. In Costa Rica, Guatemala and the State of Guerrero, Mexico, the shape which serves as the basis for most of these figures is that of the celt. Indeed, some of the ornaments must be regarded simply as decorated celts. In other cases celts have been halved or quartered to get material for ornaments. The explanation of this may be that stones of the finest color and texture were hard to obtain, and that the celts which turned out after polishing to be of the desired material were simply transformed into figures with the least possible labor. It must be pointed out that the region in Guatemala from which these stones come is upon the western frontier, where the lapidary's art was not so highly developed as in the great cities of the lowlands.

In the working of jadeite and other stones [1] drills and cords were used for boring and cutting. The larger stones were sawn into flat slabs. Sometimes, as has been said, celts were neatly halved or quartered by sand and water grinding in grooves probably through the agency of a cord drawn back and forth. Frequently irregular but some-

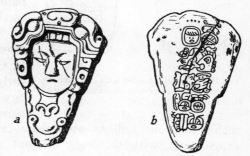

FIG. 195. — Carved jadeite amulet with inscription.

what flat pieces of stone were smoothed off or carved upon one side, while the other side was left in the original rough state. Indeed nearly all the carved jadeite objects from Mexico and Central America show portions of the original weathered surface, which is a good indication that the material was found only in small pieces. The cruder specimens have straight incised lines to mark out the details of the figures. Many of the finer objects, however, are freely carved in the graceful curves characteristic of Maya art, often with marked relief and with modeled surfaces.

Perhaps the most famous piece of worked jadeite from the Maya area is the Leiden Plate.[2] This is a thin oblong slab with rounded corners, having upon one side an incised drawing of an elaborately attired human being holding a Ceremonial Bar in his arms. Upon the other side is a column of hieroglyphics. Further discussion of this specimen is reserved for a later section. Another important though less artistic piece is the San Andres Tuxtla Statuette,[3] which will also be treated later.

A well-known jadeite amulet belonging to the famous Bishop collection [4] of jades, now installed at the Metropolitan Museum of Fine Arts, New York, is reproduced in Fig. 195. Upon the front is represented a human face in front view, with a headdress consisting of the upper portion of an animal head. The relief is rather high. Upon the back, which shows the natural weathered surface, are a number of glyphs. Dr. Förstemann attempted a tentative interpretation of the inscription as follows: "From the day 4 Ahau, the 7th of the month Zip,

---

[1] Sahagun, 1880, pp. 585–587; Seler, 1890, pp. 418–425; Holmes, 1895–1897, pp. 304–309; Saville, 1900, b, pp. 106–107.

[2] Leemans, 1877; Holden, 1879–1880, pp. 229–230; Valentini, 1881, b.

[3] Holmes, 1907.

[4] Bishop Collection, No. 309, p. 100.

when the god K ruled, lived (the person whose face is shown on the other side) until the year which begins with 8 Kan on the 13 of the month Zec." According to this the deceased person lived fifty years, two months and six days. Although it is evident enough that jades were often buried with the dead or used as votive offerings in the temples, it is unsafe to consider them as examples of portraiture.

A jadeite amulet comparable to this in having an inscription (Fig. 196) on the back was found by Maler on the Island of Jaina near the city of Campeche and is now in the American Museum of Natural History. The grooves on the front show traces of red paint and there are eight incised glyphs on the back.

A number of finely carved ornaments, mostly obtained at Ocosingo, Guatemala, by E. G. Squier, have been described[1] by that early student of Central American archaeology. The larger pieces are pierced for suspension as amulets. A flat slab about four

FIG. 196. — Jadeite amulet with red paint on front and inscription on back: Island of Jaina.

inches long and half as wide shows a human figure seated cross-legged, with the body in front view and the face in profile. Beneath the figure is a conventionalized face. The drawing is rather poor and the relief is flat. More rounded relief is shown in another specimen, roughly triangular in shape, which bears upon the front a human face in front view, with a simple headdress probably representing a conventionalized animal head. The ear plugs at the side of the human face have flaring featherlike appendages, that fill the two upper angles of the triangle. One of the most interesting pieces is reproduced in Fig. 95. This is a thin plate of translucent jadeite representing in stencil-like profile view a typical grotesque face of a Sun God. The carving is the same on both sides of the plate, and the four divisions of the "kin sign" on the forehead and the curve that indicates the pupil of the eye are cut through from one side to the other.

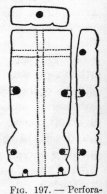

FIG. 197. — Perforations of a jadeite amulet from Chichen Itza.

FIG. 198. — Jadeite amulet from Chichen Itza.

Fig. 197 gives three diagrammatic views of a typical jade to show the perforations. One perforation traverses the entire length of the jade and another crosses from side to side. Six dowel holes enter from the side and issue at the back. These were probably used for the attachment of feathers. In Fig. 198 we have the design on the front of the specimen.

In the Squier collection is a globular head with three inscribed glyphs and several kinds of ear plugs, such as are commonly represented in the sculptures. Fig. 199 shows a well-carved square ear plug and Fig. 200 reproduces a clay figurine of a woman found near Coban with ear plugs identical in shape and design. The excavations at Copan by the Peabody Museum revealed a number

[1] 1870. The collection is now in the American Museum of Natural History.

of burials in which were found jadeite beads and other ornaments of stone and shell. The beads were of two kinds, globular and cylindrical. According to the necklaces represented on the stone sculptures these two kinds of beads were frequently strung alternately.

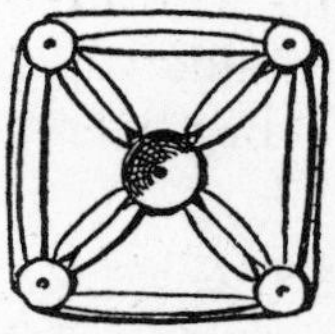

Vessels of alabaster and marble are occasionally found. A fine cylindrical jar of marble is figured by Hamy[1] and described as coming from Honduras, on the southern frontier of the Maya area. Two small bowls of very similar appearance were obtained by Dr. Gordon[2] on the Uloa River in northern Honduras and are now in the Peabody Museum. A small and a large

Fig. 199. — Jadeite ear plug: Ocosingo.

bowl of the same type, the latter with a perforated ring base, belong to the Squier collection in the American Museum of Natural History. All these stone jars have a very characteristic decoration, consisting of short scrolls carved in low but rounded relief, and knob handles carved into animal heads. The large one in the Squier collection has a face on each side (Fig. 201) enclosed in spirals of the same character as those on the smaller pieces. A fine alabaster vase cylindrical in shape and with a simple but pleasing geometric decoration was found by Thompson in the so-called High Priest's Grave at Chichen Itza. This is now in the Field Museum at Chicago.

Fig. 200. — Clay figurine showing use of jadeite ear plugs: Coban.

Metal Working. A large part of the Maya area is very young geologically and does not contain ores of any sort. Upon the southern and western frontiers metals are found, in addition to which small quantities may have been obtained in trade. Owing to this lack of material, within the region of the highest culture, objects of metal are rare. Such as do occur are fully equal to the metal work of the Valley of Mexico or the more distant Costa Rica. Gold and copper and sometimes silver were worked by hollow casting and by hammering. The making of wire filigree is found from Colombia to Central Mexico,[3] and the distribution of this interesting technical process goes farther to show cultural contact than any number of fanciful resemblances in decorative art. The objects to be cast were modeled in wax, pitch, or

Fig. 201. — Portion of design on marble vase from Honduras.

some such substance. If hollow, an inner form, probably of clay, was used. Decoration was added by rolling out a wire of the wax or pitch and applying

---

[1] 1896, pp. 10–11, and pl. 2.

[2] 1908, *a*, pp. 25–26 and pl. 12, *e* and *f*. Dr. Gordon comments on the distribution of this type of object, which seems pretty definitely limited to Honduras.

[3] References on metal working are McCurdy, 1911, pp. 189–226 (Chiriqui); Peñafiel, 1890, pls. 109–113 (Nahua and Zapotecan); Seler, 1890, pp. 401–418 (Nahua); Lumholtz, 1902, II, pp. 296, 413–416 (Tarascan, etc.); Valentini, 1879, *a*.

this to the surface in whatever design was desired. The whole was then inset in à clay mould and the wax or pitch melted out. In the metal object as cast the wire decoration has the appearance of having been attached by some metallic cement. Sometimes the entire object was built up by coiling and folding over the wire.

FIG. 202.—Copper bell with appliqué decoration: Honduras.

The most widespread object of metal is the bell, which is similar to the common sleigh bell. Cogolludo [1] states that copper bells were used among the Maya as a medium of exchange. Copper and gold bells similar to those from the Maya area have been found in Zapotecan, Nahua and Tarascan ruins. Fig. 202 is a sketch of a copper bell with coarse wire filigree coming from northern Honduras. It is one out of a very large number found in a cache and subsequently melted down for the small percentage of gold in the metal. Other caches showing similar bells are described by Blackiston.[2] Copper bells, mostly plain, were found in the High Priest's Grave at Chichen Itza. A few gold bells have been found in the Maya territory. Small ornaments of gold and copper are fairly common in Chiapas and Tabasco.

Bernal Dias speaks of the scarcity of gold among the Maya, but mentions a few objects. In the curious narrative called the "Letters of the Companions of Grijalva"[3] some interesting descriptions of objects

a   *b*

FIG. 203. — Baskets represented in sculptures: *a*, Yaxchilan; *b*, Chichen Itza.

made of precious stone (probably jadeite) and metals are given. While the general enthusiasm of these discoverers must be discounted, there is no reason to distrust their specific references. There is doubt, however, whether these objects were seen in Yucatan, as stated, or in southern Vera Cruz. In any case the list is instructive.

"Two round disks, one of fine gold, the other of fine silver, handsomely worked with beautiful figures drawn with a free hand. . . . The former measures seven spans and the silver one is smaller by about a little finger.

"Further, a head of a great serpent or dragon: a figure of very fine gold with golden teeth that are easily a span wide and three fingers thick; gather for yourself how large the head is; the eyes are of precious stones and are adorned with very costly feathers.

"Further, a great disk of precious stone completely covered with tiger hide, the hide being highly valued.

"Further, four necklaces with many precious stones set in gold.

"Further, a horn of a seafish, of gold, two spans long and about two palms wide, all of gold.

"Further, a head of gold and many other pieces of gold, silver and precious stone."

Basketry. A basket of simple twilled weaving is held in the arms of a kneeling supplicant shown on one of the lintels of Temple 21 at Yaxchilan.[4] A similar

[1] 1688, p. 181.   [3] Muller, 1871, pp. 29–30. See also Valentini, 1879, *a*, p. 97.
[2] 1910, *b*.   [4] Maudslay, 1889–1902, II, pl. 83.

but more elaborate basket is shown in Fig. 203, *a*, which is also represented on a lintel at Yaxchilan. The upper portion of this basket is executed in twilled weaving; the middle portion shows a finer weave, with designs of stepped frets and small rectangles in groups of three. The bottom of the basket seems to be ornamented with feather-work. The shape of these two baskets is somewhat unusual on account of the straight sides and flaring rim. Fig. 203, *b*, apparently represents a basket with colored decoration consisting of ribbons and other adventitious ornament. The drawing is taken from the sculptured wall of the Lower chamber of the Temple of the Jaguars, at Chichen Itza. Basket-work fans are shown in the hands of the figures on the Chama [1] vase.

Braided bands are sometimes represented in headdresses, as in the case of Stela A at Copan and Stela 10 at Seibal. It seems probable that some sort of

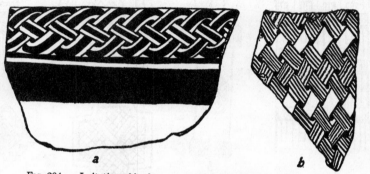

FIG. 204. — Imitation of basket weaves on painted pottery: Uloa Valley.

basket foundation may have been used to support the elaborate feather-work. A type of ceremonial staff found at Yaxchilan on Lintels 6 and 43 consists of a woven object similar to an inverted waste-paper basket which is carried on a pole. The Long-nosed God with the serpent appendage is seated on top.

Simple basket weavings appear as painted ornamentation on potsherds from the Uloa Valley (Fig. 204). Complicated braided patterns are common as the rim decoration on pottery from this region, and may have had their origin in the imitation of wicker-work basketry. It is probable that basketry was not of much importance as an art among the Maya, owing to the high development of ceramics.

Textiles. The textile art of the ancient Maya must be studied mostly at second hand from designs sculptured or depicted on the garments of figures represented on stelae and lintels or in mural decorations and codices. There is a strong probability of certain survivals in the modern art of the Indians of Yucatan and Guatemala, but little information is available. The native women of northern Yucatan still embroider their dresses with floral and sometimes geometric patterns which may be pre-Spanish. In 1765 Lieutenant Cook, afterwards the famous captain who explored the Pacific, made an overland trip from Bacalar to Merida. His report contains an excellent description of the appearance of the natives and the country. He comments on the comeliness of the women, who, he said, wore white cotton smocks embroidered with flowers in needlework at the bottom.[2] The present mode is then at least one hundred

---

[1] Dieseldorff, 1894, *a*, pl. 8; Bulletin 28, pl. 48.   [2] Cook, 1769, pp. 29–30.

and fifty years old. The Quiché and other Indians living on the highlands of Guatemala[1] still make their own textiles, but European influence seems to be pretty strong. For instance, silk is widely used for embroidery. The designs are mostly stripes of simple geometric figures, although some pieces show birds and other life forms finely conventionalized. Careful field study among these peoples might result in the determination of many of the ancient designs and their meanings.

The early explorers and historians[2] comment on the beautiful garments worn by the natives of Yucatan. Cogolludo[3] says the cotton cloth of Yucatan made

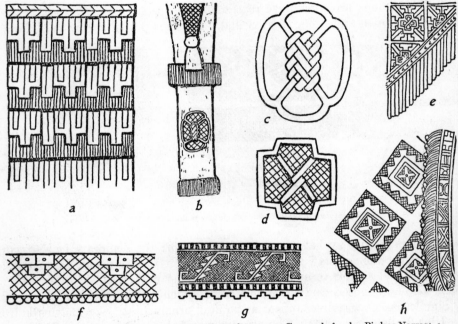

FIG. 205. — Details of textile ornament from the sculptures: a, Copan; b, f and g, Piedras Negras; e and h, Yaxchilan.

in various colors was traded over all of New Spain. Aguilar[4] likewise comments on the extent of the textile industry. Much of the tribute[5] demanded by the Spaniards was in cloth.

The every-day dress of the men was a sort of breech cloth that passed around the hips and had end flaps hanging down in front and behind. In the ancient sculptures these apron-like flaps are often embellished. The apron with a grotesque face between two serpent heads conventionalized in the form of frets (Fig. 15) may have been purely a ceremonial elaboration possible in sculptures but not used in real life. It has, however, a remarkably wide distribution among the southern cities of the Maya area. Often aprons have a sort of openwork

---

[1] Stoll, 1889, pp. 96–101; Maudslay, A. C. and A. P., 1899, pp. 41–43.

[2] Landa, 1864, pp. 117 and 182–184; Muller, 1871, p. 28; Relaciones de Yucatan, II, pp. 29, 46–47, 104–105, 123, 154, 211–212, etc. For a modern discussion see Schellhas, 1890, pp. 214–228.

[3] 1688, p. 173.

[4] 1639, p. 94.

[5] References to tribute are numerous; see Relaciones de Yucatan, 1900, II, pp. 57, 67–68, 150; Relacion de los Conquistadores, 1870, pp. 193–195, etc. Besides mantas, the tribute matter included wax, cocoa, and, in ancient times, green stones, red shell beads, etc.

design in the center and a fringe at the bottom, as may be seen in Fig. 205, *b*.
Aprons of greater width and more elaborate decoration occur, such as the one
shown in *a*, drawn from one of the statues on the Hieroglyphic Stairway at Copan.
A most beautiful apron is found on Stela 7 at Piedras Negras.[1] The design
consists of a symmetrical arrangement of small frets around a Greek cross.

FIG. 206. — Garments represented on sculptures and in codices: *a* and *b*, Chichen Itza; *c–e*, Dresden Codex.

A garment in the form of a short skirt reaching half-way down the thigh is
sometimes seen upon figures which evidently represent men. Often this skirt
has the characteristic markings of a jaguar skin, as may be seen on Stelae P, 2,
etc., at Copan. The belt at the top of this short skirt receives the greater part
of the decoration, which is usually of a geometric style. Fig. 206, *a*, reproduces
the skirt of one of the processional warriors
from the Lower chamber of the Temple of
the Jaguars at Chichen Itza. This short skirt
is marked with crossbones, which may represent painted rather than woven decoration.

The most elaborate textile patterns are
found on a sort of blanket which usually
envelops the entire body, although in some
cases it seems to have been bound around
the waist so that the corners hang down on
either side. Fig. 207, taken from one of the
lintels of Yaxchilan, represents a kneeling
supplicant. The entire body of this person
is enveloped in a robe having an all-over geometric decoration in squares, a rich border
at the bottom and a tasseled fringe along
the edge. It is possible that this dress represents the sacklike garment still worn by
the Maya women. Similarly gowned figures
occur on a number of the lintels of Yaxchilan and upon several stelae from Piedras
Negras. As a rule, these figures are of smaller

FIG. 207. — Woman richly attired: Yaxchilan.

size than those on the same lintels which have the usual masculine dress.

The geometric designs on these robes are applied in horizontal stripes, in
diagonal stripes and in all-over patterns. Very often the border of the bottom
is differentiated from the design on the blanket as a whole. Fig. 205, *f* and *g*,

[1] Maler, 1901, pl. 16.

shows two such border decorations, and *h* a fringe border marked with the common planet symbols. Fig. 205, *e*, reproduces the design on a garment which hangs over the shoulder of a male figure. Robes somewhat like these which have just been described are represented in the codices upon figures which are clearly masculine (Fig. 206, *c* to *e*).

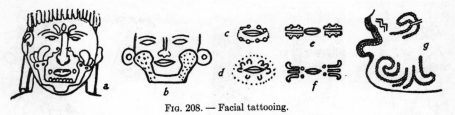

FIG. 208. — Facial tattooing.

What might be called an inset lace medallion often occurs as an evenly distributed design in the body of a garment. The details of two of these inset medallions are given in Fig. 205, *c* and *d*.

Tattooing. Dr. Schellhas[1] has already commented on the evidences of tattooing among the peoples of Central America. These evidences are found upon figurines and in the codices as well as on the sculptures. In Fig. 208, *a* to *f* are taken from the examples that Dr. Schellhas gives. Of these, the first (*a*) is a sketch of the head of a Yucatan figurine representing a man with the cheeks and chin tattooed with a drawing of a jaw bone. There is also a simple design in the center of the forehead. A simpler example of the jaw-bone design is seen in *b*. More often, however, the tattooing consists of simple markings made either around or at the side of the mouth, such as are shown in *c*, *d* and *e*. Fig. 209 presents a terra cotta head with raised designs on each cheek, and on the lips as well, that doubtless represent tattooing.[2] The most elaborate tattooing seems to have consisted of spiral scrolls at each corner of the mouth; examples of this type of facial decoration are seen on the lintels of Yaxchilan (Fig. 208, *b*). The splendid head formerly at Uxmal, and now in Mexico City (Fig. 182), has similar markings upon one side of the face.

FIG. 209. — Pottery whistle showing tattooing: Tecolpa, Tabasco.

There are no certain objective evidences of tattooing upon the body. The markings which occur on the legs of many of the grotesque figures of gods may simply indicate reptilian affinities. The human beings represented in the fresco paintings of Santa Rita,[3] British Honduras, usually have all bare portions of the body covered with minute geometric markings. Circles surrounded with dots, short hooks and short parallel lines are the prevailing motives. It is doubtful whether these markings represent real body ornamentation or merely adventitious elaboration by the artist.

Minor Carvings. A remarkable drawing made on the skull of a peccary is reproduced in Fig. 210. The engraved skull was found in a tomb at Copan,

---

[1] 1890, pp. 212–213; Landa, 1864, p. 120.
[2] Other examples of tattooing on figurines might be given. See, for instance, Batres, 1888, pls. 1–3.
[3] Gann, 1898–1899, pls. 29–31.

along with a number of pottery and bone objects, during the excavations conducted by the Peabody Museum. The drawing is here shown as if spread out
flat and no account taken of the uneven surfaces. In the upper left-hand corner
are shown three running peccaries, drawn with a considerable degree of naturalness. The hair is represented by short lines not very close together, which give
an excellent idea of the general grizzled appearance of the animals. In the corresponding right-hand corner are represented a jaguar and a monkey in profile,
back to back. The jaguar is well drawn
without any marked divergence from the
natural form. The monkey wears a breech
cloth, a necklace, ear plugs and a simple
headdress. In his right hand he holds a
rattle, apparently made from a gourd,
marked with three small crosses. The expression on the face of the monkey is very
realistic. In the center of the skull within
a quadrifoil medallion are two men seated,
facing each other, in easy conversational
attitudes, one with the face in profile and
the body in front view, and the other with
both face and body in profile. Both these
men wear rather elaborate headdresses.
Their breasts are bare and their belts have
for decoration a simple face. Between the
men and arranged one above the other
appear at the bottom a grotesque head, at
the top a group of four glyphs and in the
middle an oblong object with interlacing
bands which may represent an altar. In
the lower left-hand corner of the skull is
drawn a deer wearing a loin cloth and
standing in erect human attitude. In
front of this deer is a stooping figure with
a death's head. He carries on his back,

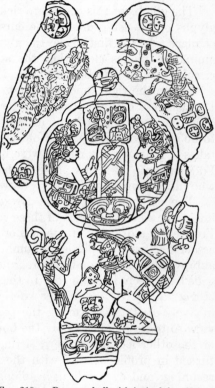

FIG. 210. — Peccary skull with incised drawings:
Copan.

by means of a tump line, a bundle tied by a number of broad bands. Over
this bundle hovers a bird with wings outstretched. Besides the drawings of
men and animals which have here been briefly enumerated, there are a number
of glyphs scattered about. These glyphs may be name glyphs referring to
the nearest figure. This drawing is remarkable for its freedom, its naturalness
and its lack of conventionality.

A fragment of a carved animal skull picked up on the river front at Copan
is reproduced in Fig. 60. It has already been commented upon at some length.

Shells carved with glyphs have been found at a number of sites. Some interesting examples come from the Island of Jaina. A large shell with a fine inscription has been figured by Thomas,[1] with the statement that it was secured in
British Honduras. A beautiful carved shell of Maya manufacture was found
during the excavations of Tula. A seated human figure is upon one side and

[1] 1894–1895, pl. 69.

four Maya glyphs upon the other. This specimen has been reproduced by Peñafiel.[1] It is now in the Field Museum at Chicago.

Illuminated Manuscripts. The three Maya codices[2] are of unequal value as objects of art. The Dresden is by far the best. The drawings of some parts are of exceeding delicacy and smoothness, while other pages show much rougher work. This difference in finish may be explained by difference in paper or in authorship. The codex treats of a variety of subjects, and it is possible that each subject was written out by a different hand.

The glyphs of this codex are rich in detail and similar in most features to the glyphs of the sculptures. The cursive style of representation has caused some changes. In the first place, the glyphs are tilted slightly toward the right. Examination makes clear that the stroke for outlining faces and other oval or circular bodies was begun at the lower left-hand corner and carried over and around to the right, ending a slight reverse curve that produces a sort of beak. Details were doubtless put in after the outline had been made. The columns of glyphs were marked out in faint lines to guide the scribe, and the numbers to be set down were marked on lightly. Certain erasures are in evidence. Mistakes of more serious nature were made in some of the calculations, according to Förstemann. It seems possible that there were professional scribes or copiers who did not understand very well what they were transcribing.

The oblong pages of the Dresden Codex are usually divided horizontally into three zones, and each of these zones subdivided vertically into three sections. Frequently a drawing of one or more figures is shown in each of the nine sections, associated with glyphs and numbers. The glyphs often show an intelligible abbreviation of the main figure, and by this means the glyphs of nearly all the gods have been determined. In these uniform spaces all the men and women are of a certain height, no matter whether standing or sitting. The figures are drawn in lively attitudes. Among the poses shown may be mentioned sitting in side view so that of the legs only the bottom of one foot and the foreshortened thigh of the other leg are in view, sitting with legs in front view but with the head turned in profile; sitting with the knees up, squatting and stooping, walking, reclining, and even falling headlong with the body curiously twisted. Objects held in the hand or placed before the figure indicate the attributes and powers.

While most of the more finished drawings are in simple black and white, many others show the use of color for the background, and a few resemble pictures in that several colors are combined to mark out the details of dress and ornament.

The probable connection of some of the gods shown in this and other codices, with those represented by other means, has already been discussed. From the prevalence of glyphs of the southern type, and especially the occurrence of the period glyphs, this codex has been referred to the southern or western part of the Maya area.

Förstemann[3] believes that the codex comes from the region of Palenque. It is significant that neither the Ceremonial Bar nor the Manikin Scepter, the two principal ceremonial objects in the Maya cities of the great period, is seen in this codex. The dates given in the Dresden Codex will be considered in another

[1] 1899, pl. 80, and 1890, pl. 169. See also Charnay, 1885, p. 74.
[2] A revised pagination for these documents is given on page 260. [3] 1897, p. 48.

section. If the last of these dates is historical, the Dresden Codex comes down from the time of the Transition, and may have originated in the region south of Uxmal or perhaps in Tabasco. There are a few remarkable similarities between this codex and others that are ascribed to the Zapotecans. An instance in point is the staff with a hand[1] at the upper end that occurs likewise in the Codex Borgia (Fig. 211).

The Peresianus Codex, now, unfortunately, in a very fragmentary condition,[2] seems also to be an old manuscript that may antedate the coming of the Spaniards by several centuries. The drawing is very fine, and there is reason to believe that in its prime it was equal to the Dresden Codex. The details of the codex show certain rather definite similarities to the sculptures of Naranjo, Quirigua and Piedras Negras, and it seems likely that the manuscript originated in the general region of these cities or was copied from an earlier manuscript having such an origin. A crocodile-like animal with its head hanging over the edge of a throne and with its feet bound to the body is seen on Plates 3–11 of the de Rosny reproduction. An apparently human figure is seated on this throne, and a god, that varies from page to page, stands before the throne holding a head in his hands, which usually appears to be that of God K, while before his face flutters a bird and before his feet is an offering of maize. The idea of a figure seated on a throne is common on the stelae of the Peten region. Here also the figure is usually human in appearance. One or more other figures, also in human guise, are sometimes arranged before this person, and these frequently hold the Manikin Scepter or some other ceremonial object

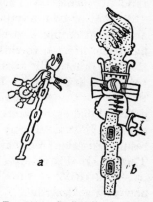

Fig. 211. — Staff ending in hand: a, Dresden Codex; b, Codex Borgia.

in their hands. In other cases the seated figure himself holds the Manikin Scepter or the Ceremonial Bar. The throne or niche in almost all instances has a bound animal placed across it. Sometimes the animal assumes the characteristics of the Two-headed Dragon. Sometimes two animals, one above the other, are represented, the upper one being highly conventionalized. Illustrations of the thrones in the Peresianus Codex and on Stela 32 of Naranjo have been already presented in Fig. 6, d, f and g. For comparative study reference is made to Stelae 5, 6, 11, 14, 25 and 33 at Piedras Negras, and Stelae 22 and 32 at Naranjo. The technique of the sculptures is very different from that of the manuscripts, and this fact should be taken into account. The form of the astronomical band on Plate 22 of the Codex is almost identical with the astronomical band on the back of Stela H at Quirigua (Fig. 6, a and c). The face of the Roman-nosed God attached to the body of a bird appears on Plates 4 and 8 of the manuscript and on the top of Stela 5 at Piedras Negras. Although the resemblances which have just been pointed out are not conclusive, yet they are more so than those shown by either of the other codices for any particular region.

The Tro-Cortesianus Codex is much inferior to the other two in artistic skill, and may be a late work or at least a late copy. The difference in style is

---

[1] This object also is seen in the Tro-Cortesianus Codex, p. 89.
[2] For the romantic history of this manuscript see Léon de Rosny, 1876, p. 6.

well shown by the drawings given in Figs. 77, 78, etc. The most striking similarity of the Tro-Cortesianus to the sculptures is in the curious representation
of the two birds with interlocked necks (Fig. 102, *i*), which resembles in subject
a rather crude carving at Labna. The glyphs are cruder and simpler than those
of the other two codices, and are inclined to be angular. The glyphs of the Books
of Chilan Balam, which belong to the Spanish epoch, are very much more angular. The Tro-Cortesianus Codex may with some assurance be assigned to
northern Yucatan and to a date not much later than 1200 A.D It contains no
representations of the sun disk and other Nahua and Zapotecan features which
appear in the late sculptures of Chichen Itza. The forms of the gods are similar
in detail to those of the other two codices. All three of the Maya codices are quite
clearly marked off from the ancient books of the neighboring peoples, although
random resemblances occur, as has already been noted.

A word or two may be given to the subject matter embodied in these codices
and the attempts at decipherment. Since the days of Kingsborough [1] attention
has been directed to this field of study. Most of the early attempts at elucidation are practically worthless and even in modern times much has been written
that is of little value. Brasseur de Bourbourg,[2] for instance, began his translation of the Codex Troano at the wrong end of the manuscript, and used the so-
called alphabet of Landa,[3] which is now known to be no alphabet at all. Charen-
cey and Léon de Rosny worked in a careful and painstaking manner and their
results deserve credit as pioneer efforts. The most important contribution of
Thomas, in his Study of the Manuscript Troano, was his demonstration that
pages 34 to 37 of the Tro-Cortesianus Codex referred to the ceremonies of the
new year as described by Landa, and his comparison with these pages of an analogous passage in the Dresden Codex (pages 25–28). Undoubtedly the greatest
single contribution to the subject in hand is Förstemann's Commentary on the
Dresden Codex. Many valuable papers on definite subjects relating to the
codices have been contributed by Bowditch, Schellhas, Seler, Fewkes, Gates,
etc. Many of these have already been referred to in this text.

The contents of the three manuscripts are largely religious and astronomical,
although the Tro-Cortesianus Codex also casts considerable light on the every-
day life of the Maya. The Tonalamatl [4] or 260-day period is frequently indicated,
usually in a much more abbreviated form than in Nahua and Zapotecan codices.
This time period, with its varying divisions, is employed in connection with
gods, ceremonies, avocations and events. The representation of the new year
ceremonies in the Tro-Cortesianus and Dresden Codices has already been mentioned. Possibly the same subject is contained in Plates 19 and 20 of the Codex
Peresianus. Several pages of the Dresden Codex are devoted to intricate astronomical calculations in which the lunar, solar and Venus calendars are correlated
in a wonderful manner. It is possible that some historical references are contained in the Dresden and Peresianus Codices, although this is not very likely. In
the former there are a number of dates that can be expressed in the same system
that was used on the ancient monuments. It is probable, however, that the true
historical records were among those destroyed by Landa and other Spanish priests.

---

[1] The Dresden Codex was first reproduced by
Kingsborough, 1831–1848, III.

[2] 1869–1870.

[3] 1864, pp. 316–322.

[4] Bowditch, 1910, pp. 266–274; Förstemann,
1895.

CHRONOLOGICAL SEQUENCE

FIRST EPOCH.

Statement of the Problem. In the analysis of any great national art the determination of the chronological sequence of forms is of first importance. How difficult a problem this may become, even in the full light of a civilization continuous to our own times, is seen in the years of labor that were necessary to arrange in such an order the remains of Greek art.

Although the pre-Columbian peoples of Central America had reached what may properly be called the historic stage of civilization, yet their history is unknown to us because we cannot decipher the inscriptions on their monuments. Only in so far as these inscriptions deal with the absolute relationships of numbers have they been satisfactorily explained. It has long been thought that the many glyphs which contain no numbers were used to carry the historical narrative, to give the names and attributes of chiefs and deities, or to make clear the exact nature of the ceremonies connected with each particular monument or temple. The glyphs which do contain numbers are found in series that express one or more dates in the wonderful system of the Maya calendar. But unfortunately these dates were measured in cycles from an imaginary beginning of time in the distant past. Mr. Bowditch,[1] speaking of this beginning date, says:

"If it were possible to connect with certainty the date 4 Ahau 8 Cumhu, from which all these other dates are counted, with our own chronology, we could easily reach a clear knowledge of the dates on which these monuments were erected and these inscriptions were carved, always provided, however, that the dates so given are records of the dates of the erection of the monuments, or at least of the buildings in which the inscriptions are found; and this, I think, is now generally conceded to be the case in almost all instances."

It must be admitted, however, that the attempts which have been made, upon the sole basis of the recorded dates to reconstruct the ancient history of the Maya have not proved over successful. We will now consider the evidence indicating the historical sequence of monuments and cities which a careful study of the art is able to furnish. Such a sequence, even after it has been determined, cannot be put on a basis of actual years until the historical character of at least some of the dates in the inscriptions has been established. The easiest method of presentation is to take up one city after another, beginning with those that show the most archaic forms.

Copan. In western Honduras is situated the ancient city of Copan.[2] The principal monuments of this pre-Columbian capital were first made known to the world through the descriptions of Stephens and the drawings of Catherwood. More recently the splendid plates that illustrate Maudslay's work and the reports

[1] 1903, *b*, p. 3.   [2] See Table of Nomenclature, p. 251.

of the detailed explorations of the Peabody Museum, unfortunately prevented from being carried to completion, have furnished additional information. The hundreds of unpublished photographs taken by the Museum expeditions, as well as the fine collection of original sculptures which are now available for study at this institution, were indispensable aids in the present work.

At Copan there are about twenty-five stelae. At least fifteen of these fall into a remarkably homogeneous series presenting the human figure in ceremonial attire. In connection with some of the stelae occur altars also decorated with carvings. There are, in addition, a considerable number of altars that are independent of the stelae. There are abundant remains of temples which had elaborate façade and interior decorations. An attempt will be made to throw this mass of sculpture into its proper chronological sequence.

The stelae of the homogeneous series, already mentioned, will now be considered. Each monolith shows on the front and sometimes on the back also a human figure considerably larger than natural size and richly attired that holds in its arms an object which has already been described as the Ceremonial Bar. This human being stands in a perfectly symmetrical pose, with the heels together and both arms held at the same angle. The figure wears an elaborate headdress, frequently consisting of one animal head over another. At the side of the face are ear plugs with ornaments attached; upon the wrists and ankles are decorative bands, usually carved to represent serpent heads; about the waist is a heavy girdle to which are attached small human or grotesque faces and a fringe of sea shells. From the center of the girdle hangs an apron which is also elaborately ornamented.

In the course of this study the stelae were first arranged in groups according to the proportions of the human figures carved upon them. It was found that this simple method threw them into a definite series in which other progressive variations were easily noted. For instance, the details of dress, of pose, and the degree of relief, all pass through a similar harmonious modification.

A brief description of a number of typical stelae will serve to indicate some of the progressive changes. The drawings in Maudslay's great work may be used to advantage in following this description, because they show the details of dress and ornament so clearly, but it must be stated in advance that the delineation has been more or less standardized. The cruder sculptures are frequently overdrawn in the style of the better ones. The face of Stela P, for instance, is very much overdrawn.

Stela P shows a tall slender figure wearing a jaguar skin skirt and standing with the heels together and the feet turned straight outward. A portion of the torso is distinctly visible above the girdle. In the arms, which are held with the elbows close to the body and the forearms nearly vertical, there is supported the Ceremonial Bar, which in this case has a pendent body (Fig. 46, a). About the neck of the personage represented on this stela is a collar consisting of a grotesque face, and upon the breast is a small face which probably represents a stone or shell pendant. The ear plugs are circular objects to which are connected a number of serpent heads. The purely ornamental details of this monument show very neat and careful work that does not seem at all archaic. But the carving of the legs, arms and face is flat and crude, with sharp edges. The face in particular is very badly done, and the eyes protrude in the same way as on the archaic Greek sculptures.

Stela 2 is another slender stela, although the slenderness is not so marked as in the preceding one. The body maintains the same pose, except that the forearms are not held nearly so vertical. The details of dress are remarkably similar, although in general somewhat more complicated. The torso is broader and the legs shorter and more muscular. The relief is somewhat higher than on Stela P, but is hardly less angular. Both of these stelae show the outlines of the shoulders and waist clearly.

The carvings on Stela I are much more complicated. The figure wears a mask over the face. The Ceremonial Bar is of the pendent type, but represents a dead snake. The girdle is heavier than heretofore, and the outlines of the upper portion of the body are entirely concealed. The figure is decidedly stocky and is sculptured in rather high but angular relief. Certain details of dress and ornament are similar to those of Stelae P and 2, particularly the ear ornaments with attached serpent heads (Fig. 41) and the grotesque face under the chin.

In Stela B a great change is to be noted. Many details of dress and ornament are new or modified. The pose is in general the same, but the feet are turned slightly inward in a more comfortable position and the forearms are held horizontally. The Cere-monial Bar no longer has a pendent body, but consists of a straight panel terminated by much-elongated serpent heads (Fig. 46, *b*). The girdle is exceedingly cumbersome. No part of the torso is visible. The face is visibly larger in proportion to the rest of the body than in the preceding stelae. The legs also have increased in

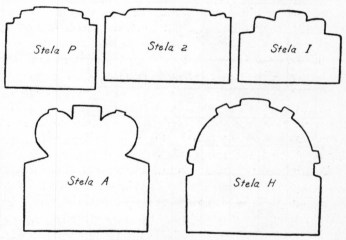

FIG. 212. — Cross-sections of Copan stelae.

length and the middle part of the body has been much reduced. The face is carved with a fair degree of modeling in almost natural relief. The arms and legs are also well rounded and stand out in high relief from the background.

Stela N presents a confused mass of superficial ornament very deeply undercut, but shows much the same pose as Stela B. The face is carved with a fair degree of naturalness, so that the cheeks show delicately rounded contours. The eyes do not protrude, although they are not very deeply sunken. The nose is carved in good relief. The legs and arms are in the full round and are carved almost free from the block. The feet are turned out, but not so much as in the case of Stela B.

The marked increase in relief is illustrated in Fig. 212, which gives the cross-sections of five stelae taken at the height of the thighs. In each case the central projection is that of the apron, while on either side of this is seen the projection of the legs (except in Stela H, which represents a skirted figure). It is readily

seen from the cross-sections of Stelae P and 2 that the relief of these sculptures
is low and angular and practically confined to one face of the quarried block.
The relief on Stela I is higher, but still angular. On Stela A (which is very similar
to Stela B, already described) the legs are not only pretty well rounded, but are
carved almost free from the block. The sculpture requires about one-half of
the plinth. The personage on Stela H is carved in such high relief that the greater
part of a very massive block is required.

In Fig. 213 is given a table of proportions for all the figures on stelae of which
reasonably complete measurements could be secured. The headdress is such a
variable feature that no account is taken of it. It will be observed that the face
is at first about twelve per cent of the length of the body, but later increases

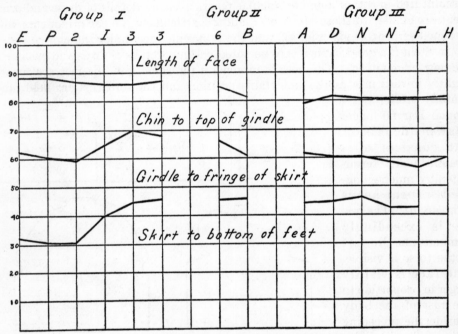

FIG. 213. — Proportions of the body on Copan stelae.

to about twenty per cent. The distance from the chin to the top of the girdle
is considerably greater in the case of the first three stelae than in the succeeding
ones. The distance from the top of the girdle to the fringe of the skirt decreases
considerably. But as a matter of fact the skirt disappears entirely in the later
sculptures, and the measurement represents the width of the girdle, which shows
decided increase. The distance from the fringe of the skirt or girdle to the bottom of the feet, which represents the visible length of leg, increases nearly one-
half over the proportions shown in Stelae E, P and 2.

So, instead of an increase of accuracy in the representation of the natural proportions of the human form, there is a marked falling off. This is due undoubtedly to the heavy ornaments which overlie the body. In the later stelae these
are given such high relief that they distract attention from the human form
beneath; all the hidden portions of the body are dwarfed. In contrast, the bare
portions have an exaggerated importance and are carefully treated. It will be

remembered that the face, arms and legs of the later badly proportioned stelae show much more skillful modeling than do those of the earlier and more properly proportioned ones.

Photographic reproductions are perhaps more convincing than drawings to indicate the range of changes which have been noted. In Plates 18 and 19 are given eight examples of sculptured stelae at Copan. Stela 7 (Plate 18, fig. 1) is probably the earliest stela at this city which bears a sculptured representation of a human figure.[1] The carving is very low, and much of it has disappeared. Stela E (Plate 18, fig. 2) is in higher relief. The forearms are almost vertical. There seems to be no doubt that both monuments antedate Stela P. Next in order is Stela P (Plate 18, fig. 3), which has already been described. Note the flat angular face with the protruding eyes. Stelae 2, 1 and I proceed in order, but are not shown in the series of reproductions. Of these Stela 1 is interesting because it introduces a different type of subject characterized by a turban headdress and a body with little elaboration. This new type is developed in Stela 6 (Plate 18, fig. 4). Two fragments of Stela 5 are given (Plate 19, figs. 1 and 2), one presenting a human face and the other a grotesque. The sculpture is considerably more advanced than in the preceding examples. Stela 3, like Stela 5, has a figure upon both front and back, the best preserved one being shown in the reproduction (Plate 19, fig. 3). This stela probably is the latest one having a Ceremonial Bar of the pendent type. Stela J may be placed with these two sculptures. It has no full-length figure, but instead a grotesque face curiously conventionalized. The new style is ushered in with Stelae A, B and D in the order named. The minor criteria of sequence in the sculptures of the last group are, 1st, the placing of the feet; 2d, the increasing use of feather drapery; 3d, the shape of the eye. The feet of Stela A are turned straight outward, although the relief of the heavy apron would have permitted the more natural pose seen in Stelae B and D. The feather trimming on Stela A is insignificant, but in D and the later monuments it plays a much more important part (Fig. 106, a, d, e and f). The eyes likewise change, although those of these three stelae are almost the same. The most excellently sculptured stelae at Copan are M, N, F, H, C and 4. The feet are in all cases turned in as far as practicable. The use of feather drapery is developed into a splendid decoration. The eyes assume more and more the form with the nearly straight top. The eyes of Stela F have circular markings to indicate the iris. Stelae N and H are reproduced in Plate 19, figs. 4 and 5, and the remaining ones may be examined in Maudslay's photographs and drawings.

Even in the latest stelae the Copan sculptors did not correct the inaccuracies in proportions that have been noted. To the last the original plinth shape of the quarried block makes itself seen in the finished monument. The face projects as far outward as does the chest (except in Stela F). These anatomical errors are not apparent in the small nude busts from the frieze of Temple 22.

Besides the artistic development which has been indicated, there are other reasons for placing these monuments in the order named. Most of the early stelae lie outside of the limits of the great plaza of the city, while the later ones are set up in this plaza. But the strongest proof is furnished by the inscriptions on the sides and back of the monuments. Many of these inscriptions present

[1] Fragments of a stela showing a still earlier style were found by the writer in Copan village in January, 1912. A low relief headdress of a large figure remains on one block.

decipherable dates in the Maya system. The sequence of the dates, when they occur, is the same as the sequence that has already been indicated by the style of sculpture. This was an unexpected confirmation, and permits the time rate of change to be accurately measured. The interval between Stela 7 and Stela N is about one hundred and fifty years. This interval of time is approximately the same as that which has been marked in the course of Greek art, between the crude metopes of the Temple of Selinus and the magnificent frieze of the Parthenon. Further reference to the dates will soon be made.

A study of the glyphs carved upon the backs of the stelae shows that the style of drawing in those glyphs goes through a series of changes parallel to that of the greater sculptures. We are able by a comparison of the glyphs to place a number of stelae which have no large human beings carved upon them. Some of these stelae having only glyphs are undoubtedly earlier than the stelae which have sculptured figures. Stela 9 bears the earliest definitely settled date at Copan, and the style of carving of the glyphs is very similar to that of Stela 7, which is the earliest stelae with a sculptured body. One side of Stela 9 is now plain, but this may once have been decorated with a painting or a very low relief sculpture.[1]

The early glyphs of Copan are flat and rectangular, with many details given in fine incised lines. The drawing is often more vigorous and lifelike than in the later forms. Each glyph is treated as a design and made to fill exactly a rectangular space. The bars that stand for the numeral five are sharp-cornered and often have diagonal markings. There is a marked use of ornamental double outlines on faces. Gradually the glyphs lose their sharpness of outline and richness of detail and become more rounded and simplified. The relief becomes much greater, so that there is often considerable modeling. Perhaps the most advanced carving of glyphs is seen on the Hieroglyphic Stairway, where the forms are very well modeled in high relief. In Plate 20 is given a series of inscriptions from the earliest to the latest. The sequence of the examples is as follows: 1, 5, 6, 2, 7, 8, 3, 4, 9 and 10. The last two examples are from Quirigua.

Probably the earliest stela at Copan is that which has been numbered 15 (Plate 23, fig. 2). This valuable monument has been broken in two pieces in recent years, and now adorns the entrance to a pig-pen in the modern village of Copan. It bears glyphs on all four sides, and on one side is what appears to be a date. Stela 12, the eastern Piedra Pintada, has glyphs which are in very low relief. In fact, they are scarcely more than incised. They have, however, rounded outlines and so may not be so very early. Stela 10, the western Piedra Pintada, has very well-carved glyphs on all four sides. It also has a date which has so far escaped decipherment. Although the relief is rather low, the details of the glyphs are fairly well rounded, and the monument may fall about the time of Stela I or even later. Stela 13 also is more or less indeterminate and probably belongs to the middle period. It has, however, a very primitive drum-shaped altar. Stela 8 appears to be rather late. From this it seems clear that the stelae without full-length sculptures of human beings do not as a group precede the sculptured ones, although most of them are early.

In connection with each stela there was probably an altar, although most of the earlier stelae do not at present show such altars in position. Stela 13 has a

[1] Unfortunately this important monument along with Stela 8 was broken into a thousand pieces in January, 1912, and used in the foundation of an adobe wall around the cemetery of Copan village.

very crude drum-shaped altar with two glyphs carved upon the side. Altar 14 is also a drum-shaped object (Fig. 214). A knotted band encircles it, to which are attached a number of water symbols or "cloud balls," and a crudely drawn bird. From available information it is impossible to tell with what stela this altar was correlated. Stela I has an altar (Fig. 215) still in position. It is drum-shaped and marked with broad knotted bands that pass around each rim of the circumference and over the top and bottom in two directions. The whole is

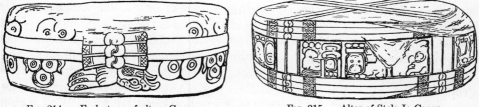

FIG. 214. — Early type of altar: Copan.   FIG. 215. — Altar of Stela I: Copan.

doubtless intended to represent a bundle. Glyphs are placed around the circumference between the bands. These glyphs are of the same type as those on the stela with which the altar is associated. Broken altars of the same kind but somewhat simpler decoration are found in connection with Stelae E and 1. These are doubtless still earlier than the one just considered. Two drum-shaped altars are connected with Stela 5, one for each sculptured face.

It is probable that the rectangular sculptured blocks X and Y found buried under Stela 5 and Stela 4, respectively, are altars of earlier stelae which were placed under later ones for some ceremonial purpose. The carving upon these rectangular altars (Fig. 216) is very similar to that of the glyphs of the earliest period, and knotted bands are present as in the circular altars. A fragment of a similar rectangular altar (Plate 20, fig. 1) was used as one of the steps in the Hieroglyphic Stairway.[1] The old carving was turned in and so preserved.

The altars of the later stelae are of diverse form, and most of them have already been described. There are a number of independent altars that are richly sculptured. Most of these can be placed pretty accurately in their proper sequence by the technique of the carving as illustrated by the stelae.

FIG. 216. — Early rectangular altar (Sculpture Y): Copan.

It has already been noted that most of the early stelae are no longer in position. Stela E, placed on the platform west of the Great Plaza, was probably in conjunction with Mound 1. If the monument was originally set up here, the mound must have been one of the first large structures. Stela I was apparently in position before the eastern wall of the Great Plaza was begun, because the wall was continued around and beyond the monument and a niche made for it. The northern end of the Great Plaza was probably only completed when Mound 2 (with the correlated Stela D) was erected. The minor hieroglyphic stairway

[1] Gordon, 1902, *a*, p. 19.

on the front of this mound may have served as the original suggestion for the great Hieroglyphic Stairway of Mound 26. Most of the monuments and sculptures found in connection with the Great Mound or the Acropolis seem to date from the latest period of the city, following Stela A. An exception is Stela P, which seems to have been reset in the western court without its altar. The altar of this stela may be the one found under Stela 4 in the Great Plaza (Sculpture Y).

Stela M is correlated with the Hieroglyphic Stairway and probably dates from the same time. It is set up directly opposite the base of the stairway. Stela N is correlated with Temple 11 in a similar manner. The carvings on the interior step of this building are of the same style as those on some of the independent altars, notably Altars T and Q, and are probably the work of the same sculptor. The most beautiful and perfect sculptures at Copan are those that served to decorate the facade of Temple 22. A splendid example now in the Peabody Museum is given in Plate 26, fig. 3. Other excellent sculptures, not quite so perfect (Plate 26, fig. 1), occur in connection with Structures 21, 26, 32 and 36, while the rather crude faces (Plate 26, fig. 2) found in the debris of Structure 41 are apparently considerably earlier.

A table that shows in a somewhat graphic manner the sequence and relationships that have just been discussed is herewith presented. Nothing seems to need further explanation except the column that gives the dates in the Maya system. Since frequent reference will be made to the dates on the monuments, it seems best to give a brief description. The subject is complex, and only a few points will be considered. A complete treatment of this difficult subject may be had in a recent work by Mr. C. P. Bowditch entitled "The Numeration, Calendar Systems and Astronomical Knowledge of the Mayas."

The periods in the first column of the table are indicated by position, the digits increasing in value toward the left. Thus the date on Altar K, written 9–12–16–7–8, may be read 9 cycles 12 katuns 16 tuns 7 uinals 8 kins. The system is based on twenty, except in the third position (tun), which is only 18 times the preceding period (uinal), so as to approximate the length of the year. Expressed in days and arranged in ascending values, the periods are as follows:

$$Kin = 1 \text{ day.}$$
$$Uinal = 20 \times 1 = 20 \text{ days.}$$
$$Tun = 18 \times 20 \times 1 = 360 \text{ days.}$$
$$Katun = 20 \times 18 \times 20 \times 1 = 7200 \text{ days.}$$
$$Cycle = 20 \times 20 \times 18 \times 20 \times 1 = 144,000 \text{ days.}$$

In the inscriptions the periods are indicated by glyphs, usually grotesque faces, and the numbers that tell how many periods are taken are indicated either by bars and dots, which usually precede the period glyphs, each bar meaning 5 and each dot 1, or by definite face glyphs representing numbers from 1 to 20.

Expressed in days, the date of Altar K, given above, is :

$$
\begin{aligned}
9 \times 144000 &= 1,296,000 \\
12 \times 7200 &= 86,400 \\
16 \times 360 &= 5,760 \\
7 \times 20 &= 140 \\
8 \times 1 &= \underline{8} \\
& 1,388,308 \text{ days.}
\end{aligned}
$$

This vast number of days is added to a constant beginning day which is named 4 Ahau 8 Cumhu and leads to a resulting day which in this case is 3 Lamat 16 Yax. These resulting days are omitted in this table and in most of the other dates which are used in this paper. The quadrinomial system of fixing days which is seen in the names 4 Ahau 8 Cumhu and 3 Lamat 16 Yax is briefly as follows. The Maya year consisted of 18 months of 20 days each plus 5 days that did not fall in any month but which were added to fill out the year. Each of the 20 days was given a number which ran from 1 to 13, and then repeated, so that the same day and number, for instance 4 Ahau, recurred every 260 days. But in addition each numbered day was further specified as occupying a certain place in a certain month. Thus 4 Ahau 8 Cumhu means, in full, the day Ahau with the number 4 falls on the 8th day of the month Cumhu. Of course each named day would occupy a fixed place in each month were it not for the 5 days added to fill out the year. This addition advances the list of days 5 days each year, with the result that each day can occupy on different years 4 places in each month. With the permutation system thus established any day whose number is given and whose place in a month is stated must occur once every 52 years, neither more nor less. This period of 52 years is known as the calendar round. Dates which have only the quadrinomial designation are referred to as being in the short count. They are accurate enough if one can be sure of the particular cycle of 52 years in which they fall.

Most of the dates given in the first column belong to the class known as initial series and are definitely fixed for a very long period of time. Nearly all such dates fall in the ninth cycle, but a few will be considered later that fall in the eighth and tenth cycles. The ninth cycle is approximately 400 years long and is divided into 20 katuns each of about 20 years. The katun will be used more than any other period in comparing dates, because monuments falling about 20 years apart usually show differences that may be ascribed to the advance of culture. The tun period of about one year will be used for more specific datings.

Still other methods than those given were used by the Maya. Sometimes a certain day is declared to fall on the first day of a tun or katun with a certain number and is thus fixed in the long count without a very large element of doubt. The method used in the Books of Chilan Balam and at the time of the Spanish Conquest will be described later.

The second column gives the lapse of years between the first accurately dated monument and the monument before which the date in question appears.

A few notes on doubtful dates are perhaps in order. Stela 15, which from artistic criteria has been placed first in the list of monuments, seems to have an initial series on one side (Plate 23, fig. 2). The inscription, however, is incomplete. Face numerals are used instead of bars and dots, and these occur in the left-hand column, while the period glyphs occupy the right-hand one. The period glyphs are indistinct except the uinal, which represents an entire frog, as on Stela D. The cycle number may be the usual 9. The face for the katun number, which is the significant number, if this is a ninth cycle date, strongly resembles the face for 4 which represents the Roman-nosed God with a kin sign in front of the ear plug. The number before the tun clearly shows a bleached bone and so must be 10 or above. The uinal is preceded by a face with a hand for the lower jaw, one of the regular signs for zero. The kin glyph and number are wanting. The inscription, then, may be read 9–4–10 (or over)–0–? Since there is a strong tendency to express only even, half and quarter katuns, the most probable date is 9–4–10–0–0. This would be about 40 years earlier than the date of Stela 9 and would agree with the style of the carving.

Stela 13 bears an initial series which, according to a rather poor photograph, seems to be 9–11–0–0–0. Stela 10 also probably has an initial series inscription, but the glyphs are partly defaced and Maudslay's drawing may be slightly inaccurate. The upper part of the first glyph should probably be the face for 9 with the dots around the mouth rather than the face given with the hand for a lower jaw. The katun seems to bear the number 15, the tun the face for 10 (?) the uinal the number 16 or 17 (the 18 is impossible) and the kin 0. But any date in the fifteenth katun is 40 years or more too late for glyphs of the style shown on this monument.

The date on Stela 7 is given in face numerals and was deciphered by Mr. Morley. The early use of face numerals at Copan is worthy of note; it shows that even during the archaic period the calendar and the glyphs were already highly developed. The inscription on Stela 2 is partly defaced, but the top of the katun glyph shows a bleached bone, the usual indication of 10, and in view of the place that this monument occupies in the artistic sequence, it seems pretty certain that the date falls in the tenth katun. There is an undeciphered initial series (owing to the imperfect photographs) on the Altar of Stela 1.

The dates of Stelae 3 and 5 have not yet been deciphered. The initial series on the former is largely destroyed. An important fragment showing the beginning of the initial series of Stela 5 was discovered by the writer on a recent visit to Copan. The glyphs are much worn, but with the aid of the inscriptions on the two circular altars the date of this monument stands in a fair way to be deciphered. In the stylistic sequence these monuments lie between Stelae 1 and 6 on the one hand and A and B on the other. The date of Stela 5 probably falls in the thirteenth katun and that of Stela 3 in the early part of the fourteenth. The inscriptions on the two early rectangular altars, X and Y, seem to be too incomplete to admit of an exact placing in the chronology.

There are, or rather were, a number of initial series on the Hieroglyphic Stairway, perhaps recording the history of the city or the lives of its rulers. The first three that are given by Gordon [1] seem to be trustworthy. They are as follows:

$$9 - 5 - 19 - 12 - 0.$$
$$9 - 8 - \ \ 8 - \ \ 6 - 5.$$
$$9 - 9 - 14 - 17 - 4.$$

The last definite date at Copan is 9–16–10–0–0. To be sure the beginning of the tenth cycle, 70 years distant from this date, is declared on Altar S and possibly also on Stela 8. The style of the former monument is much more nearly in accord with its own initial series, which marks the beginning of the fifteenth katun. As for Stela 8, the style of sculpture would place this still earlier. These two declarations may have had some prophetic significance. The dates [2] on Altars

[1] 1902, a, pp. 21–25.   [2] Bowditch, 1910, Table 29.

G1, G2, G3, and Q are rather doubtful. They are given only in the short count, but each date falls in one of its possible positions at the beginning of a quarter katun. The dates of Stela H, F, C and 4 are as yet undeciphered. The last three have long inscriptions with an introducing glyph that resembles that of the regular initial series.[1] Stela H simply states a day in the short count which recurs every 52 years.

The chronology of Copan may be summed up as follows. The earliest monuments are very crude and archaic particularly in regard to the carving of the human face. A steady improvement is noted extending from the ninth to the fifteenth katun. By the beginning of the fifteenth katun almost the last trace of archaic treatment had vanished. The brilliant period lasted until the middle of the sixteenth katun and possibly somewhat longer.

Tikal. The chronological sequence of the sculptures of Copan has been pretty definitely established. That of Tikal, a city at a considerable distance from Copan and in a different environment, will be presented in much the same way. Differences dependent upon the physical nature of available material account for only a small part of the dissimilarity between the monuments of these two cities. Both inherited the same culture, but each developed it along individual lines.

Each Maya city has what may be called its personal equation. In each the same traditional ideas are presented in a somewhat different way and with a different emphasis upon details. New ideas radiated from the points of origin, becoming more or less modified in transit. Undoubtedly some cities were more progressive than others of the same period, or more fortunate in possessing artists of greater originality and builders of greater daring. Some cities were regal and others provincial. Some were great centers of wealth lying in fruitful lands, while others were poor in resources and perhaps held in tribute. Some were creators in fashion, and others mere imitators. Thus, at the same point of time a number of cities might show an unequal advance in technical skill. Some might be found still clinging to old fashions which had passed away in the more progressive centers of art. A personal equation of time must be added to, or subtracted from the apparent time of the styles of sculpture. Besides this inequality of cities really contemporaneous, there is the further perplexing problem of real sequence in cities not contemporaneous; for many settlements were doubtless colonial offshoots of earlier centers of population or were new establishments of older cities, whose people had migrated *en masse*.

Tikal, like Copan, furnishes examples of archaic workmanship in many pieces of sculpture. Here, however, there is no long homogeneous series of monuments, but instead a number of small groups. It is somewhat difficult to argue the line of development from one of these groups to another, because the groups, as such, were probably not strictly successive. When results are cast up, it is found that out of a mass of surmise and conjecture a small number of facts have been definitely established. These seem distinctly worth the trouble.

---

[1] For attempts at decipherment see for Stela F, Goodman, 1897, p. 131; for Stela C, Goodman, 1897, p. 130; Seler, 1899, p. 708; Thomas, 1897–1898, pp. 776–777; Bowditch, 1910, pp. 134, 195–196; for Stela 4, Bowditch, 1910, p. 135. It is important to note that the late monuments often show calculations much more complicated than the early ones; for instance, Stela N, Bowditch, 1910, pp. 186, 320–321, and Altar U, Bowditch, 1910, pp. 206–207, Altar Q, Bowditch, 1910, pp. 135 and 185.

The stelae[1] may be arranged stylistically in the following groups:

Group 1 — Stelae 3, 7, 8, 9, 13.   Group 3 — Stelae 4, 10, 12.
Group 2 — Stelae 1, 2.   Group 4 — Stelae 5, 11, 16.

Group 1. In this group the human figure is represented in a style strikingly different from that which has been noted in Copan. The entire figure is shown in profile and in low relief. The proportions of the body are slender, and there is usually no cumbrous mass of dress and ornament. The pose is natural, one foot being placed slightly in advance of the other, so that the rather slender legs are somewhat separated below the short garment. The figure faces either right or left, and one hand grasps a ceremonial staff which rests upon the ground, while the other hand carries a decorated pouch. The blocks of stone upon which the figures are carved do not show careful quarrying, since in all cases the tops are roughly rounded off and the sides more or less irregular. Within this group the stelae may be arranged tentatively in the following chronological sequence: 7, 8, 13, 9, 3. Stela 9 is in the finest state of preservation and is really a very delicate and graceful piece of sculpture. It seems later than the other stelae of the same general style, but the glyphs are certainly less perfect than those of Stela 3. Of this series of stelae numbers 7 and 9 are reproduced in Plate 21, figs. 1 and 2.

Group 2. Stelae 1 and 2 may be put in a class by themselves, although in point of time they probably fall within the limits of Group 1. Both show the same style of carving and both are broken and partly destroyed. The top of Stela 1 is missing and the bottom of Stela 2; between the two, however, the design can be made out very nicely. The two stones stood side by side before a small temple somewhat apart from the main plaza[2] in which were set up most of the other Tikal monoliths. There is one feature that seems to indicate that these sculptures were broken rejects. The lowermost hieroglyphs on the back of Stela 1 were never finished, but were merely blocked out in the rough. The carving of the principal figure on each monument fills the two sides as well as the front, the design being simply bent round the corners of the rectangular block. The pose as far as the head and feet are concerned is the same as in the previous group. But the shoulders and the breast are by necessity shown in front view since, instead of staff and pouch, the Ceremonial Bar is held in the arms after the manner of Copan (Fig. 58). This Ceremonial Bar has a straight central panel, and each serpent head shows the complete manikin god, ventral appendage and all, sitting upon the lower jaw. The sides of the stelae present a confused mass of supernumerary heads attached to a chainlike object that may represent a serpent body. The front of Stela 1 is reproduced in Plate 21, fig. 3.

Group 3. Stela 4 in Group 3 is an irregular stone upon which a figure is rather crudely carved with the face in front view and in very low relief. It is different from any other stela and so cannot be accurately placed, but the style of the glyphs is that of the early period. Stelae 10 and 12 show figures carved in high relief, with the body in front view and the face in profile. In general style these two stelae are comparable to the first group of stelae at Copan, except that the

[1] The stelae referred to are all reproduced by Maler, 1911. For a correlation of nomenclature see page 256.

[2] The location of the stelae in this plaza is shown by Tozzer, 1911, p. 119, and outside of it in pl. 29 of same memoir.

relief is much higher. The legs and other parts of the body have the blocklike character and the dominant angularity already noted in the archaic sculptures of Copan. The feet are turned straight out with the heels together, and the waist is surrounded by a very heavy belt. A new feature that will be frequently met with in other cities not yet considered is the captive who lies on the ground just behind the standing figure.

Group 4. The three stelae in this group are carved upon large blocks of stone with straight sides and rounded tops, which have been carefully trimmed to shape. With a certain degree of assurance, these stelae may be placed in the following order: 16, 11, 5. Stela 16 (Plate 21, fig. 4) represents an elaborately dressed figure standing, with the body in front view and the head in profile and supporting horizontally in the two hands a Ceremonial Bar of unusual type (Fig. 65). The figure stands out clearly against the plain sunken background which is broken only by three short columns of raised glyphs. The carving is very flat, but the space relations of the third dimension are indicated by slightly differentiated planes. This stela is set up in the western part of the city at some distance from the main plaza, and before it lies the beautiful Altar 5. The style of sculpture on the altar is very similar to that on the stela, although the subjects are quite distinct.

Stela 11 presents a pose somewhat similar to that of Stela 16, except that the Ceremonial Bar, which is of the same type, is held by one hand diagonally across the body, while the other hand is outstretched. The relief is low and the detail rich. The headdress shows a fine free use of feathers drawn in sweeping curves. The raised margin of the stela has a simple pattern decoration.

On Stela 5 (Plate 22, fig. 1) the figure stands in pure profile, with the feet close together, one behind the other. The nearer hand hangs at the side and holds a decorated pouch, the farther hand holds up a Manikin Scepter by its usual serpentine appendage. The carving of the figure is in fairly high relief, with a considerable degree of careful modeling. Details of the dress are undercut. In particular the elaborate feather ornament which hangs down at the back shows a skillful foreshortening of the feathers. There seems no room for doubting that this stela dates from the same period as the splendidly carved wooden lintels of Tikal.[1] The glyphs carved on the sides of this stela are identical, in style and the handling of decorative details, with the glyphs carved on the lintels. There is also a remarkable similarity between this stela and several at Yaxchilan, particularly in matter of dress.

Concerning the decipherable dates of Tikal the following detailed information is contained in a letter from Mr. C. P. Bowditch under date of August 3, 1910.

"Stela 3 is surely 9–2–13–0–0, 4 Ahau 13 Kayab. If this is a historical date, it is one of the earliest known and gives evidence of Tikal having been occupied before the other cities and perhaps being the center of Central American civilization.
"On Stela 10, lower part, we find 9–3–6(or 11)–2–?
9–3–6–2–0 would be 6 Ahau 8 Pax.
9–3–11–2–0 would be 11 Ahau 3 Muan.
The 0–11–19 over this series are not, I think, 'period' glyphs.
"On Stela 17 we read by means of the two dates 9–6–3–9–15, 10 Men 18 Chen.

---

[1] Maudslay, 1889–1902, III, pls. 71–74, 77 and 78.

"On Stela 16 we have 7 Ahau 13 ? and on A4 we have what looks like the 'end of tun 14,' but no 7 Ahau appears at the end of a tun 14 in cycle 9 except 9–11–14–0–0, 8 Ahau 18 Mol, and the month number in the inscription is 13. If, however, A4 is 'end of uinal 14,' we should have 9–2–4–14–0, 8 Ahau 13 Muan, and the month looks more like Muan than anything else.

"The Altar 5 has no means of determining its place in the long count. The dates run

1 Muluc 2 Muan
     11–11–18
13 Manik 0 Xul
     8–9–19
11 Cimi 19 Mac
    No distance number, — 3 is needed.
1 Muluc 2 Kankin.

From 1 Muluc 2 Muan to 1 Muluc 2 Kankin is 20×364 days = 7280 days = 20 years less 20 days = 1–0–4–0 = 4(5–1–0).

"So far the dates are early. But on Stela 5, if the reading of A5 is 'end of tun 13,' as it seems to be, there can be but one date in Cycle 9, namely, 9–15–13–0–0, 4 Ahau 8 Yaxkin, though possibly the month may be something else than Yaxkin."

From this conservative account it is evident that the dates of Tikal are few in number and difficult to place definitely. According to style of carving we have already seen that Stela 3 probably belongs to the end of Group 1 and that there are a number of similar monuments of cruder workmanship and apparently earlier date. If the initial series of Stela 3 is accepted as historical, it must follow that the art of Tikal in its beginnings antedates that of Copan. The date on Stela 3 is about 76 years previous to that on Stela 9 at Copan and about 125 years before that on Stela 7, which is the earliest Copan stela, yet discovered, having a sculptured human figure.

These unexpectedly early dates at Tikal need not militate against the sequence that has been established at Copan. We have seen that on the first monuments of Copan the hieroglyphs were excellently carved and in point of design were even better than on the later ones. They were sharply defined, and each was made to fill exactly a given rectangular space. The line of change was not toward more excellent glyphs but simply toward more rounded lines, higher relief and a greater amount of modeling. We have also seen that the earliest Copan subjects were elaborately attired. No figures showed simple dress except Stelae 1 and 6, and these represented a new departure during the middle period.

Now at Tikal we find what was lacking at Copan; namely, glyphs that seem truly archaic, and figures with simple attire. The method of carving in profile is much easier than carving in front view. It is to be noted, however, that the only stela at Tikal which exhibits a mastery of modeling and foreshortening is Stela 5, that bears the date 9–15–13–0–0 and is contemporaneous with the best period of Copan.

The stylistic development of the hieroglyphs of Tikal should be presented at this time, because so much of the tentative chronological arrangement of the monuments and buildings depends on the evidence they furnish. The crudest form of glyph may be seen on Stelae 8, 13 and 9. The glyphs are placed in a single vertical column, although this fact may have no special significance. They are not evenly spaced and are not of uniform size. The contours (see Plate 22, figs. 2 and 3, for examples of glyphs from Stelae 13 and 9) show a lack of refinement and artistic quality, and the masses do not neatly fill out a rectangular space. On Stela 3 and on one side of Stela 10 the hieroglyphs are in double columns and exhibit more order in sizing and spacing and are better drawn. Some of the glyphs on Stela 10 have decorative detail expressed in fine, incised lines. This use of decorative etching is still more evident on Stela 12. In fact, many of the glyphs on this stela resemble markedly the earlier glyphs of Copan, but, in general, do not show such angular blocking as is seen at the latter city. The glyphs at the top of Stela 1 are well blocked out and show considerable detail. Those at the bottom were apparently never finished (Plate 22, fig. 4). The inscriptions on Stela 16 and Altar 5 have well-chosen detail and better qualities of design than any examples so far described. They have, however, the same flat surface as all the forms that have preceded. On these latter monuments we see the first use of raised strips of glyphs introduced into the field of the composition itself. Previously the glyphs have occurred only on the sides or the back of the monument. The most skillful use of blocks of glyphs to vary the design and balance the composition will be seen at Yaxchilan and Palenque.

From this consideration it becomes pretty evident that the suggested date of 9-2-4-14-0 is altogether too early for so well-sculptured a monument as Stela 16. The date 9-11-14-0-0 seems much more credible, although still very early, and the simple mistake of leaving out a bar over the month sign glyph is one that might easily occur.

A reading more in agreement with the apparent date of the sculpture is offered by Mr. Morley, namely, that the inscription declares katun 14 rather than tun 14. Katun 14 begins with the day 6 Ahau 13 Muan. Owing to the use of ornamental dots to fill out glyphs, it is very easy to mistake 6 for 8. The lowest dot in A1 appears to be crescent-shaped rather than round, and if this is the case the upper dot must be the same, so that the bar and three dots are cut down to a bar and one dot. This emendation [1] leads to the date 9-14-0-0-0.

The dates on Altar 5 might well fall within the 52 year period that includes the date on the correlated Stela 16. In fact, the final date on this monument would then fall just 31 days short of the date on the stela.

We now come to the final and finest stage of glyph making at Tikal, — the inscriptions on the sides of Stela 5 (Plate 22, fig. 5) and on the beautifully carved temple lintels. Although not carved in high relief, the glyphs are delicately modeled and escape the dead flatness of the earlier forms. The ornamental detail is extremely rich and consists in the skillful use of double-lining, cross-hatching and beading. Under all this, however, there is a strong note of suggestive realism.

It seems probable that the dates in the short count on the wooden lintels fall near the date of Stela 5, which shows the same type of carving. The reading suggested by Mr. Bowditch [2] for two of these lintels is 9-15-10-0-0, which is within three years of the date on the stela.

[1] Mr. Bowditch also seems to concur in this; 1910, p. 184.

[2] 1910, Table 29. Elsewhere (p. 295) he suggests the position to be 10-0-15-8-0. The earlier date seems the better one. The lintel of Temple I (Maudslay, 1889-1902, III, pl. 71) begins with 9 Ahau 13 Pop, which may be 9-13-3-0-0.

The dates of Tikal seem to agree with the sequence as indicated by the style of carving. The summary of the known dates covers a period of exactly 13 katuns or about 257 years, as follows:

Stela 3	$9 - 2 - 13 - 0 - 0$	Stela 16	$9 - 14 - 0 - 0 - 0$
Stela 10	$9 - 3 - 6$ (or 11) $- 2 - ?$	Lintel, Temple II	$9 - 15 - 10 - 0 - 0$
Stela 17	$9 - 6 - 3 - 9 - 15$	Lintel, Temple IV	$9 - 15 - 10 - 0 - 0$
Altar 5	$9 - 13 - 19 - 16 - 19.$	Stela 5	$9 - 15 - 13 - 0 - 0.$

Mr. Maudslay [1] makes the suggestion that the location of the principal temples of Tikal may indicate their sequence in construction. New temples may have been erected when the fairway of the old ones had become obstructed. A safer method of chronological classification concerns the methods of construction. All the temples of Tikal have a definite type of ground-plan with very little variation in the essential parts. In all cases the room space is a very small proportion of the area covered by the walls. The roof structures are responsible for the heavy construction, but the study of these is incomplete. Dr. Tozzer found inclosed rooms in one of them. A careful plan of every part of all the temples would doubtless give data upon which the structures could be arranged in their proper sequence. Only a suggestion can be made at the present time; namely, that the temples with the largest proportion of room space are the latest in construction. The width of the rooms is especially significant. However, the size and character of the roof structures may explain the differences in floor space in the various temples rather than real advance in the building art.

Upon the basis of comparative floor space the five principal temples fall into the following order of construction: V, IV, III, I and II. The difference in floor space between the two extremes of this list is well marked.[2] The well-known carved lintels which show close technical resemblances to Stela 5 probably were taken from Temples I, II and IV. There are other temple structures besides the five upon the lofty pyramids. Most of these have ground plans very closely resembling those of the principal temples, but executed on a smaller scale. As regards the residential buildings at Tikal it may be noted that the rooms are very narrow, seldom more than six feet in width, and that the walls are thicker than the walls of similar structures at Palenque and in northern Yucatan. The narrowness may be in part due to the frequent use of a second story, which in northern Yucatan was rarely built over the room beneath but over a solid core.

It seems certain that Tikal was one of the first Maya cities to become a center of art and culture. Its monuments illustrate the archaic period as well as the period of greatness. The dates, however, are few and the latest ones so far known do not extend into the sixteenth katun of the ninth cycle. It cannot safely be said that Tikal was abandoned at this time, but it is very significant that such a large city does not show the structures with the superior construction that will presently be described in neighboring cities with later dates.

Earliest dated Objects. The earliest remains of Maya art which bear dates in the long-time count are two small objects of jadeite — the Tuxtla Statuette [3] and the Leiden Plate.[4] The former piece of carving was dug up near

---

[1] 1889-1902, III, p. 48.

[2] Maler gives a table of heights of these temples, 1911, p. 50.

[3] See Holmes, 1910, for symposium.

[4] Leemans, 1877, p. 299; Holden, 1879-1880, p. 229; Valentini, 1881, b; Bowditch, 1910, p. 121.

San Andrés Tuxtla in the southern part of the State of Vera Cruz, Mexico, and the latter was found during the excavation of a drainage ditch near San Filippo and the Graciosa River on the frontier of British Honduras. Unfortunately this town and river are not shown on any maps that have come to hand. Upon the back of the Tuxtla Statuette is a somewhat imperfect inscription which has been carefully examined by a number of authorities. The date seems to be 8–6–2–4–17, which, if contemporaneous with the carving of the statuette, would make this object of art 403 years earlier than Stela 9 at Copan. The inscription on the Leiden Plate is 8–14–3–1–12 which is 160 years after the date on the Tuxtla Statuette and 243 years before that of Stela 9. As has been seen, the date on Stela 3 at Tikal is 9–2–13–0–0, which is 76 years earlier than the first certain date at Copan.[1] Moreover, there are a number of stelae at Tikal which are apparently earlier than Stela 3, thus reducing considerably the time to be accounted for.

FIG. 217. — Glyphs from San Andrés Tuxtla Statuette.

It must be accepted as self-evident that the Maya calendar could not have sprung suddenly into being, based as it is upon exact astronomical facts and intricate mathematical calculations. There was no earlier civilization in the American field sufficient to furnish even the fundamental concepts of the calendar. No one can tell how long a period of observing, recording and correcting was necessary before the Maya year count was made nearly as accurate as our own, and far superior to the best that the classical culture of Greece and Rome could offer. Furthermore, other features of Maya culture must have passed through a long process of selection and evolution before

FIG. 218.—Introducing glyph on Leiden Plate.

the beginning of the period of recorded history. The simple pictographs of the American Indian, the only prototype that research has offered, could not in a moment have developed into a complicated hieroglyphic system. Government and religion must also have had time slowly to muster its control over the masses of the people before the great pyramids, some of which probably antedate even the most archaic monuments, could have been attempted.

On the Tuxtla Statuette the initial glyph is of a very simple form, with a trifoil at the top. There are no period glyphs, the periods being indicated by position as in the Dresden Codex. If this inscription is really an initial series, calculated from the normal 4 Ahau 8 Cumhu, the resulting day and month would be 8 Caban 0 Kankin. There is a glyph at the bottom of the column which has before it the number 8, but this glyph is different from any known form of Caban. The other glyphs on the Tuxtla Statuette are exceptionally angular and lack the usual rich ornamental detail. Examples of these glyphs are shown in Fig. 217. Somewhat similar glyphs were made in northern Yucatan at the time of the Spanish conquest.[2] But it is often difficult to distinguish the crudity of first and last attempts, which in the one case arises from inexperience and in the other from decadence.

---

[1] Or 36 years earlier than Stela 15 if the suggested date is correct.

[2] See Bowditch, 1910, for plates giving the range of day, month and period glyphs; also Brinton, 1882, d. The late demotic forms given by Landa show no angular treatment.

The initial glyph of the Leiden Plate (Fig. 218) is comparable to the usual run of initial glyphs in the inscriptions. It shows the common hassock-shaped figure at the base, which seems to be a spread-out tun sign, as well as a head with a kin sign for the ear plug and the ribbon ornament at the top which corresponds to the trifoil of the Tuxtla Statuette. The comb-shaped figures which commonly occur at the side of initial glyphs are wanting on that of the Leiden Plate. In minor details the initial glyph under discussion seems most to resemble the initial glyph of Stela 9 at Copan.

Period glyphs occur on the Leiden Plate, but they differ from those in the inscriptions. The cycle and katun glyphs seem to be turned about, since the latter rather than the former shows a hand for the lower jaw of the grotesque face. The tun glyph is of unusual form and seems to represent a fish, judging by the tail-like appendage. A very similar tun glyph appears on Stela 3 at Tikal, which is nearest to the Leiden Plate in point of time. The uinal glyph

FIG. 219. — Head of the San Andrés Tuxtla Statuette.

shows the characteristic curled fang at the back of the mouth. The differences in the form of glyphs from those on the stelae are such as might naturally be expected in early specimens of a complicated art. After all, the method of indicating periods of numeration by position was entirely sufficient for the needs of the time count. The period glyphs simply gave an extra artistic flourish. The same marked fondness of the Maya for unnecessary complexity led to the use of face numerals instead of bars and dots, and to cryptograms such as occur on Stela J at Copan and Stela H at Quirigua. From this examination it seems justifiable to consider the Tuxtla Statuette and the Leiden Plate as very early examples of Maya art. The dates may tentatively be considered contemporaneous with the making of the objects.

The character of the drawings upon these objects deserves some slight attention. The Tuxtla Statuette is thus described by Holmes:[1]

"The upper part represents a human head with somewhat pointed crown, and with features well defined but primitive in treatment. The lower part of the face is masked with the beak of a bird, suggesting that of a duck or other water-fowl, carved in relief and extending like a beard down over the chest; while covering the cheeks and passing half-way down the sides of the beak are two mustache-like devices in low relief. The idea of the bird suggested by the beak is further carried out by wings covering the sides of the figure, the lower margins of which are engraved with alternating lines and rectangles to represent feathers. Beneath the wings in incised outline are the legs and feet of the bird."

The question might be raised whether the "bird-beak" on the lower part of the face (Fig. 219) may not have been intended to represent the nose of a serpent. There is a narrow tongue-like projection at the end. The statuette would then represent a complex of human, bird and serpent elements quite in keeping with the later developments of Maya art.

The drawing on the Leiden Plate is of the utmost interest, and certain features have already been repeatedly referred to. The drawing represents a richly dressed figure standing with the head and lower part of the body in profile and

[1] 1910, p. 692.

the breast turned nearly in front view. The feet are placed one behind the other. In the arms is held a Ceremonial Bar (Fig. 45), with pendent body such as is seen on the early stelae at Copan (Fig. 46, *a*). The grotesque heads in the serpent mouth at each end of the bar show the characteristic features of the Sun God. In many details of dress a close connection is shown between the drawing on the Leiden Plate and the monumental sculptures. The headdress has several heads, one above the other; the ear plugs have serpentine ornaments; the belt is adorned by small faces and large shells arranged in threes; a decorated apron hangs down from the waist, and the ankle bands show the common ser-

Fig. 220. — Foot of figure on Leiden Plate showing serpent-head ankle ornaments.

a   *b*   *c*

Fig. 221. — Feet of Copan stelae showing serpent-head ankle ornaments.

pent form. Compare, for instance, the ankle ornament in Fig. 220 with those from Copan in Fig. 221. A prostrate figure with the hands tied lies on the ground behind the principal figure.

It seems hardly likely that the heroic figures on the stelae could ever have been attempted without a preliminary development of the designs upon a smaller scale. The Leiden Plate is valuable as showing such an early development.

Quirigua. Quirigua, distant about twenty-five miles from Copan as the crow flies, naturally shows remarkable similarity in assemblage and in monumental remains to the latter city. The agreement at Copan between the dates on the monuments and the stylistic development of the carving encourages the trial use of the dates in arranging and studying the sculptures of Quirigua. Omitting a few dates which are so far removed from the historic period that they probably had merely a traditional or mythological significance, and taking usually the latest date on the monument when there is a choice to be made, the list is as follows:

9–16–0–0–0 . . . . Stela H [1]		9–17–10–0–0 . . . . Altar B	
9–16–5–0–0 . . . . Stela J		9–17–15–0–0 . . . . Altar G	
9–16–10–0–0 . . . . Stela F		9–18–0–0–0 . . . . Altar O	
9–16–15–0–0 . . . . Stela D		9–18–5–0–0 . . . . Altar P	
9–17–0–0–0 . . . . Stela E		9–18–10–0–0 . . . . Stela I	
9–17–5–0–0 . . . . Stela A		9–18–15–0–0 . . . . Stela K	
9–17–5–0–0 . . . . Stela C			

The choice of the quarter katun dates as the historical ones is admittedly arbitrary. Fuller details are given below.

Stela J. The initial series is 9–16–5–0–0, 8 Ahau 8 Zotz. From this is made a subtraction of 1–11–13–3 leading back to 9–14–13–4–17, 12 Caban 5 Kayab. The katun coefficient of the subtrahend is apparently zero rather than 1, but if this were really the case the glyph would have been omitted entirely.

[1] The date of Stela H is given on the verbal authority of Mr. S. G. Morley, who recently examined the original monument.

Seemingly independent of this is a second subtraction from the same 9–16–5–0–0, 8 Ahau 8 Zotz, of 18–3–14 leading to 9–15–6–14–6, 6 Cimi 4 Tzec. Both of these resultant dates appear on Stelae E and F and on Altar G.

Stela F. The initial series on the west side is 9–14–13–4–17, 12 Caban 5 Kayab. To this is added 13–9–9 leading to 9–15–6–14–6, 6 Cimi 4 Tzec. The date 3 Ahau 3 Mol, which falls on 9–15–10–0–0 is also stated but apparently is not directly reached by addition or subtraction. 4 Ahau 13 Yax which falls on 9–15–0–0–0 is also declared. Then comes the distance number 1–16–13–3 which when added to 9–14–13–4–17, 12 Caban 5 Kayab, carries us to the concluding date 9–16–10–0–0, 1 Ahau 3 Zip. On the east side this last date is declared in the initial series.

Stela D. The initial series on the west side is 9–16–13–4–17, 8 Caban 5 Yaxkin. Near the bottom is a secondary series of which the last two digits, 13–3, are clear. These are sufficient to raise the date to an even tun whatever the rest may be. The initial series on the east side is 9–16–15–0–0, 7 Ahau 18 Pop.

Stela E. The initial series on the west side is 9–14–13–4–17, 12 Caban 5 Kayab, a date we have seen twice before. To this several additions are made. There are a number of manifest errors which are overcome by the double check of distance numbers and quadrinomial dates as pointed out by Goodman, 1897, pp. 125–127. The first addition is of 6–13–3 and leads to 9–15–0–0–0, 4 Ahau 13 Yax. A second addition of 6–14–6 carries us to the familiar date 6 Cimi 4 Tzec. A third addition of 1–4–16–15 brings us to 9–16–11–13–1, 11 Imix 19 Muan, and a fourth of 8–4–19 to the concluding date 9–17–0–0–0, 13 Ahau 18 Cumhu. On the east side the initial series gives us this last date in full. The date 13 Ahau 13 Uo is also declared, but its position is not stated. This date falls at the end of a quarter katun in 10–0–5–0–0.

Stela A. The initial series is 9–17–5–0–0, 6 Ahau 13 Kayab. In another place is a quadrinomial date, 6 Ahau 13 Zac which may fall at 9–7–10–0–0. No subtraction is in evidence, although the date in this position would hark back nearly 200 years.

Stela C. On the east side the initial series declares 13–0–0–0–0, 4 Ahau 8 Cumhu. This date marks the beginning of the grand cycle and is over 3,000 years earlier than 9–15–0–0–0 around which the really historical dates cluster. On the west side the initial series is 9–1–0–0–0, 6 Ahau 13 Yaxkin. Later an addition of 17–5–0–0 is declared to lead to 6 Ahau 13 Kayab. This date actually occurs at 9–17–5–0–0 rather than at 9–18–5–0–0, showing that the secondary series was either added to 9–0–0–0–0 or that the katun value was intended for 16 rather than 17.

Altar B. The hieroglyphs on this monument are very difficult to read because they represent entire figures. Mr. Bowditch makes the initial series 9–10–0–0–0, 1 Ahau 8 Kayab, but Dr. Seler and Mr. Morley offer the reading given above (9–17–10–0–0, 12 Ahau 8 Pax). The katun glyph seems to show the Roman-nosed God with the twisted nose ornament. This head is characteristically used for 7 and 17. The declaration of the day and month is partly destroyed.

Altar G. The initial series is clearly 9–17–15–0–0, 5 Ahau 3 Muan. The calculations that follow are complicated and the glyphs partly destroyed. It seems indisputable, however, that the date 10–0–0–0–0, 7 Ahau 18 Zip, is declared.

This might be considered to refer to the future rather than to the past. Mr. Bowditch suggests that 10–1–0–0–0, 5 Ahau 3 Kayab, might be intended in another glyph. On the other hand the familiar dates 12 Caban 5 Kayab and 6 Cimi 4 Tzec that on Stelae J, F and E occupied the positions 9–14–13–4–17 and 9–15–6–14–6, respectively, also occur although the long distance numbers given do not seem to lead to them directly.

Altar P. The initial series is clear but the succeeding calculations which may run forward into the future or backward into the past are much destroyed.

The remaining monuments listed, Stelae H, I and K and Altar O, bear initial series dates with little or nothing in the way of addition or subtraction. Altar L may have a partial initial series, but the forms are very unusual. Altar M has a distance number, 3–2–0 running from 4 Ahau 13 Yax to 6 Ahau 18 Zac. The former date falls at 9–15–0–0–0.

From this detailed account it is seen that the choice of an even quarter katun as the date of erection for some of the monuments rests upon a rather slender basis. Calculations run forward and backward. The dates which might have a real historical value may be those which do not fall on an even quarter katun but are reached by calculations. Two of these occur, as we have seen, at least four times. But dates which are important in the city's history may, after all, have no direct bearing upon the erection of the monuments.

From this list it is seen at once that with a few exceptions the dates at Quirigua are later than those at Copan; furthermore, that they occur at quarter katuns or intervals of about five years. Quirigua was apparently founded well along in the historic epoch, possibly by a colony from Copan, and it may have been the place of refuge for the people of Copan if that city was really abandoned, as seems to have been the case. The course of development of the stelae and altars may be said to begin at Quirigua where it leaves off at Copan.

None of the sculptures of Quirigua shows the flat archaic carving of the face that characterizes the early stelae at Copan. Instead the faces of the principal figures are carved in the full round, with eyes well sunken and noses in marked relief. The stone at Quirigua is much harder than at Copan. There is, except for the face, an evident reversion to the less laborious method of low relief. A recession at the shoulders, which frequently extends to the top of the stela, throws the face and the central portion of the headdress into full relief, but the arms, the legs and the details of body ornament follow the plinth-like outlines of the quarried block and have neither the high, rounded relief nor the deep undercutting of the later stelae of Copan. This reversion to flat relief occurs also at other late cities, and may be called archaistic to distinguish it from the truly archaic.

While the stelae are, as a rule, taller than those of Copan, yet the proportions of the human body, as represented by the heroic figure, show the same defects or dwarfing the parts that happen to be covered with clothing or ornament. Indeed, the dwarfing is carried much farther than at Copan. The headdress is much elongated, and a decorated panel is placed beneath the feet so that the design as a whole is lengthened. The poses have greater freedom and variety, frequently departing from the strict observance of bilateral symmetry in the disposition of the limbs. Instead of the Ceremonial Bar the Manikin Scepter is often the principal religious object. This is held in one hand by the appendage so that it extends diagonally across the body. Feather drapery, skillfully and freely applied, adorns the top of most of the stelae.

It must not be imagined that the artists of Quirigua drew all their ideas from Copan. There are features found there which occur at Tikal, Piedras Negras and other cities, but not at Copan. One of these is a peculiar ornament placed over the ankle (Fig. 222). This occurs widely in the Peten and Usumacinta regions. Another is the Manikin Scepter (Fig. 42, b) with the characteristic ventral appendage in the form of a serpent. This was doubtless known to the artists of Copan, but it does not appear on any of the monolithic sculptures. The method of representing a figure sitting in a niche, which characterizes the sculptures of Piedras Negras, is seen on the back of Stela I at Quirigua (Plate 23, fig. 2). The band of planet symbols that arches over the niche is also a feature prevalent at Piedras Negras. The apron-like ornament below the figure in the niche finds its closest analogy on the back of Stela H at Copan.[1]

FIG. 222. — Conical ankle ornament: Quirigua.

So much for the general features of the stelae of Quirigua. Chronological sequence at Quirigua is difficult to determine from the art alone. The best evidence is that of increasing complexity, and this is seen in the altars rather than in the stelae. The earliest stela seems to be Stela H, which shows on the front a human figure standing upon a grotesque head and holding a Ceremonial Bar (Fig. 84, a) in the same manner as is seen at Copan, and on the back an inscription in a braided cryptogram somewhat like that on the back of Stela J at the latter city. The heads of the bar are represented on the sides of the monument. After its occurrence on this monument the Ceremonial Bar is seen only in decadent forms at Quirigua. No significant difference in style of carving between Stela H and Stela J is noted. The latter appears to be in somewhat higher relief and to have somewhat richer feather drapery.

Stelae F, D and E are the finest monuments of this sort at Quirigua. All three are over twenty-five feet in height and are characterized by extreme elaboration of dress and by splendid use of feather drapery at each side of the headdress. Each stela has a full-length figure on both front and back. The figures on these three stelae as well as those on the fronts of the Stelae A and C wear a small beard. This is likewise seen on some of the later monuments of Copan (Stelae B, C, D, etc.). These three stelae are given in the order of the dates carved on the sides. Except for a slight increase in height there seem to be no features indicating any advance from one monument to the other. The lapse of time represents only ten years, and much change is not to be expected.

Stelae A and C are almost identical in style and subject. Both show a rather simply attired figure on the front and a complicated low-relief design on the back representing a figure with the face turned in profile. They were doubtless carved by a different sculptor than the three stelae just considered.

The quarter katun monuments for the next five periods are monolithic altars. After these come two more stelae, I and K, both being much dwarfed in their proportions. The first of these has already been commented upon. The second is often called the Dwarf. The face is large and the body broad and short. It seems pretty clear that no real dwarf is represented, and that the bad proportions

[1] Maudslay, 1889–1902, I, pl. 61.

are to be explained by the overlying ornamentation of the body which caused a similar distortion at Copan and elsewhere.

The earliest altar is doubtless Altar L, which is of the circular type, with a figure sitting cross-legged in front view but with the face in profile carved upon the top. This altar seems to be the earliest monument so far found at Quirigua. The style of carving might almost be called archaic. There is a curious and apparently incomplete inscription on this monument which, according to Mr. Bowditch, may be 9–14–10–?–?. Another sculpture at Quirigua which may be an altar is described as an alligator's head (Altar M). It appears to be much later than the circular altar, although the date inscribed upon it may be 9–15–0–0–0.

The remaining altars of Quirigua (Plates 1 and 2) are all large and important sculptures that have already been described in some detail. One of them, Altar G, represents a jaguar with a greatly modified body, the other altars present the much elaborated body of the Two-headed Dragon. Animal altars, as these may be called, are known to occur only at Copan and Quirigua, and so offer very strong evidence concerning the connection between these two cities. The last of the altars

FIG. 223. — Altar N: Quirigua.

and by far the most complex, although all are complex enough, is Altar P The simplest animal altar at Quirigua and the one nearest to those of Copan in style is Altar N (Fig. 223).

Practically nothing is known concerning the temples of Quirigua, but it is presumed that they were of the same character as those of Copan with much less decoration.

From this survey of the dates and the monuments it becomes evident that Quirigua flourished after the archaic period had passed. The changes which have been recorded witness the struggles of the artists for new effects which they hoped to obtain by complexity of form and ornament.

Naranjo. The important ruins of Naranjo lying east of Tikal and near the boundary of British Honduras only recently have been made known to archaeologists through the descriptions and photographs of Maler.[1] On account of the large number of well-preserved stelae, most of which bear decipherable dates in the native reckoning, the remains of this ancient city are of especial value in the study of the history of Maya art.

The buildings of Naranjo are in such an advanced state of ruin that they furnish little evidence on questions of sequence of construction. The general features of ground-plan and elevation are determined with difficulty, while nothing is known concerning the interior and façade decorations. The sculptured stelae set up before the temples must, however, have been intended to serve a secondary decorative function. It is the distribution and character of these monuments that demand attention. As has been explained, the chief structures of Naranjo are assembled around courts or plazas and orientated according to the four directions. Each court thus constitutes a natural unit, and with its associated temples and stelae might be expected to correspond to a definite period in the

[1] 1908, *b*, pp. 80–127.

growth of the city. At least three courts inclosed by important secular or religious buildings appear upon Maler's map of Naranjo.[1] In the western court are Stelae 6–11, in the middle court Stelae 12–19 and in the eastern court Stelae 20–32. Stelae 1–5 lie in the western part of the city near the acropolis and are not comprised in a regular court.

As a whole, the sculptures on the stelae of Naranjo bear a greater resemblance to those of Tikal than to those of Copan and Quirigua, but in the character of subject, dress and ceremonial regalia they serve to emphasize the common basis of the culture of all these cities. The figures are carved in very low relief rather than in high relief or full round. As a consequence of the method of low relief the face and headdress are always turned in profile, although the rest of the body is shown in front view. Small faces on girdles are alone represented in full view.

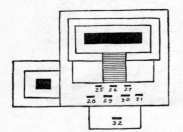

FIG. 224. — Plan of Main Temple, Naranjo, showing placing of the stelae.

The usual subject portrayed is an heroic figure, standing with his feet somewhat apart and turned out, who holds in his arms the Ceremonial Bar. The distortion of the feet and the frequency of the Ceremonial Bar recall the sculptured figures of Copan. But in a number of cases the Manikin Scepter or some sort of ornamented staff or pouch replaces the Ceremonial Bar. The apron with a grotesque face between two serpent heads conventionalized in the form of a fret occurs here, as in most of the cities of the southern Maya area. A number of figures, possibly intended to represent women, wear the long network skirt such as is seen on Stela H at Copan. An important feature at Naranjo, which has been observed at Tikal and on the Leiden Plate but not at Copan or Quirigua, is the presence of a bound captive beneath the principal figure. At Naranjo the principal figure stands on the back of the bound captive, while at Tikal he stands before it. These bound captives have been taken by Maler as conclusive and harrowing evidence of human sacrifice. But they may as well symbolize success in war, even as the foot of the king on the neck of the captive stands for conquest on the ancient monuments of the Far East.

At the eastern end of the city stands the structure that Maler calls the Main Temple. On two terraces before this temple (Fig. 224) are arranged eight stelae. Nearest the temple are Stelae 25, 26 and 27, while in front of these on the same terrace are Stelae 28, 29, 30 and 31. Stela 32 occupies the medial position on a lower terrace, which seems to have been specially constructed to support this monument. It is pretty clear, from an examination of the sculptures, that before this one building is displayed the full chronological range of sculptural art at Naranjo. Of the three stelae in the upper row, namely, 25, 26 and 27, only the first was found in condition to be photographed. This stela (Plate 24, fig. 1) is by all odds the crudest and most archaic in the city. The figure represented upon it holds in an almost vertical position a straight Ceremonial Bar. The figure is carved very simply and there is a noticeable lack of ornamentation. The relief is very low and flat. Stelae 25 and 27 were probably similar in style to this, and the three may well have been taken from some earlier temple

---

[1] 1908, *b*, p. 83. See also Morley's map, 1909, p. 544, on which the principal structures are numbered as in this text.

to be set up again in front of this one. Stelae 28, 29, 30 and 31 are much more elaborate. Of these four monuments, Stelae 28 and 29 seem to show the least advance in sculptural art. Stela 30 (Plate 24, fig. 2) is admirably preserved, and many of the incised details of the dress come out clearly in the photograph. This stela, however, presents no real advance in the representation of the human form over the sculptures of Group I at Copan or at Tikal. Stela 32, which stands on the lower terrace, has been so much destroyed by the flaking off of the sculpture that little of the design can be made out. Apparently a figure was represented seated upon an elaborate throne and holding diagonally a Ceremonial Bar. It is still possible to make out the end of this Ceremonial Bar (Fig. 225), which consists of a very complicated scroll-work representing the highest elaboration of the serpent head. This stela is an extreme example of the general process of change leading toward flamboyant curves and complicated detail. It is undoubtedly the latest work of art that has yet come to light at Naranjo.

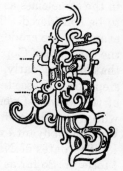

FIG. 225. — One end of Ceremonial Bar of Stela 32: Naranjo.

On the northern side of the same Eastern Court is a temple before which are set up Stelae 21, 22 and 23. Stela 22 shows a style of sculpture apparently much later than the ones that flank it. As on Stela 32, the sculpture represents a figure seated on a throne and holding a Ceremonial Bar. This object does not show the exaggerated scroll-work seen on Stela 32, but the carving of the throne, the lower part of which represents a complicated grotesque profile, is in an advanced style.

FIG. 226. — Ceremonial Bar, Stela 6: Naranjo.

In the Western Court before a temple facing the south are alligned Stelae 6, 7 and 8. From a stylistic comparison it seems perfectly clear that Stela 6 is earlier than Stela 8 and the latter, in turn, earlier than Stela 7. The increasing use of flamboyant lines in delineation from the date of Stela 6 to that of Stela 32 may be readily seen by comparing the Ceremonial Bar on the earlier stela (Fig. 226) with that on the later (Fig. 225). Intermediate stelae (numbers 7, 12, etc.) present an intermediate elaboration.

The evidence furnished by the monuments attached to these three temples shows that correlated monuments in Naranjo, at least, are of doubtful value in determining the time of construction of the temples themselves. The placing of a number of stelae before a building seems in itself to have been a rather late development. In each of the cases so far considered the middle stela appears to be the latest.

Owing to the lack of homogeneous series, it would be unwise to attempt to arrange all the stelae of Naranjo in their chronological sequence. Many are so badly weathered that the style of sculpture can no longer be determined with assurance.

Stelae 2, 3 and 5 would be early monuments at Tikal, but here they are rather late. Stelae 12 (Plate 24, fig. 3), 13 and 14 before a temple in the Middle Court apparently belong to the later period of the city. Stela 10, located in the same court, has glyphs of late form, but no sculptured figure. This court as a whole seems to be the latest at Naranjo, although the latest single monument is found in the Eastern Court.

Dominating the Western Court is a structure that Maler terms the Palace of the Tiger Head Stairway. This large building has at its base a hieroglyphic stairway. The glyphs on this stairway are beautifully carved in the most advanced style. One of the blocks is broken and half is missing. In its place is a fragment of a lintel covered with glyphs of a much earlier style.

Although a large and important city, Naranjo does not deserve to be placed in the same class as Copan, Quirigua, Tikal and certain other cities which remain to be considered. The art of this city has a provincial character. The earliest examples are crude, but their crudity lacks the vital quality which distinguished the early art of Copan and Tikal. None of the monuments of Naranjo bear dates that are very early. In nearly all cases the calculations show many additions or step-ups. These step-up dates do not seem to occur on the very early monuments of the Maya. Over a long period the sculptures of Naranjo show a dead level with a few signs of progress. Toward the end there is a rapid development toward flamboyant exaggeration that in itself was a type of degeneration.

The dates of Naranjo have been deciphered by Mr. Bowditch[1] and by Mr. Morley.[2] So far as known there are eight initial series dates and a few additional dates which are fixed in the long count by the declaration of a definite katun. In all other cases the dates are given in the short count and may recur at intervals of 2–12–13–0 (52 years). When such recurring dates are encountered, the choice of the most probable positions in the long count are made according to two methods. First the date is chosen on which the named day marks the beginning of a whole, half or quarter katun. Failing to find such a one, the second method is to accept the date nearest the ascertained date of related monuments.

The dates in the long count are as follows:

Hieroglyphic Stairway	9–10–10–0–0.
Old lintel in the Stairway	Katun 10 declared.
Stela 24	9–12–10–5–12.
Stela 29	9–12–10–5–12.
Stela 22	9–12–15–13–7.
Stela 23	Katun 14 declared.
Stela 30	Katun 14 declared.
Stela 13	9–17–10–0–0.
Stela 14	9–17–14–4–3.
Stela 8	9–18–10–0–0.
Stela 7	Katun 19 declared.

The final or latest dates on each of the stelae of Naranjo, grouped according to the structures before which the monuments are erected, will now be given.

Main Temple (Structure 29).

Stela 28	9–12–19–0–0.
Stela 29	9–14–3–0–0.
Stela 30	9–14–3–0–0.
Stela 31	9–14–10–0–0.
Stela 32	9–19–10–0–0.

The dates of the three crude stelae that form the upper row are unknown. The next four stelae date from what corresponds to the last portion of the archaic

[1] 1910, pp. 102, 118–119, 129, 143, etc. Tables 29 and 31.   [2] 1909, pp. 545–550.

period at Copan. They are much later than the stelae of corresponding style at Tikal, but show scarcely any more advance in sculpture. Stela 32 is the latest monument of any city so far considered. The style is the most advanced at Naranjo, but not nearly so remarkable as the sculptures of Quirigua. The date on this stela was decided by Mr. Morley [1] largely upon a consideration of the sequence of style as presented in this paper, but, apart from this line of argument, the fact that a half katun is reached in the calculation is much in its favor.

Structure 27.	
Stela 24	9–13–10–0–0.
Structure 26.	
Stela 21	9–13–9–3–2.
Stela 22	9–13–10–0–0.
Stela 23	9–14–0–0–0.
Structure 23.	
Stela 20	9–13–2–8–16.

The style of Stela 22, as has been already stated, is more advanced than that of Stelae 21 and 23, and its date seems to be altogether too early when the sculptures of this city are taken as a whole. In fact, all the early dated monuments of the Eastern Court are better than might be expected in a city whose later sculpture is so mediocre.

Structure 21.	
Stela 19	9–17–10–0–0.
Structure 17.	
Stela 12	9–18–10–0–0.
Stela 13	9–18–0–3–0.
Stela 14	9–18–0–0–0.

These dated monuments of the Middle Court are seventy years or more later than those of the Eastern Court, but some of them show little if any advance.

Structure 15.	
Stela 10	9–19–0–3–0.
Stela 11	9–17–18–0–0.
Structure 14.	
Stela 6	9–17–1–0–0.
Stela 7	9–19–0–3–0.
Stela 8	9–18–13–0–0.

The monuments of the Western Court bear uniformly late dates. Stela 10 has no sculptures except a double column of glyphs. These are of a well-rounded type and justify the extremely late date. Stela 11, however, is a reversion in style and subject. The style is not very different from that of Stela 30 (Plate 24, fig. 2) and the subject is close to that of Stela 21, which is dated about ninety years earlier. Judging by this evidence, the increase of skill during this period was almost nil. The very late character of the beautiful hieroglyphs of the Tiger Head Stairway is evident at a glance. The early date that appears in the inscription must have a memorial significance. The piece of a lintel which replaces part of one of the sculptured steps is important for several reasons. In the first place, it is valuable as an early fragment, although it may not be so very early after all. In the second place, its presence in the step to com-

[1] 1909, p. 559.

plete a broken sculpture may indicate occupation and use of the building for a long time after it was finished. Why did not the builders carve a new block and put it in place of the broken one? Stela 9 has no decipherable date. It is located on the north side of the Tiger Head Stairway. Subjectively it is one of the most interesting monoliths at this city, since it shows five figures, one larger than the others. The serpent heads of the Ceremonial Bar are decidedly flamboyant, so the stela probably dates from the eighteenth or nineteenth katun. As for the stelae belonging to Structure 14, the marked difference in style, which corresponds to the considerable difference in the dates, has already been pointed out. Stela 6 is very flat and angular. Stela 7 is, next to Stela 32, the most complicated and flamboyant sculpture in the city. Stela 8 has more rounded contours than Stela 6, but is far behind Stela 7.

Structure 9.
Stela 5   9–17–13–2–8.

This monument in the western part of the city shows the earlier style before flamboyancy came into vogue. Stelae 1, 2, 3, and 4 of Structure 8 have no de-

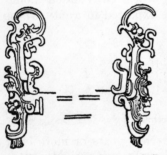

FIG. 227. — Ceremonial Bar, Stela 7: Naranjo.

cipherable dates. Judging by the style of Stelae 2 and 3, the date may be close to that of Stela 5. This ends the list of dated monuments. The most significant fact to be gathered from this rather tedious survey is that while Naranjo started well it remained stagnant during the period from the fifteenth to the eighteenth katun, which was the most brilliant period in Copan and Quirigua. There seems to have been a sudden development during the eighteenth katun that was directed toward complicated curvilinear effects. Taken by and large, the latest dates on the monuments agree very well with the artistic sequence.

There are many other sites in the Peten region where further exploration will vastly increase our store of information. Some of these sites have rather crude provincial sculptures, probably far inferior to the sculptures of the same period in the great cities. Examples of these crude works are seen in several of the stelae of Yaxha.[1] However, one or two monuments at this city are worthy of much praise. The Stela of Benque Viejo[2] is a good piece of work, probably of the later period. A city that might prove to be of first importance is Ixkun.[3] Only one monument from this city is available for study. This is a very interesting one, having a very early initial series date. A portion of the sculpture on this stela representing a bound captive is given in Fig. 228. The relief

FIG. 228. — Bound captive: Ixkun.

is low, but the carving is spirited and seemingly well along toward the great period. The recently illustrated stela of Motul de San Jose[4] is apparently another late piece of work. In regard to correlating the scattered monuments good

[1] Maler, 1908, b, pls. 15, 16, 17 and 18, fig. 1.   [3] Maudslay, 1889–1902, II, pls. 68 and 69.
[2] Maler, 1908, b, pl. 19   [4] Maler, 1910, pl. 45.

use can be made of identities in ceremonial regalia such as staffs. Some of the more common staffs are given in Fig. 229.

Seibal. At Seibal there are a number of interesting monuments that have been figured and briefly described by Maler.[1] The forest growth is very heavy over the ruins of this city, and only a meager plan of the principal temple groups was obtained. The stelae are set up in definite relationship to mounds upon which temples formerly stood. An interesting example of correlation is seen in the case of a square mound with a splendid stela opposite the center of each side (Stelae 8–11). Before an oblong mound are arranged Stelae 5 and 7, while the shattered remains of Stela 6 lie between.

All but one of the sculptures represented by photographs are carved in low, delicate relief with the faces in profile. The exception (Stela 2) is a rather clumsy figure in front view. The artistic quality of the Seibal monuments varies widely. Stelae 1, 3, 8, 9, 10 and 11 are among the most beautiful examples of art in the Maya area, while Stelae 2, 5 and 7 are notably crude.

A careful examination of the later two monuments seems to indicate that their crudity must be explained by provincial inefficiency rather than by truly archaic ignorance. The drawing is bad; the eyes, however, are of the late form and the glyphs are rounded. Stelae 6 and 7 (Plate

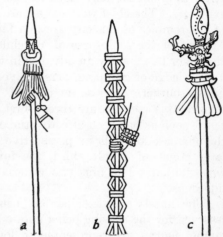

FIG. 229. — Ceremonial spears: *a* and *b*, Chichen Itza; *c*, Palenque.

25, fig. 1) bear, according to Mr. Bowditch,[2] the comparatively late date 9–17–0–0–0. It seems possible that Siebal was a city that came into power long after Tikal and Copan.

Mr. Morley obtained interesting results, as yet unpublished, from an examination of moulded fragments of Seibal monuments, some of which are reproduced by Maler as fragments of Stela 6 and of Stelae 12–15. He was able to piece together several parts of a calculation running from 9–15–15–0–0, 9 Ahau 18 Xul, to well up towards the beginning of the eighteenth katun.

Stela 1, which stands alone at the end of a ruined oblong structure, is a splendidly preserved and exquisitely carved monument. The relief is low with an archaistic flatness, but the details of dress are shown on different planes. The first two glyphs are apparently 3 Ahau 3 Yax, corresponding to the quarter katun at 9–18–15–0–0–0.

The four stelae numbered 8 to 11 are very similar in technical skill. Of these Stela 10 (Plate 25, fig. 2) is in almost perfect state of preservation. The sculptures all exhibit the flamboyancy that was noted in the late carvings of Naranjo and show moreover a number of definite points of resemblance to the latter city in details represented. In two cases a markedly decadent form of the Ceremonial Bar is given. In the second line of glyphs at the top of Stela 11 we see the date 7 Ahau 18 Zip, which ushers in the tenth cycle declared in the following glyph.

[1] 1908, *a*, pp. 10–27 and pls. 3–10.　　　　　　[2] 1910, table 29.

Next comes the sign for 1 katun, and in the column of glyphs in front of the human figure is the date 5 Ahau 3 Kayab followed by the ending sign with 1 katun. This 5 Ahau 3 Kayab is doubtless 10–1–0–0–0. The same date introduces the calculation on the remaining three monuments of this very important group. It may be stated here that these sculptures are the latest accurately dated examples of high art, that have so far come to light. There are two or three other tenth cycle dates that are a few years later than the ones above recorded, but they are not associated with sculptures of great merit.

Yaxchilan. Yaxchilan, situated on the western bank of the Usumacinta River at about 17° north latitude, has been visited and described by a number of explorers. The chief works of art are sculptured stone lintels and stelae.[1] Many of the temples of this city are in a fair state of preservation.

Few of the sculptures of Yaxchilan offer evidence of archaism. Many, on the other hand, show an advance in the representation of the human figure and a knowledge of grouping, perspective, and foreshortening beyond anything seen in the southern cities so far treated. The principal criteria of chronological sequence at Yaxchilan are three: first, development of rounded relief out of flat relief, such as has been already studied at Copan, Quirigua, Tikal, etc.; second, the increase of skill in perspective and foreshortening, briefly noted in the later stelae of Tikal; third, the invention of safer and lighter methods of construction. The first two criteria concern the sculptures, and the last the buildings.

The lintels at Yaxchilan are usually carved on the under side, the space reserved for the carving being approximately square. In this space two or more human figures are represented in low relief. Blocks of glyphs commonly fill the corners and occupy most of the open space between the figures. One of the persons represented is, as a rule, somewhat larger than the other. They commonly face each other, one being drawn in pure profile, while the other has the body in front view and the face in profile. The feet of the person shown in front view are turned directly outward in the awkward pose so frequently noted in other cities, while the figure in profile stands in a soldierly attitude with one leg concealed behind the other.

The attempt to represent the human body in side view, after the front-view method had been established, seems to have led to a fair understanding of the difficult feat of foreshortening, especially in the details of breast ornaments and aprons. It should also be noted that lintel sculptures have the character of a design limited to a given space, and as a natural development of this limitation there results a feeling and an expression of that subtle balance in the grouping of points of interest which is commonly called composition.

The earliest lintels of Yaxchilan seem to be those which show the carvings in low, flat relief, with details of dress and of glyphs simply incised. In the more advanced sculptures the relief is considerably higher and there is more of a feeling for well-rounded-out contours. Also there is a marked increase in artistic quality. As a rule, there are several lintels in each temple, and these commonly show a similar style of carving. The tentative order of some of the principal temples of Yaxchilan on the basis of lintel classification will now be given. There is really little choice among the first five or six positions.

[1] For the notation and nomenclature see p. 259.

Structure 1	Lintels, 5, 6, 7, and 8.	Structure 21	Lintels 15, 16, and 17.
Structure 20	Lintels 12, 13 and 14.	Structure 2	Lintel 9
Structure 33	Lintels 1, 2 and 3	Structure 42	Lintels 41, 42, 43.
Structure 10	Lintels 32 and 33.	Structure 44	Lintels 44, 45 and 46.
Structure 16	Lintels 38, 39 and 40.	Structure 23	Lintels 24, 25 and 26.

In addition to these there are some lintels with only glyphs which are not easily placed. Lintel 10 of Structure 3 seems to show rather archaic carving. Lintels 18, 19, 20, 21, 22 and 23 of Structure 22 are not uniform in style of carving or in appearance. Lintel 18 has incised glyphs; Lintel 21 has glyphs in low relief; Lintel 22 has glyphs in rather high relief, hardly a single one of which is recognizable. The glyphs on this stone resemble somewhat those on Lintels 35 and 37 from Structure 12, but the latter have much more artistic quality. Lintels 27 and 28 of Structure 24 are so badly weathered that it is difficult to judge their style. They resemble the lintel which is now in the Berlin Museum.[1] It is possible that this lintel was taken from the same much destroyed structure.

The stelae of Yaxchilan are arranged before temples much after the manner of those at Naranjo. As a rule, the temples which have carved lintels do not have associated stelae. Stelae 1 and 2 are apparently correlated with Temple 33, which is built upon the greater acropolis while they stand below upon the river bench. This temple also has Lintels 1, 2 and 3 and is one of the largest and best preserved buildings in the city. Stelae 3, 4, 5, 6 and 7 are aligned in front of Temple 20. Stela 3 is at a considerable distance opposite the center of the stairway, while the other four stelae are set up on the lower terrace of the temple. This important temple likewise has three carved lintels. The three Temples 39, 40 and 41 are situated upon the back portion of the greater acropolis. Before Temple 39 is a single stela, No. 10, that is placed directly in front of the doorway. Before Temple 40 are Stelae 11, 12, 13 and 14, arranged symmetrically. Temple 41 has Stelae 15, 16, 17, 18, 19 and 20, three being placed upon the upper terrace and the other three upon the middle terrace of the temple. The two remaining stelae are placed before two of the so-called sepulchral pyramids. As a rule, the stelae of Yaxchilan have sculptures upon both front and back faces, and before each face is a drum-shaped altar. According to Maler,[2] the side which faces the temple has a religious significance and the side away from the temple a secular one.

It will be remembered that when several stelae are arranged before a building at Naranjo they are not all of the same style and period. The same situation exists at Yaxchilan. Stelae 1 and 2 are correlated with the central axis of Structure 33, but are some distance from the structure and on lower levels. Stela 2 is nearer the temple, while Stela 1 occupies the commanding position. The latter monument is splendidly carved in a style far superior to that of the former stela and of the three lintels in the temple itself. Similarly in the case of Structure 20, the monument that occupies the position of honor, namely, Stela 3, is undoubtedly a late work. There are four other stelae before this structure. The two flanking monuments, Stelae 4 and 7, are excellent pieces, and may belong to the same period as Stela 3, but the two middle sculptures are much inferior in design and are carved in lower, flatter relief. Curiously enough, the fragment that according to Maler is the upper part of Stela 5 has

[1] Maudslay, 1889–1902, II, pl. 98.   [2] 1903, p. 126.

been published by Maudslay as a part of a lintel from Structure 44 (House M). Probably some confusion in notes occurred, because it is pretty evident that the fragment did not form part of a lintel and the two buildings in question are at opposite sides of the city. The three lintels of Structure 20 seem to be earlier in style than the three fine stelae, but may belong to the same period as the two crude ones.

In front of Temple 39 is a single monument showing careful carvings in intermediate relief. Before Temple 40 were four (or perhaps only three) stelae. Of these Stela 11, which occupies the important position, has splendidly carved and excellently preserved designs upon front and back. The sculptures are in high but somewhat flat relief and show excellent composition. The remaining monuments, judging by Stela 13, are of a much earlier period.

None of the six stelae in front of Structure 41 is stylistically of the latest period. The sculpture in most cases seems to be very low. Stela 16 is something of an exception, but the carving is much inferior to that of Stela 11 before the neighboring temple.

Stelae 8 and 9 remain to be considered. No photographs of the former could be secured. The latter is a carefully executed piece with much grace. The relief is low, but the finish is smooth.

The placing of these monuments in a definite order cannot safely be attempted at this time. Suffice it to say that Stelae 1, 3, 4, 7 and 11 represent the latest and best work, next in order appear to be Stelae 2, 5, 9, 10 and 16, while the remaining known monuments, including Stelae 6, 13, 15, 18, 19 and 20, are in the earliest group.

Under the previous section devoted to architecture many progressive changes in construction were pointed out. As a rule, the crude beginnings were seen in the southern cities of the Maya area and the finished products in the western and northern ones. At the time the statement was made that such structural developments probably indicated chronological sequence. It is almost axiomatic that a sound principle of construction once thoroughly mastered is seldom forgotten. Esthetic art ebbs and flows, but utilitarian art rises steadily and conserves its positive gains. This is particularly true of architecture, as may be seen from the long history of this art in Europe.

The development of roof structures has been explained in some detail (see page 110), from the cumbersome first attempts at Tikal to the airy superstructures at Palenque and in northern Yucatan. At Yaxchilan three or four stages are shown in as many groups of buildings.

The simplest examples show the roof structure, in the form of a narrow wall perforated by windows, placed over the ridge pole of a one-roomed building. The weight is supported for the most part by heavy interior buttresses which divide the long narrow room into a number of compartments and necessitate a number of doorways in the outer walls. Structure 39 is an example with very heavy walls and a heavy roof crest. The room in this temple is very narrow, resembling the rooms in the temples of Tikal. The roof comb is lightened, and the proportion of wall space to room space is reduced in Structures 25, 40 and possibly 41. The attempt to lighten the load by throwing the roof comb off center is seen in Structures 20, 42 and 44. In these buildings the width of the room is increased considerably over the structures of the earlier group. The buttresses become more prominent. According to Maler's plan, the roof wall in Structure 21 was built directly over the front wall of the building in the form of a flying façade.

In the next group the roof structure rises over the medial partition of a two-roomed building. There are at least two examples of this stage, namely, Structures 23 and 30. In the first of these the interior buttresses are still seen in one of the rooms in spite of the direct support that the roof crest receives. The superstructure is still a single wall with perforations.[1]

The final stage of development shows a roof structure consisting of two walls sloping inward and bonded by cross beams of stone. Each of these walls contains rows of windows. In the case of Structure 33 this double roof wall is placed over a single room and the old interior buttresses are again called into play. It may be remarked, however, that the outer walls of the temple support most of the weight and that this roof crest is much grander and more substantial than any that preceded it. According to Maler's diagram the roof wall of this temple consists of but one wall, but the photographs and Maudslay's sketch prove the opposite to be the case (Fig. 148, b and c). Of course it is uncertain whether this stage came before or after the stage just given showing the mechanical use of a medial wall. It is important to note that the temples of Palenque present a combination of the double-walled roof crest with the medial wall support.

Another example of the double roof structure is seen in Structure 6. Here the two walls rise above the two longitudinal partitions of a three-roomed building. The roof structure may be said to straddle the narrow interior room. There are no interior buttresses. A third example is seen in Structure 19.

The correlation of these different lines of evidence with each other and with the dates given on lintels and stelae is difficult, and the conclusions are far from satisfactory. In many cases the inscriptions are incomplete, and there are no means of knowing whether or not the latest date has been deciphered. Frequently the calculations run from one lintel to another. It has been shown that the different stelae before a single building were probably set up at different times; hence the dates on these stelae are of doubtful value in determining the age of the structure.

Mr. Bowditch[2] has carefully worked over the inscriptions of Yaxchilan, and the following list of dates is compiled from his results. Only the latest date in the inscriptions connected with each building is taken. The arrangement is chronological.

Structure	Names of sculptures	Latest date
24	Lintels 27, 28	9–10–18–16–17.
44	Altar, Lintels 44, 45, 46	9–12–9–8–1.
20	Lintels 12, 13, 14 } Stelae 3, 4, 5, 6, 7 }	9–15–10–0–1.
21	Lintels 15, 16, 17	9–16–?–?–?.
22	Lintels 18, 19, 20, 21, 22, 23	9–16–1–0–9.
1	Lintels 5, 6, 7, 8	9–16–1–8–6.
16	Lintels 38, 39, 40	9–16–3–3–6.
42	Lintels 41, 42, 43	9–16–4–1–1.

[1] It must be confessed that Maler's plans are hardly convincing on this point. Further field work must be carried on before the art history of the Usumacinta Valley can be made stable and satisfactory. Single wall roof combs are found in Peten.
[2] 1903, a, pp. 27–29.

Structure	Names of sculptures	Latest date
33	Lintels 1, 2, 3. Stelae 1, 2	9–16–6–0–0.
23	Lintels 24, 25, 26	9–17–?–?–?.
10	Lintels 29, 30, 31, 32, 33	9–18–0–0–0.
39	Stela 10	9–18–9–12–1.
40	Stelae 11, 12, 13, 14	9–18–13–13–0.
41	Stelae 15, 16, 17, 18, 19, 20	9–18–17–17–6.

Structure 24, which according to this list has the earliest final date, has two lintels carved on the outer edge but not on the under surface. There are no sculptures on these lintels, except a double row of weathered glyphs. The style, however, seems to be reasonably advanced and the true date of the building may fall in the fifteenth or sixteenth katun. The temple itself is in utter ruin. In the case of Structure 44 the inscriptions on the three splendid lintels, which are of the last type of lintel carving, are undecipherable. The date given is obtained from a rectangular sculptured block which may have served as a sort of altar. The initial series date is clear enough, but certainly does not give the true date of the monument.

FIG. 230. — Head on fragment of Lintel 41: Yaxchilan.

With these two exceptions the dates on the lintels agree in the main with the grouping of these works of art upon a basis of the style of sculpture. It seems that the low-relief style flourished in the first part of the sixteenth katun. In the case of Structure 10 the lintels are accredited with a later date than the style of sculpture warrants. The calculations on these lintels are apparently accurate and specific, and lead to the beginning of the seventeenth katun if not to the eighteenth. Maler considers that the building has an older and a newer part. The first three lintels have only glyphs carved in low relief. The outlines of the glyphs are fairly well rounded, but the style does not seem at all advanced. The other two lintels are carved with figure compositions in low relief. These lintels, which are situated in an L-shaped addition to the building, have glyphs that are apparently of a later type than those of the first three instances.

The dates which are given to Structures 39, 40 and 41 seem to be too late, particularly in the case of the last, where the sculptures are all rather poor and in the earlier style. The interpretation of these dates in the eighteenth katun instead of the sixteenth depends upon the value of a glyph which occurs with unusual frequency at Yaxchilan. This is the katun sign, surmounted by the Ben-Ik sign and preceded by a bar. This sign has been read as meaning 18 katuns, but this reading is admitted to be more or less of a moot point. After the late dates encountered at Quirigua, Naranjo and Seibal the dates of Yaxchilan are fairly early. But probably they all occur after the close of the archaic period. A close resemblance in style is to be noticed between Stela 5 of Tikal and the best group of stelae at Yaxchilan. The method of representing the eye at Yaxchilan (Fig. 230) is the same as seen on the later stelae of Copan.

The dates of Yaxchilan are noteworthy because of the comparative scarcity of even quarter katuns. The declarations of odd days are obviously more apt to refer to definite events than those which fall at the end of a recurring five-year period. The earliest date at Yaxchilan is an initial series on Lintel 21 that registers 9–0–19–2–4, 2 Kan 2 Yax. This date precedes any known date at Copan or Tikal, and while it may refer to the traditional history of the people of Yaxchilan it is not possible to associate it with any archaic sculptures. A secondary series of 15–1–16–5 brings the final count of this lintel into the sixteenth katun. Stela 1 may read 9–11–12–0–0, 3 Ahau 8 Chen, and may likewise advance into the sixteenth katun. An early initial series is found on an altar near Structure 44. The date reads 9–12–8–14–1, 12 Imix 4 Pop. Although this date does not count forward more than a few months in the secondary series, there is good reason to believe that the true date of the carving is at least fifty years later. Most of the increase in the count on the other monuments covers a comparatively short period and usually falls in or after the sixteenth katun. Maler mentions a hieroglyphic stairway in connection with Structure 5 but gives no photographs of the inscriptions. From this inconclusive survey it is evident that Yaxchilan promises splendid results to the archaeologist of the future.

Piedras Negras. Piedras Negras [1] is situated on the Guatemalan side of the Usumacinta River, about half-way between Yaxchilan and Tenosique. At this city Maler photographed a considerable number of stelae and a few lintels and large table altars. The stelae vary widely in subject and appearance, but are remarkable for the common use of high-relief sculpture showing the face in front view. In a number of cases a small seated figure is carved in high relief in a sunken niche. The sides of the niche are decorated in delicate low-relief sculpture. Most of the stelae bear figures on both faces, but usually one side is almost destroyed. These monuments are placed in front of buildings, as at Naranjo and Yaxchilan. The buildings, however, are mostly in utter ruin.

The dates which have been deciphered at Piedras Negras are all rather early. The inscriptions in most cases are incomplete, however, and it is possible that there are much later dates than any so far discovered. The latest certain date is that of Stela 3, which registers the beginning of the fourteenth katun. It is possible that 4 Ahau 13 Yax given on Stela 6 may announce the beginning of the fifteenth katun, although Mr. Bowditch prefers the reading 4 Ahau 13 Uo which falls on 9–2–0–0–0. The problem that presents itself at Piedras Negras is the same that we shall find at Palenque. The known dates are much too early to accord with the advanced style of the art. In each case there is urgent need of further exploration.

The earliest and latest dates on the monuments of Piedras Negras that have been deciphered with a degree of assurance are:

Altar 1	13–0–0–0–0,	4 Ahau 8 Cumhu,		
Stela 25	9–8–10–6–16,	10 Cib 9 Mac	to 9–8–15–0–0,	10 Ahau 8 Tzec.
Stela 36	9–10–6–5–9,	8 Muluc 2 Zip	to 9–11–15–0–0,	4 Ahau 13 Mol.
Lintel 2	9–11–6–2–1,	3 Imix 19 Ceh	to 9–11–15–0–0,	4 Ahau 13 Mol.
Stela 1	9–12–2–0–16,	5 Cib 14 Yaxkin	to 9–13–14–13–1,	5 Imix 19 Zac.
Stela 3	9–12–2–0–16,	5 Cib 14 Yaxkin	to 9–14–0–0–0,	6 Ahau 13 Muan.
Stela 6	9–15–0–0–0,	4 Ahau 13 Yax	or 9–2–0–0–0,	4 Ahau 13 Uo.

---

[1] Maler, 1901, is the only original authority on the monuments of this city.

The following dates appear twice and may have some special significance.

Stela 36 and Lintel 2	9–11–15–0–0, 4 Ahau 13 Mol.
Stela 1 and Stela 3	9–12–2–0–16, 5 Cib 14 Yaxkin.
Stela 1 and Stela 3	9–13–14–13–1, 5 Imix 19 Zac.

It has been suggested that the series of dates on Stelae 1 and 3 might very well refer to the life of some individual.

Before what was probably the principal temple at Piedras Negras are eight splendid stelae (Nos. 1–8), each with one well-preserved face. No two of these are alike. The first one is artistically of less interest than the others, but even here it is seen that the face and headdress are excellently carved in the full round, although the body is given in low relief. This recalls the reversion from the late method of Copan that was noted at Quirigua. The figure is that of a woman wearing a skirt with an all-over decoration of lace insertions in the form of a Greek cross. The glyphs are carved in low, delicate relief, but with well-rounded outlines and many details of enrichment. In the cases of Stelae 2, 4 and 5 the face of the principal figure is turned in profile. Stela 4 is a splendid example of flat, sharp-cornered relief with much fine detail. The headdress is sculptured on several differentiated planes, so that the overlay of one detail by another is clearly indicated. Stela 5 is sculptured in somewhat higher and much more rounded relief. The subject is a man seated on a canopied throne. The canopy is a grotesque head upon the top of which sits a bird, while from the eye issues a grotesque figure that probably represents a god. Other grotesque figures are seen at the back. The personage on the throne holds in one hand a staff bearing the head of the Long-nosed God. A human being in ordinary dress stands facing him. Stelae 3 and 6 present seated figures in fairly high relief. All the features are given in low relief. The latter stela furnishes an excellent example of the figure in a niche. A strip of astronomical symbols combined with the Two-headed Dragon and the Serpent Bird frames in the seated person. A similar design from this city has already received comment (Fig. 57, d). Stelae 7 and 8 show standing warriors in front view. The relief is rather high, and certain details are treated in the full round, while certain others are treated in low relief. The enrichment of the dress is remarkable.

Space forbids a complete survey of the wonderful monuments of this little-known city. Careful study of the sculptures available for study fails to disclose any truly archaic specimens unless Stela 29 should be such a one. The glyphs on this broken stone resemble somewhat those on the earlier stelae of Copan.

The artistic evidences indicate that Piedras Negras flourished after the fifteenth katun, which may be taken as marking the end of the archaic period. The mastery of the full round seen here is comparable to that of Copan and Quirigua. The developed form of eye is found here as at Yaxchilan, Quirigua and Copan. The course of development of this feature may be studied on the later monuments of the last-named city and thus pretty accurately dated. Another detail, the development of which may be studied in the light of a known chronology, is the placing of the feet. On Stelae 7 and 8 the feet are turned outward, but the heels are placed as far back as possible, so that the outer angle is less than a straight angle. This is likewise seen on the stelae at Copan erected after 9–15–0–0–0 and on Stela K at Quirigua. Often the relief is so low at Quirigua and Piedras Negras as not to permit this adaptation, but the sculptors took advantage when given the chance. It was noted at Copan and Quirigua that the elaboration of dress tended to destroy the proportions of the body. At Piedras Negras this malformation is very little in evidence, although the dresses are extremely ornate. The close resemblance between the little seated figure on the back of Stela I of Quirigua and figures in niches at Piedras Negras is another bit of oblique evidence on the lateness of this city. The date of Stela I is 9–18–10–0–0.

It will be remembered that the poses on the larger monuments at Copan are stiffly symmetrical, while at Quirigua this symmetry is more or less broken up. The profile sculptures of Tikal and Naranjo are also formal, although a pose showing bilateral symmetry is naturally impossible. The grouping of two or more human figures is seen on some of the stelae at Yaxchilan as well as on most of the lintels. In the earlier cities a single human figure is represented upon each monument or upon each sculptured side. Now at Piedras Negras not only are the poses greatly relaxed in many cases, but there are also excellent examples of compositions containing several figures. The pose of the figure sculptured on Stelae 13 (Plate 25, fig. 3) is a remarkable exhibition of ease. The turning out of the feet is the only awkward feature. Real action is indicated by seeds or other objects that are thrown downward from the open right hand. The rich details of the dress, illustrating feather-work, beadwork, carved faces, sea-shell fringes and jaguar-hide garments, come out with the utmost sharpness and fidelity. Note, for instance, the plain inside foundation of the feather cloak that hangs down the back. In its triumphs over traditional defects this monument is far beyond anything yet presented in this historical consideration.

Stela 14 shows a human figure, apparently a woman, standing before another figure seated in a niche upon a high throne. To combine a richly attired person in low relief with another in high relief so that the effect is harmonious is no easy problem. The ornate apron of the seated figure lies loosely and naturally across the knees and hangs down in front. Stela 12 is perhaps not so effective, but is an even more ambitious attempt. A chieftain richly attired and holding a decorated spear in one hand sits looking downward in an easy position on a lofty throne. Below him two soldiers, one at either side, keep guard over nine miserable captives bound with ropes. The soldier on the right-hand side is excellently carved, with the torso in three-quarters view. The new desire for realism appears in the graceful disarray of the girdle fringes.

It is interesting to note that Stela 1 at El Cayo,[1] an ancient city situated between Yaxchilan and Piedras Negras, is almost identical in pose with Stela 13, that has just been described and figured. A sculptured lintel from the same building at El Cayo before which this and another stela are placed bears an inscription that clearly runs up into the seventeenth katun.[2] In the same connection it should be stated that the remarkable Stelae 1 and 2 of La Mar,[3] which present the closest analogies in grouping and freedom of action to Stela 12 of Piedras Negras, date from 9–17–15–0–0 and perhaps later.

Other evidence pointing to the same conclusion of a late date for Piedras Negras is seen in the nature of the objects portrayed or omitted. It is significant that the Ceremonial Bar, which appears upon some of the earliest monuments of

[1] Maler, 1903, pp. 83–89 and pls. 34 and 35.
[2] Bowditch, 1903, a, p. 2.
[3] Maler, 1903, pp. 93–96 and pl. 36; Bowditch, 1903, a, pp. 2–3.

the Maya area, is absent from this city. The monuments of Quirigua show that this object fell into disuse during the last quarter of the ninth cycle and that its place was taken by the Manikin Scepter and other objects. It occurs, however, at Naranjo and Yaxchilan. The form of the Manikin Scepter that is found at Piedras Negras is very advanced. The body is absent and the head appears on a staff. On the other hand, the Two-headed Dragon that is of late development elsewhere is very common at Piedras Negras in a phase that is far from realistic.

The architecture of Piedras Negras is too far destroyed to be studied effectively, but the excessive use of stelae as a supplementary architectural feature is a pretty good evidence of late date. The main temple at Naranjo is a very late example of such a development which may serve for comparison.

Palenque. Palenque has long been famous for its temples and sculptured tablets. Early descriptions of its antiquities appear in the works of Antonio del Rio, Dupaix, Waldeck, Stephens, etc. Mr. Maudslay and Mr. Holmes have presented excellent and fully illustrated accounts of the best known buildings. And yet this site has never been fully explored. Certain problems connected with its position in the general chronological sequence cannot be settled until exploration has been carried much farther than it has at the present time. Broken fragments are sometimes more significant than perfect specimens.

The criteria of the age of Palenque are of two kinds — first, artistic; second, architectural. Most of the general remarks devoted to the art of Piedras Negras hold true of Palenque. To be sure, the monuments are of very different sorts. Stelae are unusual at Palenque. A single monument of this sort has been noted. It is apparent that the stone available at Palenque was difficult to work, for very few examples of stone sculpture in the full round have come to light. These few, however, are of excellent workmanship. The stone tablets set up in the sanctuaries are carved in extremely low relief. The finish, however, judging by the Tablet of the Temple of the Sun in the Museo Nacional at Mexico City, is very smooth and the contours well rounded. Lacking easily worked stone, the artists of Palenque fell back on stucco as a material to embody their ideas. The stucco work is in both high and low relief, and shows the finest modeling seen anywhere in the Maya area.

The chronological significance of the growing mastery of foreshortening and composition has already been explained. The handling of the pure profile is seen at its best at Palenque. The anatomy of the human body receives more careful and exact treatment at this city than elsewhere. Likewise there is a distinct appreciation of the contrast value of the open background at Palenque. We have seen that the whole tenor of Maya art in the earlier cities is toward complexity rather than simplicity. A slight subordination of certain details is evident at Yaxchilan and Piedras Negras, but there is little in the way of blank space on the sculptured stones of these cities. The sculptures of Palenque are definitely limited to rectangular spaces. There is considerable elimination in the matter of dress, so that a large part of the body is nude while the headdresses are much less cumbersome than heretofore. The human figures stand out against a plain background, or at least a background relatively plain when the natural exuberance of Maya art is considered.

Certain objective similarities and differences between Palenque and other cities might be noted. In Fig. 231 we see a short-handled wand bearing the head of the Long-nosed God; *a* is from Palenque and *b* from Yaxchilan. Striking similarities with Piedras Negras in other forms derived from the Manikin Scepter might be noted as well as in the elongated phase of the Two-headed Dragon. The Ceremonial Bar, which was absent from the latter city, is also absent from Palenque. However, in Fig. 66, *b*, is given an object which occurs on the Tablet of the Cross, and which is almost identical with an object that has evidently replaced the Ceremonial Bar on Stela F at Quirigua (Fig. 66, *a*). The Serpent Bird on Stela 5 at Piedras Negras resembles the Serpent Birds on the Tablets of the Cross and the Foliated Cross in all features except the face. This difference is not especially significant. A striking detail in the headdress of Stela 10 at Seibal represents a bird head with a fish in its mouth. In a headdress at Palenque an entire bird with a fish in its mouth is seen. The lateness of Seibal is clearly indicated by the inscriptions.

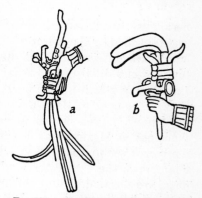

FIG. 231. — Short wands with Long-nosed God: *a*, Palenque; *b*, Yaxchilan.

Perhaps the strongest evidence of the lateness of Palenque is seen in the architecture. In Palenque are found the widest rooms, the thinnest walls, the most refined shapes and the most ideal interior arrangements to be found anywhere in the southern and western part of the Maya area. Certain of these qualifications are equaled in northern Yucatan, but the structures there belong to another and still later epoch. The crowning contributions of Palenque to the development of the roof structure, the sanctuary and the portico have already been briefly explained in the section devoted to architecture. When discussing Yaxchilan a more detailed consideration of the roof structure was attempted as an evidence of chronology.

The roof structures of Palenque show a great improvement over those of Yaxchilan. But the solutions of mechanical problems worked out at the latter city were accepted by the builders of Palenque. The two-walled roof crest is uniformly supported upon a medial longitudinal partition which is more massive than any other wall in the building. The weight is reduced to a minimum by making the roof structures over into a mere trellis work carefully bonded together. The interior walls of the building are also reduced by perforations, the like of which appear at no other city. Since it is perfectly clear that there was extensive intercourse between the various Maya cities, and since the building art would naturally progress toward more safe, economic and beautiful construction, it follows that the structures of Palenque are later in time than those of Tikal and Yaxchilan that furnish analogous but cruder forms.

The development of the sanctuary at Palenque seems to follow the suggestion furnished by Yaxchilan. As a rule, the temples of Yaxchilan have four interior buttresses, two on each side. The two attached to the back wall are near the center, and between these is a deep niche which seems to have been considered the "holy of holies" or the true sanctuary (Fig. 148, *a*). In one temple a carved figure was found in this sanctuary, and in others were found altars. This niche, no longer the result of necessity in the Palenque temples, seems to have been idealized into a sanctuary of the highest type. This process of development may not all have taken place at Palenque. Mr. Maler [1] describes a temple at Xupa with the same plan and style of decoration as the temples of this city but with heavier walls.

The initial series of Palenque are

Temple of the Cross	12–19–13–4–0,	8 Ahau 18 Tzec.
Temple of the Sun	1–18–5–3–6,	13 Cimi 19 Ceh.
Temple of the Foliated Cross	1–18–5–4–0,	1 Ahau 13 Mac.
Temple of the Inscriptions	9–4–0–0–0,	13 Ahau 18 Yax.
Palace Steps.	9–8–9–13–0,	8 Ahau 13 Pop.

The first three dates are some 3000 years before the beginning of the great period at Copan, and the next two dates are in the first part of the archaic period as established by the sculptures. Long distance numbers are plentiful at Palenque. The latest date reached on the closely connected inscriptions of the first three temples is 9–13–0–0–0, 8 Ahau 8 Uo. The calculations in the Temple of the Inscriptions touch all the even katuns from 9–4–0–0–0 to 9–12–0–0–0 and then skip to the opening date of Cycle 10.

A finely carved slab collected by Dupaix and now believed to be in the Museo Nacional in Mexico City bears the date 9–11–0–0–0, 12 Ahau 18 Ceh. This piece was set in the wall at the head of a stairway leading to a subterranean chamber in the " great temple " at Palenque. Two other similar slabs containing dates are also figured, but the drawings are inaccurate.[2] Another specimen which may have been taken from Palenque is a sculptured disk showing a seated figure surrounded by glyphs. This excellent piece is now in the Museo Nacional at Mexico City and has been figured by Peñafiel.[3] Many writers have credited Palenque with being inhabited at the coming of the Spaniards. Förstemann [4] himself believed that the dates referred to the fifteenth century. Schmidt and Meye [5] thought the chronological order was Quirigua, Copan, Palenque. They note that the finest work of Palenque has " freed itself from all fantastic, unintelligible elements, winning its way to freedom of movement based upon a fuller knowledge of anatomy." Bancroft [6] confesses his own inability and admits a shade of skepticism concerning the ability of others to form a well founded judgment of chronology on the basis of art. Dr. Gordon [7] contents himself with the conclusion that the historical movement was from the south towards the north.

As the matter stands, there seems to be little doubt that Palenque is one of the latest cities of the first great epoch of Maya culture. But perhaps an early occupation might also be revealed by careful observation. No help can be obtained from the dates given in the inscriptions, because these are few in number and altogether too early. Some of them are clearly mythological. The inscriptions of Palenque are extensive and may prove to treat largely of calendarical calculations especially as regards the revolutions of the planet Venus and intercalary days.[8] The suggestion might be made that the knowledge of mathematics increased along with the other phases of culture, and that long

---

[1] 1901, p. 19.
[2] Antiquités Mexicaines, II, p. 80 and pls. 39–41.
[3] 1910, pl. 118.
[4] 1899, p. 78; Bull. 28, p. 576.
[5] 1883, Last page of Introduction.
[6] 1875–1876, IV, p. 361.
[7] 1904.
[8] Bowditch, 1910, pp. 204–205; 1906, pp. 5–11.

calculations may themselves be an indication of the late date of the monument upon which they occur. It is certain that the very early monuments do not show long secondary series of dates.

It is unnecessary to fix upon an exact date for the period of Palenque. The buildings seem to be pretty clearly of one type, and it seems likely that there was a short, brilliant period that may have fallen either just before or just after the beginning of the tenth cycle. Of course the city need not have been altogether abandoned at the close of this brilliant career.

Other Sites. Two cities which show striking similarities to Palenque in architectural forms and decorative art are Comalcalco and Ocosingo. Both of these cities are on the frontier of the Maya area, the former in the lowlands near the coast and the latter nearly due south of Palenque upon the highlands.

The ruins of Comalcalco have been described by Charnay.[1] While extensive, they hardly deserve the extravagant praise bestowed upon them. The cross-section of one of the buildings shows a type very close to that of Palenque, with comparatively light walls, a simple cornice and a sloping upper zone. Evidence concerning the roof comb is wanting. Square towers occur at this site, another detail suggesting connection with Palenque. Of architectural embellishment only fragments of stucco work remain. These, again, resemble the refined and graceful art of the aforementioned city.

To the west of Comalcalco, along the coast of Tabasco and Vera Cruz, minor objects of Maya art in the form of clay figurines, whistles, etc., have come to light. Batres[2] reproduces a number of these specimens. It was near the western end of this coastal strip that the jadeite statuette of San Andrés Tuxtla, bearing what appears to be a very early Maya date, was found. It must be noted, however, that no remains of sufficient importance have been discovered to justify the belief that this region was an early seat of Maya power. On the contrary, most of the artifacts resemble closely those of Campeche, and it is possible that they were obtained during the later periods of Maya history.

Between Comalcalco and Palenque, near the mouth of the Grijalva River, are the ruins that Brinton[3] identifies as those of Cintla. It was with the natives of Cintla that Cortes fought his first important battle. The artifacts from these sites will be discussed later. At Jonuta, on the banks of Usumacinta, there are earthen temple mounds and pottery remains. Figurines from this site are of a fine and purely Maya type. In the Museo Nacional of Mexico City there is a broken but splendidly carved slab that shows a kneeling human figure carved in low relief with a bird fluttering behind his back. Upon this slab is painted the name Jonuta.[4] If the legend is exact, it proves beyond doubt that Jonuta belonged to the same period as Palenque. The fluttering bird is one of the most remarkable pieces of realistic carving from the Maya area.

The ancient ruins near Ocosingo are sometimes referred to under the name Tonina. They are described by Stephens[5] as of considerable extent.

The ground-plan of one of the temples shows an arrangement of rooms very similar to the highly developed temples of Palenque. In particular, there is an inner shrine on the walls of which Stephens found remains of painted stucco

[1] 1885, pp. 163–177.
[2] 1908, pls. 45–56.
[3] 1896.

[4] Batres, 1888, p. 17, says the slab was found in the State of Campeche.
[5] 1841, II, pp. 258–262.

decoration representing monkeys and human beings, in a style strongly resembling the stucco work of Palenque. Over the doorway of this shrine were remains of a representation of the Serpent Bird which likewise occurs over a doorway at the latter city. Unfortunately Stephens misinterpreted the partly destroyed design as a Winged Globe, thereby furnishing a piece of evidence that has been much used by speculative writers seeking to establish connections between Central America and Egypt.[1] The sketch plan of the elevation of the temple gives the sloping upper zone but shows no roof comb. The walls of the building are light and the chambers wide. Altogether there seems to be little doubt that Ocosingo belonged to the same period as Palenque for at least a part of its existence.

According to Mrs. Seler [2] the painted stucco found by Stephens has since been destroyed by the elements. She figures, however, some stones having excellently carved hieroglyphs and animal heads, and two small stelae representing human figures in the full round with glyphs on the backs. On both pieces the dress, as seen from behind, seems to be a sort of loose cloak with vertical grooves for folds. Dr. Seler [3] reproduces the four sides of a stone with inscriptions containing dates which unfortunately are not placeable in the long count. He also comments on the stelae.

Plate 25, figs. 4 and 5, reproduces the front view of two small headless stelae at Ocosingo that are doubtless of the same type as those just mentioned. These little monuments are very much like the Copan stelae and must have been modeled in miniature after these sculptures. The Ceremonial Bar is held against the breast, the heavy apron with the frets at the sides — a very widespread feature — hangs from the belt, and, most important of all, the feet are placed in a comfortable position with the heels well back of the apron flap. This last detail practically proves that the monuments were carved at a later time than the fifteenth katun because this position of the feet was not thought of at Copan until after the carving of Stela A.

In the Museo Nacional at Mexico City is a small but well-sculptured stela together with fragments of one or two others, all closely resembling the ones just described. The complete stela has been figured by Peñafiel [4] and wrongly called a God of Fire. Upon the back is a cloak like that worn by the figures which Mrs. Seler reproduces. There is a column of weather-worn glyphs down the back. This stela and the fragments of similar ones probably came from Ocosingo. Some of the finest carved jadeite ornaments in the Squier collection were found at Ocosingo and offer further evidence of the high plane of the art of that city.

There are good reasons for believing that most of the ruins on the highlands of Guatemala and the state of Chiapas date from much later than the great period of Maya art. However, there are a few towns that must have flourished near the close of that period. Ruins of the earlier lowland type extend well up the rivers. Dr. Tozzer discovered on the upper Tzendales River a small ruin with remains of several mounds and buildings. One of the buildings had a simple roof comb with windows that has already been described (page 112). A stela

---

[1] Squier, 1851, p. 248; Le Plongeon, 1896, p. 217.

[2] Seler, C, 1900, p. 147.

[3] 1901, c, pp. 192–195; see also Brine, 1894, pp. 263–265.

[4] 1903, pl. 81.

in fair state of preservation was found. This is reproduced in Fig. 232 from the hurried drawing made in the field corrected by a number of measurements. The Manikin Scepter on this monument furnishes an important link between the original form of the object and the later one consisting of a head on the top of a plain staff. The dress in many details recalls that seen on the figures of Yax-chilan and Palenque. The carving certainly be-longs to the best period, and yet in the inscription we find declared 9–13–0–0–0, 8 Ahau 8 Uo.

Dr. Seler [1] reproduces the upper part of a small stela from Salinas de los Nueve Cerros on the Chixoy River, north of Coban. This shows carv-ing in front view and high relief. Mr. Maler [2] has explored the upper Usumacinta and gives descriptions of several important sites. At the mouth of the Chixoy is the site called Altar de Sacrificios, which has a few interesting sculptures, in particular a stela with an early initial series.[3] Farther up stream at Itsimté-Sácluk are several stelae which resemble strikingly the monuments of Naranjo. At Cankuen, near the head of the river, are still other sculptures. Stela 1 at Can-cuen (Plate 25, fig. 6) is carved in the latest and best style. On one side is sculptured a skirted figure seated cross-legged on a throne or couch and holding a variant form of the Ceremonial Bar. The lower part of this figure is as well pre-served as if it were carved yesterday. The pro-jection of the knees is accurately foreshortened in low relief, and the dress is represented freely and naturally.

FIG. 232. — Stela at Tzendales.

Upon the Guatemalan highlands a few stelae have been found. For instance, one resembling the sculptures of the Usumacinta cities may be seen at Chincoltic, near the Lake of Tepan-cuapam.[4] The two fragmentary stelae discovered at Saccana [5] are of the greatest importance be-cause they bear initial series dates in the tenth cycle. Stela 1 is 10–2–5–0–0, 9 Muan 18 Zac, and Stela 2 is 10–2–10–0–0, 2 Ahau 13 Chen. The stelae have no ornamentation and the glyphs are very rudely carved.

A painted vase from the Quiché region near Huehuetenango that has part of a ninth cycle date is figured by Brinton. [6] The original vase is in the Museum of the University of Pennsylvania. The Chama vase and other pieces of elab-orately decorated pottery from the environs of Coban may also date from the end of the great period. This is indicated, in particular, by a portion of a pottery

[1] 1902–1908, III, p. 576, pl. 1. [2] 1908, a.
[3] Mr. Bowditch makes this date 9–10–3–17–0, 4 Ahau 8 Muan.
[4] Seler, C. 1900, pl. 54. [5] Seler, 1901, c, pp. 17–23. [6] Brinton, 1894, b, p. 140.

box with decoration by a nicely modeled relief that represents a seated figure holding in his lap a Ceremonial Bar (Fig. 63).

The many great ruins in northern Yucatan will be considered in another section. In all that region there is only one initial series date that has been definitely deciphered. This date is in the second katun of the tenth cycle and is found at Chichen Itza. If this region was inhabited during the great period, its culture was of a provincial character.

Summary of First Epoch. We have seen, from this survey of the principal cities of the southern and western portion of the Maya area, that considerable dependence may be placed upon the historical character of some of the dates on the monuments, but that some other dates must be regarded as referring to the past or the future. The historical dates seem to indicate a general movement of culture from the south towards the north and west. The correlation of the period covered by this culture with Christian chronology will be attempted later.

Our examination of the first great age of Maya art is ended. It is now necessary to begin again and establish new criteria for the second great age that reached its height several hundred years later. Perhaps a word of warning is necessary. It must not be thought that Maya culture in its most peculiar features was not continuous through both these ages and even after the close of the second. Learning and religion were maintained as before, doubtless through the aid of books and an organized priesthood. The complicated calendar, as has been demonstrated by Mr. Bowditch and others, remained the same in substance from the founding of Copan until the time of Bishop Landa. Unfortunately for us, however, the use of initial series inscriptions expressing dates in the long count seems to have fallen into disfavor and to have been largely supplanted by the shorter counts of the 52 and the 260 year cycles. The mechanics of architecture and other features of purely utilitarian arts seem hardly to have suffered a set-back. Only esthetic art in its most spiritual and imaginative phases was blotted out by some potent social change.

The explanation of the eclipse of all that was finest in Maya civilization is not far to seek. Any long-continued period of communal brilliancy undermines morals and religion and saps the nerves and muscles of the people as a whole. Extravagance runs before decadence, and civil and foreign war frequently hasten the inevitable end.

THE SECOND EPOCH

The most important cities of the second great age are located in northern Yucatan. In these cities there are admirably preserved temples, as has already been seen, but a general lack of monolithic stone sculptures. The façade ornamentation is a mosaic of small carved stones presenting either geometric or highly conventionalized designs. There are few examples of relief or full round carvings upon which to base any stylistic order. The architectural forms furnish the best evidence of chronological sequence, but these are not figured and described accurately enough to make conclusions certain. Moreover, there is practically nothing to serve as a check upon the theoretical results and to make clear the rate of change except the traditional history embodied, for the most part, in the so-called Books of Chilan Balam. This traditional history makes no reference to definite buildings and, indeed, only refers by name to the cities of Chichen Itza, Uxmal, Mayapan and Izamal. All the other great cities must be correlated with these four. It may be said, in passing, that the names applied to most of the ruins in northern Yucatan and elsewhere in the Maya area are of modern origin. Many are purely descriptive.

As Copan was the key to the chronology of the south, so Chichen Itza is to that of the north. Not only does this city have many more carvings and excellently preserved structures than any other city, not excepting Uxmal, but its architectural styles are capable of being differentiated, and the traditional accounts refer to it more specifically than to any other center of power. Chichen Itza was probably the last Maya city to fall and one of the earliest to be founded in the northern region. The initial series date which connects this city with the chronology of the earlier cities far to the south and west has already received brief comment and will presently be considered more in detail.

The difficulties of presenting in short space the evidences of chronological sequence after the end of the Great Age are considerable. There is much to be examined, and the facts brought out are only significant when carefully correlated. The results are suggestive rather than definitive. Frequently the occupation of a city extended over two or more periods, and we find materials that were taken from old buildings and used again in new ones. Similarly in minor art pottery vessels, jadeite ornaments, etc. were passed down as heirlooms and finally buried or broken. The different periods will be taken up seriatim instead of the different cities. It seems possible to distinguish the following periods.

I. Period of the Transition.

II. Period of the League.

III. Period of Influence from the Valley of Mexico.

IV. Period extending from the Fall of Mayapan to the Present Time.

The second and third periods together make up the Second Great Age of Maya art.

The Period of Transition. The period that followed the Great Age may be called the Period of the Transition, because it marks a cultural and a geographical shifting. It is not well defined, but evidence of it exists in a few cities of northern Yucatan which seem to have been founded before all the southern cities were abandoned. The most important connecting links are enumerated below:

1st. Initial Series Inscriptions.

    (a) Chichen Itza, Temple of the Initial Series.

    (b) Xcalumkin, Temple of the Inscriptions.

2d. Manikin Scepter.

    (a) Santa Rose Xlabpak, sculptured panel.

    (b) Sayil, stela.

3d. Wooden lintel with sculptures showing survivals of the old style.

    (a) Kabah.

4th. Stelae.

    (a) Xcalumkin

    (b) Sayil

    (c) Tabi.

In a somewhat detached portion of Chichen Itza, that is commonly known as

Old Chichen Itza, Mr. E. H. Thompson discovered a stone lintel bearing the only date in northern Yucatan that has so far been deciphered. The date is 10-2-9-1-9, 9 Muluc 7 Zac, which falls within a generation of dates in some of the southern cities. The temple in which this lintel was found is briefly described by Seler.[1] It consists of a single room with entrances on the south, the west and the north. The doorway on the west is the principal one, and over it was placed the inscribed lintel. The two door posts are atlantean figures similar in general form to many others in Chichen Itza. At the foot of the temple mound is a half-reclining figure of the Chacmool type. Now, although the lintel itself seems to be old, the two features just mentioned undoubtedly date from the latest building period of the city. It is probably safe to conclude that the lintel was taken from the ruins of an early building and set up in a late one.

A near-by building is the Temple of the Phalli concerning which no definite information is available. The structure takes its name from a series of projecting stones. Although phallic worship was not important in the Maya area, there is some evidence that it existed sporadically. It may have arisen during the decadence that followed the golden age. Brinton [2] has commented on the insufficiency of the evidence of its existence at the time of the Spanish Conquest. Maya art throughout its entire course is remarkably free from anything that might offend the most prudish. The picotes or cylindrical columns in the middle of the courts at Uxmal and elsewhere have been given [3] a phallic significance, but it seems more likely that they are a late modification of stelae. However, an unmistakable phallic column was found at Labna,[4] while Maler [5] records the occurrence of phalli as cornice ornaments at Chacmultun. The building on which these occur is a well-developed example of late Maya construction that can hardly date from as far back as the time of the Transition.

The Temple of the Inscription at Xcalumkin [6] is a two-storied structure, but little now remains of the upper story, or, for that matter, of the northern series of rooms belonging to the lower story. On the southern side there are two small rooms and one fairly large room in good interior preservation. The upper zone of the façade shows remains of lattice work, and it is likely that other ornamentation once existed. On the walls of the principal chamber are traces of paintings, but only scrolls and bands can now be discerned. On the back wall, extending from the apex of the roof to the floor, is the aforementioned initial series inscription with the glyphs arranged in a double column. The doorway of the chamber is a wide one, with two piers or rectangular pillars which have glyphs upon their outer faces. Glyphs also appear upon the capitals, or rather abaci, of the pillars and upon the first course of stones above the lintels.

According to Dr. Seler,[7] the initial series inscription records a ninth cycle date. But a careful examination shows that this conclusion is open to serious doubt. It seems more likely the face numeral of the cycle period is 10 instead of 9. The so-called maggot sign, which resembles the common percentage symbol and is a much used Maya method of indicating death, occurs a number of times in this inscription. It seems to occur on the numeral face that precedes the cycle glyph. The face for 9 is characterized by dots around the month, that for 10

---

[1] 1908, p. 237.

[2] 1882, a, p. 156; also pp. 130-131.

[3] Orozco y Berra, 1880, II, p. 456.

[4] Peabody Museum photographs.

[5] 1895, p. 249; 1902, p. 199.

[6] Maler, 1902, p. 203.   [7] 1908, p. 239.

represents a death's head. The marks on the face are partly destroyed, but one reading is as good as the other. There is one other glyph in the secondary series where the face with the same death sign means 10. The katun glyph is peculiar, but may be 18. The fourth glyph shows the kin signs that characterize the number 4, and the last one is 9 by the bar and dot system. According to Mr. Morley, the most probable reading is 10–18–10–4–9, 7 Muluc 2 Yaxkin. This falls several hundred years later than any other date and is of course open to serious question. Thomas[1] makes a point in regard to this inscription that a shift of one day in the system of counting is shown by the date 8 Caban 4 Zotz. This shift makes the inscription agree with the calendar in vogue in northern Yucatan at the time of the Spanish Conquest.

The life history of the Manikin Scepter has already been given. This object, with a ventral appendage in the form of a serpent, is exceedingly common in the sculptures of the Great Age. It does not occur in the codices or in the obviously late sculptures. It is, however, seen on a stela[2] at Sayil and on a sculptured panel at Santa Rose Xlabpak.[3] The presence of this figure certainly shows a more intimate connection with southern art than is indicated by the generality of northern figures. Its occurrence in one case upon a stela is an added proof of age. Stelae are rarely encountered in northern Yucatan. The sculptured panels of Santa Rose Xlabpak suggest the wall decorations of Palenque. The temple in which they occur is of a developed type and has already been described on page 102. There is evidence that the carved stones forming these panels were taken from an earlier building, because they do not fit together exactly as they are now placed.

The wooden lintel which Stephens[4] found at Kabah is interesting, because it shows a strong survival of the early style of sculpture. The sculptured door jambs[5] from this city probably date from a later time.

The sporadic occurrence of stelae is an evidence of the survival of early ideas. These stelae are not found in correlation with any of the great structures at Chichen Itza, Uxmal, etc., and seem to belong to a different epoch. The sculptures on the stelae are crude, but resemble in certain details the noble monuments of the south. Upon a platform mound at Sayil, Maler[6] found three stelae and a number of small pillars grouped about a circular altar. Two of the former are figured in the account of his explorations. The sculpture is very flat and crude, but the free and easy postures indicate that the crudity comes from decadence rather than inexperience. Careful search might reveal many more examples of these monuments, and enable a reconstruction of the little-known period that followed the great age of Maya art. The stelae of Tabi are very crudely executed. They are known through casts made by Charnay. Maler[7] mentions a monument at Xcalumkin that falls into this category, as do others elsewhere which are referred to by Stephens.[8] The so-called Pillars of Ben[9] in the State of Chiapas may mark a contemporaneous dying out of early forms upon the western frontier.

The historical evidence of the Period of the Transition will be considered in another place. At this time it may be stated that this evidence points to the

[1] 1900–1901, p. 253.
[2] Maler, 1895, p. 278.
[3] Stephens, 1843, II, p. 164; Maler, 1902, p. 223.
[4] 1843, I, pp. 403–407.
[5] 1843, I, pp. 411–413.
[6] 1895, pp. 277–278.
[7] 1902, p. 202.
[8] 1843, I, p. 364.
[9] Brinton, 1897. Le Plongeon, 1881, p. 253, figures a crude stela at Mayapan.

region inland from Campeche as the probable center of the highest culture. Little is known concerning the ruins between Lake Peten and the Gulf of Mexico.

Period of the League of Mayapan. The Period of the Transition was followed by a much greater one, that in accordance with traditional history may be called the Period of the League of Mayapan. Clearly there was a second ascent to high culture caused by organized effort. The seat of this high culture was in northern Yucatan, and the area of its influence was apparently much more restricted than that of the first great age.

Artistically the most noteworthy achievements are in architecture. From a constructional point of view, as has already been stated, the architecture of the second epoch is superior to that of any of the earlier cities with the possible exception of Palenque. Walls are comparatively light, rooms are usually of the maximum width, doorways are frequently enlarged through the use of columns, and both roof combs and flying façades are economically constructed. The façade decoration is marked by the use of the formal mask panel, the geometric panel and the continuous or broken application of plain and banded columns.

The greater number of structures at the important cities of Uxmal, Labna, Kabah, Sayil, Hochob and Chacmultun probably belong to the Period of the League of Mayapan. Many smaller centers in the same region may have risen after the period was well begun and the tide of wealth and power had turned again to the Maya. At Mayapan itself there is a tower of the same type as the Caracol at Chichen Itza, but there are few other remains of consequence and these seem to be late. At Chichen Itza the following buildings probably date from this luxurious age of renaissance:

1st. Akat'cib.
2d. Casa Colorada.
3d. Group of the Monjas.
4th. Caracol.

In the first three cases the buildings show features comparable to the great mass of architecture in northern Yucatan, characterized as it is by the tridentate cornice, the mask panel, lattice work and vertical roof structures. The first three buildings have hieroglyphic inscriptions with details similar to those of the southern sculptures. The last building may belong to the next epoch, since round towers may have been associated with the cult of Quetzalcoatl introduced from Mexico.

Evidence of chronological sequence within the limits of this period are rather hard to discover in the present state of knowledge, and it is impossible from an objective study to fix the rate of change when once the sequence has been established. A theoretical sequence may be worked out in some instances from the apparent evolution in architectural construction and decoration. This, however, is a rather dangerous procedure. More exact data upon this subject may be gleaned from a careful examination of the different parts of the great agglomerate structures, such as the Monjas at Chichen Itza and the so-called palaces at Labna and other important cities.

It has often been noted that the Monjas at Chichen Itza, already briefly described on page 101, represents several periods of growth. Holmes [1] recites the evidence of two or three periods of construction. A breach in the substruc-

[1] 1895–1897, pp. 106–109.

ture exposes a considerable portion of a smaller inclosed substructure. Maudslay[1] goes still farther and finds evidences of foundation enlargements and room additions in the following order. These may be seen on the partial plan given in Fig. 139 and in Fig. 233, which shows the two inclosed substructures of the main building.

1st. The lower half of the third or inmost substructure.

2d. The upper half of the third or inmost substructure.

In connection with these there are no remains of stairways or chambers and no decoration.

3d. The second substructure. This was probably ascended by the present stairway or by a narrower stairway in the same position. The chambers were probably removed, but possibly remain as the two long chambers of the present Main Range. The second substructure has a simple cornice decoration.

4th. The enlargement of the second substructure to form the present foundation and the erection of the present Main Range of rooms (Plate 27, fig. 1). The upper part of the substructure is decorated with mask panels of several kinds (Plate 28, figs. 3 and 4), and the

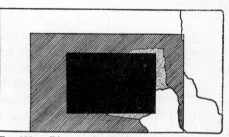

FIG. 233. — Diagram showing growth of the substructure of the Monjas: Chichen Itza.

main range is decorated with geometric panels, mouldings, etc. (Plate 28, fig. 2). There are remains of frescos that closely resemble those of the Temple of the Jaguars. These may have been painted long after the building was finished.

5th. The filling up of the long northern chamber and the erection of the upper stairway and the single room temple on the roof of the Main Range. The upper stairway is of the same type as the lower one. The walls of the upper temple are made up of miscellaneous sculptured stones that are clearly re-used material (Plate 28, fig. 1).

6th. The erection of the principal portion of the East Wing on the ground-level. This splendid structure is richly ornamented with mask panels of several sorts, and the eastern façade shows the use of a profile mask panel that has already received comment (Plates 13, fig. 2; 27, fig. 2).

7th. The addition to the East Wing fronting on the rear court. The façade of this addition is very simple, its only ornament consisting of the usual tridentate cornices and a frieze of plain columns in groups of three.

8th. The filling up of the central chambers of the East Wing for the support of an upper story that was never built.

Detailed examination of the mask panels which decorate this structure and the adjoining building, commonly called the Iglesia or Church (Plate 15, fig. 1), gives rise to certain interesting questions. The eastern façade of the East Wing (Plate 13, fig. 2) may first be examined. This narrow front is flanked by six corner masks, one half of each appearing on this face while the other half appears on the north or south façade, as the case may be. Four of these masks are symmetrically placed in the lower zone and are rather richly elaborated (Plate 28, fig. 6). The remaining two corner masks are of the same type as the six frontview masks. These front-view panels are distributed, as were the corner masks,

[1] 1889–1902, III, p. 18.

four in the lower zone and two in the upper. Each is framed in by plain strips of stone (Plate 28, fig. 5).

It has been frequently stated that the mask panels of northern Yucatan are mosaics. Now, although the elements in the eight masks on this façade are the same, yet the spaces to be occupied are not of uniform size and the parts are spaced accordingly. The elements of the two upper front-view masks are widely spaced so as to fill areas that are both longer and higher than those in the lower zone.

While the façade as a whole shows careful planning, there is evidence that an attempt was made to re-use old material probably taken from an earlier building. If the carvings had been made to order for this front, they would surely show better joining.

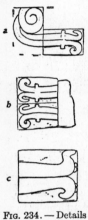

FIG. 234. — Details of re-used mask panels: Chichen Itza.

Other details support this theory of re-used sculptures. In one instance the head band was not put together properly. This head band is made of five carved stones, the center one showing a division of the beaded disks. In one case this center stone was replaced by one of the side stones. Elsewhere on the building the masks are in considerable variety, there usually being two or three of a kind. Many are very loosely fitted together, an example being given in Plate 28, fig. 3.

But the clearest example of the use of heterogeneous material is seen on the flying façade of the Iglesia. This consists of three masks, each of different size and style and each more or less incomplete. These three incomplete masks were not sufficient to fill all the space, so an asymmetrical strip of fretwork had to be introduced at one side to fill out. As an example of the make-shift character of the masks, the two lateral mouth ornaments of the central one are different (Fig. 234, b and c). That on the observer's right is made of one stone, while that on the left consists of two stones. These two stones belong to a mask of the same type as several on the frieze of the foundation mound of the Monjas (Fig. 234, a), and are undoubtedly a pair of old lateral mouth ornaments made over into one.

It seems reasonable to hold that the later additions to the Monjas Group are made up from the wreckage of several earlier buildings. The design of the eastern façade of the East Wing belongs, as we have seen (page 127), to the most advanced type showing the use of the two profile mask panels at either side of a doorway. It is undoubtedly later in time than the façades that show these features in their purity.

Similarly many other large structures in other cities give evidence of sequence of parts. Mr. Thompson, speaking of the principal edifice of Xkichmook, says:[1]

"The Palace appears to be the result of successive periods of growth. It would seem that the central portion had been completed, and that time left its mark upon the wall before the wings were added, and the eroded surface was hidden beneath a new material. The second story also appears to occupy the site of an older structure. The newer building seems to be identical in style with the old."

It seems unwise to proceed further in the lack of more definite information. It may be stated with assurance, however, that the problems of structural and

[1] 1898, p. 216.

artistic sequence in northern Yucatan are capable of accurate solutions. The buildings with the more simple and graceful decoration, particularly those showing façades with plain and banded columns, will probably be found to date from the end of the Period of the League of Mayapan.

The realistic sculptures of the Period of the League of Mayapan are few and far between. One of the finest has already been presented in Fig. 182. This sculpture certainly does not date from the latest period of Uxmal, because it was found in a wall that had been built over and concealed by another structure. A second interesting but weather-worn example is given in Fig. 235. The human being sculptured in low relief on the cavern wall in the cave of Loltun [1] may be another.

The Period of Influence from the Valley of Mexico. Following the period of pure Maya culture came one in which foreign influence was strongly felt. In particular, the results of influence from the Valley of Mexico are very evident at Chichen Itza, and are, in fact, shown in the greater number of structures of that city.

FIG. 235. — Serpent head with human head in its mouth. West Range of Nunnery Quadrangle: Uxmal.

The well-known identities between the art of Chichen Itza and that of Tula, San Juan Teotihuacan, etc., have given rise to a number of theories of migration. In particular the defenders of the so-called Toltec theory have used these identities as proof of the northwestern origin of Maya culture. Charnay's map of the Toltec migration shows these more or less mythical people passing from the highlands of Mexico to Comalcalco and thence in two bands to Tikal and Chichen Itza. But it has been seen that Comalcalco, although on the frontier, is an early Maya city showing no foreign affiliations. Tikal is the earliest and Chichen Itza the latest of all Maya centers. Much evidence besides that furnished by the art can be brought against this theory of the Toltec migration. The true significance of these similarities is not far to seek. An historical explanation will be given in a later section.

The principal structures at Chichen Itza exhibiting Nahua features are

1. Temple of the Initial Series.
2. Castillo.
3. Ball Court Group.
4. Group of the Columns.
5. Structures 9, 10, 12, 13, 14, etc.

The principal features of probable Nahua origin that occur in connection with these structures are as follows:

1st. Architectural features.
   (a) Serpent columns and serpent balustrades.
   (b) Open-work decoration on top of temple walls.
   (c) Sloping or "battered" bases of temple walls.
   (d) Platform mounds with colonnades.
   (e) Flat roofs.
   (f) Ball courts.
   (g) Atlantean supports.

[1] Thompson, 1897, pl. 6.

2d. Artistic and religious features.
   (a) "Chacmool" sculptures.
   (b) Sun disks and the "celestial eye" type of star symbols.
   (c) Speech signs.
   (d) Feathered monsters in front view.
   (e) Processional grouping of warriors accompanied by identifying glyphs.

These many features combining in different ways prove beyond doubt that all the structures named date from the same cultural period. Since Chichen Itza alone shows the complete adaptation of these forms in the Maya area while many cities on the highlands of Mexico present the same details, it follows that the culture is intrusive at Chichen Itza. This conclusion is made more certain by the fact that many other features, clearly of Maya origin, occur at Chichen Itza which are not found at the sites in question on the highlands of Mexico.

The serpent columns of Chichen Itza find their closest parallel in the great columns of Tula, which have been described by Charnay.[1] The columns are either round or square, the serpent head is thrust outward at the base, the body makes the shaft and the tail projects forward and then upward, forming a peculiar capital. The feature of the serpent tail capital seems to be a development peculiar to Chichen Itza. The temples which have serpent columns usually have pyramidal substructures with balustraded stairways on all four sides. The balustrades sometimes end in serpent heads.

This series of temples seems to have been decorated by open fretwork at the tops of the walls, and in no case is the flying façade or the roof comb present. This open-work at the top of the temple walls is represented on the clay models of Nahua temples and in the pictures of them in the codices.

The lower part of the walls of all typical Maya buildings is vertical. The group of buildings under consideration shows a sloping or battered base. This feature is found in early Mexican structures at San Juan Teotihucan, Xochicalco, etc. The use of interior columns for support of the roof is also a Nahua and Zapotecan feature that reappears at Chichen Itza.

Platform mounds with long rows of columns, usually four deep, are plentiful in the curious Group of the Columns at Chichen Itza. Although this feature does not seem to find an exact parallel in Mexico, still the use of columns is much more common there than in Yucatan. All the buildings associated with these peculiar colonnades are of the prescribed type.

Flat roofs are characteristic of Nahua and Zapotecan ruins. They do not seem to have been much used in the Maya area. The colonnades just mentioned may have served to support a flat roof. Some of the buildings attached to the back court of the Monjas probably had timber roofs, either flat or pitched. Stephens found evidence of flat roofs at Tuloom, but elsewhere in Yucatan they are rare.

Atlantean or caryatid supports, architectural and otherwise, have been found at Chichen Itza in the Maya area and at Tula, Tlascala, and Tenochtitlan in the Valley of Mexico. The first site has yielded by far the greatest number of specimens.

In the Temple of the Initial Series at Old Chichen Itza the lintel of the main entrance is supported by two atlantean figures. Each is carved in the round and is made up of five drums of limestone. Fig. 236 reproduces a drawing of one of

[1] 1885, p. 293.

these supports. As may be seen, the figure is stiff, angular and poorly proportioned. Certain details of dress are given in relief, and these details were doubtless originally marked out in color. The two arms are represented in a vertical
position, with the elbows unbent, yet the hands are only on a level with the
crown of the head. The weight of the superstructure thus rests upon both head
and hands, and the figure as a whole has the structural value of a column. Other
atlantean figures (Plate 29, fig. 4) at Chichen Itza [1] present the
same pose, but the proportions of the body are usually more
squat, allowing the whole figure to be carved from a single stone.
In at least one other small temple at Chichen Itza atlantean
columns serve as lintel supports. More commonly these curious
figures are used as legs for table-like altars. As such they
occur in the Temple of the Jaguars and in several structures of
the Group of the Columns, the most important being the
Temple of the Tables.

FIG. 236. — Atlan-
tean figure; Tem-
ple of Initial Series:
Chichen Itza.

Atlantean figures from Tlascala are described by Seler (Fig.
237). These, although lacking much of the ornament in dress
found on the Chichen Itza figures, are yet so strikingly similar
as to preclude the possibility of independent invention. The
excavations in Escalerillas Street [2] in Mexico City have yielded
two small figures of the same general type that must be referred
to Tenochtitlan. At Tula have been found the bases of large
atlantean columns well known through the descriptions of Charnay.[3]

Cultural contact is undeniably shown by such striking similarities. Since Chichen Itza alone in the Maya area presents figures
of this precise type, it might be assumed that the place of origin
for atlantean columns was in the Valley of Mexico. But there is
another kind of evidence to be considered before this conclusion is
accepted. The idea of human support is capable of being expressed
in relief sculptures as well as in the full round. That the later
pictographic device was considered as related to the former functional one seems clear from the frequent occurrence at Chichen
Itza of atlantean figures in relief (Fig. 11) on door jambs and
capitals in buildings of the same type as those which have the table
altars. Elsewhere in the Maya area the idea of human support is
expressed in a variety of ways. Thus at Naranjo and other cities of the southern region the principal figure represented on the stelae frequently stands upon
a prostrate captive. At Palenque, on the famous Tablet of the Sun, the officiating priests stand upon the backs of kneeling grotesque persons, while two other
seated men support on their shoulders the altar of the sun. This latter conception is pretty close to that of atlantean columns supporting table-like altars,
as at Chichen Itza. As a detail of façade decoration small bodies which appear
to hold the cornice upon their raised hands may be seen at Xculoc.[4] These
latter are veritable atlantean figures, but are only carved in high relief and not
in the full round. Columns with human beings carved on the front occur on
Cozumel Island [5] and at Dsecilna [6] in Yucatan.

FIG. 237. — At-
lantean figure:
Tlascala.

---

[1] See also Maler, 1895, p. 288, and Seler, 1908, pls. 10–17.   [2] Batres, 1902, b, p. 19; Peñafiel, 1910, pl. 10.
[3] 1885, p. 72.   [4] Maler, 1902, p. 208.   [5] Holmes, 1895–1897, p. 78.   [6] Maler, 1895, pp. 290–291.

From these foregoing examples it seems unnecessary to go outside of the Maya area for the origin of the atlantean conception. It is an open question whether the atlantean column passed from the Valley of Mexico to Chichen Itza or *vice versa*, but that there was a transmission either one way or the other seems clear.

The sculptured stone to which Le Plongeon [1] gave the fanciful name of Chacmool is one of a very widespread type that is more Nahua than Maya. The attitude is peculiar. The sculpture represents a human being, partially reclining upon back and elbows, with the knees raised and the feet drawn in. The head is likewise raised and is turned to one side. In the center of the body is a bowl for the burning of incense, which is held in the two hands of the figure.

The famous Chacmool of Chichen Itza is now in the Museo Nacional at Mexico City. It was excavated in Mound 13, which has been called a mausoleum

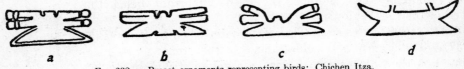

a   b   c   d

FIG. 238. — Breast ornaments representing birds: Chichen Itza.

although its purpose is not clearly established. It is important to note that this figure wears a breast decoration in the form of a conventionalized bird exactly like the breast ornaments seen in the sculptures of the Temple of the Jaguars, the Castillo, the Temple of the Tables, etc. (Fig. 238).

Minor Chacmool sculptures occur at Chichen Itza in connection with Structures 12, 18 and 25, as well as the Temple of the Initial Series that has already been considered. No other sculptures of this type have been reported from the Maya area. But very similar stone carvings have been found at Tlascala [2] and elsewhere in the Valley of Mexico. In the Tarascan area [3] of the State of Michoacan the reclining gods also occur. A drawing in the Museo Nacional at Mexico City by Don José M. Velasco, made in 1892, represents a Chacmool sculpture before a temple at Cempoalam in the State of Vera Cruz. According to a photograph furnished by Mr. E. Mosonyi, a Chacmool sculpture has been discovered in San Salvador and is now placed in the court of the university at the capital of this republic (Plate 29, fig. 5).

Prominent among the remains of the earliest high culture in the Valley of Mexico are evidences of a sun worship apparently differing from the sun worship of the Maya. Among the latter people the sun gods assume human or grotesque forms and are identified by the associated kin or sun sign. This sign may represent primarily the four directions and by extension the sun that gives rise to the conception of the four directions. In the Nahua area the face or disk of the sun is itself represented (Fig. 239, e). This disk in its simplest phase is elaborated with four markings that resemble the principal division points of a compass. In more complicated phases the division points are multiplied and other figures added, as may be seen on the well-known Calendar Stone of Mexico City. This sun disk is called Tonatiuh in the Aztec tongue. It is frequently a constituent part of Mexican place-name hieroglyphs. It is also of common occurrence in

[1] 1886; Salisbury, 1877.
[2] Sanchez, 1877, p. 278; Nuttall, 1901, a, pp. 93–96; Seler, 1908, pp. 171–173 and pl. 9.
[3] Lumholtz, 1902, II, p. 451.

Nahua and Zapotecan codices as an object of worship or of astronomical significance. It has a wide distribution as a decorative design upon minor objects of art. The sun disk does not occur in the three Maya codices, nor is it in evidence in any of the Maya cities so far known except Chichen Itza and Santa Rita.

At Chichen Itza the sun disk is distinctly represented both in the sculptures and in the frescos of the Temple of the Jaguars.[1] A human figure is represented with the sun disk. This feature is also seen in some of the more elaborate sun disks from the Nahua and Zapotecan codices. A sun disk from Mitla is shown in Fig. 239, a.

There is evidence, however, that the sun disk at Chichen Itza was identified with the elaborate astronomical symbol with the serpent heads issuing on the four diagonals. The intermediate stage is given in Fig. 129, where an undeniable sun disk inclosing a human figure shows also four serpent heads attached to the rim.

At Santa Rita, in the northern part of British Honduras, the sun disk likewise occurs. Fig. 239, d and e, gives two sun disks, each with a human head on one side, the first from Santa Rita and the second from the Codex Porfirio Dias.[2] In the first case the head is inclosed in a conventionalized serpent head, while in the second case the serpent head appears in the center and the head at the top.

FIG. 239. — Sun and star symbols of the Nahua type: a, Mitla; b, Totonacan area; c and d, Santa Rosa; e, Codex Porfirio Dias; f, Codex Fejérváry-Meyer; g, Vienna Codex; h, Chichen Itza; i, Mitla.

Associated with the sun disk at Santa Rita is the type of planet or star symbol which is characteristic of the highlands of Mexico. The astronomical symbols of the Maya have already been described on page 91. A simpler and less diversified method of indicating heavenly bodies was employed in the neighboring areas. Stars were represented as "celestial eyes." Similar examples of these celestial eyes are given in Fig. 239, a, c, f to i, including drawings at Santa Rita, Mitla, etc. What may have been intended for a celestial eye at Chichen Itza appears in h.

[1] Maudslay, 1887–1902, III, pl. 35, and Miss Breton's drawings in the Peabody Museum.
[2] Antigüedades Mexicanas, 1892.

The interesting device known as the speech sign is common throughout the Mexican highlands both on the monuments and in the manuscripts. Its occurrence in the Maya area is rare except at Chichen Itza, where it is elaborately developed. The speech sign is an object of diverse shape, often scroll-like, that is represented as issuing from the mouth to indicate sound or speech. In Fig. 101 is shown a potsherd from Copan with a painted representation of a jaguar

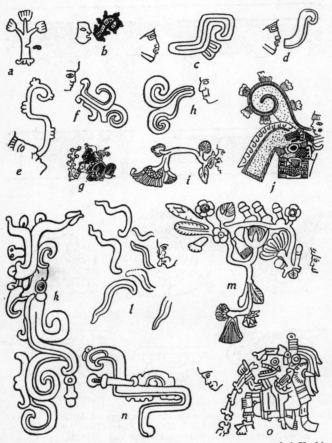

with such a sign attached to his mouth. The hieroglyph of the month Xul and the so-called Burner-period glyph also seem to indicate an animal in the act of howling. In the Maya codices the sounds of animals and of musical instruments are sometimes represented by such symbols, but the speech of human beings is not so shown. In short, the speech sign is an unusual and uncharacteristic feature in Maya art.

A selection of speech signs from different situations is given in Fig. 240. In a is shown the Mexican hieroglyph for Cuauhnahuac (Cuernavaca). In this rebus the "nahuac," which means "near," is represented by its homonym which means "speech." The same is seen in the Mex-

FIG. 240. — Speech scrolls: a and b, Nahua place names; c and d, Xochicalco; e, Santa Lucia Cosumahwalpa; f, h, i, k, l, m and n, Chichen Itza; g, Dresden Codex; j, San Juan Teotihuacan; o, Codex Chavero.

ican place-name hieroglyph, Acolnahuac, where the object endowed with a mouth and speech is an amputated arm instead of a tree. In b is given the place name for Cuicatlan, which means "the place of song." In this instance the speech scroll is elaborated with designs to indicate singing. A drawing in the Codex Borbonicus [1] represents a man beating on a drum and singing, each sort of noise being represented by appropriate symbols. Often the character of the speech sign indicates the nature of the prayer or perhaps the deity to whom it is addressed. Thus in j is probably pictured a prayer for rain and good crops. Flowers adorn the upper scroll, and symbols for running water the lower one. This example is from San Juan Teotihuacan. [2] Similar figures from Chichen

[1] Hamy, 1899, a, p. 4.   [2] Peñafiel, 1899, pp. 49–50, pls. 81–87.

Itza are shown in i and m. At Santa Lucia Cosumahualpa [1] and other sites in Guatemala are still other elaborate examples of flowery speech signs. Returning to Chichen Itza, in l is possibly represented a prayer to the fire god and in n to the serpent. Examples of serpent heads are fairly common in the speech scrolls of this city. An interesting symbol is that given in k, which apparently represents the Long-nosed God. This is shown still better in Fig. 241. In fact, we may see in these drawings the final stage of change that took place in the representation of the Manikin Scepter. The Death God is shown in one of the Mexican codices (Fig. 138, o) in the act of delivering a homily on death. From these comparisons we see that the speech signs at Chichen Itza in their high development strongly suggest influence from the Mexican highlands.

A grotesque monster, that occurs a number of times at Chichen Itza [2] as a decorative motive on structures of the last group, has been identified by Seler [3] as Kukulcan. This figure presents in front view a human face, with a terraced nose ornament, in the more or less rectangular mouth of a monstrous reptile. The inclosing reptile head is characterized by sweeping plumes and by nose plugs at the top and by a long, divided tongue at the bottom. On either side of this grotesque head appears a leg with claws. Ex-

FIG. 241. — Speech scroll representing the Long-nosed God: Chichen Itza.

amples of this figure occur on the balustrades that flank the front steps of the Temple of the Jaguars as well as upon the end wall of the sculptured chamber below. But the best preserved representations adorn the so-called Temple of the Cones. A portion of a similar sculpture from an unknown source is built into the walls of the house of the hacienda.

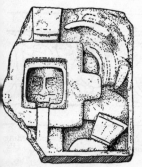

FIG. 242. — Terra cotta tile from Tezcoco.

The nearest approach to this figure in general style of presentation is the front-view reptilian form decorating the upper zone of the Temple of the Cross at Palenque.[4] But an examination shows that the modes of conventionalization do not agree. Both figures, however, probably relate to the Two-headed Dragon with its many divergent forms. The fish and water plant motive is found in intimate relation with both. While the representation of a human head in an animal's mouth is too general in and out of the Maya area to have any specific bearing on the subject at hand, still there is a marked objective similarity between the Chichen Itza sculptures and the headdresses of Stelae 7 and 26 at Piedras Negras, which will be shown later.

But in keeping with other close parallels noted between the art of the last period of Chichen Itza and that of the so-called Toltec cities of the Valley of Mexico we find this conventionalized figure almost exactly reproduced upon a small water-worn terra cotta tile from the ancient Tezcoco. This tile, which is in the American Museum of Natural History, is reproduced in Fig. 242. It practically completes the chain of evidence connecting the last flash of brilliancy

[1] Habel, 1878; Bastian, 1882; Seler, C. 1900, pl. 42.   [3] 1908, p. 235.
[2] Maudslay, 1889–1902, III, pl. 52, d and e.   [4] Maudslay, 1889–1902, IV, pl. 68, a and b.

on Maya soil with the most magnificent epoch in the Valley of Mexico that itself ended before the beginning of the fourteenth century. The peculiar terraced nose plugs that appear on the human heads in the reptile mouth also are seen in the codices from the highlands of Mexico (Fig. 243, *a*).

The method of grouping as well as the general style of delineation shown on the walls of the Lower Temple of the Jaguars and the South Temple of the Ball Court exhibits similarities to the sculptures on the famous Sacrificial Stone of Mexico City or Stone of Tizoc. But the most significant similarity concerns the accompanying hieroglyphs. Above each warrior is a glyph which probably represents the name of the individual. These glyphs are drawn in the Mexican manner, and it is not at all impossible that they are to be read in the Nahua rather than in the Maya language. The warriors which appear with the twining bodies of serpents behind them find a close parallel in the warrior from the Codex Borbonicus [1] reproduced in Fig. 243, *b*, as well as in a sculpture at Tula.[2]

FIG. 243. — Nahua subjects similar to those of Chichen Itza: *a*, head with terraced nose plug and eagle headdress. Codex Vaticanus 3773; *b*, warrior with attendant serpent: Codex Borbonicus.

The historical importance of these remarkable similarities showing intrusive ideas from the Mexican highlands will be considered presently. It must not be gathered that the art of this period was entirely Nahua, because such a conclusion would be far from the truth. The inherited features of Maya art still are seen in many sculptured figures. For instance, there are no drawings from the highlands of Mexico that show the knowledge of foreshortening that we see in Fig. 244 from the Temple of the Jaguars. The vault construction, etc., is purely Maya.

The evidence is so complete and the identities so numerous that immediate contact between these two cultures is the only explanation that can be offered. The traditional evidence of a Nahua invasion just previous to the downfall of the League of Mayapan will soon be presented. It seems clear from the sculptures alone that Chichen Itza fell under the influence

FIG. 244. — Design showing Maya mastery of foreshortening: Chichen Itza.

of foreigners who infused new spirit into the decadent art and introduced new ideas of their own. But complications arise from the fact that much of the early Nahua culture was itself derived at an earlier date from Maya sources, and still retained traces of its origin at the time of its reversion to Yucatan.

The sculptured columns and pilasters (Plate 29, figs. 1, 3 and 6) of the temples possessing the features just considered are the most important criteria of classification of the structures of this period. Many of them have been reproduced by Dr. Seler. Of especial interest is a small temple with two pilasters made of stones wrongly assembled. This structure was apparently made of waste material, but this material was from the latest period. Perhaps

[1] Hamy, 1899, *a*, p. 17.   [2] Peñafiel, 1890, pl. 154.

the finest single sculpture of this period is that of a jaguar reproduced in Plate 29, fig. 7.

Clear evidences of so-called Toltec or pre-Aztec influences are not wanting elsewhere in the Maya area. In northern Yucatan these evidences apparently relate to the same time as the foreign importations we have just noted at Chichen Itza or to a slightly later time. The ball court at Uxmal [1] may well have been modeled directly after that of Chichen Itza, for in general the structures of this city are purely Maya. The remains that Charnay [2] identifies as those of a ball court at Ake are, indeed, somewhat doubtful. But the possibility of their being such is somewhat increased by the presence of another feature that may be un-Maya. The platform with columns in three rows at Ake resembles the more complicated Group of the Columns at Chichen Itza,[3] which clearly dates from the period of foreign influence. Upon the Island of Cancun off the east coast of Yucatan there are two platform mounds facing each other, which have no walled temples on their summits but only rows of columns.[4] Neither at Ake nor at Cancun is there enough sculptural detail to allow a stylistic comparison. At the latter place, however, was found a broken heroic statue, the head of which [5]

FIG. 245. — A stucco panel at Acanceh.

shows a close resemblance to heads attached to incense burners from British Honduras, Tabasco, etc. that seem to have been in vogue just previous to the Spanish Conquest. Stephens [6] at Mayapan notes the presence of a structure with double rows of columns.

FIG. 246. — Figure that may represent Manikin God: Santa Rita.

The recently discovered wall at Acanceh [7] with its well-preserved stucco reliefs seems to show foreign influence in several details. It is possible that we have here simply a platform with ornate sides like the so-called mausoleums of Chichen Itza. But there are several vaulted chambers near by whose floors are on a lower level than the base of the wall. The ornamentation is unusual in style and subject. The upper projection of the wall presents a series of repeated symbols based upon the eye of the serpent and resembling somewhat the Mexican star signs, while the lower band shows two Maya planet signs in alternation. The middle portion of the wall between these projecting bands is largely given over to more or less humanized animal figures inclosed in panels with terraced outlines (Fig. 245). Prominent among these figures are the squirrel, the bat and the serpent. The speech scroll occurs several times.

The ruins of Santa Rita in the northern part of British Honduras are well known on account of the fresco paintings found and described by Mr. Thomas Gann.[8] The art of this place shows many of the Nahua features that have already

[1] Holmes, 1895–1897, p. 90.
[2] 1885, p. 249.
[3] Maudslay, 1889–1902, III, pp. 36–43, pl. 60.
[4] Arnold and Frost, 1909, pp. 150–151.
[5] Arnold and Frost, 1909, p. 240.
[6] 1843, I, p. 137.
[7] Breton, 1908; Seler, 1911, a.
[8] 1897–1898.

been noted at Chichen Itza. The sun disk and the celestial eyes have already been considered. In general technique the paintings resemble those of Mitla. The Maya admixture is more noticeable in subject than in treatment. It seems possible to identify the faces of both the Manikin God (Fig. 246) and the Roman-nosed God (Fig. 247), although the identification of the former is far from

certain. Likewise Maya glyphs occur, particularly numbers combined with the day sign Ahau. The paintings probably record conquests. The style of some of the pottery (Fig. 248) is characteristic of the period just before the coming of the Spaniards.

Brief mention has already been made of the common occurrence upon the highlands of Guatemala and Chiapas of parallel earthworks that Seler [1] has identified as ball courts. If the identification is correct, the presence of these structures may indicate Nahua influence in this region. Such influence must have come in after the fall of Copan and the other great cities of the lowlands, because no such remains are found at these cities.

FIG. 247. — Head of Roman-nosed Sun God: Santa Rita.

The sculptures of Santa Lucia Cozumahualpa are excellent examples of Nahua art, and according to Brinton [2] are to be attributed to the Pipiles, a Nahua tribe. The speech scroll is a prominent feature and is sometimes very elaborate. Other Nahua tribes that carried with them some of the old culture located themselves still farther south near the shores of Lake Nicaragua.

Modern Period. Little is known concerning the styles of architectural decoration in vogue at the arrival of the Spaniards. In regard to the minor arts, however, there is a type of pottery which has been pretty surely authenticated as dating from this last period. This is seen in incense burners made as a rule of a coarse sandy material and showing decoration with faces and entire human figures built up in full relief.[3] The type of face is peculiar and is characterized by a pronounced nose with a beadlike knob at the top. Examples come from Cosumel Island,[4] British Honduras and Tabasco, and are thus of wide distribution. In the last locality they seem to be associated with the so-called ruins of Cintla,[5] with whose inhabitants Cortes fought his first great battle,

FIG. 248. — Head of figurine with animal headdress: Santa Rita.

and with numerous earthen mounds near Frontera (Fig. 249). A photograph of a stone image of large size on the Island of Cancun showing the same type of face is given in a recent publication.[6]

The modern descendants of these incense burners may be seen among the Lacandone Indians of the Usumacinta Valley (Fig. 250). These vessels are crudely made, but usually have a face on the rim. This face shows the bead above the nose and the old round ear plugs at each side of the head. These features are clearly survivals of the old art. It has already been stated that

[1] 1901, c, pp. 26–32.
[2] 1885, d. See also Lehmann, 1909, p. 16.
[3] Tozzer, 1907, pp. 89–92 and pls. 15–17; Seler, 1901, c, p. 148; Seler, 1895, d, pp. 26–27.
[4] Salisbury, 1878.

[5] Brinton, 1896, p. 268. Some of the specimens collected by Berendt and mentioned herein are now in the Peabody Museum.
[6] Arnold and Frost, 1909, p. 240.

weaving, as practiced in the different parts of the Maya area, may also show certain survivals.

Correlation of Maya and Christian Chronology. Various attempts have been made to bring about a concordance of Maya and Christian chronology principally by means of the sequence of katuns given in the native Books of Chilan Balam. The earliest attempts were based upon Chronicle I, the Book of Chilan Balam of Mani. This document was discovered and first translated from the Maya by Don Juan Pio Perez. The text and a retranslation into English were published by Stephens.[1] The discoverer himself worked out the chronology on the basis of 24 years to a katun and did not correctly determine the number of periods. In these mistakes he was followed by Bishop Carrillo,[2] who drew his results from the manuscript of Perez and from a number of other Maya documents.

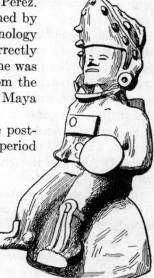

FIG. 249. — Figurine from Cerro de los Idolos: Tabasco.

It is now well established that the katun in these post-Spanish records corresponds in length to the katun or period of the fourth position in the ancient calendar and consists of 20×360 days. For ease of calculation this may be lengthened to an even 20 years. The error then accumulates at the rate of about 4 years in 300. In the Books of Chilan Balam each katun is distinguished by the number of day Ahau with which it begins. These fall in the following order: 13, 11, 9, 7, 5, 3, 1, 12, 10, 8, 6, 4, 2, 13, etc. Thus katuns with the same designation can occur only at intervals of 13×20, or 260 years. As long as these 260-year cycles are kept in their proper order the count is accurate enough. It was apparently the intention of the native historians to obviate mistakes by repeating all of the katuns in order whether or not there were historical entries opposite them. But in the chronicles as they have survived there are both omissions and repetitions.

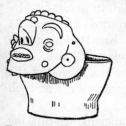

FIG. 250. — Typical Lacandone incense burner.

Abbé Brasseur de Bourbourg[3] and Don Eligio Ancona[4] based their considerations principally upon the work of Perez, the latter using 24 years as the length of the katun. Their chronologies vary somewhat in the number of katuns. What seems to be the proper sequence and number of the katuns was first established by Valentini[5] and later adopted without important change by Brinton.[6] The former worked only with the original chronicle discovered by Perez, while the latter correlated with this document four other more or less similar ones from different towns. The count is carried back 70 katuns, from the end of katun 13, which fell in the year 1541. This places the beginning of the traditional history in the year 160 A.D.

But the Books of Chilan Balam, useful as they are, cannot be regarded as a

[1] 1843, I, Appendix, pp. 434 *et seq.* The original with the commentary of Pio Perez was published by Brasseur de Bourbourg, 1864, pp. 366–429.   [2] 1871, p. 405; 1883, pp. 60–64.   [3] 1857–1859, II, pp. 1–72.   [4] 1878–1880, I, p. 138.   [5] 1879, *b.*   [6] 1882, *b.*

summary of Maya history as a whole. The historical events therein recorded may have referred originally to a single clan, the Itzas, who from a small beginning became more and more powerful till they controlled the destinies of northern Yucatan. This brief history of the most important tribe or ruling family may have later served as a basis and model for the histories of other important tribes or families. Against this supposition is the general lack of purely genealogical data. The tribal or family histories from the highlands of Guatemala furnish detailed genealogical information and give as well accounts of wars and other events.

We have seen that during the Great Period there were many cities with dated monuments and that at the close of this period the use of such dated monuments seems to have been entirely discontinued. Several attempts have been made to bring these dates into some definite relation with our own calendar. One note-worthy attempt, made by Mr. Bowditch, is based upon a date in the Books of Chilan Balam expressed in the quadrinomial system of the Maya and likewise in European chronology. The event recorded is the death of a native chief called Ahpula, which fell on the day 9 Imix 18 Tzec, six years before the completion of katun 13 Ahau, in the year of our Lord 1536. We know that 9 Imix 18 Tzec corresponded to October 21.

The year-bearer, or the 1st day of the month Pop, July 16, 1836, is variously given in these chronicles as 4 Kan[1] and 5 Kan,[2] while in the so-called chronicle of Nakum Pech the year-bearer for July 16, 1841, is given as 13 Kan.[3] No two of these agree with the necessary positions in the 52-year calendar round. The complete year given by Landa begins with 12 Kan and was probably taken down directly from a native informant as the year then passing. Landa's work was completed in 1566. Possibly other dates of this sort will be found in unpublished records. At present the confusion is very great, although the numbering of the katun periods seems to be pretty accurate.

It has already been explained that there is an apparent shift of one day be-tween the ancient and the modern Maya calendar. In fact, the date 9 Imix 18 Tzec is impossible in the long count and must be shifted to 9 Imix 19 Tzec. This change and the discrepancies above noted militate somewhat against the value of the date given for Ahpula's death. If the determination made by Mr. Bowditch[4] is correct, the inscription on Stela 9 at Copan records the year 34 A.D. This determination is certainly much more reasonable than the one made by Dr. Seler upon another date which makes Stela 9 go back to 1255 B.C. If the correlation of Mr. Bowditch is accepted, we must lengthen the Period of the Transition about 260 years to take up the slack time. The chronology at each end of this period is accurate enough.

A second method of correlating the mass of dates in the ancient inscriptions with the European system has been explained by Mr. Morley.[5] It is based upon the general sequence of historical events as outlined in the chronicles and the date in the long count which occurs on the lintel at Chichen Itza. This city is the only one mentioned by name in the chronicles at which a date in the ancient system has been found. The date itself is significant as being one of the latest

[1] Brinton, 1882, b, p. 104 (Chronicle I); p. 162 (Chronicle III).
[2] Brinton, 1882, b, p. 149 (Chronicle II).   [3] Brinton, 1882, b, p. 228.
[4] 1901, b.   [5] 1910, b.

expressed in this manner. It is 10–2–9–1–9, and thus falls in the ninth year of the second katun of the tenth cycle. Mr. Morley's determination depends upon the accepted fact that the designation of the katun by the day with which it began was common to both the old and the new calendars. Thus the first day of the tenth cycle according to the old system was 7 Ahau 19 Zip and according to the new system was simply katun 7 Ahau. 10–2–0–0–0, 3 Ahau 3 Ceh, equals katun 3 Ahau in the new system. This being known, the problem is to find a katun 3 Ahau that falls during one of the noted occupations of Chichen Itza.

The Chronological Table given in Table 2 covers the entire range of Maya history, and shows the results obtained from the study of the monuments and the native historical records. The periods of the Long Count, the Short Count and the European Count are correlated horizontally in this table. The principal events as related in the different Chronicles are set down in separate columns upon the same principle of arrangement. A synopsis of the recorded history of the Quiché and Cakchiquel is presented in a detached space and in a genealogical manner owing to the lack of definite dating.

It is evident from the table that the period which is richest in monuments is poorest in historical references. But this is hardly to be wondered at when we remember that the chronicles are post-Cortesian, while the dated monuments fall in the first centuries of the Christian era. The Tuxtla Statuette and the Leiden Plate have eighth cycle dates; the Dresden Codex has a few eighth cycle dates, a large number of ninth cycle ones and a few that fall near the end of the tenth cycle. It is very doubtful whether these dates have any historical value.

Chronicles I and II, if the correlation is correct, begin with the round number 9–0–0–0–0 as the time of departure from the mythical land of Tollan. This date is earlier than any date on an erected monument with the exception of a few mythical dates thousands of years previous to the historic period. The first date at Tikal iš, however, but 50 years later and thus precedes the stated time of arrival at Chacnouitan (or Chacnabiton) of the party under Holon Chantepeuh, for the migration lasted 81 years. Ahmekat Tutulxiu, however, seems to have arrived a few years earlier. Because, if his residence is placed a cycle later, as Brinton places it, there is little worth in the statement that the residence in Chacnouitan lasted 99 years. Bacalal is being occupied during this time. There is another slight point: the 99 years when added to the 81 years that had preceded makes exactly 9 katuns.

It is clear that there is a hiatus of 120 years at this point. This 120 years falls unfortunately in a most significant epoch, just before the Maya sculptors developed their greatest skill. Perhaps the record of other cities might have filled the gap. Most likely, however, the chroniclers did not attempt to give a résumé of the Maya nation as a whole. Zian caan or Bakhalal seems to have been discovered at the close of the archaic period, as determined by the sculptures. This region or province may be identified with the modern Bacalar. During the 60-year residence at Bacalar the more northern parts of Yucatan were colonized, in particular Chichen Itza. Probably this city and region remained an unimportant province during the brilliant florescence of the Usumacinta centers. Chronicle V indicates in one passage the dispersal of the tribes in the four directions at about this time. This may refer to the spread of Maya culture into central Honduras, western Guatemala, southern Mexico and northern Yucatan.

A detail which may settle the accuracy of the correlation is the statement that Pop (the first month of the Maya year) was counted in order. This counting in order falls about 9–17–0–0–0, and it may sometime be possible to identify the calculations referred to in the chronicle.

The Period of Transition begins with the abandonment of Chichen Itza and the conquest of Chanputun (Chakanputun). This has been commonly taken to mean the region east of Campeche. From the chronicles we may judge that it was already occupied when the Itzas arrived, and that they first founded a city and finally secured complete mastery of the country. Archaeological information concerning this region is very deficient, and it is impossible to state what city or cities may be identified with Chanputun. Iturbide, Santa Rosa Xlabpak and Xcalumkin may be mentioned as likely candidates.

After a sojourn of 260 years the Itzas abandoned Chakanputun. In Chronicle IV there is a statement that Chakanputun was destroyed by fire, which would seem to indicate that it was a city and not a province, but the date of this destruction does not agree very well with the other dates. There is some reason to believe that the Itzas were expelled. It is clear that they suffered misfortune for several decades before they finally established themselves at the old capital, Chichen Itza.

This re-establishment marks the beginning of a new epoch. Mayapan[1] probably existed before this time, and Uxmal was apparently founded a few years after by Ahzuitok Tutulxiu. The three cities combined forces, and the union was known as the League of Mayapan. It apparently existed for about 200 years, the end being marked by civil war. There is no doubt that the greater part of this period of the league was peaceful and prosperous. There are many important cities that were apparently contemporaneous yet concerning which we have no definite historical information. Izamal is involved in the wars at the end of the period.

The references to the so-called plot of Hunac Ceel are voluminous and ambiguous. This person was the ruler of Mayapan and seems to have resorted to treachery to undermine the power of Chichen Itza. The plot is mentioned in all the Chronicles, but the dates given do not agree in all instances.

The coming of warriors from the highlands of Mexico, and in all probability from the cities of Tula, Cholula and San Juan Teotihuacan, as has been shown from a study of the artistic remains, is distinctly stated in a number of historical documents. Chronicles I and II give the names of the seven men of Mayapan, all of whom bear names that are seemingly of Nahua origin. They were the allies of Hunac Ceel, and it seems likely that the vanquished Chichen Itza was turned over to them as the spoils of war. Brinton[2] translates certain pieces of testimony offered in a lawsuit at Valladolid in 1618. According to this testimony the ancestors of the interested parties came from Mexico to found cities in Yucatan. They built the great temples at Chichen Itza, and they settled likewise near Bacalar and upon the northern coast. These other localities correspond to Santa Rita and Cancun, where evidences of Nahua contact were seen in the art and architecture. Landa[3] mentions a settlement of Aztecs west of Merida. Aguilar[4] also states that there were invaders from the highlands who forced the natives

---

[1] For the traditional account of the foundation of Mayapan by Kukulcan see Landa, 1864, pp. 34–38.
[2] 1882, b, pp. 116–118.   [3] 1864, p. 54   [4] 1639, p. 86.

to construct great temples. Alonzo Ponce, in the passage already quoted (see page 7), makes a reference to the lapse of 900 years since the establishment of Uxmal. The Maya often use the number 9 in the generic sense of "many."

We may imagine, from the confusion that follows the plot of Hunac Ceel, that the course of Maya dominion did not flow smoothly. There are references in the chronicles to civil wars and to the final overthrow and destruction of Mayapan. This probably happened after the civilization had sadly declined. Landa,[1] Cogolludo, etc. make reference to the fall of Mayapan. Events subsequent to this have little interest to us because they have no bearing upon the art.

The possibility of the Dresden, Tro-Cortesianus and Peresianus codices furnishing historical data offers an interesting field for speculation. Seler claims that the Tro-Cortesianus Codex shows the calendar system in vogue at the coming of the Spaniards, because the year bearers in connection with the ceremonies of the new year (pages 20–23) are Kan, Muluc, Ix and Cauac,[2] and not Lamat, Ben, Eznab and Akbal. But Mr. Bowditch [3] points out that the only quadrinomial date occurring in the manuscript (13 Ahau 13 Cumhu on page 73) is in accordance with the ancient inscriptions. There are a number of initial series dates in the Dresden Codex counted from the normal date 4 Ahau 8 Cumhu. Most of these are in the ninth cycle, but some are in the eighth and others in the tenth. Mr. Bowditch [4] is inclined to think that present time in this codex is represented by the date 9–9–9–16–0. This hardly seems likely owing to the absence from this manuscript of the ceremonial objects characteristic of that period. This date falls well back in the archaic period about the time Stela P was erected at Copan. According to Mr. Morley there are two eighth cycle dates that fall in the sixth katun and one date that falls in the nineteenth katun of the tenth cycle. Thus a range of over a thousand years is covered almost exactly corresponding to that shown on the monuments if the inscriptions on the San Andrés Tuxtla Statuette and on the Temple of the Inscriptions at Xcalumkin are validated. Unfortunately the codex dates are difficult to read and the dates on the monuments in question are far from established.

Connection with other Cultures

Maya Influence in Nahua and Zapotecan Art. Maya art has now been studied in its crude beginnings, in its greatest brilliancy and in its phases of decadence and renaissance. It has been shown that in a late epoch there was a political and artistic transfer of culture from Mexico. This influence may be ascribed to the cities of Tula, Teotihuacan and Cholula, and others of the pre-Aztec period. Let us now treat in some detail the evidences of artistic influence that the Maya exerted upon their neighbors.

The adequate discussion of the interrelations of culture as a whole would require more space than is available. Suffice it to say that similarities in material arts, social organization and religious institutions bind the various peoples of southern and central Mexico in a firm ethnographic union with the Maya. The principle of divergent evolution is admirably illustrated in nearly all the phases

---

[1] 1864, pp. 48–52.   [2] 1902–1908, I, p. 556.   [3] 1910, pp. 78–79.   [4] 1909, p. 279.

of culture. The divergence is explained by both geographical and chronological differences. The single item of the elaborate calendar which was used with comparatively little change from the Tarascans and Otomies on the north to the tribes of Nicaragua on the south is itself conclusive evidence of ethnic affiliations throughout the region. It seems reasonably certain that the calendar was invented by the Maya who brought it to its highest stage of perfection. In Mexico it is supposed to have been introduced by Quetzalcoatl. Many names used in the Nahua calendar have the same meaning as those in the Maya calendar. As Gadow [1] points out there are five animals represented as day signs in the Aztec calendar which do not occur on the highlands of Mexico, hence it is reasonable to suppose that the calendar did not originate in that region. All of the animals, on the other hand, do occur in the Maya country. Moreover, the principal divinity of the Aztecs was a war god who had nothing to do with the calendar. Quetzalcoatl, according to most of the accounts of his origin collected by Bandelier,[2] came into Mexico from a foreign land. He it was who introduced fine weaving and the working of jade. It seems quite likely that Quetzalcoatl[3] was a Mexican adaptation of one of the principal Maya deities, probably the Long-nosed God. The fact that Quetzalcoatl was introduced again into the land of his origin by the Mexican invaders does not necessarily militate against this theory. The worship of Tonatiuh, or the sun's disk, seems, on the other hand, to have been a purely Nahua development.

The calendarical system of the Nahua ran in fifty-two-year cycles and there was no method of accurately differentiating the cycles. In this respect it resembled the calendar used by the Quiché who are a Maya tribe. Dependable chronology hardly goes back two hundred years before the conquest. Traditions of earlier times are rather full and many of them probably have a basis of fact. According to these traditions Tula and Teotihuacan were founded in the seventh or eighth century, at about the end of the Maya epoch of greatest brilliancy. But it seems probable that these cities were in their greatest splendor several centuries later, synchronous with the Maya epoch of the League of Mayapan. The early cities in the Valley of Mexico appear to have declined in the twelfth and thirteenth centuries. Other cities rose in their stead; such as Tezcoco, Tlascala, and Tenochtitlan.

From a study of the archaeological remains it is possible to prove at least three epochs in the Valley of Mexico each distinguished from the other by characteristic art, mostly ceramic. The earliest of these periods seems to show no cultural connection with the Maya. This early period will presently be treated in some detail.

The condition of superimposed cultures which characterizes the Valley of Mexico probably holds true in other parts of Mexico. In the Zapotecan area Monte Alban and Tonila certainly represent a different and much earlier period than Mitla. In fact these ruins seem to be more closely connected with the great age of Maya civilization than do the pre-Aztec centers in the north. In the far northwest, the great ruins of La Quemada, Chalchihuites and various sites extending down the Boloños Valley appear to antedate by several centuries the historical Nahua and Tarascan towns of Sayula, Colima and Tzintzuntzan,

---

[1] Gadow, 1908, pp. 302–303.   [2] Bandelier, 1884, pp. 188–198.
[3] For a commentary *variorum* on this subject see Robelo, 1905, pp. 345–437.

while still earlier remains doubtless await the spade of the archaeologist. But there is no reason to ascribe sensational antiquity to any of the famous ruins of Mexico. It seems likely that the effects of the great Maya ascendancy were felt far and wide and it will be interesting to determine some day the exact nature of the original Mexican culture upon which it reacted.

Let us now examine a few examples of art that indicate borrowings. One of the most characteristic and peculiar features of Maya art is the placing

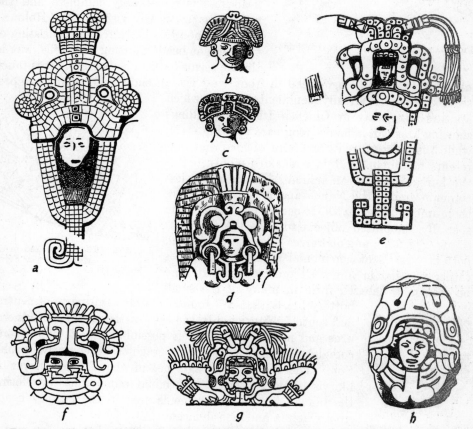

Fig. 251. — The human head in animal jaws: *a* and *e*, Piedras Negras; *b–d*, Oaxaca; *f*, Chalco; *g*, Chichen Itza; *h*, Highlands of Mexico.

of human heads in the mouths of reptiles and other animals. This feature is also seen in a few important sculptures of neighboring areas, where the sporadic cases have a very wide distribution. Highly conventionalized forms in which it is difficult to recognize the original features are much more common. Fig. 251 presents a number of heads for comparison. Of these *a* and *e* are from stelae at Piedras Negras and represent the head of a human being inclosed in a somewhat conventionalized animal's jaws. Note the hook on the outside of each eye, the double curl at the end of the nose and the forked tongue that hangs down over the lower jaw. In the second example nose plugs are seen. On the original sculptures these heads are surrounded by plumes not given in the drawings. Now comparison with *d*, the top of a small stone figure from Oaxaca, will make it clear that this human head is likewise enclosed in an animal head similar to those described above. The double curl of the nose and the hook at the back of the eye are identical in shape. Many figurines with animal headdresses which may

FIG. 252.—The human head in conventionalized animal jaws: Oaxaca.

or may not have the lower jaw come from the same general locality (b, c and Fig. 252). The head in f is drawn on a slab of onyx from Chalco. The upper jaw of the animal headdress is remarkably complete and the nose plugs are clearly visible. Mr. Holmes [1] has explained this headdress as consisting of two serpent heads meeting in profile, but in this he seems to be mistaken since it is much more likely that a single head in front view was intended. Drawing g repre-

sents a monster already commented upon which appears frequently at Chichen Itza on buildings showing Mexican influence (compare with Fig. 242), while h is a sculptured stone from Mexico that represents a human head in a snake's mouth. But the human head in an animal's jaws is much less common among the Nahua and neighboring tribes than among the Maya. It occurs most clearly on specially elaborated objects such as the Calendar Stone (Fig. 253), and on knives, spear-throwers, and pottery vessels of ceremonial significance, but is rather unusual in minor decorative art. It may be seen in a debased form in many of the small

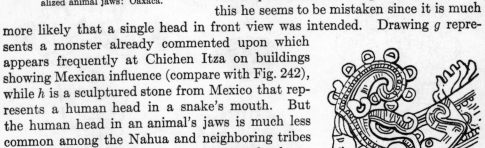

FIG. 253.—The human head in the jaws of a serpent, Calendar Stone: Mexico City.

pottery heads that are found in almost all parts of central and southern Mexico. In the case of the Zapotecan funeral urns and minor figurines it is possible to work out several complete series showing every stage of degenerative evolution. The typical clay figurines of the Totonacan region likewise show vestiges of an original animal's head enclosing the human head. The same is seen in the pottery heads from Cholula and Teotihuacan.

FIG. 254.—Serpent head
on Cholula pottery.

It must be admitted that in Aztec times there was a wide use of eagle and jaguar headdresses of a strikingly realistic character (Fig. 243, a). In some of the codices human figures are represented dressed in the entire skins of animals and birds. In the case of the latter, however, it is at once apparent that the skin of an eagle is not large enough to clothe the body of a man and that the costume must have been merely imitative. This costume may have had its origin in high antiquity and the suggestion drawn from the realm of religious art.

FIG. 255.—Serpent head on engraved
bowl from Cholula.

Animal headdresses are very widespread among primitive people in all parts of the world but the lower jaw is usually lacking. In the Maya area, however,

[1] 1895–1897, pp. 304–309.

the ideal character of the human head in the jaws of the serpent, the jaguar, etc., is beyond dispute.

The treatment of the serpent motive in Nahua art and in some other arts of Mexico shows essential similarities to the same object in Maya art. Perhaps the most elaborate examples are the plumed serpents on the Temple of Xochicalco.[1] The supraorbital plate is prominent in the representations of both areas and there are close similarities in the dentition, and in the application of foreign bodies such as nose and ear plugs. But, taken all in all, the serpent outside of the Maya area seems to lose much of its spirituality. Often it is represented as being killed and sacrificed, a condition that never appears in Maya drawings.

FIG. 256.—Serpent head painted on bowl from Cholula.

It may be worth while first to examine a few serpent

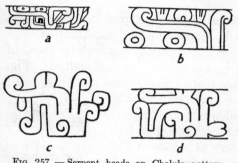

FIG. 257.—Serpent heads on Cholula pottery.

heads having the same features as the heads of the Maya area and secondly to trace the process of degeneration toward the more usual types. The most complete serpent heads are seen in the pottery of Cholula. Fig. 254 reproduces a head painted in different colors. The upper part of the upper jaw is horizontal while the lower jaw is vertical and extends downward. The tongue is attached to the end of the lower jaw and is drawn horizontally. The fang appears near the juncture of the two jaws. The eye is placed in the angle of the upper jaw near the same juncture. On the lower side of the upper jaw we see one molar and one incisor tooth, and on the upper side of the same jaw appears the nose scroll, greatly modified, with two nose plugs sloping backward. In its details of unnatural elaboration this head shows that it was derived from a Maya model (Fig. 30).

FIG. 258.—Conventionalized serpent heads arranged as a swastika.

In Fig. 255 the circular appendage at the back of the head may represent the ear ornament, the only important detail not appearing on the head first described. Otherwise the second head is much simpler. In Fig. 256 is seen the most characteristic profile of the jaws, with the lower one short and horizontal and the upper one

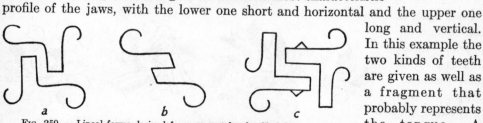

FIG. 259.—Lineal forms derived from serpent heads, Cholula pottery.

long and vertical. In this example the two kinds of teeth are given as well as a fragment that probably represents the tongue. A double fang issues from the back of the mouth. The circular body over the eye may represent a displaced ear plug.

[1] Miss Breton, 1906, makes comparisons.

Four highly modified serpent heads are shown in Fig. 257. The teeth survive in almost every case. The first example, *a*, shows the eye, the nose scroll and the ear ornament, in addition to the fully distended jaws. In the second case, *b*, the jaws are in evidence, together with two teeth and three round bodies of uncertain provenance. The two last examples are much more complicated, and some of the features are to be identified only with difficulty.

Another kind of modification is seen in Fig. 258 where the principle of assemblage is the swastika. A circular eye is placed in the center and enclosing this are two heads back to back, one being inverted. The alternating lower and upper jaws, each with its terminal hook, thus form the arms of the swastika. A single molar tooth appears on each side. A variation of this motive is given by Batres.[1]

FIG. 260. — Serpent drawn in curvilinear style: Codex Vaticanus, 3773.

Fig. 259 shows the characteristic serpent profile reduced to a line motive and manipulated by opposition and combination.

In the later drawings of the Aztec period, particularly those of the codices, the serpents show commonplace conventionalisms. Fig. 260 reproduces a rattlesnake with a winding body. The supraorbital plate is well marked. The opposite development of angularity is seen in Fig. 261. A double-headed serpent, the body making a sort of bowl,[2] is given in the next example (Fig. 262).

Serpent heads painted on ancient pottery of northern Vera Cruz are reproduced in Fig. 263. These show similarities on the one hand to the Cholula examples already given and on the other to the drawings of the Maya area. The curious scroll

FIG. 261. — Serpent head, drawn in angular style: Codex Vaticanus, 3773.

FIG. 262. — Double-headed serpent forming a bowl: Codex Vaticanus, 3773.

designs on stone yokes frequently show more or less similarity to Maya art in the choice of characteristic reptilian lines and curves (Fig. 264). Realistic details also give evidence of affiliations. Note particularly the shape of the supraorbital plate of the head given in Fig. 265.

Certain interesting sculptures from the State of Guerrero with intrusive serpentine features have recently been described,[3] and these will likewise be found to have points of resemblance to the art of the Maya, more in the processes and the subject matter than in the general appearance of the designs. Serpent forms occur very widely in Mexico, but in many regions are represented in a manner so simple and direct that the figures offer no proof of cultural contact.

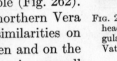

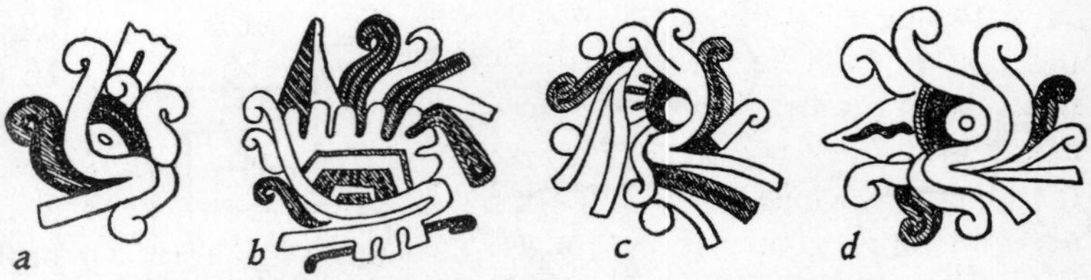

FIG. 263. — Serpent heads painted on pottery from the State of Vera Cruz.

[1] Batres, 1888, pl. 14.　　[2] Gordon, 1905, pl. 4 and Spinden, 1911, pp. 53–54.　　[3] Spinden, 1911, pp. 47–55.

As regards other subjects than the serpent there are also evidences of the debt due to the Maya by the other nations of Mexico and Central America. The foreshortening of the human body when shown in a seated position and in low relief is a case in point. Fig. 266 reproduces one of the human figures on the temple at Xochicalco, in which this pose is used. The drawing of the human eye with a straight line at the top might also be cited. This feature may be studied to advantage in the Codex Nuttall and other ancient manuscripts from the southern part of Mexico.[1]

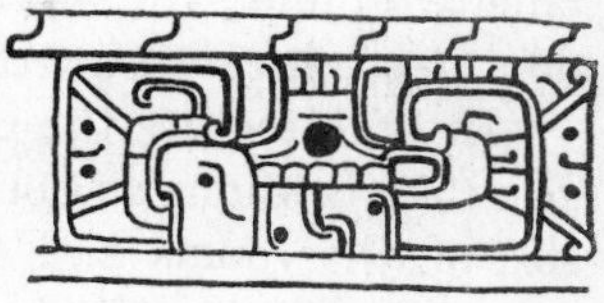

FIG. 264. — Detail of stone yoke from State of Vera Cruz.

In the representations of birds, jaguars, monkeys, etc., there are also many evidences of cultural connections. The same may be said of ceremonial regalia and sacred objects. The peculiar staff ending in a hand (Fig. 211) has already been mentioned as occurring in both the Dresden Codex and the Codex Borgia.

In his various commentaries on Mexican codices Dr. Seler has pointed out many seeming parallels in the religion of the Nahua and the Maya, basing his conclusions largely on evidence furnished by graphic art. For instance, representations of the Shell God and the Bat God occur in both areas and certain complicated passages in the codices of both areas refer to the planet Venus.

FIG. 265. — Reptile head on stone yoke from Vera Cruz.

Without belittling the established work of the eminent scientist mentioned above, it seems necessary to point out that it is very unsafe to assume subjective identities from objective similarities, and it is not too much to say that this practice has played altogether too great a part in the attempted elucidation of the ancient manuscripts. Most of the detailed accounts of religious beliefs and ceremonies that have come down to us refer primarily to the Valley of Mexico, while nearly all the really elaborate codices of a religious nature come from either the Zapotecan-Mixtecan area or from the Maya. So the situation is complicated by chronological, linguistic and environmental conditions when an attempt is made to apply Nahua names to Zapotecan deities and then to make general comparisons with the theology of the Maya. Real cultural connections seldom amount to identities.

Chronological Sequence of Art in Mexico. Having treated thus briefly the general subject of connections in art between the Maya and their western neighbors, there remain one or two points that deserve more specific notice. While it is too early to

FIG. 266.—Human figure Xochicalco.

attempt more than a tentative classification of artistic remains in Mexico upon a chronological basis, still a few facts which seem significant may be emphasized. The correlation may at least prove suggestive.

It has already been stated that the ruins of Monte Alban, near Oaxaca City, seem to show fairly close affiliation with the Maya, presumably of the earlier

[1] For a classification of the ancient manuscripts belonging to southern Mexico see Lehmann, 1905, a.

period. At this important site there are stelae and other large blocks of stone carved with rather crude figures of men, monkeys, and composite animals. These stones also carry columns of glyphs, which present a striking superficial resemblance to those of the Maya. The numbers are expressed in the bar and dot system. The pottery heads from Monte Alban likewise resemble Maya work. Many of the jadeite amulets found there follow the southern model. Some of these were doubtless obtained in trade.

In architecture the great use of lofty pyramids arrayed around plazas suggests connections as does the occurrence of small vaulted chambers. The small size of the rooms and the absence of columnar support may fairly be taken as good evidence of early date. The apparent absence of the ball court is also worthy of note. This structure, as we have seen, is absent from the early Maya sites, but appears at a later date in northern Yucatan and upon the highlands of Guatemala. In the Zapotecan region it is found at Quie-ngola according to the authority of Dr. Seler.[1] We may make a supposition — subject, of course, to future proof for or against — that Monte Alban was synchronous to the first great Maya cities or slightly subsequent. It was abandoned and in ruins when the Spaniards entered the country.

Mitla, on the other hand, apparently lasted down into the Aztec period. It was, perhaps, captured by the warlike Mexicans in 1495. The well-preserved buildings of this city, with their rich mosaic decoration in many geometric patterns, are too well known to require description. The style is peculiar and is found elsewhere only in a few nearby tombs of the cruciform type. The technique of these mosaic decorations is very close to that used on the buildings of northern Yucatan, although the subject matter is fairly distinct. The rooms are rather wide and in one important instance stone columns were used as a supplementary roof support. The doorways are also wide, this being accomplished by the use of piers. Very little in the way of pottery has been found at Mitla. None of the elaborate Zapotecan funeral urns have been discovered in the tombs although fragments of these vessels may be picked up in the fields. Perhaps the most important criteria of age at Mitla are the remains of fresco paintings.[2] These resemble very closely, both in style and subject matter, the finer Mexican codices. As before remarked, most of these codices were doubtless obtained in southern Mexico. At the advent of the Spaniards nearly all of this region was under the dominion of the Aztecs. The frescos of Santa Rita in British Honduras resemble in many details the frescos of Mitla.

So much for the two chronological extremes of culture. The rich development of Zapotecan ceramic art, as evidenced by the funeral urns of Xoxo and Cuilapa, probably falls after the period of Monte Alban and before that of Mitla. The modeling of the figures, and particularly the faces, is superb and the art of Mitla shows nothing that would have led up to this splendid development. The subject matter is various, but in many instances the human faces are masked in what seems to be a long-nosed grotesque face of serpent origin, not very different from the Long-nosed God of the Maya.

It seems quite likely that careful comparison would result in the arrangement of Zapotecan sculptures in a natural series showing development analogous to that at Copan. There is a marked difference between certain groups of sculp-

[1] Seler, 1902–1908, II, p. 191.   [2] Seler, 1895, a.

tured stones at Monte Alban.[1] In the best of these pieces there is used a characteristic assemblage of details that likewise occurs on small sculptured slabs from Etla,[2] Zachila, Tlacolula[3] and Cuilapa. Pottery urns of the elaborate funeral type are rare at Monte Alban, but are found in quantity at the sites just named. A transition from stone art to ceramic art is clearly indicated on many of the clay tablets, urns and figurines. The last decadent stage of hieroglyphic inscriptions may perhaps be seen in the curious lintels of Xoxo and Cuilapa. It seems impossible that these inscriptions could have had meanings. They resemble the purely decorative glyphs on some Maya pottery. One of the pottery pieces in the Sologuren collection[4] represents a temple in clay showing the use of offset paneling so highly developed at Mitla[5] but without geometric enrichment. From this incomplete presentation it is evident that whether the conclusions here set down are true or false, yet the archaeology of southern Mexico contains promise of great results and the life history of Zapotecan art is there for the reading.

Little is known of the art of Tonala,[6] a large ruin west of Tehuantepec and near the Pacific, but the few pieces that have been reproduced suggest the early work of Monte Alban. On the basis of the beautiful pottery with codex-like figures one is tempted to put a late date on the Mixtecan city of Nochistlan.

Farther to the north we come to the famous center whence radiated the culture of the Aztecs and their predecessors, the Toltecs. In the Valley of Mexico the succession is capable of more exact demonstration than in Oaxaca, although there are many important points still undecided and although a chronology expressed in years is a thing for the future.

Mrs. Nuttall has collected a great deal of material upon the earliest known horizon of culture in the Valley of Mexico. Bishop Plancarte has also been industrious in this field. Through collaboration with Mr. Juan E. Reyna the writer was introduced into this new and exciting study.

In 1910 many figurines of a peculiar type appeared on the curio market in Mexico City. They were obtained at Atzcapatzalco, a suburb of the capital, and a place famous in pre-Cortesian annals. At Atzcapatzalco[7] there are remains of several earthen mounds bearing relics of the Aztec and pre-Aztec periods. From these mounds have come some of the most beautiful figurines in Mexico, representing richly attired human beings, birds, monkeys, etc. The level plain also contains relic beds which have been exposed at several points by the pits of adobe and gravel gatherers.

The stratification of the plain is as follows. First comes a layer of alluvial soil some four or five feet in thickness, which towards the bottom seems to be impregnated with a whitish volcanic ash. This layer contains many sharp-edged fragments of pottery, including parts of bowls, figurines, whistles, flageolets, pipes, etc. The ware runs the gamut of the different styles of paste and ornamentation found in the neighboring sites of Teotihuacan, Tezcuco and Tenoch-

---

[1] Compare Batres, 1902, a, pls. 5 and 6 on the one hand with pls. 2 and 9 on the other, and great improvement will be noted.

[2] Seler, C., 1900, pl. 8.

[3] Seler, E., 1902–1908, II, pp. 359–361.

[4] Batres, 1902, a, pl. 25.

[5] Saville, 1909, p. 189, holds that Mitla was built by the Nahua and later was conquered by the Zapotecans.

[6] Seler, C., 1900, pp. 110–115.

[7] Mr. William Niven of Mexico City has written a number of articles in the Mexican Herald concerning the relic beds of Atzcapatzalco. Dr. Seler, in a paper which has just appeared, 1912, comments on the occurrence of the figurines of the oldest type and presents photographs of them.

titlan. Most of the ware is painted, some is rough and some is highly polished, and many of the vessels have tripod supports.

Underneath the alluvial layer which contains these objects lies a thick stratum of coarse water-bearing gravel mixed with sand. In some places this gravel layer is fifteen or eighteen feet in depth. Throughout this layer are found figurines and potsherds quite different in material and appearance from the relics in the upper bed. The material is a very hard terra cotta containing a large percentage of volcanic ash. The objects are nearly all waterworn and comprise

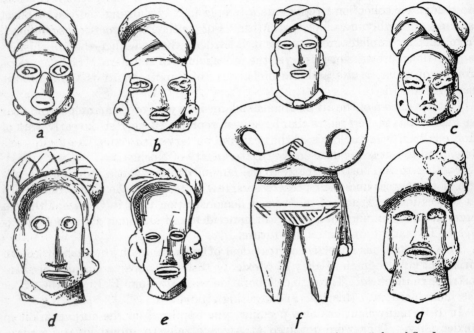

Fig. 267. — Figurines from the earliest culture horizon in Mexico: *a–c*, Atzcapatzalco; *d*, San Juan Teotihuacan; *e*, Tuxpan; *f*, Zapotlan; *g*, Cuernavaca.

figurines, disk-shaped labrets, bulbous resonator whistles, and fragments of bowls with constricted necks and globular bodies. The figurines are usually three or four inches in length. They are naively realistic and often represent nude women in sitting or standing positions with the hands upon the knees or under the breasts. Other figures represent men. The limbs are well rounded, but taper off so much that the hands and feet are much too small. The faces are characteristically long and the heads are of slight depth. The eyes are often tilted, Chinese fashion, and are made by a groove across an applied nodule of clay or by one or more gougings. The headdresses are usually of the fillet type made with little rolls of clay (Fig. 267, *a–c*).

It is probable that the scientific excavation of these beds would show a more exact and detailed stratification of remains than is here given.

It is interesting to note that Mr. Holmes [1] examined in 1884 the stratification of the remains of human handiwork in another part of Mexico City. He describes with great accuracy the superposition of the various ceramic types. Apparently

[1] Holmes, 1885.

none of the early figurines came to his notice, but the round-bodied bowls with constricted necks are mentioned.[1]

Figurines of the same strongly individualized type, referred to above, are found widely in the Valley of Mexico and in the country to the south and west. They are found, for instance, in considerable numbers in an adobe yard on the outskirts of Cuernavaca (Fig. 267, g), associated with the globular pottery. Fragments of the pottery are very plentiful in the extensive lava caves near the same city. A number of these hollow lava flumes were explored in 1910 by Mr. Reyna and the writer, and in addition to the pottery fragments there were found rough beads of green stone and pieces of shell that had evidently served as ornaments. Some of the pottery was ornamented with applied nodules of clay. Hollow tripod supports occur on the early ware.

Perhaps the most interesting point in regard to this early type of art is its obvious relationship to the elaborate funeral pottery coming from Tepic, Colima and western Jalisco. The large hollow figures from this region represent human beings, both men and women, usually engaged in every-day occupations. The expression of the peculiarly long faces with their staring eyes gives a definite character to this ancient art. The reproduction of native ornament is very complete; ear and nose ornaments, facial and body decorations that suggest tattooing, and even textile designs are given by plastic and painted additions to the figures. A very interesting series of specimens, now in the American Museum of Natural History, has been described by Lumholtz.[2] The finest pieces came from Iztlan, and were taken from a burial mound of which Dr. Seler[3] gives a plan.

Small solid figurines, almost identical with those of Atzcapatzalco are found in the same area. Fig. 267, f, reproduces one of four similar pieces from Zapotlan and a head from Tuxpan is shown in e. Dr. Seler[4] presents drawings of three typical specimens.

Figurines of this sort, although they are commonly called Tarascan, occur but rarely in the Tarascan territory. They are not associated with extensive architectural remains. It has been possible to find no detail suggesting cultural connection with the Maya. The headdresses never show, for instance, the natural or conventionalized representation of an animal head inclosing the human head. In this regard the figurines should be distinguished from those of the Totonacan area which resemble them in method of manufacture but which show highly modified animal headdresses.

It is possible that the culture briefly considered above may have continued to flourish in the far northwest after it had been displaced in the Valley of Mexico. The next definite culture in the northwestern frontier had its center somewhat farther to the north, and comprised the important cities of La Quemada,[5] Chalchihuites,[6] Totoate,[7] Estanzuela,[8] etc. At most of these sites are found extensive architectural remains including pyramidal mounds, retaining walls and wide rooms with rows of columns.

[1] Holmes, 1885, p. 73.
[2] Lumholtz, 1902, II, pp. 300–315.
[3] Seler, 1902–1908, III, p. 93.
[4] Seler, 1902–1908, III, p. 94.
[5] Bancroft, 1875–1876, IV, pp. 578–592; Batres, 1903; Seler, 1902–1908, III, pp. 545–559.
[6] A fine collection excavated by Mr. Gamio is in the Museo Nacional in Mexico City.
[7] The collection made by Dr. Hrdlička is in the American Museum of Natural History.
[8] The remarkable pottery from this site has been briefly described by Lumholtz, 1902, II, pp. 460–462 and pls. 13–15. The collection is in the American Museum of Natural History.

The most peculiar art objects are pottery vessels with encaustic or cloisonné decorations. The vessels were apparently fired in the usual manner and then covered with a thick layer of greenish or blackish sizing. This sizing was then cut away with a sharp implement to form a background for complicated geometric and realistic designs, after the fashion of a stencil. The spaces cut away were then filled in flush with paints of various colors so that the whole surface resembled a sort of mosaic. The different inlaid colors were divided off from each other by narrow strips of the original sizing material, so that there resulted a superficial resemblance to cloisonné work. Of course there was no enameling.

The culture of these cities may have been an offshoot of the pre-Aztec or Toltec. The rows of columns suggest this. The encaustic pottery resembles the fine fresco vases of the artists of Tula and Teotihuacan although the technique is really different.[1] At any rate this culture disappeared before the advent of the Spaniards.

Following this there seems to have arisen a new civilization, identified with the Tarascans of Michoacan and various Nahua tribes isolated from those of the Valley of Mexico. The Tarascan mounds are of peculiar shapes [2] and the finest art products are in clay and metal. The stone work, as a rule, is very crude.[3]

The Chacmool type of reclining figure [4] is an interesting detail connecting the art of this area with the thirteenth century products of the Valley of Mexico that were introduced, as we have seen, into Chichen Itza.

Returning to the Valley of Mexico to consider the art that followed the archaic figurines, already described, we find ourselves both helped and hindered by the preserved traditions. The problem here is capable of being solved with the greatest accuracy, but in order to do this much tedious work must be done in comparing and classifying pottery collections. The larger part of the specimens in our museums were not excavated by archaeologists, and in many cases the exact localities are unknown. However, certain peculiar styles of pottery are now pretty well established, as, for instance, the beautiful vases of Teotihuacan [5] and Tula, which after being burned were covered with a heavy white sizing and then painted in delicate colors. Following this comes the polychrome pottery of Cholula and finally the fine Aztec pieces found on the site of the Great Temple in Mexico City. Still other types might be mentioned. The miniature pottery heads should prove important for purposes of classification. The stone sculptures of the early period are few in number but many are still *in situ*, and so are of great value as definite standards of comparison. There is a great need of more archaeological work. Even the important ruins of Teotihuacan are but imperfectly known. The ruins of Xochicalco have been studied in the most superficial way, and not even the ground-plans of the buildings are available for purposes of comparison. The single well-preserved temple forms a very small part of this remarkable site. Excavations might show that this city is even more ancient than Tula and Teotihuacan.

The type of art from the Aztec period is fairly well determined through the

[1] Undoubted examples of this ware have been found in the Valley of Mexico, however. For a remarkable piece see Charnay, 1885, p. 142, and Peñafiel, 1890, pls. 62 and 63. An example in the American Museum of Natural History came from Atzcapotzalco.

[2] Seler, 1902–1908, III, pp. 127–128.
[3] Lumholtz, 1902, II, pp. 331–452, makes many references to the archaeology.
[4] Lumholtz, 1902, II, p. 451.
[5] Peñafiel, 1890, pls. 74–75.

finds that have taken place in Mexico City.[1] Tenochtitlan was founded about 1325, and its period of real greatness did not begin till nearly a hundred years later. Consequently the sculptures that have been recovered are exceedingly valuable as standards of comparison. Sculptures of the same type are found to have followed the Aztec rule into the region toward the south and east. In the south, for instance, we have Aztec sculptures at Tehuacan,[2] and in the east at Teayo.[3]

An examination of the remains in Tamaulipas and Vera Cruz shows a very confusing condition. At the north, in southern Tamaulipas, the Huasteca[4] developed a somewhat peculiar art in stone characterized by crouching and humpedback figures which lack practically every quality found in the sculptures of their kindred to the south. The pottery is more interesting and more peculiar. The finest specimens, of which there are several examples in the Peabody Museum, have narrow necks and flaring sides fluted like melons. Farther to the south, in the Totonacan[5] area, some of the pottery designs suggest Maya influence in minor details. This is particularly true of the ware from the Island of Sacrifices.[6] The use in stone sculptures of reptilian lines and curves recalling Maya handiwork has already been mentioned. It is best seen on the remarkable stone yokes, paddle-shaped stones, etc., and on large sculptured stones at Papantla.[7] The late intrusion of Aztec art is seen in well-preserved sculptures of Teayo.[8] Intrusion of Nahua culture at a somewhat earlier period may perhaps be seen in the Chac-mool figure at the Totonacan capital, Cempoalam.[9] Maya influence may be discernible in the more southerly stelae-like sculptures of Tepatlaxco,[10] Quilozintla[11] and Alvarado.[12] The use of bar and dot numerals on the sculptured boulders of Maltrata[13] furnish a suggestive detail. It will be remembered that bars and dots are found likewise at Monte Alban. This method of notation, so much more economical than the one in common use among the Nahua, was only employed in a few of the Mexican codices, particularly in those of the Fejérváry-Mayer group.

From this survey and attempted correlation of ancient Mexican art one thing at least is evident. There is no good reason to ascribe a northern (or western) origin to Maya art because in the north the art in the earliest period is independent of the Maya in all particulars; in the middle period the current set from the Maya towards the people of lower culture on the highlands of Mexico, and only in the last decadent period did influence from the Nahua make itself felt among the Maya.

Problems of Cultural Connection outside of Mexico. In concluding this study of Maya art a brief space may be devoted to certain general problems of cultural contact more or less remotely relating to the civilization developed by the Maya. The writer does not care to dignify by refutation the numerous empty theories[14] of ethnic connections between Central America and the Old

[1] Peñafiel, 1911; Batres, 1902, b; Seler, 1901, b.

[2] Seler, 1902–1908, III, pp. 788–789.

[3] Seler, 1904; another site is Xico, Fewkes, 1903–1904, pp. 245–248.

[4] Seler, 1888, b; Prieto, 1873, pp. 10–57; Fewkes, 1903–1904, pp. 271–284 and pls. 126–129.

[5] Fewkes, 1903–1904, pp. 233–244 and pls. 112–125; Strebel, 1883 and 1885. Batres, 1908, pls. 3–44.

[6] Nuttall, 1910, pls. 7–14.

[7] Seler, 1906, a.

[8] Seler, 1904.

[9] Drawing by Velasco in Museo Nacional referred to above.

[10] Batres, 1905, pl. 1, Seler, 1906, b.

[11] Batres, 1905, pl. 9; Seler, 1906, b; Fewkes, 1906.

[12] Batres, 1905, pp. 17–18.

[13] Batres, 1905, pls. 6 and 7.

[14] For a spirited reply to these theories see Brinton, 1894.

World, but to treat only the questions of cultural ramifications in the New World. Many devotees to this subject have unfortunately confused the ethnological problem of the origin and growth of human cultures with the zoological problem of the origin and dispersion of human kind. The species, man, may have originated in India or where you will. From this unknown center he spread abroad like the fox and the deer till he reached the ends of the earth. We cannot prove that before leaving his first home he had developed a single art. The most suggestive evidence of the antiquity of man in the New World is the vast number of distinct languages spoken by the aborigines, and the marked diversity of physical types. As for any particular kind of culture, it is comparatively short-lived and impermanent. The Maya culture is perhaps the oldest concerning which we have accurate evidence and yet the beginnings of this culture may not antedate the Christian era by more than a few centuries. Every group of human beings has the common inheritance of a tendency and a power to form and reform complex habits partly controlled by environment, and other natural conditions. Very often the phenomenon is presented of two groups of people who speak the same language and yet have different cultures or the obverse of two or more tribes who speak different languages and yet have similar religious, social, utilitarian and esthetic institutions. As for identities or similarities in ideas or artifacts between two or more culture areas, there are several possible explanations among which that of actual transmission is often the least likely.

One group of theories aims to connect Mexico and Central America with Peru and other South American centers. A second group tries to establish a community of interest between the so-called Mound-builders of the Mississippi Valley and the Southeastern States, the ancient and present-day Pueblo Indians of the Southwest and the civilizations of Mexico and Central America. The evidence deserves to be examined in some detail. Perhaps at the end of this examination the subject will be as open to futile speculation as at the beginning. The three principal lines of proof concern:

1st. Pyramids and other features of material culture.

2nd. Religious ideas connected with the serpent.

3rd. Similarities in symbolism and art.

Pyramids. The building of square-base pyramids had a notable distribution among the ancient centers of high culture both in the Old and in the New World. In the Old World, the most famous examples are the pyramids of Egypt. These pyramids were used primarily as tombs and as such seem to have been a development of the mastaba. They were built during the early dynasties and were later supplanted by other forms. The pyramids of Assyria were, however, intended to bear temple structures upon their flat summits. They rose in a succession of vertical steps or sloping terraces and were ascended by zigzag inclined planes or ramps and not directly by stairways. Owing to the lack of stone, Assyrian pyramids were built of sun-dried bricks. Except in the matter of stairways and methods of construction the pyramids of Assyria were not dissimilar from those of Mexico and Central America. Superficial resemblances might also be noted in the assemblage of rooms in the palace structures and in the marked use of inclosed courts.

Pyramidal substructures, or at least solid interior cores in the form of the stepped pyramid, were also used by the temple builders of the Far East. **Dr.**

Leemans has described, in an elaborate publication, the great Brahmin temple of Boro Boedoer, in the Island of Java. This temple is distinctly pyramidal in appearance. Somewhat similar temples occur in the highlands of Cambodia, and elsewhere in the Far East.[1]

Passing to the New World, pyramids are found in three large but detached areas: 1st, western Peru and Ecuador; 2nd, Central America and Mexico; 3rd, the Mississippi Valley and the southeastern portion of the United States.

The pyramids of South America cover a large area, the limits of which have never been exactly determined. Throughout this area there are many important ruins which show no remains of pyramids, and the pyramid may be called a secondary phase of Peruvian culture. The pyramids are of several types. Some are natural hills which have been leveled and terraced, some are artificial mounds of sun-dried bricks or of cut stone. The pyramid of the famous Temple of the Sun at Pachacamac,[2] near Lima, is a natural hill which has been terraced with five low, broad steps faced with well constructed walls. The ruins of the temple occupy the crown of the hill. At Vilcas Huaman,[3] situated about half-way between Lima and Cuzco, are remains of a Temple of the Sun, which is carefully oriented although the walls of the neighboring structures show no such alignment. The pyramid rises in three vertical steps admirably constructed of cut stone, and a stairway ascends it on the eastern side. Proceeding northwards, at Huanuco-viejo[4] are found ruins of an extensive city showing careful orientation throughout. The principal temple is marked by a well made platform mound having a broad stairway. The so-called Fort of Huinchuz,[5] in the region of Pomabamba, is really a temple structure. The substructure is not a rectangular pyramid, but a terraced and truncated cone rising in six steps. The great pyramid of Moche,[6] near Trujillo, resembles in plan many of the substructures of Central America. Attached to the base of the pyramid are extensive platform mounds. But the method of construction discloses differences. The pyramid is built of sun-dried bricks arranged in tiers which incline inwards. The structure upon the summit of the pyramid and upon the subjoined platforms have all disappeared. At Coyor,[7] or Incatambo, near Cajamarca in northwestern Peru, there is an oval dome-shaped outcropping of granite, the natural place of refuge in a valley subject to floods. This elevation shows nine concentric artificial terraces. Upon these terraces houses were constructed, and upon the summit a tower-like temple structure was built. There is a lack of references to pyramids in the Calchaqui area and in the southern provinces of the ancient Peruvian empire. No plans or descriptions of pyramids in Ecuador are at hand, but such remains are said to extend well into this country, and may even cross the southern boundary of Colombia.

In other phases of material culture there are but few striking similarities between Peru and Central America. Architecture is very different in the two areas. Metal working, weaving and pottery making, all of which reached a high

[1] The status of art in the great cultural province of southern Asia is remarkably like that of Central America. The civilizations were on nearly the same plane. The life history of this art has never been fully presented although the historical data available are voluminous. Perhaps it is the stupendous nature of the correlation that has prevented the work from being done.

[2] Uhle, 1903, pls. 16 and 17.
[3] Wiener, 1880, pp. 264–272.
[4] Wiener, 1880, pp. 210–217.
[5] Wiener, 1880, pp. 189–191.
[6] Squier, 1877, pp. 130–132.
[7] Wiener, 1880, pp. 130–134.

plane of development in both localities, are sharply distinguishable as regards the technical processes involved and the appearances of the products. The religious and the social organization of Peru is unlike that of the Maya in most respects, and there is evidence that its development was autochthonous and extended over many centuries.[1] The Peruvians had no system of hieroglyphic writing and no carefully elaborated calendar. Certain features of graphic art will be considered separately, but in general this too was peculiar and characteristic of the region.

Pyramidal substructures apparently do not occur in a long stretch of country from the southern part of Colombia to the central part of Honduras and Salvador. Low burial mounds exist, and well to the north there are low platforms which may have served as foundations for temples. Costa Rica has been said to belong ethnographically with South America. But the ancient metal working of northern Colombia and Chiriqui is characterized by the so-called wire technique that does not occur in Peru or Equador, but is common in Guatemala and Mexico. The marked use of tripod and ring-base pottery in the Isthmus region also suggests a northern affinity. Many of the carved celts and amulets of Costa Rica resemble roughly those of western Guatemala.

At the time of the Spanish conquest certain Nahua-speaking peoples [2] inhabited the shores and islands of Lake Nicaragua. These are said to have been emigrants from Anahuac, who left their home at the disruption of the great civilization preceding the Aztecs. The cultural connection of these southern peoples with their linguistic kinsmen of the north can readily be proved by their carvings and pottery decoration. But of the remains great pyramids and platform mounds seem to be wanting. It might be pointed out that such enormous communal structures demanded a greater organization and control of the masses of the people than would be expected among fugitives in a strange land.

In Salvador,[3] along the course of the Lempa River, platform mounds surrounding courts are known to occur and with these is said to be associated characteristic Maya pottery. Squier [4] described with considerable detail the ruins of Tenampua in Central Honduras. Pyramids and platform mounds are much in evidence. Here and at other sites in the Valley of Comayagua, pottery and other artifacts similar to those of Copan and the Uloa River ruins have been found. A number of pieces of pottery from Tenampua, collected by Squier, are in the American Museum of Natural History. Without doubt this settlement marked the real southern frontier of the Maya pyramid and other characteristic phases of Maya culture.

It might be well next to consider the pyramidal substructures of the United States and attempt to approach the Maya area from the north.

The Mound Area of the United States shows several distinct types of mounds and earthworks. Some of the types have a pretty definite limitation to certain parts of the field. Thus nearly all of the effigy mounds lie within the limits of the

---

[1] Uhle, 1902; 1903, pp. 19–45. The line of research is continued in 1904 and 1908, in different localities.

[2] Berendt, 1876, pp. 142–144; Pector, 1888, pp. 152–154; Squier, 1852, II, pp. 309, 332.

[3] Squier discusses the Nahua people of San Salvador, 1858, pp. 316–340, and gives notes on the archaeology, 1858, pp. 341–344. Other brief references are Guzman, 1904, Cruz, 1904, and Gonzales, 1906. By far the most important archaeological results are those of Lehmann, 1910. This article unfortunately came to the attention of the writer too late for fuller reference. Dr. Lehmann refers to sculptures of the Chacmool type, describes pottery, etc., and discusses linguistic and cultural questions.

[4] Squier, 1853 and 1858, pp. 133–139.

State of Wisconsin. To be sure, the famous Serpent Mound is situated in Ohio, but this mound falls in a type by itself. The complicated geometric inclosures, perhaps the most remarkable of all mound remains in the entire area, seem limited to the State of Ohio. Burial mounds, of one type or another, occur over the entire area. Pyramidal mounds likewise have a wide distribution and are common in eastern Missouri and Arkansas and in all the Gulf States with the noteworthy exception of Texas.

Of all these types of mounds only the pyramidal type would suggest any cultural connection with Mexico and Central America. These mounds are not, however, constructed of stone and mortar. They are simply built of earth and provided with ramps or inclined roadways instead of stairways. In plan and assemblage, the mound groups at Cahokia [1] in southern Illinois, at Etowah [2] in northwestern Georgia, and Moundville [3] in Alabama show decided superficial resemblances to mound groups in the Maya and Nahua domains. But these resemblances are not more striking than those furnished by the great structure at Moche in Peru already described, or to go still farther afield, by the ruins at Tello in Chaldea, where there were inclosed courts, platform mounds and seven-storied pyramids.

In other phases of material culture the ancient Mound-builders were far behind the natives of Mexico and Peru. Metal working, for instance, probably did not go beyond simple hammering of native copper. Although many of the artifacts, such as ear plugs and breast ornaments, show very careful manipulation they offer no evidences of casting and smelting. Decoration in metal was accomplished by stenciling and by repoussé work. Pottery and textiles, while developed to a noteworthy degree, can hardly be compared with the products of Mexico and Central America.

A stretch of a thousand miles by the nearest land route separates the southwestern outposts of the Mound Area of the United States and the northeastern point of occurrence of pyramids in Mexico. In all this intervening area there is no record of any culture higher than that of the Athapascan Lipan and the mysterious Jumano. The Indians of Texas and of southern Chihuahua are reported to have been completely nomadic and much given to savage warfare.

Indeed, the debatable land is not passed till we reach the territory of the Huasteca in southern Tamaulipas and northern Vera Cruz. These Indians, as we have seen, are linguistically related to the Maya and culturally bound to the civilizations of Mexico. They are lords of the northern marches. Characteristic remains of this region have been described by Prieto, Fewkes and others. Pyramidal foundations mark the sites of the ancient temples.

The most northern ruins on the uplands that clearly lay within the sphere of influence of the Valley of Mexico are those of La Quemada and Chalchihuites in the State of Zacatecas. These ruins, and a number of others in the valley of the Boloños and perhaps extending as far southward as Sayula, give evidence of a fairly distinct and localized culture. The most striking feature of this culture is a peculiar type of pottery decorated with heavily inlaid paints. It has been called encaustic or cloisonné pottery,[4] and it occurs rarely in other parts of

[1] Bushnell, 1904, p. 8.
[2] Thomas, 1890–1891, pp. 292–311.
[3] Moore, 1907, map.
[4] Lumholtz, 1902, II, pp. 460 et seq.

Mexico where it may have passed in trade. The architecture shows the use of columns, built up by slabs of stone, which probably supported flat roofs.

North of these outposts stretch several hundred miles of arid desert before the ruined pueblos of the Casas Grandes in the State of Chihuahua are reached. These prehistoric ruins are commonly considered to mark a southern extension of the great Pueblo culture which apparently centered in the States of Arizona and New Mexico, and spread to the north and to the south. There is good reason to believe that all the essential features of the Pueblo culture are indigenous.

It has been pretty definitely established by traditions and by similarities in material culture that the so-called Cliff-dwellers, as well as the builders of the numerous prehistoric structures in the open country, were merely the ancestors of the present-day Pueblo Indians. A careful comparison of pottery fabrics and architectural details throughout the area would probably demonstrate a definite cultural sequence extending over a long period of time. In fact, the researches of Mr. A. V. Kidder along this line have already borne interesting results.

No pyramidal substructures have been reported from any part of the Pueblo area. Bandelier describes [1] some interesting mounds at the Casas Grandes but does not venture the assertion that they served as substructures for temples. However, there were doubtless trade relations between the Pueblo Indians and the tribes in Mexico far to the south. Copper bells have been found at Casas Grandes and at Pueblo Bonito. At the latter site was found a fragment of encaustic or cloisonné pottery which seems to be identical with the typical pottery of La Quemada and Chalchihuites. This object, the significance of which has apparently been overlooked, is now in the American Museum of Natural History. It may serve as an important clue to the comparative chronology of the ruins of Mexico and New Mexico. The atlatl, or spear-thrower, found by Cushing in a pueblo ruin is an additional evidence of trade contact. This implement is not in use by the present-day Pueblo Indians.

Religious Ideas connected with the Serpent. It is well known that the serpent plays an important part in mythology, religion and art, the world over. To the primitive man the serpent naturally represents a great division of animal life. There are quadrupeds and bipeds, including men and birds. Then there are snakes which have no legs at all. Primitive art often lacks in any closer classification of animal life than this, so that the snake is apt to receive an undeserved emphasis in pictographs and designs. The gracefulness and simplicity of the snake's body render it an easy subject for the artist.

The body of the snake combines readily in art with certain characteristic parts of other animals. Wings, horns, feathers and claws are often seen on the grotesque and almost universal " dragons " which result from such combination. Sphinxes and griffins which lack snake features belong to the same category of unnatural beasts made by combination. Snakes and other animals are sometimes given human features according to several processes which have already been briefly discussed. This change is probably due to animistic beliefs — in particular to the application in art of what has been called the pathetic fallacy which endows lower forms of life with the spiritual and mental qualities of human beings.

[1] Bandelier, 1892, p. 550.

But the religious importance of the serpent, while considerable, is very much over emphasized by the devotees of the mystic and occult philosophies. Rarely indeed is serpent worship more than a secondary phase of any religion. When present at all it is often elaborated in art beyond its proper religious significance owing to the artistic possibilities of the subject. In many regions the importance of the serpent in religion has been assumed without good reason from its presence in art and in other regions from incidents given in the mythologies.

The serpent, usually modified by certain unnatural additions, is seen in art over a great portion of North and South America, as well as in the Old World. In mythology it may be found with similar unnatural features among nearly all the Indian tribes of the United States even where no drawings of it are made. Thus Goddard gives myths of the Indians of northern California concerning a horned snake. A similar monster, possessing antlers, and sometimes wings, is also very common in Algonkin and Iroquois legends although rare in art. As a rule among these tribes the horned serpent is a water spirit and an enemy of the thunder bird. It is important to note that the religious importance is not very great — at any rate the magical snake does not rise to the level of a culture hero.[1] In some regions the creature is considered friendly to man and in other regions decidedly unfriendly.

Among the Pueblo Indians the horned snake seems to have considerable prestige in the religious belief.[2] This prestige comes from its connection with water, the great necessity of these people. In this region it is represented on the ceremonial objects but not on the objects of every-day use. Information gathered at the different pueblos concerning the horned and plumed serpent varies in many details. As a rule, it is held that only one such serpent exists and that it is invisible. It lives in the water or in the sky and is connected with rain and lightning. There seems to be more or less of a taboo placed upon the use of the name for this serpent.

Symbolism and Art. Postponing for a moment the subject of the serpent, let us now consider some of the more general questions of cultural affiliation where decorative and pictographic art furnish the evidence. The last group of facts supposedly connecting the cultures of Central America with those in other parts of the New World concerns similarities in symbolism and graphic art.

Similarities in symbolism are always of doubtful value because the symbols are usually simple geometric forms and the authoritative interpretation of them which might furnish convincing proof of ethnic affinity is usually wanting.[3] Variations of the " ring and cross " symbol, for instance, do occur throughout all the ancient cultures of North America as well as among the modern Indians. But, for that matter, they are universal. The circle frequently represents the sun, and the cross the four directions, an idea directly derived from the sun. However, it is quite possible that the symbol may represent in some regions something quite different, — or, for that matter, it may represent nothing at all and have no use other than to embellish. It is clear that some of the so-called "cosmic

[1] Hewitt, 1889.
[2] For general accounts see Fewkes, 1894, a; 1895, a.
[3] The symbolism of skulls and bones can hardly be called esoteric, but such symbols as the hand with the eye in the palm, so common in the ancient art of the Southern States, are distinctly esoteric. The disassociated features, however, might occur anywhere.

symbols " that occur among the Maya represent definite ideas that have little to do with the cosmos as a whole.[1] The normal form of the Sun and Venus glyphs[2] are cases in point. These have already been discussed. An example of similarity in form with difference in meaning is seen in two figures given by Professor Putnam and Mr. Willoughby.[3] One is a design on a shell gorget from Tennessee which has been explained as symbolic of the universe, and the other, from Mexico, is the Nahua hieroglyph for gold.

Little reliance can be placed upon the presence of similar geometric motives to show connection between two regions when the bond is not strongly indicated by other features. The scroll, the fret, the guilloche, the swastika, the stepped pyramid, etc., occur among practically all the high cultures of the world. They form either singly or in combination the universal basis for conventionalization. In many cases they were originally developed through suggestions furnished by the structural limitations of basketry and weaving and were later transferred to other arts.

Realistic art may show relationships between two cultures principally through peculiarities in representation such as mutual deviations from the normal form of the object represented. Similarities in conventionalized art are much more significant than those of purely realistic art, but even here it is not safe to assume that they indicate transmission of ideas from one region to another. Conventionalized art is made by the amalgamation of geometric and realistic motives and since both of these original factors are liable to be the same in two areas, and since the controlling technique, as in textiles, is apt to impose the same restrictions to growth, it follows that similarities may be extended to the two independent products. Since the idealistic modification of natural forms is based upon more or less constant methods of imaginative reconstruction it must be evident that similarities in this phase of art are not necessarily proof of contact.

The examples of representative art which have been most frequently taken to show cultural affiliations in the New World are those which present the modified serpent which has already been discussed. Here again we will cast a quick glance over analogous subjects in Old World art. The reason these foreign analogies are given is to vitiate the apparent importance of the similarities in New World art. If the facts submitted prove anything they prove too much. Everyone is willing to admit the basic physical and psychical unity of man but few will admit the cultural unity.

Many of the ancient temples of India, Burmah, Java, Cambodia, etc., show a high development of the serpent in architectural embellishment. There are great diversity of treatment and a few rather close parallels to Maya art. As a rule the snake body is a simple winding motive completely overlaid by arabesque designs. The idealism does not seem to have led to even partial anthropomorphism although this is clearly shown in the case of the elephant. The hooded cobra is the snake most frequently represented and the single body often ends in a number of heads in accordance with the East Indian method of multiplying arms, legs, and heads upon the bodies of divinities. The Chinese dragon has a composite origin to which the serpent contributes. The closest parallel to Maya art in the ideal

[1] For a discussion of "symbols" in Mexican art see Preuss, 1901. Mrs. Nuttall, 1901, a, has also covered this subject.

[2] The normal or "cosmic" form of the Sun

glyph, probably, has a phonetic value in at least two of the "direction" glyphs. Bowditch, 1910, p. 255.

[3] Putnam and Willoughby, 1895, p. 321, Fig. 31.

development of the serpent is seen in Egypt. Representations of winged serpents occur in connection with a number of the Egyptian deities such as the Goddess Mersokan and the Goddess Ranne. Anthropomorphism of serpents also occurs as may be seen by the examples given by Cooper.[1]

Winged serpents occur in Greek mythology in connection, for instance, with the chariot of Demeter. A partial humanization of the serpent is seen in some of the monstrous creations. Monsters with human head and torso and with serpent legs are depicted; and

Fig. 268. — Design on interior of a bowl from Calchaqui area.

various conceptions of Medusa with snakes for locks of hair. Nowhere in the Old World is found the subtle and spiritual conception that existed among the Maya. The human head in the reptile mouth to indicate the innate human intelligence is found only in Mexico and Central America.

The general distribution of the serpent in the mythology and art of the New World has already been given. Let us now consider some of its representations beginning in the Far South. It is well known that the cultural remains of the ancient Calchaqui people of Argentina have many superficial resemblances to the artifacts of the Mound-builders and the Pueblo Indians of the United States. Snakes, with or without horn-like appendages to the head, are common in decoration of the pottery, a fair example being presented in Fig. 268, sketched from a bowl in the Field Museum. Ambrosetti[2] has treated the subject with some detail.

The serpent forms a minor motive in the exuberant decorative art of Peru. The most striking representations of it are found painted on pottery vessels from Chimbote. The serpent of Chimbote has a head that in profile view resembles that of a dog with ears erect. When the head is represented in top view the likeness to a dog's head largely disappears (Figs. 269, a and b). Composite and grotesque animals with reptilian features also occur in this area.

Fig. 269.—Snakes on vessels from Chimbote, Peru.

A splendid piece of textile art from Pachacamac that was unearthed by Uhle[3] has two rectangular panels of design each showing a human figure framed in on either side by snakes that issue from belt and headdress or are held in the hands. A small portion of this fabric is reproduced in Fig. 270 to illustrate how the reaction of textile art upon a natural form has produced a type of conventionalized head similar to some found in Central America: note the turned-back nose.

Fig. 270. — Detail of textile design: Pachacamac, Peru.

[1] Cooper, W. R., 1873. It is difficult to find any except incidental references to the serpent in art in the works of recognized merit dealing with classical archaeology. The writer does not feel justified in going deeply into the subject.

[2] Ambrosetti, 1896 and 1899.

[3] Uhle, 1903, pl. 5.

A unit of design on a polychrome vase from Pachacamac is given in Fig. 271.
A fine lot of painted pottery vessels from Nasca in southern Peru is in the
Peabody Museum. Many of the complicated designs on these objects seem
to represent some sort of reptile largely overlaid with simplified faces that might well be human.

Fig. 271. — Painted de-
sign on pottery vessel:
Pachacamac.

The decorative art of Ecuador, Colombia and Costa
Rica seems to offer little evidence that can be construed
to indicate affiliations with Mexico. On the basis of well
developed local styles this stretch of country may be divided into many art provinces. There is, however, plenty
of evidence of interchange of products and designs within
short distances. Serpents of gold with horns or feathers
attached to the head have been found in the sacred lakes
of the Colombian highlands.

The purlieus of northern art include, however, parts of Nicaragua. The
serpent heads that decorate some of the finer pieces of pottery (Fig. 272) may
easily claim a Maya or Nahua ancestry. More convincing proof is furnished

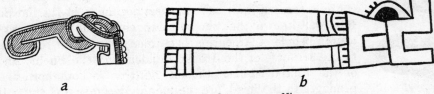

a   b

Fig. 272. — Serpent heads on pottery: Nicaragua.

by crude stone figures on Zapatero Island and elsewhere.[1] Many of these clearly
show the human head in the animal mouth, a feature that originated with the
Maya and was taken over by the Zapotecans, Nahua, etc. Fig. 273, a–c,
present carved stones of this type. It must be remembered that a considerable

part of Nicaragua
was, at the time of the
Conquest, actually
inhabited by tribes
that spoke Nahua
dialects. Bransford[2]
considers the so-
called Santa Helena
pottery as the prod-
uct of the intruding
Nahua, and thinks
the Luna ware ante-

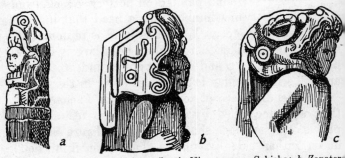

Fig. 273. — Sculptures of Nahua tribes in Nicaragua: a, Subiaba; b, Zapatero
Island; c, Pensacola.

dates their coming. Conventionalized forms, probably serpentine, occur on
both these kinds of pottery as well as on other fabrics.

A clear example of Maya stone carving that shows the style of Copan has
been found near Tegucigalpa on the head waters of the Choluteca River.[3] This
is reproduced in Fig. 274. It may have been an object of trade. The carvings of

[1] Squier, 1850; also 1852, I, pp. 301–328; II, pp. 3–
68, 87–98; Bransford, 1881; Bovallius, 1886 and 1887.

[2] 1881, p. 80.
[3] Hamy, 1896, pl. 1.

Santa Lucia Cosumalhuapa [1] have already been referred to as being more Nahua than Maya and as having probably been made by an intrusive Nahua tribe.

Highly conventionalized but recognizable plumed serpents appear on a number of beautiful bowls from the Casas Grandes now in the American Museum of Natural History (Fig. 275). Both Saville [2] and Lumholtz [3] have commented upon this occurrence. The thick-billed parrot is also represented. This bird is a native of Chihuahua but does not extend into New Mexico and Arizona. Nevertheless it is highly prized and semi-sacred among the Indians of the Rio Grande pueblos and in early times a regular trade for its feathers was maintained. It is interesting, if not significant, to find a plumed serpent and a green-feathered parrot of religious and artistic importance in the region of high culture nearest of all to the high culture of Central America where the quetzal and the serpent were combined.

FIG. 274.— Maya sculpture from Cholulteca River, Honduras.

FIG. 275.— Plumed serpents on Casas Grandes pottery.

The most important drawing to suggest connection with the south is that given in Fig. 276. The design in red and black extends around the circumference of a narrow-necked bowl from Casas Grandes. It represents a body, possibly that of a man, stretched out horizontally. Only the legs and head are reproduced in full, the torso being simply a panel of geometric figures. The head is most interesting since it shows a headdress consisting of another head.

FIG. 276.— Prostrate figure with animal head for headdress: Casas Grandes.

Plumed serpents are seen on ceremonial objects at Zuñi. Fig. 277 gives examples of them. As a rule, however, the miraculous water serpent has a back-

[1] Habel, 1879; Bastian, 1882; Strebel, 1893, etc. The strikingly similar sculptures of Palo Verde and antaleon have been described and figured by Mrs. . Seler, 1900, pp. 232–241.

[2] Saville, 1894.
[3] Lumholtz, 1902, I, p. 96 and pl. 2.

ward curving horn rising from the top of the head and is without feathers. Examples of these horned serpents may be seen on a collection of ceremonial jars from San Ildefonso Pueblo that are now in the American Museum of Natural History.

a   b

Fig. 277. — Plumed serpents of Zuñi.

That this divine creature is not a modern innovation in the region of the Rio Grande is seen from incised drawings of it in ancient cliff ruins such as those on the Rito de los Frijoles. Fig. 278 reproduces a simple horned serpent on a bowl

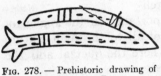

from the prehistoric ruin of Puye, that is now in the Museum of the Southwest, while Fig. 279 gives the design on one side of a small sacred meal bowl said to have been excavated at Perage, opposite San Ildefonso. Accounts differ as to whether this pueblo was abandoned just before or soon after the coming of the Spaniards. The horned snake in this

Fig. 278. — Prehistoric drawing of horned serpent: Puye.

instance resembles those still found among the Hopi where usually the object is represented in an unrealistic manner.[1] It may be stated that sacred snakes are seldom seen as a decoration on the prehistoric pottery of the western pueblo ruins.

The drawings and carvings which have been most frequently referred to as showing connection between the Mound Area of the United States and Mexico and Central America are more or less realistic in nature. They consist of representations of winged and horned serpents, of anthropomorphic birds and of human beings.

Fig. 279. — Tewa drawing of horned serpent on early historic pottery.

Many writers, including Holmes, Thomas, Putnam and Moore, have repeatedly suggested Mexican influence in these works in art but without actually coming to any hard and fast conclusions.

The homogeneity of the graphic art of the Mound Area is most remarkable. Certain characteristic details occur in drawings and carvings from one end of this vast area to the

Fig. 280. — Shell gorget with rattlesnake design: Tennessee.

other. Attention is particularly directed towards a method of representing or elaborating the eye that is widespread and peculiar. The eye-ball is represented by a single circle or by two or more concentric circles and to this is added a posterior or inferior appendage usually consisting of two or more acute angles. Examples of this decorated eye are found on drawings of birds, human beings and serpents. The appendage does not seem to represent any natural feature of eyes in

[1] Fewkes, 1894, *a*, p. 79, shows the serpent reduced to a zigzag line.

general and so is of the utmost importance in showing artistic connection between the objects upon which it does occur.

The representation of the serpent [1] may be considered first. This is frequently
seen on shell gorgets and sometimes on pottery. Nearly all the serpents have
rattles, and so may safely be considered rattlesnakes although they are not
accurately drawn in the matter of body markings. The ornamented eye is an
almost constant characteristic. Supernatural features in the nature of wings,
backward curving horns, branching antlers and feather crests are often added.
A shell gorget of common type is reproduced in Fig. 280. The ornamented eye

a   *b*

FIG. 281. — Winged and horned snakes of the Mound Area: *a*, Alabama; *b*, Arkansas.

of the snake is in evidence and the markings on the tip of the tail that indicate
rattles. Two antlered and winged rattlesnakes are figured in the next illustration (Fig. 281). The second of these shows the " heart-line," a feature common
among the present-day Indians from the upper Missouri to the Rio Grande.

In the southern part of the Mound Area there seems to be a close connection
between the eagle [2] and the serpent. This may be seen by comparing the typical
eagle heads engraved on pottery with the heads of some of the winged serpents.

FIG. 282. — Design on a bowl from Georgia.

Slight evidence of the anthropomorphism of the serpent is seen on a small
bowl from Georgia (Fig. 282). Upon this vessel are delineated four serpents,
three having the elaborated eye that has received comment. Two of these serpents have a branching horn growing out of the head while the others have heads
which approximate the human type. One of these human heads has a forehead
ornament and the other seems to have an ear plug.

The anthropomorphism of the eagle is much more developed. Representations of the so-called " eagle man " have a wide occurrence. Fig. 283 gives some
well known examples of designs done on sheet copper in repoussé. Of these *a*

---

[1] Moore, 1905, p. 136; 1907, pp. 371–377.
Holmes, 1880–1881, pp. 289–293; 1898–1899, p. 91
and pl. 119; Putnam and Willoughby, 1895, etc.

[2] For the eagle see Moore, 1901, pp. 462–463;
1905, pp. 205–206; 1907, pp. 350–351; 388–390.

The other bird, so frequently represented in incised
drawings on the pottery of the Southern States, is
the ivory-billed woodpecker or the very similar
pileated woodpecker.

represents an eagle with little modification except the zigzag lines attached to
the eye, while *c* and *e* show the eagle in human form. The beaked nose is obvious and the wings and tail are drawn in the identical manner seen in the first
instance with scallop-shaped markings on the former and parallel lines on the
latter. Copper plates
with designs compar-
able to these have been
found in a number of
sites and shell gorgets
with identical details
are not uncommon.
Sometimes the anthro-
pomorphic eagles lack
the wings and tail but
possess clawed feet.

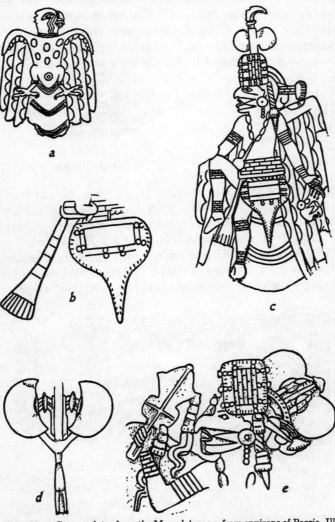

   In regard to the
dress, which is doubt-
less taken over from
that of human beings,
note the peculiar rec-
tangular object on the
front of the headdress,
the hair ornament
with crescent-shaped
wings that is worn
above this, the heart-
shaped apron (Fig.
283, *b*) resembling the
Scottish apron, and
the arm and leg bands.
A hair ornament of
the same type as those
represented on the
copper plates (Fig.
283, *d*) was found with
them in the Etowah
Mound, but Thomas
does not seem to have
understood its signifi-

FIG. 283. — Copper plates from the Mound Area: *a*, from environs of Peoria, Ill.;
b–e, from Etowah Mound, Georgia.

cance. The apron and the arm and leg bands appear on a shell gorget from
Kentucky (Fig. 284, *a*) that represents a human being with a chunkee stone (?)
in one hand. The apron and the rectangular plate of the headdress are seen on
a shell gorget from Alabama reproduced in Fig. 284, *b*. This drawing shows an
"eagle man" with claws for hands.
   A number of writers have directed attention to similarities in shell gorgets
from Mexico and from the Mound Area. For instance, Dr. Frederick Starr,
after comparing seven examples from the United States with a single piece from

[1] 1896, p. 178.

Mexico, says: "So close and striking are the resemblances that accident cannot account for them, and we are forced to the conclusion that it (the art) must be the offspring of the same beliefs and customs and the same culture as the art of Mexico." Such a conclusion is not forced upon the present writer and possibly a third person may fail to see the compelling resemblances noted by Dr. Starr. A wide range must always be allowed for opinions in matters of art.

References [1] are given below to the seven examples used in this comparison and to a number of other examples including those reproduced in Fig. 284, a and b. On the Mexican side of the question there are four shell gorgets including the one described by Starr,[2] himself, which came from Morelia. The other three are from Tampico,[3] Tuxpan [4] and an unknown site in Guerrero.[5] All four are brought together by Lehmann.[6] Only the first two resemble in subject or

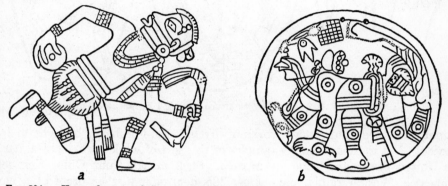

a   *b*

FIG. 284. — Human figures on shell gorgets showing heart-shaped apron, etc.: *a*, Kentucky; *b*, Alabama.

drawing the gorgets of the Mound Area, and even in these cases the similarity is easily explained. A human figure is drawn in a circular space with part of the background cut away stencil fashion. The most prominent features of dress are a belt with apron flaps at front and back, leg wrappings, a circular ear plug and an oblong nose plug. In the specimens from the Mound Area the belt and aprons are usually represented and sometimes bands are shown on the arms and legs and beads around the neck. Circular ear plugs also appear but nose plugs are not represented in a single instance. The ear plugs of Mexico and the Mound Area while they resemble each other in drawings are very different in reality. It must be admitted that the subject of the gorgets is commonplace enough and that the manner of representation might easily arise independently in two areas from the natural limitations and suggestions of the material used.

In the instances from the Mound Area just considered we have recurring features not found in Mexican art, including the ornamented eye and the heart-shaped apron or pouch. These, as we have seen, also occur on copper plates.[7] Moreover, objects of copper and shell, worked in the same manner but repre-

[1] Holmes, 1880–1881, pls. 71–74 and 1903, pl. 29. Thomas, 1890–1891, pp. 306–307, figs. 189–190. Moore, 1899, p. 336, fig. 53; 1905, p. 158; 1907, pp. 397–398, figs. 96–98. Starr, 1896, p. 175; Wilson, 1895, pl. 10.

[2] Starr, 1906, p. 177.

[3] Saville, 1900, p. 100.

[4] Lehmann, 1905, b, fig. 1.

[5] Holmes, 1903, pl. 30.

[6] Lehmann, 1905, b.

[7] On the technique of these plates see Cushing, 1894, and on copper working in general see Moore and others, 1903.

senting different subjects [1] are very common and widespread in the Mound Area. Certain details even occur in drawings on pottery vessels and fragments of bone.[2] Quite apart from this there are many other objects of art which prove a stage of art sufficiently high to account for the presence of these drawings without invoking foreign influence.[3]

Mr. Fowke [4] in a recent publication comments on a number of copper plates bearing eagle men in repoussé that were found in Missouri to the effect that they

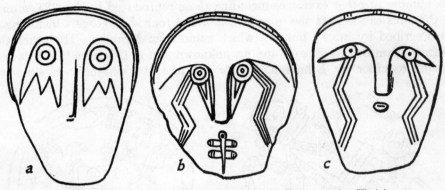

FIG. 285. — Shell marks from the Mound Area: *a*, Tennessee; *b–c*, Virginia.

cannot have been indigenous works of art but were probably brought in from Mexico! Yet there are many examples of this sort of work in the central part of the United States and none in Mexico. Shell masks from Ohio, Kentucky, Tennessee, West Virginia, etc. (Figs. 285, *a–c*) offer further proof of a close-knit unity in Mound Area art since they carry out the features of the elaborated eye. One of these masks was recently excavated from a mound in Manitoba.

FIG. 286. — Horned snake on buffalo-skin lodge, Dakota Indians.

Indeed, it seems likely that these figures of winged serpents, eagle men, etc., refer to some ancient cosmogenic myth, the episodes of which are here depicted.[5] The supernatural serpents still survive in the mythology of the area and the eagle men may be no other than the miraculous thunder birds. The zigzag lines often connected with the eyes certainly suggest lightning. Other types of Mound culture products need not be considered at this time, since enough has been shown to establish homogeneity.

The horned-serpent motive is not absent from the decorative art of the modern Indians of the Plains. Examples may be seen of its use as a house decora-

[1] Moore figures many specimens of copper, for instance, 1899, pp. 327 and 344; 1895, pp. 160–165, 195–198, 216; 1907, pp. 399–403, etc., etc. For shell carvings of geometric and realistic subjects (crosses, scalloped disks, swastikas, birds, spiders, serpents, etc.) see Holmes, 1880–1881, pp. 267 *et seq.*, and Wilson, 1894, pp. 906–920.

[2] The use of crosshatched areas on the remarkable carved bones and other objects from the Turner Group and elsewhere (see Putnam and Willoughby, 1905; and Gordon, 1907).

[3] For instance the beautiful stone disks, slabs, bowls, pipes, etc., the painted and modeled pottery of the Southern States, the clay figurines from the Turner Group, etc., all reach a high plane of workmanship.

[4] Fowke, 1910, p. 98 and pls. 15–19.

[5] Mr. Moore refers briefly to the probable religious beliefs of the inhabitants of ancient Moundville, 1907, pp. 404–405.

tion among the Blackfoot. Fig. 286 shows a horned serpent painted upon a buffalo-hide lodge of the Dakota Sioux. Among the Menomini, according to Mr. Skinner, the figure is applied to the medicine outfits of conjurors.

The elaboration of the serpent in religion and religious art, leading to certain identities in peculiar and unnatural features, has proved to be one of the most important phenomena of the native culture of the New World — and the Old World too, for that matter. In some of the principal culture areas the development seems to have been entirely independent and indigenous. Elsewhere there may have been an actual connection, often of the most flimsy sort, and entirely unimportant as concerns the larger questions of cultural evolution. For instance, these similar art products may, in some cases, be explained by a recrudescence of ideas transmitted by mythology. Word of mouth travels faster and farther than craft of hand.

Still we may see in these designs the result of a slow exfiltration, with many relays, of ideas originating among the Maya, if you will, but not passing from them directly to the ancient peoples of the Mississippi Valley. There are no trustworthy evidences of trade relations between the Mexicans and Mound-builders, nor is there any sure indication of fundamental unity of culture at any time in the distant past.

Conclusion. This brief presentation of Maya art, which is now brought to a close, leaves many important questions to be decided. In many lines of research the material available has been insufficient to permit a definitive piece of work. The results obtained are, however, suggestive enough to serve as a basis for further study. The principal facts have been blocked out in the rough. We know that the Indians of Mexico and Central America developed an autochthonous culture of a high type. We know that in point of time this culture cannot boast a sensational antiquity or even one which will bear comparison with that in classic lands or in the Far East. We know, in a general way, the course of empire; the epochs of brilliancy and decadence. And we know the end of it all, very much as the priest or Balam sang it in one of the scanty fragments of Maya poetry.[1]

> Eat, eat, while there is bread.
> Drink, drink, while there is water,
> A day comes when dust shall darken the air,
> When a blight shall wither the land,
> When a cloud shall arise,
> When a mountain shall be lifted up,
> When a strong man shall seize the city,
> When ruin shall fall upon all things,
> When the tender leaf shall be destroyed,
> When eyes shall be closed in death;
> When there shall be three signs on a tree,
> Father, son and grandson hanging dead on the same tree;
> When the battle flag shall be raised,
> And the people scattered abroad in the forest.

[1] Brinton, 1890, p. 303.

TABLE OF NOMENCLATURE

RUINS AND MONUMENTS

The following list of ruins and principal monuments is designed as an aid in fixing designations and in cross referencing the descriptions of various modern authors.   Only such ruins as are represented by published matter, including photographs of buildings and monuments, ground-plans or descriptions of noteworthy specimens, are included.   Even with these restrictions the list is probably far from complete.

ACANCEH
>   Breton, 1908; Seler, E., 1911, *a*.   Principal mound and Mound with Stucco Façade.   Other mounds and buildings not named.

AHUACHAPAN
>   Lehmann, 1910, p. 735, figures a stela showing Maya influence.

AKE
>   Stephens, 1843, II, pp. 440–443.   Charnay, 1885, pp. 246–256, gives a plan showing the following features: Ball Court, Gallery of Columns, three or more ruined buildings called Palaces, 3 pyramids called Akabna, Xnuc and Succuna.

ALMUCHIL
>   Maler, 1902, pp. 213–215.   Principal Palace, House of Two Chambers.

ALTAR DE SACRIFICIOS
>   Maler, 1908, *a*, pp. 3–9.   Circular Altar and Stelae 1–6 of which Circular Altar and Stela 4 are reproduced.   Mounds unnumbered but plan given.

ANAITÉ II
>   Maler, 1903, pp. 98–99.

ARROYO HONDO
>   Seler, 1895, *d*, pp. 49–50.   Painted pottery.

AZUCAR
>   Tozzer, 1911, p. 93.

BELLOTE
>   Charnay, 1885, pp. 157–159, gives a short description.

BENQUE VIEJO
>   Maler, 1908, *b*, pp. 73–79.   The principal building called the Castle of Two Epochs.   Stela 1 and a Rectangular Altar.

BOLONCHAC
>   Sapper, 1895, *a*, table 5.   Mounds A to E.   Location of idols shown.

BUDSILHÁ
>   Maler, 1903, pp. 89–93.   Two-roomed building.

CAKIHA
>   Sapper, 1895, *a*, table 3.

CALCETOK
>   Mercer, 1896, pp. 21–31.   Cave of the Mice, Actun Spukil.   Potsherds, etc.   Other caves in vicinity, pp. 32–44.

CANCUN ISLAND
>   Holmes, 1895–1897, pp. 63–64.   Arnold and Frost, 1909, pp. 146–152, give further information.

CANKUEN
>   Maler, 1908, *a*, pp. 36–49.   Stelae 1–2.

CAVE OF LOLTUN
>   Thompson, 1897, pp. 6–22.   Mercer, 1896, pp. 98–125.

CERRO DE LOS IDOLOS

Hamy, 1897, pl. 24, figures pottery urns. Charnay, 1885, pp. 356–357, refers to the same pieces.

CHACBOLAI

Maler, 1902, pp. 197–198, mentions the Castillo.

CHACMULTUN

A plan of the principal structures is given by Thompson, 1904, pl. 3. Edifices 1–5. Edifice No. 1 is called the Palace.

Maler also describes these ruins, 1895, pp. 249–250, and 1902, p. 199. He refers to Edifice 1 as the Temple Palace of the Phalli, to Edifice 2 as the Chamber of Justice and to Edifice 4 as the Temple-Palace Xetpol.

CHACUJAL

Sapper, 1895, a, table 4. Mounds 1–8. Maudslay, 1889–1902, II, pp. 28–30.

CHACULÁ

Seler, 1901, c, pp. 59–77. Ruins mapped.

CHÁNCALA

Maler, 1901, pp. 13–17. A temple.

CHICHEN ITZA

The usage in regard to names at Chichen Itza is very complex. Maudslay's notation is taken for the most part in the following classification (Maudslay, III, pl. 2 and pp. 13 et seq.).

No. 1. The Monjas Group consists of the Main Range on the foundation mound, the Upper Chamber on top of the Main Range and the East Wing on the ground level together with the buildings grouped around the Enclosed Court on the south side of the East Wing, the small annex known as the Iglesia or Church and the larger annex known as the Southeast Temple. The L-shaped mound east of the Iglesia has no name nor has the wall and mound attached to the northwest corner of the Monjas Group. Casa de Monjas means Nunnery, but the Spanish term is here retained as a convenient distinction from the Nunnery Quadrangle of Uxmal. The word arose from the traditional use of the buildings for the habitation of sacred virgins (Cogolludo, 1688, p. 176) and not from the use of lattice work in the façade decorations.

Nos. 2 and 3 are small mounds with serpent-head stairways.

No. 4 is the Akat'cib; the name means "the writing in the dark."

No. 5 is the Caracol, Snail or Round Tower. It has a small annex at the southwest corner of the foundation platform.

No. 6. A small temple with a sanctuary, northwest of the Caracol.

No. 7. Casa Colorada, Red House, or Chichanchob. Several unnumbered ruins are near by.

No. 8. Small nameless temple.

No. 9. High Priest's Grave. A deep shaft was found in the center leading down to a burial chamber. This was excavated by Mr. E. H. Thompson and the objects found were placed in the Field Museum at Chicago.

No. 10. Small mound with four serpent-head stairways. This and two small terraces are alligned with the eastern stairway of the High Priest's Grave.

No. 11. The Ball Court also called the Tennis Court and the Gymnasium (Maudslay, III, pl. 26). The Ball Court Group consists of Temple A, commonly referred to as the Temple of the Jaguars but also called Temple of the Tigers and the Shields, Casa del Tigre and Temple of the Ball Court Wall. This structure has a lower ground-level annex at the back called Lower Chamber of the Temple of the Jaguars. Temple B is usually called North Temple of the Ball Court and Temple C the South Temple of the Ball Court.

No. 12. Low terrace east of the Ball Court Group. This is probably the structure called Mausoleum II by Maler, 1895, p. 280, and Seler, 1908, pp. 170 et seq.

No. 13. In this mound was found the Chacmool sculpture, so-called, by Dr. Le Plongeon (see Salisbury, 1877). The mound is called Mausoleum I by Maler and Seler in the places noted. It is badly restored by Le Plongeon, 1896, pl. 57.

No. 14. The Temple of the Cones excavated by Dr. Le Plongeon. This is also called Mausoleum III (Seler, 1908, pp. 235–236).

No. 15. The Castillo or the Castle.

Nos. 16–32, comprise the Group of the Columns, Maudslay, III, pl. 60. This extensive group of closely related structures has never been thoroughly explored. It was first described by Friedericksthal in 1841. The most important structures are:

No. 17. The Temple of the Tables.

No. 21. The Arcade, so called because of an arched passage under the platform with the columns.

No. 22 is probably a ball court and may be called the Small Ball Court.

No. 25. The Temple of the Little Tables was partially excavated by Thompson. It has been described by Maler, 1895, pp. 279–281, and Seler, 1908, pp. 182–183.

No. 26. The Temple of the Stairway was also partially excavated by Thompson. Plates 5, fig. 1, and 7, fig. 2, show this building. Maudslay's plan is considerably at fault. The buildings southeast of this structure are unnumbered.

No. 30. The Sunken Court.

In the northwestern part of the city, Maler excavated two buildings which are not represented in Maudslay's notation. One of these he calls the Building of Two Columns with Changed Stones (Seler, 1908, pl. 26), because the separate stones of the columns bear designs that do not fit together. The stones are apparently re-used material from an earlier structure. The second building he calls the Temple of the Two Serpent Columns, because each column bears a serpent carved in relief upon the front side (Seler, 1908, pl. 25).

Less than half a mile south of the Monjas lie the little-known ruins of Old Chichen Itza. In this site there are many unnamed and unnumbered mounds. Two important buildings in the eastern part of Old Chichen Itza are the House of the Phalli and the Temple of the Initial Series. The latter has been briefly described by Seler, 1908, pp. 237–238. Considerable information concerning Old Chichen Itza and the Group of the Columns was furnished by Mr. S. G. Morley.

The description Stephens, 1843, II, pp. 290–324, gives of Chichen Itza is incomplete but very accurate so far as it goes. The names he uses do not vary from the names used in this classification.

CHINIKIHÁ

Maler, 1901, pp. 10–13. Sculptured table; Stela.

CHINKULTIC, TEPANCUAPAM

Seler, 1901, c, p. 187 and pl. 40. Pyramid and stela.

CHIPOLEM

Dieseldorff, 1895, b.

CHOCOHA

Périgny, 1908, pp. 71–75.

CHÚNHUHUB, CHUNHUHU

Stephens, 1843, II, pp. 130–132, several buildings figured. Maler, 1902, pp. 210–213. Principal Palace or Palace of the Figures, Annex and 1st, 2nd, and 3rd Castillos.

CHUNKATCIN

Thompson, 1888, pp. 164–166, gives a brief description of buildings.

CHUNTICHMOOL

Thompson, 1888, p. 166, mentions a chultun with stucco decoration. This may be the one figured by him in 1898, p. 225.

CHUNYÁXNIC

Described by Maler, 1895, pp. 247–248. Small temple with flying façade figured.

COBA

Stephens, 1843, II, pp. 340–341, quotes a description.

COBAN, CHAMA, ETC.

Dieseldorff, 1893, a; 1893, b; 1894, a; 1894, b; 1895, a. Seler, 1895, d, etc.

COMALCALCO

Charnay, 1885, pp. 161–177. Sketch plan. Structures named are Palace and Towers 1 and 2.

COMITAN

Seler, 1901, c, pp. 189–191.

COMITANCILLO

Sapper, 1895, a, table 9. Mounds A to E, not all mounds numbered on plan.

COPAN

The nomenclature of this city has been pretty well established by Maudslay, 1889–1902, I, pl., and by the Peabody Museum Expeditions, Gordon, 1896, pl. 1. The principal parts and structures are:

Main Structure or the Acropolis.

Great Plaza.

Eastern and Western Courts.

Structures (Mounds, Buildings, Stairways, etc.) numbered 1–56. This numbering is very incomplete, and covers only the ceremonial center of Copan.

Stelae A, B, C, D, E, F, H, I, J, M, N, P. 1, 2, 3, 4, 5, 6, 7, 8, 9, 10, 11, 12, 13 and 15.

Altars and other separate pieces. C, D, E, F, G1, G2, G3, H, I, J, K, L, M, N, O, O1, Q, R, S, T, U, X, Y, Z, 1, 4, 5 (2 altars), 13 and 14.

COPAN — *continued*

Many minor sculptures have not received names or numbers.

Stephens, 1841, I, pp. 130–160, gives a plan and reproduces many of the sculptures but without any system of naming. Some of these drawings are of value in restoring lost parts and giving original locations. A few stelae were reproduced in larger scale by Catherwood, 1844. The drawings of Meye and Schmidt, 1883, have been superseded.

Much work remains to be done at Copan but there seems to be no good reason to renumber or rename the well known sculptures. To do so would be to outlaw and invalidate much classic literature on Maya archaeology.

COZUMEL

Stephens, 1843, II, pp. 372–378. Holmes, 1895–1897, pp. 64–69. Arnold and Frost, 1909, pp. 164–184.

DSECILNA, ZEKILNA

Maler, 1895, pp. 282–284. Palace; Columns with human figures. Stephens, 1843, II, pp. 124–126.

DSEKABTUN

Maler, 1902, pp. 227–230. Principal Palace with Dependent Structures, built round a square, Temple with Roof Comb or House of the Six Chambers.

DSIBILNOCAC, ZIBILNOCAC TZÍBINOCAC

Stephens, 1843, II, pp. 180–190. Maler has also explored it and taken photographs of the structures. Sapper, 1895, *c*, pl. XXX, fig. 4.

DSIBILTUN

Maler, 1895, p. 251; 1902, p. 230. The Palace, the Temple, the Chamber of Justice.

EL CAYO

Maler, 1903, pp. 83–89. The Palace. Stelae 1–3. Lintel 1.

EL CHICOZAPOTE

Maler, 1903, pp. 100–104. A ruined structure with Lintels 1–4.

EL CHILE

Maler, 1903, pp. 96–98. A double temple.

EL MECO

Holmes, 1895–1897, pp. 69–74. Arnold and Frost, 1909, pp. 143–145.

EL SACRAMENTO

Sapper, 1895, *a*, table 5. Ball court and three idols.

HACIENDA GRANDE

Sapper, 1895, *a*, table 2. There seems to be some doubt as to the location of these ruins.

HOCHOB

Maler, 1895, pp. 278–279. Principal Structure and several other temples.

HOLMUL

Tozzer, 1911, p. 93.

HUNTICHMÚL

Maler, 1895, pp. 250–251. Palace of the Half-columns, Building of the Inscription, etc.

ICHPICH

Maler, 1902, pp. 199–202, mentions a number of structures including the Palace.

ITSIMTÉ, YTSIMPTE

Maler, 1902, pp. 215–216. Temple-Palace and Serpent-head Palace. Stephens, 1843, II, pp. 139–141.

ITSIMTÉ-SÁCLUK

Maler, 1908, *a*, pp. 28–35. Stelae 1–6, of which Stelae 1, 4 and 6 are reproduced. Mounds unnumbered but plan given.

IXIMCHÉ, TECPAN GUATEMALA, PATINAMIT

Stephens, 1841, II, pp. 146–154; Brühl, 1894; Sapper, 1895, *a*, table 7; Maudslay, 1889–1902, II, pl. 73. Bancroft, 1875–1876, IV, pp. 122–123. Maudslay's map is the best but the mounds are unnumbered.

IXKUN, DOLORES

Maudslay, 1889–1902, II, pp. 21–22, pls. 67–69. Sketch plan. Stela 1 reproduced and others mentioned.

IXTINTA

Sapper, 1895, *c*, pp. 542 *et seq.*, and pl. 30, figs. 1 and 2; Sapper, 1897, p. 360. Plans.

IZALCO

Seler, 1901, *c*, pp. 180–181. Maya pottery in western Salvador.

IZAMAL
> Stephens, 1843, II, pp. 432–439. Brasseur de Bourbourg, 1866, *a*; Charnay, 1885, pp. 259–265, identifies the pyramids with those mentioned by Lizana, namely 1st, Kinich-Kakmó, 2nd, Ppapp-Hol-Chac, 3rd, Ytzamat-ul. Holmes, 1895–1897, pp. 97–100.

JAINA
> Charnay, 1887, *b*; Norman, 1843, pp. 214–218; Hamy, 1897, pl. 26.

KABAH
> Stephens, 1843, I, pp. 384–413. Casas 1–3. Structure of the Sculptured Lintels. Structure of the Sculptured Doorjambs. The Broken Arch. Charnay, 1885, pp. 315–320, uses this numbering. Researches of the Peabody Museum at Kabah, as at Labna, are unpublished.

KALAMTÉ
> Sapper, 1895, *a*, table 8. Mounds A to H, all not numbered on plan.

KANCABCHEN
> Maler, 1895, p. 284. Grotesque sculpture.

KANTUNILE
> Grave finds of carved shell, etc., described by Stephens, 1843, II, pp. 341–344.

KEWICK
> Stephens, 1843, II, pp. 66–77. Several buildings. Painted slab.

LABNA, LABNAH
> An unpublished map of the Peabody Museum Expedition to Labna in charge of Mr. E. H. Thompson classifies the ruins as follows:
> Palace Group.
> Old Edifice Group.
> Portal Group.
> Temple Group.
> The mounds are associated principally with the last two groups and are numbered 1–20 on the map, although Mound 41 is referred to in Thompson, 1897, p. 19. Many unnumbered terraces are found in connection with the buildings of the first two groups.
> The chultunes or reservoirs that were excavated are numbered 1–34 (Thompson, 1897).
> Stephens, 1843, II, frontispiece, gives a fine panorama of the Palace Group and describes other structures, pp. 49–59.

LA CUEVA DE SANTA CRUZ
> Sapper, 1895, *a*, table 4. Mounds A–G. Seler, 1895, *d*. Bull. 28, p. 103.

LA HONDRADEZ
> Tozzer, 1911, p. 93.

LA MAR
> Maler, 1903, pp. 93–96, describes the ruins and figures Stelae 1 and 2.

LAS PACAYAS
> Sapper, 1895, *a*, table 3. Structures A–K.

LAS QUEBRADAS
> Sapper, 1895, *a*, table 3. Plazas I–VI.

LA REFORMA
> Maler, 1901, pp. 9–10.

LEMPA VALLEY
> Lehmann, 1910, pp. 691–695 and 734–741, discusses Maya influence.

MACOBA
> Stephens, 1843, II, pp. 214–219.

MANKEESH
> Stephens, 1843, II, p. 223.

MASAPA
> Sapper, 1895, *a*, table 6. Mounds A to H.

MATARÁS
> Cruz, 1904, gives brief description.

MAYAPAN
> Stephens, 1843, I, pp. 131–141; Brasseur de Bourbourg, 1866, *b*; Le Plongeon, 1881, Round Tower, Structure with columns.

MIXCO
    Maudslay, 1889–1902, II, pl. 74. Mounds are those of an ancient city between Mixco and Guatemala City. Ancient Mixco is situated north of Guatemala City and is entirely distinct.

MOTUL DE SAN JOSÉ
    Maler, 1910, pp. 131–135. Stela 1.

MUJERES ISLAND
    These ruins have been often described: see Stephens, 1843, II, pp. 415–417; Salisbury, 1878; Holmes, 1895–1897, pp. 57–63.

NACO
    Blackiston, 1910, b, describes a cache of copper bells in the vicinity.

NAKUM
    Périgny, 1910. Tozzer, 1911, p. 93.

NARANJO
    Maler, 1908, b, pp. 80–127. Stelae 1–32. Morley, 1909, p. 544, also gives the various buildings numbers which run from I to XXIX, and makes the Courts A to E.

NEBAJ
    Seler, 1902–1908, III, pp. 718–729. Painted pottery.

NOCUCHICH
    Maler, 1895, pp. 281–282. Colossal stucco face, Tower.

NOHCACAB
    Stephens, 1843, I, pp. 347–348.

NOHCACAB, 2nd.
    Périgny, 1908, pp. 81–84.

NOHOCHNA
    Périgny, 1908, pp. 79–80.

NOHPAT
    Stephens, 1843, I, pp. 362–368. This ruin may be an older part of Uxmal. The monolithic sculptures have not been numbered or photographed.

OCOSINGO, TONINA
    Stephens, 1841, II, pp. 255–262; Sapper, 1895, c, pl. 31; Sapper, 1897, p. 361, fig. 8; Seler, 1901, c, pp. 191–195. The Principal Temple follows the Palenque model. Stelae 1–2 shown in Plate 25, figs. 4 and 5 of this volume after photographs of Dr. Tozzer. Other monuments unnamed and unnumbered.

OXKINTOK, MAXCANU
    Stephens, 1843, I, pp. 212–220. Mercer, 1896, pp. 45–63. The Labyrinth, Cave, Mound called Xemtzil.

OXKUTZCAB
    Mercer, 1896, pp. 126–145. Caves with potsherds, etc.

PALENQUE
    The situation in regard to terms is very discouraging and a correlation of the many authorities cannot be attempted. The best thing to do is to accept the nomenclature of Maudslay. His large map, 1889–1902, IV, pl. 1, shows many ruins unnamed and unnumbered.
    The Palace is subdivided into:
    Houses A to I.
    The Square Tower.
    The principal temples are:
    The Temple of the Inscriptions.
    The Temple of the Cross.
    The Temple of the Foliated Cross.
    The Temple of the Sun.
    The House of the Lion. This is perhaps better known as the Temple of the Beau Relief.
    The Southern Temple (Maudslay, IV, p. 34).
    The Northern Temples, 6 in number (Maudslay, IV, p. 35).
    Mr. Maudslay, IV, pp. 7–8, refers to most of the early authorities on Palenque including Antonio del Rio, 1822; Dupaix in Antiquités Mexicaines, 1834, and Kingsborough, 1831–1848; Waldeck, 1866; Stephens, 1841, II, pp. 291–321; Catherwood, 1844, pls. 6 and 7; and Charnay, 1885, pp. 179–218. Mr. Holmes has also given us a valuable description in 1895–1897, pp. 151–209. Some new frescos were discovered by Dr. Seler, 1911, b.

PASOJON
    Sapper, 1895, a, table 8. Plan.

PETEN–ITZA, FLORES, TAYASAL
Maler, 1910, pp. 153–158. One stela in a church but may have come from some other site.

PETHÁ
Maler, 1901, pp. 30–31. Rock paintings.

PIEDRAS NEGRAS
Maler, 1901, pl. 33, has given descriptive names to the principal structures and has numbered the sculptures as follows:
Stelae 1–37.
Altars I to V.
Lintels 1–4.
The inscription on Stela 3 was drawn and commented on by Maudslay, 1897–1898, and later by Förstemann, 1901, b. The inscriptions have been considered in detail by Bowditch, 1901, c.

PLAYA DE LOS MUERTOS
Gordon, 1898, a, pp. 97 et seq. Blackiston, 1910 a.

PORVENIR
Tozzer, 1911, p. 93.

QUEN SANTO
Seler, 1901, c, pp. 97–185. Maps and plans. Structures 1–44. Caves 1–3. Nearby Casa del Sol is not included in above numeration.

QUIRIGUA
The great monuments of Quirigua have already become well known to the world through Maudslay. His system of lettering, II, pl. 2, is adopted in this paper. The only change in the nomenclature is to substitute "altar" for "animal" in the names of the monolithic sculptures carved on residual boulders. The structures are numbered by Mr. Morley, 1912, who has recently conducted archaeological work at this site.
The monuments are:
Stelae A, C, D, E, F, H, I, J and K.
Altars B, G, L, M, N, O and P.
The structures around the Temple Court are numbered 1 to 6.
The monuments illustrated by Stephens, 1841, II, pp. 118–124, and by Meye and Schmidt, 1883, are poorly done and possess only an historic interest.

RABINAL
Maudslay, 1889–1902, II, pp. 25–27 and pl. 70. Groups of buildings, A–G.

RIO BEQUE
Périgny, 1908, pp. 75–79.

SABACCHE, SABACHTCHÉ
Stephens, 1843, II, pp. 41–47; Maler, 1895, p. 248. The two buildings figured in Plate 6, fig. 2, and Plate 15, fig. 3, of this volume Maler calls Temple with the Lattice-work and Temple of the Serpent Head.

SABAKA
Mercer, 1896, pp. 146–159. Cave with potsherds.

SACBEY
Stephens, 1843, II, p. 122.

SACCACAL
Stephens, 1843, II, pp. 235–237.

SACCHANÁ
Seler, 1901, c, pp. 17–23. Stelae 1–2.

SACULEU, LAS CUYES, ZAKULEU
Sapper, 1895, table 6. Mounds A to K. Bancroft, 1875–1876, IV, pp. 128–130.

SAJCABAJÁ
Sapper, 1895, a, table 10, Mounds A, B, C, 1 and 2, D, E, F, G, H, I, 1–12, K, 1–4, L. Not all the mounds numbered.

SALINAS DE LOS NUEVE CERROS
Seler, 1902–1908, III, Art. 3, pl. 1. Stela.

SAN ANDRÉS TUXTLA
The important statuette from here as described by Holmes, 1907. A map of an ancient city nearby is given by Kerber, 1882. The ruin is probably not Maya.

San Clemente
> Sapper, 1895, *c*, pp. 541 *et seq.*, and pl. 32; Sapper, 1897, p. 362. Courts A–D. Structures I–VII, Mounds 1–10.

San Lorenzo
> Maler, 1903, pp. 203–208. Rock Carvings and one or two minor works.

Sannacté
> Stephens, 1843, II, pp. 36–38. Two ruined buildings mentioned.

Santa Cruz Quiché (see Utatlan).

Santa Rosa Xlabpak
> Stephens, 1843, II, pp. 157–168; Maler, 1902, pp. 220–228. Structures called by Maler, Temple-Palace of Tampak, House of a Room with a Half Arch, Red House, House with Serpent Heads.

Santana
> Gordon, 1898, *a*, pp. 8 *et seq.*

Santa Rita
> Gann, 1897–1898. Mounds 1–23. Frescos on walls of Mound 1.

Santiago de Maria
> Lehmann, 1910, p. 741. Pottery.

Sayil, Zayi
> Stephens, 1843, II, pp. 16–27; Maler, 1895, pp. 251–252 and 277–278. Casa Grande or Temple-Palace and many other structures. Maler describes three stelae. This ruin should be carefully explored and mapped.

Seibal, Sastanquiqui
> Maler, 1908, *a*, pp. 10–28. Stelae 1–15 of which most are figured. Fragments of last four are doubtful; may be altars. Plan given but structures unnumbered.

Silbitúk
> Maler, 1910, pp. 141–142. Sacred Island in the lake.

Sijoh
> Stephens, 1843, I, pp. 199–201. Plate stelae mentioned.

Tabasqueño
> Maler, 1895, pp. 248–249. The Temple-Palace.

Tankuché
> Stephens, 1843, I, pp. 202–206. Building with paintings.

Tantah
> Maler, 1902, p. 218. Two Palaces with banded column decoration.

Tehuacan
> Gonzales, 1906, gives a brief description.

Tenampua
> Squier, 1853; 1858, pp. 133–139. Bancroft, 1875–1876, IV, pp. 73–77.

Ticul, San Francisco
> Stephens, 1843, I, pp. 271–283. Slight excavation.

Tikal
> The notation of the Peabody Museum Expedition is employed as shown on the sketch map, Tozzer, 1911, pl. 29. The correlation of this system with that of Maler, 1911, is stated at the beginning of the paper referred to (Tozzer, 1911, p. vi). The monuments are:
> Stelae 1–17.
> Altars 1–6
> Temples I–V.
> Structures 1–89.
> The correlation with Maudslay, 1889–1902, III, pp. 44–50 and pls. 67–82, is as follows:

Stela A of Maudslay	Stela 5
" B " "	" 9
" C " "	" 10
Temple A of Maudslay	Temple I
" B " "	" II
" C " "	" III
" D " "	" V
" E " "	" IV

The correlation of the sculptured lintels with the temples in which they were originally placed is difficult and the evidence must be given in some detail.

Temple I.

Lintel 1. Plain and in place (Maler, 1911, p. 27).

Lintel 2. Sculptured, 2 beams removed and 2 in place; doorway 8 feet wide (Maler, 1911, p. 28). The missing pieces may be those shown by Maudslay, III, pls. 71 and 74, left-hand inscription. The height of the sculpture is slightly less than 8 feet, which agrees with the width of the doorway. The fragments seem to be parts of two beams. Two small pieces are in the British Museum and the others in the Museum of Archaeology at Basle, collected by Bernoulli in 1877. The pieces at Basle were splendidly reproduced in heliograph by Léon de Rosny, 1882, pl. 10, f, and pl. 12, i.

Lintel 3. Out of 5 sculptured beams, 4 removed; 1 on ground in 1895; doorway 6 feet 2½ inches wide (Maler, 1911, p. 28). The sculptured beams shown by Maudslay, III, pls. 72 and 73, could not have come from this temple: 1st, because outer lintel to which they are ascribed is plain and in situ; 2nd, there are 4 beams and hence the fragments could not have come from Lintel 2 which lacks only two beams; 3rd, the width of the third doorway which would determine the height of the sculpture on Lintel 3 is only 6 feet 2½ inches, while the carving is about 7 feet 2 inches.

Temple II.

Lintel 1. Five beams removed; possibly sculptured; width of doorway 7 feet 4½ inches (Maler, 1911, p. 29). Maudslay, III, pl. 69, is probably in error when he labels this lintel "plain." The sculptures last referred to, that Maudslay, III, pls. 72 and 73, ascribes to Temple I, probably came instead from this doorway. The originals are at Basle and the original reproductions were by Léon de Rosny, 1882, pl. 10, d (object inverted) and e; pl. 11, g and h.

Lintel 2. Originally 5 sculptured beams; 3 removed entirely; 2 found in 1895 and 1904; doorway 7 feet 1 inch wide. For the fragments see Maler, 1911, pp. 29–30, and pl. 18, fig. 2. These pieces come from the right-hand side of a tablet and so cannot form a part of any of the lintels so far considered.

Lintel 3. Plain and in place (Maler, 1911, p. 31).

Temple III.

Lintel 1. Outer doorway very wide, 12 feet 11½ inches; the 6 beams are missing and may have been sculptured (Maler, 1911, p. 37). On Maudslay's plan, III, pl. 69, this lintel bears the legend "beams fallen." If sculptured the height of this lintel would have been much greater than any lintel sculptures known.

Lintel 2. Sculptured and in place but badly mutilated (Maler, 1911, p. 37).

Temple IV.

Lintel 1. Plain and in place (Maler, 1911, p. 41).

Lintel 2. Six sculptured beams removed; width of doorway 6 feet 11½ inches (Maler, 1911, p. 41). The width of the doorway is slightly less than the height of the sculpture shown by Maudslay, III, pls. 72 and 73, and this fact makes the earlier choice of location, Temple II, Lintel 1, all the more certain.

Lintel 6. Seven or 8 sculptured beams removed; width of doorway 6 feet 4½ inches; thickness of wall 7 feet 9 inches; probable width of sculpture 7 feet 3 inches (Maler, 1911, pp. 42–43).

This lintel is undoubtedly that collected by Bernoulli and now in the Museum of Archaeology at Basle (Maudslay, III, pls. 77 and 78). The dimensions of the sculpture proper are, height, 5 feet 9 inches; width, 6 feet 19 inches. The original condition of the beams is shown in the beautiful heliographic plates of Léon de Rosny, 1882, pls. 8–9.

Thus we have accounted for all the known fragments of Tikal wood carvings except, possibly, a small piece in the British Museum collected by Mr. J. W. Boddam-Whetham in 1875 (Maudslay, III, p. 46 and pl. 71) and another fragment mentioned by Maudslay in his preliminary report, 1883, p. 193, as being in the Christy Collection.

TÓPOXTÉ, LAKE YAXHA
Maler, 1908, b, pp. 55–60. Plans of ruins.

TŠOTŠKITAM
Tozzer, 1911, p. 93.

TULOOM
Stephens, 1843, II, pp. 387–407. Plan. Many buildings, largest being the Castillo. Holmes, 1895–1897, pp. 75–78, figures the Castillo from the sea. Dr. Howe, 1911, adds some details. He reproduces a part of a stela or tablet.

TZENDALES
(See pages 111 and 196–197.)

TZULÁ
Thompson, 1904, pp. 8–9. The paintings at the end of one of the rooms are reproduced by Thompson, 1904, pl. 2. There seems to be no doubt but that this ruin and these paintings are described also by Stephens, 1843, II, pp. 92–93.

UAXAC CANAL
Seler, 1901, c, pp. 24–58. Scattered ruins in a valley.

ULOA VALLEY
(See Santana and Playa de los Muertos.)
Gordon, 1898, a. Lehmann, 1910, p. 736. Blackiston, 1910, a and b.

UOLTUNICH
Périgny, 1908, pp. 80–81.

UTATLAN, SANTA CRUZ DEL QUICHÉ
Stephens, 1841, II, pp. 169–188. Sapper, 1895, c, pl. 33. Maudslay, 1889–1902, II, pl. 72. Mounds unnumbered. Concerning the traditional names, Maudslay, 1889–1902, II, pp. 30–38.

UXMAL
In naming the buildings at Uxmal the following terms are employed:
Nunnery Quadrangle with North, East, South and West Ranges.
House of the Magician with the Annex.
Ball Court.
House of the Governor.
House of the Turtles.
House of the Birds.
House of the Old Woman.
Great Pyramid.
Southwest Group with the House of the Pigeons and the South Temple.
There are many descriptions of Uxmal, among which may be mentioned Stephens, 1843, I, pp. 163–186, 226–232, 253–256, 297–325. Stephens in most cases uses the terms given above or their Spanish equivalents. Waldeck, 1834, is so inaccurate that his plates are of little value. He calls the House of the Magician the Temple of Kingsborough. Holmes, 1895–1897, pp. 80–96, gives an interesting description with valuable drawings. His names do not vary greatly from the list given above. Morley, 1910, a, gives a detailed map of the Southwest Group. The very early description of Alonzo Ponce has been quoted in full, pp. 5–8. The description of Lorenzo de Zavala in Antiquités Mexicaines, 1834, I, is of little value.

VALLE LA JOYA
Lehmann, 1910, pp. 736 and 740. Pottery.

XAMPON
Stephens, 1843, II, p. 124. Two nearby ruins called Hiokowitz and Kuepak.

XCALUMKIN
Maler, 1902, pp. 202–206. Temple of the Initial Series. Other monuments unnumbered and unnamed.

XCAVIL DE YAXCHÉ
Maler, 1902, pp. 205–206. The Temple-Palace.

XCOCH
Stephens, 1843, I, pp. 348–357. A large cave used as well.

XCULOC, SCHOOLHOKE
Maler, 1902, pp. 208–210. Stephens, 1843, p. 134. The Palace with Figures.

XKÁLUPOCOCH
Maler, 1902, pp. 215–216, describes three structures the most important of which he calls the Palace of the Meanders.

XKANJA, CACA XKANHA
Sapper, 1895, c, pl. 30, fig. 3; Sapper, 1897, p. 360, fig. 3. Plan of two structures.

XKICHMOOK, Kich-Moo, Xkichmol
A plan is given by Thompson, 1898, pl. 26, on which are marked: Edifices 1–10. Mounds 1–3. Reservoirs or Chultunes 1–19. Edifice No. 1 is known as the Palace.
A preliminary description of this site was given by Thompson in 1888, pp. 166–170, under the name Kich-Moo. Maler calls it Xkichmol.

XLABPAK OF MALER
Maler, 1902, pp. 204–205. The Principal Temple.

XLABPAK OF SANTA ROSA
(See Santa Rosa Xlabpak.)

Xul
  Thompson, 1904, pp. 7–8.   Stephens, 1843, pp. 83–84 and 89–90.

Xupá
  Maler, 1901, pp. 17–22.   A temple of the Palenque type with engraved tablets.

Yaabichna
  Périgny, 1908, pp. 80–81.

Yakal-Chuc
  Maler, 1902, p. 219.   Structure of the Two Chambers.

Yakatzib
  Stephens, 1843, II, p. 229.   Nearby is an artificial aguada with chultunes in the bottom.   Stephens, 1843, II, pp. 224–227.

Yaxché
  Maudslay, 1889–1902, II, pp. 23–25.

Yaxché-Xlabpak
  Maler, 1902, pp. 206–208, mentions Structures I to V, calling III the Castillo.

Yaxchilan, Menché Tinamit, Lorrilard City
  The notation of Maler, 1893, pl. 39, is used and is correlated with the less complete surveys of Charnay (1885, pp. 382–399) and Maudslay, 1889–1902, II, pp. 40–47 and pls. 76–98.   The site is called Lorillard City by Charnay and Menché Tinamit by Maudslay.
  The numbering of Maler includes: Structures 1–52.   Lintels 1–46.   Stelae 1–20.
  Besides these there are several unnumbered pieces including an oblong block called an altar in front of Structure 44, and several other altars, two of which are shown by Maler, 1903, pl. 80.   A sculptured statue in Structure 33 is also without designation.
  Charnay, 1885.

First Temple, p. 385	Structure 33
Palace, p. 389	Structure 19
Second Temple, p. 390	Probably the roof comb of Structure 6
Lintel, p. 391	Lintel 2
" p. 393	" 24
" p. 399	" 25

  Maudslay, 1883, and 1889–1902, II, pl. 76

House A	Structure 6
" B	" 10
" C	" 11
" D	" 12
" E	" 20
" F	" 21
" G	" 23
" H	" 19
" J	" 25
" K	" 33
" L	" 42
" M	" 44
Lintel, shown in pl. 78, b	Lintel 30
" " " pl. 79, a, and 80, a	" 37
" " " pl. 79, b, and 80 b	" 35
" " " pl. 81	" 13
" " " pl. 82	" 14
" " " pl. 83	" 15
" " " pl. 84	" 16
" " " pl. 85	" 17
" " " pl. 86	" 24
" " " pls. 87 and 89	" 25
" " " pl. 92	" 1
" " " pl. 93	" 2
" " " pl. 94	" 3
" " " pl. 95 "North Lintel"	" 43
" " " pl. 95 "South Lintel"	" 41
" " " pl. 96	" 42

YAXCHILAN, MENCHÉ TINAMIT, LORRILARD CITY — *continued*

Lintel, shown in pl. 97, left-hand figure . . . . Lintel 45
"   "   " pl. 97, right-hand figure . . . . Stela 5
"   "   " pl. 98 . . . . Lintel 23

Mr. Bowditch, 1903, pp. 20–22, discusses most of the sculptures figured by Maudslay and not by Maler.

YAXHÁ

Maler, 1908, *b*, pp. 61–73. Sketch plan. Stelae 1–10 of which parts of 1, 2, 4, 5, 6 and 10 are figured.
Mounds unnumbered.

YARUMELA

Bancroft, 1875–1876, IV, p. 72.

YOKAT

Mercer, 1896, pp. 79–84. Two caves.

CODICES

The following table correlates the page numbers of the three Maya codices with the plate numbers of the reproductions. The numerals in parentheses belong to the reproductions. The two sides of the manuscripts, one labeled "obverse" and the other "reverse," appear in natural order in opposite columns. The top of the pages on the obverse side corresponds to the top of the pages on the reverse side in both the Dresden Codex and the Peresianus Codex (Léon de Rosny, 1887, p. 14) while in the Tro-Cortesianus Codex the top of one side corresponds to the bottom of the other except in pages 77 and 78. Here the scribe apparently had his book top side down as he wrote and consequently these two pages should doubtless be reversed in order when being read. Every student should have his copies of the codices bound in the screen form of the originals.

The Dresden reproduction given here is the second edition of Förstemann, made in 1892. In the first edition of 1880 the numbers of pages 1 and 2 are reversed as well as their opposites, pages 45 and 44 (Förstemann, 1902, p. 2). The two parts of the Dresden Codex really form one manuscript and the pagination should be continuous on each side (Bowditch, 1909, pp. 268–269). The difficulties of the problem are readily seen from Förstemann's original description translated into English by Thomas, 1884–1885, pp. 261–269. Owing to the mass of literature on the Dresden Codex it seems best not to change the references to fit the revised pagination but the latter may be of service in setting up the book from the plates.

The Peresianus reproductions of Léon de Rosny made in 1887 and 1888, the former in color and the latter in black and white, are here correlated with the actual arrangements of the sheets in screen form. The explanations of the editor are not over-lucid in spots. The plates numbered 1 and 12 of the edition of 1887 are reversed in the later one of 1888, possibly for correction, but the text references are identical. Plates 1 and 12 are clearly the outside sheets bearing the stamp of the library and plate 15 is no less certainly the reverse of plate 12 of the edition of 1888.

On the basis of a two-part interlocking series of ahau sequences on the obverse side of the manuscript, which necessitates 13 pages for its complete presentation, Rosny intended to give the numbers 1–13 to the obverse (1887 or 1888, pp. 22–27) at the same time recognizing that the natural pagination of the codex in its present state is 1–11 for the obverse and 12–22 for the reverse (1887 or 1888, p. 15). He thus added two blank pages, 13 and 14, the first to complete the obverse and the second to serve as its opposite on the reverse. But he made a curious error. The pages which he numbers 1 and 12 cannot both be on the same side of the manuscript because both are exposed on the outside of the folded codex. One has to be eliminated from the obverse leaving him still one short of the hypothetical thirteen. To get his full series he also should have added a blank sheet at the beginning which would have been numbered 1 on the obverse and 26 on the reverse.

A careful examination shows that the short page numbered 12 in the edition of 1888 is the one that apparently is devoted to the long involved ahau sequence above noted and hence belongs to the obverse. Its real number should be 11, and all the preceding pages numbered 2–11 should be shifted back one number. The sheet numbered 1 in the 1888 edition is really the last page instead of the first. The mistake probably arose from the fact that this sheet was exposed at the top of the manuscript as folded screen fashion. The ahau symbols that Rosny notes on this sheet (1887 or 1888, p. 18) are very doubtful.

That the above conclusions are correct may be seen from the recent reproductions of the Peresianus Codex by Mr. Gates (1909). The republished photographs originally made in 1864 by Duruy are numbered by Mr. Gates in an approximation of the system of Léon de Rosny in that the interpolated extra pages 13 and 14 are retained. But page 1 is renumbered page 25 and put in its proper place at the end of the codex.

The Cortesianus Codex was published in 1892 by Rady y Degado in the screen form of the original and with the pages unnumbered. The earlier photographic edition of Léon de Rosny, 1883, is very rare. The Troano was brought out as the plates to a dissertation by Brasseur de Bourbourg, 1869–1870. The first plate he gives (page 78) bears no number at all and the others are numbered backwards. The plate numbers of the reverse side are distinguished by an asterisk.

Dresden

Obverse	Reverse
First Part	
1 (1)	78 (45)
2 (2)	77 (44)
3 (3)	76 (43)
4 (4)	75 (42)
5 (5)	74 (41)
6 (6)	73 (40)
7 (7)	72 (39)
8 (8)	71 (38)
9 (9)	70 (37)
10 (10)	69 (36)
11 (11)	68 (35)
12 (12)	67 (34)
13 (13)	66 (33)
14 (14)	65 (32)
15 (15)	64 (31)
16 (16)	63 (30)
17 (17)	62 (29)
18 (18)	61 (blank)
19 (19)	60 (blank)
20 (20)	59 (blank)
21 (21)	58 (28)
22 (22)	57 (27)
23 (23)	56 (26)
24 (24)	55 (25)

Second Part

Obverse	Reverse
25 (46)	54 (74)
26 (47)	53 (73)
27 (48)	52 (72)
28 (49)	51 (71)
29 (50)	50 (70)
30 (51)	49 (69)
31 (52)	48 (68)
32 (53)	47 (67)
33 (54)	46 (66)
34 (55)	45 (65)
35 (56)	44 (64)
36 (57)	43 (63)
37 (58)	42 (62)
38 (59)	41 (61)
39 (60)	40 (blank)

Peresianus

Obverse	Reverse
1 (2)	22 (1)
2 (3)	21 (24)
3 (4)	20 (23)
4 (5)	19 (22)
5 (6)	18 (21)
6 (7)	17 (20)
7 (8)	16 (19)
8 (9)	15 (18)
9 (10)	14 (17)
10 (11)	13 (16)
11 (12)	12 (15)

Tro-Cortesiansus

Obverse	Reverse
Cortesianus	
1	57
2	58
3	59
4	60
5	61
6	62
7	63
8	64
9	65
10	66
11	67
12	68
13	69
14	70
15	71
16	72
17	73
18	74
19	75
20	76
21	77
Troano	
22 (XXXV)	78 (No number)
23 (XXXIV)	79 (XXXIV*)
24 (XXXIII)	80 (XXXIII*)
25 (XXXII)	81 (XXXII*)
26 (XXXI)	82 (XXXI*)
27 (XXX)	83 (XXX*)
28 (XXIX)	84 (XXIX*)
29 (XXVIII)	85 (XXVIII*)
30 (XXVII)	86 (XXVII*)
31 (XXVI)	87 (XXVI*)
32 (XXV)	88 (XXV*)
33 (XXIV)	89 (XXIV*)
34 (XXIII)	90 (XXIII*)
35 (XXII)	91 (XXII*)
36 (XXI)	92 (XXI*)
37 (XX)	93 (XX*)
38 (XIX)	94 (XIX*)
39 (XVIII)	95 (XVIII*)
40 (XVII)	96 (XVII*)
41 (XVI)	97 (XVI*)
42 (XV)	98 (XV*)
43 (XIV)	99 (XIV*)
44 (XIII)	100 (XIII*)
45 (XII)	101 (XII*)
46 (XI)	102 (XI*)
47 (X)	103 (X*)
48 (IX)	104 (IX*)
49 (VIII)	105 (VIII*)
50 (VII)	106 (VII*)
51 (VI)	107 (VI*)
52 (V)	108 (V*)
53 (IV)	109 (IV*)
54 (III)	110 (III*)
55 (II)	111 (II*)
56 (I)	112 (I*)

PLATES

PART I

1, ALTAR G, VIEWED FROM THE NORTHWEST.

2, ALTAR G, WEST SIDE.

3, ALTAR B, SOUTH SIDE.

4, ALTAR B, EAST SIDE.

QUIRIGUA.

PLATE 2.

1, QUIRIGUA: ALTAR P, WEST SIDE.

2, QUIRIGUA: ALTAR P, DETAIL OF EAST SIDE, SHOWING OVERLAID GROTESQUE ORNAMENT.

PLATE 3.

1, COPAN: MOUND 21, SHOWING TERRACED PYRAMID WITH STAIRWAY, AND CHAMBER WITH INTERIOR STEPS.

2, COPAN: INTERIOR WALLS OF STRUCTURE 21A, AND CORNER MASK ON SIDE OF STRUCTURE 22.

PLATE 4.

1, COPAN: SMALL VAULTED CHAMBER, SHOWING NICHES, SHELVES, AND ROOFING STONES.

2, LABNA: CROSS-SECTION SHOWING TWO CHAMBERS OF THE TEMPLE.

1, CHICHEN ITZA: EXCAVATED PORTION OF A STRUCTURE NEAR THE GROUP OF THE COLUMNS.

2, UXMAL: SEALED PORTAL VAULT IN THE HOUSE OF THE GOVERNOR. THE VENEER CHARACTER OF THE CUT STONE IS EVIDENT.

PLATE 6

1, UXMAL: HOUSE OF THE DOVES; SERRATED ROOF-COMB.

2, SABACCHE: SMALL TEMPLE WITH FLYING FAÇADE DECORATED WITH LATTICE-WORK PANELS.

PLATE 7.

1, CHACMULTUN: EDIFICE 1, SHOWING USE OF COLUMNS FOR SUPPORT AND DECORATION,
ALSO ROOF NICHES OVER DOORWAYS.

2, CHICHEN ITZA: EXCAVATED PORTION OF A STRUCTURE NEAR THE GROUP OF THE COLUMNS,
SHOWING COLUMNS WITH ABACI.

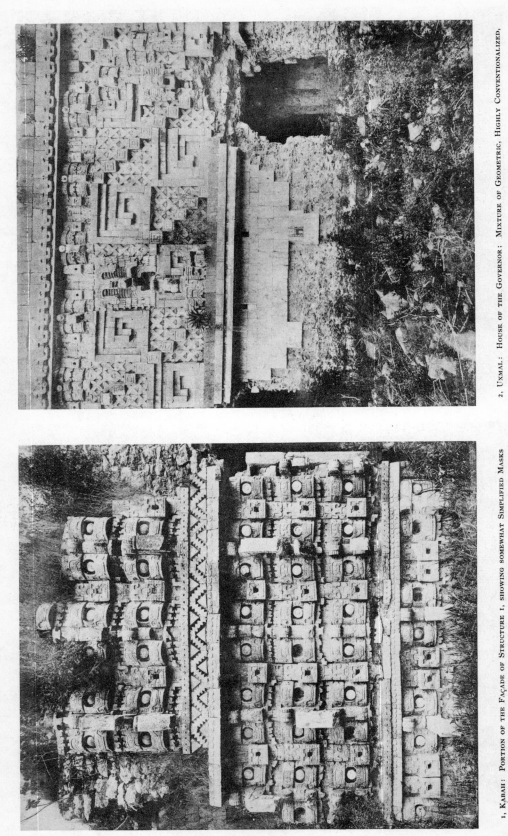

PLATE 8.

2, UXMAL: HOUSE OF THE GOVERNOR; MIXTURE OF GEOMETRIC, HIGHLY CONVENTIONALIZED, AND FAIRLY REALISTIC MOTIVES.

1, KABAH: PORTION OF THE FAÇADE OF STRUCTURE 1, SHOWING SOMEWHAT SIMPLIFIED MASKS IN THE UPPER AND LOWER ZONES.

PLATE 9.

1, UXMAL: WESTERN RANGE OF NUNNERY QUADRANGLE; MASK PANELS, GEOMETRIC DECORATION,
AND FREE USE OF WINDING SERPENT MOTIVE.

2, LABNA: PALACE, EAST WING OF UPPER RANGE; SIMPLIFIED MASK PANELS OVER WIDE DOORWAYS,
FLANKED BY LATTICEWORK AND FRET PANELS.

PLATE 10.

1, LABNA: PALACE, WEST WING, LOWER RANGE; SIMPLIFIED MASK PANELS.

2, LABNA: BUILDING NORTH OF PORTAL; MASK PANELS IN LOWER ZONE, SHOWING SUBSTITUTION
OF GEOMETRIC MOTIVES FOR THE ORIGINAL PARTS.

PLATE 11.

1, HOCHOB: LEFT WING OF PRINCIPAL STRUCTURE; MASK PANEL OVER DOORWAY.

2, HOCHOB: MIDDLE PORTION OF PRINCIPAL STRUCTURE; MASK PANEL OVER DOORWAY AND PROFILE SERPENT HEAD
AT EACH SIDE OF DOORWAY IN MIDDLE ZONE.

Plate 12.

2, Dsibilnocac (Itubide): Temple with Sealed Doorway; Mask Panel and Lateral Profile Masks.

1, Tabasqueño: North Façade of Temple; Mask Panel over Door and Profile Panel at each side of Door.

PLATE 13.

1, UXMAL: HOUSE OF THE MAGICIAN.

2, CHICHEN ITZA: CASA DE MONJAS; EASTERN FAÇADE OF THE EAST WING.

PLATE 14.

1, UXMAL: HOUSE OF THE GOVERNOR; GEOMETRIC DECORATION ALTERNATING WITH MASK PANELS IN TIERS.

2, UXMAL: EASTERN RANGE OF NUNNERY QUADRANGLE; LATTICE-WORK DECORATION OVERLAID WITH OTHER MOTIVES; ELABORATED CORNER MASKS.

PLATE 15.

1, CHICHEN ITZA: THE IGLESIA, SHOWING FLYING FAÇADE. THE MASKS OF THE FLYING FAÇADE ARE MADE OF REFUSE MATERIAL.

2, LABNA: THE PORTAL ARCH FROM THE SOUTHEAST; GEOMETRIC DECORATION.

3, SABACCHE: PRINCIPAL STRUCTURE, EAST FAÇADE; GEOMETRIC AND MASK PANEL DECORATION COMBINED.

PLATE 16.

1, KABAH: CASA 3, SHOWING SEVERE USE OF BANDED COLUMNS IN FAÇADE DECORATION.

2, XLABPAK: FAÇADE OF PRINCIPAL TEMPLE; MASK PANELS AND GEOMETRIC PANELS,

3, UXMAL: THE NUNNERY, NORTH RANGE; MASK PANELS ALTERNATING WITH ROOFED NICHES OVER DOORWAYS.

PLATE 17.

1-3, Terra-cotta Whistles from the Uloa Valley, Honduras; 4, 7, Terra-cotta Whistle and Figurine from Jonuta, Tabasco, Mexico; 5, 6, Terra-cotta Figurines from Mounds at Kamela, Rio Salinas (Chixoy), Guatemala; 8, Modern Cast from Terra-cotta Mould, Rio Salinas, Guatemala; 9-12, Terra-cotta Figurines from the Island of Jaina, Campeche.

PLATE 18.

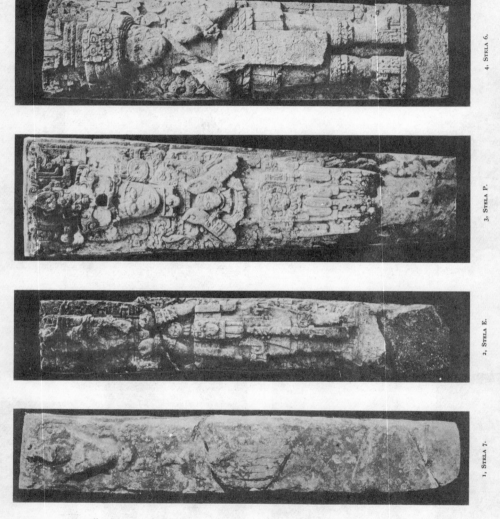

1, STELA 7.   2, STELA E.   3, STELA P.   4, STELA 6.

COPAN: SERIES OF ARCHAIC STELAE.

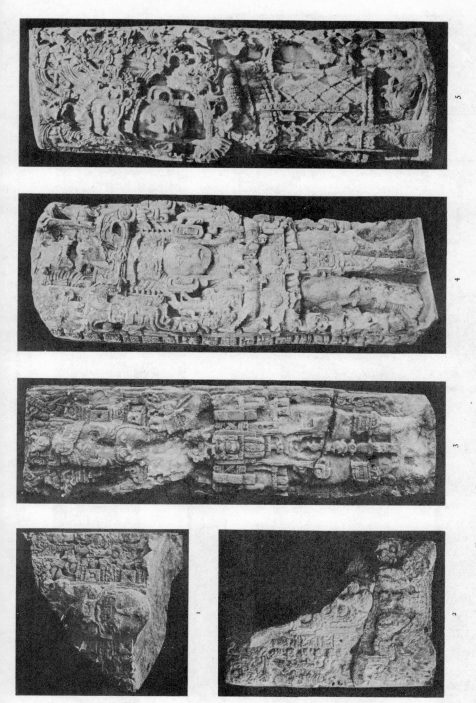

1, 2, Fragments of Stela 5, showing Sculpture on Opposite Sides; 3, Stela 3; 4, Stela N; 5, Stela H.

COPAN: SERIES SHOWING DEVELOPMENT OF SCULPTURE.

PLATE 20.

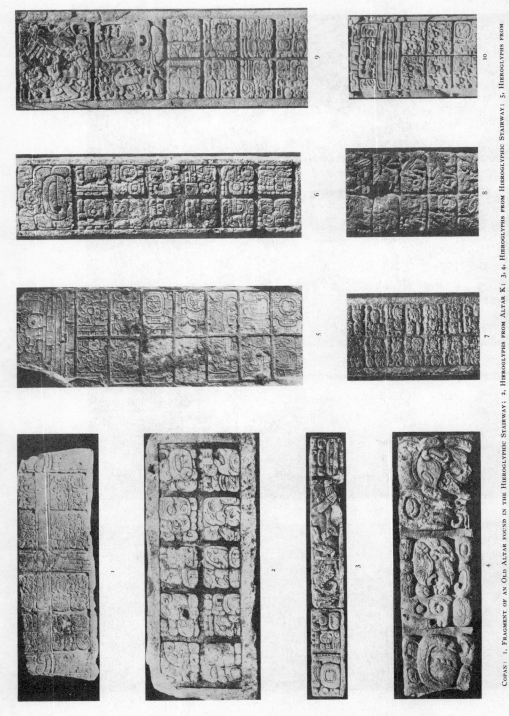

COPAN: 1, FRAGMENT OF AN OLD ALTAR FOUND IN THE HIEROGLYPHIC STAIRWAY; 2, HIEROGLYPHS FROM ALTAR K; 3, 4, HIEROGLYPHS FROM HIEROGLYPHIC STAIRWAY; 5, HIEROGLYPHS FROM STELA 9; 6, HIEROGLYPHS FROM STELA 6; 7, HIEROGLYPHS FROM STELA A; 8, HIEROGLYPHS FROM STELA D. QUIRIGUA: 9, HIEROGLYPHS FROM STELA D; 10, HIEROGLYPHS FROM STELA F.

1, STELA 7.   2, STELA 9.   3, STELA 1.   4, STELA 16.

TIKAL: SERIES SHOWING DEVELOPMENT OF SCULPTURE.

PLATE 22.

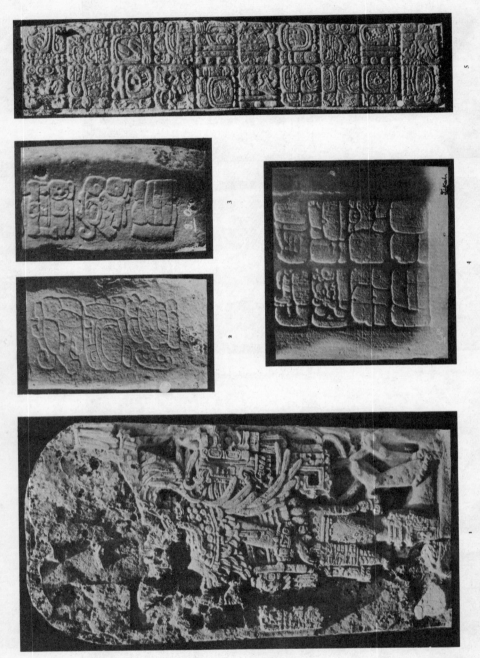

1, STELA 5. 2, THREE HIEROGLYPHS FROM STELA 13. 3, THREE HIEROGLYPHS FROM STELA 9. 4, EIGHT HIEROGLYPHS FROM STELA 1. 5, PART OF HIEROGLYPHS FROM WEST SIDE OF STELA 5.

TIKAL.

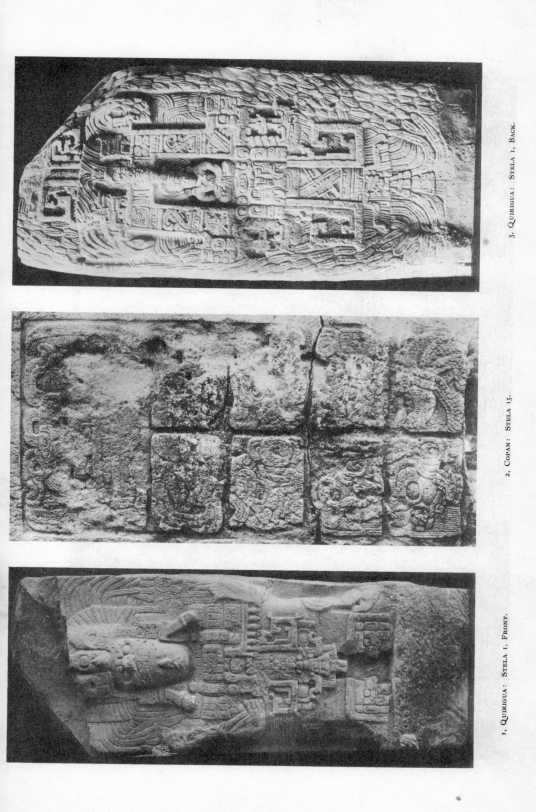

1, QUIRIGUA: STELA 1, FRONT.

2, COPAN: STELA 15.

3, QUIRIGUA: STELA 1, BACK.

PLATE 24.

3, STELA 12.

2, STELA 30.

1, STELA 25.

NARANJO: SERIES SHOWING DEVELOPMENT OF SCULPTURE.

Seibal: 1, Stela 7; 2, Stela 10. Piedras Negras: 3, Stela 13. Ocosingo: 4, Lower Portion of Stela 1; 5, Portion of Stela 2. Cankuen: 6, Lower Portion of Stela 1.

PLATE 26.

COPAN: 1, STONE HEAD FROM MOUND 32; 2, STONE HEAD FROM MOUND 41; 3, STONE HEAD FROM DEBRIS OF TEMPLE 2
PALENQUE: 4, 5, 6, THREE VIEWS OF STONE HEAD (AFTER MAUDSLAY).

PLATE 27.

1, CHICHEN ITZA: CASA DE MONJAS; SECOND RANGE.

2, CHICHEN ITZA: CASA DE MONJAS; EAST WING, FROM THE NORTH.

PLATE 28.

1, Reused Stones, Upper Chamber.

2, Geometric Panel, Second Range.

3, Mask Panel in Frieze of Foundation.

4, Mask Panel in Frieze of Foundation.

5, Mask Panel, East Façade of East Wing.

6, Northeast Corner of Façade, East Wing.

CHICHEN ITZA: CASA DE MONJAS.

PLATE 29.

1, SCULPTURED COLUMN, NORTH TEMPLE OF BALL COURT. 2, FRESCO PAINTING, TEMPLE OF THE JAGUARS.
3, PILASTER, TEMPLE OF THE TABLES. 4, ATLANTEAN FIGURE. 5, CHACMOOL FIGURE AT SAN SALVADOR.
6, SCULPTURED COLUMNS, TEMPLE OF THE TABLES. 7, JAGUAR RELIEF, MAUSOLEUM, MOUND 13.
ALL EXCEPT NUMBER 5 ARE AT CHICHEN ITZA.

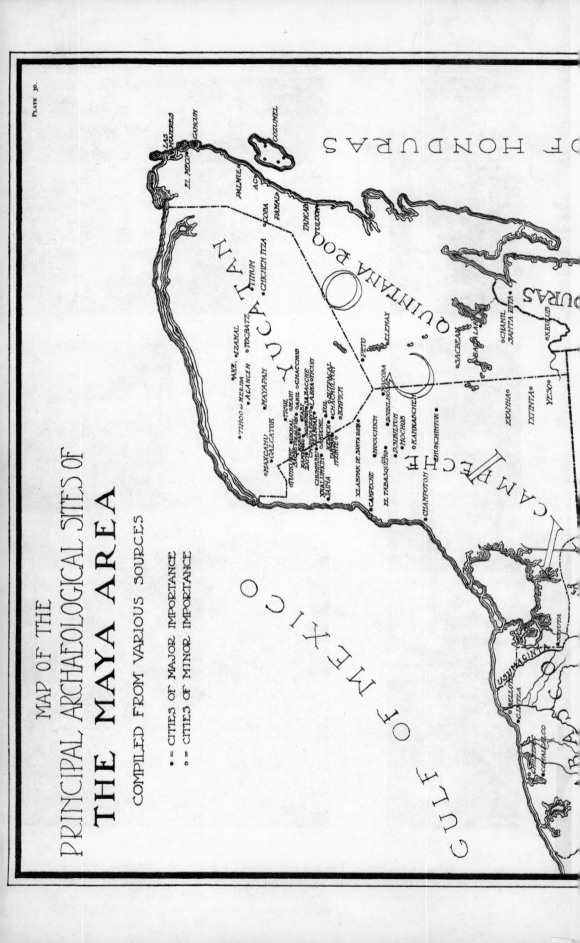

Plate 30.

MAP OF THE
PRINCIPAL ARCHAEOLOGICAL SITES OF
THE MAYA AREA

COMPILED FROM VARIOUS SOURCES

• = CITIES OF MAJOR IMPORTANCE
○ = CITIES OF MINOR IMPORTANCE

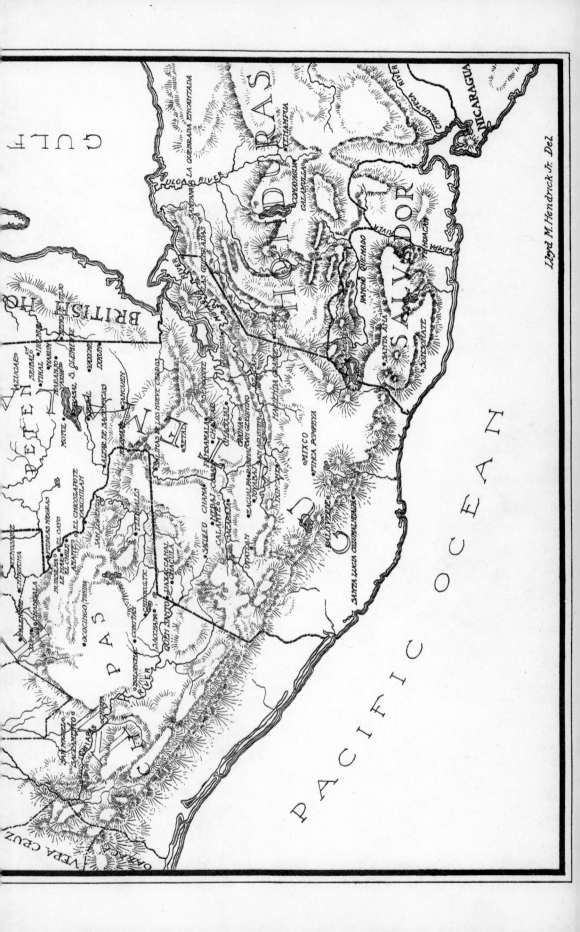

Lloyd M. Hendrick Jr. Del.

PART II

THE NUCLEAR CIVILIZATION OF THE MAYA
AND RELATED CULTURES

INTRODUCTORY NOTE*

THIS second part is intended as a general commentary and explanation of the more important phases of the ancient life and arts of the Indians of Mexico and Central America, and especially of their history. The substance of it is drawn from many sources, for the anthropologist must mould together and harmonize the gross results of several sciences. Archæology, ethnology, somatology, and linguistics all make their special contributions and we are only on the threshold of our subject. In the Mexican and Central American field we find the accumulated writings that result from four hundred years of European contact with the Indians and in addition a mass of native documents and monumental inscriptions expressed in several hieroglyphic systems.

The general method in this part will be to take up in order the recognized "horizons" of pre-Columbian history, beginning with the earliest of which we have knowledge. In relation to each horizon we will examine the records and discuss the principal developments in arts, beliefs, and social structures. The introductory chapter is designed to put before the reader such facts as may be necessary for a ready understanding of the discussions and explanations that will follow.

The Mexican Hall of the American Museum of Natural History furnishes illustrations of most of the facts given herewith. This Hall contains both originals and casts brought together by various expeditions of the Museum and of other scientific institutions. The principal patrons of science whose names should be mentioned in connection with the upbuilding of these collections are: Willard Brown, Austin Corbin, R. P. Doremus, Anson W. Hard, Archer M. Huntington, Morris K. Jesup, James H. Jones, Minor C. Keith, the Duke of Loubat, William Mack, Henry Marquand, Doctor William Pepper, A. D. Straus, I. McI. Strong, Cornelius Vanderbilt, Henry Villard, William C. Whitney. But thanks are also due to innumerable persons who have contributed single specimens and small collections as well as those who have placed information at the disposal of the scientific staff. The principal collectors have been: George Byron Gordon, Aleš Hrdlička, Carl Lumholtz, Francis C. Nicholas, Marshall H. Saville, Eduard Seler, Herbert J. Spinden, and John L. Stephens.

---

* This text generally follows that of the third edition published in 1928 and printed subsequently in stereotype until 1951. There is new material in the Epilogue. However, many developments after 1928 are not treated, including amendments in the historic periods. While the new face of Mayan and Central American history is sketched in the Epilogue, it may be pointed out here that the dates for the Early, Middle, and Great Periods are not much affected. After 629 A.D., however, several changes are required in accordance with data that cannot be treated here.

FUNERARY URN FROM A ZAPOTECAN TOMB

The cylindrical urn is concealed behind the human figure. The dress of the human figure consists of a cape, apron, and a widespreading head-dress. Over the face is worn a mask. Height, 15½ inches.

INTRODUCTION

Geography and Natural Environment. Unfortunately the terms "Mexico and Central America" are not mutually exclusive. Central America is a natural division comprised between the Isthmus of Tehuantepec and the Isthmus of Panama. Mexico is a political division that includes several states in Central America, namely, Chiapas, Tabasco, Campeche, Yucatan, and the territory of Quintana Roo. The ancient high cultures of Mexico hardly extended as far north as the Tropic of Cancer and the region beyond this is of slight interest to us. Positions south of Mexico will often be referred to the areas of the modern political units although these have no immediate relation to pre-Spanish conditions. These political units are: Guatemala, British Honduras, Honduras, Salvador, Nicaragua, and Costa Rica.

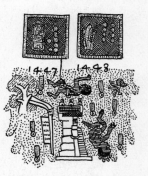

Fig. 1. The Great Snowstorm of 1447 shown in the Pictographic Record of the Aztecs called Codex Telleriano Remensis.

Although lying within the tropics, the territory extending from the Isthmus of Panama to Central Mexico exhibits great extremes of climate and topography and hence of plant and animal life. The year is everywhere divided into a wet and a dry season but the relative duration of each depends upon land form and altitude. The coast of the Pacific is considerably drier than that of the Atlantic. Three climatic zones are generally recognized, namely, the *Tierra Caliente* (Hot Land), *Tierra Templada* (Temperate Land), and *Tierra Fria* (Cold Land), and in some regions each of these has an arid and a humid strip. The change from luxuriant forests to open thorny deserts is often very sudden. On the high plateau or *Tierra Fria* the natural warmth of the latitude is largely overcome by the altitude. In the Valley of Mexico snow falls only at rare intervals, yet chilling winds are common in the winter. Much of the plateau from Mexico south into Guatemala is open farming land well suited to the raising of maize and wheat where water is sufficient. The shoulders of the mountains bear forests of pine and oak while the highest peaks are crowned with perpetual snow.

A description of the mountains, rivers, and lakes will help towards an understanding of the problems that are before us. The broad plateau, crossed by irregular ranges of mountains, that occupies the states of New Mexico and Arizona continues far south into Mexico. On the western rim the Sierra Madre lifts a great pine-covered barrier, beyond which the land drops off quickly into the hot fringe of coastal plain bordering the Pacific Ocean and the Gulf of California. The highest mountains of the western Sierra Madre are El Nevado and Colima, the first a snowy peak 14,370 feet high and the second an active volcano 12,278 feet high. On the eastern rim of the central plateau the second Sierra

267

Madre is less continuous but it culminates in the loftiest peak of all Mexico—
the wonderful cone of Orizaba. This mountain rises from the tropical jungles
well into the region of perpetual snow and attains an elevation of 18,314 feet
above the sea. Its name in Aztecan is Citlaltepetl, which means Star Mountain.
Two other famous peaks of Mexico are Popocatepetl and Iztaccihuatl, both
names being pure Aztecan. The first means Smoking Mountain and the second
White Woman. These volcanic crests rise into the snowy zone from the table-
land which is itself about 8,000 feet above the sea.

In southern Mexico the plateau area enclosed between the principal sierras
narrows perceptibly, because the shore line of the Pacific and the mountain
range that parallels it swing more and more towards
the east. At the Isthmus of Tehuantepec a low valley
separates the highland area of Mexico from that of
Central America. This second table-land is not so wide
as the one we have just considered and is more deeply
dissected by rivers. The mountains of Guatemala rise
to a considerable altitude, the highest being Tacaná
with 13,976 feet elevation. Active volcanoes are numerous and earthquakes frequent and often disastrous.
The Volcan de Agua and the Volcan de Fuego (Volcano
of Water and Volcano of Fire) look down upon Ciudad
Vieja and Antigua Guatemala, the old Spanish capitals
which each in turn destroyed. The cordillera still presents its most abrupt front to the Pacific and on the

Fig. 2. The Smoke
reaches the Stars, a
Mexican Picture of a
Volcanic Eruption in
the Codex Telleriano
Remensis.

eastern side, in Guatemala and Honduras, there are
high forest-bearing ridges between the river systems.
The Cockscomb Mountains in British Honduras are a
low outlying group. In southern Nicaragua the main
chain is broken by a low broad valley that extends from
ocean to ocean. In Costa Rica and Panama a single
range stretches midway along the narrow strip of land, with peaks that rise
above 11,000 feet.

The lowland strip on the Pacific side of our area is a narrow fringe. Like the
central plateau it is for the most part arid, but irrigation makes it productive.
The lowlands of the Atlantic side are generally wet and heavily forested. The
greatest land mass of uniformly low elevation is the Peninsula of Yucatan. In
eastern Honduras and Nicaragua there are extensive river valleys of low elevation.

The river systems of Mexico and Central America flow into the two bounding
oceans or into lakes which have no outlets. Several closed basins occur on the
Mexican table-land. The Rio Nazas and the Rio Nieves flow into salt marshes
in the northern state of Coahuila. But the most important interior basin is the
Valley of Mexico. In this mountain-enclosed valley, whose general level is 7,500
feet above the sea, there are five lakes which in order from north to south are
named Tzompanco, Xaltocan, Texcoco, Xochimilco, and Chalco. The last two
contain fresh water, since they drain into Lake Texcoco, but the rest are more
or less brackish. Lake Texcoco is by far the largest, although its area has
been greatly reduced by natural and artificial causes since the coming of the
Spaniards.

The largest river of Mexico is the Rio Lerma which takes the name Rio de

Santiago during its deep and tortuous passage from Lake Chapala to the Pacific. Farther to the south is the Rio de las Balsas which likewise flows into the western ocean. The name means "River of the Rafts" and is given because of a peculiar floating apparatus made of gourds tied to a wooden framework that is used on this stream. Flowing into the Gulf of Mexico are several large streams, among which may be mentioned the Panuco, Papaloapan, Grijalva, and Usumacinta. The last is by far the greatest in volume of water, and with its maze of tributaries drains a large area of swamp and jungle in which are buried some of the most wonderful ruined cities of the New World.

In the northern part of Yucatan there are no rivers on the surface on account of the porous limestone. Instead there are great natural wells called *cenotes* where the roofs of subterranean rivers have fallen in. Many of the ancient cities were built near such natural wells.

Passing to the south the most important river of Guatemala is the Motagua, which has cut a fine valley through a region of lofty mountains. In Honduras there are several large rivers, including the Uloa, Patuca, and Segovia. The lake region of Nicaragua is drained by the San Juan River that flows into the Caribbean Sea. Nearly all the streams of Central America that flow into the Pacific are short and steep torrents. An important exception is the Lempa River that forms part of the interior boundary of Salvador.

Concerning lakes, mention has already been made of Chapala and Texcoco, the most important in Mexico. The former is about fifty miles in length. In the state of Michoacan there are a number of beautiful lakes intimately connected with the history and mythology of the Tarascan Indians. The most famous is called Patzcuaro. In southern Yucatan the shallow body of water known as Lake Peten also has a distinct historical interest. Several lakes in Guatemala are well known on account of the rare beauty of their situation. Lake Atitlan is surrounded by lofty mountains, and Lake Izabal, or Golfo Dulce, is famous for the luxuriance of the vegetation that screens its banks. Lakes Nicaragua and Managua are well known on account of their connection with the much-discussed canal projects. The Island of Ometepe in Lake Nicaragua bears an active volcano.

In regard to the geology it is only necessary to point out a few of the more important characters. The highlands which bear so many active and quiescent volcanoes naturally show great masses of eruptive rocks, some due to recent action and others much more ancient. Porous tufa is a common material for sculptures in many parts of Mexico and Central America. In other places there are great beds of softer and finer grained material also of volcanic origin. In these places, such as Copan in western Honduras and Mitla in southern Mexico, building in stone received its greatest development. The soft greenish stone of Copan seems to be a solidified mud flow permeated with volcanic ash rather than a true lava flow of melted rock. Limestones are also common and important in the economic development. In some regions there are beds of a hard, blue limestone going back to the Carboniferous epoch. This stone makes an excellent cement after burning. The Peninsula of Yucatan is a great plain of limestone of much more recent formation. Like our own Florida it was once a coral reef which was lifted above the sea by some natural agency. This limestone gets older and more solid as we approach the base of the peninsula but at best is rather porous and coarse-grained.

The fauna and flora present great variation. In the moist lowlands the monkeys play in the tree tops and the jaguar lies in wait for its prey. Alligators and crocodiles infest the rivers and swamps. Two small species of deer and the ocellated turkey are important items in the meat supply of Yucatan, that includes also the iguana, the peccary, and various large rodents. The tapir and manatee are the largest animals of the lowlands but neither seems to have been of great significance to the natives. Bats are frequently represented in the ancient art and a bat demon appears in several myths.

Upon the highlands of Mexico the Toltecan deer is still hunted, together with the wild turkey that is the parent of our domestic birds. The turkey was, in fact, domesticated by the Mexican tribes. It probably occurred southward over the Guatemalan highlands, but is now extinct in this latter region. In the southern part of Central America the place of the turkey as an item of diet is taken by the curassow, a yellow-crested bird with black plumage. The coppery-tailed trogon, the famous quetzal, was sacred in ancient times and is now the emblem of Guatemala. This beautiful bird occurs only in the cloud cap forest zone on the high mountains of southern Mexico and Guatemala. Blue macaws, parrots,

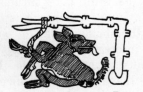

Fig. 3. Yucatan Deer caught in a Snare. From the Mayan Codex, Tro-Cortesianus.

Fig. 4. The Moan Bird, or Yucatan Owl, personified as a Demigod. Dresden Codex.

paroquets, and humming birds contributed their gay plumage to adorn head-dresses and feather-covered cloaks. These and many other birds doubtless flitted about in the aviary of Moctezuma. The black vulture, the king vulture, and the harpy eagle are other conspicuous birds often figured in the ancient art. The coyote, ocelot, and puma are the principal beasts of prey on the highlands.

Among the characteristic trees of the lowlands may be mentioned the palm, which occurs in great variety, the amate and ceiba, both of which attain to large size, as well as mahogany, Spanish cedar (which is not a cedar at all but a close relative of the mahogany), campeche, or logwood, rosewood, sapodilla, and other trees of commerce. Upon the higher mountain slopes are forests of long-leaf pine and of oak. In the desert stretches the cactus is often tree-like and there are many shrubs that in the brief spring become masses of highly-colored blossoms.

Some of the principal crops of Mexico and Central America have been introduced from the Old World, including coffee, sugar cane, and bananas. Other

crops such as maize, beans, chili peppers, cocoa, etc., are indigenous. Among
the native fruits may be mentioned the aguacate, or alligator pear, the mamey,
the anona, or custard apple, the guanabina, jocote, and nance.

History of European Contact. The great area with which we are concerned
has been in touch with Europe since the beginning of the sixteenth century.
Columbus, on his last voyage in 1502, landed on the northern coast of Honduras
and rounded the stormy cape called Gracias à Dios. Later he skirted the shore
of Costa Rica and Panama and entered the body of water which was named in
his honor Bahia del Almirante—Bay of the Admiral. He brought back sensational news of the gold in possession of the natives, which they had told him
came from a district called Veragua. After a few years of stormy warfare the
Spaniards established themselves firmly in this golden land. Vasco Nuñez de
Balboa, who emerged from the bickering mob as the strongest leader, was the
first white man to cross the Isthmus. This he did in 1513, grandiloquently laying claim to the Pacific Ocean and all the shores that it
touched in the name of Spain. The crown appointed the
greedy and black-hearted Pedrarias Davila governor of
Darien and in 1517 he succeeded in having Balboa be-
headed on a flimsy charge. Colonization and exploration
went forward rapidly. In 1519 the old city of Panama,
now in ruins, was founded. The rich region around the
Nicaraguan lakes was discovered by Gil Gonzalez Davila
and the city of Granada was founded in 1524. The exploration from the southern base came in contact with
that from the north in Salvador shortly after this event.

Fig. 5. Spanish
Ship in the Aubin
Codex.

Let us now direct our attention to the conquest of
Mexico. Perhaps the Portuguese were the first to sight
the mainland of Yucatan in 1493. There is little to prove this except one or
two charts or maps made in the first decade of the sixteenth century that show
the peninsula in its proper location. In 1511 or 1512 a ship from Darien was
wrecked and some of the sailors were cast upon the coast of Yucatan. Most of
them were killed and sacrificed, but two survived. One of these survivors was
Geronimo de Aguilar, who later was rescued by Cortez and became his guide
and interpreter.

The first accredited voyage of discovery to Mexico was one under the command of Francisco Hernandez de Cordoba, which sailed from Cuba in February,
1517. He coasted the northern and eastern shores of Yucatan. When he attempted to obtain water he was worsted in a serious battle with the Maya
Indians. His expedition finally returned to Cuba in a sad plight. The next year
Juan de Grijalva set out to continue the exploration of the new land with the
stone-built cities. He landed at Cozumel Island and took possession. He explored the eastern coast of Yucatan as well as the northern and western ones,
discovered the mouth of the large river that bears his name, and proceeded as
far as the Island of Sacrifices in the harbor of Vera Cruz.

The next year Hernando Cortez was sent out by Velasquez, the governor of
Cuba, to conquer the new land. He landed at Cozumel Island and rescued
Geronimo de Aguilar. Then he followed the coast to the mouth of the Grijalva
River where he disembarked and fought the important battle of Cintla, the first

engagement in the New World in which cavalry was used. After a signal victory Cortez continued his way to Vera Cruz. Here delay and dissension seemed about to break the luck of the invaders.

Although the Mexicans were somewhat inclined to regard the Spaniards as supernatural visitants and to associate their coming with the fabled return of Quetzalcoatl, the Plumed Serpent, still Moctezuma refused to grant an interview to Cortez. The Totonacan city of Cempoalan opened its gates and became allies of the invaders. Finally, at the instigation of their stout-hearted captain, the Spaniards destroyed their ships on the shore in order to steel their resolution through the impossibility of retreat. Then the little band of 450 white men with their retinue of natives marched towards the highlands. The route led past Jalapa and over the mountains to the fortified city of Tlaxcala. This city, after a skirmish, likewise enlisted in the Spanish cause, a course that came easy because Tlaxcala was a traditional enemy of Tenochtitlan, the ancient Mexico City, and had withstood the attacks of the Aztecs for many years. From here Cortez passed to the sacred city of Cholula where, suspecting treachery, he caused many of the inhabitants to be massacred.

Fig. 6. Cortez arrives with Sword and Cross and Moctezuma brings him Gold. Codex Vaticanus 3738.

In the Spanish histories one hears much concerning the omens, the prophecies, and the vain appeals to the gods that became more and more frequent and frantic as the invaders approached the capital. Arriving at Ixtapalapan they entered upon the great causeway leading out to the Venice-like city in the lake. Accepting the inevitable, Moctezuma and his nobles met the Spaniards and conducted them to the Palace of Axayacatl, which was prepared for their habitation. This took place in November, 1519. The fears of Moctezuma were soon fulfilled, for he was taken prisoner and held as a hostage of safety in his own capital.

Meanwhile Velasquez, convinced of the unfaithfulness of Cortez, dispatched Narvaez to capture the rebellious agent. But Narvaez was himself captured and his soldiers went to augment the army of the victor.

Alvarado had been left in command of the garrison at Tenochtitlan during the absence of Cortez. The time approached for the great feast of Tezcatlipoca and the Spaniards, fearing the results of this appeal to the principal Aztecan god, resolved to be the first to strike. The multitude assembled in the temple enclosure was massacred and after this deed the soldiers fought their way back to the stronghold in which they were quartered. The Aztecs were thoroughly aroused by this unwarranted cruelty as well as by the cupidity of the Spaniards. Cortez hastened back to take personal charge; but in spite of victories in the storming of the pyramids and in other hand-to-hand contests, the invaders were so weakened that their condition was truly alarming. Moctezuma died in captivity and the last restraint of the natives was removed.

The night of June 30, 1520, is famous as La Noche Triste—The Sad Night— for on this night the Spaniards attempted to steal out of the city that had become untenable. The natives were warned by a woman's shriek and a desperate encounter took place on the narrow causeway leading to Tlacopan. The bridges were torn down and the Spanish soldiers in armor were hemmed in between the deep canals. At last, however, the firm land was reached. Here, instead of following up the victory, the natives permitted the Spaniards to re-form their ranks. A few days later Cortez was able to restore something of his lost prestige by the decisive victory at Otumba, after which he continued his retreat to the friendly Tlaxcala.

A year was spent in recuperation, in building boats for an attack from the lake, and in putting down the Aztecan outposts. In the meantime the natives were suffering from a dreadful visitation of smallpox, introduced by the Spaniards, and Cuitlahuac, the successor of Moctezuma, had died of this disease after a rule of eighty days. Finally Tenochtitlan was besieged again. The buildings were leveled to the ground as the Spaniards advanced. The brave defense of Cuauhtemoc availed for naught against cannon and steel armor. On the 13th of August, 1521, the conquest of Tenochtitlan was achieved and the spirit of a warlike people forever broken.

The Valley of Mexico having been taken, numerous expeditions were sent out to subdue the more distant provinces and to establish colonies. Alvarado invaded the south and by 1524 he had captured Utatlan and other native strongholds on the highlands of Guatemala and had invaded Salvador. Cortez himself undertook a wonderful march from Vera Cruz to the Gulf of Honduras to punish

Fig. 7.   Aztecan Canoe.   Lienzo de Tlaxcala.

an unruly subordinate. His course lay through the swamps and jungles of the Usumacinta Basin, thence across the savannahs of southern Yucatan to Lake Peten, and, finally, over the mountains to Lake Izabal and the Motagua River. Even today much of his route would be called impassable for an army. Puerto Cortez, on the northern coast of Honduras, was founded at the conclusion of this expedition. The exploitation of Yucatan and Tabasco was granted to Francisco Montejo, who began the conquest of this low-lying territory in 1527. The first campaigns were disastrous and heartbreaking. Several short-lived Salamancas were founded, one of them at Chichen Itza. But the odds were too great and by 1535 all the Spaniards had been killed or expelled. The son of Montejo renewed the struggle. In 1540 Campeche was founded and early in 1542 the city of Mérida was established upon the site of an earlier Mayan town.

Progress was also rapid in the north. Nuño de Guzman departed in 1529 on a mission to conquer Michoacan and the great northern province known as New Galicia. His rule was marred by many acts of cruelty. In 1538 Coronado, the successor of Guzman, led his army northward to the land of the Pueblo Indians and then out into the Great Plains. Before the first English settlement was made in North America the power of Spain was firmly established, not only throughout Central America and Mexico, but also in the southwestern part of the United States.

The spiritual conquest was no less remarkable than the territorial. The priests accompanied and even preceded the armies with the doctrine of the cross. The rough and ready characters that enliven the wonderful drama of this period had the vices of greed and cruelty, but nearly all were imbued with a pride of religion, if not with the true flame. The firmness and bigotry on the one hand and the open sympathy on the other with which the Catholic fathers met the practical problems before them resulted in vast achievements. Either by accident or design certain patron saints and efficacious shrines of special interest to the natives were not long in becoming known. The Virgin of Guadeloupe and the Black Christ of Esquipulas brought many converts to the foreign faith. Church building was carried on apace. The various religious orders became rich and powerful and exerted a strong influence upon civil administration.

The later history of this great region can be passed over briefly. Cortez was the first governor general of Mexico but he was soon shorn of his power as dictator at large. The First Audiencia was appointed in 1528 and is noteworthy simply by reason of its misrule. The Second Audiencia, beginning two years later, put through some excellent reform laws. The first Viceroy, the great and good Mendoza, arrived in 1535 and for fifteen years the land prospered under his rule, which was benign without being weak. He was succeeded by Luis de Velasco, who emancipated many of the enslaved Indians. The long line of viceroys continued until 1821, when Spain was forced to relinquish her provinces in America. Among the greatest of the viceroys was Bucareli, the forty-sixth in line, who ruled Mexico from 1771–1779 while the United States of America were just beginning to feel the pulse of life.

During the viceregal period in Mexico the region to the south was ruled by the captain general of Guatemala. The dominion was subdivided into five departments corresponding to the modern republics of Guatemala (which then included the Mexican state of Chiapas), Honduras, Salvador, Nicaragua, and Costa Rica. Panama was ruled from the South American province of New Granada.

Weakened by Napoleonic wars and rent by internal dissensions, Spain found herself in the first two decades of the nineteenth century unable to maintain her waning power in America. Bolivar and his brother patriots raised the standard of revolt in South America in 1810 and in the same year war for independence broke out in the north. Hidalgo, the parish priest of Dolores, rang the liberty bell of Mexican freedom on the 16th of September, 1810. This beloved patriot was captured the year following, and shot, but the revolution, once begun, was continued under Morelos and other leaders. After 1815 the cause seemed hopeless, but in 1820 there was a new uprising and General Iturbide, who was sent to put it down, turned his army against the government and established himself as emperor. Central America was also included in this Mexican empire. The rule of Iturbide soon became unpopular and in 1823 he abdicated his throne. The Mexican republic that was then instituted continued until the French intervention in 1861. During this time the most noteworthy events were the war with the United States in 1846–47 and the passing of the reform laws under Benito Juarez that freed Mexico from the oppressions of the church.

As a result of the French intervention Maximilian of Austria was made emperor. This unfortunate ruler, who did much to beautify Mexico City, was dethroned and shot in 1867. The republic was then re-established.

The other republics of Central America formed a federal union at the time the first Mexican empire came to an end in 1823. This union was preserved till 1839 and several later attempts were made to restore it. The five republics have had such tempestuous careers as a result of warfare, usurpation, and political brigandage that their material and social development has been stunted. Several are now, however, on the high road to stability.

Panama was until 1903 a part of Colombia. British Honduras had its origin in the concessions given to English logwood gatherers and due to the fact that pirates found refuge behind the coral reefs that line the shores. The English claim to the Mosquito Coast rested upon a similar flimsy basis, and was finally abandoned.

Languages. The twenty distinct stocks of related languages formerly recognized in Mexico and Central America have now been greatly reduced. Of those that remain, some occupied small areas and had little in the way of dialectic variation, while others stretched over wide territories and were divided into many mutually unintelligible tongues, which, in turn, were subdivided into well-defined dialects. Several stocks are now approaching extinction through the substitution of Spanish. A number of languages, however, are still spoken by hundreds of thousands of natives.

The language having the greatest geographical extension within the area under consideration is the Mexican, or Nahuan, now consolidated with the Piman, Shoshonean, etc., in a great stock called the Uto-Aztecan. In its extent this stock may be compared to the Indo-Iranian of the Old World which comprises most of the modern and ancient languages of Europe as well as those of a large part of Asia. Within the United States are the numerous Shoshonean tribes found as far north as Idaho, reaching into California on the one hand and into Texas on the other. In southern Arizona and northwestern Mexico come the Piman group. East of the Sierra Madre are the Tarahumare and the Tepehuane. These languages are mutually unintelligible, although morphologically related, and all are subdivided into dialects. The relationship is proved through laborious comparison and analysis of the words and grammar, in the same way as the philologist proves that Persian, Greek, Russian, English and Welsh are all cognate tongues. Farther to the south are still other divisions of the stock, including the Huichol and Cora of the mountainous region north of Guadalajara and the Mexican or Aztecan of the Valley of Mexico and adjacent country. The Mexican language is still spoken by a million or more natives and is divided into a number of dialects. Properly the Aztecs are a single tribe whose chief city was Tenochtitlan, the ancient Mexican City. They first appear on the page of history as the Mexitin, along with the closely related Chalca, Xochimilca, etc. The people of Central Mexico called their language Nahuatl, meaning "clear speech," and nicknamed their relatives to the south, Pipil, or "boys," because they spoke awkwardly. Mexican colonies were widespread before the coming of the Spaniards and during the Conquest the distribution of this nation was made still greater. The Mexicans, and especially the natives of Tlaxcala, accompanied the Spaniards on military expeditions against other tribes and as a consequence many place names in southern Mexico and Guatemala were translated into their language. There were, however, large groups of Indians of Mexican stock already located in southern Guatemala and in Salvador. Still farther south were the Niquirao of Nicaragua and a little-known group called the Sigua in Costa Rica.

The wide geographical distribution of Uto-Aztecan languages has an undeniable historical significance. The numerous tribes represent a very wide range in culture albeit nearly all are dwellers of arid or semi-arid regions. Some, like the Paiute, are miserable "diggers" willing to eat anything that will support life; others like the Comanche are warlike raiders; more progressive tribes like the Hopi have adopted agriculture and developed interesting arts and customs; while the highest members of the group are among the most civilized nations of the New World. It seems clear that language can be used as a basis of classification over a much greater stretch of time than can other social habits summed up as "culture." Particular phases of art, religion, and government develop and disappear, but the grouping of sounds used to express ideas remains as proof that peoples now far apart geographically, as well as in their habits and achievements, were once close together. The peculiar distribution of the Uto-Aztecan languages may indicate a general southward movement of the stock.

The second most important linguistic stock is the Mayan, now spoken by over half a million people. This stock has only one outlying member, namely, the Huasteca of northern Vera Cruz. The other twenty-one languages cover a continuous area in the Mexican states of Yucatan, Tabasco, and Chiapas, and in the republic of Guatemala. The most important language of the group is the Maya proper, which is spoken by the natives of Yucatan and by the Lacandone Indians of the Usumacinta Valley. The Tzental, Quiché, Cakchiquel, Chol, and Chorti are other prominent languages.

In the region of the Isthmus of Tehuantepec are the Zapotecan and Mixtecan stocks, which differ widely in sound and structure from the Mayan and Nahuan tongues that hem them in. West and east of the Valley of Mexico are, respectively, the Tarascan and Totonacan stocks, which show no great amount of subdivision. In Honduras, Nicaragua, and Costa Rica are several language groups that have never been carefully studied. It seems likely that some of these will be consolidated when words and grammatical structures are better known. The Chiapanecan languages were spoken in three localities on the Pacific side of Nicaragua and Costa Rica, while a fourth division occupied a small area far to the northwest on the banks of the Chiapas River. It is now believed that the Otomi group, as well as a number of minor languages, including the Mazatecan, belong in a single stock with the Chiapanecan. If this supposed connection should prove true a northern movement of the stock would be pretty surely indicated. Several members of the Subtiaban stock show the same south to north movement and here there is evidence that the migration took place some three centuries before the coming of the Spaniards. Parts of the Isthmian region were held by tribes having linguistic affiliation with South America and it is not unlikely that a considerable back flow from South America made itself felt along the Atlantic coast of Central America, if we may judge by ethnological features and by suggested linguistic connections.

The great Hokan stock has now been extended from California across northern Mexico to Texas, taking in the Seri and numerous other tribes of low culture. For the most part these tribes are extinct or at least have lost the ancient speech.

Ethnology. To a less extent than the native languages the old-time customs still hold out against the tide of European influence. In regions not easily accessible on account of deserts, mountains, or tropical jungles, there are a number of Indian tribes that preserve in a large measure their ancient arts and ideas. But the study of these remnant peoples has not been very thorough.

Fig. 8. Design on Modern Huichol Ribbon.

Fig. 9. Woven Pouch of the Huichol Indians showing Two-Headed Austrian Eagle.

The Pima, Seri, Tarahumare, Tepehuane, and other tribes of the extreme north and northwest of Mexico have until recent times been comparatively unmodified by Spanish influences. Basketry, textiles, and pottery have been maintained by them as well as many religious ceremonies. Farther south among the Cora and Huichol there also are surviving arts. The woven fabrics of these Indians are very beautiful but introduced ideas are frequently seen. For instance, a very common motive in Huichol textile art is the two-headed Austrian eagle evidently taken from the coins of Charles V. Crowns similar to those worn by the two-headed eagle are often shown on the heads of rampant animals. But most of the motives are doubtless of native origin.

Among the Huichol and Tarahumare the curious *peyote*, or *hikule* worship, may be studied. A small variety of cactus is eaten, which induces ecstasy or stupor accompanied by color visions and peculiar dreams. Elaborate ceremonies are associated with the eating and gathering of this plant. The religious cult of the peyote has swept over a large portion of the Great Plains Area of the United States and is known even to Indians in the neighborhood of the Great Lakes. There can be no doubt that the narcotic action of the peyote was known to the Aztecs, who made a ceremonial use of it under the name *teonanacatl*. An intoxicating drink called *teswin* is commonly made in northern Mexico from the heart of the mescal plant. It takes the place of the famous *pulque*, the ancient beverage of the Mexican highlands. Hunting dances in which are employed regalia and ceremonial objects of great interest occur among the Huichol and neighboring tribes. The so-called "god's eyes" made of yarn strung spider-web fashion over crossed sticks are practically identical with the "squash blossoms" of the Pueblo Indians. There are also real temple structures, or "god houses," which are very significant when we consider the former importance of the temple among the more highly civilized peoples to the south. In these and other respects the Huichol culture is about midway between the culture of the Southwestern Pueblo tribes and that which formerly existed in central Mexico.

Elsewhere in northern and central Mexico it is possible to find many suggestions of ancient Indian ways of living. In nearly all the outlying villages the old-time thatched huts are still used, while baskets, gourd vessels, wooden bowls, earthen pots, and other household objects hark back to native origins, although often modified by European contact. For instance, glazing is commonly seen on the modern pottery. Many travelers in Mexico bring away as souvenirs pieces of pottery from Guadalajara and Cuernavaca. These wares are made by Indians, but in decoration they have only slight traces of the ancient art of the Mexicans.

In dress there are noteworthy survivals. The *serape* made either on the narrow hand loom or on a crude form of the Spanish tread loom is a picturesque element in the national dress that is rapidly disappearing from view. Time was when the rich plantation owner wore a gayly colored blanket on *fiesta* days. The most famous centers for the manufacture and sale of blankets were the cities of Saltillo and San Miguel. The Saltillo pattern shows a medallion consisting of concentric diamonds in various colors upon an all-over design in stripes. The motives are minute geometric figures skilfully interlocked. The colors are rich and permanent and are combined in a very pleasing manner. Saltillo blankets must be classed among the finest textile products of the world. The best period was before 1850. San Miguel blankets show characteristically a rosette instead of a diamond in the center. Many beautiful blankets come from other localities in Mexico. The Chimayo blankets have the same part Indian, part Spanish origin and are made by the Spanish-speaking natives in the mountain valleys of New Mexico.

In southern Mexico there are many towns of Indians where the women still wear the finely embroidered huipili. This old-time garment varies considerably in different towns but as a rule it is a simple sack-like gown cut square at the neck and with short sleeves. Sometimes it is shortened to a blouse, and is worn with a skirt; at other times a short huipili is worn over a longer one. An easily visited town where the natives still wear the old-time dress is Amatlan, within an hour's walk of Cordova. The women of the Isthmus of Tehuantepec have a gorgeous costume of which the most remarkable feature is a wide ruff worn around the neck or on the back of the head. The Mayan women of Yucatan wear white huipili with needlework in color around the bottom. On the highlands of Guatemala the huipili is usually a blouse. The skirt sometimes consists of a strip of cloth wrapped several times around the body.

An interesting ceremony which survives in some parts of Mexico and Guatemala has as its principal feature a lofty pole with a swivel arrangement at the top to which long ropes are attached. These ropes are wound round the swivel and performers, who may be dressed like birds, attach themselves to the rope ends. During the process of unwinding the performers whirl dizzily around the pole descending lower and lower and swing in a wider and wider circle till they reach the ground.

The Lacandone Indians live in the marshy jungles that border the winding Usumacinta. They speak the same tongue as the Maya Indians of Yucatan but in the matter of culture they have acquired little from the Spaniards. They still weave simple garments and make pottery vessels. In hunting they use the bow and arrow, the latter usually tipped with a point of stone. In their religious practices they use incense burners which are comparable to those of the sixteenth century.

The Caribs occupy the greater part of the north coast of Guatemala and Honduras, running east from the port of Livingston on the Gulf of Amatique. These people, originally of South America and later of the West Indies as well, were deported by the English from the Island of St. Vincent in 1796. They have now established themselves in the new land where they raise the manioc or cassava root and press out the poisonous juice in a basketry tube as do their kindred in the Orinoco Valley. Long before the forcible immigration it is likely that the Caribs, who were cannibalistic in habit, had raided the shores of Central America in their seagoing canoes. A significant passage in the chronicles of the Mayas states that naked man-eating savages visited Yucatan long before the coming of the Spaniards.

The Mosquito Indians of the east coast of Nicaragua and Honduras have a very considerable Negro admixture. They are fishermen of low culture. Farther inland are found the Sumo who flatten the heads of their children and who hold strange feasts in honor of the dead in which the dancers are masked so that none may be recognized. A string is stretched over the tree tops from the grave to the feasting place and over this string the ghost of the dead person is supposed to walk. When everyone has fallen in a drunken stupor from *mishla* the ghost of the dead man departs for the land of the dead. These Sumo Indians build large houses with open sides and are very skilful at fishing with bow and arrow and steering their canoes through white rapids. They practise polygamous marriages, weave cotton, and make interesting beadwork ornaments.

In the narrow Isthmian region there are tribes of Indians that resist manfully the inroads of civilization. Perhaps the best known of these are the San Blas Indians who inhabit the mountain fastnesses east of the Canal Zone. In northern Costa Rica the Guatuso and Talamanca tribes still maintain to a considerable degree their old native character.

Physical Types. Minor physical differences in stature, head form, and facial expression mark off pretty clearly the tribes of this area from each other. The stature is lowest among the Mayas and Mazatecs, the average being about 5 feet 1 inch, while among the Tarascans, Tlaxcalas, and Zapotecs, it averages about 5 feet 3 inches. The other tribes of Central America and of central Mexico fall between these extremes. In northern Mexico the stature increases considerably, average measurements for the Yaqui being in excess of 5 feet 6 inches. To make up for their lack of height the southern Indians are sturdy and heavy muscled, with deep chests. Their hair is usually black and straight, but occasionally wavy. Light beards and mustaches are sometimes worn, especially by the Mayas. The eyes are so dark brown as to appear black to the casual observer. They are set rather wide apart and while usually horizontal they seem, in some instances, to have a slight Mongoloid tilt. Noses vary greatly but are often finely aquiline. The cephalic index (obtained by dividing the breath of the head by its length and multiplying the result by 100) is rather high. The Mayas are strongly round-headed with an index of 85.0 while their linguistic relatives, the Tzendals, have a medium index of 76.8. The other tribes of southern Mexico fall between these extremes. No long-headed peoples are found in this area although in northern Mexico some tribes approach the long-headed type.

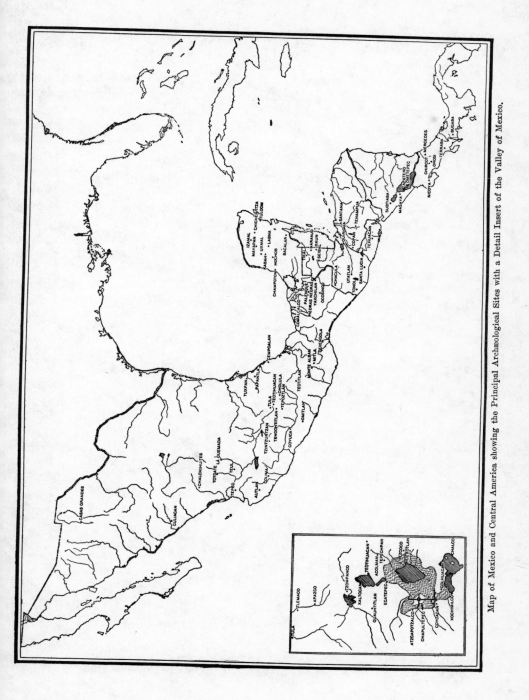

Map of Mexico and Central America showing the Principal Archæological Sites with a Detail Insert of the Valley of Mexico.

THE ARCHAIC HORIZON

IN 1910 an actual stratification of human products was found in the environs of Mexico City in which three principal culture horizons could be readily discerned. A collection made at the time, illustrating the objects characteristic of the three strata, is on exhibition in the American Museum of Natural History. In parts this stratification verified theories of culture succession already held by students working in this field. Since that time careful research in several localities has been carried on and many authentic specimens from the three layers have been brought together.

The stratigraphic series concerns sedentary life after the invention of agriculture. Presumably a nomadic horizon preceded that of the first farmers, but few traces of this have so far been reported from southern Mexico and Central America. The earliest known specimens of the lowest level are not rudimentary but are well stylized, and opinions vary as to the length of time necessary for a theoretical formative stage. It seems necessary to consider this old civilization as a stratigraphic unit admitting the probability that true beginnings await the archæologist's spade.

The culture of the lowest stratum is here called archaic, a word meaning old, but not necessarily primitive. The word "horizon" carries an implication of chronological succession, but it would not be wise to insist that archaic remains everywhere represent a dead chronological level. Archaic art is oldest in its place of origin, the highlands of Mexico and Central America, and in or near this general region, it was first succeeded by higher types. On the margin of its distribution archaic art, or at least the most striking traits of archaic art, lasted into much more recent times, and in some places may even have survived till the coming of the Spaniards. Even when every allowance is made for independent expressions which may find nearly the same form, it seems that remarkable homogeneity and continuity can be demonstrated for products of the archaic civilization of the New World.

Most of the evidence of the old civilization consists of ceramic objects, but there is also some stonework including implements, ornaments, and crude statues. Common household pottery shows local variations, but as a rule the archaic wares can be recognized as such by qualities of paste, shape, and decoration. The motives are simply geometric or realistic and there is a lack of formalized designs. One process of decoration has wide distribution and seems to have been invented well along in the archaic period.' This is the process of negative painting in which the lines of the decorative pattern, originally applied in wax or pitch, stand out in the natural surface color of the pot against an over-painted background. This "batik" pottery extends from central Mexico to northern Peru.

The most interesting and important objects of archaic art in clay are human

281

figurines executed in peculiar styles. These not only reflect details of dress, etc., but also seem to stand for a set of religious ideas. Especially a type of figurine representing a nude female appears to be an agricultural fetish, symbolizing the fecundity of Mother-Earth.

Stratification of Remains. Atzcapotzalco was once an important center of the Tepanecan tribe situated on the shores of Lake Texcoco. It was an early rival of Tenochtitlan, the Aztecan capital, and was conquered and partly destroyed in 1439. The principal modern industry of Atzcapotzalco is brick-making, and several mounds and much of the surface of the plain have been removed for this purpose. In the mounds are found many pottery objects of the late Toltecan period, while on the surface of the ground are encountered fragments of the typical Aztecan pottery in use when the Spaniards arrived.

Fig. 10. Atzca-potzalco Destroy-ed. The temple burns at the Place of the Ant

The stratification of the plain varies in different places so far as the thickness of the different strata is concerned, but the order is always the same. At one locality it is as shown in Fig. 11. First comes a layer of fine soil of volcanic ash origin, probably deposited by the wind. This is five or six feet in thickness, yellowish at the top, and much darker towards the bottom, with streaks and discolorations. The Aztecan pottery is found close to the surface, while Toltecan pottery occurs in the middle and lower sections. Underneath the soil layers lies a thick stratum of water-bearing gravel mixed with sand. This gravel stratum is possibly the old bed of a stream that formerly entered Lake Texcoco near this point. In some places it is fifteen or eighteen feet in thickness. Scattered throughout the gravel are heavy, waterworn fragments of pots as well as more or less complete figurines of the archaic type.

At other sites, such as Colhuacan, the Toltecan layer is of greater thickness and the archaic layer of lesser thickness. The remains extend below the present level of the water and may indicate that considerable changes have taken place in the level of the lake. But we must remember that many of the ancient settlements were built over the water and that land was made in ancient times, as it is today in the gardens of Xochimilco, by deepening canals. Archaic remains are also common on the denuded tops of hills which may once have been covered by soil.

A stratification of archæological remains has recently been determined in Salvador.

The Cemetery under the Lava. An ancient cemetery lying under lava has recently been explored in Copilco, a suburb of Mexico City. The lava swept down from Mount Ajusco in some cataclysm perhaps 3000 years ago, covering many square miles of territory to the depth of thirty or forty feet, and burying such villages as chanced to lie in its path. (See Pl. VIb). The discovery of human remains was made several hundred feet back from the original front of the lava flow in a quarry where lava rock was being removed to build roads. Tales of clay figurines found under the lava in this quarry had been current for years, but no serious investigation was made until human burials were met with in the earth under the great lava cap. Then a series of tunnels was dug and a considerable number of ancient burials were uncovered, but not moved from their original position. One now enters an electric-lighted graveyard and sees human bodies lying exactly as they have lain for untold centuries, with the funeral offerings beside them. This enormously important find gives us an historical level in mid-Archaic.

Another site, at Cuicuilco, on the opposite side of the lava flow, has received attention from archæologists. Here a great round mound rises in terraces faced with cobblestones. It is surrounded by the lava flow and some persons have

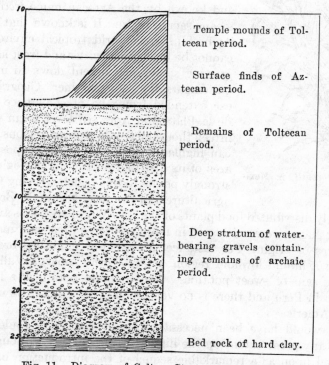

Fig. 11. Diagram of Culture Strata at Atzcapotzalco.

assumed that the mound was already abandoned and in decay when the lava flow took place. Perhaps, however, the mound was built on a piece of land that the lava flow had spared. There are no contacts between the lava and the mound except at the ends of two projecting aprons or causeways. The pottery at this site is sufficiently different from that found at Copilco.

Invention of Agriculture. Before examining in greater detail the art of the Archaic Horizon let us consider its real significance. It is generally admitted that America was originally populated from Asia, but on a culture level no higher than the Neolithic. The simple arts of stone chipping, basketry, fire-making, etc., were probably brought over by the earliest immigrants, but there is abundant evidence that pottery-making, weaving, and agriculture were independently invented long after the original settlement. The cultivated plants in the New World are different from those of the Old World and there is a vast area in northwestern America and northeastern Asia, upon the only open line of communication, where agriculture and the higher arts have never been practised.

Now the invention of agriculture is an antecedent necessity for all the high cultures of the New World. It is equally clear that this invention must have taken place in a locality where some important food plant grew in a wild state.

Fig. 12. *Teocentli* or Mexican Fodder Grass.

By far the most important food plant of the New World is maize. While this plant has changed greatly under domestication, botanists are inclined to find its nearest relative and possible progenitor in a wild grass growing on the highlands of Mexico and known by the Aztecan name *teocentli*, which means sacred maize. It is known that maize is at its best in a semi-arid tropical environment. It cannot be brought to withstand frost although the growing season can be cut down to meet the requirements of a short summer. Geographically its use extended from the St. Lawrence to the Rio de la Plata and from sea level to an elevation of fifteen thousand feet in tropical regions. The Mexican highlands occupy the central position in the area of its distribution and archæological evidence strongly points to this region as being the cradle of agriculture and the attendant arts. Besides maize, the most widely distributed food plants of the New World are beans and squashes. Certain other plants were cultivated in more restricted areas and may have had different places of origin. For instance, manioc was doubtless brought under cultivation in a humid lowland region, probably the Amazon Valley, and the same may be said of sweet potatoes. The common potato was found under domestication in Peru and there is no very good evidence that its use extended into Central America.

Irrigation would have been necessary before agriculture could have been developed to any great extent on the highlands of Mexico. Although irrigation is often looked upon as a remarkable sequel of the introduction of agriculture into an arid country, yet from the best historical evidence at our command we should rather regard it as a conception which accounts for the very origin of agriculture itself. The earliest records of cultivated plants are from Mesopotamia, Egypt, Mexico, and Peru where irrigation was practised. In these regions are also seen the earliest developments of the characteristic arts of sedentary peoples, namely, pottery and weaving, and the elaborate social and religious structures that result from a sure food supply and a reasonable amount of leisure.

If this theory is true we must admit that below the Archaic Horizon we should find traces of a horizon of non-agricultural peoples, living a nomadic life without pottery. Unfortunately, such peoples make fewer objects and scatter them more widely than do sedentary agriculturists.

No one on the basis of present knowledge can offer more than an opinion concerning the date of the invention of agriculture in the New World. The thick deposits left by the sedentary peoples argue great age and the wide area of homogeneous products argues slow change. In the most favored regions archaic art may have been succeeded by higher forms shortly before the time of Christ, and perhaps 5000 years is not too long a time to allow for the diversities of the domesticated plants of America.

Archaic Figurines. Archaic art is characterized by figures of men and women

Fig. 13. Archaic Figurines from Central Mexico. The first three specimens are from under the lava at Copilco.

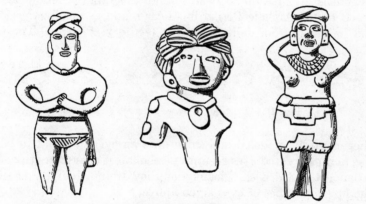

Fig. 14. Archaic Figurines—Zapotlan, Jalisco; Tampico, Vera Cruz; and Cuesta Blanca, Salvador.

modeled in clay and sometimes painted. The forms are peculiar and the technique well standardized. Most are modeled in a flat gingerbread fashion into a gross shape. Upon this gross shape special features are indicated by stuck-on ribbons and buttons of clay and by gougings and incisings with some pointed instrument. Modeling was done entirely by hand, moulds being as yet unknown. The figurines are usually from two to five inches in height and often represent nude women in sitting or standing positions with the hands upon the knees, hips, or breasts. The heads are characteristically of slight depth compared with their height, the limbs taper rapidly from a rather plump torso and hands and feet are mere knobs with incised details. When the figures are intended to stand erect, as is often the case, the feet show signs of having been pinched between the thumb and finger of the potter so that they have a forward and backward cusp and a broad base of support. Groovings are seen in connection with the hair, eyes, mouth, fingers, toes, and details of dress and ornament. Paint is often added to this surface to indicate tattooing, textile patterns, etc.

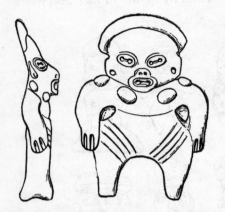

The eyes of the archaic images—and the mouths as well—are made according to several methods. First, there is the simple groove; second, a groove across an applied ball or button of clay; third, a round gouging made by the end of a blunt implement held vertically; fourth, a round gouging in an applied ball or button of clay; fifth, two gougings made with a round or chisel-edged implement held at an angle. The second form of eye, which resembles a grain of coffee, and the fifth form with the double gouging made from the center outward, are found from the northern limits of archaic art in Mexico as far south as Colombia and Venezuela.

Fig. 15.   Archaic Figurine from Salvador.

The technique of manufacture naturally changes somewhat with the increase in size. There is also reason to believe that the largest hollow figures come from the end of the Archaic Period in Mexico, and especially those that have been found in the state of Jalisco and the territory of Tepic. The eyelids are

Fig. 16.   Types of Eyes of Archaic Figurines.

often rather carefully modeled and sometimes an eyeball is put in between the lids. These and perforated eyes seem to be the latest characters to be developed in the archaic art and it is significant that they are not found over such a wide area as the first five types of eyes given above.

Ancient Customs. We may gather much of an ethnological nature from the study of these quaint figures. Articles of dress and adornment are shown as well as musical instruments, weapons, etc. Headdresses may consist of fillets, turbans, and objects perched on one side of the head. Noserings and earrings are abundantly represented and in considerable variety. We may be sure that weaving was rather highly developed because many garments such as shirts, skirts, and aprons are painted or incised with geometric designs. Body painting, or tattooing, appears to have been a common usage. Among weapons the *atlatl*, or spear-thrower, was already known and knobby clubs seem to have been popular. Men are shown beating on drums and turtle shells, while women nurse children and carry water. Since the large figures of clay are often found in tombs it is not impossible that they were intended to be portraits of the dead. Many have a startling quality of caricature.

Archaic art is a pretty certain index of the religion then in vogue. There is a notable absence of purposely grotesque or compounded figures representing divinities such as will be found in the later horizons. We miss entirely the

characteristic Mexican gods such as Tlaloc and Ehecatl. Dogs are frequently
modeled in clay and were apparently developed into a rather special domestic
breed. Snakes are sometimes found as a plastic decoration on pottery but there

Fig. 17.   Textile Designs painted on Archaic Effigies.

are few signs of serpent worship. We can find no evidence that human sacrifice
was practised. The presence of human figurines in graves has already been
mentioned and the suggestion made that some of them may have been intended
as portraits of the dead. Nude female figurines in sitting or standing positions
have an unbroken distribution from Mexico into South America and it is not
unlikely that the primitive agriculturists associated them with fertility and
used them as amulets to secure good crops. The male figurines may have been
votive offerings for success at arms.

Archaic Pottery. The ordinary pottery of the Archaic Period from Mexico
and Central America is heavy and simple in shape. The globular bowl with

Fig. 18.   Typical Tripod Vessels of the Archaic Period, from
Morelos, Mexico.

a constricted neck is a common form as well as wide-mouthed bowls with or
without tripod supports. Lugs and handles are very common. When plain, the
tripods are large, hollow and rounded, with a perforation on the under side, but
they are often modified into faces and feet. Many vessels are decorated by the
addition of modeled faces enabling us to make a direct connection with the figures
in clay already described.

In fact the decoration of pottery of this early period is predominantly in relief.
Paint is sparingly used and then only in the simplest geometric fashion. There
is a general lack of conventionalized motives presenting animals and other natural
forms in highly modified ways. In later ages the painted decoration is much

concerned with the serpent, but except for a few winding serpents in relief, this motive is not seen on the pottery of the Archaic Period.

Stone Sculptures of the Archaic Period. The earliest stone sculptures are recognized first by resemblance to the ceramic art just described and second by a quality which they possess of being archaic in an absolute sense. The greater difficulty of working stone as compared with clay and the longer time required in the process make stone art less subject to caprice than ceramic art. Perhaps the most primitive examples of stone sculpture are boulders rudely carved in a semblance of the human form with features either sunken or in relief. The arms and legs are ordinarily flexed so that the elbows meet over the knees. The eyes and mouths in the most carefully finished pieces protrude, but the face has little or no modeling. Many celts are modified into figures by grooves, and faces are frequently represented on roughly conical or disk-shaped stones.

We know very little from actual excavations concerning houses of the Archaic Period. It is likely that they were small and impermanent, possibly resembling the modern huts. The pyramidal mound as a foundation for the temple may have been developed towards the end of the Archaic Period. It would be inter-

Fig. 19. Series showing the Modification of a Celt into a Stone Amulet. State of Guerrero, Mexico, probably late Archaic.

esting to determine whether adobe moulded into bricks was known at this time, as it was at a later time in the same region, or whether walls were built up out of fresh mud possibly reinforced by slabs of stone.

Extensions of the Archaic Horizon. The curious objects of ceramic art that we have found deeply buried under the débris of higher civilizations in the Valley of Mexico can be traced far and wide. They are encountered, for the most part, in arid and open country, and since we have every reason to belief that the earliest agriculture was developed under irrigation, it is but natural to find the use of agriculture spreading first into other arid regions. And if there was an association between the fertility of Mother-Earth and little fetishes representing women then these fetishes would spread as part of the agricultural complex.

It now seems possible that the cult of the female figurine reached our Southwestern states on the earliest level of agricultural life. In sites belonging to Basket-Maker III—the archæological level of the first Pueblo pottery—little female fetishes are found and, indeed, are symptomatic of this early culture.

They are cruder than anything as yet found in Mexico, but not necessarily older. With them occurs a primitive maize doubtless introduced from the south.

In the Isthmian region, on the other side of the Mexican and Central American cradle of New World agricultural civilization, there are small figurines quite similar to the archaic figurines of Mexico and Salvador as regards pose and bodily proportions. These are mostly on the level of the first Mayan civilization even in cases where the coffee-grain eye is used. Around the Nicaraguan lakes the figurines of nude females were cast in moulds, a device entirely unknown on the Archaic Horizon in Mexico. In the Nicoya Peninsula of Costa Rica the figurines are skilfully modeled with painted designs in black on a dark brilliant red, which may represent tattooing. In the Chiriqui Province of Panama the figurines belong in a ceramic group characterized by the use of highly conventionalized alligators or crocodiles. It has already been stated that designs of the Archaic Horizon in Mexico are either geometric or naïvely realistic. There is another matter that deserves attention: some of these southern types of the female fetish occur in distinctly humid lands and this, by itself, is a strong argument against great antiquity.

The Isthmian female fetish must have been implanted on the Archaic Horizon even though the present examples are mostly from post-archaic times. Perhaps future archæological investigation will reveal early stations of a purely archaic type in desert parts of Costa Rica and Panama. Till then a controlling fact is that Mayan religious art avoids all references to sex and cannot, therefore, possibly be held responsible for the culture trait of the female fetish. But this fetish does agree with a pre-Mayan concept, as we have seen.

The ancient gold work of Costa Rica and Panama also reflects the technique of archaic art, although most of it, to judge by the religious significance of many of the subjects and designs. was made long after the Archaic Period. Just as the pottery figurines were built up by the addition of ribbons and buttons of clay to a generalized form so the patterns for gold castings were made by adding details in rolled wax or resin to a simple underlying form of the same material.

In Colombia and Venezuela archaic art is common in arid and mountainous territory. Local developments confuse the issue of time. Various cultural successions took place here, the Quimbaya, Sinu, and Tairona Indians having developed civilizations with possible Mayan affiliations in some features. The archaic figurines of Colombia are decorated with designs made by the process of negative painting through the medium of wax. This process is pretty generally distributed from central Mexico to northern Peru. The indications are that it was invented long before the rise of the Mayas, and once invented remained popular.

As regards Venezuela the figurines of men and women from the Eastern Andes are often strikingly similar to those of Mexico, especially in such matters as eyes made by double gougings. As a rule, these figurines are painted. Around Lake Valencia they are made without paint, but in combination with pottery designs showing the beginnings of conventionalization. Here there is added the circumstance that wild Carib tribes, coming down the Orinoco, drove the earlier inhabitants out over the West Indies. This flight must have taken place centuries before the coming of the Spaniards.

The archæology of the lower Amazon is best known from the remains found on the Island of Marajo where female figurines exhibit close similarity in pose to specimens from Venezuela and Mexico. This culture of Marajo seems to have been disrupted before the coming of Europeans. But it may be significant that crude fetishes representing women are used at the present time by tribes on the margins of the old Amazonian culture area. The earliest level at Ancon, Peru, yields ware recalling northern products. Nude females, apparently of somewhat later time, however, are in standing rather than sitting pose. It seems, then, that the trail of dissemination of agriculture and the ancillary arts can be followed across the northern part of South America and southward along the Andes to Peru. The greatest similarities must be sought in the oldest objects and some leeway granted in the case of marginal survivals.

It is proper to speak of agriculture, pottery-making, and weaving as the great civilizing complex. Few inventions could break down the ordinary boundaries of language and environment, as these had done. Yet, after the discovery of America, the horse, introduced by the Spaniards, spread rapidly through native tribes, modifying their lives greatly. It is capable of demonstration that with the horse went two types of saddle—the pack saddle and the riding saddle. Similarly in the first rapid spread of agriculture went pots and woven garments.

Two maps of the New World are given herewith: the first showing the extent of the Archaic Horizon and the second the final distribution of pottery among the American Indians and the final distribution of agriculture. The agricultural area is subdivided according to, first, the arid land type where irrigation is generally practised; second, the humid land type; and third, the temperate land type. The first type of agriculture appears to be the earliest and the range coincides, for the most part, with the range of the archaic pottery art.

Summary. In concluding this section let us sum up the general facts of ancient American history as these appear in relation to the archæological evidences of the Archaic Horizon.

I. Pre-Archaic Horizon

The peopling of the New World from Asia by tribes on the nomadic plane of culture.

II. The Archaic Horizon

Invention and primary dissemination of agriculture, together with pottery-making and loom-weaving. Homogeneous culture with undeveloped religion and unsymbolic art adjusted to arid tropics.

III. Post-Archaic Horizon

Specialized cultures in North, Central, and South America dependent upon agriculture. Strong local developments in esthetic arts, religious ideas, and social institutions. Agriculture extended to humid tropical and temperate regions.

We will now make an effort to analyze still further the historical levels in the Post-Archaic Horizon.

THE MAYAN CIVILIZATION

THE wonderful culture of the Mayan Indians to which we will now turn our attention was developed in the humid lowlands of Central America and especially in the Yucatan Peninsula. Artists are everywhere of the opinion that the sculptures and other products of the Mayas deserve to rank among the highest art products of the world, and astronomers are amazed at the progress made by this people in the measuring of time by the observed movements of the heavenly bodies. Moreover, they invented a remarkable system of hieroglyphic writing by which they were able to record facts and events and they built great cities of stone that attest a degree of wealth and splendor beyond anything seen elsewhere in the New World.

The Mayan culture was made possible by the agricultural conquest of the rich lowlands where the exuberance of nature can only be held in check by organized effort. On the highlands the preparation of the land is comparatively easy, owing to scanty natural vegetation and a control vested in irrigation. On the lowlands, however, great trees have to be felled and fast-growing bushes kept down by untiring energy. But when nature is truly tamed she returns recompense many fold to the daring farmer. Moreover, there is reason to believe that the removal of the forest cover over large areas affects favorably the conditions of life which under a canopy of leaves are hard indeed.

The principal crops of the Mayas were probably much the same as on the highlands, with maize as the great staple. Varieties favorable to a humid environment had doubtless been developed from the highland stock by selective breeding as agriculture worked its way down into the lowlands. Archaic art appears along the edges of the Mayan Area in the state of Vera Cruz, Mexico, and in the Uloa Valley, Honduras. In both these regions are also found clay figurines that mark the transition in style between the archaic and the Mayan, as well as finished examples of the latter. There can be no doubt, then, that the archaic art of Mexico marks an earlier horizon than the Mayan. Whether or not it was once laid entirely across the Mayan Area cannot be decided on present data but it seems unlikely. We have already seen that this first art was distributed primarily across arid and open territory.

With their calendarial system already in working order the Mayas appear on the threshold of history 600 years before the Christian Era, according to a correlation with European chronology that will be explained later. The first great cities were Tikal in northern Guatemala and Copan in western Honduras, both of which had a long and glorious existence. Many others sprang into prominence at a somewhat later date; for example, Palenque, Yaxchilan or Menché, Piedras Negras, Seibal, Naranjo, and Quirigua. The most brilliant period was from 300 to 600 A. D., after which all these cities appear to have been abandoned to the forest that soon closed over them. The population moved to northern Yucatan, where it no longer reacted strongly upon the other nations of Central America and where it enjoyed a second period of brilliancy several hundred years later.

Architecture. The idea of a civic center is admirably illustrated in Mayan cities, particularly those of the first brilliant period. The principal structures are built around courts or plazas and there is usually an artificial acropolis which is a great terraced mound serving as a common base or platform from which the individual pyramidal bases of several temples rise. At some sites this acropolis is a natural hill which has been trimmed down or added to, but at other sites it is entirely artificial. At Copan there is an especially fine example of artificial platform mound rising from one end of the Great Plaza and affording space for several temples, as well as for sunken courts with stepped sides that

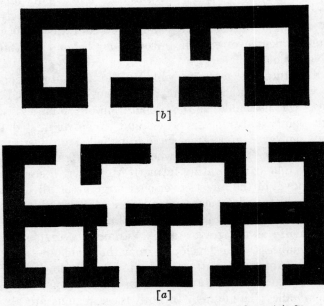

[b]

[a]

Fig. 20. Groundplans of Yaxchilan Temples: (a) Structure 42; (b) Structure 23.

may have been theatres. The river washing against one side of this great mound has removed perhaps a third of it and made a vertical section that shows the method of construction. It is apparent that the mound was enlarged and old walls and floors buried.

Mayan buildings are of two principal kinds. One is a temple pure and simple and the other has been called a palace. The temple is a rectangular structure crowning a rather high pyramid that rises in several steps or terraces. As a rule the temple has a single front with one or more doorways and is approached by a broad stairway. The pyramid is ordinarily a solid mass of rubble and earth faced with cement or cut stone and rarely contains compartments. Some temples have but a single chamber while others have two or more chambers, the central or innermost one being specially developed into a sanctuary. The so-called palaces are clusters of rooms on low and often irregular platforms. These palaces may have been habitations of the priests and nobility. The common people doubtless lived in palm-thatched huts similar to those used today in the same region.

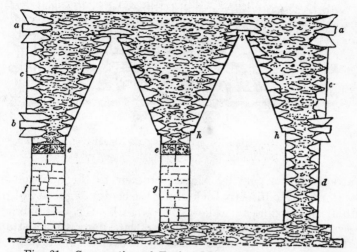

Fig. 21. Cross-section of Typical Mayan Temple in Northern Yucatan: *a*, upper cornice; *b*, medial cornice; *c*, upper zone; *d*, lower zone; *e*, wooden lintels; *f*, exterior doorway; *g*, interior doorway; *h*, offset at spring of vault; *i*, cap stone.

The typical Mayan construction is a faced concrete. The limestone, which abounds in nearly all parts of the Mayan Area, was burned into lime. This was then slaked to make mortar and applied to a mass of broken limestone. The facing stones were smoothed on the outside and left rough hewn and pointed on the inside. It is likely that these facing stones were held in place between forms and the lime, mortar, and rubble filled in between. The resulting wall was essentially monolithic. The rooms of Mayan buildings are characteristically vaulted but the roof is not a true arch with a keystone. The vault, like the walls, is a solid mass of concrete that grips the cut stone veneer and that must have been held in place by a false work form while it was hardening. The so-called corbelled arch of overstepping stones was doubtless known to the Mayan builders but was little used. Taking the single rectangular room as the unit of construction the width was limited to the span of the vault, which seldom exceeded twelve feet, while the length was indeterminate.

The first variation from the temple with one rectangular room was the two-roomed structure with one chamber directly behind the other. In this case there were two vaulted compartments separated from each other by a common supporting wall pierced by one or more doorways. The inner room was naturally more dimly lighted than the other one and as a result was modified into a sanctuary, or holy of holies, enhanced by sculptures and paintings, while the outer room developed gradually into a portico. The outer wall was cut by doorways till only pier-like sections remained, and finally these piers were replaced by square or round columns. The development of the Mayan temple may be traced through a thousand years of change and adjustment.

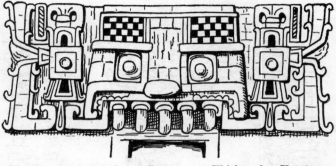

Fig. 22.   Mask Panel over Doorway at Xkichmook.   Yucatan.

Much attention was paid by Mayan builders to the question of stability, which was accomplished directly by keeping the center of gravity of the principal masses within the supporting walls rather than by the use of binding stones. The cross-section of a two-roomed temple of late date will illustrate how this was done. There are three principal masses, one over the front wall, one over the medial partition, and one over the back wall. The roof where these sections join is of no great thickness. The central mass is symmetrical and, if the mortar has the proper cohesiveness, very stable. For the front and back masses the projection of the upper or frieze zone tends to counterbalance the overhang of half the vault. In the earlier temples the upper zone of the façade often slopes backward so that the balance is not so perfect.

So far we have given brief space to the question of elevations. Taken vertically there are three parts to the Mayan building: first, the substructure or pyramidal base; second, the structure proper; third, the superstructure. In the case of temples the structure proper is one story in height. Two and three stories are rather common in palaces, but the upper stories are in most cases built directly over a solid core and not over the rooms of the lower story. The upper stories, therefore, recede, so that the building presents a terraced or pyramidal profile. One building at Tikal is five stories in height, in three receding planes, the three uppermost stories being one above the other. In a tower at Palenque we have an example of four stories but this is unusual.

On top of the building proper, especially if it is a temple, we frequently find a superstructure. This is a sort of crest, or roof wall, usually pierced by windows. When this wall rises from the center line of the roof it is called a roof comb or roof crest, and when it rises from the front wall it is called a flying façade. The highest temples in the Mayan Area are those of Tikal that attain a total height of about 175 feet, counting pyramid and superstructure.

Massive Sculptural Art. The decoration of Mayan buildings may be considered under three heads: first, interior decoration; second, façade decoration; third, supplementary monuments. In many temples at Yaxchilan, Tikal, etc., are found splendidly sculptured lintels of stone or wood. At Copan we see wall sculptures that adorn the entrance to the sanctuary and at Palenque finely sculptured tablets let into the rear wall of the sanctuary. Elsewhere are occasional examples of mural paintings, sculptured door jambs, decorated interior steps, etc.

The façade decorations of the earlier Mayan structures are freer and more realistic than those of the later buildings. In many cases they consist of figures

Fig. 23. Design on Engraved Pot representing a Tiger seated in a Wreath of Water Lilies. Northern Yucatan.

Fig. 24. Painted Design on Cylindrical Bowl showing Serpent issuing from a Shell. Salvador.

of men, serpents, etc., modeled in stucco or built up out of several nicely fitted blocks of stone. Grotesque faces also occur. In the later styles, decoration consists largely of "mask panels," which are grotesque front view faces arranged to fill rectangular panels, but there is an increasing amount of purely geometric ornament. The masked panels represent in most instances a highly elaborated serpent's face which sometimes carries the special markings of one of the greater gods. These panels, considered historically, pass through some interesting developments. Angular representations of serpent heads in profile are sometimes used at the sides of doorways.

The supplementary monuments are stelæ and altars. These are monolithic sculptures that are often set up in definite relation to a building either on the terraces or at the foot of the stairway. The stelæ are great plinths or slabs of stone carved on one or more sides with the figures of priests and warriors loaded down with religious symbols. The altars are small stones usually placed in front of the stelæ. Many stelæ and altars are set up in plazas and have no definite architectural quality.

Minor Arts. While the richly ornamented temples and the great monoliths attract first attention as works of art, the humbler products of the potter, the weaver, and the lapidary also attained to grace and dignity.

The Mayas were expert potters and employed a variety of technical processes in the decoration of their wares, such as painting, modeling, engraving, and stamping. We can only take time to examine a few examples of the best works, leaving the commoner products practically undescribed. Suffice it to say, that tripod dishes were much used, as well as bowls, bottle-necked vessels, and cylindrical vases, and that the common decorative use of hieroglyphs serves to mark off Mayan pottery from that of other Central American peoples. The realistic designs are drawn in accordance with the highest principles of decorative art. Serpents, monkeys, jaguars, various birds, as well as priests and supernatural beings, are used as subjects for pottery embellishment. Geometric decoration is also much used.

The polychrome pottery is rare and exceptionally beautiful, with designs relating to religious subjects. The background color of these cylindrical vases is usually orange or yellow, the designs are outlined in black, and the details filled in with delicate washes of red, brown, white, etc. The surface bears a high polish made by rubbing. Plate XVIII reproduces the design units on two vases from Chamá, Guatemala. The first example pictures a seated man with a widespreading headdress made of two conventional serpent heads from the ends of which issue the plumes of the quetzal. The hieroglyphs are Mayan day signs—Ben and Imix on the left and Kan and Caban on the right. The second example presents a god before an altar. This god has the face of an old man and his body is attached to a spiral shell. This divinity was probably associated with the end of the year.

Fig. 25. Mayan Basket represented in Stone Sculpture.

In the next illustration an engraved design on a bowl from northern Yucatan is given. A jaguar attired in the dress of man is seated in a wreath of water lilies. After the vessel had been formed, but before it had been fired, this design was

made by cutting away the background and incising finer details on the original
surfaces. Other designs in relief were obtained by direct modeling or by stamping.
The stamps were moulds or negatives made from bas-relief patterns.

The textile arts of the ancient Mayas can be recovered in part from a study
of the monuments since the designs on many garments are reproduced in delicate
relief. The designs are mostly all-over geometric patterns, but borders repro-
ducing the typical "celestial band," a line of astronomical symbols, are also seen.
The techniques of brocade and lace were understood by the ancient weavers.
In the minor textile art of basketry the products must also have ranked high;
a typical basket pictured on a lintel is given in Fig. 25.

Jade and other semi-precious stones were carved by the Mayas into beautiful
and fantastic shapes. There was a considerable use of mosaic veneer on masks
and other ceremonial objects. Metal was unknown during the first centuries of
Mayan florescence, later it was rare and could not be used for tools, but the
working of gold and copper in the manufacture of ornaments was on a high plane.

Having now passed in brief review the objective side of Mayan remains, let
us turn our attention to the subjective.

The Serpent in Mayan Art. Mayan art is strange and unintelligible at first
sight, but after careful study many wonderful qualities appear in it. In the

Fig. 26. Typical Elaborated Serpents of the Mayas. The serpent with a human head in its mouth is from Yaxchilan. In this
example the writhing movements of the serpent's tail are probably
intended by the added scrolls. The plumed serpent is from Chichen
Itza.

knowledge of foreshortening and composition, the Mayas were superior to the
Egyptians and Assyrians. They could draw the human body in pure profile and
in free and graceful attitudes and they could compose several figures in a rectangular panel so that the result satisfies the eye of a modern artist.

But, unfortunately for our fuller understanding, the human form had only
a minor interest because the gods were not in the image of man and the art was

essentially religious. The gods were at best half human and half animal with grotesque elaborations. The high esthetic qualities were therefore wasted on subjects that appear trivial to many of us. But, as we break away more and more from the shackles of our own artistic conventions, we shall be able to appreciate the many beauties of ancient American sculpture.

The serpent motive controlled the character of Mayan art and was of first importance in all subsequent arts in Central America and Mexico. The serpent was seldom represented realistically, and yet we may safely infer that the rattlesnake was the prevailing model. Parts of other creatures were added to the serpent's body, such as the plumes of the trogon or quetzal, the teeth of the jaguar, and the ornaments of man. The serpent was idealized and the lines characteristic of it entered into the delineation of many subjects distinct from the serpent itself. Scrolls and other sinuous details were attached to the serpent's body and human ornaments such as earplugs, noseplugs, and even headdresses were added to its head. Finally, a human head was placed in the distended jaws.

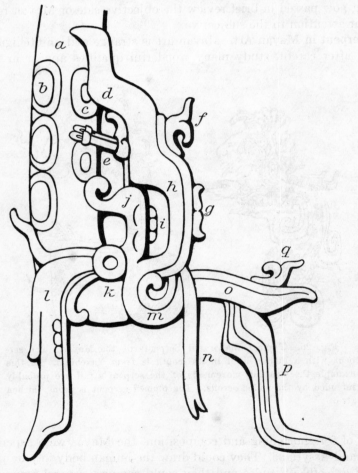

Fig. 27. Conventional Serpent of the Mayas used for Decorative Purposes: a, body; b, ventral scale; c, dorsal scale; d, nose; e, noseplug; f, incisor tooth; g, molar tooth; h, jaw; i, eye; j, supraorbital plate; k, earplug; l, ear pendant; m, curled fang; n, tongue, o, lower jaw; p, beard; q, incisor tooth.

The Mayas may have intended to express the essential human intelligence of the serpent in this fashion. The serpent with a human head in its mouth doubtless belongs in the same category as the partly humanized gods of Egypt, Assyria, and India. It illustrates the partial assumption of human form by a beast divinity. The features combined are so peculiar and unnatural that the influence of Mayan

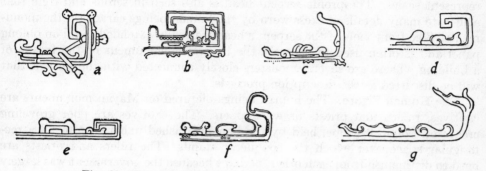

Fig. 28. Upper Part of Serpent Head made into a Fret Orna- ment; a, Ixkun; b, Quirigua; c, d, g, Copan; e, Naranjo; f, Seibal.

Fig. 29. Sculpture on Front of Lintel at Yaxchilan showing Man holding Two-Headed Serpent with a Grotesque God's Head in each of its Mouths.

Fig. 30. Types of Human Heads on the Lintels of Yaxchilan.

art can be traced far and wide through Central America and Mexico by com- parative study of the serpent motive.

A typical serpent head in profile (with the human head omitted) as developed by the Mayas for decorative purposes is reproduced in Fig. 27 with the parts lettered and named. It will be noted that the lines of interest in this design are either vertical or horizontal, although the parts themselves have sinuous outlines. Two features of the typical serpent's body enter widely into the enrichment of all kinds of subjects. One of these is the double outline which is derived from the line paralleling the base of the serpent's body and serving to mark off the belly region. The second feature is the small circle applied in bead-like rows to represent scales. The profile serpent head is also seen in scrolls and frets that elaborate many details of dress worn by the human beings carved on the monuments. The front view of the serpent's head is usually extended to fill an oblong panel and is often used to decorate the base of a monument or the façade of a building. There are several monsters closely connected with the serpent that will be discussed as the description proceeds.

The Human Figure. The human beings pictured on Mayan monuments are captives, rulers, and priests or worshippers. The captives are poor groveling creatures, bound by rope, held by the hair or crushed under foot to fill a rectangular space over which the conqueror stands. The rulers and priests are hard to distinguish from each other, perhaps because the government was largely theocratic and the ruler was looked upon as the spokesman of divinity. The spear and shield of war served to mark off certain human beings from others who carry religious objects such as the Ceremonial Bar and the Manikin Scepter.

Elaborate thrones on several monuments are canopied over by the arched body of the Two-headed Dragon that bears symbols of the planets. Over all is seen the great Serpent Bird with outstretched wings. Upon the throne is seated a human being who may safely be called a king and a line of footprints on the front of the throne may symbolize ascent. On other monuments the commanding personage wears the mask of a god and wields a club to subdue or scatters grain to placate. On the great majority of monuments the human beings, richly attired in ceremonial regalia and carrying a variety of objects, possibly present the great warriors and priests of the day. Many of the early sculptures are stiff and formal, but in a number of instances the quality of actual portraiture is convincing.

Design, Composition, and Perspective. It is difficult to compare directly the graphic and plastic arts of different nations where the subject matter is diverse unless we compare them in accordance with absolute principles of design, composition, and perspective drawing. The Mayas produced one of the few really great and coherent expressions of beauty so far given to the world and their influence in America was historically as important as was that of the Greeks in Europe. Set as we are in the matrix of our own religious and artistic conventions, we find it difficult to approach sympathetically beauty that is overcast with an incomprehensible religion. When we can bring ourselves to feel the serpent symbolism of the Mayan artists as we feel, for instance, the conventional halo that crowns the ideal head of Christ, then we shall be able to recognize the truly emotional qualities of Mayan sculptures.

It is generally recognized that design to be successful must contain order of various sorts (in measurements, shapes, directions, tones, colors, etc.). In the simpler forms of decorative art the restrictions of technical process, as in basketry, may impose order, but in freehand sculpture it must come from an educated sense of beauty involving selection and the reproduction of the finest qualities. Design at its highest is embodied in the Mayan hieroglyphs. Given spaces had to be filled with given symbols and the results attained were uniformly excellent. Although the influence of the serpent led to the great use of tapering flame-like masses in nearly all Mayan designs, still dominant vertical and horizontal lines of interest were maintained.

The panel and lintel sculptures show composition achieved by simple and subtle methods. The sweeping plumes of headdresses were skilfully used to fill in corners, while blocks of glyphs were placed in open spaces that might

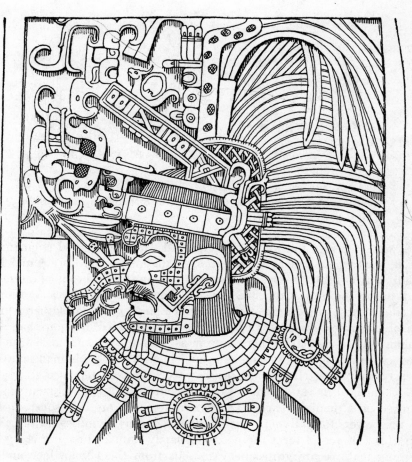

Fig. 31.   Sculpture on Upper Part of Stela 11, Seibal.   The man wears an inlaid mask, an elaborate headdress, and a collar of shell and jade.

otherwise distract the attention. Many compositions appear overcrowded to us, but this fault decreases with knowledge of the subject matter. Also, the Mayas appear to have painted their sculptures so that the details were emphasized by color contrast.

In perspective as applied to the human figure the Mayas were far ahead of the Egyptians and Assyrians, since they could draw the body in front view and pure profile without the distortions seen in the Old World. They were even able to make graceful approximations of a three-quarters view, as may be seen in Plate XIX, where the raising of the nearer shoulder has a distinct perspective value.

The Mayan Pantheon. We have seen that during the earliest culture of Mexico and Central America there were no figurines of individualized gods, simply straightforward representations of human beings and animals. With the Mayan culture, however, we enter upon an epoch of rich religious symbolism. The serpent, highly conventionalized as we have just seen, and variously com-

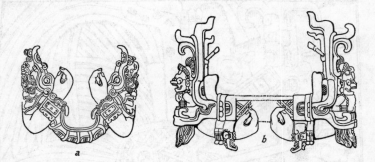

Fig. 32. The Ceremonial Bar. A Two-Headed Serpent held in the Arms of Human Beings on Stelæ: *a*, Stela P, Copan; *b*, Stela N, Copan.

bined with elements taken from the quetzal, the jaguar, and even from man himself, appears as a general indication of divinity. The Ceremonial Bar, essentially a two-headed serpent carrying in its mouths the heads of an important god, is one of the earliest religious objects. The heads that appear in the mouths are usually those of a Roman-nosed or of a Long-nosed god. Other representations of divinities are combined with the Two-headed Dragon that also has reptilian characters; still others appear as headdresses and masks on human figures. Strange to say, the gods are supplementary to the human figures on all the early sculptures. In the codices, however, they are represented apart from man, as engaged in various activities and contests. Mayan religion was clearly organized on a dualistic basis. The powers for good are in a constant struggle with the powers for evil and most of the benevolent divinities have malevolent duplicates. In actual form the gods are partly human, but ordinarily the determining features are grotesque variations from the human face and figure. While beast associations are sometimes discernible, they are rarely controlling. Sometimes, however, beast gods are represented in unmistakable fashion, good examples being the jaguar, the bat, and the *moan* bird. All of these have human bodies and animal heads.

The head position in the Mayan pantheon may with some assurance be given to a god who has been called the Roman-nosed god and who is probably to be identified with Itzamna. According to Spanish writers Itzamna was regarded by the Mayas as the creator and father of all, the inventor of writing, the founder of the Mayan civilization, and the god of light and life. This Zeus of the Mayas is represented in the form of an old man with a high forehead, a strongly aquiline nose, and a distended mouth, toothless, or with a single enlarged tooth in front. On the ancient monuments he is frequently seen in the mouths of the Ceremonial Bar and also in association with the sun, moon, and the planet Venus. In the codices he is shown as a protector of the Maize God and in other acts beneficial to man. There is, however, a malevolent aspect of this god or possibly another being who imitates his features but not his qualities. This being may be an old woman goddess who wears a serpent headdress and who is associated with destructive floods, the very opposite of life-giving sunshine.

Of almost equal importance to the Roman-nosed god is a god whose face is a more or less humanized serpent. His proper name is Ah Bolon Dzacab.

On the early monuments this god is shown in connection with the Ceremonial Bar. He also appears at a somewhat later date as the Manikin Scepter, an object in the form of a manikin that is held out by a leg modified into a serpent's body. Since a celt is usually worn in the forehead of the manikin it has been suggested that this curious object represents a ceremonial battle-ax. The face of the Long-nosed god is frequently worn by high priests and rulers either as a headdress or, more rarely, as a mask. It is possible that this divinity was regarded as primarily a war god but in the codices he is evidently a universal deity of varied powers. Especially he is shown in connection with water and maize and it seems likely that his principal function was to cause life-giving rain. A malevolent variant of the Long-nosed

Fig. 33. The Manikin Scepter, a Grotesque Figure with one Leg modified into a Serpent.

god has a bare bone for the lower jaw, a sun symbol on his forehead, and a headdress consisting of three other symbols. This head is associated with the Two-headed Dragon, a monster which brings calamity at times of the inferior conjunction of Venus and the Sun.

Fig. 34. The Two-Headed Dragon, a Monster that passes through many Forms in Mayan Sculpture. It apparently symbolizes calamities at inferior conjunction of Venus and the Sun. Copan.

Ah Puch, the Lord of Death, was the principal malevolent god. His body as figured in the codices is a strange compound of skeletal and full-fleshed parts. His head is a skull except for the normal ears. His spinal column is usually bare and sometimes the ribs as well, but the arms and legs are often covered with flesh. As added symbols black spots and dotted lines are sometimes drawn upon his body and a curious device like a percentage sign upon his cheek. The Death God in complete form is rarely shown in the earlier sculptures, although grinning skulls and interlacing bones occur as temple decorations. As has already been pointed out, Mayan religion was strongly dualistic and the evil

powers are usually to be identified by death symbols such as a bare bone for
the lower jaw, or the percentage symbol noted above on the cheek. Death
heads of several kinds are frequent in the hieroglyphic inscriptions.

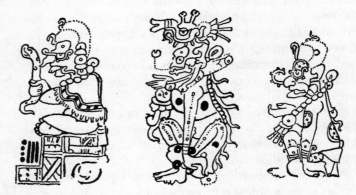

Fig. 35. Gods in the Dresden Codex: God B, the Long-
Nosed God of Rain; God A, the Death God; God G, the Sun
God.

The Maize God, figured so frequently on the ancient monuments and in the
Mayan codices, may be the same that in the time of the Conquest was called
Yum Kaax, Lord of the Harvest. He is represented as a youth with a leafy
headdress that is possibly meant to represent an opening ear of maize. The *kan*
sign, a grain of maize, is constantly associated with him. He appears to be at
the mercy of the evil deities when not protected by the good ones.

Space considerations forbid a further study of Mayan gods. Suffice it to say
that several other divinities are shown in the sculptures and codices including
a somewhat youthful appearing war god, as well as a more mature and grotesque
war god called Ek Ahau, the Black Captain. There is an old god with a shell
attached to his body, a god with the face of a monkey who is associated with
the North Star, a god in the form of a frog and another in the form of a bat.
In the Spanish accounts we can also glean scanty information concerning Ixchel,
Goddess of the Rainbow and mate of Itzamna; Ixtubtun, patroness of jade
carvers; Ixchebelyax, patroness of the art of weaving and decorating cloth, etc.

How Mayan History has been Recovered. The arrangement of Mayan remains on a time scale is now an accomplished fact thanks to a correlation which
permits us to read the dates on ancient monuments in terms of the Gregorian
calendar and the Christian era. Early attempts to achieve this result met with
widely varying results. Most of these attempts were made by developing a
single line of evidence and some were based on assumptions that can now be
disproved. But no single line of evidence should be deemed sufficient to decide
this all important question.

The general course of Mayan history is indicated unmistakably by four
principal lines of evidence capable of being correlated with each other. These
are:—

1. Stratigraphic sequences in pottery, stylistic sequences in sculpture, structural sequences in architecture, etc.

2. Traditional history preserved in the Books of Chilam Balam and representing a knowledge of past events at the time of the Spanish Conquest.

3. Dates inscribed on a great number of monuments in terms of the ancient Mayan time counts.

4. Astronomical checks on these inscribed dates.

The artistic position of a monument may be used to validate the contemporaneous character of an inscribed date, otherwise interpretable as referring to the past or future, or it may serve to fix a repeating date in a single historical setting. The events in the traditional history of the Books of Chilam Balam, meager enough when taken alone, have the valuable quality of reaching back into the

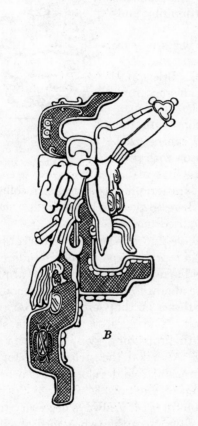

Fig. 36. The Front Head of the Two-Headed Dragon on Stelæ at Piedras Negras showing the Increase in Flamboyant Treatment. The interval between (a) and (b) is 125 years, that between (b) and (c) is 45 years.

time of the First Empire when the use of dates on temples and monuments was much in vogue. They permit a richly documented past to be tied in, as it were, to a poorly documented terminal period.

Before the matter of the ancient inscribed dates can be understood, however, the somewhat complicated mechanism of the Mayan calendar must be explained,

as well as the system of hieroglyphs
and the notation of numbers. Then
there is the problem of correlation
which necessitates delicate adjudica-
tions of evidence. Finally we must
take up the proofs which demonstrate the astronomical achievements
of the Mayas which, in reverse, provide checks upon the correctness of
the day for day correlation itself. We
must proceed slowly and carefully,
without much following of by-ways,
however attractive they may appear.
We will begin with stratigraphy and
stylistic sequence.

Sequences in Art. The study of
Mayan ceramics reveals developments as regard shapes, fabrics, and
designs. Specimens recovered from
sealed cysts under stelæ at Copan
establish true associations with the
higher forms of art and can be used
far and wide in comparison with pottery finds in Salvador, Guatemala,

Fig. 37. Grotesque
Face on the Back of
Stela B, Copan.

Fig. 38. Jaguar in
Dresden Codex with
a Water Lily at-
tached to Forehead.

etc. Vaillant has found stratigraphic sequences in a collection of funerary vessels
obtained at Holmul, where graves occurred under the floors and within the
filled-in chambers of a buried temple.

As regards sculpture we find at Copan a remarkably homogeneous series of
stelæ on which a royal or priestly personage stands erect and in front view.
A Ceremonial Bar is held symmetrically in the two arms and the body is partly
covered with rich and elaborate ornament. The amount of relief, the proportions of the body, the forms of the Ceremonial Bar, etc., all pass through a
harmonious development. The earliest monuments show a crude block-like
carving of the face, with protruding eyes, while the latest monuments have
fully rounded contours. At Tikal the stelæ show, for the most part, human
figures in profile, but unmistakable development can be seen in general quality
of carving as well as in specific details.

In making comparisons in art it is always necessary to consider similar things.
At many other Mayan cities than the two named above it is possible to obtain
satisfactory evidence of sequence in art forms by cutting out similar details from
different masses. Thus at Naranjo, when we examine all the Ceremonial Bars,
we find a remarkable development of flamboyant detail on the later monuments.
At Quirigua the faces on the tops of the altars may be compared with the same
result. At Piedras Negras the heads of the Two-headed Dragon that occur in
exactly similar positions on four monuments likewise show a steady modification
towards flamboyancy as may be seen from Fig. 36, where the front heads are put
side by side.

Still other lines of evidence on historical sequence are to be gained from a study of architecture. Not only is it possible to determine the general developments that hold true of the entire Mayan Area but also in a given city it is sometimes possible to arrange the buildings in their order of erection according to dependable criteria, both decorative and structural.

The earliest temples have narrow vaulted rooms, heavy walls, and a single doorway. The rooms increase in width, the walls decrease in thickness, the doorways multiply till the spaces between them become piers and finally columns. The support for the heavy roof comb taxed the structural ingenuity of the Mayan architects. The solving of this problem is marked by successive advances and since mechanical science goes forward rather than backward the relative order of structures is fairly certain. Moreover, many buildings are closely associated with dated monuments, tablets, lintels, or stelæ. Still another evidence of architectural sequence is seen in structures that have been enlarged by the addition of wings or by the enclosing of the old parts under new masonry.

Books of Chilam Balam. We now turn to a very different kind of history, the digests of ancient chronicles in the Mayan language but in Spanish script which managed to survive in the so-called Books of Chilam Balam along with other texts, ceremonial and medical. There are five chronicles, the two longest covering 68 katuns before the coming of the Spaniards in 1517. We now know that these katuns were time units consisting of 7200 days, or nearly 20 years, and that they were designated by their final day which was always a day called Ahau associated with a number, 1 and 13, in a peculiar sequence. A katun with the same designation returns in 13 × 7200 days or about 256 years. Such a completion, counted especially from a Katun 8 Ahau, was called the "doubling back of the katuns" or, as we would say, the completion of a cycle. The count of the katuns used in the chronicles was really part and parcel of a fuller count just as a year '22 implies a position in one of the centuries of our Christian era.

The chronicles unfortunately give few names of chieftains and cities and few outstanding events. Chichen Itza is the city most fully concerned and an early occupation is recorded, then an abandonment for some two and half centuries. After its re-establishment the Toltecs enter Yucatan and capture this capital. The first part of the chronicles has the atmosphere of myth rather than history, but a calendarial adjustment of some kind is mentioned in one place. This was an event which took place in 503 A. D. as we shall see in another place.

The first rough correlation between the time count on the ancient monuments and the time count in the chronicles was made on the theory that a dated lintel at Chichen Itza had to be placed in the first occupation of the city: when this was done the beginning of the chronicles was found to proceed from an important round number in the old day count while the abandonment of Chichen Itza coincided with the abandonment of all the cities of the Mayan First Empire. We must now turn attention to the famous calendar.

The Mayan Time Counts. The passage of time, seen in finer and finer degree in the course of human life, the succession of summer and winter, the waxing and waning moons, the alternation of day and night, the upward and downward sloping of the sun, and the swinging dial of the stars, are phenomena that no human group has failed to notice. Longer periods than those included within the memory of the oldest men (presenting an imperfect reflection of the memory

Fig. 39. Late Sculpture from Chichen Itza. The headdress resembles that worn by the rulers on the highlands of Mexico.

of men still older) are found only in those favored centers where a serviceable system of counting has been developed. Mythology has a content of history but hardly of chronology. Tradition, when organized by the priesthood, may be reasonably dependable for perhaps two hundred years.

The year and the month are the basis of all primitive time systems, the former depending on the recurring seasons, the latter on recurring moons. Both of these are expressed in days. Unfortunately, the day is not contained evenly in either the month or the year, nor do these larger time measures show any simple relation to each other as regards length. The history of the calendar is one of compromise and correction.

The Mayan calendars were made possible by, first, the knowledge of astronomical time periods; second, the possession of a suitable notation system; third, the discovery of a permutation system of names and numbers.

Elements of the Day Count. There is reason to believe that the Mayas had first a lunisolar calendar of twelve months of thirty days each, making a year of 360 days, and that they reduced the number of days in the formal month to 20 and raised the number of months in the year from 12 to 18. These changes permitted a close adjustment of the units of time with their vigesimal system of counting. With a truer knowledge of the length of the year an extra five day month was added to make a year of 365 days. Beyond this the "leap year" error was calculated but not interpolated. As proof that the lunar month of thirty days preceded the formal month of twenty days, it need only be pointed out that the name for this period, *uinal*, seems to be connected with the name for moon, *u*,

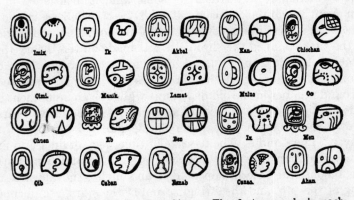

Fig. 40. The Twenty Day Signs. The first example in each case is taken from the inscriptions and the second from the codices.

and that the hieroglyph for moon has the value, twenty, in the inscriptions and ancient books.

Before entering into a fuller discussion of the astronomical and notational facts let us turn for a moment to the third fact, the permutation system. The origin of the cycle[1] known by the Mayan name *tzolkin* and the Aztecan name *tonalamatl*, book of the days, has never been satisfactorily explained. It is a permutation system with two factors, 13 and 20. The former is a series of numbers (1–13) and the latter a series of twenty names as follows:—

1. Imix	6. Cimi	11. Chuen	16. Cib
2. Ik	7. Manik	12. Eb	17. Caban
3. Akbal	8. Lamat	13. Ben	18. Eznab
4. Kan	9. Muluc	14. Ix	19. Cauac
5. Chicchan	10. Oc	15. Men	20. Ahau

These two series revolve upon each other like two wheels, one with thirteen and the other with twenty cogs. The smaller wheel of numbers makes twenty revolutions while the larger wheel of days is making thirteen revolutions, and after this the number cog and name cog with which the experiment began are again in combination. Thus, a day with the same number and the same name recurs every 13 × 20 or 260 days.

PERMUTATION TABLE

		1	2	3	4	5	6	7	8	9	10	11	12	13	1
1	Imix	1	8	2	9	3	10	4	11	5	12	6	13	7	1
2	Ik	2	9	3	10	4	11	5	12	6	13	7	1	8	2
3	Akbal	3	10	4	11	5	12	6	13	7	1	8	2	9	3
4	Kan	4	11	5	12	6	13	7	1	8	2	9	3	10	4
5	Chicchan	5	12	6	13	7	1	8	2	9	3	10	4	11	5
6	Cimi	6	13	7	1	8	2	9	3	10	4	11	5	12	6
7	Manik	7	1	8	2	9	3	10	4	11	5	12	6	13	7
8	Lamat	8	2	9	3	10	4	11	5	12	6	13	7	1	8
9	Muluc	9	3	10	4	11	5	12	6	13	7	1	8	2	9
10	Oc	10	4	11	5	12	6	13	7	1	8	2	9	3	10
11	Chuen	11	5	12	6	13	7	1	8	2	9	3	10	4	11
12	Eb	12	6	13	7	1	8	2	9	3	10	4	11	5	12
13	Ben	13	7	1	8	2	9	3	10	4	11	5	12	6	13
14	Ix	1	8	2	9	3	10	4	11	5	12	6	13	7	1
15	Men	2	9	3	10	4	11	5	12	6	13	7	1	8	2
16	Cib	3	10	4	11	5	12	6	13	7	1	8	2	9	3
17	Caban	4	11	5	12	6	13	7	1	8	2	9	3	10	4
18	Eznab	5	12	6	13	7	1	8	2	9	3	10	4	11	5
19	Cauac	6	13	7	1	8	2	9	3	10	4	11	5	12	6
20	Ahau	7	1	8	2	9	3	10	4	11	5	12	6	13	7

This 260 day cycle corresponds to no natural time period and is an invention pure and simple. It is the most fundamental feature of the Mayan time count and of the time counts of other nations in Mexico and Central America. We may perhaps assume that the twenty names were originally those of the twenty days in the modified lunar months. But the thirteen numbers have no recognized prototype. The formal book of days generally was considered to begin with 1

[1] The word *cycle* is applied in this book to re-entering series, or wheels, of days. These all contain the *tzolkin* or *tonalamatl* without a remainder. The word *period* is applied to fixed numbers that do not contain the *tonalamatl*.

Imix for the Mayas and with a corresponding day for the other Mexican and Central American nations. But it can be made to begin anywhere and proceed to an equivalent station that is always 260 days removed.

The Conventional Year. It has been stated that the Mayas arrived at a conventional 365 day year made up of eighteen months of twenty days each plus a short period of five days that fell after the eighteen regular months had been counted. The Mayan month names are as follows:—

1. Pop	6. Xul	11. Zac	16. Pax
2. Uo	7. Yaxkin	12. Ceh	17. Kayab
3. Zip	8. Mol	13. Mac	18. Cumhu
4. Zotz	9. Chen	14. Kankin	19. Uayeb (five
5. Tzec	10. Yax	15. Muan	additional days)

Since there are twenty days or positions in the month and likewise twenty distinct day names in the *tzolkin*, falling in regular order, it follows that each day would always occupy the same month position were it not for the offset at the end of each year caused by the short Uayeb period. As it is, any day name occupies the same month position during the course of an entire year and a position five days in advance during the course of the following year. Since five is contained four times in twenty there can be only four shifts, the fifth year showing the same arrangement as the first. The following table gives the month

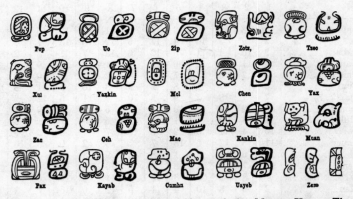

Fig. 41. The Nineteen Month Signs of the Mayan Year. The first example in each case is taken from the inscriptions and the second from the codices. The last details are signs for zero.

positions of each day name during the changes of four consecutive years as these are recorded in the ancient inscriptions.

Ik	Manik	Eb	Caban	0	5	10	15
Akbal	Lamat	Ben	Eznab	1	6	11	16
Kan	Muluc	Ix	Cauac	2	7	12	17
Chicchan	Oc	Men	Ahau	3	8	13	18
Imix	Cimi	Chuen	Cib	4	9	14	19

Thus Ik occupies 0 position the first year, 5 the second year, 10 the third,

15 the fourth, and 0 the fifth. While Manik that belongs to the same set has position 5 the first year, 10 the second, etc. It will be noted that Imix, the first day of the formal permutation of the *tzolkin*, is never the first day of a month.

The Calendar Round. But this assignment of particular day names to particular places in the month does not close the problem. Each day name is associated in the *tzolkin*, or permutation, with a day number. While it is true that each day can occupy only four month positions in as many years, it must be remembered that the day numbers associated with these names can run the whole gamut of 13 changes. Thus, although Ik must always occupy the fifth position in the months during a certain year, nevertheless it will have numbers which fall in the sequence 1, 8, 2, 9, 3, 10, 4, 11, 5, 12, 6, 13, 1, etc. The complete cycle of variations must run through the least common multiple of 260 (the permutation) and 365 (the conventional year) or 18,980 days. This cycle is commonly known as the Calendar Round. A Mayan day fixed in a month, or let us say a calendar round date, has four parts to its name, thus, 11 Ahau 18 Mac. We describe a day as Tuesday, July 4, meaning "Tuesday the third day of the seven day week occupies the fourth position in the month of July." Similarly the Mayan date 11 Ahau 18 Mac may be read "the day named Ahau as eleventh day in a thirteen day week occupies the eighteenth position in the month Mac." Owing to leap year corrections the European date given above does not recur at regular intervals, but a Mayan day recurs infallibly in 52 calendar years, never sooner, never later.

So far we have considered two kinds of Mayan dates, first the *tzolkin* date, recurring every 260 days, secondly the calendar round date recurring every 18,980 days. Before we can understand a third and much more important kind of date, namely a date which states, in addition to the calendar round designation, the total number of days since a beginning day called 4 Ahau 8 Cumhu, located far in the past, we must direct our attention to the matter of numbers and notation.

Mayan Numbers. The three most common numerical systems in use in the world are all derived from man's anatomy. The quinary system is based on counting the fingers of one hand, the decimal system on counting those of both hands and the vigesimal system, which prevailed in Central America, is based on counting all the fingers and all the toes. The vigesimal system is seen in imperfect form in our count of scores, where seventy years are three score and ten.

The Mayan name for one was *hun:* they had simple names to 9 and composite ones from 10 to 19, much as in English, and twenty was *hun kal*, one score. The ascending values in the vigesimal scale were as follows:—

Mayan Numbers		Arabic Equivalents
	hun	1
20 hun	= 1 kal	20
20 kal	= 1 bak	400
20 bak	= 1 pic	8,000
20 pic	= 1 cabal	160,000
20 cabal	= 1 kinchil	3,200,000
20 kinchil	= 1 alau	64,000,000
20 alau	= 1 hablat	1,280,000,000

They invented signs for zero and discovered the principle of "local value" in the writing down of numbers centuries before these ideas (which are fundamental

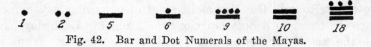

Fig. 42.   Bar and Dot Numerals of the Mayas.

to higher mathematics) were known in the Old World. The notation of numbers had its simpler and more complicated phase. In the simpler phase 1 was represented by a dot, 2 by two dots, 5 by a bar, 6 by a bar and dot, 15 by three bars, etc. The commonest sign for zero was a shell while a picture of the moon stood for twenty. In the more elaborate notation a series of twenty faces of gods represented the numerals from 0 to 19.

The straight vigesimal system was doubtless used by the Mayas in ordinary counting, but in counting time a very important change was introduced in the third position. Also the names were modified: *hun* was called *kin* which means sun or day. In the second position *kal* was called *uinal* which means month and 18 of these were taken to form a *tun*, stone, which was the third unit. The *tun* then had a value of $18 \times 20 = 360$ days, making a conventional year about five and a quarter days less than a true year. Twenty *tuns* made a *kaltun* or *katun* and above this period the numeral system proceeded as before and in the ascending values the names already given were merely combined with *tun*, if Gates is right in his clever suggestion. For years it has been customary to speak of the fifth period as cycle for want of a native term: this will now be called *baktun*. One *hablatun*, the highest period with a name, has the astonishing value of 460,800,000,000 days. However, the highest numbers fall considerably short of this potential limit.

In our decimal system the number 347,981, for instance, is really:—

$$
\begin{aligned}
3 &\times 100000 \\
4 &\times 10000 \\
7 &\times 1000 \\
9 &\times 100 \\
8 &\times 10 \\
1 &\times 1
\end{aligned}
$$

When written out in a horizontal line each "position" has a value ten times that of the "position" to the right of it. It is understood that a digit which stands in a "position" is to be multiplied by 1, 10, 100, 1000, etc., as the case may be. The Mayas, using the principle of position, ordinarily write their bar and dot numerals in columns. But we can partially transcribe a Mayan number in imitation of our own system by putting dots or dashes between the positions or periods. The number in five positions given below is transcribed as 9.12.16.7.8.

9×144000	1,296,000
12×7200	86,400
16×360	5,760
7×20	140
8×1	8
	1,388,308

We read this day: 9 baktuns, 12 katuns, 16 tuns, 7 uinals, and 8 kins. It is convenient to remember that a tun is a little less than a year, a katun a little less than 20 years and a baktun a little less than 400 years. But the count is really of days, not years.

Fig. 43. Face Numerals found in Mayan Inscriptions. In most cases these are the faces of gods. Reading from left to right: the values are 1, 3, 4, 5, 6, 9, 10.

Fig. 44. The Normal Forms of the Period Glyphs. Reading from left to right: baktun, katun, tun, uinal, kin.

Fig. 45. Face Forms of Period Glyphs. From left to right: introducing glyph, baktun, katun, tun, uinal, kin.

Although the numerical values are expressed by position alone in some cases, in other cases use is made of Period Glyphs to make assurance doubly sure. These Period Glyphs represent the basic value of the positions which are to be multiplied by the accompanying numerals. For examples, see Figs. 44 and 45.

The Long Count. Many early monuments of the Mayas have inscriptions with an enlarged Introducing Glyph containing a variable element indicating the title or principal subject matter of the inscription. Next follows the number of elapsed days from the epoch of a Mundane Era. This starting point is uniformly the day 4 Ahau 8 Cumhu and the complete Initial Series date not only states the number of elapsed days, but also the name and number of the day reached and its position in a Mayan month.

The Initial Series is normally followed by a Supplementary Series which concerns the lunar calendar, and often there are numbers of days to be added to or subtracted from the Initial Series date: these are called Secondary Series. Also Period Ending dates are used, these being merely abbreviated dates which correspond to indicated round numbers in the day count.

The Initial Series analyzed in Plate XXIII actually records the number 1,401,217. This number does not, however, reach the day 12 Caban declared immediately after it or the month position 5 Kayab recorded in glyph 10b. When 13 tuns are corrected to 12 tuns on the theory that the sculptor did not follow copy, we do reach 12 Caban 5 Kayab. Another check comes when we add the Secondary Series of 2423 days and reach 4 Ahau 13 Yax ending an even katun.

Dates of Dedication. Initial Series dates are especially common on stelæ at cities of the First Empire, mostly located in the southern part of the Mayan Area. While it is impossible to read much of the texts which accompany these dates, nevertheless it is a remarkable fact that when we arrange the monuments in their artistic order we find that the inscribed dates in the great majority of cases fall in the same order. This leads us to conclude that the dates are practically contemporaneous with the carving and setting up of the monuments. Now the above is especially true when the inscription gives a simple Initial Series date. When more than one date is given the historic one appears in most instances to be the latest, but in a few instances it appears to be a specially emphasized intermediate date. In addition, then, to contemporaneous dates there are some that refer to the past and others that refer to the future.

Some writers have assumed that the stelæ and other inscribed monuments were primarily time markers set up at the end of hotun (or five year) periods. This seems an unnecessarily narrow view. We can demonstrate that some inscriptions deal with astronomical facts covering long stretches of time. It is also apparent that many of the sculptures represent conquests and it is extremely likely that portraits of actual rulers are to be seen in certain carvings. It would be too much to expect events to happen regularly at the end of time periods and as a matter of fact we find at different cities repeated dates that do not occupy such positions. These repeated dates would seem to recall events of special importance to the city in question.

The running co-ordination between the apparent order of the artistic styles and inscribed dates permits us to measure very accurately the rate of change in art which was rapid, indeed, at certain times. The style of carving, on the other hand, enables us to put into definite 52 year periods many of the calendar round dates—if these are to be regarded as contemporaneous. The result is that for the First Empire, as it has been called, there is an exceedingly accurate chronology. After the fall and abandonment of the great southern cities dates are rare and we have to fall back upon remnants of history preserved after the coming of the Spaniards.

Hieroglyphs. Mayan hieroglyphs resemble the Egyptian and Chinese hieroglyphs only in being "sacred writing" that is not based upon an alphabet. The styles and symbols are entirely different. No Rosetta Stone has yet been discovered to give us inscriptions in more than one system of writing in Central America. The great use of hieroglyphic inscriptions on monuments was characteristic of the earlier period of Mayan history and at a later time the writing was reduced to books. Bishop Landa obtained what he supposed was a Mayan alphabet, but what he really obtained was a list of signs representing among other sounds the particular sounds he had asked for.

The phonetic use of syllables rather than of simple sounds or letters is probably an important feature of Mayan writing. Many hieroglyphs are pictographic and consist of abbreviated pictures of the thing intended or of some object connected with it. Often a head stands for the entire body. The following list practically exhausts our knowledge of Mayan hieroglyphs:—

1. The signs for the twenty named days of the calendar.
2. The signs for the nineteen months of the Mayan year.
3. The face signs for numbers from zero to nineteen inclusive.
4. Period glyphs in two styles for place values in the numerical notation.
5. The symbols for the four directions and for the colors associated with them.
6. The hieroglyphs of several gods and ceremonies.
7. The symbols of Heaven and Earth, the Sun, Moon, Venus, Mars, Jupiter, and a few astronomical phenomena such as conjunctions.
8. Hieroglyphs for special times of the year such as solstices and equinoxes.
9. Signs meaning era, or base from which a numerical count is made, completion, etc.

Some of these have recently been solved, thanks to mathematical and astronomical calculations, others rest on the calendarial forms given by Landa. There are some phonetic elements in Mayan writing and some ideographic elements. It seems likely that the gist of the Mayan inscriptions which deal with history will be solved in somewhat the same fashion as those that deal with astronomy. The matter is, however, most perplexing. So far not a single place name or personal name has been definitely recognized and translated. In spite of the hundreds of glyphs recovered at the sites called Copan and Palenque, for instance, we do not know the real names of these cities or even their symbols. We may expect to find signs referring to tribute and common objects of trade and others referring to birth, death, establishment, conquest, destruction, and other fundamentals of individual and social existence. These signs, taken with directives, connectives, and dates, would make possible the recovery of the main facts of history. There seems no possibility of purely literary inscriptions. While progress necessarily will be slow there is no reason for despair and without doubt the greater portion of Mayan inscriptions will finally be deciphered.

Fig. 46. Hieroglyphs of the Four Directions: East, North, West, South.

As an example of the phonetic use of signs in the building up of hieroglyphs let us take the common sign *kin*, meaning "sun." This sign appears regularly in the glyphs for the world directions east and west, the Mayan names being *likin* and *chikin*, and also in the month sign *Yaxkin*, and sometimes in that for

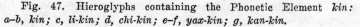

Fig. 47. Hieroglyphs containing the Phonetic Element *kin*: a–b, *kin*; c, *li-kin*; d, *chi-kin*; e–f, *yax-kin*; g, *kan-kin*.

Kankin. It also appears as the sign for the lowest period in the time count having the value of a single day and called *kin* (Fig. 47). Now this kin sign also appears in many undeciphered hieroglyphs and in some of these it seems likely that it has a phonetic value. Other signs with definite values in several glyphs are *yax, tun, zac,* etc. This general method of writing is seen in more decipherable form among the Aztecs. The glosses of the early priests that have proved so great a help in the case of the Aztecan writing are absent from the few Mayan documents.

Codices. Only three ancient Mayan books or codices are known to exist and these are more or less incomplete. They have all been reproduced in facsimile and are known by the following names: Dresden Codex, Peresianus Codex, Tro-Cortesianus Codex.

These illuminated manuscripts are written on both sides of long strips of amatl paper, folded like Japanese screens. The paper was given a smooth surface by a coating of fine lime and the drawings were made in black and in various colors. From the early accounts we know that books were also written on prepared deerskin and upon bark. Concerning their subject matter we are told that the Mayas had many books upon civil and religious history, and upon rites, magic, and medicine. The three books named above have been carefully studied. They treat principally of the calendar and of associated religious ceremonies.

A page of the Dresden Codex containing some interesting calculations is reproduced herewith. The numbers with the digits one above the other are transcribed in two diagrams. In the upper diagram the bar and dot numerals are simply put over into Arabic numerals and the Mayan system of periods or positions is retained. In the lower diagram these numbers are reduced entirely to the Arabic system. The columns are lettered at the top, the hieroglyphs are counted off in sixteen rows at the left and the separate groupings of numbers are shown in five sections at the right.

Among the hieroglyphs the Venus sign is especially prominent. At the base of column B is given a number in five periods that, counted from the normal beginning day 4 Ahau 8 Cumhu, leads again to this day which is recorded at the bottom of column A. The long number in column C, similarly counted from 4 Ahau 8 Cumhu, leads to 1 Ahau 18 Kayab, recorded at the bottom of B. The day 1 Ahau 18 Uo is reached by another calculation which will be explained later. At the base of A is a number in three periods which amounts to 2200. Not only is this the difference between the long numbers in B and C $(1,366,560 - 1,364,-360 = 2200)$ but it is also the number of days by which 1 Ahau 18 Kayab precedes 4 Ahau 8 Cumhu. In other words we deal in this passage with the end of the seventy-second calendar round after the original 4 Ahau 8 Cumhu and with a new point of departure 2200 days earlier, which is some way involved with the calendar of Venus.

Let us now make a new beginning in the lower left hand corner of this page. In G5 we find the number 2920 which as we have already seen is exactly the number of days consumed in eight years of 365 days or five synodic revolutions of Venus of 584 days. We will now see how the Mayan scholars arrived at 13×2920 or 37,960, the calendar round of Venus. If we proceed towards the left in section 5 we find the second number, F5, is 5840 which equals 2×2920, the third is 8760 or 3×2920, and the fourth is 11,680 or 4×2920. The addition is continued in sections 4 and 3 till we reach 35,040 or 12 × 2920. To be sure the scribe made a slight error in one place, writing a 5 for an 8, but this is caught up by the day signs 9 Ahau, 4 Ahau, 7 Ahau, 12 Ahau, etc., that fall at regular intervals of 2920 days.

Fig. 48. Mayan Ceremony as represented in the Dresden Codex. The figure at the left beats a drum while the one on the right plays a flageolet. The sound is indicated by scrolls. The head on the pyramid is that of the Maize God and it rests upon the sign *caban*, meaning earth.

From section 3, the calculation jumps to section 1 where the numbers in the original are partly destroyed. They have, however, been restored with perfect assurance since the days in all instances are 1 Ahau and therefore must be separated by multiples of 260 days. The number in G1 has been restored as 5-5-8-0 or 37,960 or 13 × 2920. It contains 260 an even number of times and therefore every successive period of 37,960 days begins with the same day, 1 Ahau. It also equals 13 × 8 × 365 days or 104 years and 13 × 5 × 584 days or sixty-five revolutions of Venus.

The three numbers to the left in F1, E1, and D1 are respectively 2, 3, and 4 times 37,960. The last number, 151,840 days is therefore equal to 416 years or exactly 8 calendar rounds of 18,980 days.

The numbers in section 2 are more difficult to explain but they possibly have to do with corrections and correlations of astronomical periods. If we add to 1 Ahau 18 Kayab the number of days in E2 (68900), we arrive at a day 1 Ahau 13 Mac. This day is prominent in more detailed calculations elsewhere in the Dresden Codex. If we add to the same 1 Ahau 18 Kayab the number in D2 we arrive at 1 Ahau 18 Uo recorded at the bottom of C. Space permits no further explanation but the reader will see from the foregoing the method of experiment and cross checking that must be applied to the decipherment of the Mayan manuscripts. Fortunately, the relationships of numbers are absolute and the coincidences between the recorded numbers and astronomical periods are too close and frequent to be dismissed as accidental.

In addition to rational calculations dealing with astronomy one sees in the Mayan manuscripts many arrangements of the *tzolkin* supposed to bring to light good and bad days and to forecast events. A section of the Dresden Codex showing a condensed *tzolkin* is presented along with a diagram of its parts. At the top and right are seventeen hieroglyphs containing the symbols of the four directions, and of at least three of the principal gods. At the right is a column of five day signs with the number 3 at the head of the column. The permutation is divided into five parts of fifty-two days each and each part is subdivided into four groups of three days each. It begins with 3 Akbal, the day sign at the top of the column, and after the four subdivisions of thirteen days each have been counted we arrive at the day 3 Men, the second day sign in the column. The count is repeated till the 260 days have been exhausted and we come back again to 3 Akbal. In the diagram the red numbers of the codex are represented by Roman numerals and the black numbers by Arabic numerals. Since the count in this example begins with 3 and the addition is always 13, or exactly one round of numbers, the resultant days always have the number 3.

The three pictures of gods give us an inkling into the significance of this particular table of chances. All of the gods carry the *kan* or maize sign in their hands. The first god is the benevolent rain god and the third is the benevolent sun god. Between them is seated the malevolent goddess of floods with a serpent on her head. The maize god is not shown but his hieroglyph is given. This *tzolkin* probably deals with agriculture and may be an attempt to determine lucky days for planting.

Correlation with Christian Chronology. The day for day correlation rests broadly on the placing of the date on the Lintel of the Initial Series at Chichen Itza in the first occupation of that city according to the chronicles. More specifically it rests upon statements in Mayan and Spanish documents relating to the completion of tuns and katuns in the never-languishing day count. Also consideration must be given the so-called Year-Bearers, these being the first days of current years which furnish the designations for such years. Bishop Landa has a specimen Mayan year with its equivalent days in the Spanish calendar; this is the year 12 Kan corresponding to 1553–1554 A. D. and the day 12 Kan is found in the Long Count position 12.9.17.9.4, 12 Kan 2 Pop, July 26, 1553, Gregorian Calendar.

The Mayan Eras. The zero of the Mayan day count, reached by subtracting 12.9.17.9.4 or 1,799,104 days from the position declared above, is shown to be October 14, 3373 B. C. in the backward projection of the Gregorian calendar. The Gregorian readings are preferable to the Julian because they preserve the actual times in the tropical year, but it is sometimes useful to use the days of the Julian Period which can always be found by adding 489384 to the Mayan number.

Now Mayan history does not reach back to the zero date which must be regarded as a theoretical beginning or Mundane Era. The earliest object with a contemporary date is the Tuxtla Statuette with May 16, 98 B. C. It appears, however, that the really historic beginning of the day count was 7.0.0.0.0, 10 Ahau 18 Zac, August 6, 613 B. C. The calendar of months was probably inaugurated in 580 B. C. when 0 Pop, New Year's day, coincided with the winter solstice. A third era, 9.0.0.0.0, 8 Ahau 13 Ceh, February 11, 176 A. D., is the one used in the Mayan chronicles.

Astronomical Checks on the Correlation. The first astronomical checks which develop from the correlation explained above are dates which reach the equinoxes, solstices, etc., further marked by special hieroglyphs which are to be explained as ideographs of these stations in the natural year. For instance the most emphatic date in the three famous temples of the Sun, the Cross, and the Foliated Cross at Palenque is one written 9.12.18.5.16, 2 Cib 14 Mol, September 23, 430 A. D., which coincides with the autumnal equinox. In connection with this repeated date we find two glyphs both of which are admirable ideographs of the equinox. One is Ahau, a face explained as that of the Lord of Day, but here half covered with starry eyes, and the other is the Kin or sun symbol, half darkened with cross-hatching. At Comitan a round number date exactly coinciding with the equinox has a variant of this second ideograph.

Other strong proofs concern Venus and the moon. Hieroglyphs of these heavenly bodies are found in combination with dates and these later actually reach significant phases of the planets in question. For Venus the phase chosen is commonly the first appearance as morning star four days after inferior conjunction, or what is known as the heliacal rising. Records of the moon are prominent when a new or full phase coincides with a round number in the day count.

Astronomical Observatories. One of the most interesting pieces of evidence in support of the correlation explained above has to do with a giant sun dial at Copan. Two stelæ stand on opposite sides of the valley establishing a line which runs about 9 degrees north of west. When observation is made from the eastern marker the sun sets behind the western stone two times during the course of a year, once shortly after the vernal equinox and once shortly before the autumnal

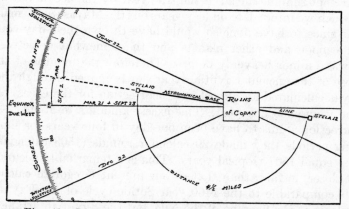

Fig. 49. Diagram of the Astronomical Base Line at Copan giving readings at April 9 and September 2. Slight shifts were made in this line: at an early time it was arranged to read April 5 and September 6 and at a later time April 12 and August 30.

equinox. Now the Mayan chronicles state that the calendarial New Year was "counted in order" during a certain Katun 13 Ahau which extended from 491 A. D. to 511 A. D. Altar U at Copan was observed to record two New Year's dates equaling April 9 in conjunction with another date, equaling September 2, 503 A. D., and falling in the required interval covered by Katun 13 Ahau. These dates were such as might be reached by just such a base line as exists at

Copan and it was first believed that they were exactly reached by it. Careful reconsideration of the evidence in the inscriptions and a re-survey of the line of sight led to the interesting conclusion that the sun dial of Copan was originally set up in 392 A. D. to give sunset coincidences on April 5 and September 6. About 490 A. D. the stones were readjusted to give the April 9 and September 2 which are recorded on Altar U and still later a third and present arrangement was effected giving April 12 and August 30. Each pair of dates is "reciprocal" in the sense that one member marks the same interval after the Spring equinox that the other does before the Fall equinox. The shifting seems to have been decided upon by astronomical congresses, and the purpose was to fix propitious times of planting the crops.

Other Mayan observatories at Uaxactun and Chichen Itza have lines of sight which mark exactly the positions of the sun (the summer solstice, etc.), and all in all the evidence deduced from these observatories is in complete agreement with the correlation of the Mayan and Christian time counts originally effected on the evidence in sixteenth century documents.

The True Year. The base line at Copan yielded accurate data on the exact length of the tropical year, a period varying by a difficult fraction from 365 full days. The tropical year is the time measured by the revolution of the earth around the sun and by the recurring seasons. No agricultural people could neglect this natural time period with its obvious relation to planting and harvest.

Reference has already been made to the notational 360 day year (tun) of the Mayas and to their formal calendar year (haab) of exactly 365 days. The calendar year kept running ahead of the true year by the accumulating amount of the days which we intercalate on leap years but the Mayas wisely made no such intercalations since to have done so would have thrown their day count out of gear with the moon and other planets and the somewhat defective calendar based upon these minor heavenly bodies. Therefore the months of the Mayan year like those of the ancient Egyptian year slowly moved through the seasons. But the Mayas calculated an almost exact correction for the excess of the true year over the vague 365 day year. This excess amounts to about .24 of a day and their correction seems to have been one day in four years for short periods while for long periods they made 29 calendar rounds (1508 calendar years or 550,420 days) equal 1507 tropical years. This is a remarkably accurate adjustment, much closer, in fact, than that of our present Gregorian calendar. This great cycle is comparable to the 1460 year Sothic cycle of the Egyptians in so far as that relates to the flooding of the Nile, but the Egyptian arrangement has an error of about twelve days for the cycle while the Mayan arrangement is accurate to a very small fraction of a day.

In the calendars of various Guatemalan and Mexican tribes the slow shifting of the months is attested by actual statements of early Spanish writers. But the conventional 365 day year was, after all, sufficiently accurate for most purposes since associations between the months and the seasons would hold reasonably true for the average lifetime.

The Lunar Calendar. The apparent revolution of the moon around the earth was taken by the Mayas as the basis of a lunar calendar distinct from the civil calendar, but used in combination with it for various ceremonial purposes. Now the average duration of a lunar revolution is 29 days, 12 hours, 44 minutes, 2.87

seconds. Twelve lunations amount to a little more than 354 days and are therefore far short of a true year. Primitive peoples whose principal interest is to keep the moon in adjustment with the seasons have an occasional thirteenth month in their lunisolar calendars.

The Metonic cycle of the Greeks, an equation of 19 tropical years, 235 lunations and 6940 days, has been regarded as a remarkable achievement in observation. The Mayas discovered the same equation and with their system of designating days were able to use it with much greater ease than the Greeks since one katun minus one tzolkin gives exactly the required number of days:—

$$
\begin{aligned}
1.\ 0.\ 0.0 &= 7200 \text{ days} \\
13.0 &= \ \ 260 \text{ days} \\
19.\ 5.0 &= 6940 \text{ days}
\end{aligned}
$$

This interval is used prominently in several calculations at Copan and Quirigua.

On pages 51 to 58 of the Dresden Codex is found a remarkable lunar calendar covering 405 lunations or nearly 33 years. The lunar revolutions are arranged in groups of five or six, the former calculated at 148 days and the latter at 177 or 178 days. These are the necessary intervals between eclipses. The total amounts to 11,960 days which exactly contains the tzolkin and therefore forms a cycle. It is a remarkable fact that 405 lunar revolutions amount, according to modern calculations, to 11,959.888 or only 0.112 of a day less than the Mayan lunar calendar. Therefore this re-entering series can be used nine times, or nearly 300 years, before an error amounting to one whole day has accumulated. There is also evidence that the Mayas used the great cycle of 29 × 52 calendar years, or 1507 tropical years, in connection with the moon and here the error for 18,639 lunations is about .64 of a day.

The Supplementary Series in Long Count dates is probably to be interpreted as the statement of the day reached by the Initial Series in a lunar calendar with an accumulated error; that is, the Mayas had an uncorrected lunar count as well as an uncorrected calendar year. Glyph C records a number of complete lunations which is never in excess of six; Glyph D gives the number of days in the current lunation when these are 19 or less and Glyph E, which has the basic value of 20, finishes the count of a current lunation. There is some evidence that

Fig. 50. Representations of the Moon: *a*, sun and moon hieroglyphs; *b*, moon from a ''celestial band''; *c*, moon hieroglyph used for 20 in codices.

the Mayan lunar calendar in the fifth century A. D. had receded about four days from the true positions of the moon, the count being made from the new or conjunctional phase. When, however, a new or full phase actually coincided with an important round number in the day count special record of the fact was made.

The lunar table in the Dresden Codex does not apply precisely to records of the First Empire but possibly may be adjusted to the times of the Second Empire. The indications are, however, too complicated to be examined in detail.

Fig. 51. The Last Glyph of the Supplementary Series: *a*, moon glyph; combined with the numeral 9 or 10 to indicate a 29 or a 30 day lunar month.

Venus Calendar. Mayan astronomers reached a remarkable knowledge of the movements of the planet Venus and evolved a Venus calendar based essentially on the correspondence between 8 calendar years of 365 days each and 5 apparent or synodical revolutions of Venus of 584 days each. Venus whirling on an inside orbit actually makes thirteen revolutions around the sun in very nearly the same time that the earth makes eight revolutions and therefore passes between the earth and the sun five times (the difference between 13 and 8) during the course of this astronomical period of 2920 days. Just before inferior conjunction the planet disappears as evening star and a few days later emerges as morning star. The mean length of the synodical revolution of Venus is 583.92 days and the actual length may vary about four days from this mean. While the Mayas standardized the Earth year at 365 days and the Venus year at 584 days, they were fully aware of the amount of error in each case, and made proper correction for it without resorting to the devices of intercalation or excision.

We have seen that the Mayas manipulated the year and the lunation in combination with the tzolkin or permutation of 20 days and 13 numbers. They also found a round of these elements in combination with the phases of Venus. Since the period of 2920 days is divisible by 20 but not by 13 it had to be taken 13 times before the round of the Venus calendar was reached.

In the Dresden Codex five pages are devoted to this round of the Venus calendar. Each Venus year of 584 days is divided into four parts of 236 days for the phase of morning star, 90 days (superior conjunction), 250 days (evening star) and 8 days (inferior conjunction). These divisions agree closely enough with actual appearance. But we must remember that the observations were made without instruments and that the planet cannot be seen by the naked eye when close to the sun. Moreover we must expect beliefs as to the nature of this planet, personified as a god, to supplement the knowledge gained from actual observations. The obscuration of Venus at inferior conjunction seems to have been greatly dreaded especially when a round number in the day count fell within the eight days of its duration. A grotesque two-headed monster apparently ruled this fatal period: on the front head is seen the symbol of Venus and on the rear head the symbol of the sun, both associated with elements of death.

The Venus calendar seems to have taken form in the sixth century B. C. on the basis of heliacal risings of the planet as morning star in sets of five making an eight year cycle. The dates in the Mayan calendar especially emphasized in connection with Venus are 19 Xul, 18 Kayab, 12 Yax, 6 Zip, and 5 Kankin standing exactly 584 days apart, while the corresponding dates in the Gregorian calendar are April 12, November 17, June 24, January 29, and September 5. When these sets of dates, one in a fixed and the other in a vague calendar, are carried back to a common focus they are found to correspond very closely with the proper astronomical phase of Venus. The maximum difference of the true positions of Venus from the positions in the Venus calendar is then only two days, plus or minus.

The coincidences of the 8 day period of obscuration of Venus at inferior conjunction with the following round numbers in the day count was memorialized by important monuments:—

9.14.0.0.0,	6 Ahau	13 Muan,	Feb. 4, 452 A. D.	Venus rises as morning star
9.17.0.0.0,	13 Ahau	18 Cumhu,	Mar. 27, 511 A. D.	Venus invisible during conjunction
10. 0.0.0.0,	7 Ahau	18 Zip,	May 17, 570 A. D.	Venus invisible during conjunction
10. 3.0.0.0,	1 Ahau	3 Yaxkin,	July 6, 629 A. D.	Venus about to set as evening star

The Venus table in the Dresden Codex, the introductory page of which has been explained in an earlier section (see Plate XXIV), emphasizes the same Mayan and Gregorian positions of Venus as the ancient monuments but this table was evidently intended to be used between the tenth and thirteenth centuries A. D. The point of departure for the table is 9.9.9.16.0, 1 Ahau 18 Kayab, April 12, 363 A. D., which does not coincide with an heliacal rising of the planet, although April 12 and 18 Kayab occur in other connections at the time of the inauguration of the Venus calendar in the sixth century B. C. But in the lunar table we find 10.19.6.1.0, 4 Ahau 18 Kayab, November 20, 950, which does reach an heliacal rising of Venus as morning star.

Summary of Mayan History. A brief summary of Mayan history is given below:—

PROTOHISTORIC PERIOD

613 B. C. to 176 A. D.   7.0.0.0.0 to 9.0.0.0.0

The counting of days apparently began on August 6, 613 B. C. and the civil calendar in perfected form was inaugurated about 580 B. C. when 0 Pop coincided with the winter solstice, while the Venus calendar emerged half a century later. The calendarial inventions, the numerical notation and the hieroglyphic system may, perhaps, be credited to the genius of one man afterwards deified as Itzamna. The earliest contemporary Mayan date occurs on a jade statuette from San Andres Tuxtla, and is May 16, 98 B. C. The next earliest one is on the jade tablet known as the Leyden Plate and is November 17, 60 A. D., having reference to the Venus calendar. This is followed almost immediately by several contemporary dates on monuments at Uaxactun which also are of astronomical import. The design on the Leyden Plate shows that the characteristic details of Mayan drawing had already been developed and we may surmise that during the protohistoric period the early carvings were on wood instead of stone and that the peculiar religion of the Mayas was even then beginning to crystallize around the serpent, the jaguar, etc.

EARLY PERIOD

176 A. D. to 373 A. D.   9.0.0.0.0 to 9.10.0.0.0

During these ten katuns the great cities of the south make rapid strides towards grandeur. Pyramidal mounds are erected and temples built upon them. Public squares are laid out and in these are set up stelæ and altars. The leading early cities are Palenque, Tikal, and Copan, where the dated monuments and temples mark rapid progress in the arts of sculpture and architecture while the subject matter of inscriptions reveals growing ability in astronomy and mathematics. Low angular relief characterizes stone sculptures and the profile presentation of the human figure is now handled more skilfully than front view.

MIDDLE PERIOD

373 A. D. to 471 A. D.   9.10.0.0.0 to 9.15.0.0.0

Some of the most beautiful monuments of the Mayas belong to this middle period. While archaism does not entirely disappear there is freshness, purity of style, and straightforwardness of presentation about the sculpture of this age. Flamboyancy is not apparent. At Copan the Great Mound was practically carried to completion during this period, an enormous undertaking which absorbed so much energy that few stelæ were set up. The best series of monuments from the middle period are seen at Naranjo and Piedras Negras.

GREAT PERIOD

471 A. D. to 629 A. D.   9.15.0.0.0 to 10.3.0.0.0

Many cities flourished in the culminating years of Mayan civilization. In addition to those already mentioned Quirigua, Ixkun, Seibal, Nakum, Cancuen, Yaxchilan, Toniná, and Cobá were important centers while a complete list of the sites with dated monuments would show many more names. The territorial extension reaches from northern Yucatan to the Guatemalan highlands and from southern Vera Cruz to central Honduras. Art passes through interesting changes with tendencies towards flamboyancy. Architecture makes great advances: rooms become wider, walls thinner and forms more refined and pleasing. The calculations deal more and more with complicated astronomical subjects and dates belong less and less in the category of contemporary history. The first age of Mayan civilization, called the First Empire, comes to an end with Katun 3 of Cycle 10, a date registered at Uaxactun which, strangely enough, also boasts the earliest stela with a contemporary date. It is indicated that Uaxactun was occupied for 561 years while the range of dates at Tikal is 394 years. Abandonment of all the sites of the First Empire took place within something like fifty years. What caused this collapse? Civil war? Social decadence? Failure of food supply? Or perhaps some overwhelming epidemic? There is good reason for believing that the sudden appearance of yellow fever may have had a part in the catastrophe. References in the Chronicles to the First Empire are very brief and do not help us find the answer to this mystery.

TRANSITION PERIOD

629 A. D. to 964 A. D.   10.3.0.0.0 to 11.0.0.0.0

Most of the Mayas surviving the collapse of the First Empire seem to have found a second home in western Yucatan, especially in the region called Chakunputun in the Chronicles. Here the rainfall is much less and the forest environment not nearly so luxuriant. Certain cities, which probably date from this transitional period, such as Hochob, Dzibilnocac, Rio Bec, etc., have very beautiful architecture showing advances over that of the First Empire in some features. Dated documents are so rare as practically to be non-existent. It seems probable that Mayan learning had been reduced to books for there is ample evidence from the succeeding period that astronomical and calendarial knowledge had been conserved from ancient times. At the end of these lean centuries, the Mayas made their way still farther north. Chichen Itza which had been a provincial city of the First Empire was reoccupied and the Mayan renaissance known as the Second Empire began.

PERIOD OF THE LEAGUE OF MAYAPAN

964 A. D. to 1191 A. D.   11.0.0.0.0 to 11.11.10.0.0

The first phase of the Mayan renaissance was pretty clearly centered in Chichen Itza although the earliest date which may be contemporary is probably that of the Temple of the Initial Series at Holactun. The inscription shows a survival of the ancient method of counting time and is now believed to treat of the interval between March 9, 1012 A. D. and November 14, 1016 A. D. Other cities rising to splendor during the Second Empire are Kabah, Labna, Sayil, and Izamal. The time of foundation for Uxmal is rather difficult to determine. According to tradition it was the capital of Toltec immigrants into Yucatan, but when or how they arrived cannot be answered definitely. The League of Mayapan was organized as an alliance between Chichen Itza and Uxmal in the second half of the twelfth century, and Mayapan was built as a neutralized capital of church and state under the inspiration of a Toltec noble named Quetzalcoatl. Finally, Izamal and Chichen Itza rebelled and Inetzalcoatl conquered the latter city in 1191 and made it the capital of a Maya-Toltec state.

PERIOD OF MEXICAN INFLUENCE

1191 A. D. to 1437 A. D.   11.11.10.0.0 to 12.4.0.0.0

The helpers of Hunac Ceel bore Mexican names and belonged to the Toltec nation. Hunac Ceel is identified in one place with Kukulcan, the name meaning "plumed serpent" in the Mayan language, and in another place with Quetzalcoatl which has the same significance in the Mexican language. In Chichen Itza sculptural art and architecture have many clear analogies to works in the Valley of Mexico. The building called the Castillo seems to have been built by Quetzalcoatl, being the first structure in which serpent columns and other structural ideas of this ruler were given expression. The Temple of the High Priest's Grave is a developed example of the new style bearing the date December 31, 1339 A. D. The elaborate Group of the Columns, with the famous Temple of the Warriors, may be still later.

In the first half of the fifteenth century civil war and epidemic disease brought about a second depopulation of the stone-built cities including Chichen Itza, Mayapan, Uxmal, and probably also numerous other sites in the region of Uxmal. The last monument at Mayapan may declare the date September 28, 1437.

Modern Period

1437 A. D. to the present day.

After the second general abandonment of urban life the Mayas seem to have been divided into many warring factions. Temples were still regarded as sacred and some constructions in stone and mortar were still made, as we know from the first Spanish descriptions of towns on the east coast of Yucatan. Tulum probably represented this last phase and this site on a cliff overlooking the Caribbean is probably the city compared to Seville by the coasting expedition of Grijalva in 1518. A monument at Tulum is believed to record the last setting up of a katun stone by the Mayas on 12.8.0.0.0, 2 Ahau 3 Pop, August 5, 1516, almost exactly 2129 years after the Mayas began to count every day in order.

At the present time certain ancient ideas still persist among the Lacandone Indians of the lowlands and among the Quiché, Cakchiquels, and several other tribes of the highlands. But the old glory of the Mayan civilizations has passed away never to return. A prophetic vision of this end is found in one of the Mayan Books of Chilam Balam which relates to events immediately after the founding of Merida.

"It was then that the teaching of Christianity began, that shall be universal over our land. Then began the construction of the church here in the center of the town of Tihoo: great labor was the destiny of the katun. Then began the execution by hanging, and the fire at the ends of our hands. Then also came ropes and cords into the world. Then the children of the younger brothers (the Indians) passed under the hardship of legal summons and tribute. Tribute was introduced on a large scale and Christianity was introduced on a large scale. Then the seven sacraments of the word of God were established. Let us receive our guests heartily: our elder brothers (the white men) come!"

THE MIDDLE CIVILIZATIONS

THE influence of the Mayan civilization when at its height (400 to 600 A. D.) may be traced far beyond the limits of the Mayan area. Ideas in art, religion, and government that were then spread broadcast served to quicken nations of diverse speech and a series of divergent cultures resulted. Most of these lesser civilizations were at their best long after the great Mayan civilization had declined, but one or two were possibly contemporary. It will be the aim in the present chapter to emphasize the indebtedness of these lesser civilizations to the Mayas as well as to comment upon their individual characters.

We will first proceed northwest into Mexico and then southeast into the Isthmus of Panama. The environment under which the Mayas developed their arts of life continues in narrowing bands westward along the Gulf of Mexico and southward across the Isthmus of Tehuantepec. The most westerly Mayan city of importance seems to have been Comalcalco. But there is also a large ruin near San Andres Tuxtla and it may be significant that the earliest dated object of the Mayas (the Tuxtla Statuette) came from this region. In other words, the cradle of Mayan culture may have been in this coastal belt where arid and humid conditions exist side by side and where the figurines of the archaic type are found together with those of the Mayas. Unfortunately, the archæology of this part of Mexico has been little studied.

The Olmeca or Rubber People. The Olmeca may be placed in the humid region of southern Vera Cruz and western Tabasco which the Aztecs of later times called Nonoalco. This region is frequently mentioned in the most ancient of the Mexican traditions, doubtless symbolizing in a general way the civilizing contacts with the Mayas. Rubber is called *olli* in the Mexican language and while the earliest known specimens of rubber are those found in the Sacred Cenote at Chichen Itza, the ceremonial and practical uses of the material are mostly mentioned in connection with the Olmeca and Totonac peoples. Rubber was used for incense, for water-proofing purposes, to tip drumsticks, etc. A large rubber ball was also used in a sacred game which may be compared to basket ball since the goals were rings set high up in the parallel walls of a specially constructed court.

According to Ixtlilxochitl's history the Olmeca came before the Toltecs and were the first to extend their civilizing rule over parts of the Mexican highlands. Some authorities think the Olmeca were a Mayan tribe but it is quite possible that they spoke Mexican. They may have fled south at the breakdown of the Toltec empire for we find in Nicaragua at the time of the Conquest a group of this name with traditions pointing to the far north. The ruins found in 1927 by the writer at Cerro de las Mesas, west of Alvarado Lagoon, may possibly be ascribed to this people. The site contains seventeen monuments, several of which are dedicated to Quetzalcoatl and must be referred to the thirteenth century. Bars and dots are used in connection with day signs to record dates which may belong to the calendarial system appearing on Zapotecan monuments.

Zapotecan Culture. In the State of Oaxaca the Zapotecan Indians attained to a high degree of civilization, but a study of their culture shows they were profoundly indebted to the Mayas for many ideas. Monte Alban, the White Mountain, overlooking the modern City of Oaxaca is the principal archæological site in point of size and may have been the ancient capital. It was abandoned before the coming of the Spaniards, however, and Mitla appears to have taken its place.

Fig. 52. Comparison of Mayan and Zapotecan Serpent Heads. The first two examples are from Palenque and the second two from Monte Alban.

Unfortunately no extensive traditions have come down to us to help in the restoration of Zapotecan history, or in that of the neighboring Mixtecs. Although the art, hieroglyphic writing, and calendar system were pretty clearly derived from the Mayas, nevertheless there was time and opportunity for these to develop interesting characters of their own. It is impossible to tell from the record whether the Zapotecs ever embarked on a career of empire: the area in which the full complex of the characteristic products occurs is practically limited to the area at present occupied by the tribe. It is quite possible that the Zapotecs were conquered by the Toltecs in the twelfth century and that such similarities as exist between the forms of Zapotecan sculptural art and those of the Toltec cities of Xochicalco and Teotihuacan in central Mexico, on the one hand, and those of Pipil and Chorotegan sites in Guatemala and Salvador, on the other hand, are to be explained by intercommunications under the Toltec régime.

Fig. 53. Bar and Dot Numerals combined with Hieroglyphs on Zapotecan Monuments.

Monte Alban and Mitla stand in strong contrast to each other, the first crowning a mountain ridge, the second occupying a valley site. Monte Alban has no buildings intact, but shows a vast assemblage of enormous pyramids and platforms. Mitla has only one small pyramid, but boasts a series of finely preserved temples on low platform bases. In Monte Alban we find monolithic monuments comparable to the stelæ of the Mayas, and carrying hieroglyphic inscriptions; also pottery figurines and jade amulets in a style which follows rather closely the models developed in the early cities of the humid lowlands.

At Mitla there are none of these things; instead, the architectural decoration shows a most interesting use of textile designs treated in a mosaic of cut stones. It is apparent then that a long record of high culture is to be found in the Zapotecan field.

At Monte Alban there are one or two narrow vaulted chambers in mounds, but on the tops of the mounds the few excavations have disclosed only simple cell-like rooms which probably had flat roofs. Some hints of ancient architectural decoration can be picked up here and there. Figures similar to those modeled in bold relief on the fronts of the cylindrical funeral urns (see frontispiece) seem to have been used over doorways, somewhat after the fashion of the Mayan mask panels.

The hieroglyphs that are found on the stelæ of Monte Alban and on stone slabs from other sites resemble the Mayan hieroglyphs in the use of bar and dot numerals, but the day and month signs have never been identified with either the Mayan or Aztecan system, although almost certainly dealing with the same type of calendar. Lintels with lines of hieroglyphs on the outer edge have been found in burial chambers at Cuilapa and Xoxo. The forms at the former site are clearly and beautifully drawn, while at the latter site they are degenerate and probably merely decorative.

In Zapotecan funerary urns a close connection with Mayan art can easily be demonstrated. The urns are cylindrical vessels concealed behind elaborate figures built up from moulded and modeled pieces. Many of these built-up figures clearly represent human beings while others represent grotesque divinities or human beings wearing the masks of divinities. The purely human types have a formal modeling in high relief, the head usually

Fig. 54. Detail of Wall Construction at Mitla, showing the separately Carved Stones.

being out of proportion to the rest of the body. The pose is ordinarily a seated one with the hands resting on the knees or folded over the breast. Details of dress are very clearly shown including capes, girdles, aprons, or skirts and headdresses. Necklaces are often worn with a crossbar pendant to which shells are attached. Headdresses are made of feathers and grotesque faces and are often very elaborate. As for the divine types the jaguar and a long-nosed reptile are the most common. The latter has a human body and may possibly be an adaptation of the Mayan Long-nosed God.

The funerary urns are found in burial mounds called *mogotes* which contain cell-like burial chambers. The urns are not found within these cells but on the floor in front of them, in a niche over the door, or even on the roof. They are frequently encountered in groups of five and seem never to contain offerings.

Other Zapotecan pottery is mostly made of the same bluish clay used in the urns. This clay is finely adapted to plastic treatment but never carries painted designs. The pottery products include pitchers of beautiful and unusual shapes, dishes with tripod legs modeled into serpent heads, incense burners, bowls, plates, etc. Of the same clay are also made whistles in realistic forms, and moulded figurines. Painted pottery also occurs in forms and designs of rare beauty, but it is much less characteristic of the Zapotecan province than the unpainted ware.

Carved jades of splendid workmanship have been recovered in the Zapotecan region and there is reason to believe that this semi-precious stone was obtained here in the natural state. Many of the pieces are smoothed only on the front, while the back retains its old weathered and stream-worn surface. Beautiful examples of gold work found in this region must be given a late date.

Splendid manuscripts were obtained by the Spaniards in the Zapotecan region, but the pictures of the gods as well as the hieroglyphs show strong Aztecan influences. These will be discussed briefly in a later section. Some accounts have been preserved of the special features of Zapotecan religion which mark them off rather sharply from the Aztecs, however.

The high priests of the Zapotecans were called "Seers" and the ordinary priests were "Guardians of the Gods" and "Sacrificers." There was a sort of priestly college where the sons of chiefs were trained in the service of the gods. The religious practices included incense burning, sacrificing of birds and animals, and letting of one's own blood by piercing the tongue and the ear. Human sacrifice was made on stated occasions and was attended by rites of great solemnity. The Zapotecs never went to the blood excesses that stain the annals of the Aztecs.

The 260 day cycle of the time count was subdivided into four periods of 65 days and each period was under control of a single god and was associated with one of the cardinal points. Each period of sixty-five days was further divided into five groups of thirteen days for a ceremonial reason. Some authorities have considered that the general form of the Central American calendar originated in the region of the Isthmus of Tehuantepec and spread to the north and to the south. But dependable history in the Mayan area goes back much farther than in the Zapotecan region and renders such a guess extremely hazardous.

Mitla. The famous temples of Mitla are the best-preserved examples of architecture on the highlands of Mexico and are peculiar in form and decoration. The word Mitla is a corruption of the Aztecan word *Mictlan*, place of the dead.

Fig. 55. Wall Paintings of Mitla, resembling in style the Pictographic Art of the Codices from Southern Mexico.

This site was the burial ground of Zapotecan kings and may have been a place of pilgrimage. It was conquered by the Aztecs in the last decade of the fifteenth century. While the architecture belongs in a class by itself the frescoes have the distinct character of the Aztecan period.

The remains at this site have already been contrasted with those at Monte Alban. There is one fairly large mound at Mitla but it has no surviving superstructure. The temples are placed on low platforms which usually contain cruciform tombs. The buildings are carefully oriented and are assembled in groups of four which almost enclose square paved courts. The heavy walls have surfaces of cut stone and a filling of concrete or rubble and are ornamented with longitudinal panels of geometric designs arranged according to a carefully worked out plan. The geometric patterns are based on textile art and the mosaics of separately carved stones which fit neatly together preserve for us the ancient designs on belts and mantles. The chambers are long and narrow and formerly had flat roofs which have completely vanished. The wide doorways usually have two piers which help to support the lintel blocks. These are carefully trimmed stones of great length and weight. All the outer surfaces of the Mitla temples were sized with plaster and painted red and the frescoes, traces of which can still be seen in several buildings, are in red and black upon a white base. Various gods and ceremonies are represented in these frescoes, but only the upper portion of the bands can be made out in detail.

Cruciform tombs are found under several of the temples at Mitla as well as at a number of neighboring sites such as Xaaga and Guiaroo. In these tombs the designs in panels appear on the inside and are carved directly on large blocks of stone. Pottery remains are rare in the cruciform tombs of the Mitla type but a few examples of gold work have been discovered in them.

Within a short distance of Mitla is a fortified hill with several heavy walls that still stand to the height of perhaps twenty feet. In the flat valley between this hill and the ruins a considerable number of potsherds are plowed up in the field.

Totonacan Culture. In the central part of the state of Vera Cruz are found the remains commonly referred to the Totonacan Indians. These Indians are southern neighbors of the Huastecas who are an outlying Mayan tribe. The Totonacan language is according to some authorities thrown into the Mayan stock. If not truly Mayan it contains many loan words. This apparent connection in language is all the more interesting in view of the character of Totonacan art which also shows a strong strain of Mayan feeling and technique in certain products but an unmistakable likeness to the archaic art of the Mexican highlands in certain other products. The pottery faces in the archaic style

Fig. 56. The Eyes of Totonacan Figurines.

are advanced beyond the average of such work and probably represent a late phase.

A series of eyes showing Totonacan modifications of the styles prevalent on the archaic pottery heads of the Highlands is given in Fig. 56. In some cases we find the simple single or double groove eyes and in other cases these eyes are made more conspicuous by the use of black bituminous paint. The eyeball is developed at the end of the series.

The smiling or laughing faces have a much higher technique and are perhaps the finest examples of clay modeling from the New World. These heads have tubular extensions at the back and were possibly set into temple walls. The faces and foreheads are broadened in accordance with the esthetic type of a forehead flattening people. While the faces vary so much in minor details as to create the impression that they are portraits of actual persons they are alike in method of modeling. Nearly all are laughing or smiling in a very contagious fashion. Sometimes the tip of the tongue is caught between the teeth, sometimes the corners of the mouth are pulled down as if the smile were reluctant, and there are other individual variations in the expressions of lively and unrestrained mirth.

Perhaps the most famous objects found in Totonacan territory are the so-called "stone collars" or "sacrificial yokes." In size and shape these resemble horse collars, but in contrast to somewhat similar objects from Porto Rico they are usually open while the latter are closed. Nothing is really known concerning their use but there has been no lack of fanciful surmises. The most popular explanation is that the yokes were placed over the necks of victims about to be sacrificed. It is evident that the yokes were intended to be placed in a horizontal position because there is a plain lower surface and the ends are frequently carved with faces that are right side up only when the plain side is down. These yokes represent the richest and most elaborate works of art in the entire region since they are carved in the most finished manner from single blocks of exceedingly hard stone.

Other peculiarly shaped stones are found in the Totonacan area and are carved according to the same splendid technique. The "paddle-shaped" stones have been found in considerable numbers and their use, like that of the stone yokes, is absolutely unknown. It is evident from the carving that they were intended to be stood on end.

The designs on the sacrificial yokes and paddle stones are largely reptilian, but there are examples where the turkey, the coyote, as well as the human motive are treated somewhat after the manner of the Mayas. Plumed serpents, monkeys, centipedes, and crocodiles are interestingly drawn on pottery. An important site is Papantla where a remarkably ornate pyramid rising in six terraces may be seen, as well as massive sculptures in the same style as the works of art described above. The front wall of each terrace on all four sides of the pyramid, except for the space occupied by the stairway, is divided into a series of niches neatly made of cut stone. Formerly each of these niches may have served to shelter the statue of some god. Many fine remains of Totonacan art have been recovered from the Island of Sacrifices in the harbor of Vera Cruz. This island retained its ancient sacrificial character in the time of the Spanish conquerors. It is apparent, however, that the culture had already changed greatly if we may judge by the ruins of Cempoalan, the Totonacan capital in the sixteenth century. The art of this city is largely Aztecan.

The Toltecs. Mexican history is greatly concerned with the Toltecs, the name meaning People of Tula, or Tollan, "place of the reeds." Evidence is accumulating that this Tula was not the comparatively insignificant ruin on the northern edge of the Valley of Mexico, but instead was the great city of San Juan Teotihuacan. The lesser Tula may have been founded about 1200 A. D., just before the collapse of Toltec power.

Archæology tells a more detailed and convincing story of the Toltecs than does recorded history. In the stratified remains at Atzcapotzalco, the objects accredited to the Toltecs overlie those of the first potters of the Archaic Period and are in striking contrast to them. The principal motives of Toltec decorative art are obviously related to the earlier more brilliant work of the Mayas. The pyramids of the Toltecs exceed in size those of the Mayas but are of inferior construction, adobe bricks with concrete facing taking the place of rubble and cut stone. The temples that crowned these pyramids were also of less solid construction and no single example is now intact. Vaulted ceilings were replaced by flat timbered ceilings or high pitched roofs of thatch. Sometimes in wide rooms columns were used as additional support for roof beams. The groundplans of buildings other than temples show small rooms arranged in an irregular fashion round courts.

The ceremonial game of *tlachtli*, resembling basket ball, was an important feature of Toltec religion. It may have been obtained from the Olmeca, but at any rate spread far and wide under the Toltec régime. Another feature of Toltec religion was the worship of the sun's disk which is reflected in various sculptures. Also this people are supposed to have invented *pulque*, made from the fermented sap of the agave. The reclining type of sculpture known as Chacmool, after the famous example found at Chichen Itza in northern Yucatan, may be a relic of a peculiar Toltec cult in which drunkenness figured. Human sacrifice was another feature of the religion of the Mexican highlands in contrast to that of the lowland Mayas. On the economic side Toltec culture rested on the earlier Archaic civilization, but on the artistic and ceremonial side it was largely inspired by the Mayas through the mediation of the Zapotecs, Olmecs, and Totonacs, but with new emphasis on certain aspects and several important innovations. The language of the Toltecs seems to have been essentially the same as that of the Aztecs who succeeded them.

The Toltecs made a radical departure in social policy in that they took to war and expropriation as a means of building up national wealth, thereby paralleling, somewhat ineffectively to be sure, the political methods of Europe and Western Asia. There had been war before their time in Central America, but not apparently for aggrandizement. The Mayas, and most other Mexican and Central American nations, developed excess food supply which released many persons for the pursuit of art and science. Perhaps it was pressure of population upon food supply in an arid land that directed the Toltecs towards tribute taking. At least the fact is reasonably clear that this people did embark upon a short-lived career of conquest and that they levied tribute of precious stones and precious metals and secured by the same means an augmented food supply.

There is confusion and reduplication in the lists of Toltec rulers and only three great names in succession can be regarded as certain. These are Huetzin, Ihuitimal, and Quetzalcoatl, although it seems probable that there was a still earlier chieftain named Mixcoatl or Mixcoamazatl and that two successors of

Quetzalcoatl were Matlaxochitl and Nauyotl, the last-named also figuring as the first lord of Colhuacan. Then follow various dynastic lists for several Mexican tribes which flourished between the downfall of the Toltecs and the coming of the Spaniards.

Quetzalcoatl and the Toltec Era. The chronology of the Toltecs and their successors is greatly dilated in several historical compilations made after the Spanish conquest by intelligent natives who interpreted fragments of ancient pictographic year counts then surviving in Mexico. Thanks to a modern survey of materials much more extensive than those which Chimalpahin, Ixtlilxochitl, etc., had at their disposal, we are now able to avoid the errors of these writers.

In the original pre-Spanish chronicles important events are recorded in connection with fifty-two year signs falling in regular order and then repeating. In the well-intentioned attempts to restore Mexican history entire cycles are interpolated in several places and the rulers are given lives of impossible length. In the case of Ixtlilxochitl we possess, fortunately, the principal documents which this descendant of the Texcocan kings attempted to interpret. Also in the case of the Annals of Quauhtitlan, an early compilation made by a nameless student of ancient history, we are in position to adjudicate wide erros in chronology. There is an annotation on this manuscript reading "6 times 4 centuries, plus 1 century, plus 13 years, today the 22nd of May 1558." The "centuries" are the native cycles of fifty-two years and the total on this basis would amount to 1313 years. Subtracted from 1558 the beginning would be found in 245 A. D., while the years set down by the compiler in an unbroken series reach back to 635 A. D. But there is no pre-Spanish support for written history, outside the Mayan area. of anything like this antiquity.

The Toltec Era was established by Quetzalcoatl, after a simplified model of the Mayan calendar, on August 6, 1168 A. D., this date corresponding to a day 1 Tecpatl (1 Flint) in the first position of a month Toxcatl. This day gave its name to the entire year and its hieroglyph was one of a series of fifty-two used to designate years in the pictographic records. Most of the Mexican year counts begin with the particular sign 1 Tecpatl which corresponds to 1168–69 A. D. In others there is reference to a day 7 Acatl 1 Panquetzaliztli in a year 2 Acatl (February 16, 1195 A. D.) upon which a new fire ceremony, established by Quetzalcoatl in accordance with Mayan usage, was celebrated at intervals of fifty-two years.

The conclusions are supported by evidence in Guatemalan chronicles and also in records of the Mayas for we have already seen that Quetzalcoatl conquered Chichen Itza in 1191 A. D. The three great Toltec emperors, Huetzin, Ihuitimal, and Quetzalcoatl, swept over an area extending from Durango to Nicaragua, the three seats of their government being Teotihuacan in the Valley of Mexico, Chichen Itza in Yucatan, and Iximché in Guatemala.

Quetzalcoatl probably spent his youth in Yucatan, returning to his highland home with strange religious and social ideas. His opposition to the Toltec idea of human sacrifice was followed by a war of cults. Quetzalcoatl began the construction at Tula with serpent columns like those of his lofty temple in Chichen Itza. Also he appears to have founded Cholula as a special center for his humane religion. His death occurred in connection with a prognostication in the Venus calendar of the Mayas, for the year 1 Acatl, 1207–08 A. D.

Quetzalcoatl, perhaps the most remarkable figure in ancient American history, was emperor, artist, scientist, and humanist philosopher. He established orders of knighthood as well as the coronation ceremony used by the later Mexican kings. He developed the various industrial arts and built up a wide trade in cotton, cacao, and other products. As a patron of the peripatetic merchant he appears under the name Nacxitl, which means Four-way Foot. Apotheosis being an idea strongly fixed among the Toltecs, Quetzalcoatl was deified as Ehecatl, God of Winds, on account of his support of the Mayan god of rainstorms, and for his astronomical work he was further deified as God of the Planet Venus.

San Juan Teotihuacan. This name Teotihuacan means Where the Gods (i.e., the deified dead) Dwell. This enormous ruin is located on the eastern margin of the Valley of Mexico. The principal features of Teotihuacan are two great pyramids and a straight roadway lined with small pyramids. There are also several groups of buildings of which the lower walls and the bases of the piers are still to be seen as well as some interesting fragments of fresco painting. The smaller of the two great pyramids is called the Pyramid of the Moon. It is located at the end of the roadway which is commonly called the Pathway of the Dead. The Pyramid of the Sun is situated on the east side of the roadway. This pyramid is about 180 feet in height and rises in four sloping terraces. The temple which formerly crowned its summit has entirely disappeared. Explorations conducted by the Mexican government showed that this pyramid was enlarged from time to time and old stairways buried under new masonry. On the south side of the small stream that flows through the ruins is a group of buildings called the Citadel.

In 1921 the Mexican Government undertook a restoration of the Citadel, following the discovery of remarkable sculptures on the principal pyramid. It appears that in ancient times this pyramid was enlarged by an addition to one side and the richly ornamented terraces and stairway buried (Plate XXXIII). The sculptured stones from the other three sides of the temple were allowed to fall into neglect by the Toltecs or were carried away and put to other uses, but the portion buried was kept in its original state. The colors are still bright in many places and the great heads of plumed serpents and obsidian butterflies sometimes retain their inset eyes of obsidian. The decoration is a repeated motive. The head of the feathered serpent projects outward from the terrace walls and from the balustrade of the stairway, while the body is in low relief. The tail of the serpent has a rattle, and the body is covered with feathers. Shells are seen below the serpent where the body arches and just in front of the tail is a massive head with two rings on the frontal. This doubtless represents the Obsidian Butterfly, a divinity of great importance among the Toltecs, which is represented unmistakably in frescoes at Teotihuacan as well as on pottery. The Citadel well deserves its name, since it is a great enclosure, much like a fort, with buildings upon its bulwarks, and with steep outer walls, which could easily be defended.

A few large sculptures have been found at Teotihuacan. But the site is chiefly remarkable for pottery figurines and heads that are picked up by thousands. The heads present such a marked variety of facial contour and expression that it would seem as if every race under the sun had served as models. It is very likely that these heads formed part of votive offerings, being attached to bodies made of some perishable material. The heads were seldom used to adorn pottery vessels, although many modern and fraudulent vases are so adorned. Dolls with head and torso in one piece and with movable arms and legs made of separate pieces were known. The face of Tlaloc, the Rain God, is fairly common in Teotihuacan pottery but other deities have not surely been identified. It is not improbable that the God of Fire is personified as an old man with wrinkled face, but somewhat less likely that Xipe is represented in the faces that look out through the three holes of a mask. The jaguar, the monkey, the owl, and other animals are also modeled with excellent fidelity. The Mayan convention of the human face in the open jaws of the serpent is not unknown.

Fig. 57. Jointed Doll of Clay from San Juan Teotihuacan.

A number of beautiful vases painted in soft greens, pinks, and yellows have been recovered at Teotihuacan. These colors would not stand the kiln and they were applied after the vessel had been burned. According to one method, the outside of the vessel was covered with a fine coating of plaster upon which the design was painted exactly as in fresco. According to a second method the effect of cloisonné was cleverly achieved. This technique is most characteristic of the region northwest of the Valley of Mexico and will be described later. Incised or engraved designs are commonly met with on pottery vessels at Teotihuacan. No inscriptions have been found at this ruin, in spite of the many years of exploration.

Xochicalco. Let us now pass over in brief review several ruins which belong to the Toltecan period. Xochicalco, the House of the Flowers, is a large ruin near Cuernavaca. The position seems to have been chosen primarily for defense. The rounded ridge that drops off into deep valleys on either side is laid out in courts, terraces, and pyramids. Only one building offers evidence of the sculptural skill of the ancient habitants. It is a temple, standing upon a rather low platform mound. The sides of the platform mound are decorated with great plumed serpents, seated human figures, hieroglyphs, etc. Parts of the sculptures also remain on the low walls of the temple itself which is now roofless. The stone carving at Xochicalco resembles that of Monte Alban especially as regards the hieroglyphs and is probably of somewhat later date than Teotihuacan. All in all the conclusion seems safe that writing was unknown outside the Mayan area before Quetzalcoatl devised ways and means.

Tula. Building stone of good quality was available at this site and in consequence sculptures are plentiful. Particularly famous are the great sculptured columns which represent feathered serpents and gigantic human figures. The drums are mostly mortised and the columns are crowned by true capitals. These architectural features at Tula find their closest counterpart at the Mayan city of Chichen Itza in northern Yucatan. The *tlachtli* or ball court occurs at Tula and the groundplans of complicated "palaces" can also be made out.

Cholula. The sacred city of Cholula, in the environs at Puebla, is chiefly famous for its great pyramid. This structure is more or less irregular in shape but the base averages more than a thousand feet on the side and the total height, now somewhat reduced, was probably close to two hundred feet above the plain. Compared with the Pyramid of Cheops, it covers nearly twice as much ground and has a much greater volume, but lacks, of course, in height. As already noted, the pyramids of the New World are simply foundations for temples and thus

Fig. 58. Pottery Plates from Cholula with Decorations in Several Colors. The pottery of Cholula ranks high in design and color.

always have flat tops. The great mound of Cholula is a solid mass of adobe bricks of uniform size laid in adobe mortar. The pyramid was evidently faced with a thick layer of cement of which a few patches still remain. Two other large mounds exist at Cholula. One of these has been partially destroyed and now stands as a vertical mass of adobe bricks while the other is overgrown with brush and cactus.

Unlike the other Toltecan cities Cholula was still inhabited and a place of religious importance when Cortez arrived in Mexico. But the figurines and pottery vessels that are found at this site belong for the most part to an epoch earlier than that of the Aztecs. Quetzalcoatl was the patron deity of Cholula and in the decorative art the serpent is finely conventionalized. A pottery shape frequently met with at Cholula is the flat plate bearing polychrome designs.

The Frontier Cities of the Northwest. An important culture area is located upon the northwestern limits of the area of high culture in ancient Mexico. The best known and most accessible ruin is La Quemada, "The Burned," which is situated a day's ride from the city of Zacatecas. This site was found in a deserted and ruinous condition by the Spaniards in 1535 and there is little doubt that it had been abandoned several centuries previous. La Quemada has been popularly associated with Chicomoztoc, "The Seven Caves," a place famous in Aztecan mythology, but this association rests upon no scientific basis. It is simply an unauthoritative attempt to invest a forgotten city with a legendary interest. Chicomoztoc, where the Aztecs came out of the underworld, might be compared with our own Garden of Eden and its exact location is just as much an eternal riddle. La Quemada is a terraced hill resembling Monte Alban and Xochicalco. The retaining walls of terraces and pyramids as well as the walls of buildings are still well preserved. These walls consist of slabs of stone set in a mortar of red earth. Perhaps the most noteworthy structure is a wide hall containing seven columns built of slabs of stone in the same manner as the walls. All in all the architectural types as well as the observed contacts in art point to a late epoch of the Toltecan period. Other ruins of the same character as La Quemada occur at Chalchihuites on the frontier of Durango and at Totoate, etc., in northern Jalisco.

The most important artistic product from this northwestern region is a peculiar kind of pottery which might be described as cloisonné or encaustic ware. Examination shows that this pottery was first burned in the usual way so that it acquired a red or orange color. Then the surface was covered with a layer of greenish or blackish pigment to the depth of perhaps a sixteenth of an inch. A large part of this surface layer was then carefully cut away with a sharp blade

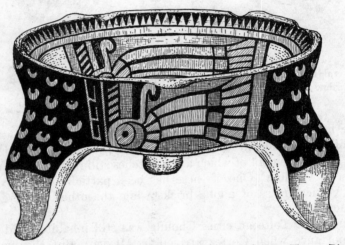

Fig. 59. Vessel with "Cloisonné" Decoration in Heavy Pigments. This example comes from a mound at Atzcapotzalco and dates from late Toltecan times. Trade pieces of this ware have been found at Pueblo Bonito in New Mexico and Chichen Itza in Yucatan.

in such a way that the remaining portions outlined certain geometric and realistic figures. The sunken spaces, from which the material had just been removed, were then filled in flush with red, yellow, white, and green pigments. The designs on this class of pottery are thus mosaics in which the different colors are separated by narrow lines of a neutral tint. The geometric motives show a marked use of the terrace, the fret, and the scroll. The realistic subjects are presented in a highly conventionalized manner and have few stylistic similarities to the figures from the Valley of Mexico. Representative collections of this ware from Totoate, already referred to, and from Estanzuela, a hacienda near Guadalajara, are on exhibition in the American Museum of Natural History.

Cloisonné pottery of a somewhat different style sometimes occurs at Toltecan sites in the Valley of Mexico, such as Tula, Teotihuacan, and Atzcapotzalco, but fresco pottery, which resembles it at first glance, is more characteristic. It appears that the cloisonné process was taken over from the embellishment of gourd dishes in connection with which it still exists over a large part of Mexico and Central America.

Another common method of ceramic decoration taken over was that of negative painting similar to the process used with cloth in making batik designs. This process still exists in Central America as regards gourd dishes although discontinued on pottery. Negative painting appears to be an ancient process of exceedingly wide distribution. It is especially common in Jalisco and Michoacan,

Fig. 60. The Turtle Motive as developed in Negative Painting with Wax at Totoate, Jalisco.

the Valley of Toluca, Nicaragua, Costa Rica, Panama, and Colombia, and sometimes occurs in Yucatan and Peru. The design was painted in wax or some other soluble or combustible paint, then the entire surface was covered with a permanent paint. When the pot was burned the design came out in the natural color of the clay against a black or sometimes a red field. The design was often made two layers deep by applying simple masses of red over the sizing before the impermanent paint of the design proper was put on. In the northwestern region of central Mexico now under consideration the negative painting technique is associated with conventionalized designs representing turtles (Fig. 60). Another ware with designs in white is concerned with derivatives of the turtle motive. Then there are the remarkable copper bells in the form of turtles made by coiling that have been found in nearby Michoacan.

It is difficult to place time limits for the artistic styles that once existed in this northwestern region. The archaic culture seems to have lasted longer here than farther south; next followed the northern flow of Toltecan culture which later receded and finally came a rather thin layer of Chichimecan or Aztecan culture. We may tentatively conclude that the forgotten cities of the Zacatecan subculture flourished after 1000 A. D. The question should be settled because of its connection with the dating of Pueblo ruins farther north.

Santa Lucia Cozumalhualpa. The zonal distribution of rain forests in southern Mexico and Central America is especially important, as has been pointed out, in connection with the spread of Mayan-type civilizations. The Olmeca and Totonacs who were among the first to feel the cultural effects of the Mayan ascendency

Fig. 61. Jaguar Head on Disk-
Shaped Stone. Salvador.

occupied lands of heavy precipitation. The Zapotecan and Mixtecan areas were partly wet and partly dry. The Toltecs seem originally to have been desert dwellers but they extended their conquests over tribes living in the humid tropics and made much of cacao, rubber, copal, etc., obtained by trade and tribute from such subject peoples.

Along the Pacific coast below the Isthmus of Tehuantepec lies a rain belt containing ruined cities which flourished between 1000 to 1300 A. D., or on the historical level of the Toltec expansion. The sculptural art at these sites resembles the works attributed to the Olmecs in Tabasco and Vera Cruz on the one hand and the works of the Chorotega of lower Central America on the other. One such ruin is Quiengola near the modern city of Tehuantepec, another occupies a ridge above Tonalá and there is a cluster of sites in the environs of Santa Lucia Cozumalhualpa in southern Guatemala, extending into western Salvador.

Whether or not the sculptures of Santa Lucia Cozumalhualpa are to be credited to the Pipil, a Mexican tribe, is far from certain, but human sacrifice and other Toltec religious ideas are plainly presented. We find here elaborate speech scrolls comparable to those of Xochicalco and the Toltec work at Chichen Itza. Also there is evidence of the ceremonial importance of cacao in this region, the god of this economic plant being pictured in the form of a jaguar.

A peculiar type of pottery centered in southern Guatemala and western Salvador from which region it was distributed far and wide by trade. Although a few examples of this ware are found at Copan it is clear from the designs that most of the pieces belong to a time subsequent to the abandonment of this Mayan city. The ware has a semi-glaze which is the result of lead in the clay. Because paint could not be applied to this ware, the esthetic idea of shape was allowed to develop itself without hindrance. This pottery is now referred to as plumbate ware.

The Chorotegan Culture. Passing south and east from the Mayan area we find remains of a rich and in many ways peculiar art, consisting mostly of pottery and stone carvings, to which the name Chorotegan is applied. This name means

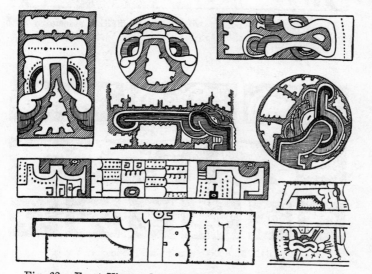

Fig. 62.   Front View and Profile View Serpent Heads in Chorotegan Art.   Although derived from Mayan models they have undergone great changes and have become highly conventionalized.

Driven-out People. It was first used in connection with several tribes of the Chiapanec-Otomi stock dispossessed of a fertile area about Lake Nicaragua by the intrusive Mexican-speaking Nicarao. The Chorotega were not, however, totally dispossessed since they continued to hold the Peninsula of Nicoya in Costa Rica as well as other pieces of territory. In an archæological sense the name Chorotegan fittingly can be extended to eastern parts of Costa Rica, Nicaragua, and Honduras, since the inhabitants of this stretch of land were also dispossessed some time before the coming of the Spaniards. Or perhaps they voluntarily migrated northward towards the end of the Toltec rule and are to be identified with the Otomi, Tlappaneca, and Mazateca of southern and central Mexico. The Tlappaneca and Otomi are definitely associated with introduction into Mexico of the peculiar cult of Xipe, God of the Flayed. This cult was clearly of southern origin and indeed still survived at Nicaragua at the time of the Spanish Conquest. The Mazateca were found in transit by Cortez, in the southern part of the Peninsula of Yucatan, living in palisaded villages. Similar palisaded villages once flourished in Honduras. The wild South American tribes who replaced the eastern Chorotega exhibit a cultural non-conformity with the archæological remains of the region they now occupy.

Fig. 63. Jaguar Design with Mayan Affinities associated with Figurines that still retain Archaic Characters. Costa Rica.

Fig. 64. Jaguars from painted Nicoyan Vases.

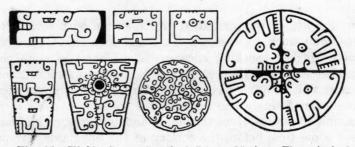

Fig. 65. Highly Conventionalized Jaguar Motive. The principal features of the head as well as the outline of the leg survive in highly modified form. From the southern end of Lake Nicaragua.

Close analysis shows that many of the decorative motives in Chorotegan art were developed from those of the Mayas. The serpent and the monkey furnish the majority of the designs that are surely Mayan but each of these is carried so far away from the original that only an expert can see the connections. The arms and legs of the monkeys are lengthened and given an extra number of joints while the heads degenerate into circles. The tongues of the serpents are elongated and bent downward at the end. All the open spaces are treated with scallops or fringes of short lines.

There is also in Chorotegan art a crocodilian motive that may be peculiar to the Isthmian region although it has Mayan affinities. The jaguar is also important in this ancient art. Among the most interesting vases are those that have a modeled head projecting from one side (jaguar, monkey, or bird) and two of the three legs of the vessel modified into animal legs. On these elaborate vessels there are bands of painted decoration mostly concerned with the crocodile.

The extremely elaborate metates (stones upon which maize was ground) from southern Nicaragua and northern Costa Rica probably were made by the producers of the peculiar pottery art already described. These were carved out of solid blocks of lava with stone tools. It is not unlikely that these elaborate metates were used as ceremonial seats since few of them show signs of use. The jaguar is perhaps the most common motive used in the decoration of these metates.

Fig. 66. Simple Crocodile Figures in Red Lines on Dishes from Mercedes, Costa Rica.

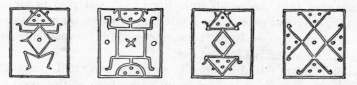

Fig. 67. Panels containing Crocodiles painted in White Lines on Large Tripod Bowls from Mercedes, Costa Rica.

Fig. 68. Simplified Crocodile Heads in the Yellow Line Ware of Mercedes, Costa Rica.

The back is broad and slightly dished, the head projects from the center of one end and the tail swings in a curve from the other end to one of the feet.

At Mercedes remarkable stone slabs were found during the excavations conducted by Mr. Minor C. Keith. These are now on exhibition in the American Museum of Natural History. The sculptures in relief on these slabs are by all odds the finest from the Isthmian area. Human beings, crocodiles, monkeys and birds are all used to decorate these carefully and laboriously made pieces whose use is entirely unknown. Statues in the full round have also been unearthed in quantity at Mercedes which gives every evidence of having been a large city with a long career.

We may be reasonably sure that the stone slabs date from a fairly late epoch because an undoubted "Chacmool" exhibiting the same style of carving has been discovered here. The "Chacmool," a half reclining figure with the knees drawn up, the body supported in part upon the elbows and a bowl for incense or other offerings in the pit of the stomach, gets its fanciful name from Le Plongeon who discovered the original at Chichen Itza. But the unmistakable sculptures of this type were apparently developed by the highland tribes and the cult was introduced into northern Yucatan during the period of Mexican influence. In addition to Chichen Itza examples have been found at Cempoalan, the historic Totonacan capital near Vera Cruz, at Texcoco, in the Valley of Mexico, at Jhuatzio in the Tarascan region, as well as at Chalchuapa far to the southeast in Salvador. All of these occurrences indicate a late Toltecan horizon for its distribution.

Isthmian Gold Work. Metal-working was unknown to the Mayas of the First Empire, but is abundantly illustrated in cities of the Second Empire, especially Chichen Itza where the pieces are predominantly of Costa Rican and Colombian manufacture evidently secured in trade. We are therefore justified in concluding that the splendid Isthmian gold work came into being after 630 A. D. and was typically developed by 1200 A. D. The "wire technique," essentially a cast rather than a soldered filigree, characterized metal working as far south as southern Colombia and is also the dominant mode in Mexico. In addition to plain and hollow casting, two kinds of gold plating were carried to perfection by the ancient metal workers: one a heavy plating over copper and the other a thin gilding. The manner in which this plating was done is still uncertain. It has been suggested that the molds were lined with leaf gold or sprinkled with gold dust before the baser copper was poured in. Also acids are said to have been used to dissolve out copper from the surfaces. Many ornaments are of pure beaten gold and have designs in *repoussé*.

The gold objects are found in stone box graves along with pottery and stone carvings. Gold is taken from only a small percentage of the graves, probably those of chiefs. A systematic rifling of the ancient cemeteries has been going on since the arrival of the Spaniards, but the finds have mostly been thrown into the melting pot. The burial places are sometimes marked by low platforms built over a group of graves. An iron rod, giving forth a hollow sound when the stone cysts are struck, is used by the searchers. Human bones are found in these graves, but seldom in a state of good preservation.

Mr. Minor C. Keith's collection of gold work from Costa Rica and Panama is unexcelled and illustrates the range of technical processes as well as of ornamental forms. Human forms are represented with peculiar headdresses and with

Fig. 69. Conventional Crocodiles from Costa Rica and Panama.

various objects carried in the hands and often they are joined in pairs. Many of the most beautiful amulets are frogs arranged either singly or in groups of two or three. These figures are all provided with a ring on the under side for suspension. Lizards, turtles, and crocodiles are frequently modeled as well as clam shells, crabs, and monkeys. But perhaps the most frequent amulets are those that picture birds with outspread wings among which may be recognized vultures, harpy eagles, gulls, man-of-war birds, and parrots. The larger and more elaborate pieces of gold work cast considerable light on the ancient religion of the natives since beast gods are figured in half human form. Bells of copper and gold were much used in gala dress and were doubtless an object of trade with the tribes farther north.

THE AZTECS

The Aztecs were the dominant nation on the highlands of Mexico when Cortez marched with his small army to conquer New Spain. The horrible sacrifices that they made to their gods and the wealth and barbaric splendor of their rulers have often been described. But their history in point of time covered short space and their art and religion were based in a large measure on achievements of the nations that had preceded them.

Mayas and Aztecs compared to Greeks and Romans. A remarkably close analogy may be drawn between the Mayas and Aztecs in the New World and the Greeks and Romans in the Old, as regards character, achievements, and relations one to the other. The Mayas, like the Greeks, were an artistic and intellectual people who developed sculpture, painting, architecture, astronomy, and other arts and sciences to a high plane. Politically, both were divided into communities or states that bickered and quarreled. There were temporary leagues between certain cities, but real unity only against a common enemy. Culturally, both were one people, in spite of dialectic differences, for the warring factions were bound together by a common religion and a common thought. To be sure the religion of the Mayas was much more barbaric than that of the Greeks but in each case the subject matter was idealized and beautified in art.

The Aztecs, like the Romans, were a brusque and warlike people who built upon the ruins of an earlier civilization that fell before the force of their arms and who made their most notable contributions to organization and government. The Toltecs stand just beyond the foreline of Aztecan history and may fitly be compared to the Etruscans. They were the possessors of a culture derived in part from their brilliant contemporaries that was magnified to true greatness by their ruder successors.

The Chichimecas. The term Chichimecas was applied by the more civilized tribes of the Mexican highlands to those nomads outside the pale who dressed in skins and hunted with the bow and arrow. Some of these wandering groups spoke Nahuan dialects, but the term was also applied to the Otomis who spoke a distinct language. Possibly through having been reduced in war certain of these wandering groups were drawn into civilization and when the Toltecan cities began to decline, they advanced to considerable power and prestige. In fact, the Aztecs may be considered as originally Chichimecan, along with the people of Texcoco. In later times, these city-broken nomads looked back with considerable pride on their lowly origin. The early life in the open is pictured interestingly in several documents including the Map of Tlotzin and the Map of Quinatzin.

We have already seen how the splendid culture of the Toltecan cities broke down under the weight of civil war about 1220 A. D. To be sure, Cholula appears to have kept alive the flame of Toltecan religion and art up to the advent

346

of the Spaniards. Atzcapotzalco, Colhuacan, and other towns near the lakes that had been established during the Toltecan period were able to hold their own for a time against the newer order.

Xolotl, founder of the dynasty of Texcoco, makes his first appearance in the Valley of Mexico in 1225, five years after the dispersion of the Toltecs, according to the Codex Xolotl. He viewed the abandoned cities but neither he nor his immediate successors chose to lead a sedentary life. The first date appears too early because it seems unlikely that the reigns of Xolotl and his son actually covered ninety years. The foundation of Texcoco took place in the reign of Techotlala and Ixtlilxochitl, his son, fell a victim to the murderous policy of Tezozomoc, the famous tyrant of Atzcapotzalco. Nezahualcoyotl, who regained the throne in 1431, was a great poet, philosopher, and law maker. The rulers of Texcoco were as follows:—

THE DYNASTY OF TEXCOCO

NOMADIC CHIEFTAINS

Xolotl	1225–1284
Nopalli	1284–1315
Tlotzin	1315–1324
Quinatzin	1324–1357

SEDENTARY CHIEFTAINS

Techotlala	1357–1409
Ixtlilxochitl	1409–1418
(Interregnum)	1418–1431
Nezahualcoyotl	1431–1472
Nezahualpilli	1472–1515
Cacama	1515–1520

Aztecan History. The history of the Aztecs has a mythological preamble in common with other nations of Mexico. The Chicomoztoc or Seven Caves must not be considered historical but simply man's place of emergence from the underworld. The general conception of an existence within the earth that preceded the existence upon the earth is found very widely among North American Indians. It is likewise impossible to locate the Island of Aztlan, that served, according to several codices, as the starting place of the Mexican migration. The northern origin for the Aztecan tribe to which so much attention has been paid need not have been far from the Valley of Mexico, since in their entire recorded peregrination they hardly traveled eighty miles.

Owing to the ineffectiveness of the Mexican time count Aztecan chronology is far from fixed. The year was known by the day with which it began and as this day ran the permutation of four names and thirteen numbers a cycle was fifty-two years in length. No method of keeping the cycles in their proper order seems to have been devised except the laborious one of putting down every year in sequence whether or not an event occurred in it. According to different authorities the year 1 Stone which begins the historical account in the Aubin Codex was 648, 1064, or 1168 in the European calendar, each date differing from the others by multiples of fifty-two years. The last base, 1168, is correct; this being the epoch of the Toltec Era established by Quetzalcoatl.

The wandering tribes, among which may be mentioned the Chalca, Xochimilca, Tlahuica, Huexotzinca, Tepaneca, and Azteca, pushed their way into the region of the lakes and were allowed to live in less desirable locations as vassals to the established tribes. The "peregrinations" relate the succession of stops and the length of each stop. The Aztecs themselves made twenty or more stops lasting from two to twenty years. Finally, about 1325, they reached Chapultepec and for a number of years lived in comparative peace and quiet.

Fig. 70. Pictographic Record of fighting near the Springs of Chapultepec, "Hill of the Grasshopper." Aubin Codex.

Their bad manners and growing power excited the enmity of several nearby towns and in 1351 the Aztecs, under their chieftain Huitzilihuitl, were worsted in a fierce battle. Remnants of the tribe, including Huitzilihuitl and his daughter, sought the protection of Cozcoztli, king of Colhuacan. They soon were able to repay his support in a war with Xochimilco. The first actual settlement on the site of the future Tenochtitlan was made in 1364 and in 1376 Acamapictli, a noble allied to the royal house of Colhuacan, was elected to be the first war chief of the new city.

One of the first improvements undertaken by the new city was in the matter of water supply. Rights were secured to the famous spring of Chapultepec, an important gain because the brackish waters of the lake were not fit to drink. A double water main of terra cotta was laid from the springs to the town. New land was made, probably after the manner still to be seen in the famous floating gardens of Xochimilco by throwing the soil from the bed of the shallow lake into enclosed areas of wattle work. Gradually a Venice-like city, traversed by canals and admirably protected from attack, rose from the lake. At the coming of the Spaniards there were three causeways leading to the shores of the lake and each of these was protected by drawbridges. There was a city wall upon which were lighthouses for the guidance of home-coming fishermen. There were palaces and market places and a great central plaza called the Tecpan, where were situated the principal temples.

The Spaniards destroyed the ancient city, blocking up the canals with the débris of temples, and building the new City of Mexico over the leveled ruins. Ancient relics are brought to light wherever excavations are made. In 1900 many sculptures and ceremonial objects were uncovered in Escalerillas Street near the Cathedral. Recently a building near the National Museum was torn down for replacement and in digging for new foundations part of the base of the great pyramid was found. This had been enlarged several times, as could be seen by the stairways successively buried under new walls. At the bottom of the balustrade of one stairway a great serpent head of stone was found in its original position (Plate XL).

The Aztecs count their history as a great people from their first war chief Acamapichtli who commenced his rule in 1376 (Codex Aubin). The names and the order of the succeeding war chiefs are the same in several records, but the dates are found to vary slightly.

Acamapichtli	1376–1396	Moctezuma I	1440–1469	Moctezuma II	1502–1520
Huitzilihuitl	1396–1417	Axayacatl	1469–1482	Cuitlahua	1520
Chimalpopoca	1417–1427	Tizoc	1482–1486	Cuauhtemoc	1520–1521
Itzcouatl	1427–1440	Ahuitzotl	1486–1502		

After throwing off the yoke of their early overlords, the Tepanecas, by the subjection of Atzcapotzalco at the beginning of the brilliant reign of Itzcouatl, the Aztecs of Tenochtitlan entered into a three-cornered league with Texcoco and Tlacopan (Tacuba). This was an offensive and defensive alliance with an equal division of the spoils of war. Soon the united power of these three cities dominated the Valley of Mexico and began to be felt across the mountains on every side. Tenochtitlan gradually assumed the commanding position in the league, and although Texcoco continued to be an important center the third member was apparently much reduced. The great votive stone of Tizoc records some of the earlier conquests of the Aztecs. At the arrival of Cortez only a few important cities such as Tlaxcala retained their independence. But the crest of power had then been passed and it seems pretty certain that the remarkable city in the lake would in time have suffered the fate of other self-constituted capitals both in the Old World and the New.

Social Organization. Spanish historians often liken Tenochtitlan to the seat of an empire and speak of the ruler as one who had the power of an absolute monarch while other and more recent writers have declared that the tribal organization of the Aztecs was essentially democratic. The truth doubtless lies between these extremes. The people were warlike by nature and all men, except a few of the priesthood, were soldiers. Honors depended largely upon success in war and warriors were arranged in ranks according to their deeds. The common warriors formed one rank and next came those who had distinguished themselves by definite achievements which gave the right to wear certain articles of dress or to bear certain titles. The chiefs were elected for an indefinite term of office from the most distinguished fighters and could be removed for cause.

But while the offices of state were elective there was, nevertheless, a tendency to choose from certain powerful families and at least the foundation of an aristocratic policy. A chief was succeeded by his son or brother except when these candidates were manifestly unfit. In the actual succession of the great war chiefs of Tenochtitlan, a peculiar system seems to have been followed in that the candidates from the older generation were ordinarily exhausted before the next lower generation became eligible. Thus Huitzilihuitl, Chimalpopoca, and Itzcouatl were all sons of Acamapichtli, and the last and greatest was born of a slave mother. Then followed Moctezuma Ilhuicamina I, the son of Huitzilihuitl. This chief had no male heirs but the children of his daughter ruled in order: Axayacatl, Tizoc, and Ahuitzotl. Moctezuma II was the son of the first of these as was Cuitlahua, while Cuauhtemoc, the last Aztec ruler, was the son of Ahuitzotl. This peculiar succession was not in vogue in Texcoco, where son succeeded father and the lawful wife was chosen from the royalty of Tenochtitlan. In the various annals, the genealogies are often indicated and the evidence that aristocracies existed is too strong to be overthrown. There are even cases of queens who succeeded to the chief power after the death of the royal husband.

It is extremely doubtful whether the Aztecs ever had what might be called clans. We have seen that there were originally eight closely related tribes constituting the Mexica or Mexici nation. The Aztecs themselves are said to have been divided into seven groups that were first reduced to four or five and then increased to about twenty. It is not clear that these were exogamic kinship groups. They were probably military societies taking into their membership all the men of the tribe. The name *Calpolli*, or "great house," which was applied to them seems to have referred to a sort of barracks or general meeting place in each ward or division of the city where arms and trophies were kept and the youth educated in the art of war. The title in land was held by the *calpolli* and the right of use distributed among the heads of families who held possession only so long as the land was worked. Each *calpolli* seems to have had a certain autonomy in governmental matters as well as a local religious organization. It is curious to find in Salvador, far to the south, the word *calpolli* applied to the platform mounds that surround courts in the ancient ruins. This use of the word may indicate that the "great houses" of the different societies were ordinarily the principal buildings of the city and that they were used for civil, military, and religious purposes.

In forming judgment on the fundamentals of social organization among the Aztecs we must remember that no clear case of kinship clans has been reported south of the area of the United States. Among the Cakchiquels, a Mayan tribe of the Guatemalan highlands, two royal houses are reported from which the ruling chief was alternately drawn. The Zotzils have been explained as a bat clan because their name is associated with the word for bat and because a bat god appears to have been their patron deity. The Mazatecas and Mixtecas, Deer people and Cloud people, also have clanlike names but in all cases these are designations of entire tribes, not of subdivisions of tribes.

Tenochtitlan was divided into four quarters and each quarter subdivided into a number of wards. An under chief was elected from each of the subdivisions which are doubtless to be identified with the *calpolli*, and an over chief from each of the four quarters. Above these stood the war chief of the entire tribe who was likewise elected, but within the limits of a fixed aristocracy. A second great chief, who seems to have been a peace officer with some important relation to the priesthood, was nominally equal to the war chief, but practically much less powerful. The real center of the home government was a council made up of all the chiefs. In time of war the war chief was in supreme command and could either delegate his rights or act in person. Just how much the priesthood intervened in governmental affairs cannot be definitely put in words, but their power was doubtless great. Certain lands were cultivated in common for the officers of church and state and much of the tribute from conquered provinces was devoted to their needs.

The Tecpan or Temple Enclosure. The ceremonial center of Tenochtitlan has been transformed into the civic center of Mexico City. The Cathedral, the National Palace, and the Zocolo, or Plaza Mayor, mark the site where once stood the famous Tecpan or temple enclosure. Within the serpent walls, according to Sahagun, there were twenty-five temple pyramids, five oratories, sundry fasting houses, four bowl-shaped stones, one disk-shaped stone, a great stepped altar, a "star column," seven skull racks, two ball courts, two enclosed areas, a well, three bathing places, two cellar-like rooms, a dancing place, nine priest houses, a prison for the gods of conquered nations, arsenals, work places, etc. A native plan of the Tecpan, much simplified, occurs in the Sahagun manuscript. The great pyramid rose in several terraces and was surmounted by two temples each three stories in height, one dedicated to Huitzilopochtli and the other to Tlaloc. Each temple contained an image of the god to which it was dedicated and a sacrificial altar. The walls were encrusted with blood of human victims whose hearts, still beating, had been torn out for divine food and whose bodies had been rolled down the steep flight of temple stairs. The foundations for the great pyramids were laid in 1447 by Moctezuma I, the pyramids were completed in 1485 while Tizoc was war chief and the final dedication ceremonies were held in 1487.

Several very interesting large sculptures and many minor objects have been unearthed on the site of the Tecpan. In 1790 and 1791 were found three famous monoliths, the Calendar Stone, the Stone of Tizoc (Sacrificial Stone), and the Statue of Coatlicue. Since 1897 many fine pieces of pottery and several sculptures have been excavated near the Cathedral and placed in the Museo Nacional.

The Calendar Stone. The great sculptured monument known as the Calendar Stone, or Stone of the Sun, is the most valuable object that has come down intact from the time of the Aztecs. It is a single piece of porphyry, irregular except for the sculptured face. It now weighs over twenty tons and it is estimated that the original weight was over twice as much. The sculptured disk is about twelve feet in diameter. This great stone was transported by men over many miles of marshy lake bottom before it could be placed in position in front of the Temple of the Sun in the temple enclosure that has just been described. The stone was doubtless thrown down from its original position by the soldiers of Cortez and may have been lost to sight. We know, however, that it was exposed to view about 1560 and was then buried by order of the archbishop of Mexico City lest its presence should cause the Indians to revert to their original pagan beliefs. It was rediscovered in 1790 and was afterwards built into the façade of the Cathedral where it remained until 1885, when it was removed to the nearby museum.

The Calendar Stone is not only a symbol of the sun's face marked with the divisions of the year but it is a record of the cosmogonic myth of the Aztecs and the creations and destructions of the world. In the center is the face of the sun god, Tonatiuh, enclosed in the middle of the symbol called Olin. Tonatiuh is often represented by a much simpler sign of a circle with four or more subdivisions resembling those of a compass which are intended to represent the rays of the sun. Olin is one of the day signs and means movement, or perhaps earthquake. It has also been explained as a graphic representation of the apparent course of the sun during the year. The history of the world, according to the Aztecan myth, is divided into five suns or ages, four of which refer to the past and one to the present. The present sun is called Olin Tonatiuh because it is destined to be destroyed by an earthquake. The day signs of the four previous suns are represented in the rectangular projections of the central Olin symbol beginning at the upper right hand corner and proceeding to the left. They are 4 Ocelotl (jaguar), 4 Ehecatl (wind), 4 Quauhtli (rain), 4 Atl (water), and they refer to destruction, first, by jaguars, second, by a hurricane, third, by a volcanic rain of fire, fourth, by a flood. It is claimed by some that the year 13 Acatl (reed) recorded at the top of the monument between the reptile tails refers to the first year of the present sun. The fifth sun will end with the day 4 Olin that is expressed in the central symbol already described. For this reason a fast was held on each recurrence of this day. Outside of the Olin symbol but between its arms are four hieroglyphs of uncertain meaning. Next to this area dealing with the great ages of the world comes a band of the twenty day signs of the Aztecan month. Outside of this band are several others which probably represent in a conventionalized manner the rays of the sun and the turquoise and eagle feathers with which the sun disk was believed to be decorated. Finally, outside of all, are two plumed monsters meeting face to face at the bottom of the disk. In each reptile face is seen a human face in profile. These reptiles are probably to be identified as the Xiuhcoatl or Fire Serpents.

The newly discovered National Stone pictures the Calendar Stone in vertical position on a mound and at the head of a flight of steps. The dates on the side of the stairway are 1 Tochtli and 2 Acatl, 1506 and 1507, indicating that the Calendar Stone was dedicated in connection with the New Fire Ceremony. The design on the back of this new-found monument pictures the eagle on the cactus, symbolic of the founding of Tenochtitlan. Other sculptures adorn the sides, the top, and the bottom of the stone.

Stone of Tizoc. The Sacrificial Stone or Stone of Tizoc is believed to have been carved by order of Tizoc, the war chief who ruled from 1482–1486, as a memorial offering to Mexican arms on the completion of the great temple to the Mexican God of War. The stone was a *quauhxicalli*, or "eagle bowl." This name was given to large bowls which were used to hold the blood and the heart of human victims sacrificed to the gods. The same name was extended to the large drum-shaped stone, under consideration, which has a pit in the center and a sort of canal running from the center to one side which may have been intended to drain off the blood. Human sacrifice actually took place on this stone but it is pretty certain that it was not one of the *temalacatl* or "gladiator stones" on which were staged mortal combats as ceremonies. According to description the gladiator stones were pierced by a hole in the center so that one or more captives could be bound fast by a rope.

Fig. 71. Details from the Stone of Tizoc: *a*, Huitzilopochtli, Aztec War God; *b*, Figures representing a captured town; *c*, Name of the captured town (Tuxpan, place of the rabbit).

On the top of the Stone of Tizoc is a representation of Tonatiuh, or the sun's disk, much less complex than that which we have seen on the Calendar Stone but with many similar parts. On the sides of the stone are fifteen groups of figures, each group representing a conqueror and his captive. The victorious soldier appears each time in the guise of the war god, Huitzilopochtli, or his wizard brother Tezcatlipoca. The left foot of the figure ends in two scroll-like objects that may represent the humming bird feathers that formed the left foot of Huitzilopochtli. But Tezcatlipoca also had a deformed foot. Moreover, on the side of the headdress is a disk with a flame-shaped object coming out of it. This may represent the smoking mirror of Tezcatlipoca. The captive wears costumes that change slightly from one figure to the next. Over the head of the captive in each instance is the hieroglyph of a captured town or district.

Nearly all the place name hieroglyphs have been deciphered. The list is interesting historically because it gives the principal conquests up to the reign of Tizoc. Starting at the side directly across the stone from the groove or drain we see that the figure of the victor has behind his head a hieroglyph that represents a leg. This is the hieroglyph of Tizoc and the victim in this case represents the district of Matlatzinco in the Valley of Toluca. This district was brought under subjection by Tizoc himself. Among the other conquered cities are such well-known ones as Chalco, Xochimilco, and Colhuacan in the vicinity of Lake Texcoco and Ahuilizapan (Orizaba) and Tuxpan that are more distant.

Coatlicue. The famous statue of the Earth Goddess, Coatlicue, "the goddess with the serpent skirt," is one of the most striking examples of barbaric imagination. The name Teoyamiqui is often given to this uncouth figure, but the identification is faulty. Like the other great sculptures we have just examined, it doubtless occupied an important place in the great ceremonial center of Tenochtitlan, but no ancient reference to it is extant. This goddess is reported to have been the mother of the gods.

The statue may be described as follows: The feet are furnished with claws. The skirt is a writhing mass of braided rattlesnakes. The arms are doubled up and the hands are snake heads on a level with the shoulders. Around the neck and hanging down over the breast is a necklace of alternating hands and hearts with a death's head pendant. The head of this monstrous woman is the same on front and back and is formed of two serpent heads that meet face to face. The

Fig. 72. Detail showing the Construction of the Face of Coatlicue from Two Serpent Heads meeting End to End.

forked tongue and the four downward pointing fangs belong half and half to each of the two profile faces.

Mexican Writing. The means of record employed in Mexican codices are in

Fig. 73. Hieroglyphs of Precious Materials: left to right, gold; turquoise; mosaic of precious stones; *chalchihuitl*, or jade; mirror of obsidian.

part pictographic and in part hieroglyphic. The sequence of the historical events in these native manuscripts is often indicated by a line of footprints leading from one place or scene of action to another. Historical records of this type resemble old-fashioned maps and some are actually called maps. The names of towns in these documents are represented by true hieroglyphs and often the character of the country is indicated by pictures of typical vegetation, such as maguey plants for the highlands and palms for the lowlands. The day or the year in which took place the foundation of the town or whatever event is intended to be recorded is usually placed in conjunction with the hieroglyph or picture. Conquest is indicated by a place name hieroglyph with a spear thrust into it or by a temple on fire, while warfare is a shield and bundle of lances encircled by footprints.

A few examples of Nahuan hieroglyphs will now be given to illustrate this interesting method of writing. It must be remembered that there is nothing in the nature of a connected narrative. The hieroglyphs or word pictures are limited to geographical and personal names, including the names of gods, to months, days, numbers, objects of commerce and a few objects or ideas of ceremonial import. Some of the signs are in no degree realistic and have a definite meaning by common consent alone, such as the symbol for gold (Fig. 73). Others are abbreviated and conventionalized pictures of objects. Thus the head of a god

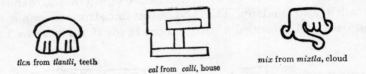

tlcn from *tlantli*, teeth   *cal* from *calli*, house   *mix* from *mixtla*, cloud

Fig. 74. Phonetic Elements derived from Pictures and used in Mexican Place Name Hieroglyphs.

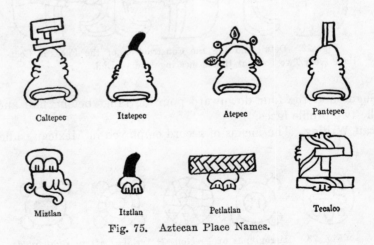

Caltepec   Itztepec   Atepec   Pantepec

Miztlan   Itztlan   Petlatlan   Tecalco

Fig. 75. Aztecan Place Names.

or of an animal frequently appears as the sign of the whole. But the most important and interesting word signs are rebuses in which separate syllables or groups of syllables are represented by more or less conventionalized pictures. The whole word picture is a combination of syllable pictures which indicate phonetically the word as a whole. Very often advantage is taken of puns on whole or partial words, while color and position are also employed to indicate sounds and syllables.

In Fig. 74 are given a few of the more common syllable pictures. The name of the object represented is cut down by the elimination of *tl*, *li*, etc., that form the nominal endings. Thus, the picture of water, *atl*, becomes the sign for the sound *a*, that of stone *tetl* is cut down to the syllable *te*. Several of these syllable pictures are combined to represent a whole word.

The hieroglyphs of the twenty days of the month (see Fig. 76) are frequently

Fig. 76. Aztecan Day Signs.

Cipactli	*Ehecatl*	*Calli*	*Cuezpallin*	*Coatl*
Crocodile	Wind	House	Lizard	Snake
Miquiztli	*Mazatl*	*Tochtli*	*Atl*	*Itzcuintli*
Death	Deer	Rabbit	Water	Dog
Ozomatli	*Malinalli*	*Acatl*	*Ocelotl*	*Quauhtli*
Monkey	Herb	Reed	Jaguar	Eagle
Cozcaquauhtli	*Olin*	*Tecpatl*	*Quiahiutl*	*Xochitl*
Vulture	Movement	Stone	Rain	Flower

a   b   c   d   e   f

Fig. 77. Variant Forms of Aztecan Day Signs: *a*, *acatl*, arrow; *b*, *mazatl*, deer foot; *c*, *malinalli*, jaw bone; *d*, *itzcuintli*, dog's ear; *e*, *ozomatli*, monkey's ear; *f*, *ocelotl*, jaguar's ear.

represented, but those of the eighteen months are not nearly so well known. As for the gods, the faces are usually pictured, especially when these are grotesque, but sometimes details of dress or an object connected with a special ceremony is sufficient to recall the divinity. The Mexican system of numbers was based on twenties. The units were figured by dots, the twenties by flags, the four hundreds by a device like a tree that represented hair, and the eight thousands by the ceremonial pouches in which copal incense was carried.

Aztecan Religion. The religion of the Aztecs, like that of the Mayas, was a polytheism in which special divinities controlled the powers of nature and the activities of men. The gods were perhaps further advanced towards human form and attributes than were those of the earlier culture to the south, but definite characterization was still accomplished by grotesque features and certain animal connections were still evident. The matter is confused beyond the point of analysis. The mythologies often ascribe different origins to the same deity. One god is addressed by many names, descriptive or figurative, that are intended to bring out the various aspects of his power. Overlapping functions make it impossible to assign each god to his special province. There are universal gods, there are special gods, and there are patron gods of trade guilds. Moreover, there are foreign gods, some recent, some ancient.

Fig. 78. Aztecan Numbers and Objects of Commerce: *a*, 1; *b*, 20; *c*, 400; *d*, 8,000; *e*, ten faces carved from precious stone; *f*, twenty bags of cochineal dye; *g*, one hundred bales of cocoa; *h*, four hundred bales of cotton; *i*, four hundred jars of honey of tuna; *j*, eight thousand leaf bundles of copal gum; *k*, twenty baskets each containing sixteen hundred ground cacao nibs; *l*, four hundred and two blankets.

The religion of central Mexico had its objective, ritualistic side, which appealed directly to the understanding of the masses, and its more subtle theological or philosophical side seen, for instance, in the poems written by priests and rulers. It was a mixture of spirituality and the grossest idolatry. The ceremonial calendar, with a description of the feasts and sacrifices occurring at different times of the year, has been preserved in a number of documents. Pageants, incense-burning, and human sacrifice gave a strong dramatic quality to the religious rites.

The conception of a supreme deity is seen in *Ometeuctli*, the Lord of Duality, a vague god-head and creator who is sometimes addressed in some of the religious poems as the "Cause of All." In the background of the popular religion was the belief in the Earth Mother and the Sky Father and in the divinity of the Sun, the Moon, the Jaguar, the Serpent, and whatever else was beautiful, powerful, and inexplicable. Tezcatlipoca, by reason of his magic and his omniscience, was placed at the head of the pantheon of active gods. Huitzilopochtli was, however, the favorite god of the Aztecs through his relation to war. Tlaloc, the god of rain, was naturally of great importance to agriculturists living in a rather arid region. Tonatiuh, the Sun God, was a more or less abstract deity who acted in part through other gods. But the list is too long to be repeated here.

The special gods of five principal Mexican cities were as follows:—

Tenochtitlan	Huitzilopochtli
Texcoco	Tezcatlipoca
Tlaxcala	Camaxtli
Cholula	Quetzalcoatl
Cuauhnahuac	Xochiquetzalli

Of gods with a foreign origin perhaps the most important were Quetzalcoatl and Xipe. The former was introduced long before the Aztecs raised their banner of war and was the Long-nosed God of the Mayas, introduced under the patronage of Quetzalcoatl, the powerful emperor of the Toltecs. The worship of Xipe is said to have originated in a town in southern Mexico. It had certainly taken a strong hold on the Aztecs of Mexico City and was likewise known as far south as Salvador. It has recently been demonstrated that the people of Yopico, specially given to the worship of Xipe, originated in Nicaragua.

Conceptions of the Universe. Cosmogonic myths, the world over, are unscientific attempts to explain the creation of the universe, to outline the powers of the gods and to trace the development of nature. The cosmogonic myths of Mexico and Central America are characterized by multiple creations. The Aztecan belief in five suns each standing for a world epoch is paralleled in fragments of Mayan mythology. Creation is not emphasized so much as destruction. The sequence of the suns is figured on the Calendar Stone, and in one of the codices, besides being explained in some of the early writings of Spanish priests and educated natives. The first sun was devoured by a jaguar and in the resulting darkness the inhabitants of the earth were devoured by jaguars. The second sun was destroyed by a hurricane, the third by a rain of fire, and the fourth by a flood.

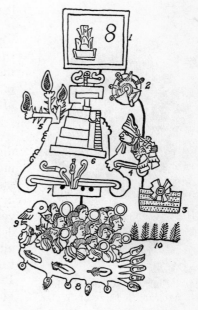

Fig. 79. Analysis of Mexican Record. 1, the year Two Reed, 1507; 2, eclipse of the sun; 3, earthquake at place pictured at 4; 5, the town of Huixachtitlan. In the temple (6) was held (7) the new-fire ceremony at the beginning of a 52-year period. In this year were also drowned in the River Tuzac (8) two thousand warriors (10) which the vultures devoured (9).

One human pair escaped each cataclysm and lived to repopulate the world. The fifth or present sun will be destroyed by an earthquake.

Notions of the shape and character of the universe are pretty well defined in Aztecan lore. The widespread belief that the universe consists of three superimposed worlds, the upper or sky world, the middle world of living men and the under world of the dead, is found in a developed form. The upper world is divided into thirteen levels. The uppermost four levels are called *Teteocan*, the abode of the gods, and are considered to be invisible. The creator of all, Ometeuctli, Lord of Duality, dwells with his spouse in the highest heaven and under him in order are the Place of the Red God of Fire, the Place of the Yellow Sun God and the Place of the White Evening Star God. The inferior heavens, called *Ilhuicatl*, are given over to the visible celestial activities. There is one heaven for the storms, another for the blue sky of the day, the dark sky of the night, the comets, the evening star, the sun, the stars, etc.

The under world is *Mictlan*, the Place of the Dead. Nine divisions are commonly given and in the lowermost of these lives *Mictlanteuctli*, the Lord of Death, and his mate. The idea of future blessing or punishment is not entirely absent from the minds of the Aztecs. Warriors killed in battle go to the House of the Sun, in one of the upper worlds, as do women who die in childbirth. *Tlalocan*, the lowermost heaven, is a sort of terrestrial paradise for others. *Mictlan* is, however, the common abode of the dead, and the wretched soul can reach it only after a journey set with horrors.

Fig. 80. Chalchuihtlicue, Aztecan Goddess of Water.

The cult of the quarters is intimately associated with the concept of the universe. With the four cardinal points a number of others are sometimes taken including the zenith, the nadir, and the middle. The sacred numbers 4, 5, 6, and 7 may thus conceivably be derived from the points of space, but it would be very unsafe to assume that they are necessarily so derived. The general concept of a universe divided into quarters, fifths, or sixths is a powerful conventionalizing factor in mythology, religion, and art. Prayers, songs, and important acts are repeated in identical or in systematically varied form for each point of space. In Mayan and Aztecan codices the symbolism of the four directions is often manifest.

Ceremonies. Ceremonialism was intensely developed in Mexico and the dramatic quality of many Aztecan rites of human sacrifice has probably never been equaled. We are apt to think only of the gruesome features of human sacrifice and to overlook the spiritual ones. The victim was often regarded as a personification of a god and as such he was fêted, clothed in fine garments, and given every honor. Efforts were made to cause the victim to go willingly to his death uplifted by a truly religious ecstasy. It was considered unlucky that he should grieve or falter.

The religious calendar was given over to fixed and movable feasts. The fixed feasts were eighteen in number and each came on the last day of a twenty-day period and gave its name to that period. These eighteen periods correspond with the Mayan uinals or months, but since dates were rarely given in relation to them, they do not have the same calendrical importance. The five days that rounded out the 365-day year were considered unlucky.

Each of the eighteen feasts of the year was under the patronage of a special divinity and each had a set of ceremonies all its own. In some cases the ceremonies were really culminations of long periods of preparation. Thus, on the last day of the month Toxcatl there was sacrificed a young man, chosen from captured chieftains for his beauty and accomplishments, who for an entire year had been fitting himself for his one turn on the stage of blood and death. This intended victim, gayly attired and accompanied by a retinue of pages, was granted the freedom of the city. When the month of Toxcatl entered he was given brides, whose names were those of goddesses, and in his honor was held a succession of brilliant festivals. On the last day there was a parade of canoes across Lake Texcoco and when a certain piece of desert land was reached, the brides and courtiers bade farewell to the victim. His pages accompanied him by a little-used trail to the base of an apparently ruined temple. Here he was stripped of his splended garments and of the jewels that were symbols of divinity. With only a necklace of flutes he mounted the steps of the pyramid. At each step he broke one of the flutes and he arrived at the summit, where the priests waited, knife in hand, a naked man whose heart was to be offered to the very god he had impersonated. This ceremony is given only as an example, but it illustrates two characteristics that are seen in several other sacrifices, namely, the paying of homage and honor to the intended sacrificial victim, and, secondly, the necessity of keeping the victim in a happy frame of mind.

The eleventh feast of the year was called Ochpaniztli, "the feast of the broom," and was celebrated in honor of the goddess known as Toci, or Teteoinnan. The first of these names means "our female ancestor" and the second one means "the mother of the gods." She was a goddess of the earth and her symbol was the grass broom with which the earth was swept. She also exerted an influence over the arts of the hearth, such as weaving. Her pictures in the codices show her with a broom in one hand and a shield in the other while about her head is a band of unspun cotton into which are stuck spindles wrapped with thread.

During this month the roads were repaired, the houses and plazas swept, and the temples and idols refurbished. According to the text in the Codex Magliabecchiano there were human sacrifices in the temples which fronted on the roads and there were great dances and carousals. Those sacrificed were afterwards flayed as in the feast of Xipe and their skins worn by dancers. The picture that accompanies this revolting admission is itself devoid of any morbid symbols. It shows a kneeling woman holding out the broom and shield. She wears a white dress and a neckless of jade beads with golden bells for pendants. Below her are two standing men who bear in their hands offerings of ripe fruit.

Sahagun gives details of a terrible drama that was enacted during this twenty-day month. For the first eight days there was dancing without song and without the drum. After this prologue a woman was chosen to impersonate the patron goddess and to wear her characteristic dress and ornaments. With her was a retinue of women skilled in medicine and midwifery. For four days these persons divided in opposing ranks and pelted each other with leaves and flowers.

While this harmless ceremony and others like it were being acted out, the greatest care was taken that the woman who played the role of the goddess and who was marked for death should not suspect her fate. It was considered unlucky, indeed, if this victim wept or was sad. When her time to die had come she was clothed in rich garments and given to understand that she should be that night the bride of a rich lord. And under such a beguiling belief she was led silently to the temple of sacrifice. There without warning an attendant lifted her upon himself, back to back, and her head was instantly struck off. Without delay the skin was stripped from her warm body and a youth, wearing it as a garment, was conducted in the midst of captives to the temple of the War God, Huitzilopochtli. Here in the presence of this mighty god the youth himself tore out the hearts of four victims and then abandoned the rest to the knife of the head priest. Thus closed the terrible drama which began with an innocent battle of flowers and ended in an orgy of blood.

The twelfth month passed under two names. It was called Pachtli after a plant with which the temples were decorated and Teotleco which signifies "the arrival of the gods." The principal feast was held, as usual, on the twentieth day when the great company of gods was supposed to return from a far land. One god, very youthful and robust, arrived on the eighteenth day, being able to outwalk the others, while a few very old and infirm divinities were late in getting to the feast. The one who arrived first was called Telpochtli or Titlacauan but in reality he was the great Tezcatlipoca in disguise.

In anticipation of this return, the temples, shrines, and household idols were decorated with branches. The youths who did this work were repaid in corn, the amount varying from a full basket to a few ears. A novel manner of attesting the earliest presence of divinity is related. Some cornmeal was spread in a circular mass upon the ground. During the night the high priest kept vigil and from time to time visited this circle of cornmeal. When he saw a footprint in the center he cried out, "Our master has come." Then there was a burst of music and everyone ran to the great feast in the temple. Much native wine was drunk, for this was considered equivalent to washing the tired feet of the travel-worn gods. As a final act of the celebration there was a dance in costume around a great fire and several unfortunates were tossed alive into the flames.

Space will not permit a further examination of the eighteen fixed feasts. The movable feasts were mostly in definite relation to the *tonalamatl* and were thus subject to repetition every 260 days. The permutation of twenty day names and thirteen numbers is pictured in Mexican codices in two or more stereotyped forms, but these are very complete. In the commonest form the entire cycle is divided into twenty groups of thirteen days each and each group is presided over by a special divinity. There are other repeating series of gods, sacred birds, etc., that preside over the individual days in these groups. The *tonalamatl* was much used in Mexico in connection with foretelling events. The days were lucky, indifferent, or unlucky, and the future life of a child was believed to be locked up in the horoscope of his birthday.

Other feasts were held in relation to longer time periods. There were important festivals held in connection with the planet Venus with especially elaborate ones falling at intervals of eight years. Still another ceremony was held at the completion of a fifty-two year period, when the set of years were figuratively bundled up and laid away and a new sacred fire lighted.

Poetry and Music. The languages of Central America were capable of considerable literary development. This is seen especially in the songs that were used in different religious ceremonies of the Aztecs, as well as in the reflective poems written by educated natives. Several very fine pieces have been preserved, and while there is no rhyme, there is much rhythm. When recited by a person speaking fluently the native tongue these poems are very impressive. Of course, translation is always hazardous, and fundamental differences in language, such as exist between English and Aztecan, make it almost impossible. The most famous poet whose name has come down to us was Nezahualcoyotl, or Famishing Coyote, who was a ruler of Texcoco and died at the advanced age of eighty years in 1472. A few verses from one of his poems on the mutability of life and the certainty of death have been translated as follows:—

All the earth is a grave, and naught escapes it; nothing is so perfect that it does not fall and disappear. The rivers, brooks, fountains and waters flow on, and never return to their joyous beginnings; they hasten on to the vast realms of Tlaloc, and the wider they spread between their marges the more rapidly do they mould their own sepulchral urns. That which was yesterday is not today; and let not that which is today trust to live tomorrow.

The caverns of earth are filled with pestilential dust which once was the bones, the flesh, the bodies of great ones who sat upon thrones, deciding causes, ruling assemblies, governing armies, conquering provinces, possessing treasures, tearing down temples, flattering themselves with pride, majesty, fortune, praise and dominion. These glories have passed like the dark smoke thrown out by the fires of Popocatepetl, leaving no monuments but the rude skins on which they are written.

Another example will serve to emphasize the strain of sadness and the vision of death that characterize so many Aztecan poems.

Sad and strange it is to see and reflect on the prosperity and power of the old and dying King Tezozomoc; watered with ambition and avarice, he grew like a willow tree rising above the grass and flowers of spring, rejoicing for a long time, until at length withered and decayed, the storm wind of death tore him from his roots and dashing him in fragments to the ground. The same fate befell the ancient King Colzatzli, so that no memory was left of him, nor of his lineage.

The Aztecs held concerts in the open air where poems were sung to the accompaniment of the drum and other simple instruments. Songs were also sung at banquets and in the stress of love and war. The common musical instruments of the Aztecs vary but little from those in use elsewhere in Mexico and Central America. There were two kinds of drums. One was a horizontal hollowed-out log with an H-shaped cutting made longitudinally on its upper surface so as to form two vibrating strips which were struck with wooden drumsticks having tips of rubber. The second sort of drum was an upright log also hollowed out and covered with a drumhead of deerskin. Conches were used for trumpets. Resonator whistles with or without finger holes were made of clay in fanciful shapes. Flageolets were constructed of clay, bone, or wood and flutes were made of reed. Resounding metal disks and tortoise shells were beaten in time. Many sorts of gourd and earthenware rattles were employed as well as notched bones which were rasped with a scraping stick. Copper bells of the sleigh bell type were exceedingly common. The marimba, however, that is such a favorite musical instru-

Fig. 81. A Mexican Orchestra: 1, log drum; 2, kettle drum; 3–4, flageolets; 5, gourd rattle; 6, turtle shell. Manuscrit du Cacique.

ment today in Central America is of African origin and fairly recent introduction. No stringed instruments were known to the ancient Mexicans nor does the pan-pipe appear to have been used in this area although common in Peru.

Minor Aztecan Arts. Some of the great sculptures of Tenochtitlan have already been described and references have been made to the native books painted in brilliant colors on paper and deerskin. Objects of minor art comprise pottery vessels, ornaments of gold, silver, copper, jade, and other precious materials, textiles, pieces of feather work, etc.

The best known ceramic products are made of orange colored clay and carry designs in black that sometimes are realistic, but more often not. The tripod dishes with the bottoms roughed by cross scoring were used to grind chili. Heavy bowls with loop handles on the sides and a channel across the bottom were seemingly made to be strung on ropes. They may have held pitch and been used for street lights. The pottery figurines of the Aztecan period are nearly all moulded and lack the sharp detail of the earlier examples. They often represent deities wearing characteristic dress and carrying ceremonial objects.

Comparatively few specimens of ancient gold work in Mexico escaped the cupidity of the Spanish conquerors, but these attest a remarkable proficiency in casting. The moulds were made of clay mixed with ground charcoal and the melting of gold was accomplished by means of a blow pipe. The technique seen in Costa Rican gold work, according to which details falsely appear to be added by soldered wire, was followed in Mexico. Modern Mexican filigree bears little relation to the ancient Indian work, but is probably of Moorish origin. The examples of Aztecan gold work include finger rings, earrings, nose and lip ornaments, necklaces, and pendants.

Among the precious and semi-precious stones known to the Aztecs, the most valuable in their eyes was turquoise. This was probably obtained by trade from the Pueblo Indians. It was mostly cut into thin plates and used in the manufacture of mosaic objects. Red jasper, green jade, jet, gold, and shell of various colors were also used in these mosaics. Jade was highly prized and was known as *chalchihuitl*. Ornaments of obsidian, a black volcanic glass, and of crystal quartz are fairly common and others of opal and amethyst have been found. Pearls and emeralds were secured in trade from the south.

Fig. 82. Mexican Blanket with the Design that represents interlacing Sand and Water called "Spider Water."

The textile decorations in vogue at the coming of the Spaniards can be restored from the pictures in codices. Mantles were often demanded as tribute and the designs are given on the conventional bundles in the tribute lists. Garments with certain designs served as insignia of office for several of the priesthoods. Feather mosaic was highly prized and was made according to several methods. Capes as well as shields and other objects were covered with brilliant feathers so arranged as to bring out designs in the natural colors.

The Tarascans. The Aztecs while by far the most important tribe in the fifteenth century did not dominate all the surrounding peoples. For instance, most of the State of Michoacan was controlled by the Tarascan tribe who defeated every expedition sent against them. The list of Tarascan towns is a long one but Tzintzuntzan, which means the "Place of the Humming Birds," was the capital and principal stronghold. The ancient history of the Tarascans is little known. Large and striking specimens of archaic art were formerly accredited to this people, but without good reason. It is likely that archaic characters in art were maintained in Michoacan after they had passed away in central Mexico, but we cannot be sure that the Tarascans were the ancient inhabitants. There is some evidence, however, of culture which can be associated with them. The peculiar T-shaped mounds called *yatacas*, which rise in terraces and are faced with stone slabs laid without mortar, may have been built by this tribe. Sculptures of rather fine quality are occasionally found, an example being a reclining god of the type made famous by the "Chacmool" of Chichen Itza. Many fine copper celts have been unearthed in this highly mineralized mountain region. When the Spaniards came the Tarascans were skilled in weaving and were particularly famous for feather mosaics and feather pictures made largely of the brilliant plumage of humming birds. The use of the *atlatl* or spear-thrower survives among the present-day Indians who also make gourd vessels covered with colored clays in pleasing geometric and floral designs.

The Otomis are a tribe of central Mexico even less cultured than the Tarascans and there is some evidence that they entered this region from the south only a few centuries before the Spaniards. Their relatives, the Matlatzincas of the Valley of Toluca, had more interesting arts.

Southern Mexico. Somewhere about the middle of the fifteenth century Moctezuma I planted an Aztecan colony at Uaxyacac on the edge of the Zapotecan territory to protect the trade route to Tabasco. This name gave rise to the modern Oaxaca. From this point expeditions were sent out which harassed the Zapotecs to the south and the Mixtecs to the west. In the Tribute Roll of

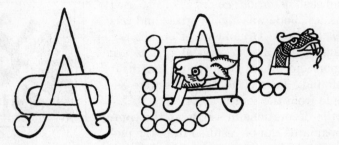

Fig. 83. The Year Symbol of southern Mexico. It is combined with the four year bearers, House, Rabbit, Reed, and Stone. In the second detail the day 6 Serpent in the year 12 Rabbit is recorded.

Moctezuma II more than twenty Zapotecan towns are listed as paying tribute that consisted of gold disks and gold dust, jadeite beads, quetzal feathers, cochineal dye, fine textiles, etc. Very little is preserved concerning the traditional history of southern Mexico, but it is presumed that the Zapotecan culture before the Aztecan ascendency was a development of that implanted many centuries

Fig. 84.   Year Bearers in the Codex Porfirio Diaz ascribed to the Cuicatecan tribe: Wind, Deer, Herb, and Movement.

before when Monte Alban flourished and which we have already examined. As for the Mixtecs we only know that they produced pottery of great beauty somewhat similar to that of Cholula.

Some of the finest pre-Cortesian codices that have come down to us are probably of Zapotecan and Mixtecan origin although reflecting to some extent the religion of the Aztecs. Several of these have been interpreted by Doctor Seler in terms of Aztecan religion and art. Among the documents from southern Mexico that belong to the late period are:—

Codex Borgia	Codex Féjervary-Mayer
Codex Vaticanus 3773	Codex Vindobonensis
Codex Bologna	Codex Nuttall or Zouche

Several *lienzos* or documents written on cloth are also from this region. The Lienzo of Amoltepec which is a fine example of this class is conserved in the

American Museum of Natural History. The documents from southern Mexico are distinguished by details of geometric ornament that resemble the panels of geometric design on the temples of Mitla. They record historical events, give

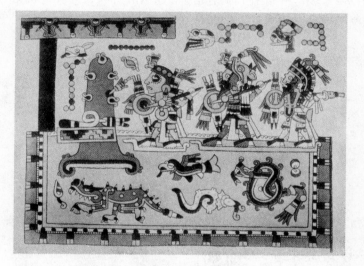

Fig. 85.   A Page from the Codex Nuttall, recording the Conquest of a Town situated on an Island of the Sea.   The conquerors come in boats and the conquest is indicated by a spear thrust into the place name hieroglyph.   The crocodile, flying fish, and the sea serpent are represented in the water.

astronomical information and present much pictographic evidence on various ceremonies and religious usages. In giving a date a somewhat different method is used than we have seen in the historical records from the Valley of Mexico. There is a definite year sign (Fig. 83) and with it is combined the year bearer, or initial day of the year, and often the particular day of the event. Unfortunately, this is not entirely satisfactory because no month signs are recorded and a day with a certain name and number frequently occurs twice in one year. The year bearers are the same as among the Aztecs for most of the documents, namely, Knife, House, Rabbit, and Reed, but in a manuscript ascribed to a tribe in southern Mexico called the Cuicatecs, the year bearers are Wind, Deer, Herb, and Movement (Fig. 84). Conquest of a town is shown by a spear thrust into the place name. Individuals are often named after the day on which they were born. Thus 8 Deer is a warrior hero in the Codex Nuttall and 3 Knife is a woman who also plays a prominent part. In some of the manuscripts from southern Mexico we see details that are very close to those in the codices of the Mayas.

Aztecan Influence in Central America. The influence from the late Mexican cultures can be traced far to the south. Decorative motives that show affiliations to those of the Aztecs and their immediate predecessors are found as far south as Costa Rica but the strain is thin and not to be compared with the evidences of culture connection over wide territories that are found on earlier horizons. There was clearly a brisk trade in gold in Aztecan times between the Isthmus of Panama and Mexico.

After the breakdown of the civilization of the humid lands of Central America, following the Mayan cataclysm, the abandoned regions appear to have been re-populated by a stream of tribes from South America who swept up the coast of the Caribbean Sea and across the peninsula of Yucatan, as far as Tehuantepec.

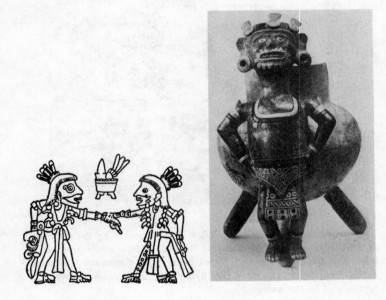

Fig. 86. The God Macuilxo-chitl, Five Flower, as shown in a Mexican Codex and in Pottery from southern Mexico.

There was also a strong northern movement of tribes along the Pacific Coast seen most clearly in the distribution of languages belonging to the Chiapanecan or Chorotegan stock. The early historic records show the Mazateca in transit from their old home in Costa Rica to their new one in northern Oaxaca. Cortez in 1526 found these Indians in Yucatan.

A CROSS-SECTION OF NEW WORLD HISTORY

This survey of ancient history in Mexico and Central America discloses a condition which doubtless holds true of the archæological record in other parts of the world. The earliest sedentary culture was by far the most homogeneous and widespread. This means it modified slowly and lasted for ages. At the same time, owing to the connection of the archaic complex with agriculture, the initial spread may have been rapid. The plants domesticated by the American Indians were developed far beyond the wild types, much farther, indeed, than the domestic plants of the Old World. This development must have extended over many centuries. The first horizon of agriculture was based on plants of an arid high-land environment. The second horizon of agriculture was based on these same plants after they had been slowly modified to fit a humid lowland environment, as well as on certain new plants of humid lowland origin.

The Mayan civilization was specialized to the wet lowlands of the tropic zone and while the influence exerted by this dominant culture of the New World was felt over a great area, the exact characters were not reproduced elsewhere. Trade relations can be traced from Yucatan to Colombia on the one hand and on the other to New Mexico. The cycle of the Mayan civilization was comparatively short and the cycles of the resultant civilizations were even shorter. All New World history must be referred ultimately to the horizons of culture described above, with the standard chronology of the Mayas as the only definite scale.

In the cross-section of New World history presented herewith the horizontal measures represent space and the vertical measures represent time. The line A–B–C–D begins at Victoria Island and ends at Cape Horn, cutting across the culture areas named on the diagram. Over a large part of this cross-section the "horizon of recorded history" is in fact the time of the first European exploration, but in Colombia and Peru, there are well-defined traditions giving lists of kings, while in Central America there is exact chronology going back 2000 years before the coming of the white man. Below this and within it there are archæological records of culture sequence which in some regions, such as the Pueblo Area, have been nicely classified. On the basis of trade relations and diffused ideas in material and esthetic arts the marginal chronology can be tied in with that of the central standard section of history. Of course, all dates earlier than the first recorded ones are theoretical. The beginning of agriculture in America is put at 4000 B. C. —it may be earlier, but can hardly be much later.

In the Pueblo or Southwest Area a single type of flint corn, doubtless intro-duced from the south, appears on the first agricultural level. Contacts with Mexico and Central America are inferable during Basket Maker II and III, the latter stratum having female fetishes roughly comparable with those of the Archaic Horizon of Mexico. Later Southwest evolution is autochthonous until the end of Pueblo III when the concepts of the Plumed Serpent, the Eagle Man, Four-direction symbolism, etc., come from Mexico with Toltec trade. Culture sequence in the Southwest is about as follows:—

Pueblo V	Modern	1692 to present time
Pueblo IVb	Early Historic	1538 to 1692
Pueblo IVa	Protohistoric	1200 to 1538
Pueblo IIIb	Toltec Trade	1000 to 1200
Pueblo IIIa	Urban Developments	
Pueblo II	Small House	
Pueblo I	Proto-Pueblo	
Basket Maker III	First Pottery	
Basket Maker II	First Agriculture	
Basket Maker I	Nomadic	

In Colombia, Ecuador, and Peru culture successions are now being worked out. The best criterion of age is found in metals, which enter Central America from South America after the fall of the First Mayan Empire, i.e., after 630 A. D. The technology of metal working is continuous from southern Colombia to central

Mexico. Negative painting with wax has a wider and perhaps earlier distribution, reaching Ecuador and Peru in association with tripod pottery which is otherwise rare in the Andean region. Various motives of design link the two continents, especially on the Toltec-Chorotegan level. Between 1000 and 1200 A. D. civilization seems to have been generally stabilized, but this halcyon age was followed by disorganization and far-reaching migrations. The pre-Spanish horizons of southern Peru are tentatively arranged as follows by A. L. Kroeber, the apparently earlier material of Ancon being omitted for lack of the cross-ties.

III.	Inca
IIc.	Late Ica
IIb.	Middle Ica
IIa.	Epigonal
Ib.	Late Nasca
Ia.	Early Nasca

The early Nasca civilization was far from primitive, being characterized by pyramids, fine textiles, and some metal. Mayan strains have been recognized in Chavin and Recuay in Peru and various sites in Ecuador.

The dynamic forces in the history of man in the New World have a tremendous bearing upon the present and future state of the world. The debt which we owe to the ancient civilizations of Mexico and Central America becomes apparent when we list the more important agricultural plants, fibers, gums, dyes, etc., which were taken over by Europeans from the American Indians.

Food Plants Cultivated by American Indians

Maize	Pineapples	Cashew nut
Potatoes	Nispero	Jocote
Sweet potatoes	Barbados cherry	Star apples
Tomatoes	Strawberries	Paraguay tea
Pumpkins	Persimmons	Alligator pear
Squashes	Papaws	Chirimoya
Lima beans	Guava	Sour sop
Kidney beans	Arracacha	Sweet sop
Peppers	Peanuts	Custard apple
Cacao	Oca	Cassava

Important Economic Contributions of American Indians

FIBERS	MEDICINES
Cotton	Tobacco
Henequen	Cinchona (Quinine)
Pita	Cascara Sagrada
	Cocaine
	Ipecac
	Sarsaparilla

DOMESTICATED ANIMALS	GUMS	DYES
Alpaca	Rubber	Añil (Indigo)
Llama	Copal	Cochineal
Guinea pig	Peruvian Balsam	Logwood
Dog (perhaps Old World)	Chicle	Fustic
Muscovy duck		
Turkey		

EPILOGUE

MAYA DYNAMIC DATING AND THE FALLACY OF TIME

A chronological viaduct or Throughway built by Maya science runs backward and forward from a historical initiation in the eighth century before Christ. On the basis of experience and analysis, certainty was reached early in the Christian era, when accurate knowledge of celestial dynamics was projected into vast stretches of both past and future by Maya astronomers. They had discovered that time is neither an endless flowing nor a senseless whirligig, but an intelligible interrelation of changing states throughout the universe. They had directed their attention to the repetition of phenomena, and had found that time is change possessing natural regulations even though it passes forward to become the measurement of history, natural and political.

The Maya day count, first and last, extends along the ecliptic as the axis of eclipses and other astronomical phenomena. Noting synchronizations in terms of named and numbered days, astronomers found that these fall properly in order when granted the flexibility of things that live and freely respond.

Mathematics helped, especially their tzolkin, which had the virtue of a catalyst. The Maya word means something like "appraiser of days." It has within itself the ingredients of a tripod jack, or Maya lifting engine, accomplishing approximations which ascend in betterments. This tzolkin was invented or first exemplified on April 1, 749 B.C., under control of eclipse phenomena. This amounts to an absolute synchronization with the invariable time clock that ticks off astronomical days.

Any mnemonic record of beads upon a string safely held in place by a knot becomes an original cyclic zero when it marks a phenomenon. Against it rest the counting beads recording intervals in days till the next phenomenon of the same sort, when another knot is added. At first, then, only beads on a string mark the flight of time with knots or nodes for recurring events.

The Maya enriched and extended this designation through their tzolkin of thirteen digits and twenty words in the combining cycle of 260 designations. Long before month positions in a calendar year were tied in, various synchronizations became apparent as regards the succession of eclipses and the relation of solar and lunar ones on a certain cyclic day, soon to be identified as 12 Lamat, then as 12 Lamat 1 Muan, then as 957,328 from Maya zero, then by the addition of 489,384 to Julian Day 1,446,712, which Europeans understand as November 10, 752 B.C., in Scaliger's system adjusted to a Maya-Gregorian calendar. This unfolding of knowledge has no break in temporal continuity, and its simple tabulation in terms of 12-Lamat eclipses reveals how the Maya mathematicians modified straight vigesimal counting to achieve their special system which counts by 360-day tuns.

369

I. The Maya Ephemeris Begins

Day	Count	Tzolkin	Maya-Gregorian	Event
A	0	12 Lamat	Nov. 10, 752 B.C.	1st solar eclipse
B	177	7 Chicchan	May 6, 751 B.C.	2nd solar eclipse
C	272	11 Ahau	Aug. 9, 751 B.C.	1st base for tuns
D	872	13 Ahau	Apr. 1, 749 B.C.	1st lunar eclipse
E	873	1 Imix	Apr. 2, 749 B.C.	tzolkin begins

The problem of ex post facto amplifications should be dealt with charily. Contemporaneity of record must be assumed simply because continuity is undeniable all along the line of historical transmission. Presumably the first counting was unmodified vigesimal, but on this point and many others archaeologists have not as yet been able to locate any lowland Maya site of the Formative Period, 752 B.C. to 58 A.D.

The principal business of the early Maya astronomers was the problem of eclipses, and in particular the co-ordination of those that fall on repetitions of 12 Lamat on a 2-tzolkin scale. It happens that $2 \times 260 = 520$ is very close to three crossings of the apparent solar path by the apparent lunar path, and that these crossings define the draconic period or eclipse season. The 520-day formula becomes effective on its 23rd multiple, when approximate synchronizations of important factors produce the usable eclipse cycle of the Maya, which amounts to both solar and lunar phenomena when dynamic factors agree. The experience of the early Maya, recoverably recorded, furnishes the great criterion of static insistence on mathematical rigidities. They point the way to dynamic exits from destructive blocking which has grievously affected the course of human civilizations. The bed of Procrustes kills its victims.

Early Maya experience with 12-Lamat eclipses is summed up in a tabulation of a first series of visible phenomena (marked by stars) which count from Date A as cyclic zero, first for solar eclipses, then for lunar ones 7,280 days later. Analysis of the intervals discloses that Maya day-count numeration is really based on the eclipse factors in chronology. Rectifications to recover dynamic reality, when the static series broke, were accomplished long before any 12-Lamat eclipses were again experienced.

Solar Eclipse + 7280 Days	Lunar Eclipse + 4680 Days
0*	7,280*
11,960	19,240*
23,920*	31,200
35,880	43,160
47,840	55,120*
59,800*	67,080*
71,760*	79,040*
$4,680 = 9 \times 520 = 13 \times 360$	(18 tzolkin = 13 tun)
$7,280 = 14 \times 520 = 20 \times 364$	(28 tzolkin = 20 zodiacal years)
$11,960 = 23 \times 520 = 5 \times 2,392$	(46 tzolkin = 1 eclipse cycle)

* Starred eclipses were visible to the Maya.

Also concerned are the Palenque and Copan whole-day formulas for lunations. Respectively, 81 are 2,392 days, and 149 lunations are 4,400 days.

This concatenation of astronomical events is most unusual, for rarely do total eclipses lie so close together in space and time as A and B. We may conclude that a preliminary interest in eclipses already existed and that permutations of things in shamanistic dealing preceded those of numbers in a time sense. Most divination is unrelieved gambling, but synchronization is scientific when circuitous dealing has a proper purpose and leads to a measurement of recurrence. Many tzolkin arrangements in the Maya codices develop into synchronic interlaces or graphic formulas. The upspiraling of time is an aspect of dynamics seen in the phyllotaxy of plants and the planetary overcycles. On the other hand, static abstractions are unproductive.

A second Maya Throughway event is back-dated on Altars H' and I' at Copan, the statement being made in the precise form of place values counted from a Maya zero yet to be invented. It is here for the first time that a general calendar of 365 days was organized, with months at contemporary places by name and symbolism in a tropical year. This departs from a sunset on the winter solstice with 0 Pop as its cyclic designation. At the same time, 0 Yaxkin was 120 days after, or 245 days before 0 Pop. At the earlier placement, it was in touch with morning-star phenomena of Venus every eight years. The addition of month places produces Station II on the Maya Throughway.

II. Maya Benchmark—Altars H' and I' at Copan

Date	Maya Calendar		Maya-Gregorian	Event
A	9 Ik	0 Yaxkin	Apr. 25, 581 B.C.	Inferior conj. of Venus
B	7 Chicchan	18 Kayab	Nov. 26, 580 B.C.	Inferior conj. of Venus
C	9 Ahau	13 Cumhu	Dec. 11, 580 B.C.	Mass conj. of planets
D	8 Eb	0 Pop	Dec. 23, 580 B.C.*	Sunset at winter solstice

* Their December 23 is our December 22, the Maya day beginning six hours earlier than ours.

It is a pleasure to state that the original calculation for the mass conjunction which anchored Maya calendars was made by Charles A. Muses, then a student of astronomy and its history, as also the dynamic diagram of the Maya Year Dial at Uxmal, for publication by me at the XXVIII Congress of Americanists in Paris, 1947, and more fully in the Smithsonian Annual Report for 1948.

Here E and F are simply A and B of Station I advanced three Venus octennials to places later emphasized in Maya calculations:

E	7 Ik	0 Yaxkin	Apr. 13, 557 B.C.	Inferior conj. of Venus
F	5 Chicchan	18 Kayab	Nov. 16, 556 B.C.	Inferior conj. of Venus

We proceed to the most important calculations of all, for which the data represent the accumulation of about 800 years.

III. ESTABLISHMENT OF MAYA ZERO AND THE THEOCRATIC STATE

Maya Long Count	Maya-Gregorian Calendar	Event
A 8–14–0–17–7	3 Manik 5 Tzec Oct. 14, 58 A.D.	Inferior conj. of Venus
8–14–0–17–7		(−3,431 tropical years)
B 13– 0–0– 0–0	4 Ahau 8 Cumhu Oct. 14, 3373 B.C.	Maya zero*

* This Baktun 13 is Maya zero, a cyclic point of time. J. I. Goodman, in his *Archaic Maya Inscriptions* (1897), calls it Great Cycle 54, that is, the 54th completion within a round of 73 times 13 baktuns which had begun at 4 Ahau 13 Yax. Early Maya theocrats had their initial series start counting days from 4 Ahau 8 Cumhu. They made subsequent changes in numeration, the first extending the number system of vigesimal place values (beginning with the tun), and the second drastically simplifying the presentation while amplifying the scope. Their real sequence of counted days was carried back to Maya zero by adding 957,328 days to the ceiling solar eclipse of their ephemeris.

The outward manifestation of the establishment of Maya zero as an integration of the tropical, draconic, and sidereal years is the use of place-value dates in inscriptions on stone monuments celebrating the apotheosis of theocrats. The first actual date is that on the Leyden Plate, a beautiful jade plaque showing a Maya theocrat holding the ecliptic in his arms. The date is:

C   8–14–3–1–12   1 Eb   0 Yaxkin   November 17, 60 A.D.

The intention must be to hark back to II, Dates E and F, with 0 Yaxkin and November 17 in relation to Venus phenomena.

We count from that zero by a number, a day name, and a month position such as are restored above in II. A great mass of argumentative detail must be passed over.

Precisely, Maya zero is a point of time which puts Saturn behind the sun at superior conjunction, with Mars close beside Saturn. The ascending node of the moon is at Aldebaran, brightest star of the ecliptic. Besides, the significant phases of the planets are fixed in the Dresden Codex by ring-form numbers giving dates before the Cosmic Point of Time.

This positive anchorage the Maya wrote as 13 baktun ($13 \times 20 \times 20 \times 360$) as a basis for dynamic comparisons. Historically concerned is the schematic addition of $7 \times 20 \times 20 \times 360 = 1,008,000$ days, leading to another cyclic zero positively intended to establish a sixth or pictun order.

13–0–0–0–0	4 Ahau 8 Cumhu	Oct. 14, 3373 B.C.
7–0–0–0–0		($7 \times 144,000$ days)
0–0–0–0–0	10 Ahau 18 Zac	Aug. 6, 613 B.C.

This is a date in historic time which astronomically is Midsummer Day, halfway between the summer solstice and the autumnal equinox. By the initial-series method, depending on the explained integration from October 14, 58 A.D., this is simply Baktun 7, which much later the Toltecs decided might well serve for their creation of the world. But it is not even the beginning of historical time for the early Maya according to the beads of their ephemeris. I think its selection was influenced by a backward extension of round numbers. For instance, 6–13–0–0–0, 11 Ahau 8 Yax, August 9, 751 B.C., is nested within the earliest historic Throughway dates (Station I, C). From August 9, 751 B.C., to August 6, 613 B.C., the convenient calculating formula, 140 tuns + 3 days = 138 tropical years, was probably used.

Initial-series dates concern the Maya theocracy when rulers were identified at death with the gods of a chronocracy, or rule of time. When theocratic government crashed in 629 A.D., the initial-series method ceased to be used, but there was no break in true chronology.

When Maya zero was calculated, astronomers and mathematicians had before them the accumulated observations of 800 years. Their master record of days may at first have been no more than one string of identified beads, carefully tagged and guarded. This was manifolded, undoubtedly, so that separate compilations, with proper days and numbers, could be used for special planetary counts departing from important phenomena. Alignments of planet, earth, and sun were construed with alignments of earth, planet, and zodiacal star. Carried far enough, these observations produced more correlatable overcycles and different explanations than Old World astronomers ever obtained. Each planetary axis, like those of earth and moon, became straight lines.

It is as though bamboo poles of varying joint lengths were used in combination with others of even joint lengths. In other words, straightened-out planetary records are correlated with designations to tzolkin and day-count chronology. In contrast, the Old World method produces zigzag courses on which separate averages, commonly called means, are constructed. The Maya developed mathematically, through their ephemeris, the principle of the coaxial cable concretely and concurrently available for object, time, and place.

Then, just as data on eclipses was extended both ways from the observer to produce two-way alignments of solar and lunar black-outs along the ecliptic, the Maya established a variety of comparable planetary reciprocities. In the original case of eclipses, their 11,960-day eclipse cycle gave the good rule: solar eclipse + 7,280 = lunar eclipse + 4,680 = solar eclipse. Other tzolkin synchronizations were sometimes available. Similarly, in the case of inferior conjunctions of Venus, the rule, 8 years = 5 synodical phenomena = 13 sidereal phenomena, was subsequently refined to 251 years = 157 synodical phenomena = 408 sidereal phenomena; but handled concretely, not abstractly.

The Maya base line put April 13 opposite October 14, with March 7 opposite August 30, and developed the Venus Wicket to average inferior conjunction between the last and first appearance in the twilight. Each 251-year overcycle of Venus broke down into 113 + 138 = 251, a further modification ultimately being required. Even with good consistency of registration, the problems of continuous change inevitably must be met for science's sake: dynamics is a property of reality.

Reciprocal alignments on the ecliptic were an unusual observation. The invention of mathematical facilities for orderly counting and the naming of the days in contact with phenomena also were important achievements. Neither was accomplished by any Old World nation before the discovery of America. While dynamic truth may be inherent in any true record, the extraction of the principle behind it is another matter.

Maya tripodal calculations have many applications. The true analysis of three eclipse seasons = 520 days = 2 tzolkin was made in reference to a lifting machine of simple application in Maya housebuilding. Only recently, since rigid tripods require level floors, have we been using adjustable tripods on surveying instruments and cameras. Many adjustments merely put off the settlement, with extrapolation a compromise. French astronomers of the eighteenth century developed a tripod calculation without the coaxial cable to extend its usefulness. That operation of Laplace's time was not truly dynamic.

Between their first solar eclipse (Throughway, I, A) and Maya zero (Throughway, III, A and B), the difference is $957,320 + 8$ days, for 4 Ahau and 12 Lamat respectively. The rectification of the eclipse season in whole days on the 12 Lamat schedule is:

$$5,523 \text{ Eclipse seasons} = 957,180 + 130 \ (\tfrac{1}{2}T) = 957,320$$
$$80 \text{ Eclipse cycles} = 956,800 + 520 \ (2T) = 957,320$$
$$3,642 \text{ Maya tzolkins} = 957,060 + 260 \ (1T) = 957,320$$

This is an accurate but not too rigid calculation which is supported by many others. Ring numbers define planetary phases for observation, such as the beginning or end of retrograde motion before zero, which have been carried backward from historical observations by the tripod calculation. For this purpose standard multiples, so called, are exact multiples of the Maya tzolkin (260) and haab (364), and also approximate multiples of incommensurate astronomical periods reaching whole-day totals. Neither 4 Ahau nor 12 Lamat strikes an eclipse at Maya zero on the ascending lunar node placed at Aldebaran, our Eye of the Bull. In the Dresden Codex the following ring numbers are before zero except the first, which refers to the moon.

THE LUNAR BASE, MAYA ZERO, AND RING NUMBERS BEFORE ZERO

1 plus	8 days	12 Lamat	Eclipse calendar
2 exact	0	4 Ahau	Integration at zero
3 minus	17	13 Akbal	Venus and Jupiter
4 "	30	13 Oc	Mercury
5 "	86	9 Ix	Mercury
6 "	121	13 Cauac	Saturn (Venus, Mars in conj.)
7 "	208	4 Eb	Jupiter, Venus
8 "	235	5 Chicchan	Venus, Mars, and Jupiter*
9 "	251	13 Muluc	Saturn calendar, Part 1
10 "	352	3 Lamat	Jupiter calendar, see 235*
11 "	456	3 Kan	Mercury-Venus combination
12 "	511	13 Muluc	Saturn calendar, Part 2
13 "	606	9 Ix	Venus, Jupiter
14 "	1,646	9 Ix	Saturn
15 "	2,200	1 Ahau	Venus, Mars in conj.; Venus calendar
16 "	51,419	13 Imix	Mercury, Mars, Jupiter, Saturn

* Explanations are passed over except for noting that Jupiter, Mars, and Venus are joined with great accuracy through a combination of ring numbers 235 and 352. Robert Willson, Harvard astronomer, was first to suggest the possibility of before-zero epochs in planetary calculations of the Maya. He did not know where zero was, but thought the 3-Lamat table referred to Mars, with which it does start even. The distance number 1,486,980 is very close to 3,600 Jupiter revolutions in a calendarial continuity. Mars is short in timing, the difference being made up when -352 is construed with -235, putting Mars and Venus together at observable phases before zero. $1,435,980 - 117$ gives 1,435,863 days, and comparing 2,459 Venus synodical and 1,841 Mars synodical gives 1,435,862.5 and 1,435,862.2 days. This should serve as a grateful tribute to the first astronomer to study Maya records dealing with the heavens.

The construction of the distance numbers which are associated with ring numbers commonly exhibits a relationship to 260, 364, 720, and 1,820 as standard multiples, with added incommensurate meanings for treatment by the tripod calculation. The Maya use designated days and numbers instead of a serial counting of periods. The advantage of this association is that the variable places of the planets are assignable by a concurrent calculation. Presumably, the Maya formed their planetary overcycles directly on their ephemeris instead of by multiplying fractional mean values. Their method is obviously older than the integration of 58 A.D. for Maya zero. In the first special case the base used is the benchmark date, or Throughway Station, II, C, December 11, 580 B.C. This was a mass conjunction of planets.

PRINCIPAL STANDARD MULTIPLES

Where Found	Title	Numbers	T(260)	ZY(364)	T3(780)	T7(1,820)
Copan,	Sp.	364,000	1,400	1,000		200
		1,820	7	5		1
Altars H' and I'		365,820	1,407	1,005	468	201
Dresden Codex 70	A	1,201,200	4,620	3,300	1,540	660
63	B	1,234,220	4,747			
31	C	1,268,540	4,879	3,485		697
62	D	1,272,544		3,496		
62	E	1,272,921				
	F	1,274,000	4,900	3,500		700
45	G	1,274,240				
58	H	1,278,368		3,512		
45	I	1,278,420	4,917		1,639	
58	J	1,386,580	5,333			
58	K	1,386,840	5,334	3,810	1,778	762
	L	1,394,120	5,362	3,830		766
	M	1,395,160	5,566			
	N	1,426,360	5,486			
	O	1,426,620	5,487		1,829	
43	P	1,435,980	5,523	3,945	1,841	789
20	Q	1,437,020	5,527			

Several examples beyond Q are much more difficult, since they apply to the Serpent Numbers. The special example is on Altars H' and I' at Copan and the others in the Dresden Codex. E and G are connected indirectly with F.

Saturn, directly behind the sun at Maya zero, is concerned in seven different ring numbers and several standard multiples. These ring numbers of Saturn emphasize its conjunction with the sun at Maya zero:

0	Conjunction with the sun
−17	Disappearance before conjunction
−121	End of retrograde motion
−251	Beginning of retrograde motion
−511	End of retrograde motion
−1,646	Conjunction with the sun
−51,419	Conjunction with the sun

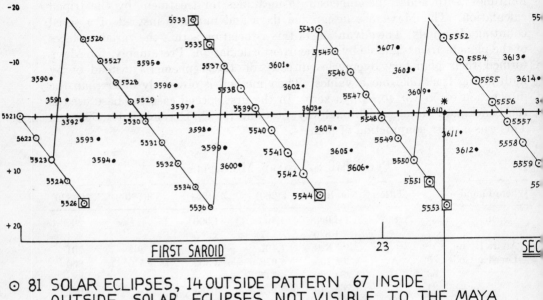

FIRST SAROID   23   SEC

⊙ 81 SOLAR ECLIPSES, 14 OUTSIDE PATTERN 67 INSIDE
 OUTSIDE SOLAR ECLIPSES NOT VISIBLE TO THE MAYA
 ECLIPSE NUMBERS ARE THOSE OF OPPOLZER'S CANON

53 LUNAR ECLIPSES COVER LIST

 IN ECLIPSELESS LANES ARE PICTURED "FATALITIES"

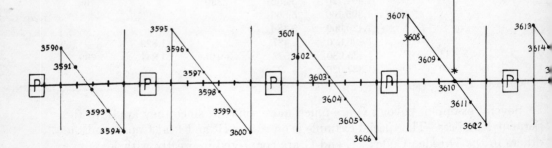

RESTATEMENT OF LUNAR CALENDAR SHOWING THE "PICTUR
LAMAT TABLE BEGINS BEST FROM OPPOLZER LUNAR ECLIP

2128692, GREG. CAL. JAN. 23, 1116 A.D.   ALL ECLIPSES

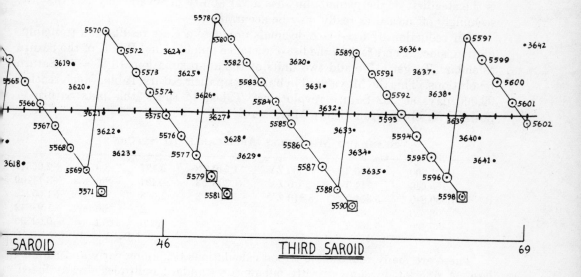

SAROID   46   THIRD SAROID   69

SCALE:

VERTICAL   1 inch   10 DAYS
HORIZONTAL 9/10 ll. of inch = 520 DAYS = 3 ECLIPSE SEASONS

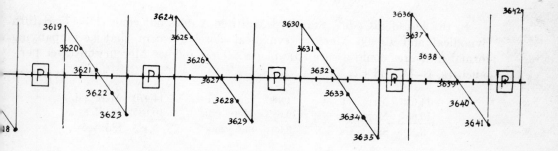

NO-ECLIPSE LANES OF 11, 12 and 23 LUNATIONS   THE 12th
10 OR 2600 DAYS LATER FROM ECLIPSE 3627

These must be judged dynamically, not statically. An exploratory method devised by Ludendorff uses A and A' indices which need not be exact. Saturn is the steadiest of the planets, but has a variability of several days, so that the seemingly off measures really may be accurate.

Our reduction by five-place decimals produces a close result open to manipulation, since A here is A in the list of distance numbers and B is K of the Saturn calendar. To get C we add two units of the approximation, 16 T = 11 Saturn revolutions. This the Maya used in building up their Saturn Table, which reaches 99,060 days as 262 Saturn revolutions. Taken 14 times, this puts Saturn in position for observation before Maya zero.

Standard Multiples Applicable to Saturn

A	1,201,200	4,620 T	3,300 ZY	1,540 T3	3,177	Sat. syn. +2.06547
	185,640	714 T	510 ZY	238 T3	491	Sat. syn. −3.11799
B	1,386,840	5,334 T	3,810 ZY	1,778 T3	3,668	Sat. syn. +1.05252
	8,320	32 T			22	Sat. syn. −1.97842
C	1,395,160	5,366 T			3,690	Sat. syn. −0.92590

There are many remarkable tripod calculations beginning early and running late. A fine lot develops directly out of the standard multiples already listed, as it reaches the environs of Maya zero and points for planetary observation which carry forward. Mostly these are found in connection with calendarial tables, but the tablets of the three related Palenque temples of the Sun, the Cross, and the Foliated Cross furnish fine examples. Mars, with its variabilities, is always difficult, but the Temple of the Sun gives us a very good tripod:

1,781	Mars syn. rev.	1,389,066.0
2,022	Mars sid. rev.	1,389,072.2
3,803	Sid. years	1,389,069.9

In the Dresden Codex, Standard Multiple A does not concern 3,177 Saturn Synodical and 10,366 Mercury synodical closely, except that accompanying formal measures could assure true places. Then follows Mercury in three periodicities, B, D, and E:

14,030	Merc. sid.		14,466	Merc. sid.		14,470	Merc. sid.
10,651	Merc. syn.		10,982	Merc. syn.		10,985	Merc. syn.
3,379	Sid. years		3,384	Sid. years		3,485	Sid. years

But wait—that last number is for Venus, too:

5,665	Venus sid.
2,180	Venus syn.
3,485	Sid. years

An extra word or two about this case. Ring number 456 and day 3 Kan are associated with 1,272,921 days. This is 13 days in excess of 3,494 ZY and therefore does not qualify as a normal standard multiple. But it does qualify as a double tripod for Mercury and Venus with its take-off well placed for effective observation. The distance number is 3 days short of 3,485 sidereal years, and 5 and 7 days more than an approximate common multiple of two kinds of Mercury revolutions, sidereal and synodic; also it is 9 and 25 days less than a common multiple of the comparable Venus rounds. This is certainly near for a double incommensurate adjustment. We think of two tripods which support the level rooftree of a house.

Things become really close, moving in on 3,500 sidereal years, a round number. E is irregular, as is G, the next to function (but both are important), and the numerical axis we call F is 1,774,000 = 4,900 tzolkin = 3,500 haab = 700 common multiples between. Then come H and I, in which 3,500 sidereal years are straddled by a Mercury combination on one side and a Jupiter combination on the other.

$$H \quad 1,278,368 = 3,512 \text{ haab} \quad - 29 \text{ days} = 3,500 \text{ sid. years}$$
$$52$$
$$I \quad 1,278,420 = 4,717 \text{ tzolkin} + 23 \text{ days} = 3,500 \text{ sid. years}$$

Written another way:

14,532	Merc. sid.	3,205	Jup. syn.
11,032	Merc. syn.	295	Jup. sid.
3,500	Sid. years	3,500	Sid. years

To be sure, none of these are perfectly carpentered mortise joints. The Maya had a living subject (as they saw it), and one mends a table leg differently from the leg of something living.

Standard Multiple J is joined with K in the Saturn Table, the separation being a single tzolkin, which also applies 39,780 days later in N and O, as follows:

$$J \quad 1,386,580 + 39,780 = N \quad 1,426,360$$
$$260 \qquad\qquad\qquad 260$$
$$K \quad 1,386,840 + 39,780 = O \quad 1,426,620$$

These numbers are counted from bases 251 and 511 days before zero when Saturn is at stationary points, with Mercury also at an observable phase in one case. The result is four historic dates in the 13-Muluc table of special closeness as regards Saturn, but also concerning Mercury and with statements which involve the Serpent Numbers in ways that call for explorations.

The 3-Lamat table of Jupiter has already received some attention. As P with 1,435,980, it is the last perfect example of the Standard Multiple device. It should be apparent that the Maya knew their astronomy.

Both Saturn and Jupiter had their movements calendarized in whole-day patterns of 378 and 399 days, respectively, then skillfully rectified for long-time accuracy. In connection with the calendars are tables of working numbers used in constructing intervals between phenomena. The average man may wonder why the Maya worked so hard on things unconnected with the practicalities of life. Originally, they may have been interested in controlling weather. Later they realized that knowledge is power and that the man capable of foretelling celestial events must be feared and respected. Living in difficult terrain, the Maya became a cultured people who developed some of the world's most important food, plants, fibers, and medicines. But without skill and organization the Maya would have been a have-not people. Small population is found today in the rainfall regions where their largest cities were located.

The rise of Maya theocrats, on compelling evidence, dates from the Station III of the Maya Throughway, but that was not the last station. Very shortly after 58 A.D. we have good evidence of several calculations which carry lunar precisions back to Maya zero. These old anchor dates are joined with much later ones in the Eclipse Table of the Dresden Codex to define factors important in eclipse calculations.

The tripodal calculations on Jupiter are most remarkable, with betterments which imply dynamic comprehension only possible at long intervals because of the wide difference between the synodical and sidereal periods of the planet. The following statement concerns three problems. First is the calendarial one, which produces 3,600 Jupiter revolutions divisible in whole days down to its sixtieth part, where the whole error of two and one-half days becomes negligible in its usable fraction. The second calculation equates the real and calendarial lengths of the Jupiter revolution. The third presents a tripodal calculation. The Maya used whole-day periods, which check the calculation by 5-place decimals for 200 A.D.

A	1,435,980 days	= 3,600 Jupiter syn. rev.	− 2.50800 days
B	1,371,600	= 3,437 Jupiter Calendar	+237.00000
		= 3,438 Jupiter syn. rev.	+236.70486
			.29514
C[1]	1,096,134	= 3,001 Sid. years	+.33630
		= 2,748 Jupiter syn.	+.68556
		235 Jupiter sid.	− 11.24976

Nowhere else in the world before 1750 A.D. would it be possible to find three calculations on Jupiter, or any other planet, running over three millennia and tailored to such perfect chronological fits as these three Maya statements. How did they do it? By playing knowledge against knowledge, one must suppose.

MAN AND DYNAMICS

Man's problems, even before he became conscious of them, were those which we group together as engineering, which, for me at least, means ultimate utility. For this he had fitted himself by successive generalizations brought about by changes in environment. As an animal he shared increasingly in the betterments of higher evolution as regards organs of awareness. His most important lift was that to arboreal life, which made him a primate with freedom of motion and growth of mind power. On his way he used natural forces, daring even to invade air and water, although normally terrestrial. His first tools were static, but he himself, as their operator, was dynamic. That means he recognized change of place and difference of time as essential somethings which must be co-ordinated. The things he sought gradually took the comprehensive form we call expression. In this, force directed against substance with a purpose needs time, which requires society to be a going concern. He found that nature made suggestions and responded in its make-up to innate qualities of energy and resistance. Man

---

[1] This is not the closest betterment on Jupiter. A preceding combination is 1,459 sid. years = 1,336 Jupiter syn. = 123 Jupiter sid., with a scope of less than two days.

learned to imitate. He learned to apply the free dynamics of air, water, and fire to move boats, turn wheels, and heat furnaces. Without some driving energy, boats, wheels, and ovens are as static in their nature as the stone tools through which man had learned to apply the energy of his own muscles, building up the strength of those muscles by digestive conversion of food. Man is a motor that runs on food as fuel.

As culture advanced, man tamed his food and harnessed natural energy without loss. A creative restoration was effected, offsetting impairment. Later, and this is still the case, the reservoirs of natural conservation were attacked and adversely dissipated. Depletion caused the fall of Rome in spite of every human instinct for frugality. Was the Roman fallacy of time largely to blame?

Throughout all matter runs creative growth, plus noncreative division and multiplication, even before life begins. What Archimedes idealized was balance— a two-armed lever of equal parts, each holding evenly against the other. But time is movement which breaks that balance in escapements, as the clock ticks. The mechanical problem of eliminating time as a factor of existence was beyond the Greek and Roman mind, for the simple reason that such logic is not the entire truth.

Archimedes was a dominant person at a crucial time in Old World history. There is no denying his greatness. He restored, it is said, the correct order of celestial bodies as farthest from the earth, arriving at Saturn, Jupiter, Mars, sun, Mercury, Venus, moon. On this order the naming of our weekdays depends, in an Egyptian permutation of seven bodies and twenty-four hours, as a correct, and Mayalike, chronocracy. That has been Europe's only dependable time-marker, surviving all intercalations and excisions. Pythagoras had been correct in the first place, working through harmonics with his music of the spheres. Heraclides of Pontus, Pytheas of Massilia, Aristarchus of Samos, Eratosthenes of Alexandria, and several other creative thinkers had been equally on the right track when the didactic injunction of Archimedes prevailed in the Greek court of public opinion. Practical philosophy took the easy, wasteful way, and imaginative metaphysics was cast into the outer darkness. There the stars insisted on telling another story, which only great artists could envision.

The fallacy of time, the Greco-Roman elimination of time as a factor in actual existence, is the cruelest untruth that plagues the world today. We cannot even discuss it in the armored resistances of our own cultural tradition. However, the true relationship is demonstrable in the Central American record, first, in the Maya achievement of space-time science; second, in the opposite destructive policy as developed by Ihuitemal-Tezcatlipoca. That frustrated emperor, like another Caesar, became the Aztec god of war. But first he was merely a nativist Toltec feeling chagrin in the presence of an artful civilization.

The syllogism which summarizes the fallacy of time may sound foolish, yet the error involved is of transcendental importance. It runs as follows: (1) *What we bought yesterday we eat today.* (2) *Yesterday we bought raw meat.* Conclusion: *We eat raw meat today.* The error, of course, is that something happened between 1 and 2: the propositions moved. Seemingly trivial, the fallacy of time denies dynamics, the characteristic of life itself, and enthrones statics, where there is no life. The tremendous application comes in the irresponsibility of sovereignty, of Caesar's ivy crown, where good and bad are at mortal issue.

We have seen, or will see, in the logical Throughway of the Maya, that engagements with celestial timing advance from calligraphic statements, linked to theocratic honors, to enlarging simplicities that seek to plumb both past and future. To a remarkable degree Maya efforts in dynamic calculation succeed as order is disclosed with measurements in definite recapitulations. There were social difficulties. The expansive psychology of tyrannical rulers, degrading all the cosmic powers and privileges bestowed upon them by society, is much the same on the Usumacinta as upon the Nile, the Euphrates, or the Ganges. As for Maya theocrats, it is very certain that their cutting down of forests to obtain fuel for reducing limestone to lime in their building operations was a factor in economic deterioration and the wide collapse of theocracy. Slowly the Maya citizenry rebuilt their commonwealth, retaining art and science, but eliminating ostentation.

The great contribution of the ancient Maya is mathematically controlled chronology which plainly registers dynamics. Owing to a faulty conception of time, the Greeks and Romans had no science of dynamics, as David Ray recognized in his *History of Mechanics*. The consequences of this deficiency go much deeper than most persons realize; for dynamics is at all times the property of experience, since forces operate as time passes. Therefore, logic which avoids the actuality of change is dead logic, although it enters into all sorts of modern deductions.

If life on earth is the single diffusion that the photosynthesis of plants suggests, then there is a progressive mating which combines inheritance, plus an infertile and unprogressive lack of mating which multiplies by the division of an original body followed by the enlargement of each fraction. The present threefold organization of life on earth certainly is very old, yet only plants can live on inorganic substances and even they need chlorophyll, an organic catalyst. With it they react, in proper light and temperature, on water and carbon dioxide to make starch as food for other living bodies. But carbon itself is accepted as organic in origin, so where does the beginning lie? The products of life are tremendously diversified on the earth, and the elementary substances are widely identified within the universe. What we see of affinity and repulsion in chemistry is not a display of temperament. It must be the opposition of active and inactive, of positive and negative, of living and dead, which may be significant from first to last. There is change and nonchange, affinity and repulsion; and apparently there are two sorts of continuity, the first progressive, matching experience in space and time, the second unprogressive, or at least unchanging, which multiplies itself by division. Evolution is mostly creative, a survival of adjusted forms, and lack of evolution leads to nonsurvival. Let modern business consider wisely whether cheap manufacture and quick replacement are valid.

Timeless assumptions are our inheritance from classical philosophy, and we often call them abstractions. The duality of light and dark, of positive and negative, of artful and artless, of ecstatic and static, of gravitational and inertial, are aspects of the antithesis of life and death. The creative impulse requires time and naturally leads to better things, to new growths that repair losses, a truth that is eminently applicable to civilizations. Societies, if they do not live conservatively, consume themselves and pass away. The archaeologist studies the bleached bones of dead illusions and wisely tries to reassemble the objectivity, re-create the subjectivity, and report on failures for all present meanings.

THE MAYA THROUGHWAY

The Throughway began, as I have tried to explain, in a project to find what time means and how time operates in nature. The method was the simple one of counting and naming the smallest overt unit of time and catching the recurrences of its larger ones. In modern terms, Station I was a synchronization, using the night-day unit to find a rule for eclipses. Or Station I might be called the Hub by a reconnaissance engineer, after he had got his bearing and found true north.

Station II was a benchmark. Five small planets, wanderers, came together in the morning twilight to hang like a drooping string of pearls before the sun which was rising to erase them. Benchmarks fix knowledge as points of reference.

I remember when, as a boy on a Northern Pacific Railroad survey of Hell's Canyon of the Snake River, I was chosen to be stake man and drove a cedar plug from which the transit man and leveler could make departure. It was where the Salmon joins the Snake in Idaho canyons that I wrote, upon that cedar stake, "Line A, Station 0." Then the chain men started out to measure and the topographer to map surroundings. Heavenly lights and earthly standards were necessary to the pathfinder of railroads (though that one was never built). Without them most persons in a wilderness might get lost, especially in daytime.

At Station III, the Maya raised their rooftree to the top of heaven, as we have considered. At Station IV, new knowledge came and with it simplification, for simplification is the best artistry and tends to become the embodiment of perfection. The last station on the Maya Throughway registered, in a way, human limitation at the margin of cultivation as minds groped for new starts in growing competition. But Station V, with its Astronomical Congress and its Serpent Numbers, was not really termination.

For those who have a true conception of perfection, the best progress is that which leads to a broadening simplification. The streamlining of a thought, a social purpose, or a harmonic score is like the streamlining of a tool or a ship. It is furtherance of a good design, asking economy of material and fidelity of production—something very different, indeed, from our endless multiplications of modern waste.

When the Maya reached an expression of primary integration at Station III of their Throughway, the social management we call theocracy took over. That is, leadership and followership joined forces in the spring tide of success to incorporate a gain in nationalism in spite of urban government.

The establishment of Baktun 9, 8 Ahau 13 Ceh, February 11, 176 A.D., as a new base for counting, to be written simply as Tun 8 Ahau, Katun 8 Ahau, etc., made the system of the Ukahlay Tunob, Katunob, ultimately inevitable. The recapitulation in astronomy between the old Baktun 13 point of time of Maya zero and the new Baktun 9 point of time was remarkably close. It brought back Mars and Saturn into conjunction at Alpha Tauri and reached other important conformities. It proved that the heavens keep an orderly procedure in spite of multiple systems of change.

IV. The Era of the Sacred Fire: Dynamic Simplification

October 14, 3373 B.C. + 1,286,000 days = Feb. 11, 176 A.D.

	Latitude	Longitude	Latitude	Longitude
Aldebaran	355°.4	−5°.6	44°.3	−5°.6
Mars	200°.1	0°.2	48°.7	+1°.7
Saturn	200°.4	1°.8	49°.0	−1°.7

In other words, there is much more here than measurement by a static rule of three. Instead, we get an actual dynamic correspondence so close as to establish, not an abstraction, but a universalization that accepts continued growths and vital changes within the scope of space, yet keeps the stride of time. This, I insist, was the Maya contribution with the ethical conclusion: if there be order in the affairs of heaven, there should be order in the affairs of men.

The Codex Peresianus, even in its ruinous condition, is an invaluable document, perhaps belonging to an early stage of scientific recovery under the Maya Renaissance. Its Ukahlay sequence occupies one side of the folded manuscript, except that one page is missing. The tun Ahaus are presented in the middle of an upper zone A, between gods and animals seated on tun glyphs. They run along the manuscript from left to right, with coefficients which decrease by fours toward the right and by sixes vertically. There may have been another row at the top, but nothing remains legible. As it stands, the two sequences of tuns construct a katun by overlapping.

The more important zone B of the Ukahlay sequence shows Ahaus which decrease by twos, with large blocks of explanatory glyphs containing some short dates. Standing gods present offerings to other gods seated on celestial thrones. A bird flutters between the two divinities.

The organization of the Ukahlay statement in relation to the initial-series statement is as follows:

	Initial-Series Statement	Greg. Date	Ukahlay Statement
A	9– 0–0–0–0, 8 Ahau 13 Ceh	Feb. 11, 176	Tun 8 Ahau, Katun 8 Ahau
B	9–13–0–0–0, 8 Ahau 13 Uo	May 19, 432	Tun 8 Ahau, Katun 8 Ahau
C	10– 6–0–0–0, 8 Ahau 8 Yax	Aug. 25, 688	Tun 8 Ahau, Katun 8 Ahau
D	10–19–0–0–0, 8 Ahau 8 Cumhu	Dec. 1, 944	Tun 8 Ahau, Katun 8 Ahau
E	11–12–0–0–0, 8 Ahau 3 Mol	Mar. 9, 1201	Tun 8 Ahau, Katun 8 Ahau
F	12– 5–0–0–0, 8 Ahau 3 Pax	Jun. 15, 1457	Tun 8 Ahau, Katun 8 Ahau

This organization is purely cyclic, with the emphasis put on tuns instead of on quarter-katuns and katuns. The day-naming tzolkin doubtless carried most of the burden of timekeeping, with calendar years available after 580 B.C. in the formal round of $73 \times 260 = 52 \times 365 = 18,960$ days, of separate designation. Years were never numbered serially, although they were capable of being grouped by thirteens. Thus the Ukahlay system took over as a cyclic mechanism, without our device for sequence. Indeed, seriation was not used by the Maya except in the case of tuns, where it was inherent in the name. The Ahau-Imix combination linked cyclic and ordinal counting of this people from first to last, under both democratic and theocratic governments. Specific dates were possible at any time by day, name, and month position within designated time blocks, such as tuns and katuns. Obviously, day names alone were sufficient for many purposes. For instance, birthday celebrations were clocked 260 days apart. I have never thought it likely that the Maya calendar was ever used as a gambling setup, with luck or mere chance unmitigated by a scientific probability. When the Toltecs and the Aztecs came along, they contaminated the problems of repetition in nature with the fallacy of time. This departure from security was not permanent; the correct procedure was recovered under the enlightened leadership of Nezualcoyotl of Texcoco.

The Ukahlay statement operates as a plaiting machine, a ribbon loom, to produce patterns of threaded time in relation to recurring events. Indeed, the flat braid is the very symbol of the theocrat. When the astronomers met at Copan on September 2, 503 A.D., to consider their great date, each wore upon his breast a beaded breastplate, tied at the top with serpents and with a dangling fringe. If we analyze the patterns produced by regarding time as a string of beads, variegated in color, according to recurrence of events, we are surprised at the many designs produced. The loom frame may have a vertical warp, prepared with double strands into which the weft is caught, then turned back, when the proper width is reached. This gives a plain and sturdy record of astronomical happenings as registered in cyclic counting.

The three Maya codices give us many tzolkin tables with different spacing and syncopations. These divide the 260 tzolkin, or some multiple of it, into halves, fourths, fifths, or tenths, and the marked string passes over and under to be caught again. The many zero signs used by the Maya are generally a planetary subject, giving results in the final patterns—not only the plain weaving, but diagonal arrangements, too. In the Codex Peresianus, the thirteen animal constellations of the zodiac are manipulated on the interplay of 13 and 28, providing 364 days, which are taken five times to get the least common multiple of 5, 7, and 13; or of 7 tzolkin and 5 haab, which is 1,820. Only here the count is from 12 Lamat, just eight days after Maya zero, and concerns the constellation of the Plumed Serpent, whose eye is Aldebaran. In other words, the pattern represents a real engagement; and while 364 is 1.25634 days less the sidereal year, the advancing pattern synchronizes approximately, with the residual error carried forward even though the sidereal year slowly changes in secular pulsation.

The Ukahlay permutations relate such cycles, in long runs of countertiming, to check the pulse rates of reality. The named days have true places restorable at any time in the tzolkin, the calendar round, and the counted time blocks which the tun produces. If one accepts the primitive idea that nature lives—"as far as our Earth Mother's breathing reaches," say the Tewa—then the Ukahlay is a cardiograph.

That is only true, of course, where living sequences are intact. The arithmetical processes of these Indians, besides adding and subtracting where the intervals connect events, also rectify all differences between the actual and the schematic at the point of time where formality and reality synchronize. Not safely to bridge the vital differences which separate statistics from dynamics is to fall into a bottomless pit—the Roman fallacy of time.

V. THE ASTRONOMICAL CONGRESS AND THE SERPENT NUMBERS

Baktun 9 as the New Era of the Sacred Fire was established on our February 11, 176 A.D., with initial series already in use for about 118 years. Stela 10 at Tikal put down 1,841,639,800 days, presumably resting on 9–3–6–2–0, 5 Ahau 8 Pax, which turns out to be our April 10, 241 A.D. This time rocket shot into the past had science behind it, and the manner in which it is written is the first example of Maya enumeration extended beyond the Maya zero point of time. The text, as it stands, is incomplete, but Morley, who studied it carefully in 1915, presents good arguments for it. It does not violate the conditions of Goodman's Grand Cycles 53 and 54, the latter being Maya zero, but incorporates them as part of an overriding vigesimal system, as follows:

1–11–18– 7–0–0–0–0	4 Ahau 8 Zotz
13–0–0–0–0	(add)
1–11–19– 0–0–0–0–0	4 Ahau 8 Cumhu, Maya zero
9–3–6–2–0	(add)
1–11–19– 9–3–6–2–0	5 Ahau 8 Pax

Morley's logic is good, but the place for the Maya zero was then unknown. However, vigesimal place values in extended series were already known in the Dresden Codex and in other inscriptions. Especially, there were Serpent Numbers written in six-place values and attached to a calendar round 9 Kan 12 Lamat, which Morley decided might be identified historically as initial series 9–15–9–9–4, 9 Kan 12 Kayab, historical position then unknown. It was recognized as the key date of the Serpent Numbers. When 6,768 days were added, this resulted in a first real interval from a shadowy backstage of 652 calendar rounds, or 4–4–18–15–15–0 in vigesimal statement. The other Serpent Numbers fitted into a series of ending dates. As now correlated these run forward from March 7, 481 A.D., one of four terminal points on the tropical standard of the Maya Year Dial. Basic 9 Kan 12 Kayab is disclosed among dates which concern the Astronomical Congress at Copan.

9–15–8–10–12	2 Eb 0 Pop,	Apr. 9, 480 A.D.
7–10		
9–15–9– 0– 2	9 Ik 10 Mol,	Sept. 6, 480
9– 2		
9–15–9–9– 4	9 Kan 12 Kayab, Mar. 7, 481	
1–13		
9–15–9–10–17	3 Caban 0 Pop,	Apr. 9, 481
1–2–13– 0		
9–16–12–5–17	6 Caban 10 Mol, Sept. 2, 503	

This 9 Kan 12 Kayab is placed as a cosmic take-off place between two 0 Pop or New Year's statements for "counting Pop in order," an idea which is repeated in later chronicles. The 9 Ik 10 Mol date is a "diamond-ring" phenomenon, a lunar eclipse with Jupiter in opposition close beside the moon. September 2, 503 A.D., is the date of the Astronomical Congress at Copan. The problem then was, apparently, that of two-way alignments or reciprocities across the universe.

The Serpent Numbers of the Dresden Codex

This tabulation begins with a starred number in six-place values, which is the 652nd multiple of the calendar round; when 6,768 days are added, we get the number which begins the lettered series. My system ties in with statements of both Beyer and Thompson in general, while agreeing with Morley's original arrangement. It has, in addition, historical engagements.

	A. Beyer			B. Thompson	
	(1–11–15) 3–16–14–11–4 4– 6–11–10– 7–2	9 Kan 12 Kayab		(1–12–16) 3–16–14–11–4 4– 6–11–10– 7–2	
	(1–11–19) 10– 8– 5– 0–6	3 Cimi 14 Kayab		(1–13– 0) 10– 8– 5– 0–6	

C. Spinden

*	4–4–18–15–15– 0 = 12,374,960 = 18–14– 8 = 6,768 =	9–15– 9– 9– 4 18–14– 8	9 Kan	12 Kayab,	Mar. 7, 481 A.D.	
A	4–5–19–13–12– 8 = 12,381,728 = 1– 0– 2–13 = 7,253 =	9–16– 8– 5–12 1– 0– 3–13	4 Eb	3 Chen,	Sept. 17, 499 A.D.	
B	4–6– 0–13–15– 1 = 12,388,981 = 6–16– 9 = 2,489 =	9–17– 8– 9– 5 6–16– 9	3 Chicchan	18 Xul,	Jul. 26, 519 A.D.	
C	4–6– 1– 0–13–10 = 12,391,470 = 9– 1–10 = 3,270 =	9–17–15– 6–14 9– 1–10	9 Ix	12 Zip,	May 1, 526 A.D.	
D	4–6– 1– 9–15– 0 = 12,394,740 = 1– 8– 0 = 520 =	9–18– 4– 8– 4 1– 8– 0	3 Kan	17 Uo,	May 4, 535 A.D.	
E	4–6– 1–11– 5– 0 = 12,395,260 = 6– 0–17–10 = 43,550 =	9–18– 5–16– 4 6– 0–17–10	3 Kan	12 Yax,	Oct. 7, 536 A.D.	
F	4–6– 7–12– 4–10 = 12,438,810 = 2– 3– 8– 9 = 15,649 =	10– 4– 6–15–14 2– 3– 8– 9	3 Ix	7 Pax,	Dec. 30, 659 A.D.	
G	4–6– 9–15–12–19 = 12,454,459 = 15– 2 = 302 =	10– 6–10– 6– 3 15– 2	13 Akbal	1 Kankin,	Nov. 4, 698 A.D.	
H	4–6– 9–16–10– 1 = 12,454,761 = 1–13–15– 1 = 9,181 =	10– 6–11– 3– 5 1–13–15– 1	3 Chicchan	18 Yax,	Apr. 8, 699 A.D.	
I	4–6–11–10– 7– 2 = 12,466,942 = 3– 0–13–19 = 21,879 =	10– 8– 5– 0– 6 3– 0–13–19	3 Cimi	14 Kayab,	Dec. 18, 733 A.D.	
J	4–6–14–11– 3– 1 = 12,488,821 =	10–11– 5–14– 5	3 Chicchan	13 Pax,	Dec. 5, 792 A.D.	

Even without the cosmic placement for the Serpent Numbers and the now-recognized fact that they furnish terminal dates in historical time, Hans Ludendorff was able to show that some of them were remarkable as mere intervals. Using 365.2423 and 365.2526 as values for the tropical and sidereal years, he tested three numbers, which turned out to be:

33,900 tropical years at the given values less 0.0004
34,100   "   "   "   "   "   "   "   0.0000
34,055 sidereal years at the given values plus 0.0001

Moreover, the first brought in the synodical period of all the planets except Mars, and the second had Mars as well. The third combined the synodical and sidereal periods of Jupiter and Mercury and, less accurately, those for the other planets. It seems the astronomer was looking for a master number which would simplify the universe. He was working with reciprocal alignments.

While no examples of Maya writing antedate 58 A.D., the record of eclipses of reference in supplementary-series calculations comes out exactly in more than 180 cases. All the Maya priest did was start with a registered eclipse and carry forward with a generally true factor of anticipation, then prophesy a coming event. That was first done, it seems, on Stela 18 at Uaxactun. The round number in the already-established day count from Maya zero led to our April 5, 97 A.D., and the event, a lunar eclipse, came as scheduled on April 13, eight days later. In other words, the controlling facts were ancient, the applications new—dangerous, too, if a mistake were made.

Presumably, the Maya had business counting before astronomical counting; that, is the bak of 400 things was older than the tun of 360 days, older also than the haab or rain counts of 364 and 365. Maya zero fixed counting of tuns serially from a point of time. In fixing zero a convergence of measures was used in the tripod calculation with its dynamic adjustment. That was splendidly validated when Baktun 9 returned an important part of calculated Baktun 13—Saturn and Mars in conjunction at Aldebaran. That compliance suggested a simplified procedure, but 20 is built of 7 and 13 any way you look at it, and initial-series dates are most impressive, as Eric Thompson rightly observes.

Great Maya monuments are generally associated with fine science. I remember the Hieroglyphic Stairway at Naranjo because it was there I found the first Venus hieroglyph in proper contact with its astronomical phenomena in my correlation. Says Hans Ludendorff in one of his last papers: "The chief result of the stairway description at Naranjo is the proof offered that the Maya were well aware of the true lengths of the tropical and sidereal years and combined their knowledge to produce a formal statement counting forward from their zero and striking very close to our determinations." He notes that 3,753 tropical years = 3,743 sidereal years + 3,600 days, which are ten tuns. The reference is concrete:

Date 4, 1,367,154, 13 Ix 12 Zac,   Dec. 4, 370 A.D. (1,370,754.4)
         (+3,600)   (−3,599.8)
Date 7, 1,370,754,   2 Ix 10 Chen, Oct. 12, 380 A.D. (1,367,154.6)

In addition, Date 10, which is 1,274 days less than the last amount, is joined, for it is the amount of 3,752 calendar years (1,359,480). That the Maya knew their astronomy is witnessed in hundreds of concrete statements.

In most astronomical calculations the Maya used the 360-day tun. They were capable of using the 400-day bak instead. Thus $2 \times 160,000 + 1 \times 8,000 = 2$-1-0-0-0 vigesimal $= 2$-5-11-2-0 in the tun scale. Also it is a measure of the sidereal year in connection with Alpha Virginis.

What, in the end, is practicality? If it is not a commonwealth of ideals and enjoyments, but only the business of liquidation, we cannot "trick the arithmetic, too base of leaguing odds." Along with studying the stars, the Maya did not ship out wealth; they grew it and enjoyed it—until the Toltecs and the Spaniards came.

The crux is this in the ancient American philosophy of life. They chose the creative rather than the destructive operations. The answer, they found, was what Benjamin Franklin advises, namely, the economy of time and the furtherance of frugality. Naturally used, time and frugality make for new growth.

It may be difficult to stop a downhill career in mid-flight—but what is at the bottom of the hill? If lack of the time factor in calculation leads to a cancerous multiplication of inertias and anemias, the answer is not further dissipation.

Wholesome strength should be sought, not a vainglory of display that tempts have-nots. Oil, coal, gas, timber, and metals are conservations, limited in available supplies and not to be wasted with impunity. What we destroy today we will not have tomorrow. What we grow today we may eat tomorrow, not raw, however, but dressed and garnished. The great Maya principle was that if there is order in the universe there should be order in the affairs of mankind, since intelligence involves a natural correlation.

How Dynamic Calculation Became Feasible for the Maya

In the attainment of dynamic calculation, Maya procedure was about like this:

1. Gun-sight alignments of earth, moon, and sun developed a two-way reciprocity in phenomena along the ecliptic. This solved for them the problem of solar and lunar eclipses as occurring on one line with the observer in the middle on the earth. With this they saw cyclic completions in registered days. We must think of the ecliptic not as a reverse curve or a celestial circle, but more as a straight line joining all alignments, direct or opposite.

2. In addition, the phenomena of Mercury and Venus in connection with their inferior conjunctions were handled as alignments of earth, planet, and sun on the ecliptic as broadened to include all planetary tracks, with visibility controlled by the eight-day Venus Wicket. In this, conjunctions are halfway between the last view as evening star and the first view as morning star.

3. Also, Mars, Jupiter, and Saturn were treated as in ecliptical alignment. Reciprocity in two observations was a major consideration, doubling opposition of the outer planets before the sun with their solar conjunction behind the sun.

4. Alignments of earth, moon, planet, sun, and fixed stars ran on different schedules. The crossings of the two systems, synodical and sidereal, gave overcycles at approximate synchronizations in the day count.

5. In special tables, such synchronizations were recorded in dynamic fashion by ring numbers and standard multiples which connect historic observations when the projected epochs lie before zero.

Kinds of Ecliptic Alignments Known to the Maya

```
                    Solar Eclipse              Lunar Eclipse
             Earth       Moon        Sun       Earth      Moon
1. Ecliptic ——— ° ——— ° ——— ° ——— ° ——— ° ——— Ecliptic
     Reciprocal eclipses of sun and moon (two events, one line)

             Earth       Venus       Sun       Venus      Earth
2. Ecliptic ——— ° ——— ° ——— ° ——— ° ——— ° ——— Ecliptic
     Inferior conjunctions of Venus in reciprocity (Maya base line)

             Sun         Earth       Moon      Jupiter
3. Ecliptic ——— ° ——— ° ——— ° ——— ° ——— Ecliptic
     Lunar Eclipses; Jupiter in opposition "diamond ring" phenomena, etc.
```

4. The Venus Wicket, an Ecliptical Alignment with Lateral Displacement. The normal, inferior conjunction −4 days = heliacal setting + 4 days = heliacal rising, may be doubled for total variability of five series.

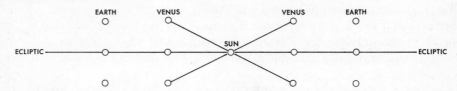

5. Maya-Toltec Year Dial, Group E, Uaxactun, by Huetzin, 1128–1147 A.D. In this the equinoctial and the ecliptic are in dynamic combination. The year dial at Copan was installed December 15, 392 A.D., with Venus and Mercury closely related. Somewhat later at Palenque a corresponding arrangement uses two stars in Gemini and two in Sagittarius to define a corresponding celestial course.

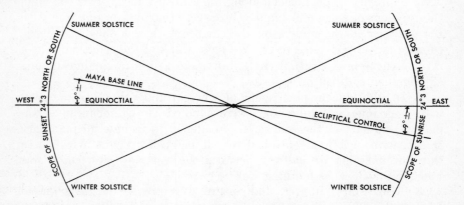

The closeness of trigonal arrangements varies, leading to ascending betterments in selection. With concomitant time scales the great inequalities between synodical and sidereal periodicities, conspicuously for the outer planets, were cleared as regards ambiguity, since true places on each leg of a tripod were approximately recoverable. Nevertheless, and this is most important, the effects of secular pulsations were absorbed in the striding record and were sufficient nearly to lock an interplay of changes.

As handled by the Maya, the tripod calculation allows for progressive changes. The scales of day names and day numbers were fixed; and when five-place decimal means are substituted with compensation, the results are comparable: ours of today and those of the Maya six centuries after Christ. Nevertheless, our decimal statements really enforce rigidity, and are superstatic. The Maya tuns and tzolkins are rigid time used to measure phenomena that are variable. The effect is final flexibility to replace a rigid bar, with a segment-and-end-cushioned vertebral column. This makes possible an animal-like elasticity in Maya mathematics, not so much arithmetic. In other words, a responsive mechanism is produced such as those in natural function.

PICTURING THE ECLIPTIC

Perception is merely seeing; apperception is seeing and understanding. An induction originates perhaps in an inspired guess which leads to an investigation for the purpose of establishing reliability. Let me take an extreme case. We can really see the ecliptic as a gossamer shimmer up and down the sky on favorable nights when that line is nearly vertical to the horizon.

The faint apparition of "zodiacal light" is pictured in the Mixtec codices as a dangling spider road down which the God of Venus walks. In one representation a celestial house is pictured; the ecliptic is here a spider thread ending in a spider. Along its course one clearly sees the sun borne by a·deer, the moon by an agouti, and the planet Venus is a jade or turquoise jewel. This representation is in keeping with sinuous, two-headed forms on sixth-century lintels at Yaxchilan, which rest across the laps of male or female theocrats. Presumably, the sinuosity is explained by the circumstance that the several planets do not hold to the central line of the zodiac, nor do the great stars with which they are conjoined occur exactly on the central line. As this conception is forwarded in the Codex Peresianus, especially, the rope falls into loops and we recover the principle of binding up time, as in altar bundles at Copan where gods tighten the ropes. Also in the Codex Peresianus, we find an almost complete Maya zodiac, where below the elongated Ecliptic Monster the sun is held in the mouths of 13 animals, while the counting-out pattern is 28 days taken 13 times for 364, and that 5 times for 1,820, which also is 7 tzolkin. The chronology of all this is discussed in another place; its ideology requires further elaboration, which starts with early Maya and ends with Aztec symbolism.

COPAN VERSUS PALENQUE

At Copan we find the physical installation of the Maya Year Dial, with Stelae 10 and 12 defining a line at which sunsets and sunrises are caught on the ecliptic and across the universe. At Palenque the same relationship is established among stars of Sagittarius and Gemini. Close to the Milky Way is Persepe, the Magellanic Cloud. There Mars and Jupiter are recorded in conjunction in the Temple of the Sun. Ludendorff developed much evidence on this celestial counterpart of the terrestrial base line in his last papers, with R. Henseling checking the calculations carefully, yet taking a somewhat different point of view. It seems that Henseling is at all times static, whereas some concept more flexible in its nature is needed.[2]

In general, the proofs are clear enough that the Palenque astronomers favored the sun and that Copan ones favored Venus. Perhaps the change of emphasis was due to the excessive humidity at Palenque, with more sunlight needed, while the reverse was true at Copan. At any rate the suggestion of John E. Teeple that Copan and Palenque destroyed each other in a celestial rivalry may well be true. The top dates at both places are about 530 A.D., or a century before the theocratic collapse. However, the archaeological evidence, especially in architecture, indicates a late reoccupation of Palenque, with the three great temples of the Sun, the Cross, and the Foliated Cross at last rebuilt to house the famous tablets in the most advanced style of the First Empire.

The crucial proofs of this situation at Palenque are seen in the Temple of the Inscriptions, with its narrow chambers and heavy walls, dated about 430 A.D. Its inscribed tablets are not very different as regards hieroglyphic detail from those of the three temples of greatly advanced architecture.

---

[2] But not so irresponsibly dramatic as Muck's use of Henseling's figures in *Atlantis-gefunden*.

Like the slightly more developed Temple of the Beau Relief, the Temple of the Inscriptions had a small chamber below its floor. When the much wider sepulcher was inserted below the temple into the pyramidal base by skillful engineering, it appears that vertical retaining walls first were built in trenches to guard against collapse. Then a new architectural feature, stone struts to support the undervault, was inserted in the rubble and mortar. While the front of the pyramid, indeed, may have been breached till the sacred burial chamber was finished with the sarcophagus in place, it is necessary to understand that this exposure was again sealed and that final exit was through the subterranean chamber of the original building by means of a stairway which ascended from the tomb. The co-operative excavation of this First Empire burial was archaeologically admirable in every way. The amplifying explanation that the theocrat was indeed a master of Mercury depends on the analysis of astronomical dates, while constructural analysis of the Palace Group at Palenque and critical examination of several stone tablets within or outside the sepulcher are corroborative.

The guardian burials of the theocrat's sepulcher at Palenque represent not human sacrifice so much as companionate suicide, and the complex of this tomb is much the same as that of Huetzin Tepeuh at Holmul, presumably supervised by Nacxitl Quetzalcoatl in 1164 A.D.

THE TOLTECS RE-INVENT THE ROMAN FALLACY

We must recognize an important difference between Maya and Toltec reckoning of time. The Maya counted by the method of full zero, naming tuns, katuns, etc., by their last days. The Toltecs, in contrast, had the Roman fallacy which we retain in Christian-era dates, as though a year was complete from its first moment rather than its last. The error accumulates at the rate of each whole unit: one day, one month, one year, one century, one millennium, etc. The implications of calling this the twentieth century are clear enough, but an easy connivance relieves the minds of many persons.

As for the Maya and Toltec divergence in this matter, Quetzalcoatl's ages are Maya baktuns departing from Baktun 7 of his creation. The tiered universe then has seven underlevels and thirteen overlevels, and each baktun submerges a level as new supports are set up for heaven.

Baktun 7	10 Ahau	18 Zac	Aug. 6, 613 B.C.	Creation
Baktun 8	9 Ahau	3 Zip	Nov. 7, 219 B.C.	First Age
Baktun 9	8 Ahau	13 Ceh	Feb. 10, 176 A.D.	Second Age
Baktun 10	7 Ahau	18 Zip	May 17, 570 A.D.	Third Age
Baktun 11	6 Ahau	8 Mac	Aug. 18, 954 A.D.	Fourth Age
Baktun 12	5 Ahau	13 Zotz	Nov. 21, 1358 A.D.	Fifth Age
Baktun 13	4 Ahau	3 Kankin	Feb. 23, 1753 A.D.	Sixth Age

The above arrangement is chronologically valid in every Maya way, but the Toltecs of Ihuitemal-Tezcatlipoca set up a deceptive substitute for Quetzalcoatl's arrangement, counting from zero (Baktun 13) as a quantity, not a cyclic point of time.

Baktun 13	4 Ahau	8 Cumhu	Oct. 14, 3373 B.C.
7 baktuns			
Baktun 7	10 Ahau	18 Zac	Aug. 6, 613 B.C.
6 baktuns			
Baktun 13	4 Ahau	3 Kankin	Feb. 23, 1753 A.D.
7 baktuns			
Baktun 7	10 Ahau	13 Yaxkin	Dec. 17, 4512 A.D.

The Toltec Era places a year, 1 Knife, just 1,781 tropical years after the first Baktun 7, which means that August 6, 1168, should be taken as an anniversary of August 6, 613 B.C. The Itza branch of the Toltecs used 52-year calendar rounds as substitutes for baktuns, producing the following false relation:

Quetzalcoatl			Tezcatlipoca
Baktun 13	0	Oct. 14, 3373 B.C.	13 × 52 = 676 years
7 baktuns	1,008,000	Aug. 6, 613 B.C.	7 × 52 = 364
6 baktuns	1,872,000	Feb. 23, 1758 A.D.	6 × 52 = 312
7 baktuns	2,880,000	Dec. 17, 4512 A.D.	13 × 52 = 676

Maude Makemson has shown that the distorted historical material of the Itza Toltecs departs from a Katun 5 Ahau, named from the forward end, and the data on the death of Tezozomoc in the Codex Xolotl disclose the same reinvention of the Roman fallacy of time.

THE ROMAN FALLACY IN ITZA-TOLTEC DATES

When we speak of *now* we count cyclically, and correctly, only hours, minutes, and seconds on our watches; and incorrectly, the growing matter of days, months, years, centuries, and millennia. Our calendarial error piles up terrifically, by the amount of each ascending unit, when we start from one each time instead of the fullness of a cyclic zero with ascending day, month, year, century, millennium, etc. On the face of it, for example, January 19, 1956, is a day off, then a month off, a year off, a century off, and a millennium off. Ordinary chronologers pay no more attention to the deficit spending of natural time than ordinary economists and politicians pay to the deficit spending of natural resources. It is only a paper transaction, so many economists seem to think, yet a day of reckoning must come, as the Romans found when nature foreclosed on their empire. Science should know truth without condoning error, even though frankness may not be popular.

We obtain reality for Tezozomoc's cremation as having taken place on June 10, 1427 A.D., and a new line on Mexican dates of the Itza-Toltec school, by reduction to Maya cyclic reckoning. The better way had reached the Valley of Mexico in the Xiu-Toltec reckoning of Nacxitl Quetzalcoatl, probably through the older Uto-Aztecan immigrants called the Teochichimecs.

	12–3–0– 0– 0	12 Ahau	18 Yaxkin	Jan. 11, 1418 N.S.
	9–11–13			
13 Reed	12–3–9–11–13	13 Ben	6 Muan	June 6, 1427
1 Jaguar		1 Ix	7 Muan	June 7
2 Eagle		2 Men	8 Muan	June 8
3 Vulture		3 Cib	9 Muan	June 9
4 Movement	12–3–9–11–17	4 Caban	10 Muan	June 10

First let us note, for what it may be worth, that 13 Reed is the date at the top of the Aztec Calendar Stone, and 4 Olin is the date in its central part belonging to the Earthquake Sun. Previous suns or world destructions also have day signs, with the number 4 within the projections of the Olin symbol.

The ages of Quetzalcoatl are Maya baktuns correctly counted from Baktun 7 as his creation and point of stabilization for time levels in a space-time continuum. Baktun 7 was invented in A.D. 58 as Midsummer Day, along with Maya zero. But the original dynamic handling rests on astronomical synchronization for names and numbers with the day count in the eighth century B.C., long preceding Baktun 7 in historic time. The final integration which Maya zero represents was delayed till October 14, 58 A.D. The basic organization for sun, earth, and moon was then a space-time formula. The first Baktun 7 was zero pictun and the second was one pictun. It is apparent from the Serpent Numbers that this high date did not end the planets, let alone the stars. The picture is given of water that rises in each world level till one heaven after another founders. After each catastrophe the world trees are set up under a new heaven with a diminished totality of duration.

OLD AND NEW WORLD ASTRONOMY

The fact that overcycles were recognized in Babylonia and especially in Assyria, as Agnes Clerke demonstrated in the fourteenth edition of the *Britannica*, does not mean a very clear differentiation of sidereal and tropical years in every case. In Egypt the mathematics is most like the Maya and chronologies may be exactly correlated. There is the simple proviso: Sothis or Sirius rose sidereally and the Nile flooded tropically.

Egypt	1,459 Sothic years	= 1,460 calendar years	= 532,900 days
	48	48	17,520 days
Maya	1,507 Tropical years	= 1,508 calendar years	= 550,420 days

This is the grand calendar round of the Maya. Also the Maya, between eclipses, used what corresponds to the Egyptian lunar cycle of 25 calendar years. Eclipses were ignored in the Nile unless, indeed, they destroyed dynasties. The Egyptian 360-day period was divided differently from the Maya tun, but as employed in chronology should make a cyclic correlation possible. There was sabotage by the Decree of Canopus, of course.

The Assyrian evidence is easily correlated and with the overcycles can be treated in the manner of Maya tripods. The significance is not social contact but simply that human intelligence is no respecter of hemispheres when the same problem is written in the sky.

"The Babylonian computers," said Agnes Clerke, "were not only aware that Venus returns in almost exactly eight years to a given starting point in the sky, but they had established similar relationships in 46, 59, 79 and 83 years severally for Mercury, Saturn, Mars and Jupiter. They were accordingly able to fix in advance the approximate positions with reference to ecliptical stars which served as fiduciary points for their determinations." Her data are completed as follows:

	Sidereal Year		Sidereal Period		Synodic Period
Mercury	*46	=	191	−	145
Venus	* 8	=	13	−	5
Mars	*79	=	42	+	37
Jupiter	*83	=	7	+	76
Saturn	*59	=	2	+	57

In whole-day flexibility, the Mercury betterments effect the first item, which is F. The 13-year Mercury overcycle is E, while higher Maya ones are not represented in Old World records to the best of my belief.

	Tripodal Betterments for Mercury				
	Mercury Rev.	Sidereal Days	Mercury Rev.	Synodic Days	Sidereal Year Rev.	Days
A	4	352	3	348	1	365
B	21	1847	16	1854	5	1826
C	25	2199	19	2202	6	2192
D	29	2551	22	2549	7	2557
E	54	4750	41	4751	13	4748
F	191	16802	145	16802	46	16802
*	573	50406	435	50407	138	50405

At Palenque, 50,407 marks the disintegration of this betterment from 9–11–0–0–0, 12 Ahau 8 Ceh, Dec. 15, 392 A.D. The Maya Year Dial marks that focus of Venus and Mercury events. A difference of methods used at Palenque and Copan comes down to statistics vs. dynamics. War and mutual destructions of their cities took place between 530 and 540 A.D. Feudal dictation then lasted till 629, when theocracy was overthrown. Palenque was rebuilt at the end as a shrine, as sun worship continued to ally itself with war.

Zodiacs are different in the eastern and western hemispheres, and the Old World failed in the rectification of calendars so beautifully demonstrated in America. The Maya Zodiac has 13 divisions which combine 12 synodic with 13 sidereal months, and then the sidereal year with both by calendarial rectification. The Old World has cycles but not cyclic counting, and the zeros of India and Arabia are empty rather than replete. The definitive proof of hemispheric independence is the fact that domesticated plants, as the basis of higher civilizations, are in independent series in the New and Old Worlds.

A Maya Toltec myth of the Xiu tradition emphasizes Baktun 7 as the creation, although it is not the first Maya date. In this connection, there is a clear association of space and time on ascending planes when the statement is made that "Uuc Yabnal, he who fertilizes the maize seven times, came forth from the seventh angle of heaven and earth to fecundate the Earth Crocodile."

Nevertheless, it appears that mankind emerged from a tiered underworld in a northern lake. The Toltec obtained this idea somewhere in the Great Basin, most probably a desiccated region of Arizona or New Mexico where maize had long been cultivated. Although the tiered universe and color symbolism of the world quarters is common to both the Old World and the New, the idea of the

Earth Navel is Uto-Aztec in the south, perhaps Chichimec. In the north it exists among the Pueblo tribes. In the Valley of Mexico the place called Tlalxico, near Chalco, means the Earth Navel and is described as a place of underworld origin. But this is the familiar Shipapu or Xipapu of the Pueblo tribes. The Earth's Black Navel Hole of the Tano is described as an underground lake. It was the drying up of terminal lakes in Southwest basins which made the Uto-Aztec tribes move south seeking a haven for dust-bowl farmers.

WHENCE THE TOLTECS?

The Toltecs arrived from the north as the second of three Uto-Aztecan migration streams roughly two centuries apart: Olmec, Toltec, and Chichimec, in the tenth, twelfth, and fourteenth centuries of our era. The Olmec group followed down the eastern sierra and met the Maya in southern Vera Cruz and Tabasco. They took up the cultivation of wild fig trees and produced rubber, taking the name of that substance for their own designation. These Rubber People revived the importance of elastic gum commercially and in connection with a ceremonial game of the ancient Maya. For them, rubber had been a by-product of paper for books, which before the time of Christ was introduced deeply into South America. A great stone drum at Copan, associated with a significant date of the sixth century before Christ, is the counterpart of signal drums, now used in the Amazon Valley and still beaten with rubber-tipped sticks, as is also the Aztec teponaztli. Various rubbers were developed from Paraguay to Arizona.

The Uto-Aztecs, and perhaps the Otomi as well, originated as a cultural people in the bolsons of northern Mexico and the Great Basin farther north. It seems probable that they had developed around terminal lakes an original form of chinampa, or swamp-utilization agriculture, like that so beautifully illustrated today at Xochimilco. Maize probably originated on the Guatemalan highlands, its cultivation spreading north and south over them. Underflow irrigation as well as the more usual ditch irrigation were intensified by the Toltecs in the Valley of Mexico. There are many indications pointing to this conclusion. The origin of swamp-utilization agriculture needs a fresh and thorough investigation.

The first Archaic culture probably spread very widely after a beginning in the second, perhaps the third, millennium before Christ. Teotihuacan was an ancient center of farmers when the Toltecs arrived about 1090 A.D.

The Toltec succession of emperors, who first of all conquered the Maya, is now safely dated. The Toltecs coming from the Mapimi basin were already well acquainted with agriculture. In a few years after 1090 they had become a populous group capable of raiding wealthy neighbors. They had no horses like the Mongols, but they moved fast. It may be that the Olmec first disturbed the tranquillity of the Maya Renaissance, leading to the protective Second Theocracy of the Maya in Yucatan; they were conquered by the Toltecs about 150 years later. Chichen was founded in connection with Baktun 11 (964 A.D.).

The great trouble with lake-basin and river-delta archaeology is that human evidence gets covered up as erosion increases. If the farmer cannot hold the soil, he loses his fields. That obviously happened in the Valley of Mexico, since bare hillsides, deep lakeside deltas, and laminated beds of clay in settling basins yield Archaic figurines, broken, rolled, and often solidified by impregnation. First called the "type of the little hills" and explained as examples of agricultural magic, these were typed stratigraphically for historical succession.

The lesson of their deposition was neglected in the static view. Yet ecological change as a spur to correction engages man's best intelligence. Human aggravations doubtless contributed to the aggressive deteriorations of climate, with plants and animals more deeply sensitive than many like to think. Glacial liquidation produced an overabundance of great lakes which dried up slowly in a general upland dessication since man's arrival. Large basins without river exit developed terminal lakes or sinks, many of which are in evidence up and down the American cordilleras. One importance of these is seen in natural gardens as focal points of settlement and the amelioration and domestication of plants. Abundant natural gardens, as in Nez Percé territory, where camass meadows abound and other food plants are plentiful, may even hold back final agriculture, since seasonal hunting and fishing were preferred for men as women foraged. Also the former string of lake basins along the cordillera must be held important in connection with the natural spread of plants. Sea-bird routes explain the spread of Nicotiana, for instance, a genus with a tropical nonoccurrence zone but close affiliation from Chile to Alaska.

Maize, as a cultivated grass, is as important in the basic Maya problem as is bamboo, with its usable sections, in ceramic origins of the wet lowlands. Maize may be of highland Guatemalan origin, spreading far to the north and perhaps the south either naturally or under early human guidance. Natural gardens within the tropics supplied gourd containers on the highlands and squash foods, along with beans, peppers, and numerous seeds, roots, and greens, with good sorts soon reduced to domestication and social transfer.

While pottery of the lagenaria-gourd school may be early in arid parts of both Peru and Central America, its association with maize appears much earlier in the northern than in the southern arid focus. Its essential breakdown into a two-season crop, one at each end of the dry season, is suggested by a Maya transfer into intermediate territory as regards elevation and humidity for the Copan, Honduras, and Tikal, Guatemala, centers of later Maya theocracy, both resting on reserve food supply. Generalized climatically by the two-crop method, maize appears to have spread rapidly under domestication into both arid and humid parts of South America and the West Indies, as well as into the Mississippi Valley up to the St. Lawrence. It combined in South America with swamp crops such as manioc. Between 752 B.C. and 58 A.D. lies the great civilizing experience of the Maya. Unfortunately, the grandiose and partly destructive developments of their later theocracy receive more attention than seems fitting. The theocratic breakdown in 630 A.D. took place after inscribed monuments had reached the riverheads on the Mexican-Guatemalan frontier, and in the subsequent Maya Renaissance there was a creative democracy on the balcony above the Usumacinta.

Teocinte, then, is probably a highland Guatemalan development that assumed importance after the Toltec conquerors arrived with Mixcoatl, who put his camp at Alotenango, back of Volcan de Agua. He ruled for about fifteen years as the first Toltec emperor out of Teotihuacan, ending in 1127, when Huetzin-Totepeuh became the second emperor.

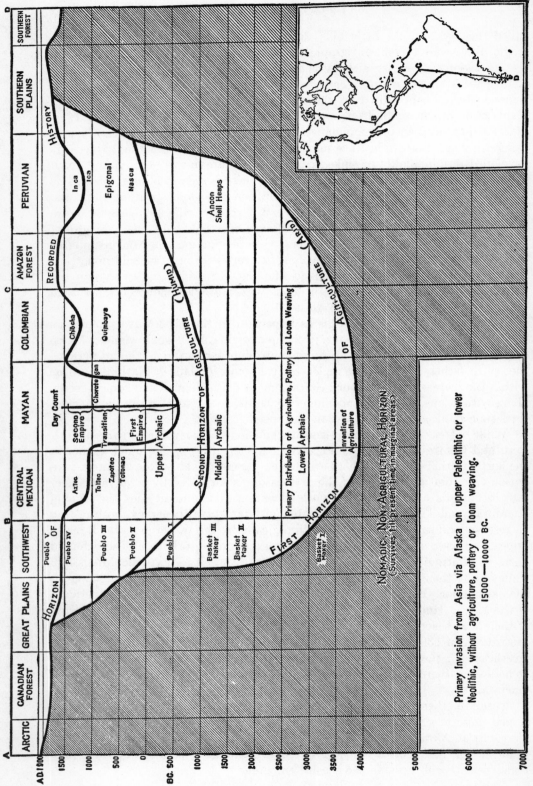

Diagram of American Chronology

PLATES
PART II

[a]

[b]

Plate I. (a) Village Scene in Arid Mexico. Cactus and other thorny shrubs are ever present. The houses of the natives are of adobe with thatched roofs. (b) In the Humid Lowlands. The view shows part of the plaza at Quirigua with one of the monuments almost concealed in vegetation of a few months' growth.

[a]

[b]

Plate II. (a) Site of Pueblo Viejo, the First Capital of Guatemala; (b) A Spanish Church at the Village of Camotan on the Road to Copan.

[a]

[b]

Plate III. (a) View of the Island Town of Flores in Lake Peten where the Last Capital of the Itzas was located; (b) The Sacred *Cenote* at Chichen Itza into which Human Beings were thrown as Sacrifices, along with Objects of Jade and Gold.

[a]

[b]

Plate IV. (a) A Guatemalan *huipili* decorated with Highly Conventionalized Animals in Embroidery; (b) Pouches of the Valiente Indians of the Chiriqui Lagoon, Panama.

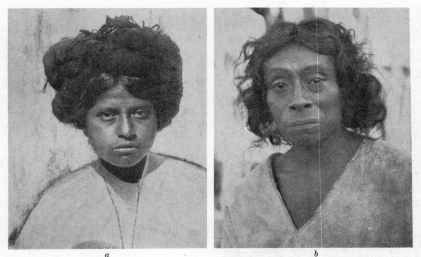

Plate V. (*a*) Zapotecan Girl from the State of Oaxaca, wearing a Turban-Like Headdress made of Yarn; (*b*) Lacandone Man from Southern Mexico. Wavy hair is sometimes seen among the few members of this Mayan tribe.

[*a*]

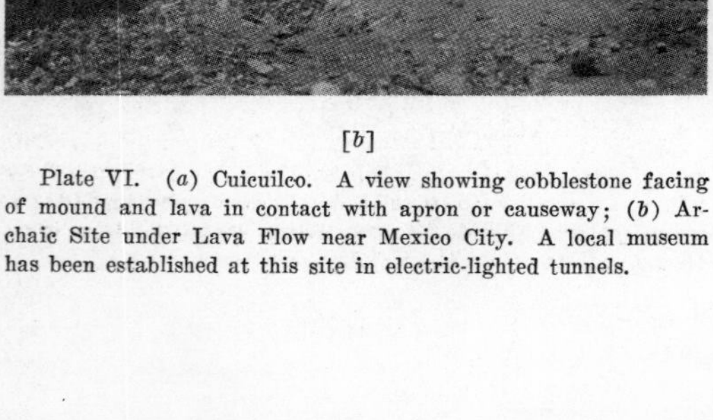

[*b*]

Plate VI. (*a*) Cuicuilco. A view showing cobblestone facing of mound and lava in contact with apron or causeway; (*b*) Archaic Site under Lava Flow near Mexico City. A local museum has been established at this site in electric-lighted tunnels.

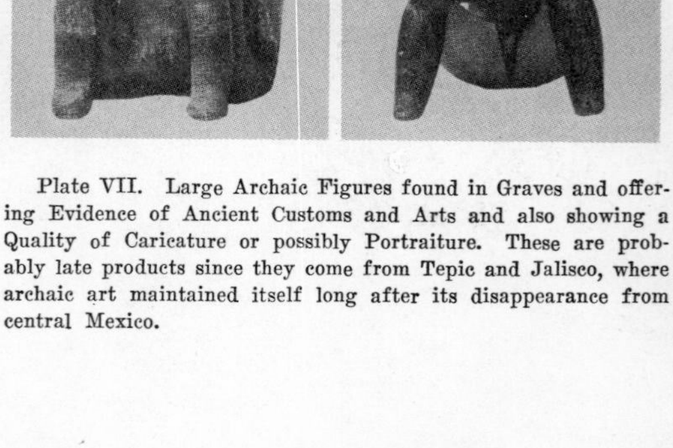

Plate VII. Large Archaic Figures found in Graves and offering Evidence of Ancient Customs and Arts and also showing a Quality of Caricature or possibly Portraiture. These are probably late products since they come from Tepic and Jalisco, where archaic art maintained itself long after its disappearance from central Mexico.

[a]

[b]

Plate VIII. Two Stages in the Stone Sculptures of Costa Rica. Note that in the first series (a) the human body is adapted to the surface of a boulder with the arms, legs, and face in low relief and with eyes, nose, and mouth all protruding, while in the second series (b) the limbs are rounded and partly freed from the body. Both are of archaic type but probably not of great age.

[a]

[b]

Plate IX. (a) Stone Sculptures of the Archaic Period. This resembles the pottery as regards style: the eyes protrude and the limbs are carved in low relief against the body; (b) Typical Site of the Archaic Period. The use of pyramids may have begun towards the end of this period.

[a]

[b]

[c]

[d]

Plate X. Widely Distributed Female Figurines: (a) Nicaragua; (b) Panama; (c) Venezuela; (d) Island of Marajo, Brazil.

Plate XI. Distribution of the Archaic Culture. The areas in solid black show the distribution of figurines of the archaic type; the areas in dots show the probable extension of pottery on the Archaic Horizon; the dotted lines give the ultimate extension of pottery.

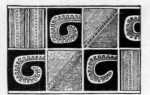

Plate XIII. A General View of the Ceremonial Center of Copan. After a model and drawing by Maudslay. The artificial acropolis with temples on pyramids and with sunken courts is in the foreground and beyond is seen the Great Plaza in which monuments are set up. The Copan River has cut into the side of the acropolis and made a natural cross-section.

Plate XII. Distribution of Agriculture in the New World. The dotted line gives the limits of pottery; solid black, agriculture in arid regions of considerable altitude, mostly with irrigation; dotted areas, agriculture under humid lowland conditions; lined area, agriculture under temperate conditions.

[a]

[b]

Plate XIV. (a) View of the Plaza at Copan from the Northwestern Corner. This view shows the monuments in position and the steps which may have served as seats; (b) View Across the Artificial Acropolis at Copan. A sunken court is shown and the bases of two temple structures of the Sixth Century. Photographs by Peabody Museum Expedition.

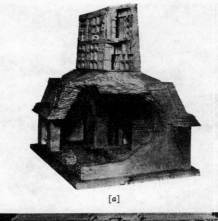

[a]

[b]

Plate XV. (a) Model of the Temple of the Cross, Palenque,
designed to show the Construction. The building has three entrances separated by piers. The middle partition is thickened
to support the weight of the roof comb which is a trellis for
stucco decoration. The sanctuary is a miniature temple in the
inner chamber. The walls are built of slabs of limestone set in
lime cement; (b) Detail of Frieze on the Temple of the Cross.
The upper band is the sky with stars and planets. A reptilian
monster occupies the main panel with human figures as supplementary decorations upon his legs. The Temple of the Cross
represents the highest achievement of the First Empire architects,
Fifth Century after Christ.

Plate XVI. A Temple at Hochob showing Elaborate Façade Decorations in Stucco. Probably ninth
century. The design over the door represents a grotesque front view face of which the eyes can still be
plainly made out. At either side of the door the design represents a serpent head in profile. Photograph by Maler.

Plate XVII. A Sealed Portal Vault in the House of the Governor at Uxmal, a Building of the Second Empire, probably Thirteenth Century. The veneer character of the cut stone comes out clearly. Peabody Museum photograph.

[a]

[b]

Plate XVIII. (a) Realistic Designs on Vases from Chamá, Guatemala, representing the Best Mayan Period in Pottery; (b) The Quetzal as represented on a Painted Cylindrical Vase from Copan. Bands of hieroglyphs are commonly found on Mayan Pottery.

[a]

[b]

Plate XIX. Stela 13, Piedras Negras. This shattered monument is one of the finest examples of Mayan sculpture, showing a fine sense of composition and a considerable knowledge of perspective. Dated March 27, 511 A. D.

Plate XX. (a) Top of Stela 1 at Yaxchilan, dealing with the Heavens. The Sky God is seen in the center with the moon at the left and the sun at the right. Below these is the Two-Headed Dragon bearing planet signs and additional heads of the Sky God; (b) Analogous Detail of Stela 4, Yaxchilan. The moon is at the right and the sun at the left. The figure in the sun is male and that in the moon, female. The faces of the Sky God hang from the lower part of the Two-Headed Dragon, being attached to it by symbols of the planet Venus.

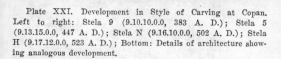

Plate XXI. Development in Style of Carving at Copan. Left to right: Stela 9 (9.10.10.0.0, 383 A. D.); Stela 5 (9.13.15.0.0, 447 A. D.); Stela N (9.16.10.0.0, 502 A. D.); Stela H (9.17.12.0.0, 523 A. D.); Bottom: Details of architecture showing analogous development.

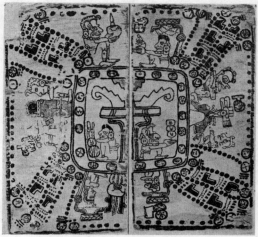

Plate XXII. Scheme of the Mayan Calendar as presented in the Codex Tro-Cortesianus. In the center is Itzamna, the God of the Sky, and his spouse, under what has been called the celestial tree. The band of hieroglyphs that frames in this picture contains the twenty day signs of the Mayan month. The figures on the outside are arranged in four groups, according to the four directions of the compass. At the top or east we again see Itzamna and his mate. In the north, or right hand quarter, human sacrifice is shown and the Death God sits opposite the God of War. In the east and in the south are also shown pairs of divinities. A series of dots running from one day sign to another covers the *tzolkin* or 260 day cycle of names and numbers.

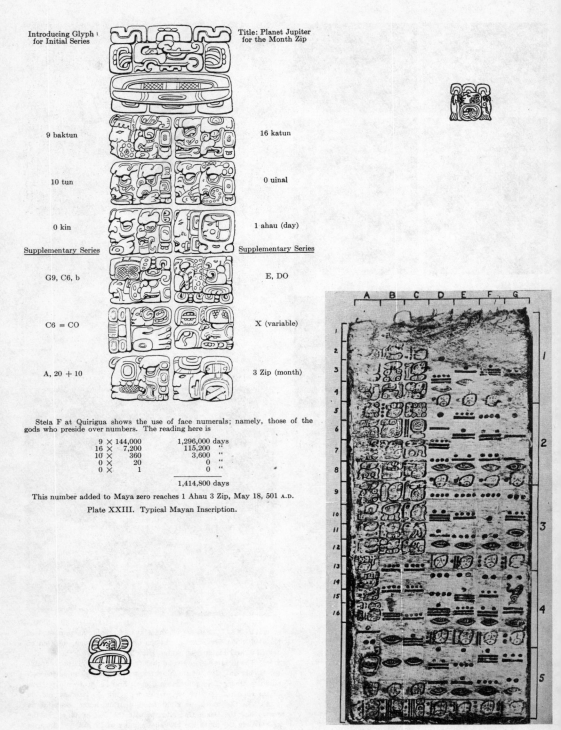

Introducing Glyph for Initial Series		Title: Planet Jupiter for the Month Zip
9 baktun		16 katun
10 tun		0 uinal
0 kin		1 ahau (day)
Supplementary Series		Supplementary Series
G9, C6, b		E, DO
C6 = CO		X (variable)
A, 20 + 10		3 Zip (month)

Stela F at Quirigua shows the use of face numerals; namely, those of the gods who preside over numbers. The reading here is

9	×	144,000	1,296,000	days
16	×	7,200	115,200	"
10	×	360	3,600	"
0	×	20	0	"
0	×	1	0	"

1,414,800 days

This number added to Maya zero reaches 1 Ahau 3 Zip, May 18, 501 A.D.

Plate XXIII. Typical Mayan Inscription.

Plate XXIV. Page 24 Dresden Codex.

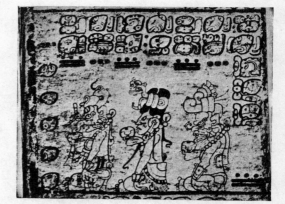

III	1 East	2 *	5 North	6 *	9 West	10 *	13 South
	3 God B	4 †	7 Woman	8 Good Days	11 God G	12 ‡	14 *
	13	III	13	III	13	III	15 God E

1 Akbal				16 Week of 13 days
2 Men	God B—rain and sky god of good powers. Holds Kan (maize) sign in his hand.	Goddess with serpent headdress possibly connected with floods. Holds Kan sign in hand.	God K—benevolent sun god. If space had been larger God E (the maize god) would probably have been drawn next.	17 Ahau
3 Manik				
4 Cauac				13

Plate XXV. (*a*) Detail of the Dresden Codex showing *Tzolkin* used in Divination; (*b*) Analysis of the above *Tzolkin*, according to Förstemann.

Diagram showing partial reduction of Mayan numbers into Arabic numbers in the calculation shown on page 24 of the Dresden Codex (Plate XXIV).

A	B	C	D	E	F	G	
			1	15	10	5	
			1	16	10	5	
Hieroglyphs			14	6	16	8	1
			0	0	0	0	
			1 Ahau	1 Ahau	1 Ahau	1 Ahau	
			1	9	4	1	
			5	11	12	5	
			14	7	8	5	2
			4	0	0	0	
			0				
			1 Ahau	1 Ahau	1 Ahau	1 Ahau	
			4	4	4	3	
			17	9	1	13	
			6	4	2	0	3
			0	0	0	0	
			6 Ahau	11 Ahau	3 Ahau	8 Ahau	
			3	2	2	2	
	9	9	4	16	8	0	
	9	9	16	14	12	10	4
	16	9	0	0	0	0	
			13 Ahau	5 Ahau	10 Ahau	2 Ahau	
6	0	16	1	1			
2	0	0	12	4	16	8	
0			5 [8]	6	4	2	5
			0	0	0	0	
4 Ahau 8 Cumhu	1 Ahau 18 Kayab	1 Ahau 18 Uo	7 Ahau	12 Ahau	4 Ahau	9 Ahau	

Diagram showing complete reduction into Arabic numbers of the calculation shown on page 24 of the Dresden Codex (Plate XXIV).

A	B	C	D	E	F	G	
			151,840	113,880	75,920	37,960	
			1 Ahau	1 Ahau	1 Ahau	1 Ahau	1
	Hieroglyphs		185,120	68,900	33,280	9,100	
			1 Ahau	1 Ahau	1 Ahau	1 Ahau	2
			35,040	32,120	29,200	26,280	
			6 Ahau	11 Ahau	3 Ahau	8 Ahau	3
			23,360	20,440	17,520	14,600	
2,200	1,366,560	1,364,360	13 Ahau	5 Ahau	10 Ahau	2 Ahau	4
4 Ahau 8 Cumhu	1 Ahau 18 Kayab	1 Ahau 18 Uo	11,680	8,760	5,840	2,920	
			7 Ahau	12 Ahau	4 Ahau	9 Ahau	5

Plate XXVI. General View of Monte Alban from the North. The mounds are arranged around courts in an orderly manner.

Plate XXVII. Detail of Monte Alban showing Wall Foundations and Small Cell-like Rooms.

Plate XXVIII. Zapotecan Art: Incense Burners, Funerary Vases of Portrait Type, Cruciform Tomb with Geometric Decoration.

[a]

[b]

Plate XXIX. (a) Stone Sculpture of the Early Zapotecan Period showing Rulers seated upon Thrones before an Altar; (b) Jade Tablets pierced for Suspension, found in Zapotecan Tomb.

Plate XXX. Laughing Head of the Totonacs, remarkable example of Freehand Modeling in Clay. Heads of this type probably
served as decorative details on temple fronts.

Plate XXXI. (a) An Elaborately Carved Stone Collar, an Example of the Best Sculpture
of the Totonacan Indians; (b) A Palmate Stone from the State of Vera Cruz. Two grotesque figures are holding snakes in their mouths.

Plate XXXII. The Temple at Xochicalco before Restoration. The lower part of the picture shows the sculptured base of the temple pyramid. The walls of the temple itself are seen above.

[a]

[a]

[b]

Plate XXXIII. Two Views of the Principal Pyramid in the Citadel at Teotihuacan. (a) General view of the original mass of the pyramid at the back with the reconstructed addition in front. (b) View of stairway and various walls covered up and preserved by the addition.

[b]

Plate XXXIV. (a) Partial View of the Great Pyramid at Cholula which rises from the Level Plain in Three Broad Terraces. A Spanish church has been built upon the top of this pyramid and a roadway leads up the badly eroded mound. (b) A View at La Quemada. Cylindrical columns built up of slabs of stone supported the roofs of some of the structures. The use of columns was characteristic of late Toltecan times.

Plate XXXV. Stone Slab from an Ancient Sepulcher in the State of Guerrero. The face at the top apparently represents a monkey, but serpents have been introduced between the eyes and the eyebrows. The other highly conventionalized faces are probably those of serpents.

[a]   [b]   [c]

Plate XXXVI. (a) Finely Carved Ceremonial Slab found at Mercedes, Costa Rica. The three large figures on the end as well as the smaller ones on the bottom represent crocodiles. Keith Collection; (b) Stone Figure from Costa Rica. This sculpture in lava rock is one of the finest pieces ever discovered in this region. The lines on the body probably represent tattoo marks; (c) Ceremonial Slab decorated with Monkeys. Mercedes, Costa Rica. These ceremonial slabs may be developments of metates or corn grinders. Keith Collection.

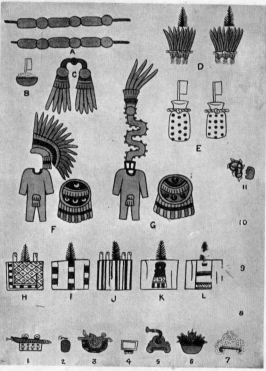

Plate XXXVII. (a) The Gold Work of the Ancient Mexicans excited the Wonder of the Spanish Conquerors. Comparatively few examples, however, have come down to us; (b) Many Ornaments of Gold are found in the Graves of Costa Rica and Panama. The Keith Collection contains a very fine series of these pieces illustrating all the forms as well as the technical processes.

Plate XXXVIII. A Page from the Tribute Roll of Moctezuma, showing the Annual Tribute of the Eleven Towns pictured at the Bottom and Right. The tribute consisted of: (a) Two strings of jade beads; (b) Twenty gourd dishes of gold dust; (c) A royal headdress; (d) Eight hundred bunches of feathers; (e) Forty bags of cochineal dye; (f–g) Warrior's costumes; (h) Four hundred and two blankets of this pattern; (i) Four hundred blankets; (j) Four hundred and four blankets; (k) Four hundred blankets. The towns are: (1) Coaxalahuacan; (2) Texopan; (3) Tamozolapan; (4) Yancuitlan; (5) Tezuzcululan; (6) Nochistlan; (7) Xaltepec; (8) Tamazolan; (9) Mictlan (Mitla); (10) Coaxomulco; (11) Cuicatlan, in the State of Oaxaca.

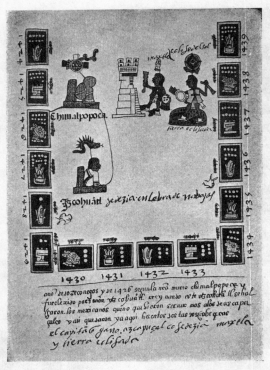

Plate XXXIX. Page from the Codex Telleriano-Remensis showing a Native Manuscript with Explication by the Spaniards. The death of Chimalpopoca and the election of his successor, Itzcouatl, is recorded, as well as the capture of Atzcapotzalco.

Plate XL. Serpent Head at Bottom of Balustrade, Great Pyramid, Mexico City. The same excavations showed that the Great Pyramid was enlarged several times and this sculpture seems to have been buried under the walls long before the coming of the Spaniards. Compare Serpent Balustrade at Chichen Itza.

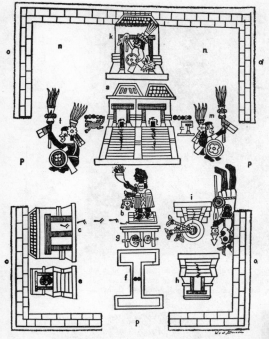

Plate XLI. Sahagun's Plan of the Tecpan in Mexico City. After
Seler. Among the details shown are: (*a*) The two great temples;
(*b*) The *Quauhxicalli* or eagle bowl; (*c*) One of the *Callimecatl*, or
priest houses; (*e*) An eagle house or warriors' shrine; (*f*) The *Te-
otlachtli* or ball court of the gods; (*g*) *Tzompantli* or skull rack;
(*h*) The temple of Xipi; (*i*) The *Temalacatl* or Gladiator Stone;
(*k*) The *Colhuacan Teocalli* or temple of Colhuacan; (*l*–*m*) The
gods 5 Lizard and 5 House respectively; (*n*) Dance courts; (*o*)
Coatenamitl or Serpent Wall, so called because it was decorated
with heads of serpents.

Plate XLII. The Calendar Stone of the Aztecs. This great stone
represents the disk of the sun and the history of the world. It may
be analyzed as follows, reading outward from the center.

Central or cosmogonic portion: The day sign 4 Olin with details
in the arms representing four epochs of the world; with the face of
the sun god in the center and minor hieroglyphs that may represent
the four directions just outside the Olin symbol.

Band of day signs beginning at the top and reading towards
the left.

Bands of conventional rays of the sun and other details such as
the embellishment of the sun with turquoise and eagle feathers.

The outer circle of two great reptiles that may indicate the
universe.

Invisible edge of the disk bears representations of Itzpapalotl,
the obsidian butterfly which is symbolical of the heavens.

Plate XLIII. The Shield Stone at Cuernavaca. This Aztecan sculpture carved upon a boulder in the City of Cuernavaca shows a shield, a bundle of war arrows, and a war banner. The sculpture records the conquest of Cuernavaca or more properly Quauhnahuac, capital of the Tlahuican nation.

Plate XLIV. The newly discovered "National Stone" of Mexico. The front view shows the Calendar Stone in position and the year signs 1 Rabbit and 2 Reed (1506 and 1507 A. D.). The sculpture on the back is an eagle on a cactus, recording the foundation of Mexico City (Tenochtitlan). On all the other surfaces priests and religious symbols are drawn.

Plate XLV. Monstrous Sculpture representing Coatlicue, the Serpent-Skirted Goddess, who was regarded as the Mother of the Gods.

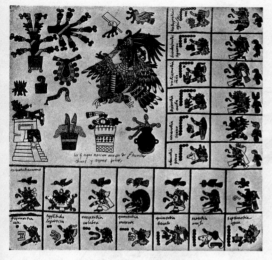

Plate XLVI. Page from the *Tonalamatl* Section of the Codex Borbonicus. The thirteen days run along the bottom of the page and up the right side of the large division. The period covered is one-twentieth of the *Tonalamatl* of 260 days. At the left of each day is seen one of the nine Lords of the Night, so-called, in orderly succession. In the divisions above or to the left of the days are the thirteen gods of the Hours of the Day in connection with the Thirteen Birds. The patron goddess of this division of the *Tonalamatl* is Itzpapalotl, the obsidian butterfly. The other pictures relate mostly to mythological instances and the details of ceremonies. For instance, the broken tree represents Tamoanchan, a legendary site, and the sacrifice of twenty birds is indicated by the flag attached to the bleeding head of a decapitated bird.

[a]

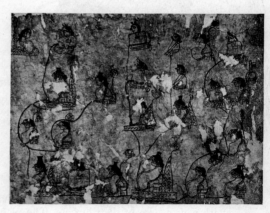

[b]

Plate XLVII. (a) Pictures of Tlaloc, the God of Rain, and of Ehecatl, the God of Winds, in the Codex Magliabecchiano; (b) Mexican Genealogical Table on Bark Paper. The names of most of the individuals are given by hieroglyphs attached to the head or the seat. Original in the American Museum.

PLATE XLVIII

NON-THEOCRATIC ART OF FARMING COMMUNITIES

This starts on an early agricultural horizon and continues till relatively recent times with a vast area of distribution. The plaque with dancing women as a man beats time is in an advanced stage of development, the earlier forms being fetishes of fecundity, dated before the Maya civilization had its start. The other detail shows Olmec laughing faces of Cerro de las Mesas in the State of Vera Cruz and approximately twelfth century A.D. Both men and women are represented as the happy dead.

Plate XLIX

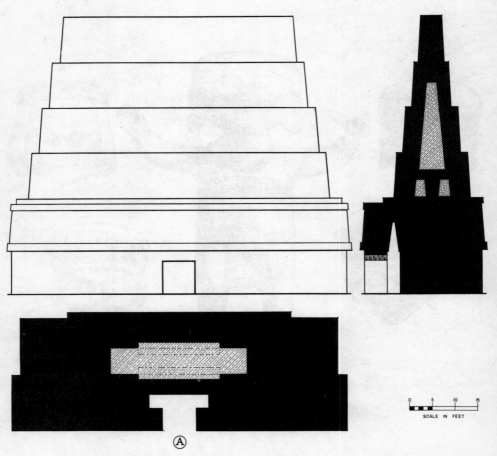

TEMPLE № 5 AT TIKAL

Development of the Maya Temple, as measured by improved handling of structural problems in the order A, B and C. The roof comb is lightened and refined; proportions of room space to wall space are greatly increased. The sanctuary becomes a miniature temple.

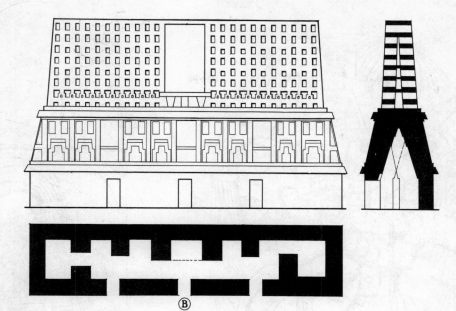

TEMPLE Nº 33 AT YAXCHILAN

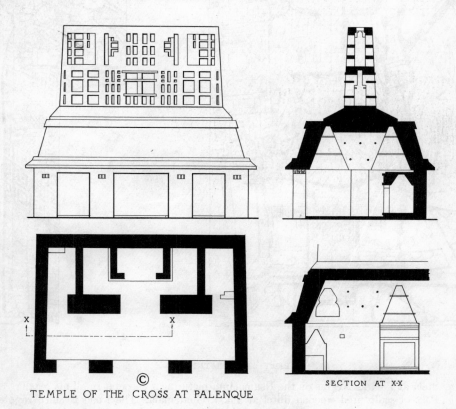

X X

SECTION AT X-X

TEMPLE OF THE CROSS AT PALENQUE

PLATE L

GREAT THEOCRATIC ART

a. Stela at Piedras Negras on the Usumacinta picturing a theocrat in all his regalia.

b. Part of sculptured wooden lintel at Tikal, Guatemala. The wood is chico zapote, which gives us chewing gum, and can be dated by Maya chronology with closely conforming radio-carbon 14 readings.

Plate LI

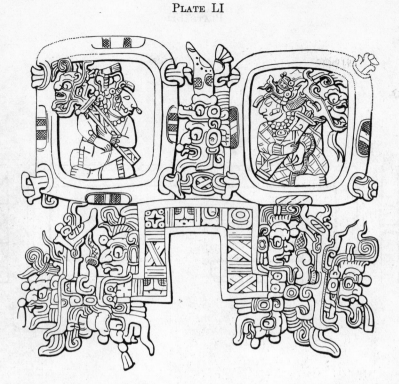

a. The Celestial Canopy, Sun, Jaguar Sky God, and Moon above the Ecliptic.

b. The Ecliptic Strip with spider thread body that moves, for male theocrat.

c. The Ecliptic Strip, for female theocrat.

PLATE LII

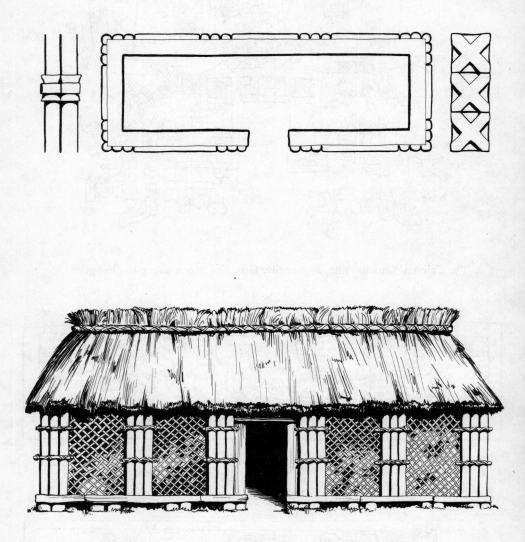

MAYA RENAISSANCE ARCHITECTURE

After the great abandonment of 629 A.D., when theocratic rule collapsed, the Maya turned to wooden architecture of poles and lattice work. The forms are reconstructed from later imitations in stone. The house shown here is based on columns and lattice work in stone buildings of the ninth and tenth centuries.

PLATE LIII

a. Rain mask at Iximche near Hopelchen, Campeche.

b. Jaguar Sun as a Warrior. Dzecab-tun, Campeche.

c. Jaguar Sun as a Warrior. Dzecab-tun, Campeche.

d. Rain mask of Venus at Xkichmul, Campeche.

THE SUN GOD TURNS WARRIOR

The Maya Renaissance buildings of the tenth and eleventh centuries have great decorative masks of both the Serpent Rain God and the Jaguar Sun God specialized as Venus and solar worship, the first in wet country, the second in dry country. With sun worship went head hunting.

PLATE LIV

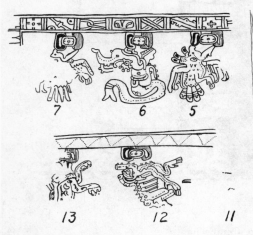
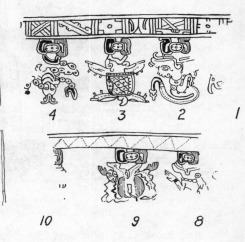

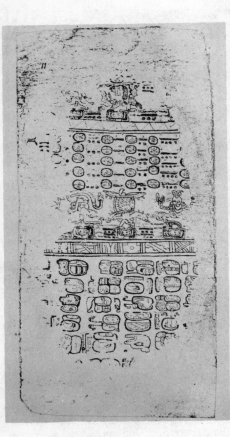
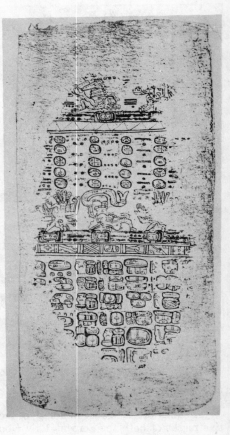

There are thirteen animal constellations in the Maya zodiac holding the sun in their mouths and twelve in the solar zodiac of the Near East, which the Greeks adopted. Originally that began in the fourth millennium before Christ with Taurus the Bull, with Alpha Taurus as the eye of the Bull. This the Arabs renamed Aldebaran. The Maya projection back to their calculated zero made that bright star the eye of the Serpent. They formed two oversized constellations confronting each other, the Jaguar based on the Great Square of Pegasus, with a paw extending across two lesser figures, and the Rattlesnake, based on Taurus, with the Pleiades as the rattle. The spacing is different, with classical Cancer equaling the Scorpion of the Maya, etc.

Our Aries is given as a Waterbird, here mostly erased, while Gemini is well identified as the Maya Turtle Stars, which fell at the summer solstice during the First Empire. Many separate constellations are pictured in the Maya codices. The two that are erased in the Codex Peresianus are Deer and Peccary. On the nunnery at Chichen Itza we have six constellations connected with the sidereal round of Venus, taking only about 225 days.

The five rows of day signs between the upper and lower rows of zodiacal constellations concern a cyclic pattern for handling phenomena in relation to the sidereal year. The zodiacal year, so called, consists of a 364-day period divided into thirteen groups of 28 days each. This period is taken five times in as many rows till 7×260 days combine with 5 times 364, or 1,820 days, for cyclic counting. On this repeating pattern are rectified incommensurate amounts on approximate common multiples, and then re-rectified as residual errors still accumulate. This was effected by attaching the table to Maya zero and a lunar base eight days later, making classical Taurus equal the Maya constellation of the Plumed Serpent.

> A. 4 Ahau 8 Cumhu, Oct. 14, 3373 B.C. Maya zero
> B. 12 Lamat 16 Cumhu, Oct. 22, 3373 B.C. Lunar base

No lunar eclipse then took place, but one did three grand calendar rounds later ($3 \times 1,507$ tropical years = 1,508 calendar years = 4,521 tropical years). This was the eclipse reached in the Dresden Codex which I call Huetzin's Eclipse. Another ordinary eclipse cycle in advance was foretold by Nacxitl Quetzalcoatl. It broke the power of Ihuitemal Tezcatlipoca and permitted the establishment of the League of Mayapan.

> C. 12 Lamat 16 Cumhu Oct. 21, 1148 A.D. (interval 4,521 years)
> D. 12 Lamat 11 Kankin July 20, 1181 A.D. (interval 11,960 days)

The interval from Maya zero to Huetzin's Eclipse corrects the sidereal year for an accumulated error of 1 Tzolkin. The table, operating continuously from Maya zero and 12 Lamat, 8 days later, has correlated the synodic and sidereal places of the planets, the conformity between 12 synodic and 13 sidereal months, and other astronomical differences.

PLATE LV

a. Huetzin's Temple, Chichen Itza, destroyed by Ihuitemal Tezcatlipoca. It was covered up by the latter's Temple of the Warriors. The destruction had followed the murder of this second Emperor of the Toltecs in 1147. He had the help of Maya artists, but invented dance platforms for military societies (the Eagles and the Jaguars especially) which he conceived as orders of knighthood with jade buttons in the nose as the ceremonial accolade. Ihuitemal converted these platforms into places of human sacrifice, where the Maya nobility were victims to honor Toltec men who died in battle and Toltec women who died in childbirth. These all went to dwell within the sun, coming out as demons when the sun was eclipsed This restoration is in the Brooklyn Museum.

TEMPLE OF THE ROYAL SEPULCHRE
DEPT OF PETEN, GUATEMALA
HOLMUL
THIS TEMPLE WAS USED AS A BURIAL PLACE FOR
IMPORTANT PERSONS, MANY PIECES OF BEAUTIFUL POT-
TERY BEING TAKEN FROM ITS SEALED CHAMBER. ALSO
THE ENTIRE EDIFICE WAS ITSELF BURIED UNDER A
MOUND OF EARTH. THE STRUCTURE SHOWS TWO PERI-
ODS OF GROWTH, AND MAY DATE FROM THE FOURTH
... CONSISTS OF GODS

b. The Temple of Reinterment, where Nacxitl Quetzalcoatl in 1164 honored the bones of his father Huetzin, murdered in 1147, is now identified as Holmul, "the hollow mound," in eastern Peten, Guatemala. This royal sepulchre was discovered by Raymond Merwin and Alfred Tozzer in 1910 on a Harvard expedition. For many years a Holmul Pottery Sequence was dilated across many centuries. It now is explained as the operation of a single ceremony. "Companionate suicide" accounts for supplementary guardian sacrifices at doors and under floors, while a bundle of weathered bones occupied the principal chamber without offerings. The pottery resembles closely that made at sites on the Guatemalan Highlands ruled by Huetzin Tepeuh, "the first who ruled with glory" in Quiché and Cakchiquel histories.

Huetzin's great achievement under Maya guidance was the Group E at Uaxactun with his famous dance platform (also buried) as the central feature of an astronomical observatory. The central temple of three in a row furnishes the prototype for the Temple of the Warriors at Chichen, as completed by Nacxitl Quetzalcoatl, and the Temple of the Magician at Uxmal, built to honor Quetzalcoatl.

PLATE LVI

Aftermath of Figurines and Portrait Statues

Clay figurines of the style called Archaic are fetishes emphasizing a psychological association between gravid females and Mother Earth as regards agriculture. They belong to the religion of early farmers over a large part of the New World, being especially common in arid territories where maize is staple. In the Old World a similar association may derive from hunters' magic, since paleolithic statuettes of ivory are found under heaps of animal bones as though to provide for the replenishment of game.

Portrait statues are theocratic among the Maya, representing exanimate rulers. Funeral whistles molded in human form make their appearance on the Usumacinta in the fourth century A.D. and become general during the democratic Maya Renaissance, as major gods are represented in proper person. The Jaguar Sun God takes to the war path, in tenth-century sculptures, while in the Jaina necropolis hundreds of humble dead clutch identifying portrait figurines in their bony fingers. In the old center near Guatemala City the Archaic figurine submits to the lowland Maya style on the Miraflores level but elsewhere survives till blotted out in the Toltec florescence.

Finally come fine portraits and imaginative compositions found in Olmec, Totonac, Toltec, Zapotec, and Chorotega tombs. Examples shown include (a) a bat patron of cylinder painting; (b) two Zapotecan aristocrats in the Royal Ontario Museum; (c) an Olmec jade of Bradley Martin's fine collection; and (d) a Mixtec gold jewel from Tomb 7 at Monte Alban in the national collections of Mexico.

PLATE LVII

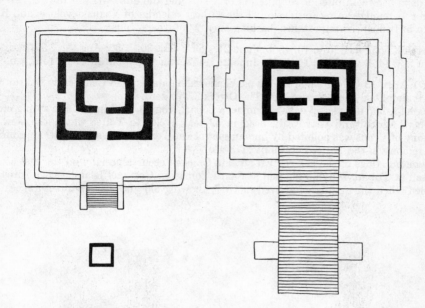

a. Temple with corner masks and low circular tower on roof at San Antonio Muyil, east coast of Yucatan peninsula.

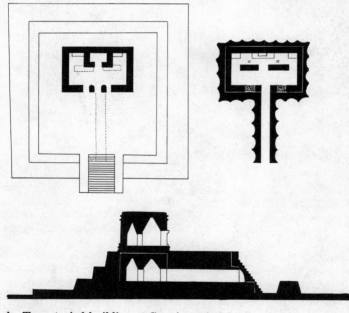

b. Two-storied building at San Antonio Muyil.

THE FINAL MAYA REVIVAL

The fall of Mayapan, Uxmal, and Chichen marks the end of Mexican control over the native Maya at Katun 8 Ahau, 1457 A.D.

The new commonwealth has as its prospectus the dedication tablet of the Temple of the Owls at Chichen reproduced as our frontispiece. This shows the Plumed Serpent as

Venus God benefiting cacao in a rain of jade and shell beads. The round number date is a few days before an inferior conjunction of Venus and the Sun. Within the next 40 years (5 Venus octennials) a recapitulation of the earliest calendar of Venus develops, and Katun 8 Ahau has enhanced importance, harking back 2,008 years, thus:

Apr. 13, 557 B.C. Nov. 16, 556: June 21, 554: Jan. 30, 552: Aug. 31, 551 B.C.
Apr. 13, 1451 A.D. Nov. 16, 1452: June 21, 1452: Jan. 30, 1456: Aug. 31, 1457 A.D.

As for 1 Ahau 13 Ceh, 1 Ahau begins all Venus calendars, and 13 Ceh recalls Baktun 9, on which a simplified chronology rests. The Owl is Maya zero.

April 13, 557 B.C., lets Venus phenomena depart from O Yaxkin and the spring crop of the Maya agricultural year. Advanced in 52-year cycles to Toltec times, the New Fire ceremony of Venus was polluted by human sacrifice as Tezcatlipoca's followers appropriated the ceremony in the Toltec Schism of 1178 A.D.

Stone buildings of the last revival outside Chichen occur especially on the east coast of Yucatan at Tulum, Muyil, etc., and at Santo Tomas on Cozumel Island. These sites were occupied when the Spaniards arrived in 1517, showing old and new architectural features.

PLATE LVIII

Two priests engaged in ritual. Bas-relief at Yaxchilan, where Maya art achieved great heights.

PLATE LIX

a. A Painful Ceremony at Yaxchilan. The woman whose tongue has been pierced has the interlaced year symbol on her headdress; the officiating male holds a bone awl in his hands.

b. Sacrificial Jade in the Codex Vienna. The triangular section taken out of the jade sign may possibly symbolize the cutting out of the heart. The four irregular fragments definitely represent sacrificial breaking of the jade offerings.

PLATE LX

a. The Sun in the Ecliptic. Aztec Carving, Fifteenth Century.

b. The Confraternity of the Eagle and the Jaguar War Societies. Aztec Carving, Fifteenth Century.

PLATE LXI

Bas-relief from Yaxchilan.
The inscription starts from
1 Imix after 13 Ahau 18 Xul.

PLATE LXII

a. Toltec Bat from Acanceh, Yucatan. Among animal motives the bat is important around the world in "decorative art," which is filled with religious meanings. These fall in historical sequences and illustrate cultural divergences and supply important data for the construction of history.

b. Chichimec Sculpture, Guatemala, Jaguar with Cacao Pods attached to the Body. In Peru the same treatment of the Jaguar Sun God is common. There, not cacao but the similarly shaped roots of the jicama, a morning glory now cultivated in Mexico, is represented. In Peru the Sun God is a jaguar who weeps rain, while the Maya gave him a water lily to wear for water. In both regions the sun has a jaguar face and serpent rays.

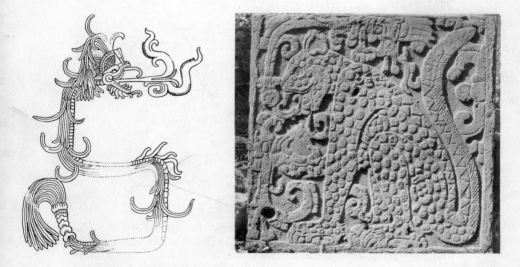

c. The Plumed Serpent, Symbol of Quetzalcoatl-Kukulcan. Chichen Itza.
d. A Jaguar Warrior of the Aztecs. Codex M, about 1300 A.D.

PLATE LXIII

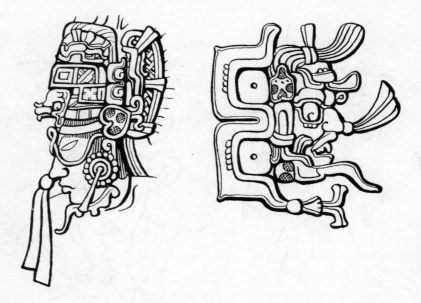

a. and *b.* Maya Carvings of the Head of a Central American Sun God with a Symbol of the Planet Venus attached, showing that the Sculpture marked an Astronomical Event, the Conjunction of the Sun and Venus. The god is frequently represented as a jaguar and when humanized shows jaguar attributes.

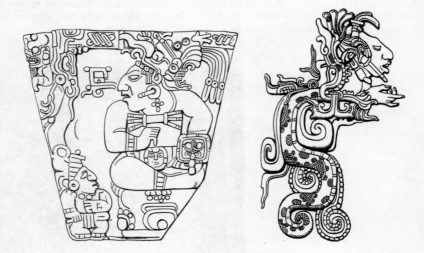

c. Jade Breastplate, carved by a Mayan Artist about 500 A.D. The principal figure, wearing the headdress of the Rain God, is seated on the hieroglyph for the rainy season. Below him is a worshiper, above whom rises a serpent with a grotesque god in its distended mouth.

d. Divine Serpent, Yaxchilan, carved with Figures of Priests on a Broad Stone used as a Lintel.

PLATE LXIV

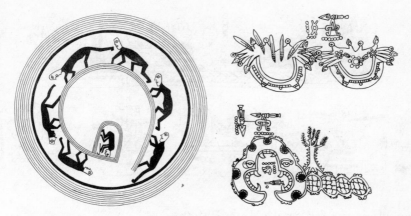

a. Man's Ascent from the Underworld. Design from ancient pottery found in New Mexico. The earth-womb concept of man's origin can be explained as a Uto-Aztec introduction into Middle America, where it combined with the space-time universe of the Maya enriched with color symbolism. Tlalxico, the Earth Navel, is in Lake Chalco, associated with Quetzalcoatl, who made the creation accord with Baktun 7, then invented a Toltec Era with Mexican Year 1 Knife as an anniversary of it. The earth's navel is important in New Mexico and Arizona origin myths. In combination with calendarial birthdays it is emphasized among the Mixtecs and Aztecs. Among the Toltecs, One Reed is the name of Quetzalcoatl as the date of his apotheosis as the Venus God. To satisfy the psychology of the Toltec spirit a fictitious One Reed is the son of Mixcoatl and Chimalman. Ascent from the underworld is not Maya except in the historical space-time sense.

b. Mixtec Place Names, Codex of the Seven Caves. (I) Feather Water; (II) Jade Water; (III) the Seven Caves with date Year 7 Reed, Day 7 Reed. Inside the cave, Day 9 Ebecatl (of Venus God) and Day 1 Reed, also of Venus God. Original MS. in the Royal Ontario Museum, Toronto, Canada.

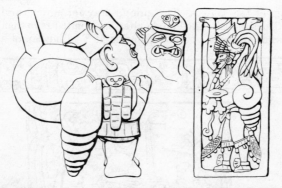

c. The Snail Man, Peru and Mexico. The Snail Man is First Empire Maya. He is Maya Renaissance, too, and Second Empire Maya. Here he is a Peruvian pot on the left with crossed tusks of a jaguar. Also he is Toltec on the right as an Atlantean device in architectural decoration. On the Gila in Arizona we get this motive as lacquer mosaic backing a marcasite mirror. This is artistic diffusion linked to different techniques. Symbolic art, like language, deals with ideas that dominate styles of expression.

PLATE LXV

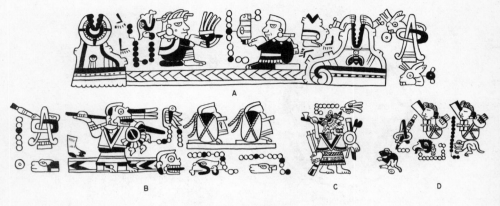

Faces, Places, and Dates make Mixtec History.
a. The Marriage of Twelve Vulture and Twelve Lizard unites Two Cities.
b. Gruesome Woman makes War. (The deerfoot sign is that of Cholula.)
c. and *d.* The Fatal Results of this War are pictured Here. The same historical matter is in two Mixtec codices.

e. Sun Worship of the Toltecs. Two priests pray for agricultural success and scatter water and seeds. The sun disk raised on an altar has pointed rays such as are characteristic of later Mexican solar symbols. A fresco painting at Teotihuacan of about 1200 A.D.

f. Carved Cylindrical Vase, Highlands of Guatemala, Period of the Maya Renaissance. Dwarfs become important after the Maya First Empire.

TABULAR VIEW OF MAYA CHRONOLOGY

ARRANGED BY H. J. SPINDEN

TRADITIONAL HISTORY

FIXED ASTRONOMY

Left scale		Right scale
1700	REDUCTION OF TAYASAL	1700
1600	RECENT	1600
1500	SPANISH CONQUEST / RESETTLEMENTS / THIRD ABANDONMENT	1500
1400	LEAGUE OF MAYAPAN DISSOLVED AFTER 14 KATUNS / TUTUL XIU LEAVES MAYAPAN (CHRONICLE V)	1400
1300	ITZAS ATTACK MAYAPAN WITH FOREIGN HELP	1300
1200	SECOND EMPIRE / ITZAS REGAIN POWER AT MAYAPAN (CHRONICLES I, III) / CHICHEN REDUCED BY QUETZALCOATL (AND TOLTECS)	1200
1100	LEAGUE OF MAYAPAN FOUNDED (LORDS OF CHICHEN ITZA HAD RULED FOR 10 KATUNS)	1100
1000	UXMAL FOUNDED (BY MEXICAN IMMIGRANTS) / CHICHEN REOCCUPIED / SECOND ABANDONMENT	1000
900	CHAKANPUTUN ABANDONED / INTERMEDIATE	900
800	CHAKANPUTUN OCCUPIED	800
700	FIRST ABANDONMENT / CHICHEN ABANDONED (CHRONICLE III) / CHICHEN ABANDONED (CHRONICLES I, II)	700
600		600
500	"POP" SET IN ORDER (ASTRONOMICAL CONGRESS AT COPAN, SEPT. 2, 503) / CHICHEN DISCOVERED	500
400	FIRST EMPIRE	400
300		300
200	ARRIVAL IN CHACNABITON / CHRONICLES BEGIN WITH MYTHOLOGICAL PREAMBLE (TOLTEC ?)	200
100		100
0		0
-100		-100
-200		-200
-300	FORMATIVE PRE-URBAN	-300
-400		-400
-500		-500
-600		-600
-700		-700
-800		-800

FOUR VENUS TABLES

I AHAU 13 MAC CALENDAR — 1227, 1123
I AHAU 18 UO CALENDAR — 1129
I AHAU 3 XUL CALENDAR — 1324
I AHAU 18 KAYAB CALENDAR — 1038, 934

ECLIPSE TABLE

"12 LAMAT" ECLIPSES

CORRELATION A
LAST DATE IN DRESDEN CODEX TIES IN WITH 18 KAYAB CALENDAR DIRECTLY, ALSO WITH 12 LAMAT ECLIPSES.

ASTRONOMICAL DATA IN OLD INSCRIPTIONS
(REACHED BY H. LUDENDORFF WITH CORRELATION A.)

A. ECLIPSES OF SUN AND MOON.

B. CONJUNCTIONS OF VENUS AND SUN, AND HELIACAL RISINGS.

C. SINGLE AND MULTIPLE CONJUNCTIONS OF SATURN, JUPITER, MARS, VENUS AND MERCURY WITH EACH OTHER.

D. CONJUNCTIONS AND OPPOSITIONS OF SATURN, JUPITER, MARS WITH SUN AND MOON.

E. INTERVALS WHICH ARE MULTIPLES OF VARIOUS SIDEREAL AND SYNODICAL REVOLUTIONS OF PLANETS.

F. INTERVALS WHICH CARRY PLANETS BACK TO SAME STAR.

G. INTERVALS WHICH ARE COMMON MULTIPLES OF SIDEREAL AND DRACONIC MONTHS.

H. DATES WHICH REGISTER EQUINOXES AND SOLSTICES.

J. DATES WHICH ARE ANNIVERSARIES (DETERMINANTS) OF OTHERS.

K. EMPHASIS ON DATES WITH MULTIPLE SIGNIFICANCE PROJECTED FAR INTO PAST.

INITIAL SERIES GIVES NUMBER, DAY NAME AND MONTH POSITION CALCULATED FROM ERA.

SUPPLEMENTARY SERIES HAS ACCUMULATED ERROR ON 4400 DAYS = 149 LUNATIONS WITH ORIGINAL ZERO AS FULL MOON.

CYCLIC ECLIPSES CALCULATED ON DOUBLE BASES:
520 DAYS = 3 ECLIPSE SEASONS
4400 DAYS = 149 LUNATIONS

	FORMAL	ACTUAL
HELIACAL RISINGS	18 KAYAB = NOV. 16	18 KAYAB = NOV. 17
	12 YAX = JUNE 23	12 YAX = JUNE 23
	6 ZIP = JAN. 27	9 ZIP = JAN. 30
	5 KANKIN = SEPT. 3	4 KANKIN = SEPT. 2
	19 XUL = APR. 10	2 YAXKIN = APR. 13

536 B.C. — VENUS CALENDAR INAUGURATED, 540 TO 533 B.C.

580 B.C. — MONTHS IN ADJUSTMENT TO SEASONS. 0 POP = WINTER SOLSTICE.

613 B.C. — DAY COUNT INAUGURATED AS 7-0-0-0-0, 10 AHAU 18 ZAC, AUG. 6. MUNDANE ERA 7 BAKTUNS EARLIER—OCT. 14, 3373 B.C., GREG. CAL.

TZOLKIN FORMED ON ECLIPSE DATA BETWEEN 751 AND 613 B.C. (THREE ECLIPSE SEASONS = TWO TZOLKIN)

751 B.C. — TOTAL ECLIPSE OF SUN ON 12 LAMAT 1 MUAN, OTHER 12 LAMAT ECLIPSES.

KATUN — 8 AHAU / 6 / 4 / 2 / 13 / 11 / 9 / 7 / 5 / 3 / 1 / 12 / 10
KATUN — 8

KATUN CYCLE
13 x 7,200 = 93,600 DAYS

5 — 8 AHAU 13 CEH
4 — 8 AHAU 13 CEH
3 — 8 AHAU 13 CEH
2 — 8 AHAU 13 CEH
1 — 8 AHAU 13 CEH

5 CALENDAR ROUNDS
5 x 18,980 = 94,900 DAYS

TABULAR VIEW OF MAYA CHRONOLOGY
ARRANGED BY H. J. SPINDEN

HOW CORRELATIONS AFFECT DATES

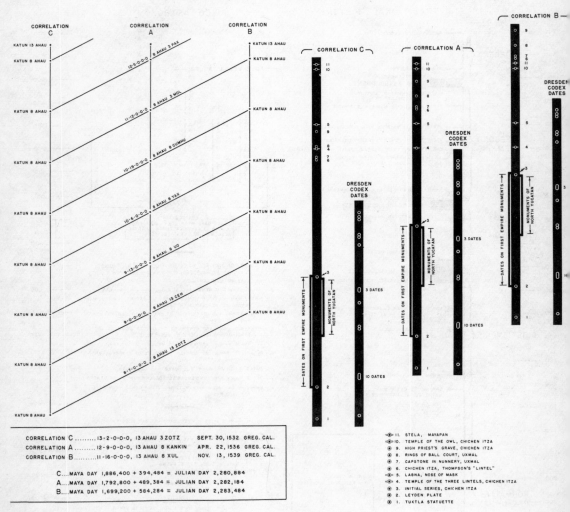

CORRELATION C .... 13-2-0-0-0, 13 AHAU 3 ZOTZ   SEPT. 30, 1532 GREG. CAL.
CORRELATION A .... 12-9-0-0-0, 13 AHAU 8 KANKIN   APR. 22, 1536 GREG. CAL.
CORRELATION B .... 11-16-0-0-0, 13 AHAU 8 XUL   NOV. 13, 1539 GREG. CAL.

C....MAYA DAY 1,886,400 + 394,484 = JULIAN DAY 2,280,884
A....MAYA DAY 1,792,800 + 489,384 = JULIAN DAY 2,282,184
B....MAYA DAY 1,699,200 + 584,284 = JULIAN DAY 2,283,484

11. STELA, MAYAPAN
10. TEMPLE OF THE OWL, CHICHEN ITZA
9. HIGH PRIEST'S GRAVE, CHICHEN ITZA
8. RINGS OF BALL COURT, UXMAL
7. CAPSTONE IN NUNNERY, UXMAL
6. CHICHEN ITZA, THOMPSON'S "LINTEL"
5. LABNA, NOSE OF MASK
4. TEMPLE OF THE THREE LINTELS, CHICHEN ITZA
3. INITIAL SERIES, CHICHEN ITZA
2. LEYDEN PLATE
1. TUXTLA STATUETTE

BIBLIOGRAPHY, PART I

BIBLIOGRAPHY, PART I

The following bibliography includes only the works referred to in the text. When two editions are given the pagination of the first is followed in the references. Most of the important contributions of original material bearing on the Maya will be found listed as well as some books which are valuable only for their illustrations or for specific statements of fact.

AGUILAR, SANCHEZ DE
    1639. Informe contra idolorum cultores del Obispado de Yucatan. Madrid. (Reprint in Anales Mus. Nac. de Mexico, 1900, VI, pp. 13–122.)

ALLEN, H.
    1881. An analysis of the life form in art. (Trans. Am. Philosoph. Soc., XV (N. s.), pp. 279–351.)

ALVARADO, PEDRO DE
    1838. Lettres de Pedro de Alvarado à Fernand Cortès. Première lettre. (H. Ternaux-Compans, Voyages, relations et mémoires originaux pour servir à l'histoire de la découverte de l'Amérique, X, pp. 107–125.)

AMBROSETTI, J. B.
    1896. El símbolo de la serpiente en la alfareria funeraria de la región Calchaqui. (Bol. del Inst. Geog. Argentino, XVII, pp. 219–230.)
    1899. Notas de arqueologia Calchaqui. Buenos Aires.

ANTIGÜEDADES MEXICANAS
    1892. Antigüedades mexicanas. Publicadas por la Junta Colombina de Mexico en el cuarto centenario de descubrimiento de América. Mexico.

ANTIQUITÉS MEXICAINES
    1834. Antiquités mexicaines. Relation des trois expéditions du Capitaine Dupaix ordonnées en 1805, 1806, et 1807 pour la recherche des antiquités du pays, notamment celles de Mitla et de Palenque, etc. 2 vols. Paris.

ANCONA, E.
    1878–1880. Historia de Yucatan desde la època mas remota hasta nuestros dias. 4 vols. Merida.

ARNOLD, C., and FROST, F. J. T.
    1909. The American Egypt: a record of travel in Yucatan. New York.

BATCHELDER, E. A.
    1910. Design in theory and practice. New York.

BANCROFT, H. H.
    1875–1876. The native races of the Pacific States. 5 vols. New York and London.

BANDELIER, A. F.
    1884. Report of an archaeological tour in Mexico in 1881. (Papers of Arch. Inst. of America. American Ser., II, Boston, 1884.)
    1887. Sources for aboriginal history of Spanish-America. (Proc. A. A. A. S., XXVII, pp. 315–337.)
    1892. Final report of investigations among the Indians of the southwestern United States, carried on mainly in the years from 1880 to 1885. Part II. (Papers of the Arch. Inst. of America. American Series, IV, Cambridge.)

BASTIAN, A.
    1882. Steinskulpturen aus Guatemala. (Veröffentlichungen der Königlichen Mus. zu Berlin.)

BATRES, L.
    1888. Civilización de algunas de las differentes tribus que habitaron el territorio, hoy Mexicano, en la antigüedad. Mexico.
    1902, a. Exploraciones de Monte Alban. Mexico.
    1902, b. Archaeological explorations in Escalerillas Street, City of Mexico. Year 1900. Mexico.
    1903. Visita a los monumentos arqueológicos de "La Quemada," Zacatecas. Mexico.
    1905. La lapida arqueológica de Tepatlaxco, Orizaba. Mexico.
    1908. Civilización prehistorica de las riberas del Papaloapam y costa de Sotavento, estado de Vera Cruz. Mexico.

BIENVENIDA, L. DE
    1877. Carta de Fray Lorenzo de Bienvenida A. S. a El Principe don Felipe dandole cuenta de varios asuntos referentes a la provincia de Yucatan. — 10 de febrero de 1548. (Cartas de Indias, Madrid. pp. 70–82.)

BISHOP, R. H.
    1906. Investigations and studies in jade. 2 vols. New York.

BLACKISTON, A. H.
    1910, a. Archaeological investigations in Honduras. (Records of the Past, IX, pp. 195–201.)
    1910, b. Recent discoveries in Honduras. (Am. Anth. (N. S.), XII, pp. 536–541.)

BOBAN, E.
    1891. Documents pour servir a l'histoire du Mexique. Catalogue raisonné de la Collection E. Eugene Goupil. 2 vols. and atlas. Paris.

BOVALLIUS, C.
    1886. Nicaraguan antiquities. Stockholm.
    1887. Resa i Central-Amerika 1881–1883. 2 vols. Upsala.

BOWDITCH, C. P.
    1901, a. Memoranda on the Maya calendars used in the Books of Chilan Balam. (Am. Anth. (N. S.), III, pp. 129–138.)
    1901, b. On the age of Maya ruins. (Am. Anth. (N. S.), III, pp. 697–700.)
    1901, c. Notes on the report of Teobert Maler, in Memoirs of the Peabody Museum, II, No. 1. Cambridge.
    1903, a. Notes on the report of Teobert Maler, in Memoirs of the Peabody Museum, II, No. 2. Cambridge.
    1903, b. A suggestive Maya inscription. Cambridge.
    1906. The Temples of the Cross, of the Foliated Cross, and of the Sun at Palenque. Cambridge.
    1909. Dates and numbers in the Dresden Codex. (Putnam Anniversary Volume, pp. 271–301. New York.)
    1910. The numeration, calendar systems and astronomical knowledge of the Mayas. Cambridge.

BRANSFORD, J. F.
    1881. Archaeological researches in Nicaragua. (Smithson. Cont. to Knowl., XXV, Art. 2, pp. 1–96.)

BRASSEUR DE BOURBOURG, C. E.
    1857–1859. Histoire des nations civilisées du Mexique et de l'Amérique centrale durant les siècles antérieurs à Christophe Colomb. 4 vols. Paris.
    1861. Popol Vuh. Le livre sacré et les mythes héroiques et historiques des Quichés, etc. Brussels.
    1864. Collection de documents dans les langues indigènes pour servir a l'étude de l'histoire de la philologie de l'Amérique ancienne. III, Paris [contains Landa, 1864, and Pio Perez, 1864].
    1866, a. Essai historique sur le Yucatan et description des ruines de Ti-Hoo (Merida) et d'Izamal. (Archives de la Commission Sci. du Mex., II, pp. 18–64.)
    1866, b. Rapport sur les ruines de Mayapan et d'Uxmal du Yucatan. (Archives de la Commission Sci. du Mex., II, pp. 234–288.)
    1869–1870. Manuscrit Troano. Études sur le système graphique et la langue des Mayas. 2 vols. Paris.

BRETON, A.

1906, *a*. The wall paintings at Chichen Itza. (Internat. Cong. of Americanists, 15th Sess., Quebec, pp. 165–169.)

1906, *b*. Some notes on Xochicalco. (Trans. Dept. Arch., Free Mus. Sci. and Art, Univ. of Penn., II, pt. 1, pp. 51–67.)

1908. Archaeology in Mexico. (Man, VIII, pp. 34–37.)

BRINE, L.

1894. Travels amongst American Indians, their ancient earthworks and temples, including a journey in Guatemala, Mexico and Yucatan and a visit to the ruins of Utatlan, Palenque and Uxmal. London.

BRINTON, D. G.

1881. The names of the gods in the Kiche myths, Central America. (Proc. Am. Philosoph. Soc., XIX, pp. 613–647.)

1882, *a*. American hero myths. A study in the native religions of the western continent. Philadelphia.

1882, *b*. The Maya chronicles. Philadelphia. (No. 1 of Brinton's Library of Aboriginal American Literature.)

1882, *c*. The graphic system and ancient records of the Mayas. (U. S. Geog. and Geol. Survey of the Rocky Mountain Region. Cont. to Am. Ethnol., V, No. 3, pp. xvii–xxxvii.)

1882, *d*. The books of Chilan Balam, the prophetic and historic records of the Mayas of Yucatan. (Penn. Monthly, XIII, pp. 261–275.)

1885, *a*. The annals of the Cakchiquels. The original text with a translation, notes and introduction. Philadelphia. (No. 6 of Brinton's Library of Aboriginal American Literature.)

1885, *b*. The lineal measures of the semi-civilized nations of Mexico and Central America. (Proc. Am. Philosoph. Soc., XXII, pp. 194–207.)

1885, *c*. Did Cortez visit Palenque? (Science, V, p. 248.)

1885, *d*. The sculptures of Cosumalhualpa. (Science, VI, p. 42.)

1886, *a*. On the ikonomatic method of phonetic writing, with special reference to American archaeology. (Proc. Am. Philosoph. Soc., XXIII, pp. 503–514.)

1886 *b*. The phonetic elements in the graphic system of the Mayas and Mexicans. (Am. Antiq., VIII, pp. 347–357.)

1887. Were the Toltecs an historic nationality? (Proc. Am. Philosoph. Soc., XXIV, pp. 229–241.)

1887–1889. On the "Stone of the Giants," near Orizaba, Mexico. (Proc. Numis. and Antiq. Soc. of Phila., pp. 78–85.)

1890. Essays of an Americanist. Philadelphia.

1894, *a*. On supposed relations between the American and Asian races. (Mem. Internat. Cong. of Anthropology, Chicago, pp. 145–151.)

1894, *b*. A primer of Mayan hieroglyphics. (Pub. Univ. of Penn., Ser. in Philol., Lit. and Arch. III, No. 2.)

1896. The battle and ruins of Cintla. (Am. Antiq., XVII, pp. 259–268.)

1897. The pillars of Ben. (Bull. Free Mus. of Sci. and Art, Univ. of Penn., I, pp. 3–10.)

BRÜHL, G.

1894. Die Ruinen von Iximche in Guatemala. (Globus, LXVI, pp. 213–217.)

BUSHNELL, D. I.

1904. The Cahokia and surrounding mound groups. (Papers Peabody Museum, III, No. 1, pp. 1–20.)

BULLETIN 28

1904. Mexican and Central American antiquities, calendar systems and history. Twenty-four papers by Eduard Seler, E. Förstemann, Paul Schellhas, Carl Sapper and E. P. Dieseldorff. Translated from the German under the supervision of Charles P. Bowditch. (Bull. 28, Bur. Am. Ethnol.)

CARRILLO, C.

1865. Estudio historico sobre la raza indigena de Yucatan. Vera Cruz.

1871. Compendio de la historia de Yucatan. Merida.

1883. Historia antiqua de Yucatan, seguida de la dissertaciones del mismo autor relativos al proprio asunto. Merida.

1895. El comercio en Yucatan antes del descubrimiento. (Internat. Cong. of Americanists, 11th Sess., Mexico, pp. 203–208.)

CATHERWOOD, F.

1844. Views of ancient monuments in Central America, Chiapas and Yucatan. Folio. London.

CASARES, D.

1905. A notice of Yucatan with some remarks on its water supply. (Proc. Am. Antiq. Soc., XVII, pp. 207–230.)

402 BIBLIOGRAPHY, PART I

CHARENCY, H. DE
1871. Le mythe de Votan; étude sur les origines asiatiques de la civilisation américaine. Alençon.

CHARNAY, D.
1884. Voyage au Yucatan et au pays des Lacandons. (Le Tour du Monde, XLVII, pp. 1–96, and XLVIII, pp. 33–48.)
1885. Les anciennes villes du nouveau monde. Voyages d'explorations au Mexique et dans l'Amérique Centrale, 1857–1882.
1887, a. The ancient cities of the New World. Above trans. by J. Gonino and H. S. Conant. London.
1887, b. Ma dernière expédition au Yucatan. (Le Tour du Monde, LIII, pp. 273–277.)
1904. Les explorations de Teobert Maler. (Jour. Soc. d'Américanistes de Paris, I (N. S.), pp. 289–308.)
1906. Les ruines de Tuloom d'après John L. Stephens. (Jour. Soc. d'Américanistes de Paris, III (N. S.), pp. 191–195.)

CHARNAY, D., and VIOLLET-LE-DUC, E.
1863. Cities et ruines américaines. Paris. One volume and collection of photographs.

CHAVERO, A.
1884. Mexico a través de los siglos. Tomo I, Historia antiqua y de la Conquista. Barcelona.
1892. Obras historicas de don Fernando de Alva Ixtlilxochitl. 2 vols. Mexico.
1900–1901. Pinturas jeroglificas. 2 parts. Mexico.

CODEX BORBONICUS (see Hamy, 1899, a).
CODEX BORGIA (see Loubat, 1898, and Seler, 1904–1909).
CODEX CORTESIANUS (see Rady y Delgado, 1892).
CODEX COLOMBINO (in Antigüedades Mexicanas).
CODEX DRESDEN (see Förstemann, 1880, 1892).
CODEX FEJÉRVÁRY-MAYER (see Loubat, 1901, and Seler, 1901–1902).
CODEX NUTTALL (see Z. Nuttall, 1902).
CODEX PERESIANUS (see Léon de Rosny, 1887 and 1888).
CODEX PORFIRIO DIAS (in Antigüedades Mexicanas).
CODEX TELERIANO-REMENSIS (see Hamy, 1899, b).
CODEX TROANO (see Brasseur de Bourbourg, 1869–1870).
CODEX VATICANUS, No. 3773 (see Loubat, 1896, and Seler, 1902–1903).
CODEX VIENNA (in Kingsborough, 1831–1848).

COGOLLUDO, D. L.
1688. Historia de Yucathan. Madrid.

COOK, J.
1769. Remarks on a passage from Balise, in the Bay of Honduras, to Merida, the capital of the province of Yucatan in the Spanish West Indies. . . . in Feb. and March, 1765. London.

COOPER, W. R.
1873. The serpent myths of ancient Egypt. London.

CORTES, H.
1868. The fifth letter of Hernan Cortes to the Emperor Charles V, containing an account of his expedition to Honduras. (Trans. by Don Pascual de Gayangos, Hakluyt Soc., London.)
1908. The five letters of relation from Fernando Cortes to the Emperor Charles V. 2 vols. New York. (Edited by F. A. Mac Nutt.)

CRESSON, H. T.
1892. The antennae and sting of Yikilcab as components in the Maya day signs. (Science, XX, pp. 77–79.)

CRUZ, F. G.
1904. Las ruinas de Matarás (antigua Texutla). (Anales del Museo Nacional, San Salvador, I, pp. 436–438.)

CUSHING, F. H.
1882–1883. A study of pueblo pottery as illustrative of Zuñi culture growth. (4th Rep. Bur. Am. Ethnol., pp. 467–521.)
1894. Primitive copper working, an experimental study. (Am. Anth., VII, pp. 93–117.)

DIAS DEL CASTILLO, BERNAL
1803. The true history of the Conquest of Mexico, 1568. (Translated by M. Keating. London.)
1908. The same, 3 vols. (Translated by A. P. Maudslay. Hakluyt Soc., London.)

DIAS, JUAN.
1838. Itinéraire du voyage de la flotte du Roi Catholique à l'île de Yucatan dans l'Inde. Fait en l'an 1518, sous les ordres du capitaine général Juan de Grijalva. (H. Ternaux-Compans, Voyages, relations et mémoires originaux pour servir à l'histoire de la découverte de l'Amérique. X, pp. 1–47.)

DIESELDORFF, E. P.
1893, a. Ausgrabungen in Coban. (Zeit. für Ethnol., XXV, Verhand., pp. 374–380.)
1893, b. Alte bemalte Thongefässe aus Guatemala. (Zeit. für Ethnol., XXV, Verhand., pp. 547–550.)
1894, a. Ein bemaltes Thongefäss mit figürlichen Darstellungen aus einem Grabe von Chama. (Zeit. für Ethnol., XXVI, Verhand., pp. 372–377. Translated in Bull. 28, Bur. Am. Ethnol., pp. 639–644.)
1894, b. Ein Thongefäss mit Darstellung einer vampyrköpfigen Gottheit. (Zeit. für Ethnol., XXVI, Verhand., pp. 576–577. Translated in Bull. 28, pp. 665–666.)
1895, a. Das Gefäss von Chama. (Zeit. für Ethnol., XXVII, Verhand., pp. 770–776.)
1895, b. Reliefbild aus Chipolem. (Zeit. für Ethnol., XXVII, Verhand., pp. 777–780.)
1895, c. Cuculcan. (Zeit. für Ethnol., XXVII, Verhand., pp. 780–873.)
1905. Jadeite und anderen Schmuck der Mayavölker. (Zeit. für Ethnol., XXXVII, pp. 408–411.)
1909. Klassifizierung seiner archäologischen Funde im nördlichen Guatemala. (Zeit. für Ethnol., XLI, pp. 862–874.)

DITMARS, R. L.
1910. Reptiles of the world. New York.

DURAN, FRAY DIEGO
1880. Historia de las Indias de Nueva España y islas de tierra firma. 2 vols. and atlas. Mexico.

DURUY, V.
1864. Comission scientifique du Mexique. Manuscrit dit Mexicain No. 2, de la Bibliothèque Impériale. Photographié sans reduction par ordre de S. E. M. Duruy, Ministre de l'Instruction publique, etc. Paris. (Reproduced by W. E. Gates, 1909.)

FEWKES, J. W.
1894, a. The snake ceremonials at Walpi. (Jour. Am. Ethnol. and Arch., IV, pp. 7–126.)
1894, b. A study of certain figures in a Maya codex. (Am. Anth., VII, pp. 260–270.)
1895, a. A comparison of Sia and Tusayan snake ceremonials. (Am. Anth., VIII, pp. 118–141.)
1895, b. The god "D" in the Codex Cortesianus. (Am. Anth., VIII, pp. 205–222.)
1903–1904. Certain antiquities of eastern Mexico. (25th Ann. Rep. Bur. Am. Ethnol., pp. 221–284.)
1906. An ancient megalith in Jalapa, Vera Cruz. (Am. Anth., VIII (N. S.), pp. 633–639.)

FÖRSTEMANN, E.
1880. Die Maya-Handschrift der Königlichen Bibliothek zu Dresden. Leipzig. Second edition in 1892.
1887–1898. Zur Entzifferung der Mayahandschriften, I–VII. (The suite of essays is translated into English in Bull. 28, Bur. Am. Ethnol., pp. 393–472.)
1892 (see 1880).
1895. Das mittelamerikanische Tonalamatl. (Globus, LXVII, pp. 283–285. Translated in Bull. 28, pp. 527–533.)
1896. Neue Mayaforschungen. (Globus, LXX, pp. 37–39. Translated in Bull. 28, pp. 537–541.)
1897. Die Kreuzinschrift von Palenque. (Globus, LXXII, pp. 45–49. Translated in Bull. 28, pp. 547–555.)
1899. Aus dem Inschriftentempel von Palenque. (Globus, LXXV, pp. 77–80. Translated in Bull. 28, pp. 575–580.)
1901, a. Commentar zur Mayahandschrift der Königlichen öffentlichen Bibliothek zu Dresden. Dresden. (For translation, see 1906.)
1901, b. Eine historische Maya-Inschrift. (Globus, LXXXI, pp. 150–153.)
1902, a. Commentar zur Madrider Mayahandschrift. Dantzig.
1902, b. Der zehnte Cyclus der Mayas. (Globus, LXXXII, pp. 140–143.)
1903. Commentar zur Pariser Mayahandschrift. Dantzig.
1905. Die Millionenzahlen im Dresdensis. (Globus, LXXXVIII, pp. 126–128.)
1906. Commentary of the Maya manuscript in the Royal Public Library of Dresden. (Pap. Peabody Mus., IV, No. 2, pp. 48–266. Translation of 1901, a.)

FOWKE, G.
1910. Antiquities of central and southeastern Missouri. (Bull. 37, Bur. Am. Ethnol.)

FRIEDERICHSTHAL, E.
1841. Les monuments de l'Yucatan. (Nouvelles Annales des Voyages et des Sciences géographiques. 4th sér., IV, pp. 297–314.)

GANN, T.
1897–1898.   Mounds in northern Honduras.   (19th Rep. Bur. Am. Ethnol., Pt. 2, pp. 661–692.)

GATES, W. E.
1909.   Codex Perez.   Maya-Tzendal.   Redrawn and slightly restored with the coloring as it originally stood, so far as possible, given on the basis of a new and minute examination of the codex itself. Mounted in the form of the original.   Accompanied by a reproduction of the 1864 photographs [see Duruy, 1864].   Point Loma, Cal.
1910.   Commentary upon the Maya-Tzental Perez Codex with a concluding note upon the linguistic problem of the Maya glyphs.   (Pap. Peabody Mus., VI, No. 1, pp. 5–64.)

GOODMAN, J. T.
1897.   The archaic Maya inscriptions.   (Part XVIII of Biologia Centrali-Americana, Archaeology, London.   See Maudslay, 1889–1902.)
1905.   Maya dates.   (Am. Anth. (N. S.), VII, pp. 642–647.)

GONZALES, D.
1906.   Arqueología Salvadoreña.   Ruinas de Tehuacan.   (Anales del Museo Nacional, San Salvador, III, pp. 45–49.)

GORDON, G. B.
1896.   Prehistoric ruins of Copan, Honduras.   A preliminary report of the explorations by the Museum, 1891–1895.   (Mem. Peabody Mus., I, No. 1, pp. 1–48.)
1898, a.   Researches in the Uloa Valley, Honduras.   Report on explorations by the Museum, 1896–1897.   (Mem. Peabody Mus., I, No. 4, pp. 1–44.)
1898, b.   Caverns of Copan, Honduras.   Report on explorations by the Museum, 1896–1897.   (Mem. Peabody Mus., I, No. 5, pp. 1–12.)
1902, a.   The hieroglyphic stairway ruins of Copan.   Report on explorations by the Museum.   (Mem. Peabody Mus., I, No. 6, pp. 1–38.)
1902, b.   On the interpretation of a certain group of sculptures at Copan.   (Am. Anth., IV (N. S.), pp. 130–143.)
1902, c.   On the use of zero and twenty in the Maya time system.   (Am. Anth. IV. (N. S.), pp. 237–275.)
1904.   Chronological sequence in the Maya ruins of Central America.   (Trans. Dept. of Arch. Univ. of Penn., I, No. 1, pp. 61–66.)
1905.   The serpent motive in the ancient art of Central America and Mexico.   (Trans. Dept. of Arch. Univ. of Penn., I, No. 3, pp. 131–163.)
1907.   An engraved bone from Ohio.   (Trans. Dept. of Arch., Univ. of Penn., II, pp. 103–104.)
1909.   Conventionalism and realism in Maya art at Copan.   (Putnam Anniversary Volume.   New York, pp. 193–197.)

GUZMAN, D. J.
1904.   Arqueologia Salvadoreña.   (Anales del Museo Nacional, San Salvador, I, pp. 381–385.)

HABEL, S.
1878.   The sculptures of Santa Lucia Cosumalwhuapa in Guatemala with an account of travels in Central America and on the west coast of South America.   (Smithson. Cont. to Knowl., XXII, Art. III, pp. 1–90.)

HAMY, E. T.
1875.   Quelques observations ethnologiques au sujet de deux microcéphales américains désignés sous le nom d'Aztèques.   (Bull. Soc. d'Anth. de Paris, X, 2e sér., pp. 39–54.)
1878.   Les premiers habitants du Mexique.   (Rev. d'Anth., I, 2e sér., pp. 56–65.)
1882.   Mutilations dentaires des Huaxtèques et des Mayas.   (Bull. Soc. d'Anth. de Paris, V, 3e sér., pp. 879–885.)
1896.   Étude sur les collections américaines réunies à Gênes à l'occasion du IVe centenaire de la découverte de l'Amérique.   (Jour. Soc. Américanistes de Paris, I, pp. 1–31.)
1897.   Galerie américaine du Musée d'ethnographie au Trocadéro.   Choix de pièces archéologiques et ethnographiques, décrites et figurées.   Paris.
1898.   Note sur une figurine Yucatèque de la collection Boban-Pinart au Musée d'Ethnographie du Trocadéro.   (Jour. Soc. Américanistes de Paris, II, pp. 105–108.)
1899, a.   Codex Borbonicus.   Manuscrit mexicain de la Bibliothèque du Palais-Bourbon, publié en fac-similé, avec un commentaire explicatif.   Paris.
1899, b.   Codex Telleriano-Remensis.   Manuscrit mexicain du cabinet de Ch. M. Le Tellier, archevêque de Reims, aujourd'hui à la Bibliothèque National (MS. Mexicain, No. 385), reprodüit en photochromographie, etc.   Paris.

HARTMANN, C. V.
  1907. Archaeological researches on the Pacific coast of Costa Rica. (Mem. Carnegie Inst., III, pp. 1–95.)

HERRERA, A. DE
  1726–1730, Historia general de los hechos de los Castellanos en las islas i tierra fierma del Mar oceano. 5 vols. Madrid.

HEWITT, J. N. B.
  1889. Serpent symbolism. (Am. Anth., II, pp. 179–180.)

HOLMES, W. H.
  1880–1881. Art in shell of the ancient Americans. (2nd Rep. Bur. Am. Ethnol., pp. 179–305.)
  1882–1883. Ancient pottery of the Mississippi Valley. (4th Rep. Bur. Am. Ethnol., pp. 361–436.)
  1884. Antiquity of man on the site of the City of Mexico. (Trans. Anth. Soc. of Washington, III, pp. 68–81.)
  1887. The use of gold and other metals among the ancient inhabitants of Chiriqui, Panama. (Bull., No. 3, Bur. Am. Ethnol.)
  1895–1897. Archaeological studies among the ancient cities of Mexico. (Field Columbian Museum, Anth. Ser., I, pts. 1 and 2.)
  1898–1899. Ancient pottery of the eastern United States. (20th Rep. Bur. Am. Ethnol., pp. 1–201.)
  1903. Shell ornaments from Kentucky and Mexico. (Smithson. Misc. Coll., XLV, pp. 97–99.)
  1907. On a nephrite statuette from San Andrés Tuxtla, Vera Cruz, Mexico. (Am. Anth., IX (N. S.), pp. 691–701.)

HOWE, G. P.
  1911. The ruins of Tuloom. (Am. Anth. (N. S.), XIII, pp. 539–550.)

KERBER, E.
  1882. Eine alte mexikanische Ruinenstätte bei S. Andrés Tuxtla. (Zeit für Ethnol., XIV, Verhand., pp. 488–489.)

KINGSBOROUGH, LORD
  1831–1848. Antiquities of Mexico. 9 vols., folio. London.

KUNZ, G. F.
  1906. New observations on the occurrences of precious stones of archaeological interest in America. (Internat. Cong. of Americanists, 15th Sess., Quebec, pp. 289–305.)
  1907. Precious stones of Mexico. Mexico.

LANDA, D. DE
  1864. Relacion de los cosas de Yucatan. This edition by Brasseur de Bourbourg is the one referred to in the text. A later edition appears in Relaciones de Yucatan, II, pp. 264–408.

LEEMANS, C.
  1877. Description de quelques antiquités américaines conservées dans le Musée Royal Néerlandais d'Antiquités à Leide. (Internat. Cong. of Americanists, 2nd Sess., Luxembourg, II, pp. 283–302.)

LEHMANN, W.
  1905, a. Les peintures Mixteco-Zapotèques et quelques documents apparentés. (Jour. Soc. de Américanistes de Paris, II (N. S.), pp. 241–280.)
  1905, b. Altmexikanische Muschelzierate in durchbrochener Arbeit. (Globus, LXXXVIII, pp. 285–288.)
  1909. Methods and results in Mexican research. Translation into English by Seymour de Ricci. Paris. (Originally published in Archiv. für Anth., VI, pp. 133–168.)
  1910. Ergebnisse einer Forschungsreise in Mittelamerika und Mexico, 1907–1909. (Zeit. für Ethnol., XLII, pp. 687–749.)

LE PLONGEON, A.
  1878. Archaeological communication on Yucatan. (Proc. Am. Antiq. Soc., Oct. 21, pp. 65–75.)
  1881. Mayapan and Maya inscriptions. (Proc. Am. Antiq. Soc., I (N. S.), pp. 246–281.)
  1886. Sacred mysteries among the Mayas and Quiches, etc. New York.
  1896. Queen Moo and the Egyptian Sphinx. New York.

LIZANA, B. DE
  1893. Historia de Yucatán. Devocionario de Ntra Sra de Itzmal y conquista espiritual. Valladolid, 1633. (Reprint by Museo Nacional de Mexico. Mexico.)

LOUBAT, DUC DE
  1896. Il manoscritto Messicano Vaticano 3773. Rome.

LOUBAT, DUC DE — *continued*.
 1898. Il manoscritto Borgeano del Museo Ethnografico della S. Congregazione di Propaganda Fide. Rome.
 1901. Codex Fejérváry-Mayer, Manuscrit mexicain precolombien des Free Public Museums de Liverpool. Paris.

LUMHOLTZ, C.
 1902. Unknown Mexico. 2 vols. New York.
 1909. A remarkable ceremonial vase from Cholula, Mexico. (Am. Anth. (N. S.), XI, pp. 199–201.)

MacCURDY, G. G.
 1911. A study of Chiriquian antiquities (Mem. Connecticut Acad. of Arts and Sci., III.)

MALER, T.
 1895. Yukatekische Forschungen. (Globus, LXVIII, pp. 247–259 and 277–292.)
 1901. Researches in the central portion of the Usumatsintla Valley. (Mem. Peabody Mus., II, No. 1, pp. 9–75.)
 1902. Yukatekische Forschungen. (Globus, LXXXII, pp. 197–230.)
 1903. Researches in the central portion of the Usumatsintla Valley. Part second. (Mem. Peabody Mus., II, No. 2, pp. 83–208.)
 1908, *a*. Explorations of the upper Usumatsintla and adjacent region. (Mem. Peabody Mus., IV, No. 1, pp. 1–51.)
 1908, *b*. Explorations in the Department of Peten, Guatemala, and adjacent region. (Mem. Peabody Mus., IV, No. 2, pp. 55–127.)
 1910. Explorations in the Department of Peten, Guatemala, and adjacent regions, continued. (Mem. Peabody Mus., IV, No. 3, pp. 131–170.)
 1911. Explorations in the Department of Peten, Guatemala. Tikal. (Mem. Peabody Mus., V, No. 1, pp. 3–91.)

MARTINEZ, J.
 1910. Los grandes ciclos de la historia maya según el Manuscrito de Chumayel. Merida.

MAUDSLAY, A. P.
 1883. Explorations in Guatemala and examination of the newly discovered Indian ruins of Quirigua, Tikal and the Usumacinta. (Proc. Roy. Geog. Soc., V (N. S.), pp. 185–204.)
 1886. Explorations of the ruins and site of Copan, Central America. (Proc. Roy. Geog. Soc., VIII (N. S.), pp. 568–595.)
 1889–1902. Biologia Centrali-Americana, or contributions to the knowledge of the flora and fauna of Mexico and Central America. Archaeology, 4 vols. of text and plates. London.
 1897–1898. A Maya calendar inscription interpreted by Goodman's Tables. (Proc. Roy. Soc. of London, LXII, pp. 67–80.)
 1908. (See Dias del Castillo.)

MAUDSLAY, A. C., and A. P.
 1899. A glimpse at Guatemala and some notes on the ancient monuments of Central America. London.

MERCER, H. C.
 1896. The hill caves of Yucatan. Philadelphia.
 1897. The kabal, or potter's wheel of Yucatan. (Bull. Free Mus. Sci. and Art, Univ. of Penn., I, pp. 63–70.)

MEYE, H., and SCHMIDT, J.
 1883. The stone sculptures of Copan and Quirigua. (Translation by A. D. Savage.) New York.

MEYER, A. B.
 1882. Jadeit- und Nephrit-Objecte aus Amerika und Europa. (Publikationen Königliches Ethnographisches Museum zu Dresden, III. Leipzig.)

MOLINA SOLIS, J. F.
 1897. Historia del descubrimiento y conquista de Yucatan con una reseña de la historia antigua de esta peninsula. Merida.

MOORE, C. C.
 1899. Certain aboriginal remains of the Alabama River. (Jour. Acad. Nat. Sci. of Philadelphia, XI, pp. 289–347.)
 1901. Certain aboriginal remnants of the northwest Florida coast. (Jour. Acad. Nat. Sci. of Philadelphia, XI, pp. 421–497.)
 1905. Certain aboriginal remains of the Black Warrior River. (Jour. Acad. Nat. Sci. of Philadelphia, XIII, pp. 125–244.)
 1907. Moundeville revisited. (Jour. Acad. Nat. Sci. of Philadelphia, XIII, pp. 337–405.)

Moore, C. C., and others
1903. Sheet-copper from the mounds is not necessarily of European origin. (Am. Anth. (N. S.), V, pp. 27–54.)

Morelet, A.
1857. Voyage dans l'Amérique Centrale, l'Île de Cuba et le Yucatan. Paris.

Morley, S. G.
1909. The inscriptions at Naranjo, northern Guatemala. (Am. Anth. (N. S.), XI, pp. 543–562.)
1910, a. A group of related structures at Uxmal, Mexico. (Am. Jour. Arch., 2nd Ser., XIV, pp. 1–18.)
1910, b. Correlation of Maya and Christian chronology. (Am. Jour. Arch., 2nd Ser., XIV, pp. 193–204.)
1911. The historical value of the Books of Chilan Balam. (Am. Jour. Arch., 2nd Ser., XV, pp. 195–214.)
1912. Quirigua, an American town 1400 years old. (Scientific American, CVII, Aug. 3, pp. 96–97 and 105.)

Muller, Frederick, editor
1871. Trois lettres sur la découverte du Yucatan et les merveilles de ce pays. — Ecrités par des compagnons de l'expédition sous Jean de Grivalja [Grijalva], Mai 1518. Amsterdam.

Norman, B. M.
1843. Rambles in Yucatan; or notes of travel through the peninsula, including a visit to the remarkable ruins of Chi-chen, Kabah, Zayi and Uxmal. New York.

Nuttall, Z.
1886. The terra cotta heads of Teotihuacan. (Am. Jour. Arch., II, pp. 157–178, 318–330.)
1901, a. The fundamental principles of old and new world civilizations. (Papers Peabody Mus., II.)
1901, b. Chalchihuitl in ancient Mexico. (Am. Anth. (N. S.), III, pp. 227–238.)
1902. Codex Nuttall. (Publication of the Peabody Museum.)
1910. The island of Sacrificios. (Am. Anth. (N. S.), XII, pp. 257–295.)

Opper, A.
1896. Die altmexikanischen Mosaiken. (Globus, LXX, pp. 4–15.)

Orozco y Berra, M.
Historia antigua y de la conquista de México. 4 vols. Mexico.

Oviedo y Valdés
1851–1854. La historia general de las Indias. 4 vols. Madrid.

Parry, F.
1893. The sacred Maya stone of Mexico and its symbolism. London.

Pector, D.
1888. Indication approximative de vestiges laissés par les populations précolombiennes du Nicaragua. (Archives Soc. Américaine de France, 2nd Ser., VI, pp. 97–125 and 145–178.)

Peñafiel, A.
1885. Nombres geográficos de Mexico. Mexico.
1890. Monumentos del arte Mexicano antiguo. 3 vols. Berlin.
1897. Nomenclatura geografica de Mexico. Mexico.
1899. Teotihuacan. Estudio histórico y arquelógico. Mexico.
1903. Indumentaría antigua. Vestidos guerreros y civiles de los Mexicanos. Mexico.
1910. Destruccion del templo mayor de Mexico antiguo y los monumentos encontrados en la ciudad, en la excavaciones de 1897 y 1902. Mexico.

Perez, J. Pio.
1864. Chronologia antigua de Yucatan y examen del metodo con que los Indios contaban el Tiempo; sacada de varios documentos antiguos. (In Brasseur de Bourbourg, 1864, pp. 366–429.)

Périgny, M. de
1908. Yucatan inconnu. (Jour. Soc. des Américanistes, V (N. S.), pp. 67–98.
1910. Les ruines de Nakcun. (Acad. des Insc. et Belles Lettres. Comptes rendus des séances. Bull., pp. 485–489.)

Popul Vuh (see Brasseur de Bourbourg, 1861)

Preuss, K. Th.
1901. Kosmische Hieroglyphen der Mexikaner. (Zeit. für Ethnol., XXXIII, pp. 1–47.)

Prieto, A.
1873. Historia, geografia y estadistica del estado de Tamaulipas. Mexico.

PUTNAM, F. W.
   1887.   Conventionalism in ancient American art.   (Bull. Essex Inst., XVIII, pp. 155–167.)

PUTNAM, F. W. AND WILLOUGHBY, C. C.
   1895.   Symbolism in ancient American Art.   (Proc. A. A. A. S., XLIV, pp. 302–322.)

RADY Y DELGADO, JUAN DE DIOS DE LA
   1892.   Códice Maya denominado Cortesiano que se conserva en el Museo Arqueológico Nacional.
      Reproducción fotocromolitográfica ordenada en la misina forma que el original.   Madrid.

RELACION BREVE
   1872.   Relacion breve y verdadera de algunas cosas de las muchas que sucedieron al Padre
      Fray Alonzo Ponce, Commissario General, en las provincias de Nueva España.   (Coleccion de
      documentos inéditos para la historia de España.   LVII and LVIII.   Madrid.)

RELACION DE LOS CONQUISTADORES
   1870.   Relacion de los conquistadores y pobladores que habia en la provincia de Yucatan, en la ciudad
      de Mérida.   25 de Julio de 1551.   (Coleccion de documentos ineditos relativos al descubrimiento,
      conquista y organizacion de las antiguas posesiones españolas en América y Oceania, sacados de los
      Archivos del Reino y muy especialmente del de Indias.   Madrid, XIV, pp. 191–201.)

RELACIONES DE YUCATAN
   1900.   Relaciones histórico-geográficas de las provincias de Yucatan.   2 vols.   Madrid.   (Coleccion
      de documentos ineditos relativos al descubrimiento, conquista y organizacion de las antiguas poses-
      iones españolas de Ultramar.   2nd Ser., XI and XIII.)

RIO, ANTONIO DEL
   1822.   Description of the ruins of an ancient city, discovered near Palenque in the kingdom of Guate-
      mala in Central America.   London.

ROBELO, C. A.
   1905.   Diccionario de mitologia Nahoa.   Mexico.

ROSNY, LÉON DE
   1876.   Essai sur le déchiffrement de l'écriture hiératique de l'Amérique Centrale.   Paris.
   1882.   Les documents écrits de l'antiquité américaine.   Compte-rendu d'une mission scientifique en
      Espagne et en Portugal.   Paris.
   1883.   Codex Cortesianus.   Manuscrit hiératique des anciens Indiens d'Amérique Centrale, conservé
      au Musée Archéologique de Madrid, photographié pour la première fois avec un introduction et un
      vocabulaire de l'écriture hiératique yucatèque.   Paris.
   1887.   Codex Peresianus, manuscrit hiératique des anciens Indiens de l'Amérique Centrale conservé
      à la Bibliothèque Nacional de Paris, avec un introduction.   Paris.
   1888.   Codex Peresianus (edition in black and white).

ROSS, D. W.
   1901.   Design as a science.   (Proc. Am. Acad. Arts and Sci., XXXVI, No. 21, pp. 357–374.)
   1907.   A Theory of pure design: harmony, balance, rhythm; with illustrations and diagrams.   Boston.

ROVIROSA, J. N.
   1897.   Ensayo histórico sobre el Rio Grijalva.   Mexico.

SAHAGUN, BERNADINO DE
   1880.   Histoire générale des choses de la Nouvelle-Espagne.   (Edited and translated by D. Jourdanet
      and Rémi Siméon.)

SALISBURY, S.
   1876.   The Mayas, the sources of their history.   Dr. Le Plongeon in Yucatan, his account of discoveries.
      (Proc. Am. Antiq. Soc., April, pp. 16–61.)
   1877.   Dr. Le Plongeon in Yucatan.   The discovery of the statue called Chac-mol and the com-
      munications of Dr. Le Plongeon concerning explorations in the Yucatan Peninsula.   (Proc. Am.
      Antiq. Soc., April, pp. 54–103.)
   1878.   Terra cotta figure from Isla Mujeres, northeast coast of Yucatan.   (Proc. Am. Antiq. Soc.,
      April, pp. 71–89.)

SANCHEZ, J.
   1877.   Estudio acerca de la estatua llamada Chac-Mool ó Rey Tigre.   (Anales del Museo Nacional,
      I, pp. 270–278.)

SAPPER, C.
   1895, a.   Altindianische Ansiedlungen in Guatemala und Chiapas.   (Veröffentlichungen aus dem Kön-
      iglichen Museum für Völkerkunde, IV, pp. 13–20 and tables 1–10.)

SAPPER, C. — *continued*

1895, *b*. Die unabhängigen Indianerstaaten von Yucatan. (Globus, LXVII, pp. 197–201. Translated in Bull. 28, Bur. Am. Ethnol., pp. 625–634.)

1895, *c*. Altindianische Siedelungen und Bauten im nördlichen Mittel-amerika. (Globus, LXVIII, pp. 165–169, 183–189. Translated in Smithson. Rep., 1895, pp. 537–555. References are to the translation.)

1896. Sobre la geografía fisica y la geología de la peninsula de Yucatán. (Bol. Inst. Geol. de Mexico, No. 3.)

1897. Das nördliche Mittel-Amerika nebst einem Ausflug nach dem Hochland von Anahuac. Reisen und Studien aus den Jahren 1888–1895. Braunschweig.

1902. Mittelamerikanische Reisen und Studien aus den Jahren 1888 bis 1900. Braunschweig.

1905. Der gegenwärtige Stand der ethnographischen Kenntnis von Mittelamerika. (Archiv für Anth., III (N. S.), pp. 1–38.)

SAVILLE, M. H.

1892. Explorations on the Main Structure at Copan, Honduras. (Proc. A. A. A. S., XLI, pp. 271–275.)

1894. The plumed serpent in northern Mexico. (The Archaeologist, II, pp. 291–293.)

1897. An ancient figure of terra cotta from the valley of Mexico. (Bull. Am. Mus. Nat. Hist., IX, pp. 221–224.)

1900, *a*. A shell gorget from the Huasteca, Mexico. (Bull. Am. Mus. Nat. Hist., XIII, pp. 99–103.)

1900, *b*. An onyx jar from Mexico, in process of manufacture. (Bull. Am. Mus. Nat. Hist., XIII, pp. 105–107.)

1909. The cruciform structures of Mitla and vicinity. (Putnam Anniversary Volume, pp. 151–191. New York.)

SCHELLHAS, P.

1890. Vergleichende Studien auf dem Felde der Maya Alterthümer. (Internat. Archiv für Ethnog., III, pp. 209–231. Translated in Bull. 28, Bur. Am. Ethnol., pp. 595–622.)

1904. Representation of deities of the Maya manuscripts. 2nd edition revised. (Translated by Miss Selma Wesselhoeft and Miss A. M. Parker, Pap. Peabody Museum, IV, No. 1, pp. 7–47.)

SELER, C.

1900. Auf alten Wegen in Mexiko und Guatemala. Berlin.

1904. Zur Tracht der mexikanischen Indianer. (Internat. Cong. of Americanists, 14th Sess., Stuttgart, pp. 419–426.)

SELER, E.

1886. Maya-Handschriften und Maya-Götter. (Zeit. für Ethnol., XVIII, Verhand., pp. 416–420. Reprinted with additions in 1902–1908, I, pp. 357–366.)

1887. Ueber die Namen der in der Dresdener Handschrift abgebildeten Maya-Götter. (Zeit. für Ethnol., XIX, Verhand., pp. 224–231. Reprinted in 1902–1908, I, pp. 367–389.)

1888, *a*. Die Ruinen von Xochicalco. (Zeit. für Ethnol., XX, Verhand., pp. 94–111. Reprinted in 1902–1908, II, pp. 128–167.)

1888, *b*. Die alten Ansiedelungen im Gebiete der Huaxteca. (Zeit. für Ethnol., XX, Verhand., pp. 451–459. Reprinted in 1902–1908, II, pp. 168–183.)

1888, *c*. Die archäologischen Ergebnisse meiner ersten mexikanischen Reise. (Internat. Cong. of Americanists, 7th Sess., Berlin, pp. 111–145. Reprinted in enlarged form, 1902–1908, II, pp. 289–367.)

1889. Die Chronologie der Cakchiquel-Annalen. (Zeit. für Ethnol., XXI, Verhand., pp. 475–476. Reprinted in 1902–1908, I, pp. 504–505.)

1890. L'orfévrerie des anciens Mexicains et leur art de travailler la pierre et de faire des ornaments en plumes. (Internat. Cong. of Americanists, 8th Sess., Paris, pp. 401–452. Reprinted in 1902–1908, II, pp. 620–663.)

1892, *a*. Some remarks on Prof. Cyrus Thomas' brief study of the Palenque tablet. (Science, XX, pp. 38–39. Reprinted in 1902–1908, I, pp. 555–556.)

1892, *b*. Does there really exist a phonetic key to the Maya hieroglyphic writing? (Science, XX, pp. 121–122. Reprinted in 1902–1908, I, pp. 562–567.)

1893. Is the Maya hieroglyphic writing phonetic? (Science, XXI, pp. 6–10. Reprinted in 1902–1908, I, pp. 568–576.)

1894. Der Fledermausgott der Maya-Stämme. (Zeit. für Ethnol., XXXVI, Verhand., pp. 577–585. Reprinted in 1902–1908, II, pp. 641–652. Translated in Bull. 28, Bur. Am. Ethnol., pp. 233–241.)

1895, *a*. Die wirkliche Länge des Katun's der Maya-Chroniken und der Jahresanfang in der Dresdener Handschrift und auf den Copan-Stelen. (Zeit. für Ethnol., XXVII, Verhand., pp. 441–449. Reprinted in 1902–1908, I, pp. 577–587.)

SELER, E. — *continued*

1895, *b.* Bedeutung des Maya-Kalenders für die historische Chronologie. (Globus, LXVIII, pp. 37–41. Reprinted in 1902–1908, I, pp. 588–599. Translated in Bull. 28, pp. 327–337.)

1895, *c.* Wandmalereien von Mitla. Eine Mexikanische Bilderschrift in Fresko, folio. Berlin. (Translated in Bull. 28, pp. 247–324.)

1895, *d.* Alterthümer aus Guatemala. (Veröffentlichungen aus dem Königlichen Museum für Völkerkunde, Berlin, IV, pp. 21–53. Reprinted with additional plates, 1902–1908, III, pp. 578–640. Translated in Bull. 28, pp. 77–121.)

1895, *e.* Das Gefäss von Chamá. (Zeit. für Ethnol., XXVII, Verhand., pp. 307–320. Reprinted in 1902–1908, III, pp. 653–669. Translated in Bull. 28, pp. 651–664.)

1895, *f.* Alterthümer aus der Vera Paz. (Ethnol. Notizblatt, I, No. 2, pp. 20–26. Reprinted in 1902–1908, III, pp. 670–687.)

1898, *a.* Die Venusperiode in den Bilderschriften der Codex Borgia-Gruppe. (Zeit. für Ethnol., XXX, Verhand., pp. 346–383. Reprinted in 1902–1908, I, pp. 618–667. Translated in Bull. 28, pp. 355–391.)

1898, *b.* Quetzalcouatl-Kukulcan in Yucatan. (Zeit. für Ethnol., XXX, pp. 377–410. Reprinted in 1902–1908, I, pp. 668–705.)

1899. Die Monumente von Copan und Quiriguá und die Altarplatten von Palenque. (Zeit. für Ethnol., XXXI, Verhand., pp. 670–738. Reprinted in 1902–1908, I, pp. 712–791.)

1900. Einiges mehr über die Monumente von Copan und Quiriguá. (Zeit. für Ethnol., XXXII, Verhand., pp. 188–227. Reprinted in 1902–1908, I, pp. 792–836.)

1900–1901. The tonalamatl of the Aubin Collection, an old Mexican picture manuscript in the Paris National Library. Introduction and explanatory text. Berlin and London. English translation by A. H. Keane.

1901, *a.* Die Cedrela-Holzplatten von Tikal im Museum zu Basel. (Zeit. für Ethnol., XXXIII, pp. 101–126. Reprinted in 1902–1908, I, pp. 837–862.)

1901, *b.* Die Ausgrabungen am Orte des Haupttempels in México. (Mittheil. der Anthrop. Gesellschaft in Wien, XXXI, pp. 113–137. Reprinted with additions in 1902–1908, II, pp. 767–904.)

1901, *c.* Die alten Ansiedelungen von Chaculá im Districkte Nenton des Departments Huehuetenango der Republik Guatemala. Berlin.

1901–1902. Codex Fejérváry-Mayer, an old Mexican picture manuscript in the Liverpool Free Public Museums. Berlin and London. English translation by A. H. Keane.

1902–1903. Codex Vaticanus, No. 3773. (Codex Vaticanus B), an old Mexican pictorial manuscript in the Vatican Library. Berlin and London. English translation by A. H. Keane.

1902–1908. Gesammelte Abhandlungen zur amerikanischen Sprach- und Alterthumskunde. 3 vols. Berlin.

1904. Die Alterthümer von Castillo de Teayo. (Internat. Cong. of Americanists, 14th Sess., Stuttgart, pp. 263–304. Reprinted in 1902–1908, III, pp. 410–449.)

1904–1909. Codex Borgia. Eine altmexikanische Bilderschrift der Bibliothek der Congregatio de Propaganda Fide. 3 vols. Berlin.

1906, *a.* Eine Steinfigur aus der Sierra von Zacatlan. (Boas Anniversary Volume, New York, pp. 299–305. Reprinted in 1902–1908. III, pp. 537–542.)

1906, *b.* Die Monumente von Huilocintla im Canton Tuxpan des Staates Vera Cruz. (Internat. Cong. of Americanists, 15th Sess., Quebec, II, pp. 381–389. Reprinted in 1902–1908, III, pp. 514–521.)

1906, *c.* Einige fein bemalte alte Thongefässe der Dr. Sologuren'schen Sammlung aus Nochistlan und Cuicatlan im Staate Oaxaca. (Internat. Cong. of Americanists, 15th Sess., Quebec, II, pp. 391–403. Reprinted in 1902–1908, III, pp. 522–532.)

1906, *d.* Studien in den Ruinen von Yucatan. (Internat. Cong. of Americanists, 15th Sess., Quebec II, pp. 414–422. Reprinted in 1902–1908, III, pp. 710–717.)

1908. Die Ruinen von Chich'en Itzá in Yucatan. (Internat. Cong. of Americanists, 16th Sess., Vienna, pp. 151–239.)

1909–1910. Die Tierbilder der Mexicanischen und der Maya-Handschriften. (Zeit. für Ethnol., XLI, pp. 209–257, 381–457, 784–846; XLII, pp. 31–97, 242–287.)

1911, *a.* Die Stuckfassade von Acanceh in Yucatan. (Sitzungsberichte Königl. Preussischen Akad. d. Wissenschaften, XLVII, pp. 1011–1025.)

1911, *b.* Brief aus Mexico. (Zeit. für Ethnol., XLIII, pp. 310–315.)

1912. Archäologische Reise in Süd- und Mittel-Amerika. (Zeit. für Ethnol., XLIV, pp. 200–242.)

SPENCE, L.

1908. The Popul Vuh. The mythic and heroic sagas of the Kichés of Central America. London. (No. 16 of Popular Studies in Mythology, Romance and Folklore.)

Spinden, H. J.
   1910. Table showing the chronological sequence of the principal monuments of Copan, Honduras. (Pub. by Am. Mus. Nat. Hist.)
   1911. An ancient sepulcher at Placeres del Oro, State of Guerrero, Mexico. (Am. Anth. (n. s.), XIII, pp. 29–55.)

Squier, E. G.
   1850. Ancient monuments in the islands of Lake Nicaragua. (Supplement to the "Literary World," March 9.)
   1851. The serpent symbol, and the worship of the reciprocal principles of nature in America. New York.
   1852. Nicaragua: its people, scenery, etc. 2 vols. London.
   1853. Ruins of Tenampua, Honduras, Central America. (Proc. Hist. Soc. of New York, Oct. — Letter dated Comayagua, Honduras, June 18, 1853.)
   1858. The States of Central America: their geography, topography, climate, population, etc. New York.
   1870. Observations on a collection of chalchihuitls from Mexico and Central America. (Ann. Lyceum of Nat. Hist., New York, IX, pp. 246–265.)
   1877. Peru. Narrative of travel and exploration in the land of the Incas. New York and London.

Starr, F.
   1896. A shell gorget from Mexico. (Proc. Davenport Acad. of Nat. Sci., VI, pp. 173–178.)
   1898. A shell inscription from Tula, Mexico. (Proc. Davenport Acad. of Nat. Sci., VII, pp. 108–110.)
   1900-1904. Notes upon the ethnography of southern Mexico. (Proc. Davenport Acad. of Nat. Sci., VIII, pp. 102–188 and IX, pp. 63–172.)

Stephens, J. L.
   1841. Central America, Chiapas and Yucatan. 2 vols. New York.
   1843. Incidents of travel in Yucatan. 2 vols. New York.

Stoll, O.
   1889. Die Ethnologie der Indianerstämme von Guatemala. (Internat. Archiv für Ethnog., I, Supplement.)

Strebel, H.
   1884. Die Ruinen von Cempoallan im Staate Veracruz und Mitteilungen über die Totonaken der Jetztzeit. (Abhandl. aus dem Gebiete der Naturwissenschaften, Naturwissenschaftl. Verein in Hamburg, VIII, pp. 1–40.)
   1885-1889. Alt-Mexico. Archäologische Beiträge zur Kulturgeschichte seiner Bewohner. 2 vols. Hamburg and Leipzig.
   1893. Die Stein-Sculpturen von Santa Lucia Cozumalhualpa, Guatemala, in Museum für Völkerkunde. (Jahrbuch der Hamburgischen Wissenschaftlichen Anstalten, XI, pp. 105–120. Translated in Rep. Smithson. Inst. for 1899, pp. 549–562.)
   1899. Ueber Tierornamente auf Thongefässen aus Alt-Mexico. (Veröffentlichungen aus dem Königlichen Museum für Völkerkunde, IV, pp. 1–28.)
   1904. Ueber Ornamente auf Thongefässen aus Alt-Mexico. Mit Unterstützung des Naturwissenschaftlichen Vereins in Hamburg. Hamburg and Leipzig.

Thomas, C.
   1881-1882. Notes on certain Maya and Mexican Manuscripts. (3rd Ann. Rep. Bur. Am. Ethnol., pp. 1–65.)
   1882. A study of the Manuscript Troano. (U. S. Geog. and Geol. Survey of the Rocky Mt. Region. Cont. to Am. Ethnol., V, pp. 1–224.)
   1884-1885. Aids to the study of the Maya codices. (6th Am. Rep. Bur. Am. Ethnol., pp. 259–371.)
   1885. Palenque visited by Cortez. (Science, V, pp. 171–172.)
   1890-1891. Report of the mound explorations of the Bureau of Ethnology. (12th Am. Rep. Bur. Am. Ethnol.)
   1892. Key to the Maya hieroglyphs. (Science, XX, pp. 44–46.)
   1893. Are the Maya hieroglyphics phonetic? (Am. Anth., VI, pp. 241–270.)
   1894-1895. Day symbols of the Maya year. (16th Ann. Rep. Bur. Am. Ethnol., pp. 205–265.)
   1897-1898. Mayan calendar systems. (19th Ann. Rep. Bur. Am. Ethnol., pp. 693–819.)
   1900-1901. Mayan calendar systems II. (22nd Ann. Rep. Bur. Am. Ethnol., pp. 203–303.)

Thompson, E. H.
   1887. A ruin at Labna. (Proc. Am. Antiq. Soc., V (n. s.), pp. 9–11.)
   1888. Ruins of Kich-Moo and Chun-kat-cin. (Proc. Am. Antiq. Soc., V (n. s.), pp. 161–170.)

THOMPSON, E. H. — *continued*

　　1892, *a*.　The ancient structures of Yucatan not communal dwellings.　(Proc. Am. Antiq. Soc., VIII (N. S.), pp. 262–269.)

　　1892, *b*.　Yucatan at the time of the discovery.　(Proc. Am. Antiq. Soc., VIII (N. S.), pp. 270–273.)

　　1897, *a*.　Cave of Loltun, Yucatan.　Report of explorations by the Museum, 1888–1889 and 1890–1891.　(Mem. Peabody Mus., I, No. 2, pp. 1–24.)

　　1897, *b*.　The chultunes of Labna, Yucatan.　Report of explorations by the Museum, 1888–1889 and 1890–1891.　(Mem. Peabody Mus., I, No. 3, pp. 1–20.)

　　1898.　Ruins of Xkichmook, Yucatan.　(Field Columbian Mus. Anth. Ser. II, pp. 211–223.)

　　1902.　Water-colors of the Maya.　(Am. Mus. Jour., II, No. 9, p. 91.)

　　1904.　Archaeological researches in Yucatan.　Report of explorations for the Museum.　(Mem. Peabody Mus., III, No. 1, pp. 3–20.)

　　1911.　The genesis of the Maya arch.　(Am. Anth. (N. S.), XIII, pp. 501–516.)

TOZZER, A. M.

　　1907.　A comparative study of the Mayas and Lacandones.　New York.

　　1910.　(With G. M. ALLEN.)　Animal figures in the Maya Codices.　(Papers, Peabody Museum, IV, No. 3.)

　　1911.　Preliminary study of the Ruins of Tikal.　(Memoirs, Peabody Museum, V, No. 2.)

UHLE, M.

　　1889.　Ausgewählte Stücke des K. Museums für Völkerkunde zur Archäologie Amerikas (veröffentlichungen aus dem Königlichen Museum für Völkerkunde, I, pp. 1–44.

　　1902.　Types of culture in Peru.　(Am. Anth. (N. S.), IV, pp. 753–759.)

　　1903.　Pachacamac.　(Univ. of Penn. Dept. of Archaeology.)

　　1904.　Bericht über die Ergebnisse meiner südamerikanischen Reisen.　(Internat. Cong. of Americanists, 14th Sess., Stuttgart, pp. 567–579.)

　　1908.　Über die Frühculturen in der Umgebung von Lima.　(Internat. Cong. of Americanists, 16th Sess., Vienna, pp. 347–370.)

VALENTINI, P. J. J.

　　1879, *a*.　Mexican copper tools.　(Proc. Am. Antiq. Soc., April, pp. 81–112.)

　　1879, *b*.　The katunes of Maya history.　(Proc. Am. Antiq. Soc., Oct., pp. 71–117.)

　　1880.　The Landa alphabet; a Spanish fabrication.　(Proc. Am. Antiq. Soc., April, pp. 59–91.)

　　1881, *a*.　Mexican paper.　(Proc. Am. Antiq. Soc., I (N. S.), pp. 58–81.)

　　1881, *b*.　Two Mexican chalchihuites, the Humboldt Celt and the Leyden Plate.　(Proc. Am. Antiq. Soc., I (N. S.), pp. 283–302.)

　　1882.　The Olmecas and the Tultecas.　(Proc. Am. Antiq. Soc., II (N. S.), pp. 193–230.)

　　1898.　Pinzon-Solis, 1508.　(Gesell. für Erdkunde, Zeitschrift, XXXIII, pp. 254–282.)

　　1902.　The discovery of Yucatan by the Portuguese in 1493.　An ancient chart.　(Records of the Past, I, pp. 45–59.)

VILLAGUTIERRE, SOTO MAJOR, J.

　　1701.　Historia de la conquista de la provincia de el Itza, reduccion, y progressos de la de el Lacandon, y otras naciones de el reyno de Guatimala, a las provincias de Yucatan, en la America septentrional.　Madrid.

WALDECK, J. F. DE

　　1838.　Voyage pittoresque et archeologique dans la province de Yucatan, pendant les années, 1834–1836, folio.　Paris.

　　1866.　Monuments anciens du Mexique.　Palenque et autres ruins de l'ancienne civilization du Mexique, etc., folio.　Paris.　(Introduction by Brasseur de Bourbourg.)

WEYGOLD, F.

　　1903.　Das indianische Lederzelt im Königlichen Museum für Völkerkunde zu Berlin.　(Globus LXXXIII, pp. 1–7.)

WIENER, C.

　　1880.　Pérou et Bolivie.　Paris.

WILSON, T.

　　1894.　The swastika.　The earliest known symbol, and its migrations; with observations on the migration of certain industries in prehistoric times.　(Rep. U. S. Nat. Mus. for 1894, pp. 757–1011.)

ZORITA, A. DE

　　1865.　Breve y sumaria relacion de los señores y maneras y diferencias que habia de ellos en la Nueva-España.　(Coleccion de documentos inéditos relativos al descubrimiento, conquista y colonizacion de las Posesiones Españolas en América y Oceanía, II, pp. 1–126.)

BIBLIOGRAPHY, PART II

BIBLIOGRAPHY, PART II

BANCROFT, H. H.
1875–1876. The native races of the Pacific States. 5 vols. New York and London.

BANDELIER, ADOLPH F.
1878. On the distribution and tenure of lands and the customs with respect to inheritance, among the ancient Mexicans. (Twelfth Annual Report, Peabody Museum of American Archaeology and Ethnology, vol. 2, no. 2, pp. 384–448.) Cambridge.

BOWDITCH, C. P.
1910. The numeration, calendar systems and astronomical knowledge of the Mayas. Cambridge.

BRANSFORD, J. F.
1881. Archaeological researches in Nicaragua. (Smithsonian Contributions to Knowledge, XXV, Art. 2, pp. 1–96.)

BRINTON, D. G.
1882. The Maya chronicles. (No. 1 of Brinton's Library of Aboriginal American Literature.) Philadelphia.
1885. The annals of the Cakchiquels. The original text with a translation, notes and introduction. (No. 6 of Brinton's Library of Aboriginal American Literature.) Philadelphia.
1890. Essays of an Americanist. Philadelphia.

BULLETIN 28.
1904. Mexican and Central American antiquities, calendar systems and history. Twenty-four papers by Eduard Seler, E. Förstemann, Paul Schellhas, Carl Sapper and E. P. Dieseldorff. Translated from the German under the supervision of Charles P. Bowditch. (Bull. 28, Bureau of American Ethnology.) Washington.

CHARNAY, D.
1887. The ancient cities of the New World. Translated by J. Gonino and H. S. Conant. London.

DIAS DEL CASTILLO, BERNAL.
1908. The true history of the conquest of Mexico, 1568. Translated by A. P. Maudslay. (Hakluyt Society.) London.

FÖRSTEMANN, E.
1906. Commentary of the Maya manuscript in the Royal Public Library of Dresden. (Papers, Peabody Museum, IV, No. 2, pp. 44–266.)

GANN, T.
1897–1898. Mounds in northern Honduras. (Nineteenth Annual Report, Bureau of American Ethnology, part 2, pp. 661–692.) Washington.

HARTMANN, C. V.
1901. Archaeological researches in Costa Rica. (The Royal Ethnographical Museum in Stockholm.) Stockholm.

HOLMES, W. H.
1888. Ancient art of the province of Chiriqui. (Sixth Annual Report, Bureau of American Ethnology, pp. 3–187.) Washington.

JOYCE, T. A.
1914. Mexican archaeology, An introduction to the archaeology of the Mexican and Maya civilizations of pre-Spanish America. New York and London.
1916. Central American and West Indies archaeology. Being an introduction to the archaeology of the states of Nicaragua, Costa Rica, Panama and the West Indies. New York.
1927. Maya and Mexican art. London.

KINGSBOROUGH, LORD.
1831–1848. Antiquities of Mexico. 9 vols., folio. London

LEHMANN, W.
    1909. Methods and results in Mexican research. Translated by Seymour de Ricci. Paris.
    1910. Ergebnisse einer Forschungsreise in Mittelamerika und Mexico 1907-1909. (Zeitschrift für Ethnologie, Band, 42, pp. 687-749.)
    1920. Zentral Amerika. Die Sprachen Zentral-Amerikas in ihren Beziehungen Zueinander sowie zu Süd-Amerika und Mexiko. (Vol. 1 of 2 vols.) Berlin.
LOTHROP, S. K.
    1926. Pottery of Costa Rica and Nicaragua. (Contributions, Museum of the American Indian, Heye Foundation, vol. VIII.)
LUMHOLTZ, C.
    1902. Unknown Mexico. 2 vols. New York.
    1900. Symbolism of the Huichol Indians. (Memoirs, American Museum of Natural History, vol. 3, part 1.)
    1904. Decorative art of the Huichol Indians. (Memoirs, American Museum of Natural History, vol. 3, part 4.)
MacCURDY, G. G.
    1911. A study of Chiriquian antiquities. (Memoirs, Connecticut Academy of Sciences, vol. 3.)
MAUDSLAY, A. P.
    1889-1902. Biologia Centrali-Americana, or contributions to the knowledge of the flora and fauna of Mexico and Central America. Archaeology. 4 vols. of text and plates. London.
MEMOIRS OF THE PEABODY MUSEUM.
    v.d. Reports on excavations and exploration by Gordon, Maler, Thompson, and Tozzer.
MORLEY, S. G.
    1915. An introduction to the study of the Maya hieroglyphs. (Bulletin 57, Bureau of American Ethnology.) Washington.
    1920. The inscriptions at Copan. (Publication 219, Carnegie Institution of Washington.) Washington.
PEÑAFIEL, A.
    1890. Monumentos del arte Mexicano antiguo. 3 vols. Berlin.
    1897. Nomenclatura geografica de Mexico. Mexico.
SAHAGUN, BERNARDINO DE.
    1880. Histoire générale des choses de la Nouvelle-Espagne. Edited and translated by D. Jourdanet and Rémi Siméon. Paris.
    1922. Historia de las cosas de Nueva España. Portfolio of illustrations from two Sahagun manuscripts copied under the direction of F. del Paso y Troncoso and issued by the Mexican Government. Florence.
SAVILLE, MARSHALL H.
    1922. Turquoise mosaic art in ancient Mexico. (Contributions, Museum of the American Indian, Heye Foundation, vol. VI.)
    1925. The wood-carver's art in ancient Mexico. (Contributions, Museum of the American Indian, Heye Foundation, vol. IX.)
SCHELLHAS, P.
    1904. Representation of deities of the Maya manuscripts. 2nd ed., rev. Translated by Miss Selma Wesselhoeft and Miss A. M. Parker. (Papers, Peabody Museum, vol. 4, No. 1, pp. 7-47.)
SELER, E.
    1901. Die alten Ansiedelungen von Chaculá im districkte Nenton des Departments Huehuetenango der Republic Guatemala. Berlin.
    1908-1923. Gesammelte Abhandlungen zur amerikanischen Sprach- und Alterthumskunde. 5 vols. Berlin.
    1902-1903. Codex Vaticanus No. 3773 (Codex Vaticanus B). An old Mexican pictorial manuscript in the Vatican Library. Translated by A. H. Keane. Berlin and London.
SPINDEN, H. J.
    1913. A study of Maya art. (Memoirs, Peabody Museum, vol. 6.)
    1924. The reduction of Maya dates. (Papers, Peabody Museum, vol. 6, no. 4.)
SQUIER, E. G.
    1858. The states of Central America: their geography, topography, climate, population, etc. New York.
STEPHENS, J. L.
    1841. Central America, Chiapas and Yucatan. 2 vols. New York.
    1843. Incidents of travel in Yucatan. 2 vols. New York.

THOMAS, C.
  1882. A study of the Manuscript Troano. (U. S. Geographical and Geological Survey of the Rocky Mountain Region, Contributions to American Ethnology, V, pp. 1–224.)
THOMAS, C., and SWANTON, JOHN R.
  1911. Indian languages of Mexico and Central America. (Bull. 44, Bureau of American Ethnology.) Washington.
TOZZER, A. M.
  1907. A comparative study of the Mayas and Lacandones. New York.
  1921. A Maya grammar, with bibliography and appraisement of the works noted. (Papers, Peabody Museum, vol. 9.)

INDEX TO PART I

[For names of authors, see Bibliography. For names of monuments, etc., see Nomenclature. For names of persons and museums given credit for use of drawings, photographs, etc., see Lists of Figures and Plates.]

Abo, 139 note
Acanceh, 85, 132, 138, 213
Acolnahuac, 210
Acropolis, artificial, 96-98
Adobe, 132, 133
Affiliations, 224, 225, 226
Affinity, cultural, 18
Ahau symbols, 59
Ahmekat Tutulxiu, 217
Ahzuitok Tutulxiu, 218
Akbal, 93
Ake, 213
Alabama, 235, 243, 245
Alabaster, 145
Alligator, 177
Alphabet of Landa, 94, 154
Altar de Sacrificios, 197
Altar on pottery, 141
Altars, animal, 59, 73, 130, 131, 177 (see also Animal)
Altars, Copan, 161-162
"   Piedras Negras, 189
"   Quirigua, 174-177
"   Tikal, 169, 170
"   Yaxchilan, 187
Alvarado, 231
American Indians, 32, 171, 235
American Museum of Natural History, v, vii, 65, 86, 138, 142 note, 144, 145, 211, 229, 230 note, 234, 236, 241
Amulets, jadeite, 143, 144, 226
Anahuac, 234
Analogies, 77
Animal altars, 59, 73, 130, 131, 177 (see Jaguar and Two-headed Dragon)
Animal and human form, in pottery, 138
Animal and human gods, 22, 35 (see Gods)
Animal form in art, 16, 20, 21, 35 et seq., 82-85 et seq.
Animal head dresses, 222, 229
Animistic beliefs, 236-247
Ankle ornaments, 173, 175
Anthropomorphism, general explanation, 34-36; in Maya art, 51-52, 57, 62, 64, 77, 79, 83-84, 135, 140; in Mexican art, 222-223; in Old World, 238-239; in Mound area, 243
Appliqué work, 137, 146
Aprons, in sculpture, 28, 44, 51, 148, 149
Arch, portal, 103-105; corbelled, 108; monolithic, 109
Archaeological sites (see Nomenclature, 249-262, and Plate 30)
Archaeological work in Mexico, 220, 227-231
Archaic Period, at Copan, Table I, 25, 156-161, 163-165, Tikal, 165-169, Naranjo, 179, 181, and Yaxchilan, 184; dates on later monuments at Quirigua, 173-175, 177, Naranjo, 181, Yaxchilan, 187-189, Piedras Negras, 189-190, Palenque, 194, Tzendales, 197, in chronicles, 217, in codices, 219; archaistic sculptures, at Quirigua, 175; lack of archaic sculptures, at Quirigua, 175-176, Piedras Negras, 190, and Palenque, 194; provincial inefficiency, at Seibal, 183 (see Tables I and II)

Architecture, 13, 96-133; in second period, 202 et seq. (see Contents for special headings)
Argentina, 239
Arizona, 236, 241
Arkansas mounds, 235, 243
Asia, southern, 233, note
Assemblage in architecture, 96, 104
Assyria, 15, 27, 35, 232
Astronomical calculations, 94
Astronomical signs, in bands, 19; wide distribution, 20-21; various occurrences, 56, 67-73, 91-93, 153, 176, 208, 213; Mexican signs, 92, 209
Astronomy, 12, et seq.
Atlantean figures, 26, 83, 100, 117, 200, 205-208
Atlatl, 236
Atzcapatzalco, excavations, 227-230
Aztec Period, 142, 218, 222, 224, 226, 227, 231

Bacalal, 217
Bacalar, 147, 217, 218
Bakhalal, 217
Balam or Jaguar Priests, 77
Bar and dot numerals, 231
Basketry, on sculptures and pottery, 146-147
Bat god, 84, 225
Bats, in sculptures and codices, 82, 84, 213, 225
Bells, copper and gold, 146; copper, in United States, 236
Ben-Ik sign, 188
Benque Viejo, 182
Berlin Museum, 185
Bibliography, 263-276
Bird, in codices, 77-82, 153, 154; hieroglyphs, 20, 21, 73, 77-82; on pottery, 65, 141, 151; sculptures, 56, 77-82, 88, 131, 153, 154, 172, 193; Mexican figurines, 227; on United States pottery and copper plates, 241-244
Birth and death symbol, 84
Bishop collection, 143
Blackfoot Indians, 247
Boloños Valley, 220, 235
Bone, carved and painted, Copan, 58
Bones, in sculpture, 40, 43, 59, 61, 85-87, 117 et seq.
Books of Chilan Balam, 154, 215, 216
Borbonicus Codex, 210, 212
Borgia Codex, 78, 84, 153, 225
Breast plates, 76 et seq.
Brilliant Period (see Great Period)
British Honduras, 1, 132, 150, 151, 171, 177, 209, 213, 214
British Museum, 31
Buddha, 129
Buildings, function of, 98-103; correlation of, 103-105 (see Contents for subheadings)
Burmah, 238

Caban sign, 73, 91, 95
Caches of copper bells, 146
Cahokia mound groups, United States, 235
Cajamarca, 233
Cakchiquel history, 217

Calcetok, 136, 141
Calchaqui, 233, 239
Calendar stone of Mexico City, 208, 222
Calendar system of Central America, studies of, 13,
    94 et seq.; beginning day of Maya calendar,
    155; general explanation of, 162–163; historical
    developmerit of, 171; correlation of Maya and
    Christian chronology, 215–220 and Table II;
    in other parts of Mexico and Central America,
                                            [220
Camara collection, 136
Cambodia, 233
Campeche, 18, 141, 144, 195, 202, 218
Cancun, 213, 218
Captives, in sculpture, 178, 182, 191, 207
Carocol Tower, 98, 115, 202
Caryatid figures, 83 (see Atlantean)
Casas Grandes, 236, 241
Casting, 145
Celestial eye, 206, 209, 214
Celts, decorated, 143
Cement, 108, 132, 146
Cempoalam, 208, 231
Ceramics, 133–142 (see Pottery)
Ceremonial Bar, explanation and types, 49–50; not
    found in codices, 49, 152, or at Palenque, 193;
    relation to Manikin Scepter and Two-headed
    Dragon, 50–57; historical changes at Copan,
    50, 156–157, Table I; on Leiden Plate, 50, 173;
    at Tikal, 166–167; Quirigua, 175–176; Naranjo,
    178–179, 182 et seq.; Seibal, 183; Piedras Ne-
    gras, 192; Ocosingo, 196; Cancuen, 197
Ceremonial objects (see Criteria)
Chacmool, 200, 206, 208, 230, 231
Chacmultun, 104, 105, 113, 118, 132, 200, 202
Chacnouitan, 217
Chacs, Rain Gods of the four quarters, 62, 77
Chacujal, 8
Chajcar, 19, 88
Chakanputun, 218
Chalchihuites, 220, 229, 235, 236
Chalchihuitl, 142
Chalco, 221
Chaldea, 235
Chama, 84, 140, 197
Chanputun, 218
Charnay casts, 201
Chavero Codex, 210
Chiapas, 1, 3, 98, 130, 146, 196, 201, 214
Chicchan God, 91
Chichen Itza, 4, 13, 14, 18 et seq.; key to chronology
    of the north, 199; initial series date, 199, 200;
    during Period of Transition, 200; during
    Period of League of Mayapan, 200–209; during
    Period of Influence from Mexico, 205–214
Chihuahua, 236, 241
Child birth, 85
Chimbote, 239
Chincoltic, 197
Chinese dragon, 238
Chiriqui, 234
Cholula, 218, 219, 222, 224
Cholulteca River, 240
Christian and Maya chronology correlated, 215
Christian Era, 217
Chronicles of Chilam Balam, 215, 216; of Nakum
    Pech, 216
Chronological classification of Maya monuments and
    cities by style of the art, 155 et seq. (see
    Contents for special headings)
Chronological sequence of art in Mexico, 225 et seq.
Chronological table of monuments at Copan, Table
    I; of Maya history, Table II
Cib, 95
Cimi, 87

Cintla, ruins of, 9, 195, 214
Classical art, compared with Maya art, 1, 11, 15–16; in-
    fluence of religion, 35; anthropomorphism, 35–
    36, 239; art sequence, 155, 160; calendar, 171;
    Old World connections, 231–233, 236, 238–239
Clawed feet on composite animals, 53, 59
Cliff dwellers, United States, 236
Cloisonné pottery, 230, 235, 236 (see Pottery)
Cloven feet on composite animals, 53, 56, 70
Coban, 18, 21, 84, 91, 95, 137, 140, 144, 145, 197
Codices, Maya, figures correlated with sculptures on
    monuments, 62 et seq.; described, 152–154;
    pagination correlated with reproductions, 160–
    161; furnish historical data, 219 (see Dresden,
    Peresianus, Tro-Cortesianus)
Codices, Mexican, 10, 153, 225 note (see Borbonicus,
    Borgia, Fejérváry-Meyer, Nuttall, Vaticanus)
Colima, 229
Colombia, 233, 234, 240
Color, 131–132 (see Painting)
Columns, development of, 113, 114; rows of, 114, 213;
    banded, 115, 128–129, 202; serpent, 115, 205,
    206; picotes, 200; phallic, 200 (see also Atlan-
    tean figures)
Comalcalco, 9, 97, 98, 195, 205
Comayagua, 1, 234
Composite ceremonial objects, 56–61; animals, 34, 88,
    236
Composition, 31–32; at Yaxchilan, 184; increase of
    skill in, at Piedras Negras, 191; at Palenque,
    192
Construction, progressive changes in, at Tikal, 170;
    Yaxchilan, 186–187; Palenque, 193; Chichen
    Itza, 202–204; Xkichmook, 204 (see Contents
    for special headings)
Conquest, memorials of, 23, 29, 212, 214 (see Spanish
    Conquest)
Contact between Maya and Mexican cultures, 1, 205–
    215, 219
Conventionalism, 33–40, 45, 49, 55, 56, 72, 73, 78, 79,
    86, 88, 118–127 et seq.
Copan, 3, 13, 17, 18, 21 et seq.; poses at, 24–25;
    monuments showing progressive changes in
    sculpture, 155–161; correlation of changes in
    sculpture with dates, 159 et seq., and Table I;
    relations with Quirigua, 175; key to chronology
    of the south, 199
Copper, method of working, 145; in United States,
    235
Copper bells, 146; in United States, 236
Copper plates, United States, 244–246
Corkscrew curl, 95
Cornices, 114–115
Corn sign, 22 (see Maize)
Corosal, 132
Correlation of bands of planet symbols, 20–21; gods,
    etc., 62–95; specific details, 152–154
Correlation of buildings, 103–105
Correlation of Maya and Christian chronology, 215
    et seq., Table II
Correlation of pagination in Maya codices and the
    reproductions, 261–262
Correlation of solar and Venus years, 93
Correlation of stelae and buildings, 161–162, 178–179,
    183, 185, 189–190, 201
Correlation of time periods of Long Count, Short
    Count and European Count, 217 and Table II
Cortes, 195, 214
Cosmic symbols, 238
Costa Rica, 133, 142, 143, 145, 234, 240
Coyor, 233
Cosumalhuapa, 214, 241
Cozumel Island, 4, 207, 214
Cranial deformation, 23, 24

Criteria of sequence in architecture:
Buried walls, enlarged foundations and additions, at Copan, 105 and Table I; Chichen Itza, 202–203; Xkichmook, 204
Correlation of stelae and buildings, at Copan, 161–162; Naranjo, 178–179; Seibal, 183; Yaxchilan, 185; Piedras Negras, 189–190; Sayil, 201
Courts, as units of city building at Naranjo, 177–178
Development, of sanctuary, 99–100, at Palenque, 193; of doorways, 100, 113, 115; roof walls, 110–113, at Tikal, 170, Yaxchilan, 186–187, Palenque, 193–194; columns, 113–114, at Chichen Itza, 206 et seq.; cornices, 114–115
Mask panels, less formal at first, 119–120; formal in Northern Yucatan, 120 et seq.; decadent forms, 123 et seq.
Profile panel, 124 et seq., at Hochob, 126; Uxmal, 127; Chichen Itza, 127
Proportion of floor space to wall space, at Tikal, 170; Yaxchilan, 186 et seq.; Palenque, 193; Comalcalco, 195; Ocosingo, 195; in Northern Yucatan, 201
Prototype, 132–133
Re-used material, at Naranjo, 181; Chichen Itza, 200, 203–204, 212
Criteria of sequence in art:
Ceremonial objects, changes in, at Copan, 49–50, 157; Palenque, 52, 58–59, 193; Yaxchilan, 57; Tikal, 166–167; Quirigua, 175–176; Naranjo, 179; Seibal, 183; Piedras Negras, 191–192; in Northern Yucatan, 201
Development of composition and foreshortening, at Palenque, 27, 192; Tikal, 28, 167, 169
Development of stelae, 129–130, at Copan, 155–159; Tikal, 166–167; Quirigua, 175–176; Naranjo, 178–182; Seibal, 183; Yaxchilan, 185–186; Piedras Negras, 190–191; Palenque, 192; Ocosingo, 196; Tzendales, 197; other sites in Guatemala, 197; Northern Yucatan, 199, 201
Development of altars, 130–131; at Copan, 160–161; Quirigua, 177
Development of lintels, at Tikal, 167, 169; Yaxchilan, 184; Kabah, 201
Eye, representation of, at Copan, 156, 159; Yaxchilan, 188; Piedras Negras, 190
Feather drapery, use of, at Copan, 159; Quirigua, 176
Feet, placing of, at Copan, 24–25, 159; Piedras Negras, 190; Ocosingo, 196
Hieroglyphs, style of, at Copan, 160; Tikal, 168–169
Human body, changes in proportion of, at Copan, 156–159; Tikal, 166; Quirigua, 175–176; Piedras Negras, 191; Palenque, 192
Increase in relief and modeling, at Copan, 156–157 et seq.; Tikal, 166–167; Naranjo, 177–179; Yaxchilan, 184 et seq.
Personal equation of cities, 165
Pose, changes in, at Copan, 156, 159; Tikal, 166–167; Quirigua, 175; Piedras Negras, 191
Subordination of detail, 32
Crocodile, 53, 153
Cross bones, 23 (see Death symbols)
Cross, diagonal, 53, 54, 55, 74
Cross, Greek, 149, 190
Cross-legged manner of sitting, 55, 144, 177, 197
Crotalus durissus, 33
Cruciform chambers, 129
Cruciform tombs, Mexico, 226
Cruller-like nose ornament, 17, 74 et seq.

Cuernavaca, 210, 228, 229
Cuicatlan, 210
Cuilapa, 226, 227
Culture periods, Maya, 155–219 (see Protohistoric Period, Archaic Period, Great Period, Period of Transition, Period of League of Mayapan, Modern Period, and Table II); in Mexico, 225–231; in Peru, 235; in Pueblo area, 236; in Nicaragua, 240
Curled fang, 40, 42
Curled nose ornament, wide distribution, 17–18; character of a god, 74
Cuzco, 233
Cycle glyph, 80, 81, 172, 200

Dakota Indians, 246, 247
Dated monuments of Great Period, 216, 217
Dates, at Copan, 156–165; at Tikal, 167–170; on Leiden Plate and Tuxtla Statuette, 171; at Quirigua, 173–177; Naranjo, 180; Seibal, 183–184; Yaxchilan, 187; Piedras Negras, 189–190; Palenque, 194; Tzendales, 197; Saccana, 197; Quiché, 197; Chichen Itza, 198, 200; Xcalumkin, 201; in chronicles, 217; in codices, 219
Dates, correlated with modern system, 216, 217
Death symbols, 23, 50–55, 66, 68, 72, 79, 81, 85–87, 90, 125, 151, 200, 201, 211
Decadence in Maya art, 9, 58, 180, 183, 198, 201, 222, 223
Decadent stage of hieroglyphic inscriptions, 227
Deer, 53, 124, 141, 151
Deformation of heads, 23, 24
Development (see Criteria)
Divinities, 11–12 (see Gods)
Dog, 85
Domiciliary structures, 96
Dragon (see Two-headed)
Drapery, 21–22, 30, 135, 148–150, 176, 178, 192, 196, 197
Dresden Codex, 19–34, 62–94, 149, 152–154, 171, 210, 217, 219, 225; described and correlated, 153, 260–261
Dress and ornament, on sculpture and in codices, 148–150; at Quirigua, 174–177; Piedras Negras, 190–192; Ocosingo, 196
Dress of native peoples, 147, 148
Drilling, 143
Dsecilna, 207
Dsibiltun, 124–127
Dualism, 66, 68
Dwellings, native, 99

Eagle, 78, 79, 81, 212, 222, 243, 244
Earliest dated remains of Maya Art, 170–173
Ear ornaments on sculpture, 24, 35, 40, 44–46 et seq.
Earthquake action, 107
East Indian art, 238
Ecuador, 233, 234, 240
Editorial Note, v
Effigy mounds in United States, 234
Egypt, 196
Egyptian art, 15, 23, 27, 49
Egyptian gods, 35
Ekchuah God, 91
Elaboration, 41–46, 54, 223
El Cayo, 191
Elevation plans, 102–103
Elimination, 38, 43, 192
El Jicaro, 140, 141
Elucidation of codices, 152–154
Esoteric symbols, 237 note
Estanzuela, 229
Etowah mounds, 235
Ethnic connections with Old World, 231
Ethnology, modern, 14

Etla, 227
Evolution, degenerative, 222; divergent, 219, 220
Excavations at Copan, 144, 145; Mexico, 207, 227–231
Explorers, accounts of, 13
Eye (see Criteria)

Façade decoration, 116
Fasciolaria gigantia, 83
Fasting, 33
Feathers, in sculpture, 28, 29, 31, 40, 42, 59, 77–82, 117 *et seq.*; feather drapery, 159, 176
Feathered serpent (see Serpent)
Feet, placing of, on monuments, 24–25, 159, 190, 191, 196
Fejérváry-Meyer Codex, 209, 231
Fetiches, 142
Field Museum of Natural History, 145, 152, 239
Figurines, 18, 138, 141, 142, 150, 195, 214, 215, 222; in Mexico, 227–229
Filigree work, 145–147
Finca Pompeya, 138
Fire God, 211
First epoch in Maya art, 155
Fish and flower, 18, 19
Fish and human, 88
Fish and water-plant, 211
Fish figurine, 88
Fish motive, 45, 64, 77, 82, 117, 193
Flageolets, Mexico, 227
Flamboyant style, 179, 182, 183
Flame-like objects, 37, 41, 63, 68, 78, 140
Flood symbols, 71
Floral motive, 45, 65, 77, 135, 136, 147
Flying façades, 113, 117, 202, 204
Foreign influence, 205
Foreshortening, 27–29, 212, 225
Fortification, 98
Four Quarters, 77, 94, 97, 177, 237
Free-hand drawing, 32
Fresco work (see Painted frescos)
Fret-work, 49, 128, 149, 196, 206, 238
Frieze, 101, 106, 116, 117, 125
Frigate bird, 78
Frog God, 91
Frontera, 9, 214
Funeral pottery, 226, 227

Galisteo Valley, 139 *note*
Gargoyles, 117
Genealogical data, 216, 217
Geometric art, 46–49, 127–130, 141, 145, 149; on native dresses, 147–149
Georgia mounds, 235, 243
Glazed paint, on pottery in Pueblo area, 138–140, *note*
Gods, anthropomorphic, 32 *et seq.;* animal, 35 *et seq.;* astronomical, 64 *et seq.*
Gods, Maya, Long-nosed, 62–69; Roman-nosed, 69–167; storm, 64; of rain and four quarters, 77; of end of year, 84; old bald-headed, 84; shell, 84; maize, 84, 88–90; Manikin Scepter, 22, 63, 64, 213–214; snail, 84; bat, 84; North Star, 90; Chicchan, 91; war, 91; frog, 91; of traveling merchants, 91; fire, 196
Gods in Maya hieroglyphs, A, 87, 90; B, 75, 90; C, 90, 93; D, 69, 73, 75, 84, 90; E, 88–90; F, 90; G, 75; H, 90; I (goddess), 71; K, 64, 153; L, 91; M, 91; N, 76, 84; O (goddess), 91; P, 91
Gods in pottery, 142
Gods of Old and New World, 35, 36
Gold bells and ornaments, 145, 146
Governments, influence of, 171
Gracioza River, 171
Graphic art, 237

Great Period, after date of Stela B, at Copan, 157–159, 165; Tikal, 167, 169–170; Quirigua, 175–177; Naranjo, 181–182; Seibal, 183–184; Yaxchilan, 188–189; Piedras Negras, 190–191; El Cayo and La Mar, 191–192; Palenque, 194; other southern sites, 195–198; Great Period, end of, 198; at Chichen Itza, 199–200; in the chronicles, 217; in the codices, 219; influence at Monte Alban, 226; earliest art in Mexico, free from influence of, 229 (see Table I and Table II)
Grecian art and mythology, 15, 35, 36, 49, 131, 132, 156, 160, 171, 239
Greek cross, 149, 190
Grijalva River, 195
Grotesque, 21, 22, 28, 31, 35, 43, 50, 51, 53, 55, 73, 87–88, 101, 176, 179
Ground-plans of buildings, 99–102
Guatemala, 1, 9, 10, 14, 18, 21, 51, 136–148, 165–170, 189, 196, 197, 211, 214, 226, 234
Guerrero, State of, 224, 245
Guilloche, 48, 49, 128
Gulf States, 235
Gymnasium or ball court, 98, 99

Hebraic type, 24
Heraldic shields, 92
Heron, 78, 79
Hervey Islands, 47
Hieroglyphs, general treatment of, 93–95; knowledge of, 155, 162, 165 *note*, 166–168 *et seq.* (see also Dates)
Hieroglyphs on monuments, verifying sequence of dates determined by style of Maya art, v, 160 *et seq.*
History, Maya, chronological table of, *facing* 216
Historical accounts, 3–11
Historical data, in codices, 219
Hochob, 113, 126, 202
Homogeneity of Maya art, 16–21, 73; of art of mound area in United States, 242
Honduras, 1, 98, 145, 146, 234 (see Copan)
Hopi Indians, 242
Horned serpent (see Serpent)
Huanucoviejo, 233
Huasteca Indians, 2, 231, 235
Huehuetenango, 197
Human form, in Maya art, 15–17, 21–24, 28, 116–127; on sculptures, at Copan, 156–165; Tikal, 165–167; on Tuxtla Statuette and Leiden Plate, 172, 178; at Quirigua, 175–177; Naranjo, 178; Cave of Loltun, 205; Mexican and Maya, 225–229
Human form, subjects represented by, 21–24
Human head in animal mouth, 35, 42, 49, 53, 54, 70, 91, 205, 239, 240; Mexican and Maya, 221, 222
Human sacrifice, 11, 12, 85, 178
Human support, idea of, 207; origin of, 208 (see Atlantean figures)

Idealization, 34, 35
Idols, 129
Illinois mounds, 235, 244
Imagery, 15
Imix symbol, 67
Incatambo, 233
Incense-burners, 131, 214, 215
Incised decoration on pottery, 51, 135
India, animal gods, 35, 238
Individuality in art, 24
Inefficiency, provincial, Seibal, 183
Influence from Valley of Mexico and other cultures, 199, 205
Inheritance, 32, 33

Initial series dates, 162–164 and Table I; at Tikal, 168; on Tuxtla Statuette and Leiden Plate, 171–175; at Quirigua, 173–175; Naranjo, 180; Yaxchilan, 188, 189; Piedras Negras, 189; Palenque, 194; Saccana, 197; Chichen Itza, 198; Xcalumkin, 201; in Dresden Codex, 219
Island of Sacrifices, 110, 231
Iturbide, 218
Itzamna, 62, 69, 92
Itzas, 216
Ixkun, 19, 28, 31, 44, 82, 84, 96, 182
Izamal, 8, 121, 218

Jade, inlaid in teeth, 24
Jadeite, 49, 74, 142–145, 196, 226
Jaguar in art, 34, 47, 74, 76, 77, 135, 137, 138, 141, 149, 151, 177, 191, 222
Jaina, Island of, 18, 136, 142, 151
Jalisco, 229
Java, 233, 238
Jemez River, 139 note
Jonuta, 138, 142, 195
Jupiter symbol, 93

Kabah, 8, 14, 82, 109, 116, 122, 201, 202
Kan sign, 67
Katun, 80, 81, 172, 174–176, 180–188, 189, 194, 196, 201
Katun periods, 215–216
Kayab, 81, 82
Kentucky, 244, 245, 246
Kin sign, 53, 54, 57, 66, 68, 69, 72, 74, 91, 92, 144, 172, 208
Knives, 58, 222
Kukulcan, 11, 62, 69, 98, 211, 218 note

Labna, 8, 14, 37, 97, 100, 109, 113, 118, 120, 123, 200, 202
Labrets, Mexico, 228
Lacandone Indians, 2, 9, 12, 214, 215
La Hondradez, 97, 111, 119
La Mar, 30
La Quemada, 220, 229, 235, 236
Lake Izabel, 3
Lapidary's art, 143
Latest Maya center, Chichen Itza, 205
Lattice work, 202
League of Mayapan, period of, 202–205, 218
Leiden Plate, 49, 143, 170–173, 178, 217
Lima, 233
Limestone, material used, 16, 206
Literature, ancient, 10
Long-nosed God, general study, 61–69; characterization by face, 62, 87; God B, and his powers, 62, 64–65; identification with Manikin Scepter God, 63; decorative use of long-nosed faces, 63–64; relation to God K, 64; Long-nosed Sun God, 66; Long-nosed Death God, 66; relation to rear head of Two-headed Monster, 66–67; flood symbols, 67; intermediate series, Long-nosed God and Roman-nosed God, 74–75; relations of God B and God D, 75–76; relations with Maize God, 90; in architectural decoration, 90; on pottery, 135; as speech scroll, 211; in fresco at Santa Rita, 213, 214; relation to Quetzalcoatl, 220; similarity of faces on Zapotecan pottery, 226 (see Manikin Scepter, Roman-nosed God, etc.)

Macaw, 78, 79, 81, 82
Madrid stela, 18
Maggot sign, 200
Maize God, 84, 88, 90
Maize symbol, 22, 26, 64, 71, 79, 153
Maltrata, 231

Manikin Scepter, general description, 50–53; combined with Ceremonial Bar, 56–57; relation to rear head of Two-headed Monster, 57–58; relation to Long-nosed God, 63; use, 65; not found in codices, 152; found at Tikal, 167, Quirigua, 175–176, Naranjo, 178, Piedras Negras, 190, 192, Tzendales, 197, and in Northern Yucatan, 199, 201; derived forms, 193; last stage of, 211
Manikin Scepter God, 22, 63, 64; at Santa Rita, 213–214 (see Long-nosed God and Manikin Scepter)
Manitoba, 246
Map of archaeological sites (see Plate 30)
Mask in sculpture, 22, 65 et seq.
Mask panels, 119–124, 202–204
Masonry, 102, 103, 107, 108, 111
Mathematics, knowledge of, 194
Mayapan, 98, 202, 213, 218, 219; fall of, 199, 219
Maya codices, 152–154 (see also Dresden, Peresianus and Tro-Cortesianus)
Maya gods, 19 (see Gods)
Maya Indian, modern, 24
Maya poetry, 247
Maya pre-Columbian books, 10
Maya temple, prototype of, 132–133
Medium of exchange, 146
Menomini Indians, 247
Mercury, signs of, 91
Merida, 8, 141, 142, 147, 218
Metal, methods of working, 145–147, 234
Methods of construction, 170, 184, 186 (see Construction)
Metropolitan Museum of Fine Arts, 143
Mexico, 9, 142, 150, 171, 192, 194, 196, 205–214, 219, 225–231; excavations in, 227, 228
Mexican art, 225–231
Mexican codices (see Codices)
Mexican influence, period of, 205–214; interrelations of culture, Mexican and Maya, 219 et seq.
Michoacan, 230
Migration, 9, 11, 217; theories of, 205
Milky Way, Lord of, 92
Miniature stelae, 196
Minor arts, 133–150 (see Contents for headings)
Mississippi Valley, 232, 233
Missouri, 235, 243
Mitla, 132, 209, 214, 220, 227
Moan bird, 79, 81
Modeling, in clay and stucco, 16
Modern Period, architecture at time of Conquest, 3–4, 214; survivals in textile art, 147–148; early historic pottery, 214; modern Lacandone pottery, 214–215; calendar system at time of Conquest, 215–216 and Table II; destruction of Mayapan, 219
Modification, 224
Monkey, 151, 196, 227
Monte Alban, 109, 220, 225; Great Period, 226
Monuments and codices correlated, 62 et seq.
Monuments, monolithic, 129–130
Moon God, 84
Moon signs, 73, 92
Moon and night God, 69
Moon or darkness, sign of, 91, 92
Morelia, 24
Mortar, 105, 107, 108, 109, 110, 133
Mosaic, 108, 110, 115, 120, 123, 127–129, 204, 226
Motagua River, 98
Motul de San José, 182
Mound area of United States, art compared with Mexico and Central America, 232–247
Mounds, pyramid and platform, 105–107
Moundville, 235

Mouth ornaments, 204
Museo Nacional, Mexico, 128, 192–196, 208, 229 *note*
Museo Yucateco, 138
Museum of the Southwest, 242
Museum of the University of Pennsylvania, 197
Museums (see American, Berlin, British, Metropolitan, Peabody)
Mythology, American Indians, 237; Greek, 239; United States, 239, 246, 247

Nahua culture, 1, 9, 10, 11, 39, 62; Toltec and Aztec features in Yucatan, 92, 94, 95, 205, 214; in Guatemala, 98, 214; historical references to Nahua invasion, 218–219; connections between Maya and Nahua culture, 219–225; earliest culture in Valley of Mexico, 227–229; Toltec culture, 230, Aztec culture, 231; Nahua culture in Nicaragua, 234, 240; in Salvador, 234; sphere of influence, 235; cosmic symbols, 238; shell gorgets, 245 (see Toltec, Aztec, etc.)
Nahua and Maya calendars compared, 220
Nahua and Zapotecan codices, 209
Nakum, 97, 111, 119, 125, 126
Name glyphs, 95, 212
Naranjo, 17, 20, 25, 44, 50, 57, 72, 82, 96, 124, 130 *et seq.;* study of sculptures, 177–182; initial series, 180; dates deciphered, 180–182
Nasca, 240
Nebaj, 19
Nephrite, 142
New Mexico, 138 *note*, 236, 241
Nicaragua, 133, 214
Niche with seated figure, 73, 118, 176, 189, 190, 191
Night symbol, 93
Nocuchich, 98, 121
Nomenclature of ruins, monuments and codices, 249–262
North Star, God of, 90, 93
Nose ornament, 17, 18, 40–46, 63, 74, 75, 126, 135, 211, 223, 224, 229
Notation, bar and dot method, 231
Numeration, 94 *et seq.*
Nuttall Codex, 225

Oaxaca, 142 *note*
Ocosingo, 50, 58, 61, 74, 97, 144, 145, 195–196
Ohio, 235, 246
Ojo Caliente, 138 *note*
Old age, 31, 70, 92
Old Chichen Itza, 200, 206
Old World art, 21, 239
Olive shell, 84
Orientation, 96, 97, 98, 177
Origin of Maya art, 1, 2
Owl, 78, 79, 81, 140
Ornaments, in precious stones, 142–146; in metal, 145, 146 (see also Dress and Ornament on Sculptures)

Pachacamac, 239
Painted frescos, 132; at Chichen Itza, 14, 30, 34, 92, 98, 99, 116, 132, 203; Xcalumkin, 200; Santa Rita, 213, 226; Mitla, 226
Painted pottery, 77, 84, 197, 210 (see Pottery)
Painted sculptures, 32 *note*, 131, 132
Painted stucco, 106, 107, 131, 132, 195, 196
Pajarito Park, 138 *note*
Palace-temple Tampak, from drawing by Maler, 103
Palenque, publications on, 8, 13; art and architecture, 16–19, 22, 24, 26, 27, 30–32, 37, 44, 45, 51, 55, 56, 58, 59, 60 *et seq.;* in chronological sequence, 192; later than Tikal and Yaxchilan, 193; one of the last cities of first great epoch, 194; brilliant period, 195

Palms, for thatching, 99
Palo Verde sculptures, 241 *note*
Panel, mask, 119–124, 202–204
Panel, profile, 124–127
Panzamala, 17, 18
Papantla, 231
Parallelism of lines, in design, 37
Parrot, 80, 81, 241
Peabody Museum, 14, 54, 58, 74, 90, 131, 135–138, 140, 141, 144, 145, 151, 156, 162, 209 *note*, 231, 240
Peccary, 53, 85
Peccary skull, engraved, 150, 151
Pensacola, 240
Perage, 242
Peresianus Codex, 20, 21, 73, 78, 79, 83, 84, 89, 90, 92; described and correlated, 153, 260, 261
Period glyphs, 80, 94, 172
Period of Influence from Valley of Mexico, theories of migration, 205; building of this period at Chichen Itza, 205; similarities between Chichen Itza and Mexican cities, 205–212; Maya elements, 212; similarities at Uxmal, 213; at Ake, 213; on Island of Cancun, 213; sculptures and pottery, 213, 214; similarities at Acanceh, 213; at Santa Rita, 213, 214; on the highlands of Guatemala, 214; references to foreign warriors, 214–215; plot of Hunac Ceel, 218
Period of League of Mayapan, second ascent to high culture, 202; cities of the period, 202; structures at Chichen Itza, 202; growth of the Monjas at Chichen Itza, 202–204; the Iglesia perhaps made of refuse of early buildings, 204; realistic sculptures, 205; historical notices in chronicles, 218; synchronous with Toltec cities in Mexico, 220 (see Table II)
Peto, 77, 135
Phallic worship, 200
Phonetic value in glyphs, 91, 94
Pictographs of American Indians, 171
Pictographic writing, 10 (see Codices)
Pictorial sculptures, 116
Picuris, 138 *note*
Piedras Negras, 2, 25, 29, 32, 46, 56, 61, 73, 82, 91, 92, 97, 131, 149, 153; problems of chronological position, 189–192; dates, 189–190; similarity of sculptures in Mexico to those of Piedras Negras, 221
Pipe, 31
Pipes, Mexico, 227
Pipiles, Nahua tribe, 214
Place-name hieroglyphs, 10, 210
Plains Indians, United States, 246
Planet symbols, 70, 93, 150, 176, 209, 213
Planet Venus, 225
Plans, ground, 99–102; elevation, 102–103
Plant and fish motive, 18, 19, 45, 64, 77, 135, 212
Plaster, 108, 131
Platform mounds, 105–107
Plumed Serpent, 11 (see Serpent)
Poetry, Maya, 247
Porfirio Dias Codex, 209
Portico, 100, 193
Pose, general description, 24–31; on an ancient skull, 151; in codices, 152–153; at Copan, 156–159; Tikal, 166–167; on Leiden Plate, 172–173; at Quirigua, 175–177; Naranjo, 178; Seibal, 183; Yaxchilan, 184; Piedras Negras, 189–190; El Cayo, 191; La Mar, 191; Palenque, 193; Tzendales, 197; Kabah, 201; Sayil, 201; Chichen Itza, 207–208, 210; Acanceh, 213
Post-Spanish Records, 10–11, 215–219
Pottery, encaustic or cloisonné, 235, 236; incised, 18, 51, 65, 84, 243; modeled, 58, 198, 214–215;

painted, 77, 84, 138, 147, 197, 210, 223–224, 239, 242; stamped, 18, 74
Pottery, making and ornamentation, 133–142
Pottery, Mexican, 222, 223, 227–231, 235, 236; Peruvian, 239; Pueblo, 138–140, note 240–241
Pottery figurines, 145, 195, 214, 215, 227–229; funeral urns, 226, 229; whistles, 150, 195, 227
Prayer signs, 211
Pre-Aztec Period, 213, 219, 220, 227
Precious stones, 142
Processional grouping of warriors, 206
Pro-Cortesian annals, 227
Profile, 27, 28, 192
Profile panel, 124–127
Protohistoric Period, objects dating from, 170–173; theoretical necessity, 171; early date in codices, 219 (see Table II)
Public works, 32
Pueblo culture, 134, 138–140, note 233–239, 241, 242
Puye, 138 note 242
Pyramid mounds, 98, 105–107
Pyramids of Old and New World, in relation to contact, 232–235

Quen Santo, 17
Quetzal bird, 34, 78, 79, 139
Quetzalcoatl, 202, 220
Quichés, 11, 148; art, 12; History, 217; Myth, 11
Quie-ngola, 226
Quilozintla, 231
Quintana Roo, 1, 12
Quirigua, 3, 8, 13, 20, 21, 23, 25, 28, 37, 41–45, 50, et seq.; chronological development of sculptures, 173–177; later than Copan, 175; historic period, 175

Rain God, 62, 64
Rain Gods of the Four Quarters, 77
Rain Symbol, 22, 67
Rat, 124
Rattle, 151
Rattlesnake, 33, 39
Realistic art, 39, 48, 77, 116–118, 137, 191, 205, 238
Religious beliefs, 11–13; influence on art, 15, 32–34, 36, 39, 171; shown in sculpture and architecture, 21, 61, 98–100; connected with serpent, 49 et seq.; dualistic, 85; compared with Nahua religion, 225
Renaissance, in art, 202
Reptilian motive, 36, 39, 45, 51, 58 et seq. (see Serpent)
Re-used building material, 181, 200, 203–204, 212
Ring and cross symbol, 53, 237
Rio Beque, 106
Rio Chixoy, 142
Rio Grande, 134, 138, 241–243
Rio Seco, 9
Rito de los Frijoles, 138, note 242
Roman-nosed God, general study, 69–76; God D of the codices, 69; connected with sun and sky, 69–70; in combination with a two-headed monster, 70; relation to front head of Two headed Dragon, 70; relation to Ceremonial Bar, 70, 72; powers of God D, 71; evil aspect and goddess I, 71; connections between Gods B, D and G, 71; Roman-nosed God as kin glyph, 72; conventionalized face, 73, 91–92; relation to Serpent Bird, 73; in sculptures, etc., 73–74; intermediate representations, 74–75; relation to God G, 75; relation to Long-nosed God, 76; relation to God N, 84; old man on Palenque panel, 86; relation with Maize God, 90; in architectural decoration, 90; in frescos at Santa Rita, 214

Rome, 171
Roof combs, 105, 108, 110–113, 186, 187, 193

Sabacche, 113
Saccana, 197
Sacrifice, human, 11, 12; in codices and on sculptures, 64, 79, 85; on pottery, 141
Sajcabaja, 142 note
Salinas de los Nueve Cerros, 197
Saltire, 57
Salvador, 234
Sanctuary, 99, 100, 193, 194
San Andres Tuxtla Statuette, 143, 170–173, 195
San Filippo, 171
San Ildefonso, 242
San Juan de Motul, 26
San Juan Teotihuacan, 205, 206, 210, 218, 228
San Salvador, 208
Santa Cruz Quiché, 51, 136, 137
Santa Helena pottery, 240
Santa Lucia Cozumahualpa, 210, 211, 214
Santa Rita, 132, 150, 209, 213, 218
Santa Rosa, 218
Santa Rose Xlabpak, 50, 102–103, 201
Saturn symbol, 93
Sayil, 50, 103, 113, 130, 201, 202
Sayula, 220, 235
Scotland, 244
Screech owl, 81
Scroll work, 53, 54, 224, 238
Sculptures (see Stelae, Lintels, Altars, etc.)
Sculptures, re-used, 204
Sealed rooms, 103, 111, 112
Sea-shell fringe, 191
Seeds, 191
Seibal, 44, 56, 57, 77, 79, 81, 91, 130, 193; provincial inefficiency of first sculptures, 183; latest accurately dated examples of high art, 189; Table II
Sepulchral pyramids, 185
Sequence of dates in inscriptions on monuments, same as indicated by style of sculptures, 159, 160
Serpent, the, 3, 7, 28, 92; general consideration of serpent in Maya art and religion, 32–76; in architecture, 92, 107, 113–114, 116–118, 120–127; in works of art, 172–173, 179, 205, 211–212; in Mexican art, 221–225; religious ideas connected with, 236, 237; representations of, in art in Old World, Peru and United States, 237–243, 246–247 (see Contents for special headings)
Serpent, feathered, 34, 59–61, 62, 77–82; horned, 236, 237, 239, 242, 243, 246; plumed, 11, 34–35, 38, 237, 241, 242; winged, 236, 237, 239, 242, 243, 246
Serpent bird, 60, 61, 77–82; columns, 113, 114, 205, 206; god, 62 et seq.; stairways, 106–107
Serpent with human head in mouth, 35 (see Human head)
Sex among the Maya gods, 71
Shell, in ornamentation, 57, 64, 82, 84, 88, 145, 156, 173, 191
Shell and human, 83, 84
Shell God, 84, 225
Shell gorgets, in Mexico and United States, 242, 245
Shell masks, United States, 246
Shell ornaments, from excavations, 145
Shell pendants, in sculpture, 28, 29
Shells, carved, from excavations, 151
Shields, in sculpture, 28, 55, 128
Shrine, with stucco work, Ocosingo, 195, 196
Silver ornaments, 145, 146
Simplification, 38–41
Sizing, on pottery, 230

Skeletons and skulls, representation of, 85–87
Skull of peccary, engraved, 150–151
Sky God, 69
Sky symbol, 93
Snail, 82, 83
Snail God, 84
Snail and human, 83, 84
Social organization, 32, 33
Sologuren collection, 227
Spanish Conquest, 171, 194, 201, 213, 214, 219, 226, 230, 234, 240, 242
Spanish epoch, 154
Spear throwers, 222
Speech scroll, 77, 132, 206, 210, 211, 213, 214
Squier collection, 144, 145, 196
Squirrel, 213
S-shape, 56
Staffs, 153, 183, 225
Stairways, 107 et seq.
Star symbols, 206, 209, 213
Statuette, Tuxtla, 171
Stela, at Altar de Sacrificios, with early series initial date, 197
   " Chincoltic, 197
   " Ixkun, with early series initial date, 182
   " Motul de San José, 182
   " Salinas de los Nueve Cerros, 197
   " Tzendales, 196, 197
Stelae, Benque Viejo, 182
   " Cankuen, 197
   " Copan, described, 156–165
   " Itsimté, 197
   " Monte Alban, 226
   " Naranjo, 177
   " Ocosingo, 196
   " Piedras Negras, described, 189–192
   " Quirigua, 173–174
   " Saccana, with important initial series, no ornamentation, rude carving of glyphs, 197
   " Sayil, 201
   " Seibal, 183, 184
   " Tabi, 201
   " Yaxchilan, 185–186
   " Yaxha, 182
Stelae and Altars, general description, 129, 131 (see Altars)
Stone, method of working, 16
Stones, precious, 142–145
Stone implements, 16
Stone ornaments, from excavations and on sculptures, 144–145
Stone yokes, Mexican, 224, 225, 231
Structural and artistic sequence in Northern Yucatan, 204–205
Stucco work, 16, 30, 31, 51, 61, 76, 85, 89, 98, 111, 115, 117, 118, 125, 192; figures in high relief, 108; painted, 106, 107, 131, 132, 195, 196
Style, of sculptors, 24
Subiaba, 240
Subordination of detail, 32, 192
Substitution, 46, 123, 124
Substructures, 105, 107
Successive periods of growth, 204
Summary of first epoch, 198
Summer solstice, 82
Sun disk, 74, 92, 206, 208, 209, 214, 220
Sun glyph, 238
Sun God, 18, 72, 74, 75, 126, 144, 173
Sun shield, 17
Sun sign, 22, 53–55, 65–70, 75, 91, 208, 209, 237
Sun worship, Maya and Nahua, 208–209
Superimposed cultures in Mexico, 220
Survivals, 12, 58, 59, 117, 127, 147, 214
Swastika, 122, 224, 238

Syllabary, 94
Symbolism, in cultural affiliation, 237 et seq.
Symbols, on Two-headed Dragon, 53, 54; astronomical, 91–95 (see Birth, Death, Fish, Flood, Flower, Maize, Rain, Saturn, Sky, Sun, Star, Tau, Water); Mexican, 209, 210, 238 note

Tabasco, 1, 9, 146, 150, 153, 195, 213–215
Tabi, 130, 201
Tabira, 139 note
Tables, I, facing 164; II, facing 218
Tamaulipas, 231, 235
Tampico, 245
Tantah, 130
Taos, 138, note
Tarascan area, 208, 220, 229, 230
Tattooing, 150; in Mexico, 229
Tau sign, 47
Tau-shaped windows, 115
Tcherigi, 138 note
Teayo, 231
Technique, 27, 143
Tecolpa, 150
Teeth, in sculptures, 51, 63, 69, 72, 74, 78, 121, 126, 127
Tegucigalpa, 240
Tehuacan, 231
Tehuantepec, 227
Temples, 98–103; prototype of, 132–133; at Palenque, 192 et seq.; Ocosingo, 195; Chichen Itza, 199; Xcalumkin, 200
Tenampua, 98
Tennessee, 242, 246
Tenochtitlan, 1, 206, 207, 220, 227, 228, 231
Tenon, 116, 128, 129
Tenosique, 189
Teotihuacan, 219, 220, 222, 227, 228, 230
Tepancuapam Lake, 197
Tepatlaxco, 231
Tepic, 229
Terra cotta (see Pottery)
Teutiercar village, 8
Textile art, 147–150; in Mexico, 229; in Peru, 239
Tezcoco, 211, 220, 227
Theocracy, 32
Theories of contact and connection, 231
Throne or niche, 153 (see Niche)
Tiho (Merida), 8
Tikal, 13, 25, 26, 28, 32, 37, 50, 53, 56, 58, 61, 68, 86, 89, 97, 100, 102, 106–112, 116–120, 125, 130–131; study of monuments, 165–170; dates deciphered, 167–170; earliest of the Maya centers, 170, 205
Tlacolula, 227
Tlaloc, 62
Tlascala, 206–208, 220
Tollan, 217
Toltec culture, 1, 211, 227; influence of, 213; migration, 205
Tonalamatl, 154
Tonatiuh of the Nahua, 74, 208, 220
Tonala, 227
Tonina, 97
Tortoise, 82, 83
Totemism, 22, 32, 33, 82
Totoate, 229
Totonacan culture, 209, 222, 229; chacmool figure, 208, 231; serpent heads and stone yokes, 224; stelae, 231
Towers, 98, 102, 202
Trade contact, 236
Traditional history, 198, 202, 215, 218 note, 220
Transition period, new conditions of study, 198–199; important links connecting with old order, 199–

200; possibility of phallic worship, 200; inscription at Xcalumkin, 200–201; Manikin Scepter, 201; stelae, 201; in chronicles, 218 (see Table II)
Tree, conventionalized, 79
Tree, cross-shaped, 60, 61
Trefoil scroll, 54, 56, 70
Trellis work, 128
Troano Codex, 154
Tro-Cortesianus Codex, 37, 63, 64, 71, 78, 83 note, 90, 219; described and correlated, 153, 260, 261
Trogan or quetzal, 78
Trujillo, 233
Tula, 114, 151, 205, 206, 207, 212, 219, 220, 230
Tuloom, 4, 12, 98, 113, 118, 206
Tun glyph, 80, 81, 84, 87, 172
Turkey, 78, 79, 82
Turkish fashion of sitting, 25, 177
Turquoise, 131
Turtle, 81
Turtle altar, 55, 83, 87
Turtle and human, 83
Tuxpan, 228, 244
Tuxtla Statuette, 143, 170–173, 195, 217
Two-headed dragon, 41–43, 53–61, 70, 71, 73, 94, 153, 190, 192, 193, 211
Two-headed dragon altar, 83, 177
Two-headed jaguar seats, 76
Types of beauty, Maya, 23
Tzendales River ruins, 52, 112, 196, 197
Tzendales tribe, 9
Tzintzuntzan, 220
Tzulá, 132 note

Uinal glyph, 91, 172
Uloa Valley, 13, 49, 74, 84, 85, 98, 137, 142, 147
Umbilical cord, 51, 89
Unity, cultural, 17
Usumacinta Valley, 2, 3, 8, 13, 25, 106, 109, 111, 114, 116, 131, 133, 138, 142, 175, 184, 187, 189, 195, 197, 214
Utatlan, 9
Utilitarian art, 186, 198
Uxmal, early description, 4–8; architectural details, 19, 21, 49, 76, 81, 86, 100–105, 109, 113, 115, 117–118, 122–124, 127, 129, 150, 200, 205; League of Mayapan, 199, 202, 205; Nahua influence, 213; historical references, 218–219

Valladolid, 218
Vandalism, 160
Variant and decadent forms, 56–61
Vaticanus Codex, 212, 224
Vaults, 108–110
Vaulted passages, 109
Velasco, José M., drawings by, 208
Veneer of cement, 132; of mosaic, 108
Ventral appendage, 63
Venus symbol, 59, 92, 93, 194, 225, 238
Vera Cruz, 2, 110, 171, 195, 208, 224, 225, 231, 235

Vertebrae, in sculpture, 87, 128
Virginia, 246
Vulture, 78, 79

Walls, 107–108
Wall of Troy motive, 128
Wands, 193
Warfare, 12, 21, 23, 26, 30, 91, 98
Water goddess, 71
Water lily, 77
Water-plant motive, 18, 211
Water-plant and fish motive, 77
Water symbols, 18, 38, 42, 53–55, 64–67, 75, 84, 210
Weaving, 215, 220
Whistles, 195; pottery, 142; Mexico, 227
Wing panel, 61, 62
Winged globe of Egypt, 61, 196
Winged serpent (see Serpent)
Winter solstice, 82
Wisconsin mounds, 235
Woman, native, 147; in sculpture, 178, 190, 228
Wood, in construction, 6, 115, 130, 132
Wooden lintels, 38, 74, 100, 115, 116, 201
Writing, hieroglyphic and pictographic, 10 (see Hieroglyphs and Codices)

Xcalumkin, 200, 218
Xculoc, 207
Xkichmook, 132 note, 204
Xlabpak, 218
Xochicalco, 206, 210, 223, 225, 230
Xoxo, 227
Xupa, 27, 194

Yaxchilan, early description of, 9; publications on, 13; plastic art, 16; in comparative study, 17, 21 et seq.; chronological sequence of monuments, 184; three different periods of art, 186
Yaxha, 50, 125, 182
Yaxkin glyph, 72
Year symbol, 84
Yucatan, 13–15, 18, 77, 82, 83, 97 et seq. (see Copan)

Zacapa, 141
Zacatecas, 235
Zachila, 227
Zacualpa, 142 note
Zapatero Island, 240
Zapotecan culture, 1, 15, 60 etc.; pyramids, 105; pottery, 137; jadeite, etc., 142; codices, 153, 225; Monte Alban early center, and Mitla late city, 220, 225–226; sculptures and figures of Oaxaca, 221–222; funeral urns, period of, 226; development of sculpture, 227; late pottery of Nochistlan, 227
Zapotecan-Mixtecan area, 225
Zapote wood (see Wood)
Zapotlan, 228
Zero sign, 68
Zotz glyph, 84
Zuñi, 241, 242

Agriculture, connection with archaic art, 367; distribution of, 288, 290; distribution in New World, 290; influence on Mayan culture, 291; invention of, 281, 283–285, 288–289; spread and development of, 288, 290, 366–367, 368, 394–395

Ah Bolon Dzacab, 303

Ah Puch, Lord of Death, 303

Aldebaran, 382, 383, 386

Alphabet of Landa, 314–315

Altars, Mayan, 296, 371, 375; Quirigua, 306

Amulets, archaic figurines as, 287; gold, 345

Animals, domestication of, 270, 287, 368

Annals of Quauhtitlan, 334

Arch, in Mayan architecture, 293

Archaic, art, 281–282, 285–286, 291, 363; art, on borders of Mayan area, 291; art, local developments of, 288–290; culture, 339–340, 366–368; culture, distribution of, 288–290; culture, figures, 287–288; figurines, 285–286; horizon, extensions of, 288–290; pottery, 281–282, 287–288; sites, 282–283; stone sculptures, 288

Architecture, early period of Mayas, 324; great period of Mayas, 324; historical sequence determined by, 307; Mayan, 292–294, 389–390; Mitla, 328–329, 330–331; Monte Alban, 328–329; period of League of Mayapan, 325; transition period, Mayan, 324–325; types of, La Quemada, 337–338; Zapotecan, 328–329

Art, archaic, 281–282, 285–286, 291, 363; archaic, characterization of, 285; archaic, Colombia and Venezuela, 289; archaic, local developments of, 288–290; bat, represented in, 270; Chorotegan, 341–344; decorative, Isthmian region, 289; high development of Mayan, 291; massive sculptural, 294–296; Mayan, 297, 323–325; Mayan, human figure in, 300; Mayan, sequences in, 306–307; Mayan, serpent in, 297–300; motives, Huichol, 277–278; Santa Lucia Cozumalhualpa, 340–341; Tarascan, 363; Toltecan, influenced by Mayan, 333; Totonacan, close correspondence to Mayan, 331–332; Zapotecan, influenced by Mayan, 328

Arts, minor, Aztecan, 362–363; Mayan, 296–297

Astronomical, base line, Copan, 319; checks, on correlation with Christian chronology, 318–319; observatories, Mayan, 319–320

Astronomical Congress, Copan, 381, 384

Astronomy, Mayan knowledge of, 291, 307–308, 316–318, 369–393

Atlatl, 286, 383

Atzcapotzalco, 347, 349; stratification at, 282, 333

Aztecan history, 347–349

Aztecs, 275–276, 346–366, 383; and Mayas, compared to Greeks and Romans, 346

Baktun, defined, 312

Bamboo, 395

Bar and dot numerals, 312, 316, 328, 329

Basketry, Mayan, 297

Bats, represented in ancient art, 270

Bells, Aztecan, 362; copper, 339; copper and gold, 345

Ben, Mayan day sign, 296

Birds, Mexico and Central America, 270

Blankets, Mexican, 278, 363

Brilliant period, Mayan civilizations, 291–292, 324

Buildings, Mayan, 292–294; Mitla, 331

Caban, Mayan day sign, 296

Cakchiquels, 326, 350

Calendar, annual, Mayan, 307, 371, 377, 383, 392, 393; Central American, 330; ceremonial, Aztecan, 356; lunar, Mayan, 320–322; lunisolar, Mayan, 308–309; religious, Aztecan, 358–359; system, Zapotecan, 328–330; Venus, Mayan, 322–323

Calendar round, Mayan, 311

Calendar Stone, 351–352, 357, 392

Calpolli, Aztecan, 350

Cannibalism, 279

Captives, as represented in Mayan art, 300

Caribs, characterization of culture, 279

Caricature, in archaic figurines, 286

Carving, development in style at Copan, 306; on Mayan monuments, 306; stone, at Xochicalco, 336

Celts, copper, Tarascan, 363; stone, 288

Cemetery, at Copilco, 282–283

Cempoalan, 272, 332, 344

Cenote, 269

Cephalic index, Mexico and Central America, 280

Ceremonial, bar, Mayan, 300, 302, 303, 306; regalia, depicted in Mayan art, 300

Ceremonies, Aztecan, 358–361; Mexican, 279

Chacmool, 333, 344, 363

Chalchuihtlicue, Aztecan Goddess of Water, 358

Chapultepec, 348

Chiapanecan languages, 276–277

Chichen Itza, 273, 307, 318–320, 325, 327, 333, 334, 336, 341, 344, 363, 394

Chichimecas, 346–347, 394

Chicomoztoc, 337, 347

Chiefs, Aztecan, 349–350; Texcoco, 347; Toltecan, 333–334; war, Aztecan, 348–349; Zapotecan, 330

Chilam Balam, Books of, 305, 307, 326

Chimayo blankets, 278

Chinampa, 394

Cholula, 272, 334, 336–337, 346

Chorotegan culture, 328, 341–344

Chronology, archaic horizon, 281; Aztecan, 347–349; bases of Mayan, 304–306; Mayan, 367; Mayan, correlation with Christian, 291, 307, 318; Mayan, established by dated monuments and style of sculpture, 305, 306; Peruvian, 367–368; Southwestern, 367; Toltecan, 334

Cities, Mayan, 291

Civilization, Mayan, 291–326, 367

Civilizations, middle, in Mexico and Central America, 327–345

Clans, kinship, 349–350

Climate, Mexico and Central America, 267

Cloisonné pottery, 336, 338–339; San Juan Teotihuacan, 336

Codex, Aubin, 347–348; Magliabecchiano, 356, 359; Nuttall, 364, 365; Xolotl, 347, 391

Codices, Mayan, 316–318, 364, 371, 383, 388; Mayan gods in, 303, 304; Mexican, 353; southern Mexico, 330, 364–365

Colhuacan, 334, 347, 348; stratification at, 282

Colonization, Central America, by Spaniards, 271; Mexico, 274

Columns, sculptured, at Tula, 336

Comalcalco, 327

Commerce, Aztecan objects of, 356

Composition in design, Mayan, 300–301

Conquest, history of Spanish, 271–275; of Mexico, 271–275; symbol for, 365

Construction of walls, La Quemada, 337–338; Mayan, 293–294; Mitla, 331

Copan, 269, 291, 292, 294, 306, 315, 319–320, 321, 324, 371, 375, 384, 394, 395; vs. Palenque, 389–390, 393

Copilco, 282–283

Cora, 275, 277

Coronado, 274

Correlations, dates with style of carving in Mayan monuments, 304–306, 307, 314; Mayan and Christian chronology, 318–319

Cortez, Hernando, 271–273, 274, 349, 351, 366

Crocodile motive, in Chorotegan art, 343, 344; Isthmian region, 344, 345

Crops, indigenous and introduced, Mexico and Central America, 270–271, 366–368; principal, Mayan region, 291

Cross-section, typical, Mayan temple, 293

Cuauhtemoc, 349

Cuicuilco, 283

Cuitlahuac, 273

Cult, of the quarters, Aztecan, 358; of Xipe, 342

Culture, Carib, 279; Chorotegan, 341–344; horizons, stratification of, 281–282; Huichol, 277–278; Lacandone Indians, 279; Mayan, 291–326; Mosquito Indians, 279; peoples speaking Uto-Aztecan languages, 275–276, 394; sequences of, 367–368; southern Mexico, 364–365; strata, Atzcapotzalco, 282; Sumo Indians, 279; Tarascans, 363; Toltecs, 332–334, 346; Totonacan, 331–332; Zapotecan, 328–330

Cycle, defined, 309

Dances, hunting, Huichol, 278

Dates, of dedication, Mayan, 314; early Mayan, 323, 327; Mayan, 305, 306, 311, 313; on National Stone, 352; Olmeca, 327–328; Toltecan, 333–334

Day, count, Mayan, 308–310, 369, 386; signs, Aztecan, 351–352, 355; signs, hieroglyphs used on Mayan pottery, 296; signs, Mayan, 308, 315; signs, Zapotecan, 328, 329

Death God, Mayan, 303

Decoration, Mayan buildings, 294–296; Mayan pottery, 296–297; pottery, archaic period, 287–288

Decorative motives, Chorotegan art, 343–344; distribution of, 367–368

Dedication, dates of, Mayan, 314

Design, composition and perspective, Mayan, 300–302; on Leyden plate, 323; on Mexican blanket, 363; motives, archaic pottery, 281, 287–288; motives, Costa Rica, 343–345

Designs, archaic horizon, 288–289; on blankets, 278; developed in negative painting, 339; geometric, at Mitla, 331, 365; Mayan pottery, 296–297; polychrome pottery, 296; realistic, Mayan pottery, 296; textile, archaic, 286; textile, Aztecan, 363; textile, Mayan, 297; Totonacan sacrificial yokes and paddle stones, 332; woven, Huichol, 277–278

Diamond-ring phenomena, 384, 387

Dogs, domestication of, 287

Draconic period, 370

Dresden Codex, 304, 316, 317–318, 321–322, 323, 372, 374, 375, 376, 378, 384, 385

Dress, shown in archaic figurines, 286; Mexico and Central America, 278–279; modern Mexican, 278

Drums, 361, 394

Dyes, 368

Dynamics, man and, 378–381; Mayas and, 387–388

Early period, in Mayan history, 324

Earrings, archaic figurines, 286

Earth Navel, 394

Eclipses, 369–371, 373, 385–386, 387, 392

Ecliptic, 369, 372, 387–389

Economic contributions, of American Indians, 368

Ehecatl, God of Winds, 287, 335

Ek Ahau, war god, Mayan, 304

Elevations, Mayan buildings, 294

Environment, Mayan, 327; Mexico and Central America, 267–271

Ephemeris, Maya, 370, 372, 373, 375

Ethnology, 277–280, 286–287

European contact, history of, 271–275

Exploration, of Central America, by Spaniards, 271; Mexico, 271, 273

Eyes, archaic sculptures, 289; color and Mongoloid tilt, 280; Totonacan figurines, 331–332; types of, on archaic figurines, 286, 289

Facade decoration, Mayan, 294–296

Face numerals, Mayan inscriptions, 312, 315

Fauna, Mexico and Central America, 270

Feast, in connection with planet Venus, 360; of twelfth month, 360

Feasts, Aztecan, 358–361; Sumo, 279

Feather mosaics, Aztecan, 363; Tarascan, 363

Fertility, female figurines associated with, 282, 287, 288

Fetishes, female, Southwestern Pueblo, 367

Fibers, 368

Figurines, archaic, 282, 285–286; archaic, at Atzcapotzalco, 282; archaic, Colombia and Venezuela, 289; archaic, Isthmian region, 289; archaic, Nicaragua, 289; archaic, Salvador, 289; clay, transition period, 291; female, Basket-Maker III, 288–289; female, distribution of, 287, 288–289;

female, Island of Marajo, 290; pottery, Aztecan, 362; pottery, San Juan Teotihuacan, 335–336

Filigree, modern Mexican work, 362

First Empire, Mayan, 307, 322, 324, 344, 367, 389–390

Flageolets, Aztecan, 361

Flora, Mexico and Central America, 270–271

Flying façade, Mayan buildings, 294

Food plants, cultivated by American Indians, 368; most widely distributed in New World, 284

Frescoes, Mitla, 331

Frontier cities of northwest, 337–340

Fruits, native, 271

Funerary urns, Zapotecan, 329, *facing* 267

Games, ceremonial Toltecan, 333; sacred, Olmeca, 327

Gardens, natural, 395

Genealogies, Aztecan, 349

Geography, Mexico and Central America, 267–271

Geology, Mexico and Central America, 269

Gladiator stones, 352

Glaze, on modern Mexican pottery, 278

Glyphs, introducing, 313; period, Mayan, 313, 315; supplementary series, 313, 321

God houses, Huichol, 278

God of War, Mayan, 304

God's eyes, Huichol, 278

Gods, Aztecan, 354, 355, 356–357; beast, Mayan representation of, 302; in Dresden Codex, 304; Mayan, 297–298, 302–304, 318; Mexican, 287, 357; represented in pottery from San Juan Teotihuacan, 336

Gold work, ancient, Isthmian region, 289; Aztecan, 362–363; in cruciform tombs, 331; Isthmian, 344–345; Mayan, 297; Zapotecan, 330

Gourd vessels, Tarascan, 363

Government, Aztecan, 349–350; theocratic, of Mayas, 300, 372–373, 378, 380, 381, 389, 390, 393, 395

Graves, Isthmian, gold objects found in, 344–345

Great Mound, Copan, 324

Great Period, Mayan history, 324

Great Pyramid, Mexico City, 348

Grooving, archaic figurines, 285–286

Groundplans, Toltecan buildings, 333; Yaxchilan temples, 292

Guatuso, 280

Gums, 368

Haab, defined, 320

Hablatun, defined, 312

Hair form, Indians of Mexico and Central America, 280

Head form, Indians of Mexico and Central America, 280

Headdresses, archaic figurines, 286; Zapotecan funerary urns, 329

Hieroglyphs, Aztecan of precious stones, 353; containing phonetic element *kin*, 315–316; decorative use on pottery, Mayan, 296, 386; of four directions, 315; Mayan, 291, 300, 314–318; Mayan, Venus and Moon, 319; Nahuan, 354; on stelae at Monte Alban, 329–330; on Stone of Tizoc, 352–353; at Xochicalco, 336; Zapotecan, 328–330

History, Aztecan, 347–349; Chichimecan, 346–347; cross-section of New World, 366–368; of European contact, Mexico and Central America, 271–275; Mayan, 318; Mayan, recovery of, 304–306; Mayan, summary of, 323–326; summary in relation to archæological evidences, on archaic horizon, 290; Toltecan, 332–334; traditional, southern Mexico, 364–365

Hochob, 325

Hokan linguistic stock, distribution of, 277

Holmul, 390

Horse, introduction of, 290

Hotun periods, 314

Houses, adobe, Mexican, 278; archaic period, 288; Mayan, 293

Huastecas, 276, 331

Huichol, 275, 277–278

Huipili, decorated, 278–279

Huitzilihuitl, 348, 349

Huitzilopochtli, 350, 352, 357, 360

Human, form, carved in stone, archaic period, 288; form, in Mayan art, 297–299, 300, 302–304

Hunac Ceel, identification of, 325

Hunting implements, Lacandone, 279

Ilhuicatl, inferior heavens, 358

Imix, day sign, Mayan, 296; first day of formal permutation, 309–310

Incense burners, Lacandone, 279

Incised designs on pottery, 297, 336

Influence, Aztecan, in Central America, 365–366; Mayan, on other civilizations, 333; Mexican, in northern Yucatan, 325

Initial Series dates, 313, 314, 318, 321, 325, 372–373, 382, 384

Inscriptions, hieroglyphic, 304; hieroglyphic, on Mayan monuments, 314; Mayan, face numerals on, 313; Mayan, Great Period, 324; Mayan, typical, 313

Invention of agriculture, in New World, 281, 283–285, 288–289

Irrigation, in New World, 268, 284, 288, 290, 394

Itzamna, 302, 304

Ixchel, Goddess of the Rainbow, 304

Ixtapalapan, 272

Ixtubtun, Mayan goddess, 304

Jade, carving of, Mayan, 297; Zapotecan, 328–330; work in Aztec mosaics, 363

Jaguar design, Chorotegan art, 343–344

Jupiter, 374, 377, 378, 379, 385, 387, 389

Kan, day sign, Mayan, 296; maize sign, 318

Katun, defined, 307, 312

Kukulcan, 325

Lacandone Indians, 276, 279, 326

Lakes, Mexico and Central America, 268, 269

Land laws, Aztecan, 350

Language, Toltecan, 333; Totonacan, 331

Languages, Central America, 361; Mexico and Central America, 275–277

La Quemada, 337–338

League, Aztecan, 349; of Mayapan, 325

Leyden Plate, 323, 372

Lienzo of Amoltepec, 364–365

Linguistic stocks, Mexico and Central America, 275–277
Lintels, Mayan sculptured, 294, 301; Zapotecan, with hieroglyphs, 329
Long count, Mayan, 313–314, 321
Long-nosed God, Mayan, 302–303, 329, 357
Lunar calendar, Mayan, 320–322
Lunisolar calendar, Mayan, 308–309

Macuilxochitl, 366
Maize, distribution of use, 284, 394, 395; most important food of New World, 284; staple, in Mayan region, 291
Maize God, Mayan, 304
Manikin Scepter, 300, 302
Manioc, cultivation of, 284, 395; use and preparation by Caribs, 279
Marimba, origin of, 362
Mars, 374, 376, 379, 381–382, 385, 386, 387, 389
Mask panels, on Mayan structures, 295–296, 329
Mathematics, Mayan, 369, 373, 388
Matlatzincas, 363
Mayan civilization, 291–326; linguistic stock, distribution of, 276
Mayas and Aztecs, compared to Greeks and Romans, 346
Mazatecas, 341–342, 350
Medicines, 368
Mercury, 374, 376–377, 379, 385, 387, 390, 393
Metal, ornaments made of, Mayan, 297; working, technology of, 367–368; Zapotecan, 330
Metates, elaborately sculptured, 343–344
Metonic cycle, Greeks, 321
Mexican influence, period of, in Mayan history, 325
Mexitin, 275
Mictlan, 330, 358
Mictlanteuctli, Lord of Death, 358
Middle Period, in Mayan history, 324
Midsummer Day, 372, 392
Migrations, Aztecan, 347–348; indicated by distribution of linguistic stocks, 276–277
Mitla, 269, 328–329, 330–331, 365
Mixtecan stock, 276
Mixtecas, 328, 350, 364, 388
Moctezuma, 272, 349, 351, 364
Modeling, archaic figurines, 285, 286; archaic sculptures, 289; clay, San Juan Teotihuacan, 335–336
Modern period, Mayan history, 326
Mogotes, Zapotecan burial mounds, 329
Monkey, in Chorotegan art, 343
Monte Alban, 328–329, 364
Month, Mayan, twenty day signs of, 308–309; signs, of Mayan year, 310; signs, Zapotecan, 329
Months, Aztecan, 355; Mayan, length of, 310; Mayan, names of, 310
Monuments, Mayan, dated, 314; sequence of Mayan determined by style of sculpture, 306–307
Moon, 370, 374, 379; representations of, 320–322
Mosaic, feather, Aztecan, 363; feather, Tarascan, 363; masks and ceremonial objects, 297
Mosquito Indians, 279
Mound, artificial, at Copan, 292, 324; at Cholula, 337; at Cuicuilco, 283
Mounds, at Atzcapotzalco, 282; foundation for temples, 292; Mayan, 324; at Monte Alban, 329; Tarascan, 363; Zapotecan, 329

Mountains, Mexico and Central America, 267–268
Multiples, standard, 375–376, 377
Music, Aztecan, 361–362
Musical instruments, Aztecan, 361–362
Mythology, Aztecan, 337, 347, 351, 356, 357–358; Mayan and Aztecan, 356
Myths, cosmogonic, 357–358

Nahuan linguistic stock, distribution of, 346
Naranjo, 291, 306, 324, 386
Nasca, 368
National Stone, Aztecan, 352
Natural gardens, 395
Negative painting, 281, 289, 339, 368
New Fire Ceremony, Aztecan, 352; Toltecan, 334
Nezahualcoyotl, 347, 361, 383
Niquiras, 276
Nose form, Indians of Mexico and Central America, 280
Noserings, on archaic figurines, 286
Notation system, Mayan, 308, 311–313
Numbers, Aztecan, 355–356; Mayan, 311–313; Mexican system of, 355–356; Zapotecan system of, 328–330

Observatories, astronomical, Mayan, 319–320
Obsidian, Aztecan ornaments of, 363
Ochpaniztli, eleventh feast of year, 359–360
Olin, Aztecan day sign, 351
Olmeca, 327–328, 340, 394
Ometeuctli, Lord of Duality, 356, 358
Organization, political, Mayan, 346; social, Aztecan, 349–350
Ornaments, precious and semi-precious stones, Aztecan, 363; shown on archaic figurines, 286
Otomi, 276, 341, 346, 363, 394

Pachtli, twelfth month, Aztecan, 360
Paddle-shaped stones, Totonacan, 332
Painting, archaic figurines, 286, 289; archaic pottery, 287–288; body, shown on archaic figurines, 286; on Mayan pottery, 296; negative, on pottery, 281, 289, 338–339, 368; Zapotecan pottery, 330
Palaces, structure of Mayan, 292–293, 294
Palenque, 291, 294, 315, 319, 324, 371, 376; vs. Copan, 389–390, 393
Pantheon, Mayan, 302–304
Papantla, pyramid at, 332
Peregrinations, Aztecan, 348
Peresianus Codex, 316, 382, 383, 389
Period, defined, in Mayan time count, 309; glyphs, Mayan, 313, 315
Permutation system, Aztecan, 360; Mayan, 308, 309
Perspective, in Mayan design, 300–302
Peyote worship, Huichol and Tarahumare, 278
Phonetic use of signs, Mayan hieroglyphs, 314, 315
Physical types, 280
Pictographic hieroglyphs, Mayan, 314
Piedras Negras, 291, 306, 324
Pima, 275, 277
Pipiles, 276, 328, 341
Place names, Aztecan, 352–353, 354
Planets, 373, 374–378, 385, 387, 389

Plants, food, cultivation of, in New World, 283–284, 366–367, 368

Poetry, Aztecan, 361

Polychrome pottery, Cholula, 337; Mayan, 296

Portraiture, in archaic art, 285–286; in Mayan art, 300, 314; in Totonacan art, 332

Post-Archaic Horizon, 290

Potato, cultivated in Peru, 284

Pottery, archaic, 281–282, 287–288, 331; Atzcapotzalco, 282; Aztecan, 362; from Cholula, 337, 364; Chorotegan, 341–343; cloisonné, San Juan Teotihuacan, 336; at Cuicuilco, 283; distribution of, 288–290; Lacandone, 279; Mayan, 296–297; Mitla, 331; modern Mexican, 278; northwestern region of Mexico, 338–339; polychrome, Cholula, 337; polychrome, Mayan, 296; San Juan Teotihuacan, 335–336; with semi-glaze, 341; Zapotecan, 328–330

Pre-Archaic Horizon, 290

Priests, in Mayan art, 300; Zapotecan, 330

Protohistoric period, Mayan history, 323

Pulque, 278, 333

Pyramid, Cholula, 336–337; Mayan, 292, 294, 390; Monte Alban, 328; San Juan Teotihuacan, 335; Toltecan, 333

Quetzalcoatl, 272, 325, 327, 333, 337, 347, 357, 390, 391–392; and Toltec era, 334–335

Quichés, 326

Quinatzin, map of, 346

Quirigua, 296, 306, 321, 324

Rank, among Aztecs, 349

Rattles, Aztecan, 361

Religion, Aztecan, 356–357; as evidenced by archaic art, 286–287; Isthmian region, 345; Lacandone Indians, 279; Mayan, 302–304, 323, 346; Toltecan, 333, 334; Zapotecan, 330

Ring-form numbers, 372, 374–375, 376

River systems, Mexico and Central America, 268–269

Roman-nosed God, Mayan, 302–303

Roof comb, on Mayan buildings, 294, 307

Roofs, Mayan buildings, 294

Rooms, Mayan buildings, 293, 294, 307

Rubber, uses of, 327, 394

Ruins, Usumacinta Valley, 269

Rulers, Toltec, 333–334

Sacred Fire, Era of, 382–383, 384

Sacrifices, Aztecan, to gods, 351; human, 351, 352, 356; human, archaic horizon, 287; human, Aztecan, 356, 358–360; human, shown on sculptures, 341; human, Toltecan, 333, 334; human, Zapotecan, 330

Sacrificial yokes, Totonacan, 332

Saltillo blankets, 278

San Andres Tuxtla, 323, 327

San Blas Indians, 279

San Juan Teotihuacan, 328, 333, 335–336

San Miguel blankets, 278

Santa Lucia Cozumalhualpa, 340–341

Saturn, 372, 374–377, 379, 381–382, 386, 387

Sculptural art, massive, 294–296

Sculptures, archaic, 288; common material for, 269; developments in, as check to chronology,

305; Mayan, Early Period, 324; Mayan, Middle Period, 324; San Juan Teotihuacan, 335; Santa Lucia Cozumalhualpa, 340–341; sequence in style, 306–307; style, correlated with dates, 314; Tenochtitlan, 362; at Tula, 336; wall, at Copan, 294; Zapotecan, 328–329

Second Empire, Mayan, 325, 344

Seibal, 291, 324

Seri, 277

Serpent, archaic pottery, 287, 288; in Chorotegan art, 343; conventional, of Mayas, 298–300; heads, comparison of Mayan and Zapotecan, 329; heads, on Mayan buildings, 296; motive, importance in Mayan art, 297–300; in religion of Mayas, 302, 303

Serpent Numbers, 375, 381, 384, 385, 392

Sky God, 304

Slabs, sculptured stone, from Costa Rica, 344; Zapotecan, 329

Smiling faces, Totonacan, 332

Social organization, Aztecan, 349–350

Songs, Aztecan, 361

Southern Mexico, culture of, 364–365

Spear-thrower, Tarascan, 363

Speech scroll, 341

Stability, Mayan buildings, 294

Standard multiples, 375–376, 377

Stature, Indians of Mexico and Central America, 280

Stelae, Mayan, 296, 306, 386, 389; Zapotecan, 328–329

Stocks, language, distribution of, 275–277

Stone, collars, Totonacan, 332; great development of building in, Copan and Mitla, 269; sculpture in, 288; yokes, 332; Zapotecan art in, 329

Stratification, archaeological, at Atzcapotzalco, 282, 333; Mexican sites, 281–282; in Salvador, 282

Structure, two-roomed, Mayan, 293–294

Subtiaban stock, 276

Sumo Indians, culture of, 279

Sun, and Palenque astronomers, 389–390

Sun God, Aztecan, 351–352, 357

Suns, sequence of, in Aztecan mythology, 357–358

Superstructures, on Mayan buildings, 294

Supplementary series, 313, 321

Swamp-utilization agriculture, 394

Syllables, phonetic use of, 314, 354–355

Symbolism, religious, Mayan, 300, 301, 302, 358, 393–394

Synchronizations, 369–371, 373, 387

Talamanca, 280

Tarahumare, 275, 277, 278

Tarascan, culture, 363; stock, 276

Tarascans, 280

Tattooing, shown on archaic figurines, 286

Tecpan, 348, 350–351

Temple, enclosure, Tenochtitlan, 350–351; structure of Mayan, 292–296; of the Sun, Aztecan, 351–352; at Xochicalco, 336

Temples, Mayan, 292–294, 307, 324, 325, 326, 376, 389–390; Mitla, 330–331; Tenochtitlan, 350–351; Toltecan, 333; Zapotecan, 328–329

Tenochtitlan, 272–273, 275, 282, 349, 350, 352, 362

Teocentli, sacred maize, 284

Teochichimecs, 391

Teocinte, 395

Teonanacatl, peyote, use of, 278

Teotihuacan, 328, 333, 335–336, 394, 395

Teotleco, twelfth month, Aztecan, 360

Tepanecas, 282, 348, 349

Tepehuane, 275, 277

Teponaztli, Aztecan, 394

Teswin, 278

Teteocan, 358

Teteoinnan, 359

Texcoco, 334, 344, 346, 347, 349, 359, 361, 383

Textile, art, Cora and Huichol, 277; art, Mayan, 297; decoration, Aztec, 363; designs, on archaic effigies, 286, 329

Tezcatlipoca, 272, 352, 357, 379, 390–391

Tezozomoc, 347, 361, 391

Theocracy, 300, 372–373, 378, 380, 381, 389, 390, 393, 395

Throughway, Maya, 369, 371, 374, 375, 378, 380, 381

Tikal, 291, 294, 306, 324, 395

Time, count, Aztecan, 347; fallacy of, 379, 383, 390–392; Mayan, 307–308; Toltecan, 334; Zapotecan, 330

Time-relations, in New World culture, 366–368

Tizoc, stone of, 349, 352–353

Tlachtli, Mexican ball game, 333, 336

Tlacopan, 273, 349

Tlaloc, God of Rain, 287, 336, 350, 357

Tlalocan, 358

Tlalxico, 394

Tlappaneca, 341

Tlaxcala, 272–273, 276, 280, 349

Tlotzin, map of, 346

Toltec era, and Quetzalcoatl, 334–335

Toltecs, 307, 325, 328, 332–334, 347, 357, 372, 383, 393; fallacy of time, 390–392; origin of, 394–395

Tomb, cruciform, near Mitla, 331

Tonalamatl, Aztecan, 309, 360

Tonatiuh, Sun god, 351, 352, 357

Topography, Mexico and Central America, 267–269

Totonacan, culture, 331–332; stock, 276

Toxcatl, Aztecan month, 359

Traditions, Colombia and Peru, 367; Mayan, 305

Transition period, Mayan history, 324–325

Trees, Mexico and Central America, 270

Tribes, Indian, Mexico and Central America, 275–276

Tribute, lists, Aztecan, 363; roll, 364; taken by Toltecs, 333

Tripod calculations, 369, 373–374, 375–378, 388, 392

Tripod vessels, archaic period, 287

Tro-Cortesianus Codex, 316

Tropical year, 320

Tula, 333, 334, 336

Tulum, 326

Tun, defined, 320

Turquoise, Aztec work in, 363

Tuxtla Statuette, 318, 323, 327

Two-headed Dragon, 300, 302, 303, 306

Tzendals, 280

Tzintzuntzan, Tarascan capital, 363

Tzolkin, defined, 309, 310–311; in Dresden Codex, 317–318; and dynamic dating, 369–371, 373, 374, 377, 388, 389; origin of, 309; permutation table, 309

Uayeb period, Mayan, 310

Uaxactun, 320, 323, 324, 386

Uinal, lunar month, 308

Ukahlay statement, 382–383

Universe, Aztecan conceptions of, 357–358; Toltec conceptions of, 390, 393

Urns, Zapotecan funerary, 329

Uto-Aztecan culture, 275–276, 394

Uxmal, 325, 371

Vault, Mayan buildings, 293

Venus, 371–374, 376–377, 386–389, 393; Aztecan festivals in connection with, 360; calendar, Mayan, 322–323

Venus Wicket, 387–388

Viceroys, Spanish, in Mexico, 274

Vigesimal system of counting, Mayan, 311–312, 370, 384

Volcanoes, Mexico and Central America, 268, 269

Wall construction, La Quemada, 337–338; Mayan, 292, 293–294; Mitla, 331; Palenque, 390

War, importance in Aztecan organization, 348–349; Toltecan, 333

War God, Aztecan, 352, 360; Mayan, 304

Weapons, shown in archaic figurines, 286

Weaving, shown in archaic figurines, 286; Cora and Huichol, 277–278; Lacandone, 279; Mayan, 297; Tarascan, 363

Whistles, Aztecan, 361

Writing, hieroglyphic, Mayan, 291; Mayan and Aztecan, 314–316; Mexican, 353–356

Xipe, 336, 342, 357, 359

Xkichmook, 294

Xochicalco, 328, 336

Xochimilco, 282, 348, 394

Xolotl, 347

Yatacas, Tarascan mounds, 363

Yaqui, 280

Yaxchilan, 291, 294, 389

Year, bearers, Cuicatecan, 365; conventional, Mayan, 310–311; Dial, Mayan, 371, 389, 393; length of Mayan, 308; Mayan, true, 360; symbol, southern Mexico, 365

Yellow fever, presence in Central America, 324

Yokes, sacrificial, 332

Yum Kaax, Lord of Harvest, 304

Zapotecan stock, 276

Zapotecs, culture of, 280, 328–330, 364

Zero, 374–376, 383, 384, 386, 390; establishment of, 372–373; invention of sign for, 312

Zodiac, 383, 388, 393

Zotzils, 350

301
pl L
LXI
PL29

stella sec.
38
17

Y